AUSTRALIAN

Signpost

MATHS

5

Alan McSeveny Rachel McSeveny Diane McSeveny-Foster

Pearson Australia
(a division of Pearson Australia Group Pty Ltd)
459–471 Church St, Level 1, Building B, Richmond, Victoria, 3121
PO Box 23360, Melbourne, Victoria 8012
www.pearson.com.au

First published 2024 by Pearson Australia
2028 2027 2026 2025
10 9 8 7 6 5 4 3 2 1

Publishers: Sophie Matta and Kerry Nagle
Project Manager: Michelle Thomas
Production Editor: Laura Rentsch
Development Editor: Rachel Elliott
Designer: Anne Donald
Proofreader: Laura Rentsch
Rights & Permissions Editor: Alice McBroom
Cover art: Michael Barter
Illustrator: Michael Barter
Publishing Services: Jit-Pin Chong
Printed in Malaysia by Vivar

ISBN 978 0 6557 0879 7
Pearson Australia Group Pty Ltd ABN 40 004 245 943

Attributions
We would like to thank the following for permission to reproduce copyright material.

Shutterstock: Eastimages, p. 105 (scales); Andrey Lobachev, p. 142 (coin); Mega Pixel, pp. 141, 143 (dice); Jeremy Red, p. 114 (pyramid); Lisa S., p. 62 (calculator); Sunnypicsoz/Geoff Childs, p. 141 (penny); Swapan Photography, p. 142 (dice).

123rf.com: Amorozov, p. 113 (didgeridoo); Shootingtheworld, p. 35 (stamps).

Acknowledgement of Country
Pearson respects and honours Aboriginal and Torres Strait Islander Elders past, present and future. We acknowledge the stories, traditions and living cultures of the Traditional Custodians of the lands on which our company is located and where we conduct our business. Pearson is committed to honouring Australian Aboriginal and Torres Strait Islander peoples' unique cultural and spiritual relationships to the land, waters and seas and their rich contribution to society.

Aboriginal and Torres Strait Islander peoples are advised that this text may contain images, voices and names of deceased persons.

What is Australian Signpost Maths?

Australian Signpost Maths is a mathematics program providing direction and support for teaching and learning. The series covers the content and skills presented in the Australian Curriculum (v9) Mathematics F–6.

A Student Book and an online Teacher Resource are provided for Foundation.

For Years 1 to 6, a Student Book, an online Teacher Resource and a Mentals Book are provided for each year level. The online Teacher Resources provide a wealth of support for teachers.

The content has been carefully sequenced within each year level and across the F–6 series to take into account students' expected mathematical development. However, from the rich and varied material provided, teachers can develop individual learning programs to meet the needs of each student.

The Student Books are designed to support explicit teaching methods. Many group activities are provided in Activity, Investigation and Fun spots within the Student Books and the online Teacher Resource.

To maximise the benefits of the program, the Student Book, the online Teacher Resource and the Mentals Book should be used together.

Student Books

Mentals Books

Teacher Resource

Structure of Australian Signpost Maths

In the Year 3 to 6 books, the worksheet pages cover all three elements: Number sense and algebra, Measurement and geometry, and Statistics and probability. These are presented in five chapters:

- Number and algebra
- Operations and algebra
- Measurement
- Space
- Statistics and probability.

This gives teachers flexibility in programming.

The contents cross-reference allows teachers to quickly find the pages where each concept has been covered.

Within the program, explicit teaching, critical and creative thinking, language development and identification and treatment of weaknesses are given high priority.

Identifying and addressing areas of need

Five progress tests are designed to identify each student's areas of need, and the follow-up program after each of the tests is designed to address these needs. A reference to the relevant worksheet page is given for each test question. A remediation record page is used to track the student's progress.

These testing resources can be found in the online Teacher Resource.

Parallel progress retests are provided for further testing after remediation has taken place.

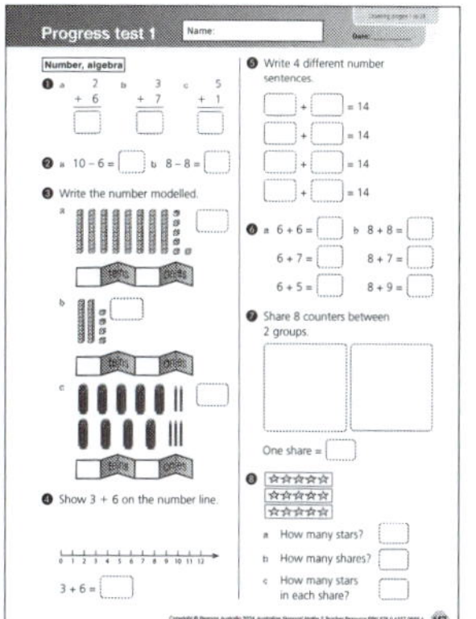

Progress test 1 Name: Date:

Number, algebra

1 a 2 + 6 = ☐ b 3 + 7 = ☐ c 5 + 1 = ☐

2 a 10 − 6 = ☐ b 8 − 8 = ☐

3 Write the number modelled.

a ☐ tens ☐ ones

b ☐ tens ☐ ones

c ☐ tens ☐ ones

4 Show 3 + 6 on the number line.

3 + 6 = ☐

5 Write 4 different number sentences.

☐ + ☐ = 14

☐ + ☐ = 14

☐ + ☐ = 14

☐ + ☐ = 14

6 a 6 + 6 = ☐ b 8 + 8 = ☐

6 + 7 = ☐ 8 + 7 = ☐

6 + 5 = ☐ 8 + 9 = ☐

7 Share 8 counters between 2 groups.

One share = ☐

8 a How many stars? ☐

b How many shares? ☐

c How many stars in each share? ☐

147

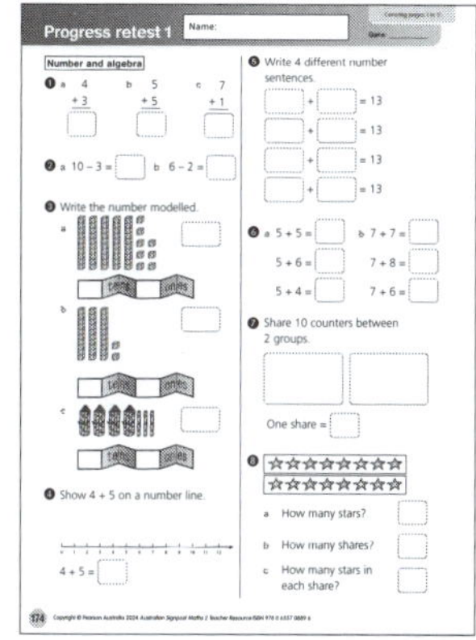

Progress retest 1 Name: Date:

Number and algebra

1 a 4 + 3 = ☐ b 5 + 5 = ☐ c 7 + 1 = ☐

2 a 10 − 3 = ☐ b 6 − 2 = ☐

3 Write the number modelled.

a ☐ tens ☐ ones

b ☐ tens ☐ ones

c ☐ tens ☐ ones

4 Show 4 + 5 on a number line.

4 + 5 = ☐

5 Write 4 different number sentences.

☐ + ☐ = 13

☐ + ☐ = 13

☐ + ☐ = 13

☐ + ☐ = 13

6 a 5 + 5 = ☐ b 7 + 7 = ☐

5 + 6 = ☐ 7 + 8 = ☐

5 + 4 = ☐ 7 + 6 = ☐

7 Share 10 counters between 2 groups.

One share = ☐

8 a How many stars? ☐

b How many shares? ☐

c How many stars in each share? ☐

174

Special features of Australian Signpost Maths

- **The traffic light icons**

  These are found on the top right of each worksheet page in the Student Books. They allow students to assess their own progress and give feedback to the teacher.

  - **Green:** I found this work easy.
  - **Orange:** I found some work on the page difficult.
  - **Red:** I don't understand the work on this page.

- **Dictionary**

  Terms used in the Student Book and terms that should be understood at this level are recorded here to provide a reference for students and teachers. This is found on pages xiv–xxiv of this book.

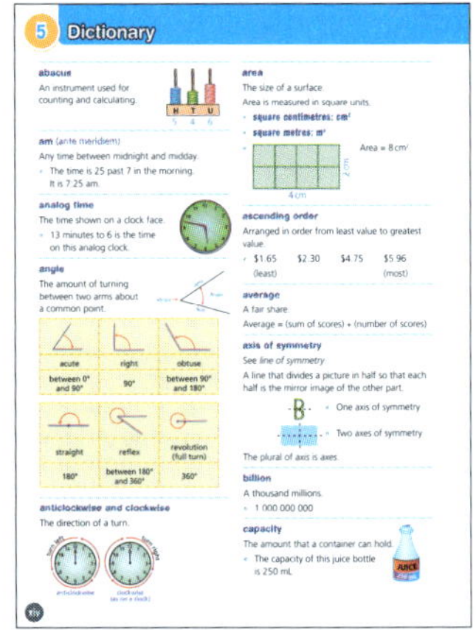

- **ID cards (Years 1 to 6)**

  These cards review the language of Mathematics by asking students to identify common terms, shapes and symbols. They are designed to be reused and are found in the online Teacher Resource and in the front of the Mentals Books.

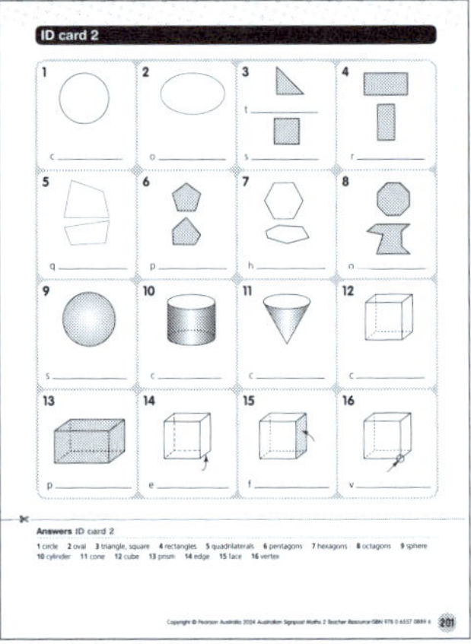

- **Progress tests**

  These allow the teacher to identify each student's strengths and needs. Cross-references for each question direct teachers and students to the pages where that work is introduced. Tables are provided to record the follow-up that takes place and parallel tests are provided for retesting. These tests can be found in the online Teacher Resource.

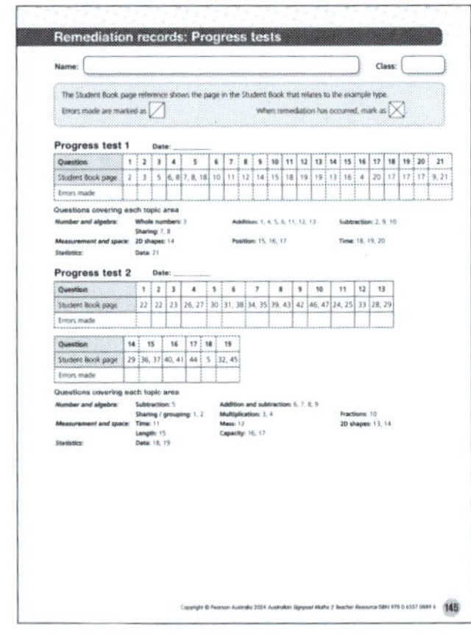

- **Year 5 Consolidation booklet**

  This 32 page booklet is found in the online Teacher Resource. It is designed to reinforce work completed in class and provides practice of important skills and addition and subtraction facts. The booklet can be used when there is limited supervision or when a student finishes classwork early.

- **Answers**

  These are supplied in the Student Book and the online Teacher Resource.

- **Blackline masters (BLM)**

  References are made to the blackline masters in the Teacher Resource suggestions provided for each student work page.

- **Differentiation**

  Each student work page has a Teacher Resource page to support it. Cross-references direct the teacher to pages where the concept is introduced and developed. These references may be from the Student Book for the previous year, the current year or the next year.

  The Teacher Resource support pages provide additional learning activities for students who need remediation or extension activities. The Blackline Masters provide activities to support students of various learning abilities.

- **Cartoons**

  Cartoons are used to motivate and instruct.

- **Extra support pages**

  Decimals, multiplication tables, factors and multiples, extended multiplication, estimation, patterns and problem solving are supported in the Extra support pages.

Australian Signpost Maths icons

Signpost icons are used throughout the book as cues to the essential nature of exercises and activities, and as a guide to ways of engaging with them. These icons often indicate alternative or more concrete approaches to dealing with concepts.

This icon highlights **important rules and concepts** occurring throughout the book. It often appears with worked examples.

Activities provide **applications and enrichment**. These activities usually involve the use of concrete materials and partner or group work.

These enjoyable activities are used to **motivate and involve** students in mathematical pursuits. They usually involve games and puzzles.

Investigations allow students to **explore and discover** maths concepts.

These activities involve the use of computers or other **information and communications** technology.

I'm on the top of each page.

Structure of the Australian Curriculum, F–6 (v9)

Numeracy elements

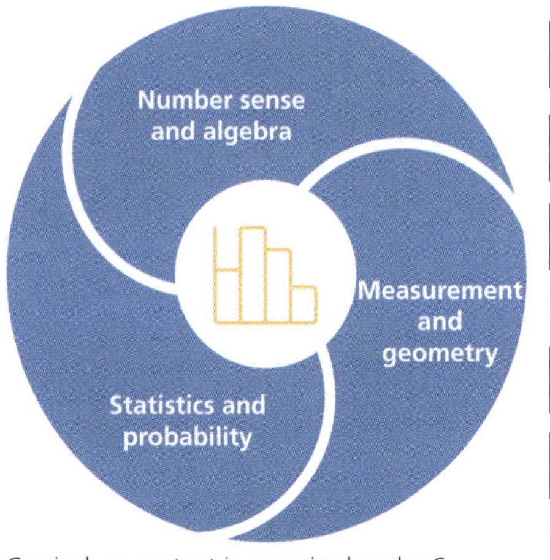

Curriculum content is organised under 6 interrelated strands: Number, Algebra, Measurement, Space, Statistics and Probability.

Sub-elements for Number sense and algebra

- Number and place value
- Counting processes
- Additive strategies
- Multiplicative strategies
- Interpreting fractions
- Number patterns and algebraic thinking
- Understanding money

Sub-elements for Measurement and geometry

- Understanding units of measurement
- Understanding geometric properties
- Positioning and locating
- Measuring time

Sub-elements for Statistics and probability

- Understanding chance
- Interpreting and representing data

The Curriculum strives to develop in students proficiency in Mathematics, highlighting Understanding, Fluency, Reasoning and Problem solving.

Mathematics content of the Australian Curriculum

- It is important that you download the **GENERAL CAPABILITIES** document from 'Downloads' in the top navigation bar of the website homepage. It contains the tables that list the progression level expectations for each Year, F to 10. It also provides the content of all progression levels.
- The LEARNING AREAS download gives a summary of Content descriptions and Elaborations. CROSS-CURRICULUM PRIORITIES can also be found there.

Contents and curriculum overview

Suggested program

This weekly program aligns with the Mentals Book, e.g. Mentals Book, Unit 9 covers work taught in the Weeks 7 and 8 of this book.

Number and algebra			Content						Suggested program	
Page	Unit	Title	Counting, number	Place value	Rounding	Fractions	Decimals	Percentages		
1	1:01	Numbers using millions	●	●					Week 3	Term 1
2	1:02	Large numbers	●	●						
3	1:03	Using large numbers	●	●	●					
4	1:04	Fractions				●			Week 4	
5	1:05	The order of unit fractions				●				
6	1:06	Mixed numbers				●				
7	1:07	Tenths and hundredths				●	●		Week 5	
8	1:08	Percentages				●	●	●		
9	1:09	Using percentages				●	●	●		
10	1:10	Fractions				●	●	●	Week 6	
11	1:11	Improper fractions, mixed numbers				●				
12	1:12	Addition of fractions				●			Week 7	
13	1:13	Subtraction of fractions				●				
14	1:14	Place value to thousandths		●			●		Week 8	
15	1:15	Place value and decimals					●			
16	1:16	Addition and subtraction of fractions				●			Week 21	Term 3
17	1:17	Equivalent fractions				●				
18	1:18	Equivalent fractions				●			Week 22	
19	1:19	Equivalent fractions				●				
20	1:20	Comparing decimals		●	●		●		Week 23	
21	1:21	Comparing decimals		●			●			
22	1:22	Subtraction from whole numbers				●			Week 31	Term 4
23	1:23	Using fractions				●				
24	1:24	Solving problems with fractions				●			Week 32	
25	1:25	Using decimals	●	●			●			
26	1:26	Patterns and percentages				●	●	●	Week 33	

- The teacher will decide when testing occurs. The Progress Tests and Retests are found in the online Teacher Resource.
- Suggested program: The first two units of the Mentals Book review the previous year and could be completed in Weeks 1 and 2.

Operations and algebra

Suggested program: This weekly program aligns with the Mentals Book, e.g. Mentals Book, Unit 9 covers work taught in Weeks 7 and 8 of this book.

Page	Unit	Title	Content: Addition	Subtraction	Multiplication	Division	Multiples, factors, divisibility	Mental strategies	Algebraic thinking	Problem solving	Suggested program	Term
27	2:01	Numbers facts, × 6, × 7, × 8, × 9			●		●				Week 3	Term 1
28	2:02	Learning your multiplication tables			●		●					
29	2:03	Division facts				●			●		Week 4	
30	2:04	Rounding						●			Week 9	
31	2:05	Strategies, + and –	●	●	●	●						
32	2:06	Addition to 999	●					●			Week 10	
33	2:07	Addition to 999	●					●				
34	2:08	Using the addition algorithm	●					●		●		
35	2:09	Subtraction with trading		●				●			Week 11	Term 2
36	2:10	Subtraction to 999		●				●				
37	2:11	Multiples			●		●				Week 12	
38	2:12	Factors			●		●			●		
39	2:13	Factors and multiples					●					
40	2:14	Addition of money	●								Week 13	
41	2:15	Subtraction of money		●						●		
42	2:16	Shopping	●	●						●		
43	2:17	Division with remainders				●				●	Week 14	
44	2:18	Division of 2-digit numbers				●				●		
45	2:19	Using division facts				●				●		
46	2:20	Subtraction to 999		●				●			Week 15	
47	2:21	Subtraction from hundreds		●				●		●		
48	2:22	Addition to 9999	●								Week 16	
49	2:23	Addition to 9999	●							●		
50	2:24	Subtraction to 9999		●						●	Week 17	
51	2:25	Subtraction from 1000s		●						●		
52	2:26	Subtraction from 1000s strategy		●				●				
53	2:27	Dividing 2-digit numbers				●					Week 18	
54	2:28	Dividing 2-digit numbers				●						
55	2:29	Dividing 2-digit numbers				●				●	Week 19	
56	2:30	Dividing 3-digit numbers				●				●		
57	2:31	Multiplying tens			●			●			Week 20	
58	2:32	Multiplying tens or hundreds			●			●				
59	2:33	Dividing 3-digit numbers by 10				●		●	●	●	Week 24	Term 3
60	2:34	Dividing with zero in the answer				●				●		
61	2:35	Divisibility				●	●					
62	2:36	Factors and multiples					●				Week 25	
63	2:37	Using factors in multiplication			●		●	●				
64	2:38	Averages	●			●				●		
65	2:39	Mental strategies for multiplication			●			●			Week 26	
66	2:40	Algebraic thinking							●			
67	2:41	Algebraic thinking							●			
68	2:42	Algebraic thinking							●		Week 27	
69	2:43	Multiplying 2-digit numbers			●			●				
70	2:44	The extended form of multiplication			●			●				
71	2:45	The extended form of multiplication			●			●		●		

- The teacher will decide when testing occurs. The Progress Tests and Retests are found in the online Teacher Resource.

Operations and algebra

Page	Unit	Title	Content	Addition	Subtraction	Multiplication	Division	Multiples, factors, divisibility	Mental strategies	Algebraic thinking	Problem solving	Suggested program This weekly program aligns with the Mentals Book, e.g. Mentals Book, Unit 9 covers work taught in Weeks 7 and 8 of this book.
												Term 4
72	2:46	The contracted form of multiplication				●						Week 28
73	2:47	The contracted form of multiplication				●						
74	2:48	Problems involving change of units		●	●	●	●				●	
75	2:49	Estimating by rounding			●							Week 29
76	2:50	Estimating by rounding		●	●	●	●		●		●	
77	2:51	Using your income		●	●						●	Week 32
78	2:52	Making a budget		●							●	
79	2:53	Using operations to solve problems		●		●	●				●	
80	2:54	Estimating products				●			●			Week 33
81	2:55	Strategies for multiplication				●			●			
82	2:56	Multiplication by 2-digit numbers				●			●		●	Week 34
83	2:57	Multiplication by 2-digit numbers				●			●		●	
84	2:58	Multiplication by 2-digit numbers				●			●		●	Week 35
85	2:59	Multiplication by 2-digit numbers				●			●		●	
86	2:60	Finding missing numbers		●	●	●	●			●		Week 37

- The teacher will decide when testing occurs. The Progress Tests and Retests are found in the online Teacher Resource.

Measurement			Content								Suggested program This weekly program aligns with the Mentals Book, e.g. Mentals Book, Unit 9 covers work taught in Weeks 7 and 8 of this book.	
Page	Unit	Title		Length	Area	Capacity and volume	Mass	Temperature	Time, duration	Problem solving		
87	3:01	Kilometres		●							Week 5	Term 1
88	3:02	Kilometres and metres		●							Week 5	
89	3:03	Perimeter		●							Week 6	
90	3:04	Perimeter		●						●	Week 6	
91	3:05	Calculating area			●					●	Week 7	
92	3:06	Square metres			●					●	Week 7	
93	3:07	Area			●						Week 8	
94	3:08	Problem solving		●	●	●		●	●	●	Week 8	
95	3:09	Time units							●	●	Week 9	
96	3:10	24-hour time							●		Week 9	
97	3:11	Using 12- and 24-hour time							●		Week 11	Term 2
98	3:12	24-hour time problems							●	●	Week 11	
99	3:13	Using measurement scales		●		●	●	●		●	Week 22	Term 3
100	3:14	Millimetres		●							Week 22	
101	3:15	Converting length measurements		●							Week 22	
102	3:16	24-hour time							●		Week 23	
103	3:17	Problems involving time							●	●	Week 23	
104	3:18	Grams and kilograms					●				Week 24	
105	3:19	Measuring mass					●			●	Week 24	
106	3:20	Perimeter		●							Week 25	
107	3:21	Exploring perimeter and area		●	●					●	Week 25	
108	3:22	Measuring volume in mL				●					Week 31	Term 4
109	3:23	Capacity and volume				●					Week 31	
110	3:24	Measuring capacity				●					Week 31	
111	3:25	Hectares			●						Week 33	
112	3:26	Square kilometres			●					●	Week 33	

- The teacher will decide when testing occurs. The Progress Tests and Retests are found in the online Teacher Resource.

Space			Content	2D space	Angles, lines	Symmetry, turning	3D objects	Position, directions	Suggested program This weekly program aligns with the Mentals Book, e.g. Mentals Book, Unit 9 covers work taught in the Weeks 7 and 8 of this book.	
Page	Unit	Title								
113	4:01	3D space					●		Week 12	Term 2
114	4:02	Prisms and pyramids					●			
115	4:03	Reflection, translation, rotation				●			Week 13	
116	4:04	Flip, slide, turn		●		●				
117	4:05	Nets					●		Week 14	
118	4:06	Describing position		●				●		
119	4:07	Using a protractor			●				Week 15	
120	4:08	Angle types in degrees			●					
121	4:09	Using a protractor			●				Week 16	
122	4:10	Classifying angles			●					
123	4:11	Compass directions						●	Week 17	
124	4:12	Reading a map						●		
125	4:13	Rotational symmetry		●		●			Week 18	
126	4:14	Measuring angles of rotation			●	●				
127	4:15	Rotational symmetry			●	●				
128	4:16	Views and nets of 3D objects					●		Week 21	Term 3
129	4:17	Coordinates on the number plane		●			●	●		
130	4:18	Using coordinates						●		
131	4:19	Drawing angles			●				Week 35	Term 4
132	4:20	Angles greater than 180°			●					
133	4:21	Mapping Australia						●	Week 36	
134	4:22	Using transformations				●		●		
135	4:23	Using angles			●					

- The teacher will decide when testing occurs. The Progress Tests are found in the online Teacher Resource.

Statistics and probability			Content					Suggested program This weekly program aligns with the Mentals Book, e.g. Mentals Book, Unit 9 covers work taught in Weeks 7 and 8 of this book.	
Page	Unit	Title		Collecting, recording data	Analysing data displays	Chance, language	Chance experiments		
136	5:01	Reading graphs			●			Week 7	Term 1
137	5:02	Drawing graphs		●	●			Week 8	
138	5:03	Drawing picture graphs		●				Week 9	
139	5:04	Surveys		●	●			Week 16	Term 2
140	5:05	Choosing at random				●	●	Week 19	
141	5:06	Fair or unfair?				●	●		
142	5:07	Comparing the chances		●		●	●		
143	5:08	Dot plots		●	●			Week 23	Term 3
144	5:09	More line graphs			●			Week 26	
145	5:10	Reading line graphs			●				
146	5:11	Drawing line graphs		●	●			Week 27	
147	5:12	Matching graphs with stories			●			Week 28	
148	5:13	Chance, as a fraction				●		Week 29	
149	5:14	Chance				●			
150	5:15	Collecting chance data		●		●	●	Week 30	
151	5:16	Collecting data		●	●	●	●		
152	5:17	Data collected over time		●	●			Week 34	Term 4
153	5:18	Data investigation		●	●				
154	5:19	Using spreadsheets		●	●				
155	5:20	Bar and sector graphs			●			Week 36	
156	5:21	Reasoning with graphs			●				
157	5:22	Selecting a graph to use		●				Week 37	
158	5:23	Comparing types of graphs			●				

• The teacher will decide when testing occurs. The Progress Tests and Retests are found in the online Teacher Resource.

Extra support pages						
159	1	Decimals	2	Place value in decimals	3	Reading and writing decimals
162	4	+ and – of fractions	5	Place value to thousandths	6	Comparing decimals
165	7	× 2, × 3, × 4, × 5, × 10 tables	8	× 6, × 7, × 8, × 9 tables	9	Factors and multiples
168	10	Extended multiplication	11	Estimating products	12	Number patterns
171	13	Problem solving with algorithms	14	Problem-solving strategies	15	Problem-solving strategies
174	16	Problem solving	17	Averages	18	Finding missing numbers
177	19	Extension: enlargements	20	Extension: enlargements	21	Decimals!

Suggested program	Term 1	Term 2	Term 3	Term 4
Number and algebra	1:01 - 1:15	-	1:16 - 1:21	1:22 - 1:26
Operations and algebra	2:01 - 2:08	2:09 - 2:32	2:33 - 2:50	2:51 - 2:60
Measurement	3:01 - 3:10	3:11 - 3:12	3:13 - 3:21	3:22 - 3:26
Space	-	4:01 - 4:15	4:16 - 4:18	4:19 - 4:23
Statistics and probability	5:01 - 5:03	5:04 - 5:07	5:08 - 5:16	5:17 - 5:23
Total number of pages:	36	45	45	32

• See the Teacher Resource for a more detailed suggested program.

Contents cross-reference

Measurement and space

Statistics and probability

abacus

An instrument used for counting and calculating.

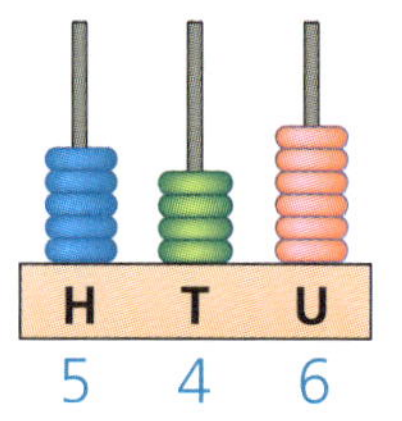

am (ante meridiem)

Any time between midnight and midday.

- The time is 25 past 7 in the morning. It is 7:25 am.

analog time

The time shown on a clock face.

- 13 minutes to 6 is the time on this analog clock.

angle

The amount of turning between two arms about a common point.

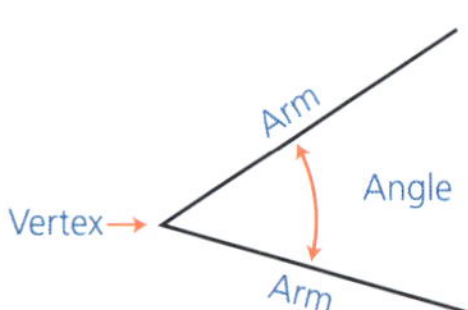

acute	right	obtuse
between 0° and 90°	90°	between 90° and 180°

straight	reflex	revolution (full turn)
180°	between 180° and 360°	360°

anticlockwise and clockwise

The direction of a turn.

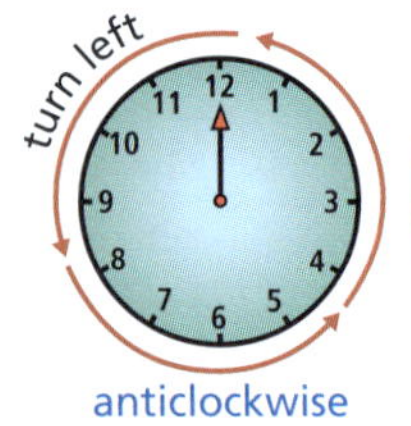

anticlockwise

clockwise (as on a clock)

area

The size of a surface.

Area is measured in square units.

- **square centimetres: cm^2**
- **square metres: m^2**
- 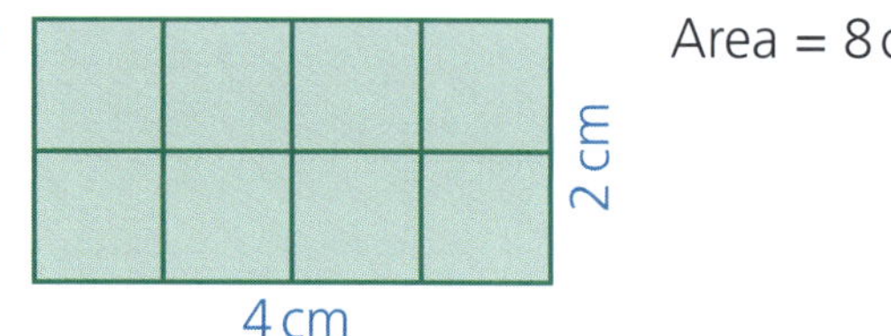

Area = $8\,cm^2$

ascending order

Arranged in order from least value to greatest value.

- $1.65 (least) $2.30 $4.75 $5.96 (most)

average

A fair share.

Average = (sum of scores) ÷ (number of scores)

axis of symmetry

See *line of symmetry*.

A line that divides a picture in half so that each half is the mirror image of the other part.

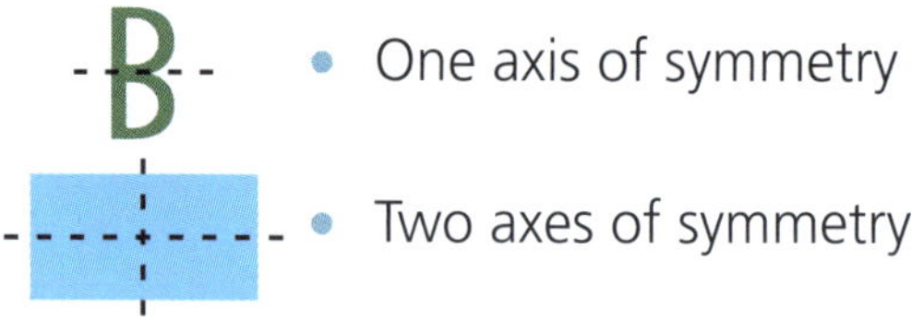

- One axis of symmetry
- Two axes of symmetry

The plural of *axis* is *axes*.

billion

A thousand millions.

- 1 000 000 000

capacity

The amount that a container can hold.

- The capacity of this juice bottle is 250 mL.

centimetre (cm)

A unit of length equal to one hundredth of a metre.

- 100 cm = 1 m, 1 cm = 10 mm

→|1 cm|←

chance

The chance (or probability) of something happening is its likelihood of happening.

- If you toss a coin, there is an even chance of tossing a head.

See *probability*.

compass directions

The needle of a compass points north (N).

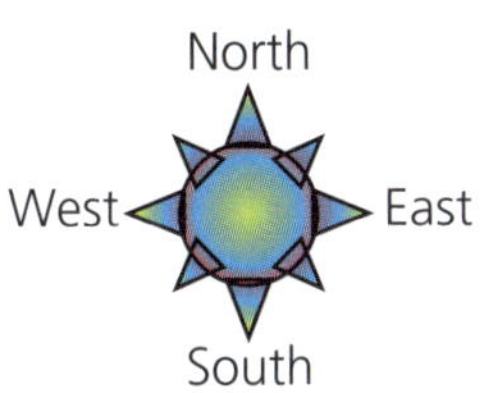

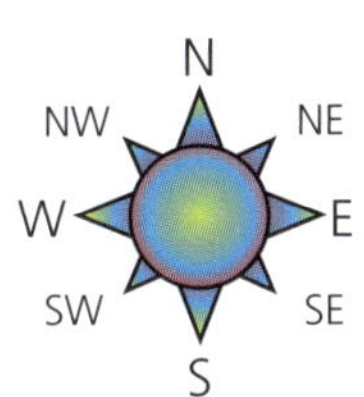

composite number

A number that has more than two factors.

- 9 is composite because it has three factors: 1, 3 and 9.

cone

A three-dimensional object with a circular base that tapers to a point.

coordinates

Pairs of letters or numbers used to show position on a grid.

- This position is D3 or (D, 3).

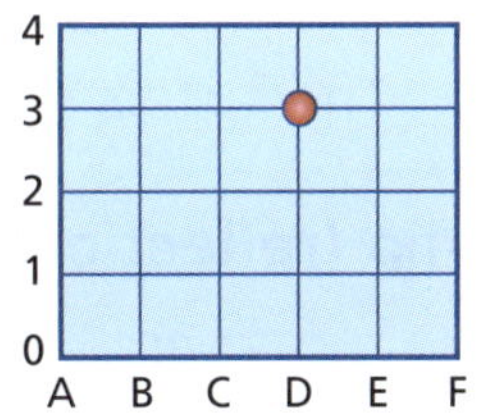

cross-section

A face that is exposed when a 3D object is cut through.

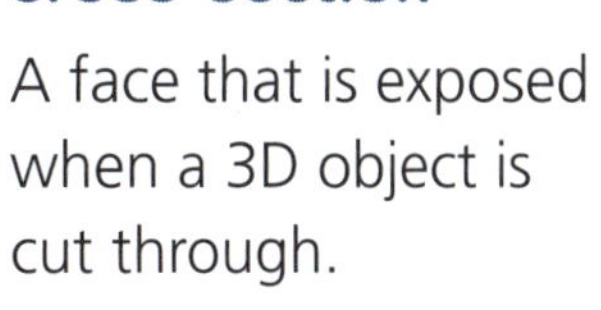
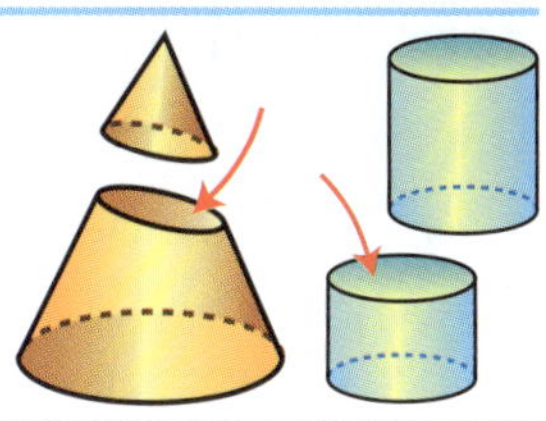

cube

A three-dimensional object that has six equal square faces, eight vertices and twelve equal edges.

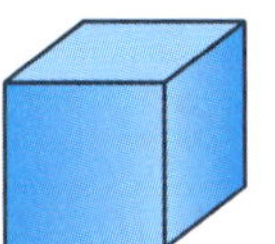

cube number

- 2 cubed = 2^3 ← Index
  = 2 × 2 × 2
  = 4 × 2
  = 8

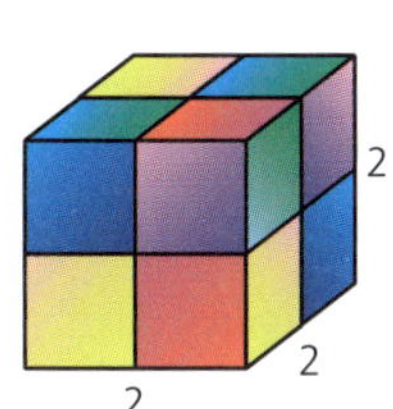

cubic centimetre (cm^3)

A unit of volume equal to the volume of a cube of side length 1 cm.

cubic metre (m^3)

A unit of volume equal to the volume of a cube of side length 1 m.

cylinder

A three-dimensional object with two equal circular faces and one curved surface.

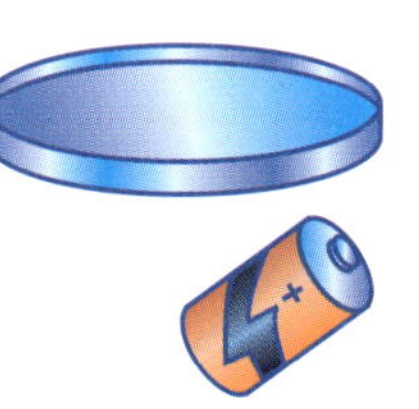

decimal notation

The decimal point separates the whole number from the fraction part.

7·5

↑

decimal point

0·7 means 7 tenths.

6·5 means 6 ones and 5 tenths.

3·07 means 3 ones and 7 hundredths.

denominator

The bottom number of a fraction.
It tells the number of equal parts there are in the whole.

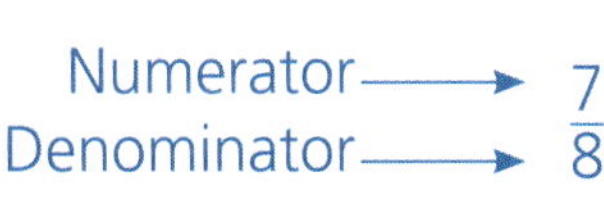

descending order

Arranged in order from greatest value to least value.

- \$5.96 (most) \$4.75 \$2.30 \$1.65 (least)

diagonal

A line that joins any two non-adjacent corners of a polygon.

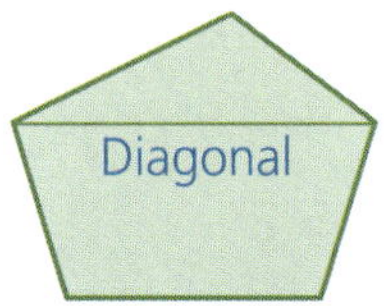

digital time

Time expressed using digits.

- This digital clock shows 24 minutes past 10.

digits

Symbols used to write a number.

- 6 Six is a 1-digit number.
- 47 Forty-seven is a 2-digit number.

divisible

To have no remainder when divided.

- 30 is divisible by 3.

division (÷)

Breaking up groups into equal parts.

- 10 ÷ 2

  a How much will each receive if you share between 2.

  b How many groups of 2 can be made?

edge

Two faces of a 3D object meet at an edge.

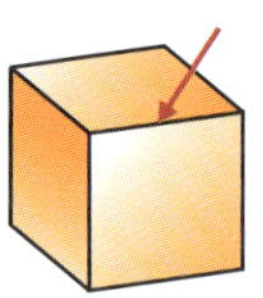

equivalent fractions

These are equal. They refer to the same part of the whole.

- 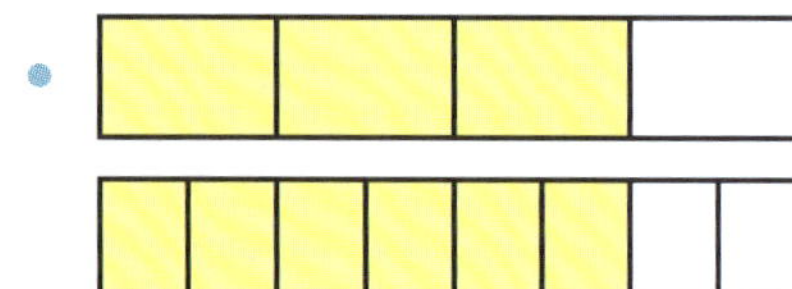

$\frac{3}{4} = \frac{6}{8}$

estimate (estimation)

A good guess.

even number

Any number that is a multiple of two and can be grouped in twos. They end in 0, 2, 4, 6 or 8.

- 16, 300, 4394

The other counting numbers are **odd**.

expanded notation

A way of writing numerals to show the place value of each digit.

- 137 = (1 × 100) + (3 × 10) + 7

face

A flat surface of a three-dimensional object that is bounded by only straight sides.

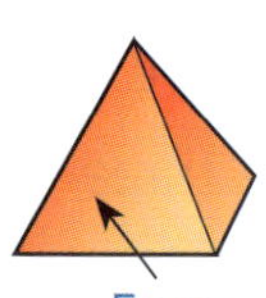

Face Face

factor

A factor of a number divides the number exactly, leaving no remainder.

- The factors of 12 are 1, 12, 2, 6, 3 and 4.

flip (reflection)

To turn over.

- A mirror image is made.

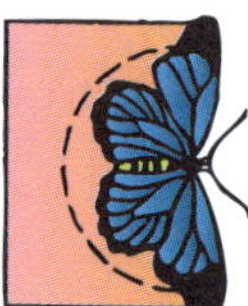

fraction

A part of a whole or group.

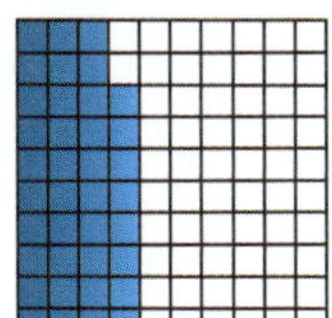

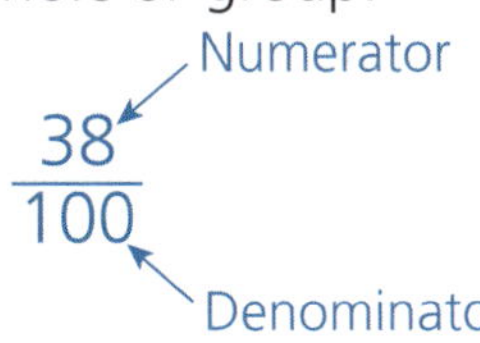

- Equivalent fraction

  Fractions of equal size.

  $\frac{1}{2} = \frac{5}{10} = \frac{7}{14} = \dots$

- Improper fraction

  A fraction which has a numerator that is bigger than the denominator.

  $\frac{9}{8}$

- Mixed numeral

  A numeral that has a whole number part and a fraction part.

  $1\frac{2}{3}$

gram (g)

A unit of mass.

- 1 kilogram = 1000 grams, 1 kg = 1000 g

graphs

- Bar graph

  A graph which uses horizontal bars to compare the size of groups.

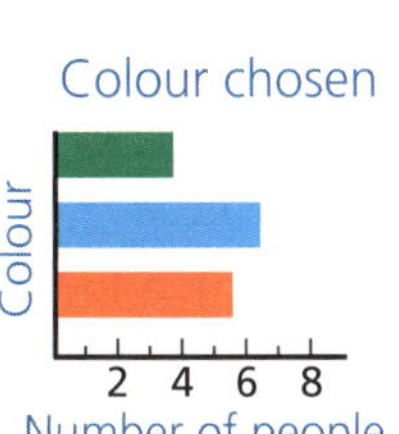

- Column graph

  Groups are compared using the heights of columns (or bars).

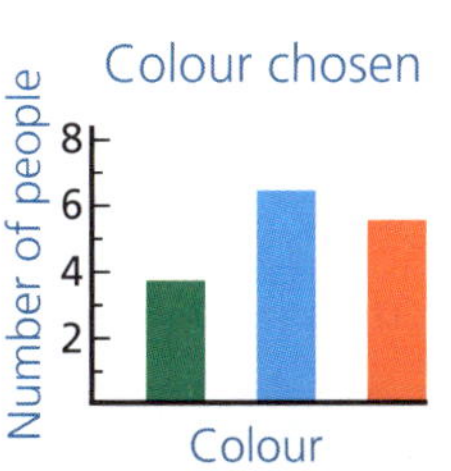

- Divided bar graph

  A bar is divided to show the make-up of the data.

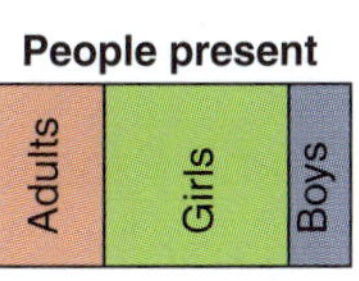

- Dot plot

  A graph which uses dots to compare the size of groups.

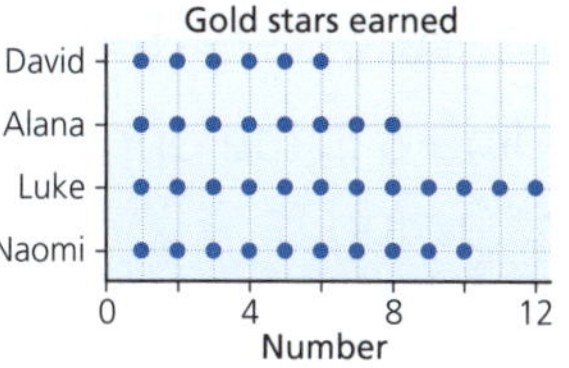

- Line graph

  A continuous line shows the connection between variables.

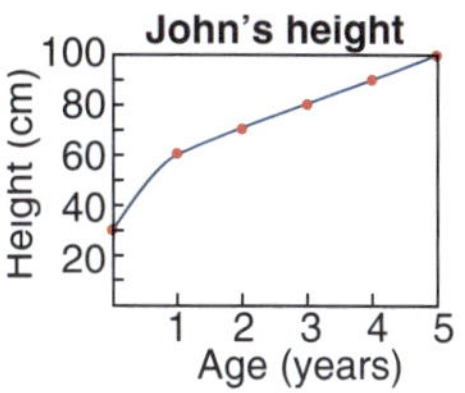

- Picture graph

  A picture is used as a unit to show how many.

- Sector graph

  A circle is cut into sectors to show the parts of a whole.

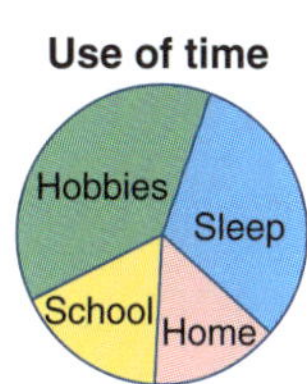

greater than (>)

A way of showing that a number is larger than another number.

- 7 > 3 means 7 is greater than 3.

See also *less than (<)*.

hectare (ha)

A unit of area equal to a square with sides of 100 m.

- 1 ha = 10 000 m^2

horizontal

- Parallel to the horizon.
- Level or flat.
- Any direction at right angles to the vertical.

inverse operations

Adding 8 is the opposite (the inverse) of subtracting 8.

- 100 + 8 – 8 = 100

Multiplying by 2 is the opposite (the inverse) of dividing by 2.

- 4 × 2 ÷ 2 = 4

jump strategy

Adding or subtracting numbers, jumping by hundreds, tens and ones.

- 52 – 14 = 38

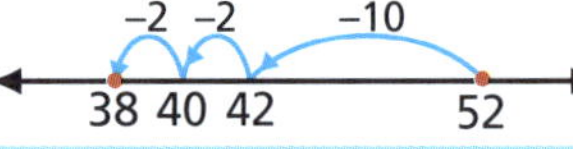

kilo (k)

Kilo means 1000.

kilogram (kg)

The basic unit of mass, equal to 1000 grams.

- 1 kg = 1000 g

kilometre (km)

A unit of length equal to one thousand metres.

- 1 km = 1000 m

less than (<)

A way of showing that a number is smaller than another number.

- 3 < 7 means 3 is less than 7.

See also *greater than (>)*.

line of symmetry

A line that divides something in half so that each half is a mirror image of the other part.

litre (L)

A unit of capacity (or volume) used for the measurement of liquids.

- 1 L = 1000 mL

map or plan

A picture of an area viewed from above.

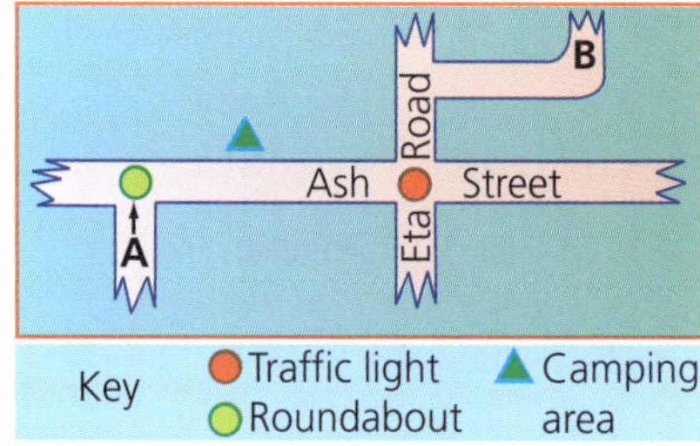

mass

The amount of matter in an object, a measure of how heavy something is.

mean

The arithmetic average.

- mean = $\frac{\text{sum of scores}}{\text{number of scores}}$

See also *average*.

metre (m)

The basic unit of length, equal to 100 centimetres.

- 1 m = 100 cm

millilitre (mL)

A unit of capacity (or volume) equal to one thousandth of a litre.

- 1000 mL = 1 L

millimetre (mm)

A unit of length equal to one tenth of a centimetre, or one thousandth of a metre.

- 10 mm = 1 cm
- 1000 mm = 1 m

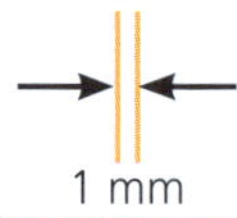

million

A thousand thousands.

- 1 000 000

mixed numeral

A numeral that has a whole number part and a fraction part.

- $4\frac{1}{8}$

mode

The number that occurs the most often in a set of numbers.

- 2, 3, 3, 3, 4, 4, 5, 7

  The mode is 3.

multiple

The result of multiplying a counting number by another counting number.

- The multiples of 5 are 5, 10, 15, 20, …

net

A flat shape that can be folded to make a three-dimensional object.

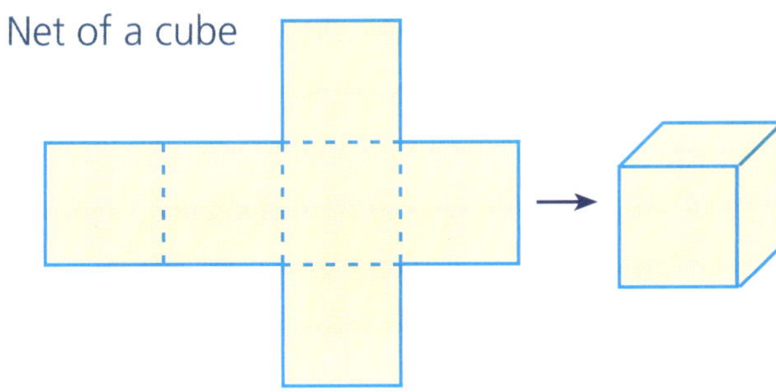
Net of a cube

object

The term used to describe a three-dimensional shape.

Hexagonal prism   Cone

octagon

A polygon with eight sides.

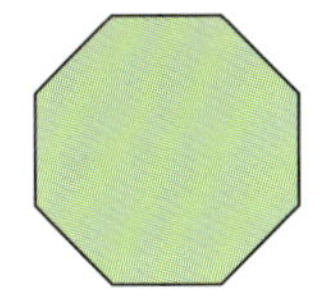
Regular octagon

Irregular octagon

See also *polygon*.

parallel lines

Straight lines on the same flat surface that do not meet.

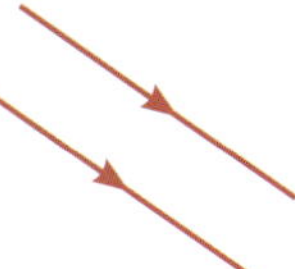

parallelogram

A shape with 4 sides such that the pairs of opposite sides are parallel and equal.

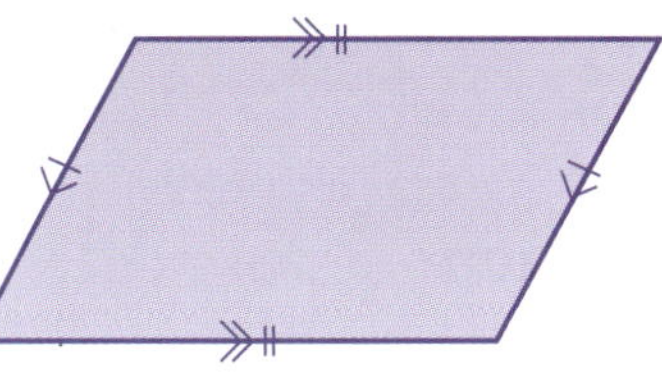

pentagon

A polygon with five sides.

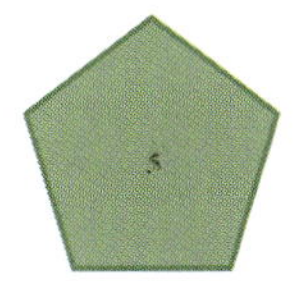
Regular pentagon

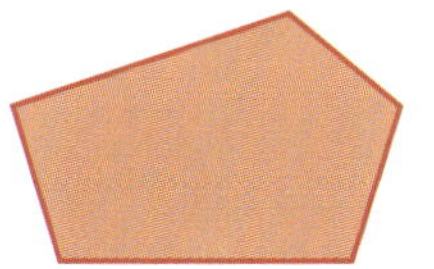
Irregular pentagon

See also *polygon*.

per cent (%)

Out of one hundred.

- $\frac{37}{100} = 0{\cdot}37 = 37\%$ or 37 per cent

perimeter

The distance around the outside of a shape; the boundary.

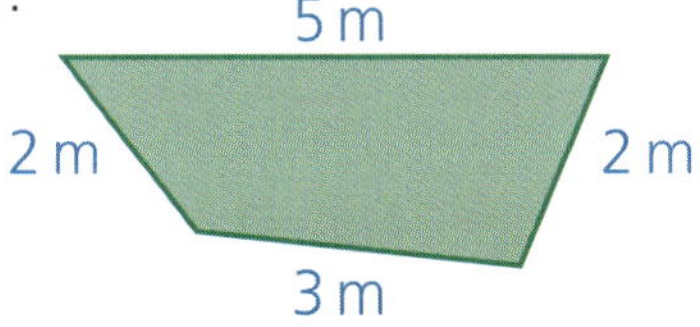

- Perimeter = 2 m + 3 m + 2 m + 5 m

  = 12 m

perpendicular lines

Lines that meet at right angles.

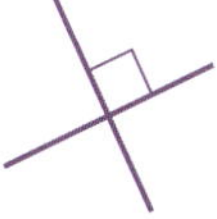

place value

The column value of a digit.

- 396 =

Hundreds	Tens	Ones
3	9	6

pm (post meridiem)

Any time between midday and midnight.

- The time is 20 past 1 in the afternoon. It is 1:20 pm.

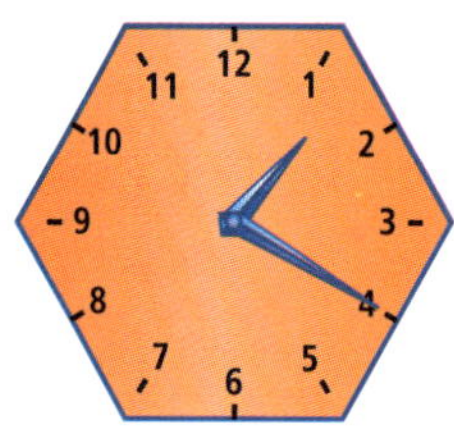

Afternoon

polygon

A two-dimensional shape with three or more straight sides, such as a triangle, quadrilateral, pentagon etc.

prism

A three-dimensional object with a uniform cross-section. The ends are identical shapes and all other faces are rectangles. Prisms are named by the shape of their ends.

Triangular prism

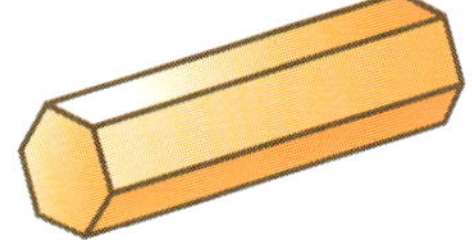

Hexagonal prism

probability

The probability (or chance) of something happening is its likelihood of happening.

- The probability of rolling an even number on a dice is 50%.

product

The answer to a multiplication question.

- The product of 8 and 9 is 72.

protractor

An instrument used for measuring and drawing angles.

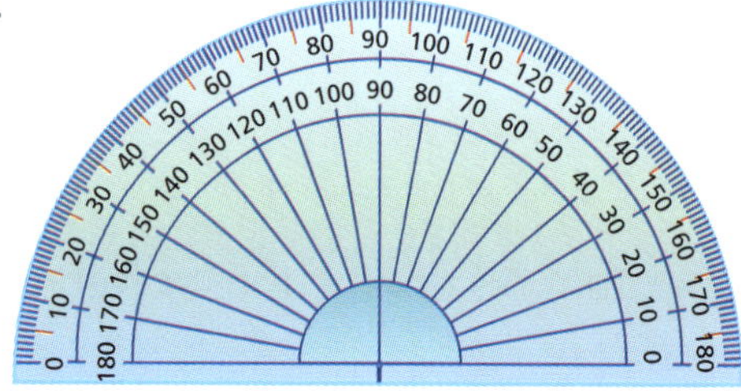

pyramid

A three-dimensional object that has a polygon for a base and triangles for all other faces. Pyramids are named by the shape of their base.

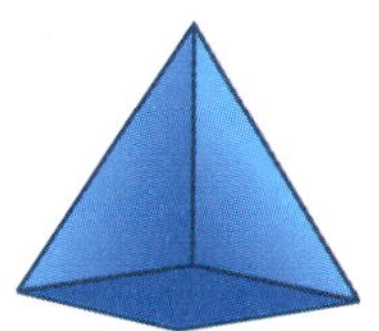

Square pyramid

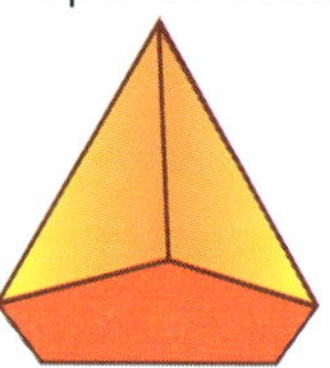

Pentagonal pyramid

quadrilateral

A two-dimensional shape with four straight sides.

quotient

The answer when one number is divided by another.

random selection

Choosing without looking.
Each item has an equal chance of being chosen.

reflection

See *flip*.

regular and **irregular shapes**

Regular shapes have all sides and all angles equal. Irregular shapes do not.

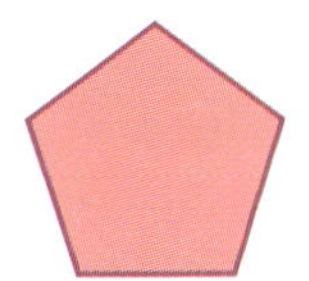
Regular shape

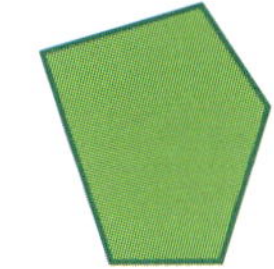
Irregular shape

remainder

The number that is left over after sharing or dividing.

- 22 cups shared among 5 people gives 4 cups each, remainder 2.

rhombus

A shape with 4 sides, opposite sides parallel, all sides equal.

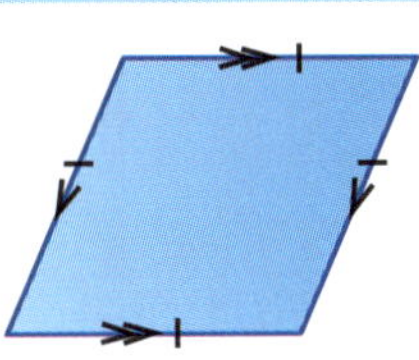

rigid shape

A model that cannot be pushed out of shape because triangles have been used in its construction.

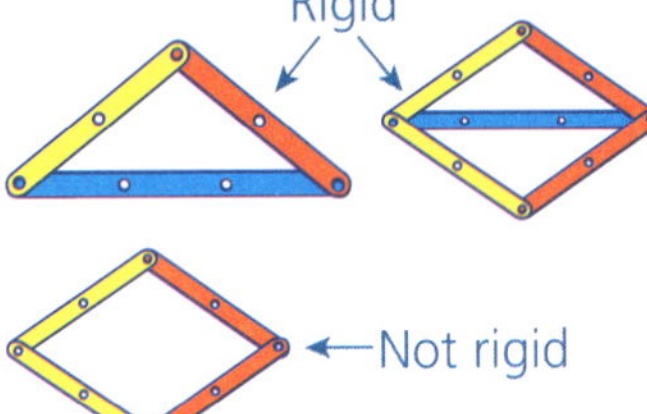

Roman numerals

A number system devised by the ancient Romans.

Roman numerals use letters for numbers:

I	V	X	L	C	D	M
1	5	10	50	100	500	1000

- XXVIII = 28

rounding

Writing a number to the nearest 5, 10, 1000, …

- 3786 rounded to the nearest 100 is 3800.
- 35 000 rounded to the nearest ten-thousand is 40 000.

skip counting

Counting on, adding the same number each time.

- 5, 10, 15, 20, 25, … is skip counting by 5.

slide (translation)

To move a shape in any direction without changing its orientation.

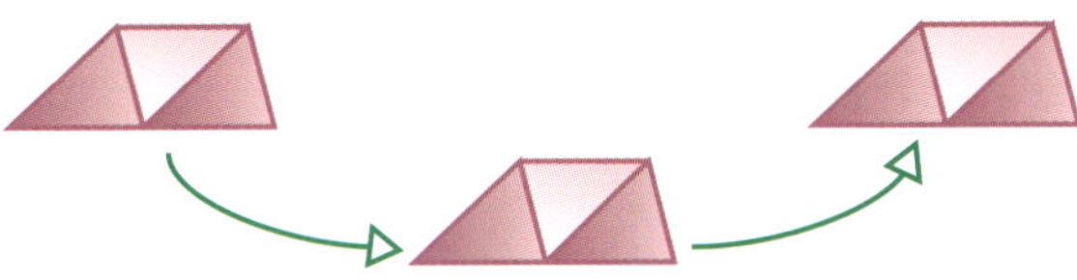

solid

A term used to describe a three-dimensional object.

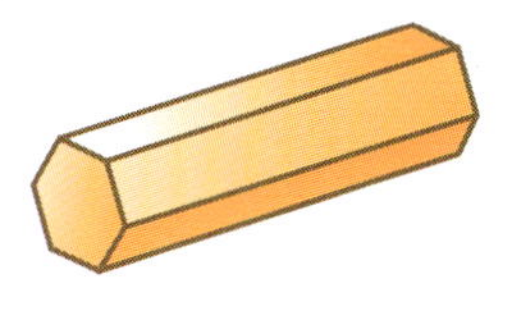
Hexagonal prism

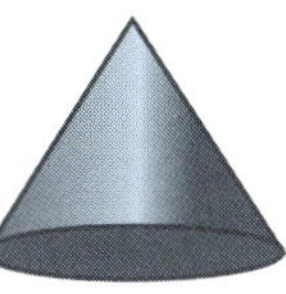
Cone

sphere

A three-dimensional object that is ball-shaped and round. All points on the surface of a sphere are the same distance from its centre.

split strategy

Adding numbers by splitting them into their parts.

- 36 + 52 = 30 + 6 + 50 + 2
  = (30 + 50) + (6 + 2)
  = 80 + 8
  = 88

spreadsheet

A table produced by a computer program used for organising data, allowing rapid calculations and the production of graphs.

square centimetre (cm²)

A unit of area equal to a square with sides of 1 cm.

square kilometre (km²)

A unit of area equal to a square with sides of 1 km.

- 1 km² = 1 000 000 m², 1 km² = 100 ha

square metre (m²)

A unit of area equal to a square with sides of 1 m.

- 10 000 m² = 1 ha

sum

The answer when you add numbers.

surface

The outside layer of a three-dimensional object. A surface can be flat or curved.

See also *face*.

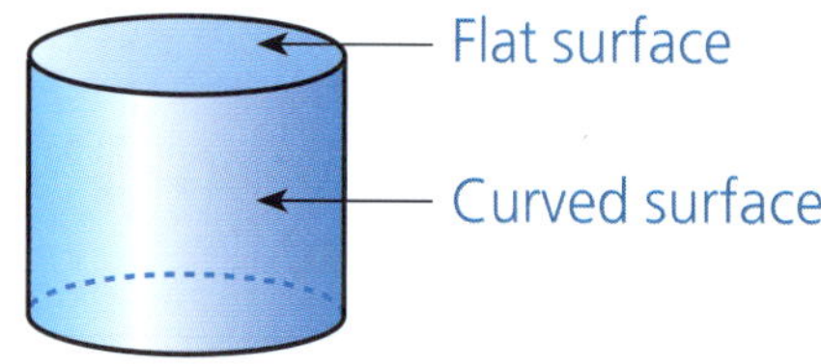

survey or **questionnaire**

A list of questions used to discover information.

symmetry

A balanced arrangement.

- Line symmetry

  A property of a figure where one half is the mirror image of the other.

- Line (or Axis) of symmetry

  A line that divides a figure into two parts that are mirror images of each other.

- Rotational symmetry

  A property of a figure where it can be spun about a point so that it repeats its shape more than once in a full turn.

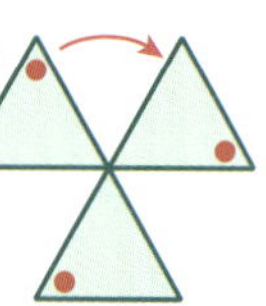

tally

To keep count by making a mark for each item. To make counting easy, the marks are drawn in groups of five with each fifth mark crossed over the other four marks.

- ~~||||~~ ~~||||~~ ~~||||~~ ||| = 18

tangram

A traditional Chinese puzzle. A square is cut into seven pieces that can be rearranged to make different pictures.

temperature

A measure of how hot or cold something is. Temperature is usually measured in degrees Celsius (°C).

- Water freezes at 0°C.
- Water boils at 100°C.

tessellation

A pattern of identical shapes that fit together without gaps or overlaps.

thermometer

An instrument used for measuring temperature.

three-dimensional (3D) object

Objects are three-dimensional. They have length, width and height.

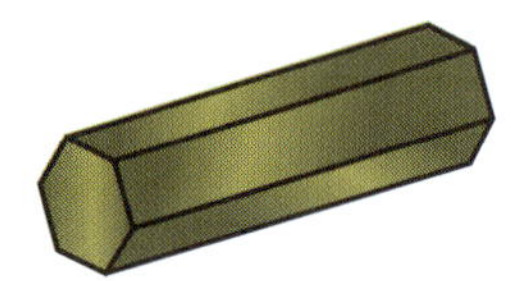

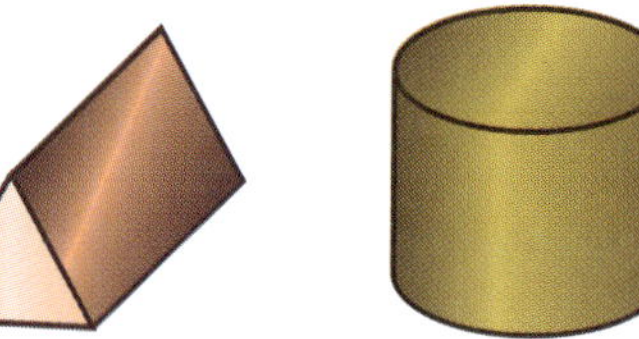

time (months of the year)

- **The number of days in each month:**

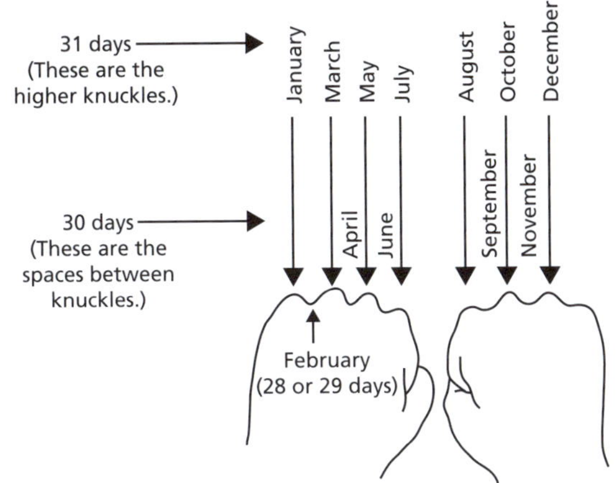

30 days has September, April, June and November. All the rest have 31, except February alone, which has 28 days clear and 29 days each leap year.

timeline

Shows a sequence of events in time.

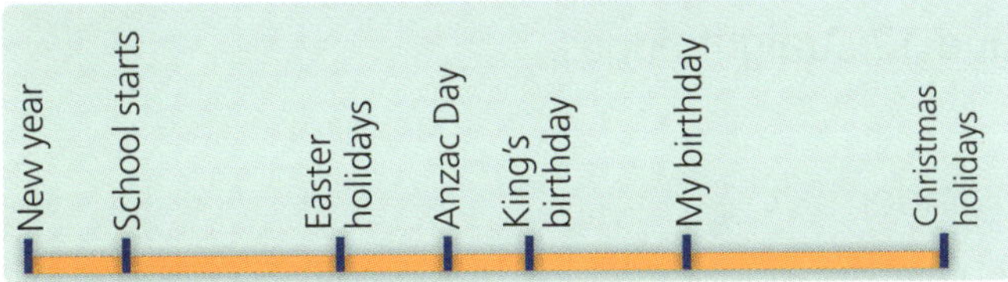

translation

See *slide*.

trapezium

A quadrilateral with one pair of parallel sides.

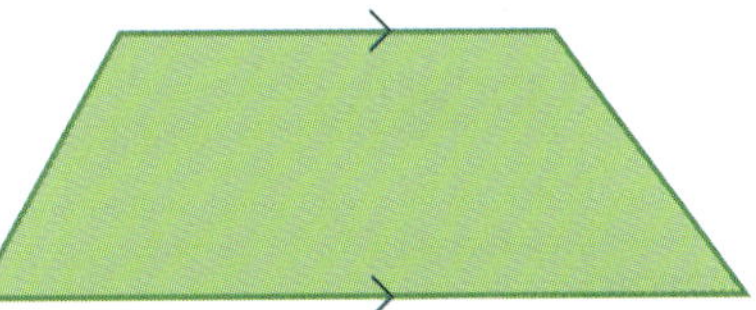

triangle

A two-dimensional shape with three straight sides and three angles.

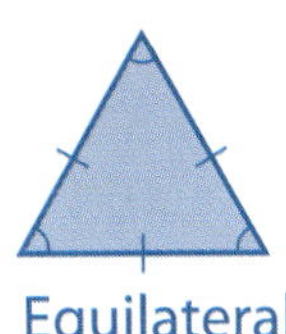

Equilateral

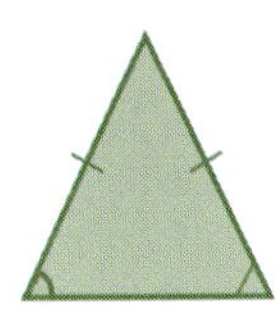

Isosceles

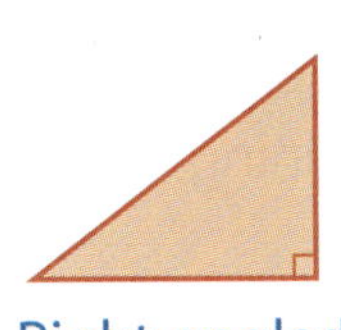

Right-angled

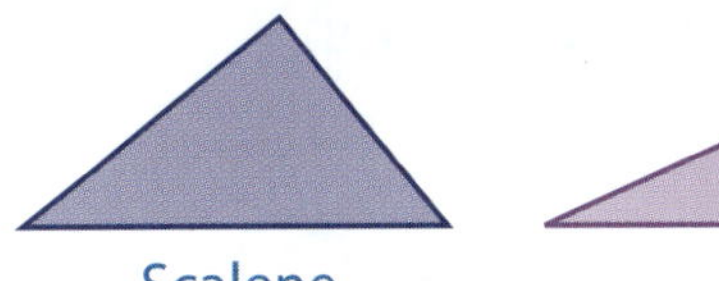

Scalene

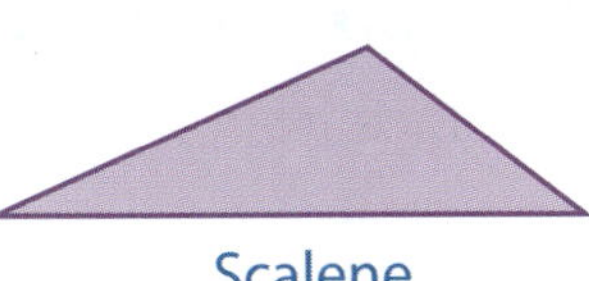

Scalene

Scalene triangles have no sides equal.

See also *polygon*.

turn (rotation)

To rotate a shape about a given point.

twenty-four hour time

Time shown as a 4-digit number, the first two digits indicating the hour and the second two digits indicating minutes.

- 13:20 is 20 past 1 in the afternoon, or 1:20 pm.

vertex

A point at which two or more lines meet to form a corner on a 2D shape or 3D object.

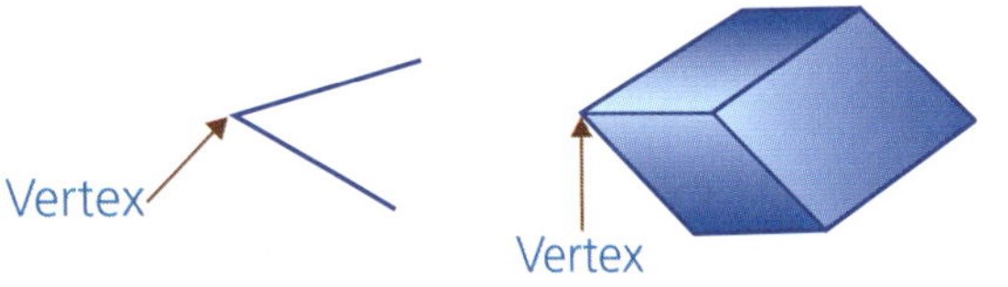

The plural of *vertex* is *vertices*.

vertical

- At right angles to the horizontal.
- Straight up and down.
- The direction in which an object falls under gravity.

volume

The amount of space occupied by a 3D object.

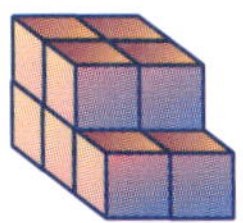

Volume = 10 cubic units

1 cubic centimetre = 1 mL

width or breadth (dimensions)

The distance from side to side.

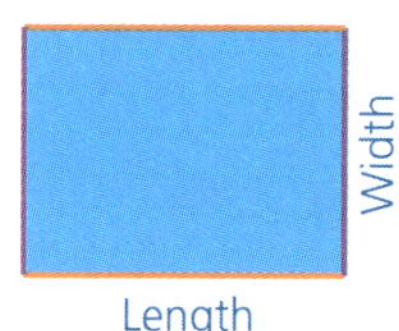

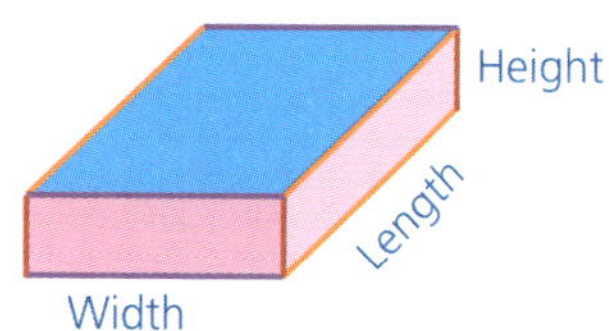

year

There are 365 days in a year and 366 days in a leap year (which is every 4th year). There are 12 months in a year.

2D (two-dimensional) shapes

Flat shapes are two-dimensional. They have length and width.

circle
1 curved side

triangle
3 sides
3 corners

square
4 equal sides
4 right angles

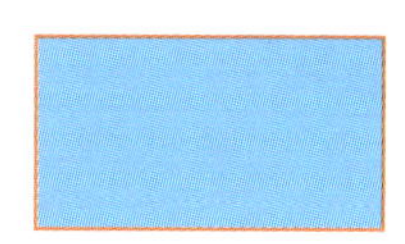

rectangle
2 equal long sides and 2 equal short sides, like a stretched square

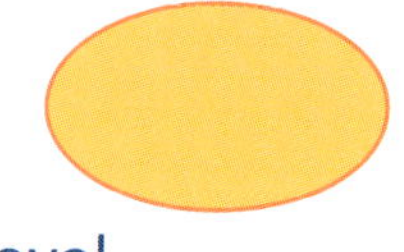

oval
1 curved side, like a squashed circle

pentagon
5 sides
5 corners

hexagon
6 sides
6 corners

octagon
8 sides
8 corners

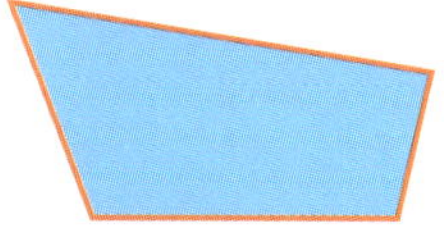

quadrilaterals
4 sides
4 corners

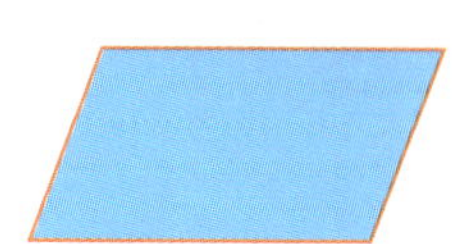

parallelogram
two sets of parallel lines
opposite sides equal

trapezium
one set of parallel lines

rhombus
all sides equal (a diamond)

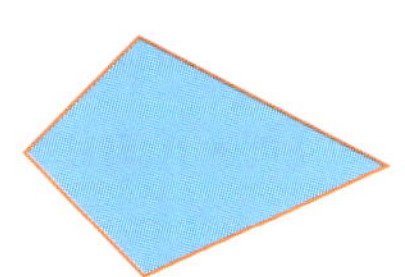

kite
two pairs of equal sides

All of the blue shapes are quadrilaterals.

3D (three-dimensional) objects

Solid objects are three-dimensional. They have length, width and height.

sphere

A sphere is curved and round.

cube

A cube has 6 square faces, 8 vertices and 12 straight edges.

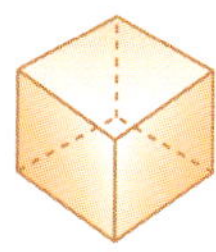

cylinder

A cylinder has 2 circular flat surfaces and 1 curved surface.

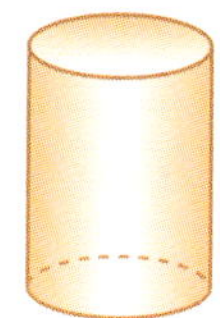

cone

A cone has 1 circular flat surface and 1 curved surface.

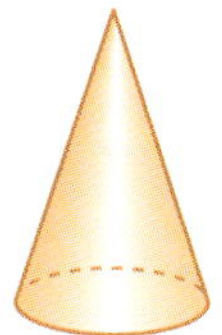

pyramid

A pyramid has triangular faces joined around a base.

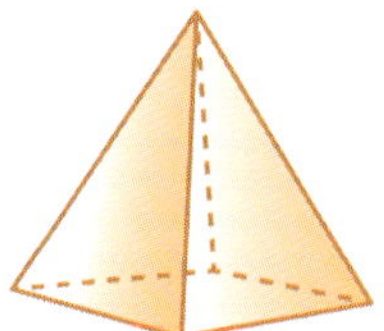

prism

A prism has rectangular faces joining two identical bases.

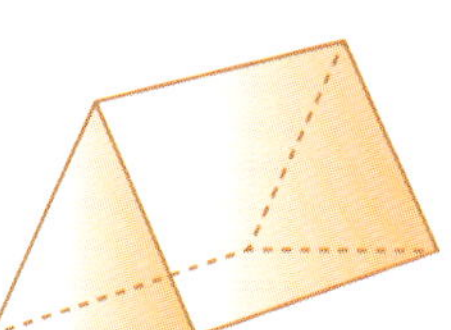

1:01 Numbers using millions

The population of Australia in 2023 was 26 million to the nearest million. (2023: 26 324 039)

CONCEPT

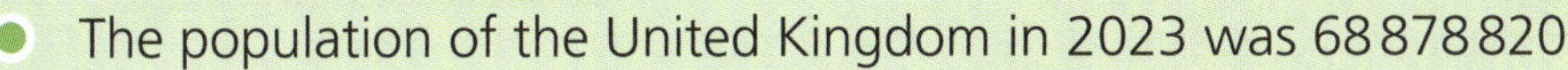

- The population of the United Kingdom in 2023 was 68 878 820

One million is 1000 thousands.

68 million			878 thousand			820		
100 000 000	10 000 000	1 000 000	100 000	10 000	1000	100	10	1
	6	8	8	7	8	8	2	0

- The population of the United States of America in 2023 was 336 406 770.

1 Read these numbers and then write them in the place-value chart.

500K is sometimes used for 500 000.

A eight hundred and sixty-nine thousand

B four million, eight hundred and one thousand, six hundred and forty-nine

C thirty-six million, three hundred and forty-one thousand, five hundred and seventy-five

D fifteen million, six hundred and fifty thousand

	Ten millions	Millions	Hundred thousands	Ten thousands	Thousands	Hundreds	Tens	Ones
A								
B								
C								
D								

a Order the numbers, in **A**, **B**, **C** and **D** of this table, from smallest to largest.

b Write the numeral that is three million more than **D**.

c Write the numeral that is one million, five hundred thousand more than **C**.

2 Write the numeral for:

a 6 000 000 + 300 000 + 70 000 + 2000 + 800 + 40

b 7 million 500 thousand

c 18 million 120 thousand 452

d (3 × 10 000 000) + (6 × 1 000 000) + (7 × 100 000) + (5 × 10 000) + (2 × 1000)

e the 2023 population of Queensland (5 million 360 thousand)

f the 2023 population of Victoria (6 million 829 thousand)

See *Extra Support 21* (Decimals!).

 • *AUSTRALIAN SIGNPOST MATHS 5* • ISBN 9780655708797

1:02 Large numbers

We say the billions, then the millions, then the thousands, and then the rest.
2 billion, 420 million = 2 420 000 000

CONCEPT

- The population of the world in 2023 was over 8 billion people.

One billion is 1000 millions

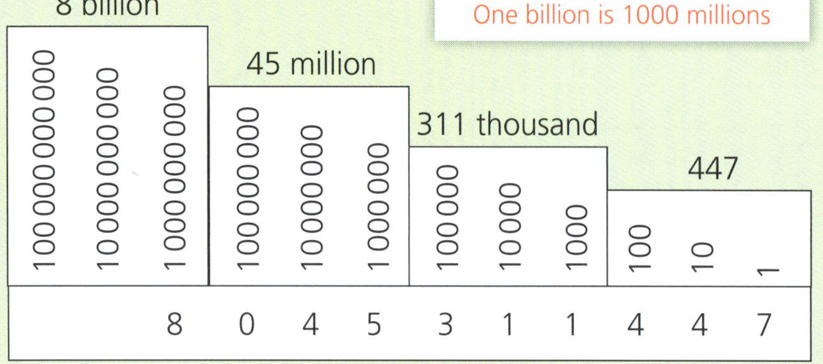

1 Read these numbers and then write them in the place-value chart.

A five hundred and sixty-four thousand and twenty-seven

B ten million, two hundred and fifteen thousand, nine hundred and eighty-two

C two hundred and fifty million, nine hundred and forty thousand

D thirty-six billion, eight hundred and fourteen million

E twelve billion, six hundred and fifty-five million, seven hundred thousand

Empty columns are filled with zeros.

	Billions			Millions			Thousands			Ones		
	H	T	O	H	T	O	H	T	O	H	T	O
A												
B												
C												
D												
E												

1 million has 6 zeros.

1 billion has 9 zeros

- Order the numbers in this table from smallest to largest.

There are 2 trillion bees worldwide.

2 000 000 000 000

2 Write the numeral for:

a 860 million

b 70 million

c 14 billion

d 2 billion

e 308 million

f 100 billion

g the distance to the Sun, 150 million 238 thousand km

h the population of India in 2023, 1 billion 417 million 792 thousand 656

i the distance to the star, Proxima Centauri, 40 billion 208 million km

j the distance light travels in one hour, 1 billion 71 million 360 thousand km

See *Extra Support 21* (Decimals!).

 • *AUSTRALIAN SIGNPOST MATHS 5* • ISBN 9780655708797

1:03 Using large numbers

Round to the nearest 1000.

5300 5400 5500 5600

Rounding to the nearest million

When rounding, look at the next figure.
If it is 5 or more, round up.

71 542 800 rounds to 72 000 000.

13 499 000 rounds to 13 000 000.

Write 3 475 040 in expanded notation.

3 000 000 + 400 000 + 70 000 + 5000 + 40

Complete: 167000 = 150000 + ▭

167 000 = 150 000 + 17 000

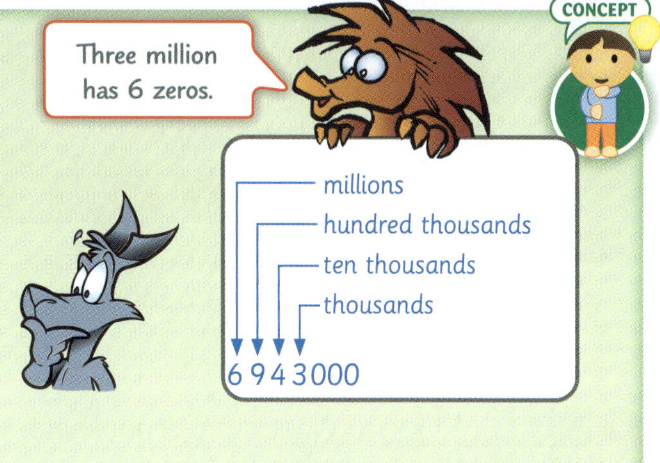

1 Write the numeral for:

a 6 000 000 + 900 000 + 40 000 + 9000 + 200 + 70 + 1

b 10 000 000 + 7 000 000 + 300 000 + 2000 + 600 + 80 + 9

c 80 000 000 + 900 000 + 5000 + 700 + 80 + 4

d 90 000 000 + 9 000 000 + 900 000 + 90 000 + 9000

2 Write the following in expanded notation.

a 3 475 600

b 847 231

c 26 809 050

d 80 520 300

3 Round each to the nearest million.

a 76 397 495

b 32 681 340

c 9 647 680

d 89 504 215

4 Complete:

a 157 350 = 150 000 + ▭

b 266 423 = 250 000 + ▭

This is called partitioning.

5 Use partitioning and doubling to answer these.

a 157 350 + 150 000 = ▭

b 250 000 + 266 423 = ▭

ICT

Find examples of large numbers on the internet.
Investigate the size of large cities.

See *Extra Support 21* (Decimals!).

Fractions

$\frac{7}{10}$ of this group is red.

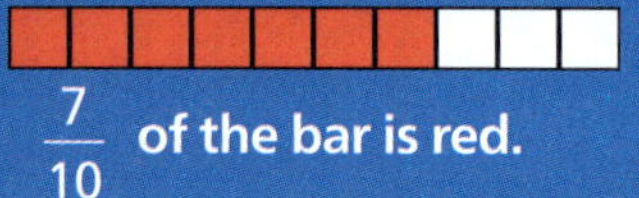

$\frac{7}{10}$ of the bar is red.

If $\frac{7}{10}$ is red, $\frac{3}{10}$ is not red,

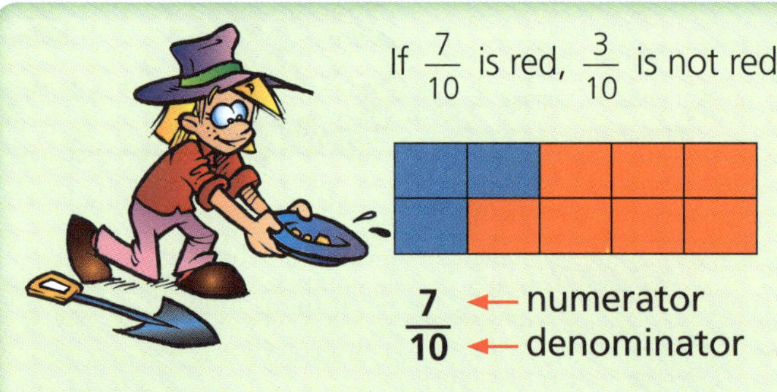

$\frac{7}{10}$ ← numerator, ← denominator

If $\frac{92}{100}$ is blue, $\frac{8}{100}$ is not blue.

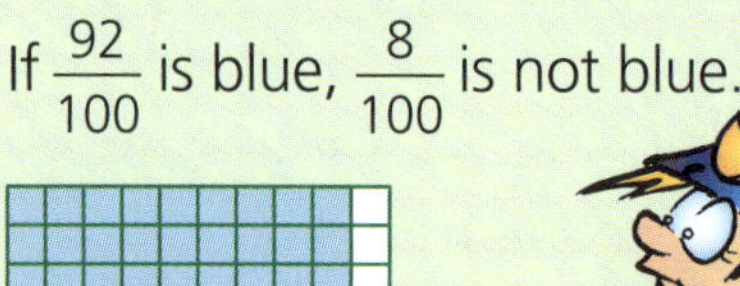

1 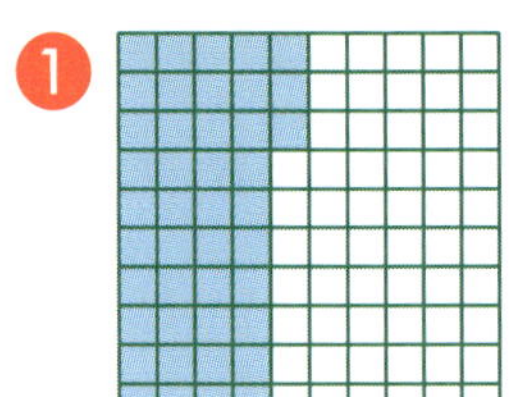

a What is the denominator of $\frac{43}{100}$? ☐

b What is the numerator of $\frac{43}{100}$? ☐

c What fraction is not coloured? ☐

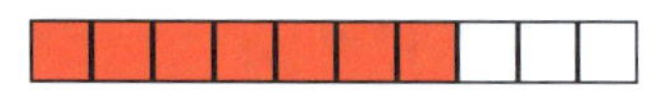

d What is the numerator of $\frac{7}{10}$? ☐

e What is the denominator of $\frac{7}{10}$? ☐

2 Complete.

a $\frac{1}{2}$ and $\frac{1}{2}$ makes ☐ whole.

b $\frac{1}{4}$ and ☐ makes 1 whole.

c ☐ and $\frac{2}{3}$ makes 1 whole.

d $\frac{2}{5}$ and $\frac{3}{5}$ makes ☐ whole.

e $\frac{3}{8}$ and ☐ makes 1 whole.

f ☐ and $\frac{4}{10}$ makes 1 whole.

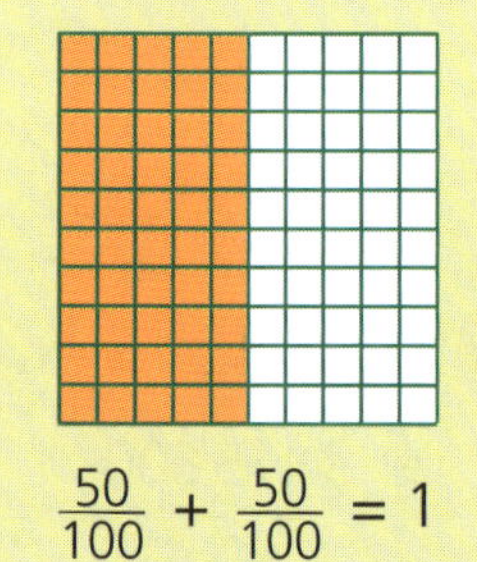

$\frac{50}{100} + \frac{50}{100} = 1$

3 a If $\frac{3}{4}$ of our class come to school by bus, what fraction does not come by bus? ☐

b If $\frac{7}{10}$ of the class is present, what fraction is absent? ☐

c If a water tank is $\frac{5}{8}$ full, what fraction of the water tank is empty? ☐

d $\frac{3}{5}$ of a pizza is left. What fraction has been eaten? ☐

e $\frac{9}{10}$ of my pavers have arrived. What fraction still needs to arrive? ☐

f If $\frac{3}{8}$ of a cake has been eaten, what fraction is left? ☐

4 

a Colour $\frac{1}{4}$ of this bar. What is $\frac{1}{4}$ of 12? ☐

b Colour $\frac{1}{3}$ of this bar. What is $\frac{1}{3}$ of 12? ☐

c Which fraction is larger, $\frac{1}{4}$ or $\frac{1}{3}$? ☐

d Colour $\frac{3}{10}$ of this bar red. Colour $\frac{5}{10}$ of this bar blue.

1:05 The order of unit fractions

1 Use dots to show the fractions on the number line. Use < or > to complete the sentence.

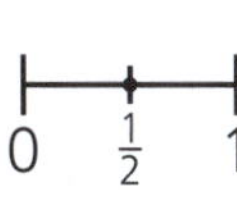

< means *is less than*.
> means *is greater than*.
2 < 7   9 > 4

a $\frac{1}{2}$ and $\frac{1}{4}$

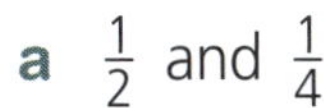
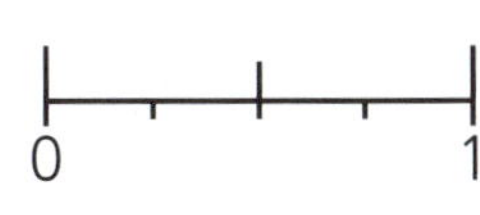

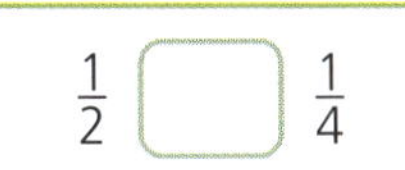
$\frac{1}{2}$ ☐ $\frac{1}{4}$

b $\frac{1}{10}$ and $\frac{1}{3}$

$\frac{1}{10}$ ☐ $\frac{1}{3}$

c $\frac{1}{2}$ and $\frac{1}{8}$

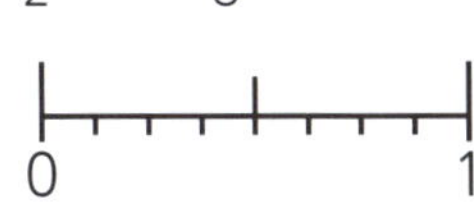

$\frac{1}{2}$ ☐ $\frac{1}{8}$

d $\frac{1}{6}$ and $\frac{1}{3}$

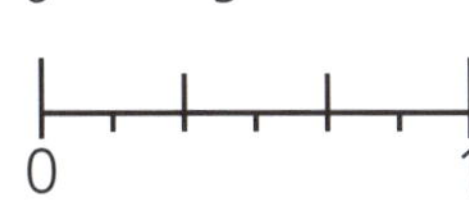

$\frac{1}{6}$ ☐ $\frac{1}{3}$

e $\frac{1}{10}$ and $\frac{1}{5}$

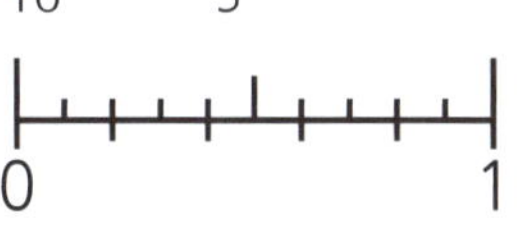

$\frac{1}{10}$ ☐ $\frac{1}{5}$

The order of unit fractions

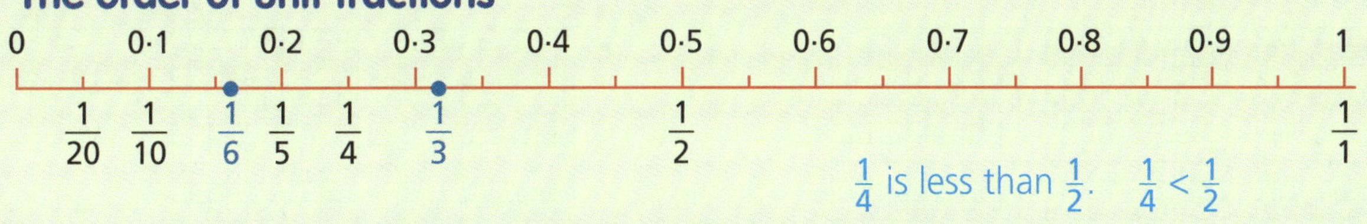

$\frac{1}{4}$ is less than $\frac{1}{2}$. $\frac{1}{4} < \frac{1}{2}$

2 Put each group of fractions in order, from smallest to largest.

a $\frac{1}{2}$, $\frac{1}{5}$, $\frac{1}{4}$ ☐

b $\frac{1}{100}$, $\frac{1}{10}$, $\frac{1}{20}$ ☐

c $\frac{1}{3}$, $\frac{1}{8}$, $\frac{1}{2}$ ☐

d $\frac{1}{4}$, $\frac{1}{8}$, $\frac{1}{2}$, $\frac{1}{12}$ ☐

3 Match each fraction with a part of the circle.

$\frac{1}{6}$

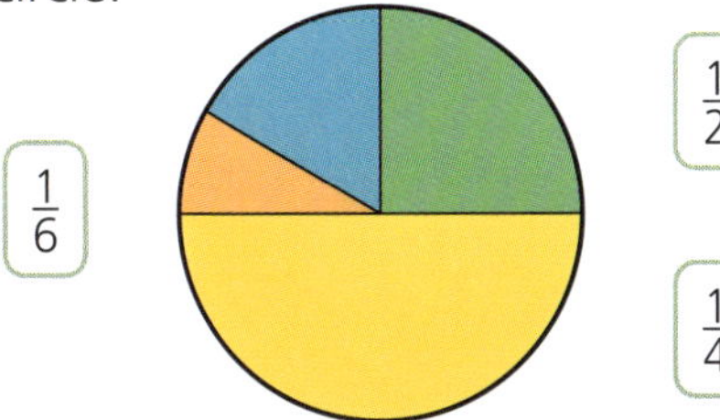

$\frac{1}{2}$

$\frac{1}{4}$

4 Match each fraction with a part of the decagon.

$\frac{1}{2}$

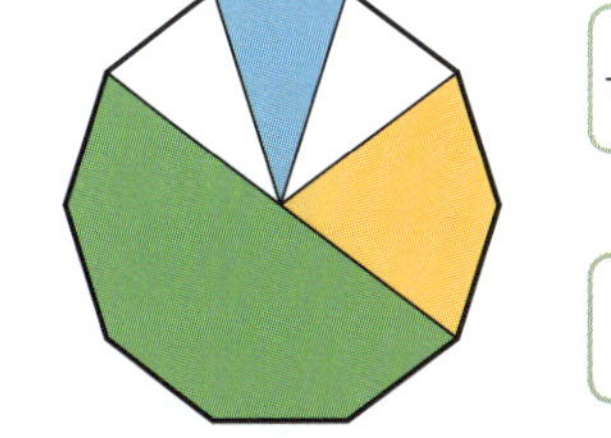

5 For unit fractions, the greater the denominator, the ☐ the fraction.

6 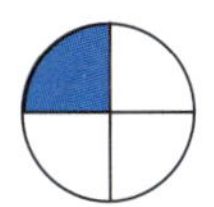 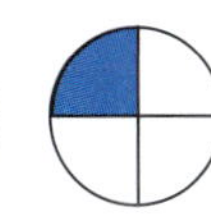 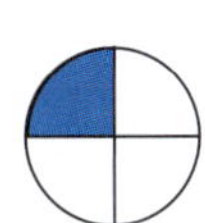 $\frac{1}{4} + \frac{1}{4} + \frac{1}{4} =$ ☐

  ISBN 9780655708797

1:06 Mixed numbers

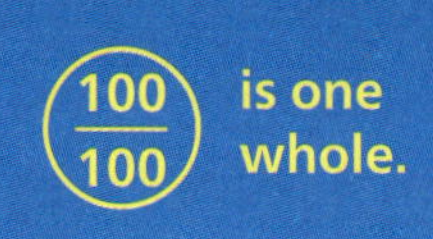

237 hundredths is 2 and 37 hundredths.

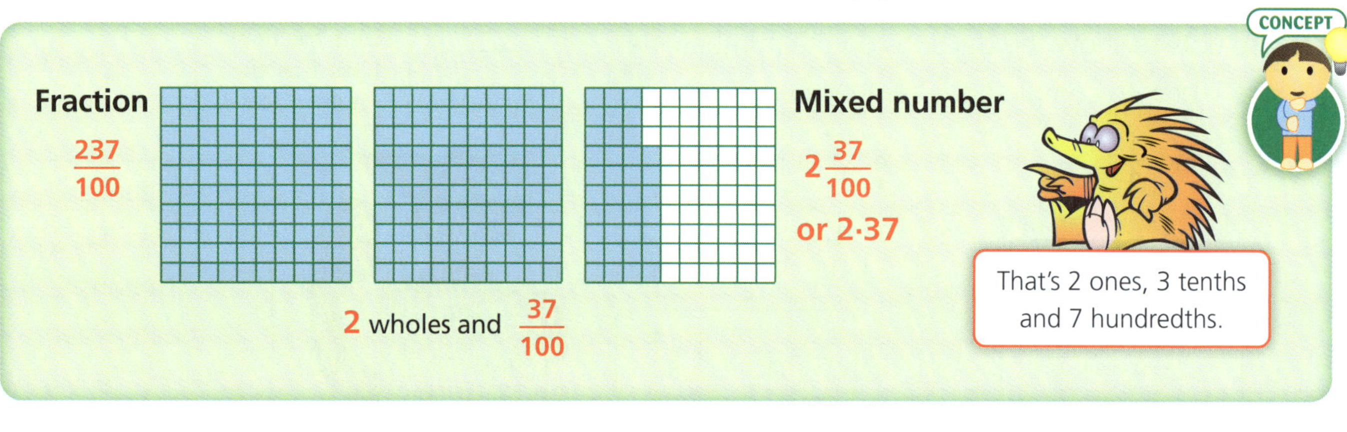

1 Write the fraction and the decimal shown in each hundred square.

a 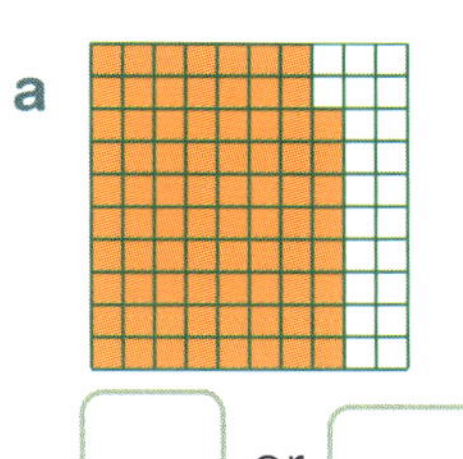 ☐ or ☐

b 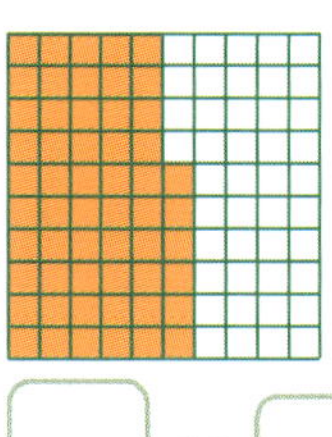 ☐ or ☐

c  ☐ or ☐

d 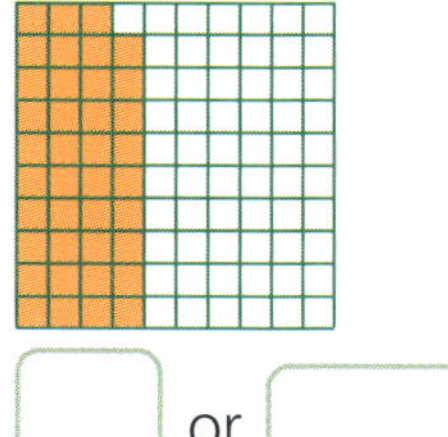 ☐ or ☐

2 Write the mixed number and the decimal for each part.

a 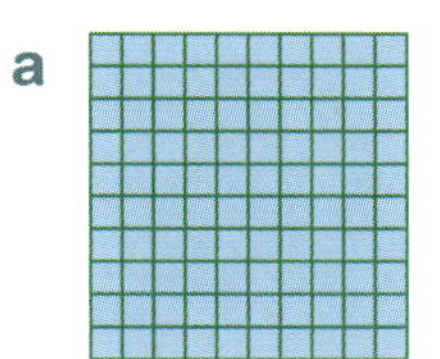 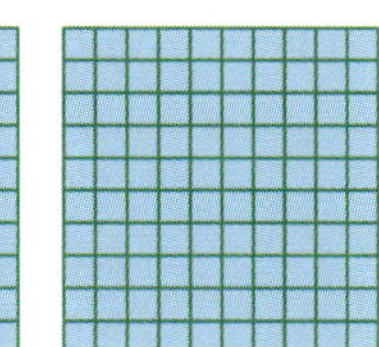 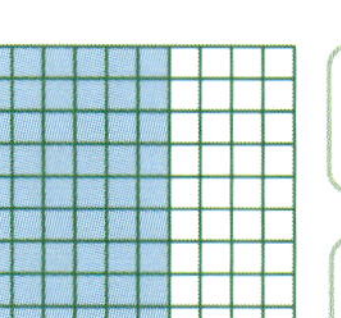 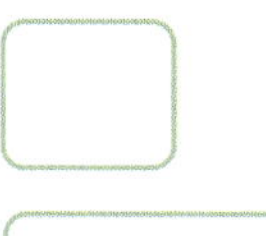 ☐ ☐

b  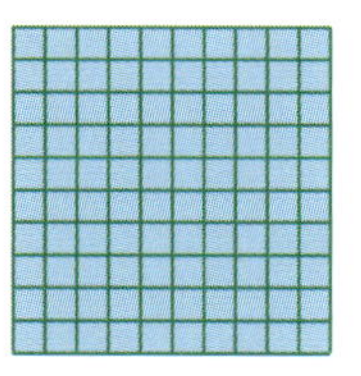 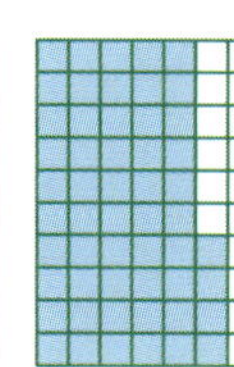  ☐ ☐

c 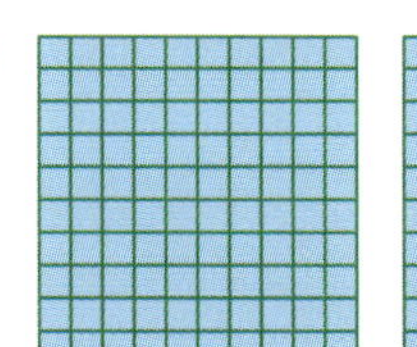 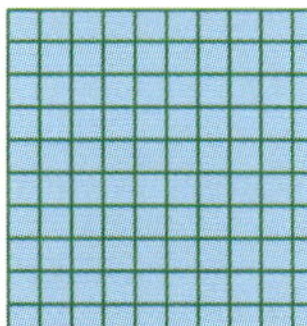 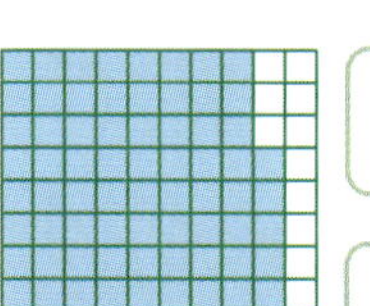 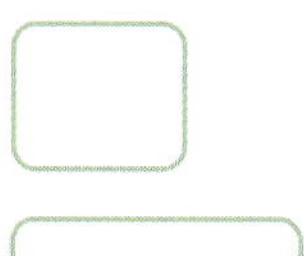 ☐ ☐

d 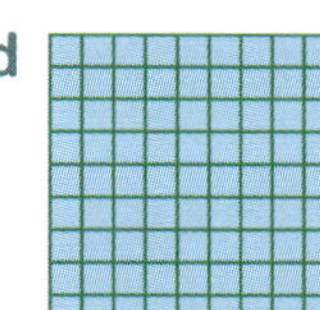 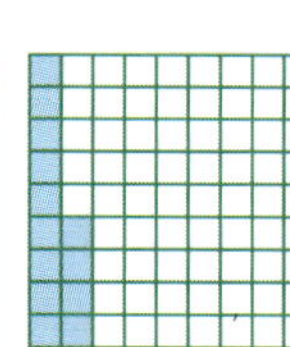 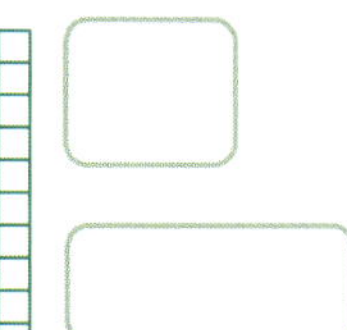 ☐ ☐

3 Write each mixed number as a decimal.

a $2\frac{37}{100}$ ☐ b $1\frac{76}{100}$ ☐ c $6\frac{8}{100}$ ☐

d $9\frac{95}{100}$ ☐ e $7\frac{81}{100}$ ☐ f $5\frac{3}{100}$ ☐

4 Write each decimal as a mixed number.

a 6·25 ☐ b 3·04 ☐ c 9·42 ☐

5 Colour 2·75 of these. Write the mixed number.

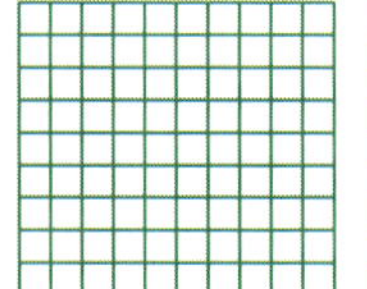 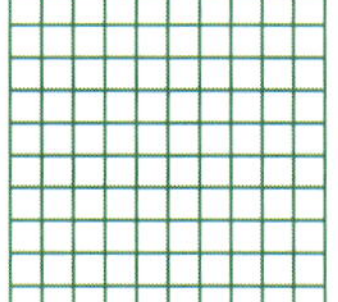 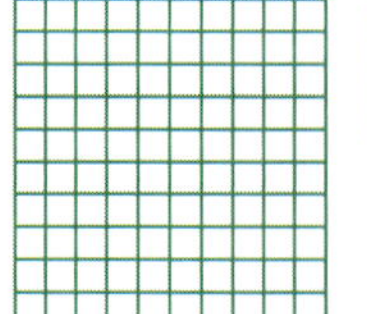  ☐

6 Colour 1·05 of these. Write the mixed number.

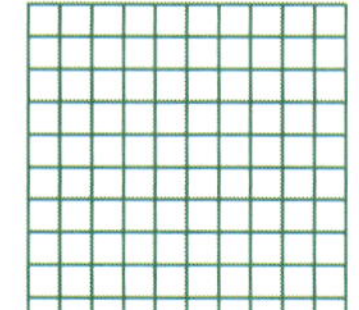 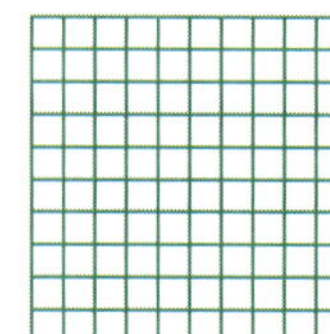  ☐

See *Extra Support 1* (Decimals).

1:07 Tenths and hundredths

0·7	
0·5	

Tick the larger decimal.

1 Use decimals to write:

a 8 tenths ____ b 3 tenths ____ c 9 tenths ____ d 4 tenths ____

e zero point eight ____ f zero point three ____ g one point zero ____

h 1 and 6 tenths ____ i 2 and 5 tenths ____ j 7 and 9 tenths ____

2 Match each fraction with the correct decimal.

a

$\frac{5}{10}$	0·5
$\frac{8}{100}$	0·2
$\frac{2}{10}$	0·08

b

$2\frac{3}{10}$	2·03
$2\frac{93}{100}$	2·93
$2\frac{3}{100}$	2·3

c

$4\frac{6}{10}$	4·5
$4\frac{5}{100}$	4·6
$4\frac{5}{10}$	4·05

3 Write the decimal for:

a $\frac{9}{10}$ ____ b $\frac{5}{10}$ ____ c $\frac{12}{100}$ ____ d $\frac{34}{100}$ ____

e $\frac{4}{10}$ ____ f $1\frac{6}{10}$ ____ g $2\frac{3}{10}$ ____ h $1\frac{12}{100}$ ____

i $3\frac{8}{10}$ ____ j $3\frac{2}{100}$ ____ k $6\frac{9}{10}$ ____ l $2\frac{87}{100}$ ____

4 Complete the number lines.

a

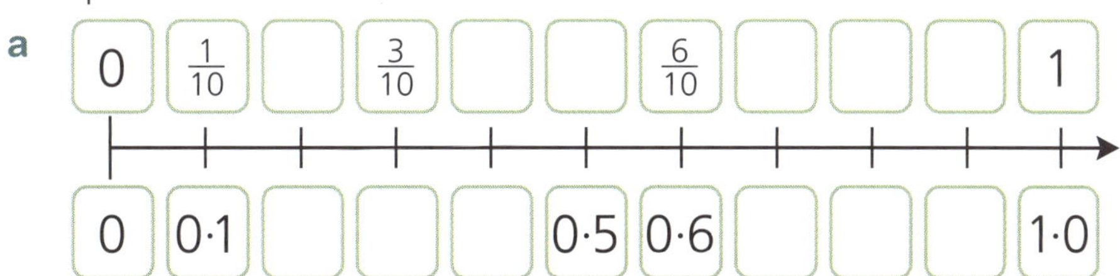

0·1 and $\frac{1}{10}$ occupy the same position on the number line.

b

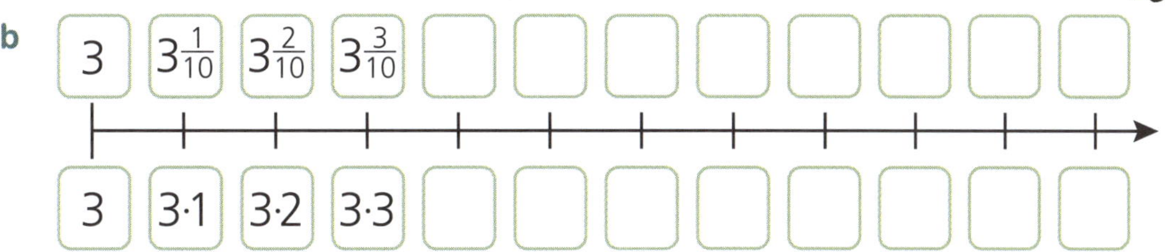

See *Extra Support 2* (Place value in decimals).

1:08 Percentages

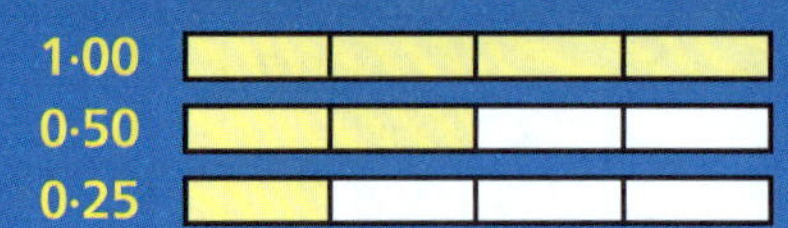

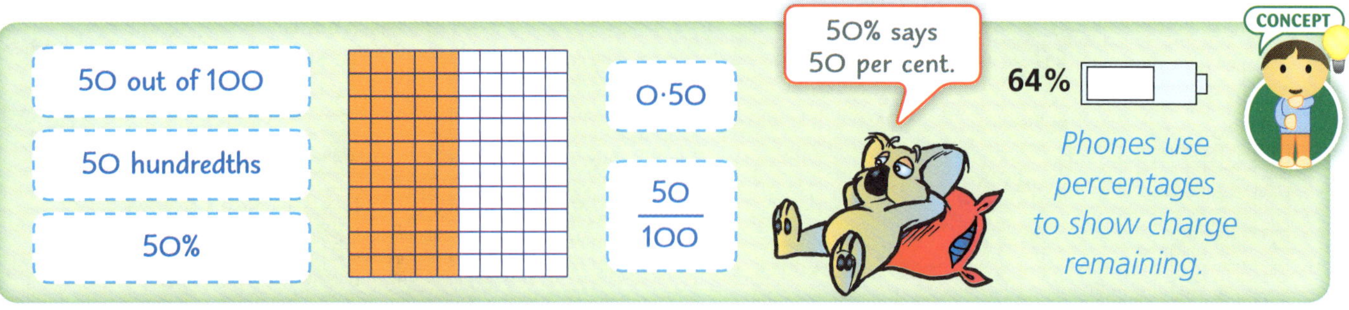

1 What percentage of each square is coloured?

a 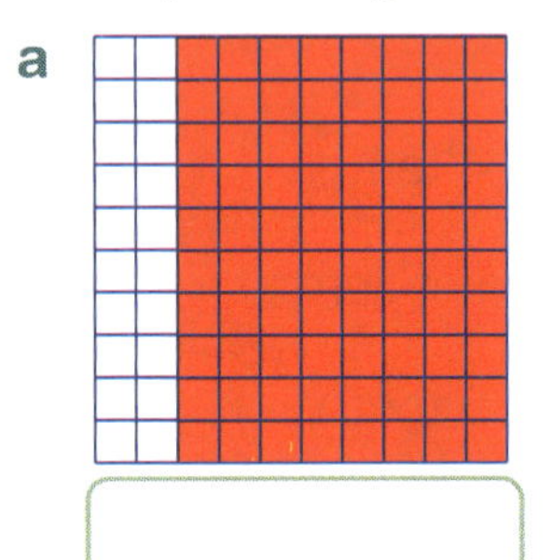

b 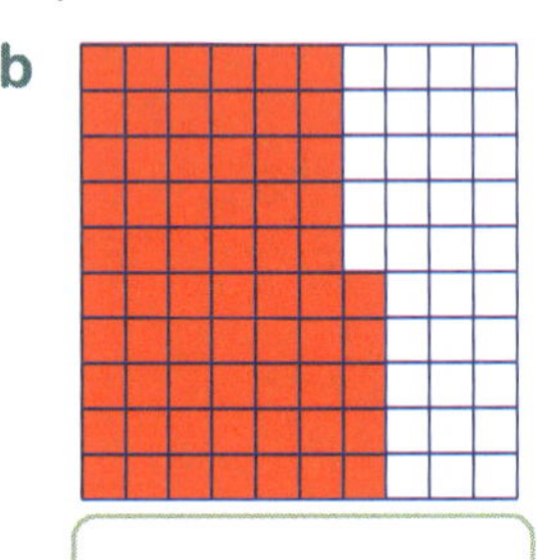

c 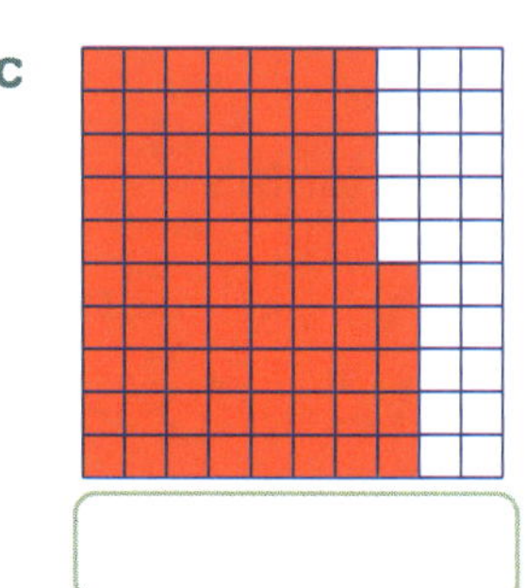

d 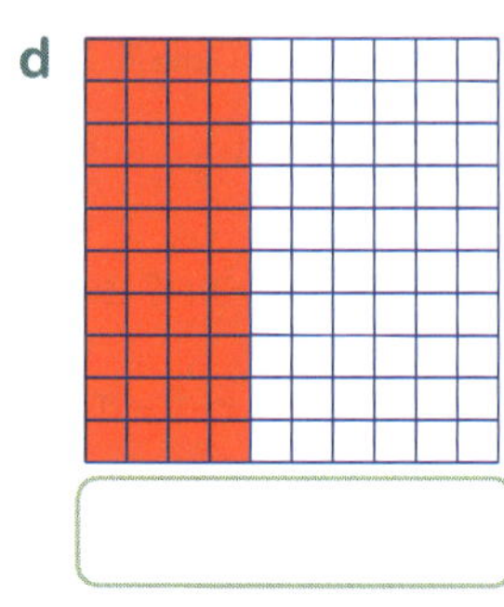

e 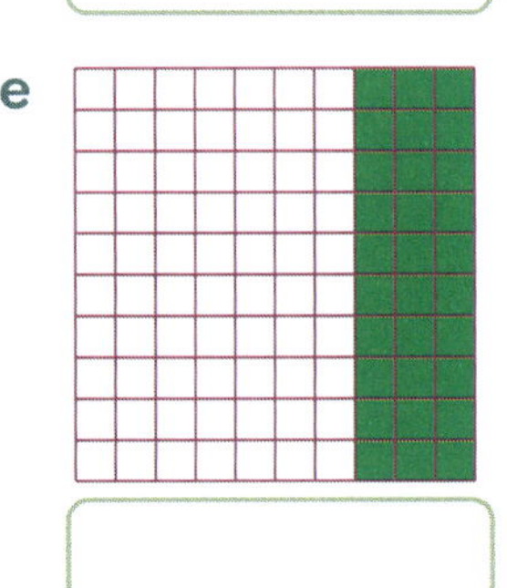

f 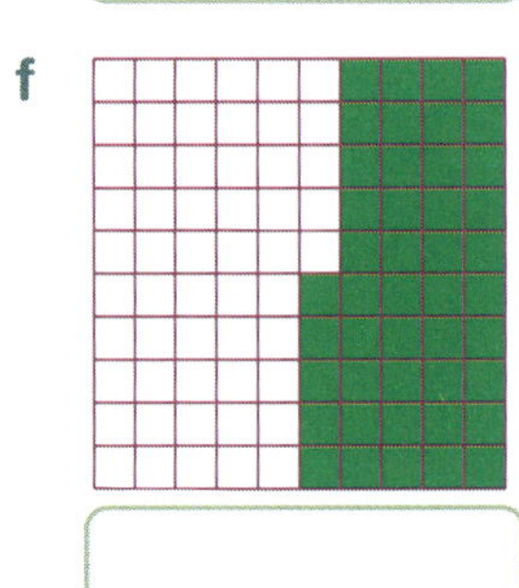

g 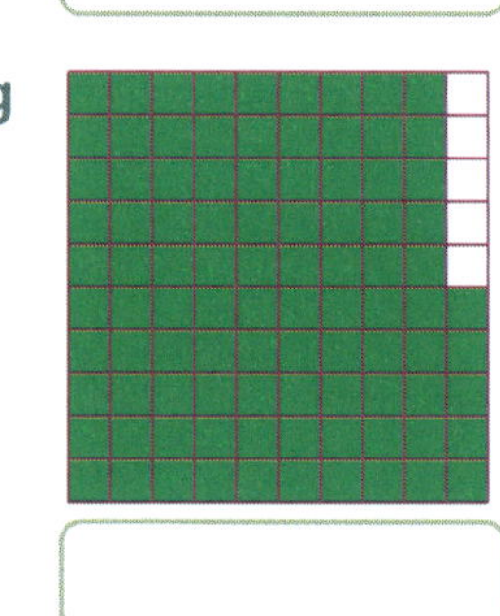

h 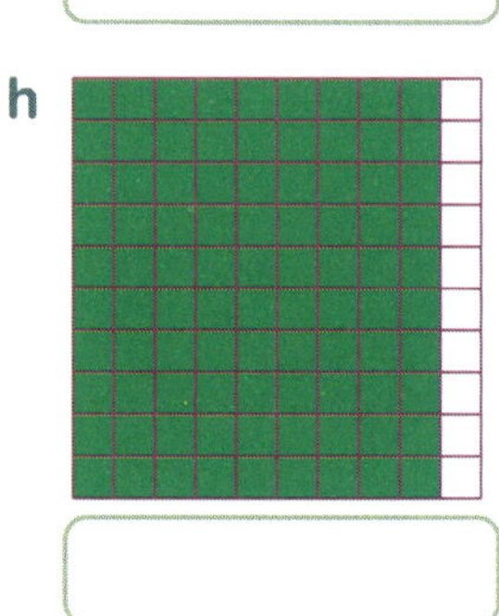

2 What percentage of each square in Question 1 is not coloured?

a ____ b ____ c ____ d ____ e ____ f ____ g ____ h ____

3 Complete these equivalents:

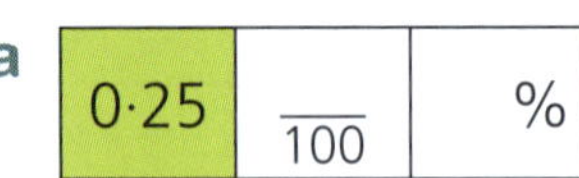

a	0·25	$\frac{}{100}$	%
b	0·65		
c	0·45		
d	0·80		
e	0·50		
f	0·20		
g	0·60		
h	0·35		
i	0·75		
j	0·55		
k	0·95		
l	0·40		

Percentages in the environment

- Collect examples of percentages from newspapers and food packages.
- Discuss different ways in which percentages are used.

See *Extra Support 2* (Place value in decimals).

1:09 Using percentages

One whole is 100%
Three quarters is ☐ %

1 For each square, colour the percentage shown.

a 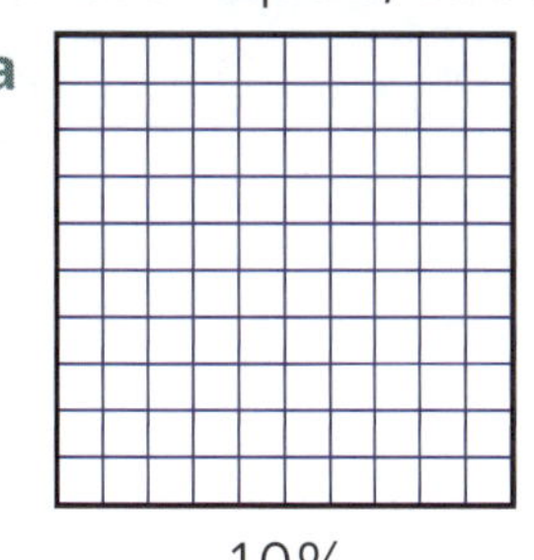 10%

b 25%

c 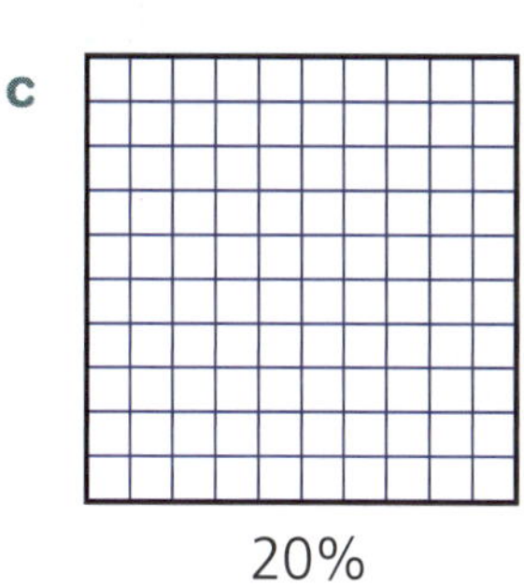 20%

d 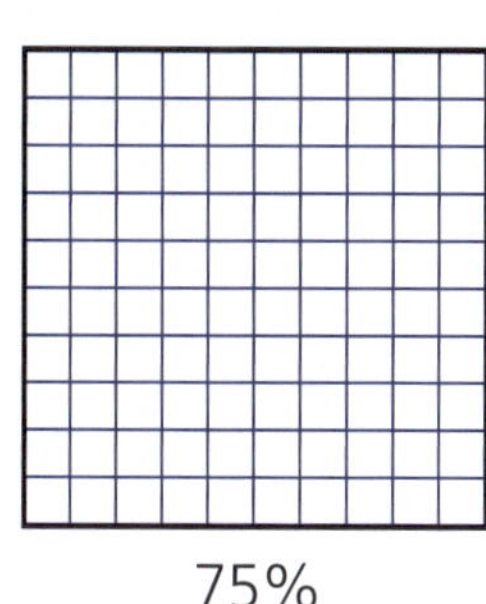 75%

e 50%

f 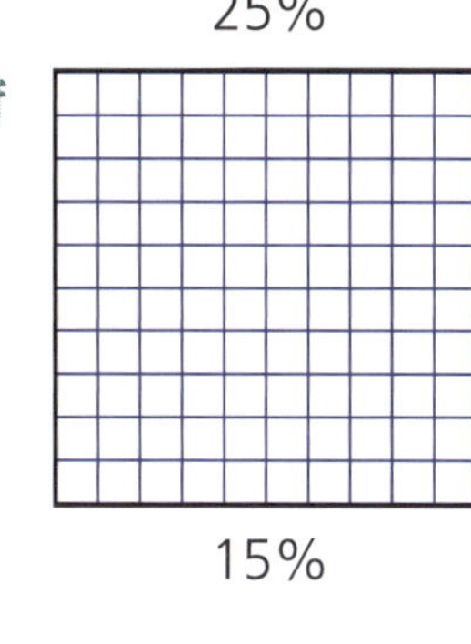 15%

g 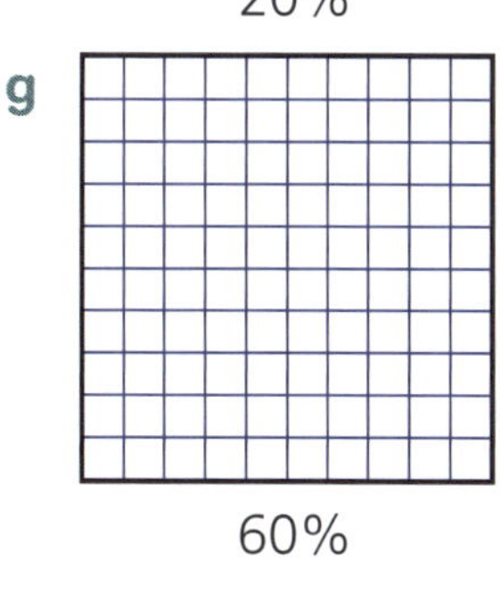 60%

h 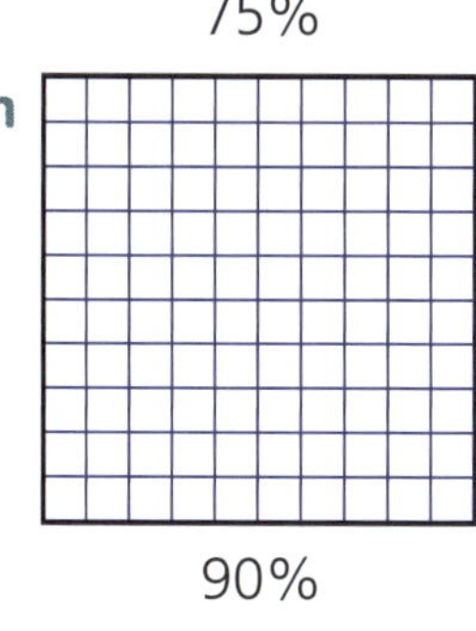 90%

2 What percentage of each square in Question 1 should be not coloured?

a  b  c 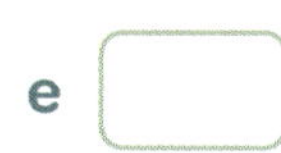 d  e ☐ f ☐ g ☐ h ☐

3 Complete the following:

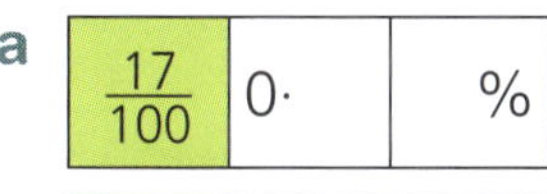
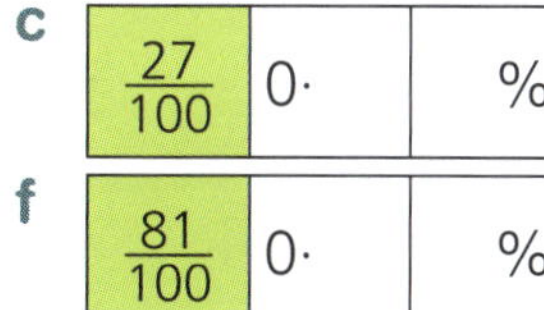

	Fraction	Decimal	Percentage
a	$\frac{17}{100}$	0·	%
b	$\frac{76}{100}$	0·	%
c	$\frac{27}{100}$	0·	%
d	$\frac{49}{100}$	0·	%
e	$\frac{98}{100}$	0·	%
f	$\frac{81}{100}$	0·	%
g	$\frac{31}{100}$	0·	%
h	$\frac{12}{100}$	0·	%
i	$\frac{34}{100}$	0·	%
j	$\frac{28}{100}$	0·	%
k	$\frac{63}{100}$	0·	%
l	$\frac{94}{100}$	0·	%

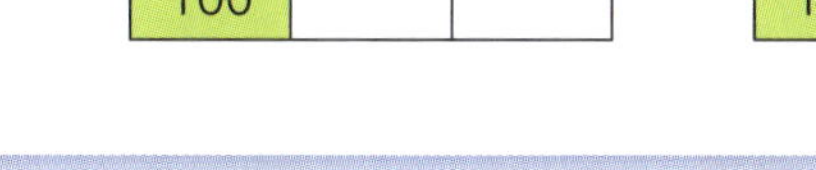

Converting fractions to decimals

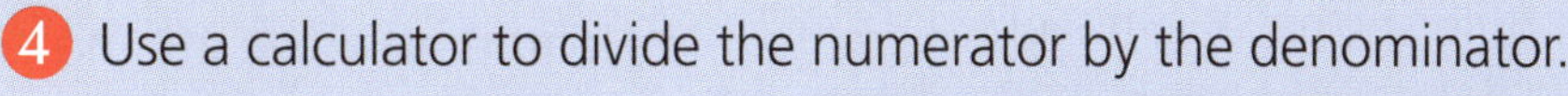

4 Use a calculator to divide the numerator by the denominator.

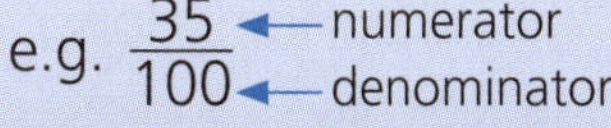

e.g. $\frac{35}{100}$ ← numerator, ← denominator is        0·35

Now calculate:

a $\frac{65}{100}$  b $\frac{15}{100}$ ☐ c $\frac{95}{100}$  d $\frac{45}{100}$  e $\frac{75}{100}$ 

f $\frac{25}{100}$ ☐ g $\frac{5}{100}$  h $\frac{60}{100}$  i $\frac{80}{100}$ ☐ j $\frac{40}{100}$ 

k $\frac{10}{100}$ ☐ l $\frac{37}{100}$  m $\frac{91}{100}$  n $\frac{20}{100}$  o $\frac{100}{100}$ 

1:10 Fractions

$\frac{2}{3}$ can mean 2 of 3 equal parts of a whole
2 of every 3 in a collection
2 wholes shared by three.

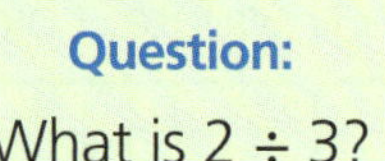

Diane, Lyn and Omar shared two chocolate bars fairly as they played cards. What fraction of a whole chocolate bar did Omar eat? ☐

Question: What is 2 ÷ 3?

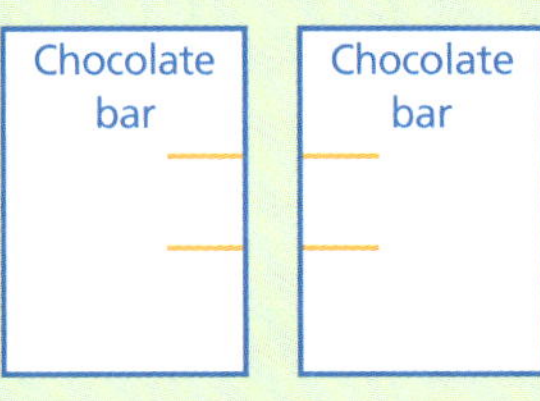

Omar ate one third of each bar, so he ate two thirds of a bar.

$2 \div 3 = \frac{2}{3}$

A fraction can be used as a division statement .

1 Students shared two chocolate bars fairly. How much chocolate would each eat if there were:

a 6 students? ☐ **b** 4 students? ☐ **c** 2 students? ☐ **d** 8 students? ☐

2 Write each of these division questions as a fraction.

a 3 ÷ 4 ☐ **b** 5 ÷ 8 ☐ **c** 1 ÷ 2 ☐ **d** 4 ÷ 5 ☐

3 Write each fraction as a division.

a $\frac{1}{2}$ ☐ **b** $\frac{3}{4}$ ☐ **c** $\frac{2}{5}$ ☐ **d** $\frac{7}{8}$ ☐

CONCEPT

- Alfie is ☐ of the way to the finish.
- Rona is ☐ of the way to the finish.

Start — 0 — $\frac{1}{3}$ — $\frac{2}{3}$ — 1 — Finish

- Niki is about ☐ of the way up the ladder.

A fraction can be used to show part of a distance.

4 **a** What fraction of the race does Rona still have to travel? ☐

b What fraction of the race does Alfie still have to travel? ☐

5 Heather ate $\frac{1}{4}$ of a cake and Tom ate $\frac{1}{2}$ of another cake. Heather said she ate more cake than Tom. How can this be so? Discuss.

$\frac{50}{100} = \frac{1}{2} = 0{\cdot}50$, $0{\cdot}5$ or 50%

$\frac{25}{100} = \frac{1}{4} = 0{\cdot}25$ or 25%

$\frac{75}{100} = \frac{3}{4} = 0{\cdot}75$ or 75%

$\frac{1}{3} = 33\frac{1}{3}\%$

 • *AUSTRALIAN SIGNPOST MATHS 5* • ISBN 9780655708797

1:11 Improper fractions, mixed numbers

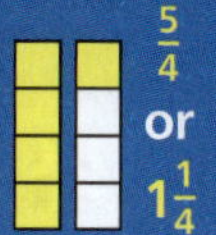

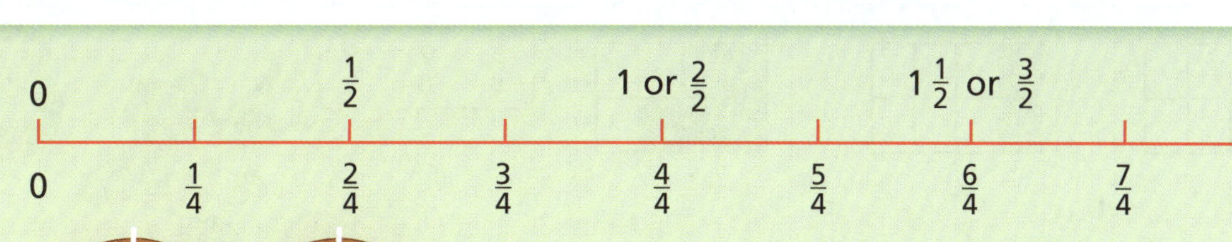

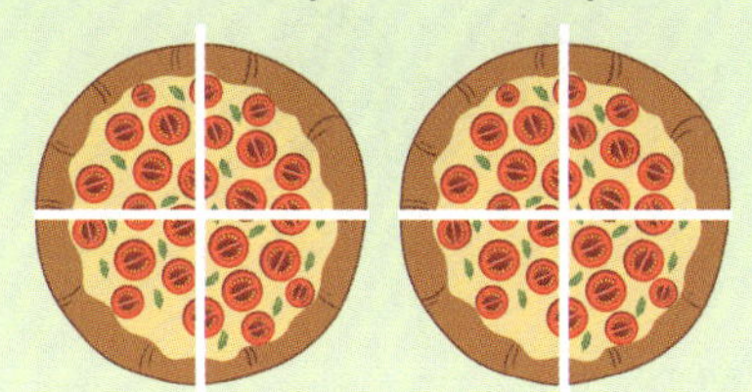

$\frac{5}{4}$ means 5 quarters and is the same as $1\frac{1}{4}$.

$\frac{3}{2}$ means 3 halves and is the same as $1\frac{1}{2}$.

When the number has a whole number part and a fraction part, it is a mixed number. $3\frac{1}{2}$

When the numerator is larger than the denominator, it is an improper fraction. $\frac{7}{2}$

- To change a mixed number into an improper fraction, multiply the whole number by the denominator of the fraction part, then add the fractions.

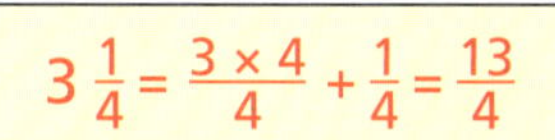

$3\frac{1}{4} = \frac{3 \times 4}{4} + \frac{1}{4} = \frac{13}{4}$

$2\frac{3}{10} = \frac{2 \times 10}{10} + \frac{3}{10} = \frac{23}{10}$

1 Change the mixed number into an improper fraction.

a $4\frac{1}{4}$ ☐ **b** $1\frac{1}{4}$ ☐ **c** $2\frac{1}{2}$ ☐ **d** $3\frac{2}{5}$ ☐

e $1\frac{4}{5}$ ☐ **f** $2\frac{3}{4}$ ☐ **g** $2\frac{2}{4}$ ☐ **h** $2\frac{2}{3}$ ☐

i $1\frac{7}{10}$ ☐ **j** $3\frac{2}{10}$ ☐ **k** $2\frac{5}{10}$ ☐ **l** $4\frac{8}{10}$ ☐

Multiply then add.

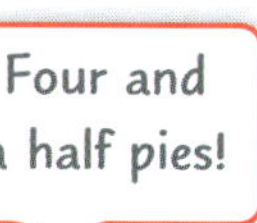

- To change an improper fraction into a mixed number, divide the bottom into the top.

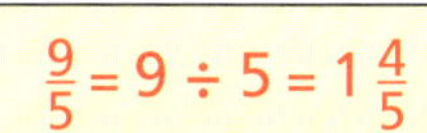

$\frac{9}{5} = 9 \div 5 = 1\frac{4}{5}$

$\frac{9}{4} = 9 \div 4 = 2\frac{1}{4}$

$\frac{9}{2} = 9 \div 2 = 4\frac{1}{2}$

2 Change the improper fraction into a mixed number.

a $\frac{9}{4}$  **b** $\frac{7}{3}$ ☐ **c** $\frac{5}{2}$ ☐ **d** $\frac{7}{4}$ ☐

e $\frac{11}{3}$ ☐ **f** $\frac{10}{4}$ ☐ **g** $\frac{14}{5}$ ☐ **h** $\frac{17}{2}$ ☐

i $\frac{17}{10}$ ☐ **j** $\frac{41}{10}$ ☐ **k** $\frac{36}{10}$  **l** $\frac{55}{10}$ ☐

Divide bottom into top.

1:12 Addition of fractions

When we add or subtract, the denominators must be the same.

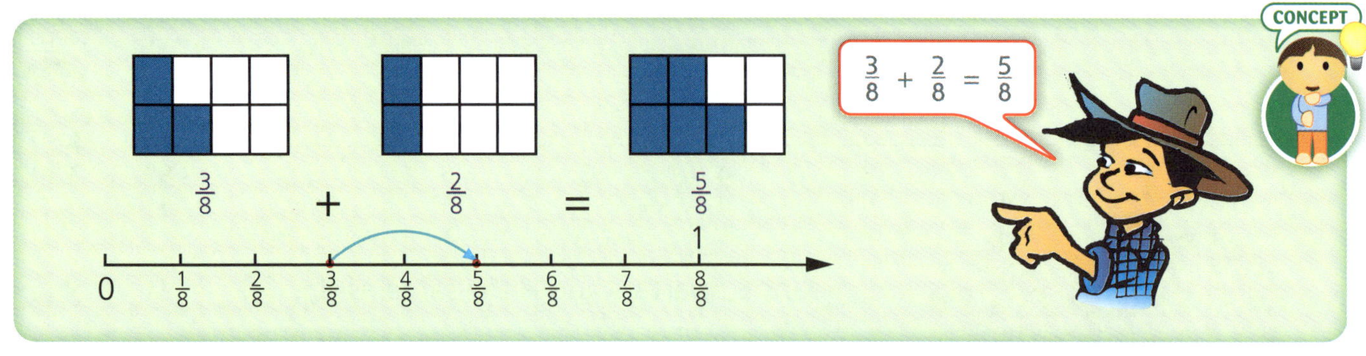

1 Add these fractions. Colour part of the last grid to match your answer.

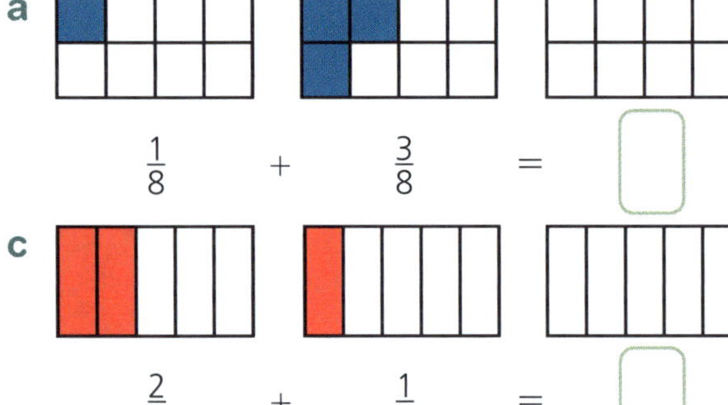

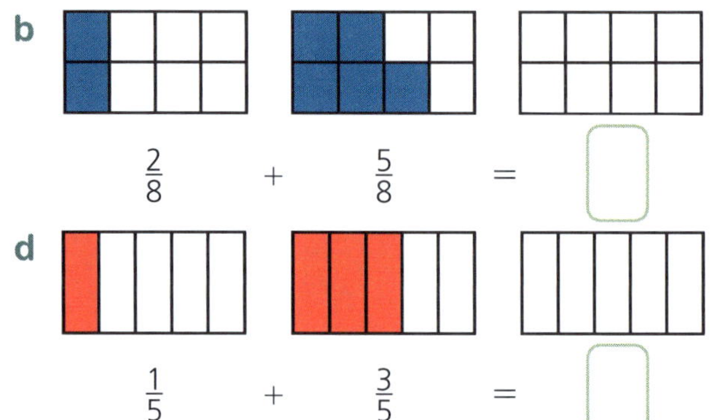

a $\frac{1}{8} + \frac{3}{8} =$ ☐

b $\frac{2}{8} + \frac{5}{8} =$ ☐

c $\frac{2}{5} + \frac{1}{5} =$ ☐

d $\frac{1}{5} + \frac{3}{5} =$ ☐

2 Use the fraction card to find the answers. (Remember: $\frac{4}{10} + \frac{6}{10} = \frac{6}{10} + \frac{4}{10}$)

a $\frac{1}{10} + \frac{5}{10} =$ ☐ **b** $\frac{3}{10} + \frac{4}{10} =$ ☐ **c** $\frac{2}{10} + \frac{7}{10} =$ ☐ **d** $\frac{6}{10} + \frac{3}{10} =$ ☐

e $\frac{5}{10} + \frac{2}{10} =$ ☐ **f** $\frac{4}{10} + \frac{5}{10} =$ ☐ **g** $\frac{7}{10} + \frac{1}{10} =$ ☐ **h** $\frac{1}{10} + \frac{8}{10} =$ ☐

3 Use the fraction cards to find the answers.

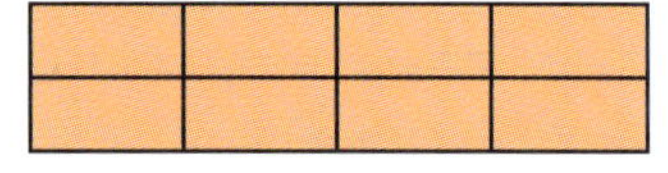

a $\frac{2}{8} + \frac{6}{8} =$ ☐ **b** $\frac{7}{8} + \frac{4}{8} =$ ☐

c $\frac{5}{8} + \frac{5}{8} =$ ☐ **d** $\frac{3}{8} + \frac{6}{8} =$ ☐

For < and >, the arrow points to the smaller number, $10 < 30$ and $100 > 40$.

< looks like an L so it means *less than*.

4 Answer **true** or **false**.

a $\frac{6}{8} > \frac{3}{8}$ ☐ **b** $\frac{7}{8} < \frac{6}{8}$ ☐ **c** $\frac{8}{8} < \frac{5}{8}$ ☐ **d** $\frac{5}{8} > \frac{9}{8}$ ☐

e $\frac{9}{10} > \frac{6}{10}$ ☐ **f** $\frac{5}{10} < \frac{9}{10}$ ☐ **g** $\frac{13}{10} > \frac{11}{10}$ ☐ **h** $\frac{8}{10} > \frac{12}{10}$ ☐

5 **a** Sharon ate $\frac{3}{12}$ of a block of chocolate and Franco ate $\frac{5}{12}$ of the same block. How much of the block did they eat? ☐

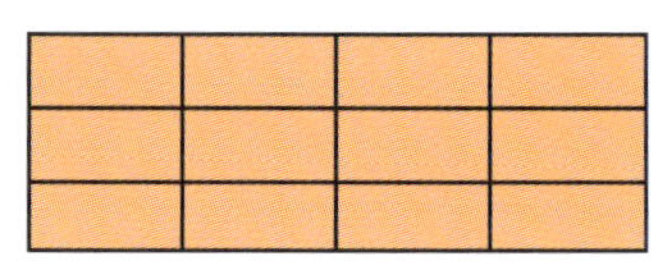

b Ron used $\frac{4}{10}$ of the paper. Eva used $\frac{5}{10}$. How much is left? ☐

 AUSTRALIAN SIGNPOST MATHS 5 • ISBN 9780655708797

1:13 Subtraction of fractions

The denominators must be the same.

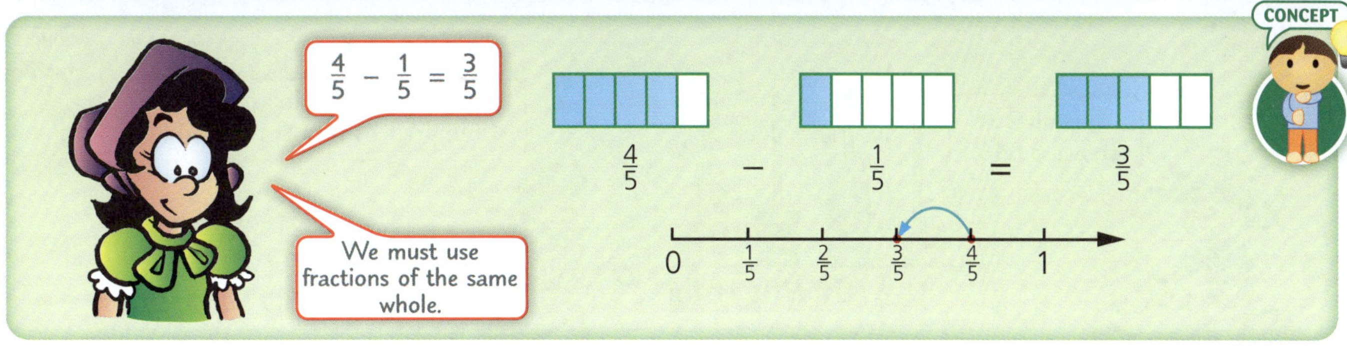

1 Subtract these fractions. Colour part of the grid to match your answer.

a 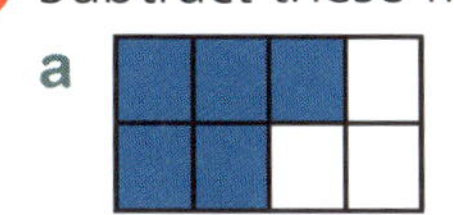 $\frac{5}{8} - \frac{1}{8} =$ ☐

b 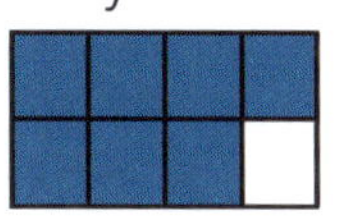 $\frac{7}{8} - \frac{2}{8} =$ ☐

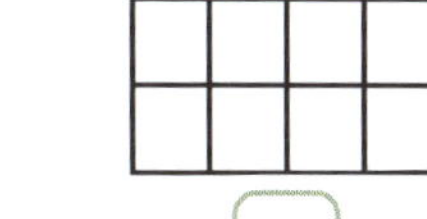

c 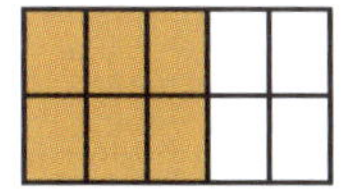 $\frac{6}{10} - \frac{3}{10} =$ ☐

d  $\frac{9}{10} - \frac{4}{10} =$ ☐

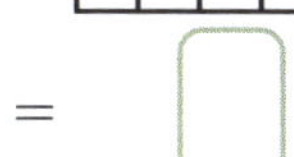

e 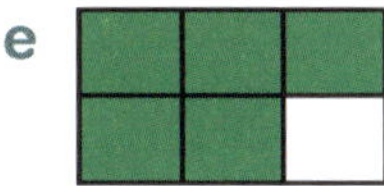 $\frac{5}{6} - \frac{2}{6} =$ ☐

f  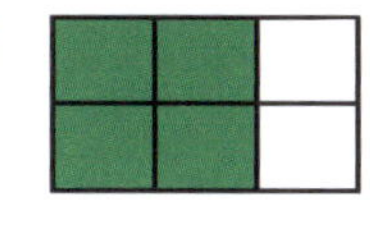 $\frac{4}{6} - \frac{1}{6} =$ ☐

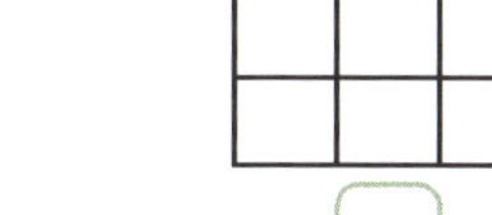

2 Use the fraction card to find the answers.

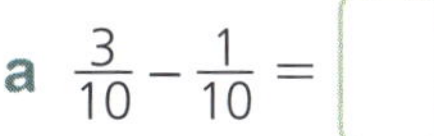

a $\frac{3}{10} - \frac{1}{10} =$ ☐ **b** $\frac{5}{10} - \frac{3}{10} =$ ☐ **c** $\frac{7}{10} - \frac{2}{10} =$ ☐ **d** $\frac{9}{10} - \frac{5}{10} =$ ☐

e $\frac{8}{10} - \frac{7}{10} =$ ☐ **f** $\frac{6}{10} - \frac{1}{10} =$ ☐ **g** $\frac{4}{10} - \frac{3}{10} =$ ☐ **h** $\frac{7}{10} - \frac{4}{10} =$ ☐

3 Use the fraction card to find the answers.

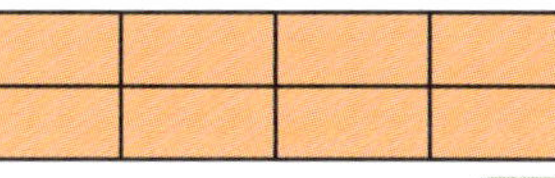

a $\frac{7}{8} - \frac{3}{8} =$ ☐ **b** $\frac{5}{8} - \frac{3}{8} =$ ☐ **c** $\frac{6}{8} - \frac{2}{8} =$ ☐ **d** $\frac{4}{8} - \frac{1}{8} =$ ☐

e Tim ate $\frac{1}{8}$ of a block of chocolate. How much was left? ☐

f Mum gave me $\frac{3}{5}$ of her money. What fraction did she keep? ☐

4 Answer **true** or **false**.

a $\frac{2}{8} < \frac{5}{8}$ ☐ **b** $\frac{6}{8} < \frac{5}{8}$ ☐ **c** $\frac{1}{8} < \frac{3}{8}$ ☐ **d** $\frac{7}{8} > \frac{4}{8}$ ☐

See *Extra Support 4* (+ and – of fractions).

1:14 Place value to thousandths

0·1 is 1 tenth
0·10 is 10 hundredths
0·100 is 100 thousandths

These are the same.

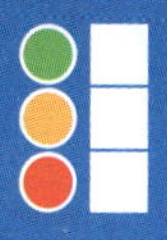

1 Write the numeral for the number shown on each abacus.

a 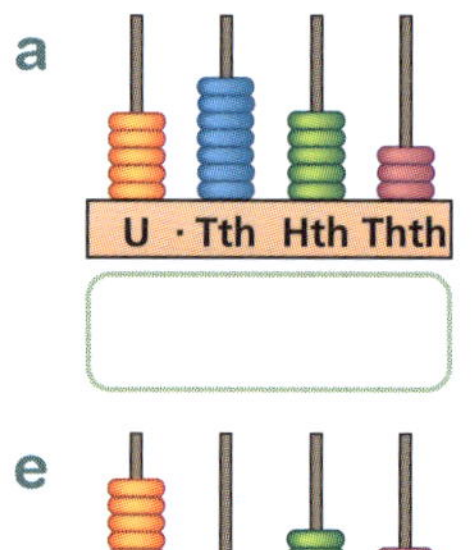

b 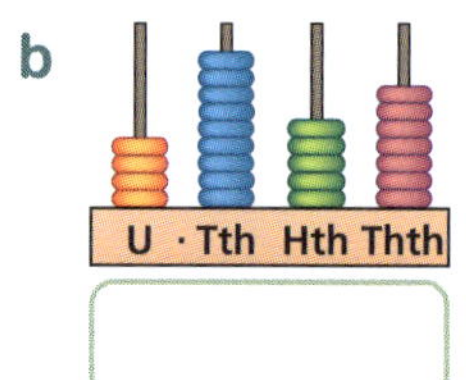

c 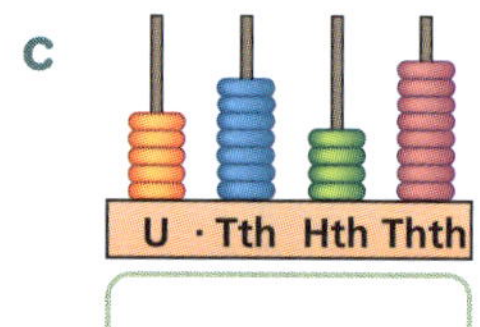

d 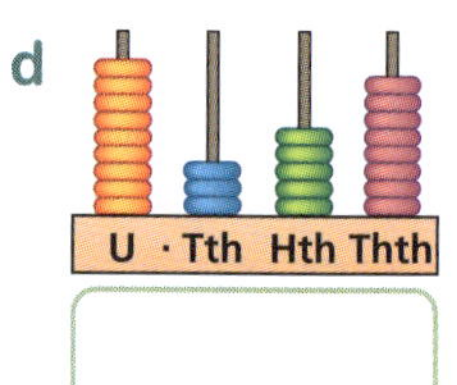

e

f 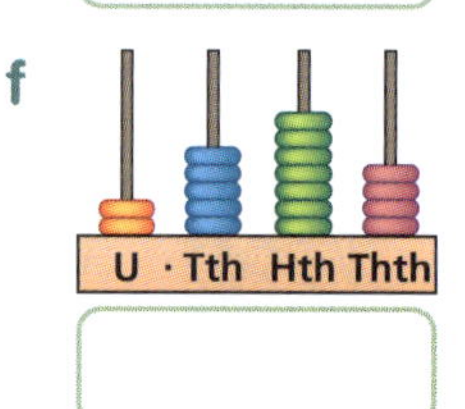

Ones		Tenths	Hundredths	Thousandths
0	·	0	1	0
			10 thousandths = 1 hundredth	
0	·	1	0	
		10 hundredths = 1 tenth		
1	·	0		
10 tenths = 1 whole				

2 Write each number on the place-value chart.

a three point one nine seven
b five point six three eight
c nine point two four nine
d six point five four eight
e eight point three five two
f two point seven one nine

Units	·	10ths	100ths	1000ths
	·			
	·			
	·			
	·			
	·			
	·			

CONCEPT

ten 1000ths = one 100th	$\frac{10}{1000} = \frac{1}{100}$
ten 100ths = one 10th	$\frac{10}{100} = \frac{1}{10}$
ten 10ths = one unit	$\frac{10}{10} = 1$

Ten of one column gives one in the column on the left.

Make the largest number

FUN SPOT

- Each player, in turn, rolls the dice and records the number in the column of their choice in the place-value card.
- The player rolls three more dice to fill the place-value card.
- The player with the largest 4-digit number wins the game.

$6{\cdot}421 = 6\frac{421}{1000}$

Units		Tenths	Hundredths	Thousandths
6	·	4	2	1

See Extra Support 5 (Place value to thousandths).

 ISBN 9780655708797

1:15 Place value and decimals

Decimals are really important.

CONCEPT

		whole number		fraction part			
larger place value ← … …	hundreds	tens	ones	tenths	hundredths	thousandths	→ smaller place value … …

hundreds	tens	ones	·	tenths	hundredths	thousandths	Meaning
		0	·	3			3 tenths
		2	·	7			2 and 7 tenths
		0	·	9	4		94 hundredths
		0	·	0	8	5	85 thousandths
8	0	8	·	6			808 and 6 tenths
	6	8	·	3	7	5	68 and 375 thousandths
1	7	8	·	8	4		178 and 84 hundredths
	$7	0	·	9	5		70 dollars and 95 cents

↑ decimal point

- 68·375 is read sixty-eight point three seven five.
- The decimal point separates the whole number part from the fraction part.

1 Write the decimal for:

a 8 tenths ______ **b** 1 tenth ______ **c** 5 tenths ______

d 7 and 5 tenths ______ **e** 4 and 1 tenth ______ **f** 9 and 3 tenths ______

g 64 hundredths ______ **h** 33 hundredths ______ **i** 25 hundredths ______

j 805 thousandths ______ **k** 65 thousandths ______

l 215 and 5 tenths ______ **m** 90 and 8 tenths ______

n 11 and 125 thousandths ______ **o** 33 and 333 thousandths ______

p 296 and 48 hundredths ______ **q** 507 and 5 hundredths ______

r 90 dollars and 15 cents ______ **s** 971 dollars and 6 cents ______

2 **a** Put blue dots on the number line, to show the positions of 5·6, 5·8, 5·9, 5·3, 5·1, 5·4.

b Circle the decimals in part **a** that are closer to 6 than to 5.

c Put red dots on the number line, to show the positions of 5·24, 5·27, 5·29, 5·21, 5·26.

d Circle the decimals in part **c** that are closer to 5·2 than to 5·3.

Number line: 5, 5·05, 5·1, 5·15, 5·2, 5·25, 5·3, 5·35, 5·4, 5·45, 5·5, 5·55, 5·6, 5·65, 5·7, 5·75, 5·8, 5·85, 5·9, 5·95, 6

See *Extra Support 3* (Reading and writing decimals).

1:16 Addition and subtraction of fractions

$\frac{5}{4} + \frac{5}{4}$

$\frac{6}{10} + \frac{6}{10}$

CONCEPT

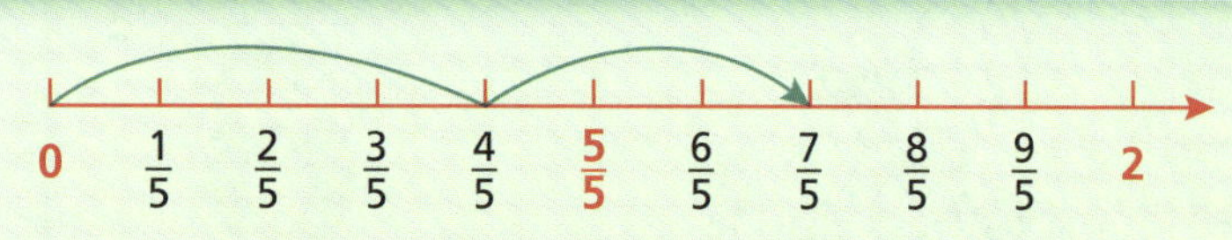

◄ $\frac{4}{5} + \frac{3}{5} = \frac{7}{5}$

0 $\frac{2}{10}$ $\frac{4}{10}$ $\frac{6}{10}$ $\frac{8}{10}$ 1 $\frac{12}{10}$ $\frac{14}{10}$ $\frac{16}{10}$ $\frac{18}{10}$ 2

◄ $\frac{16}{10} - \frac{8}{10} = \frac{8}{10}$

1 Write the improper fraction for the mixed numbers.

a $1\frac{2}{8} = \square$ **b** $1\frac{4}{5} = \square$ **c** $1\frac{3}{4} = \square$

d $3\frac{1}{2} = \square$ **e** $2\frac{3}{5} = \square$ **f** $1\frac{9}{10} = \square$

2 Write the mixed number for the improper fractions.

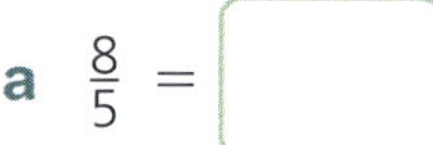

a $\frac{8}{5} = \square$ **b** $\frac{4}{3} = \square$

c $\frac{9}{4} = \square$ **d** $\frac{9}{8} = \square$

Note: $\frac{6}{4} = 1\frac{2}{4}$, $\frac{7}{4} = 1\frac{3}{4}$

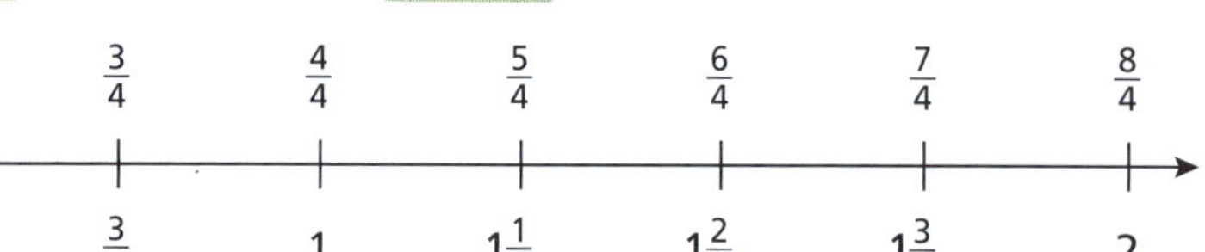

Improper fraction: $\frac{11}{8}$

Mixed number: $1\frac{3}{8}$

3 Add these fractions.

a $\frac{1}{8} + \frac{3}{8} = \square$ **b** $\frac{1}{4} + \frac{2}{4} = \square$ **c** $\frac{2}{10} + \frac{7}{10} = \square$ **d** $\frac{1}{5} + \frac{3}{5} = \square$

e $\frac{3}{5} + \frac{3}{5} = \square$ **f** $\frac{4}{5} + \frac{4}{5} = \square$ **g** $\frac{2}{5} + \frac{4}{5} = \square$ **h** $\frac{5}{5} + \frac{4}{5} = \square$

i $\frac{4}{10} + \frac{6}{10} = \square$ **j** $\frac{8}{10} + \frac{8}{10} = \square$ **k** $\frac{6}{10} + \frac{4}{10} = \square$ **l** $\frac{8}{10} + \frac{5}{10} = \square$

m $\frac{3}{8} + \frac{1}{8} + \frac{2}{8} = \square$ **n** $\frac{1}{5} + \frac{1}{5} + \frac{2}{5} = \square$ **o** $\frac{1}{10} + \frac{2}{10} + \frac{2}{10} = \square$ **p** $\frac{3}{10} + \frac{2}{10} + \frac{4}{10} = \square$

4 Subtract these fractions.

a $\frac{3}{4} - \frac{1}{4} = \square$ **b** $\frac{4}{5} - \frac{2}{5} = \square$ **c** $\frac{5}{10} - \frac{2}{10} = \square$ **d** $\frac{5}{8} - \frac{3}{8} = \square$

e $\frac{3}{5} - \frac{1}{5} = \square$ **f** $\frac{9}{8} - \frac{3}{8} = \square$ **g** $\frac{4}{3} - \frac{2}{3} = \square$ **h** $\frac{7}{4} - \frac{6}{4} = \square$

i $\frac{11}{10} - \frac{6}{10} = \square$ **j** $\frac{12}{10} - \frac{3}{10} = \square$ **k** $\frac{14}{10} - \frac{9}{10} = \square$ **l** $\frac{13}{10} - \frac{7}{10} = \square$

1:17 Equivalent fractions

$\frac{1}{3} = \frac{3}{9}$

These two fractions are at the same point on the number line.

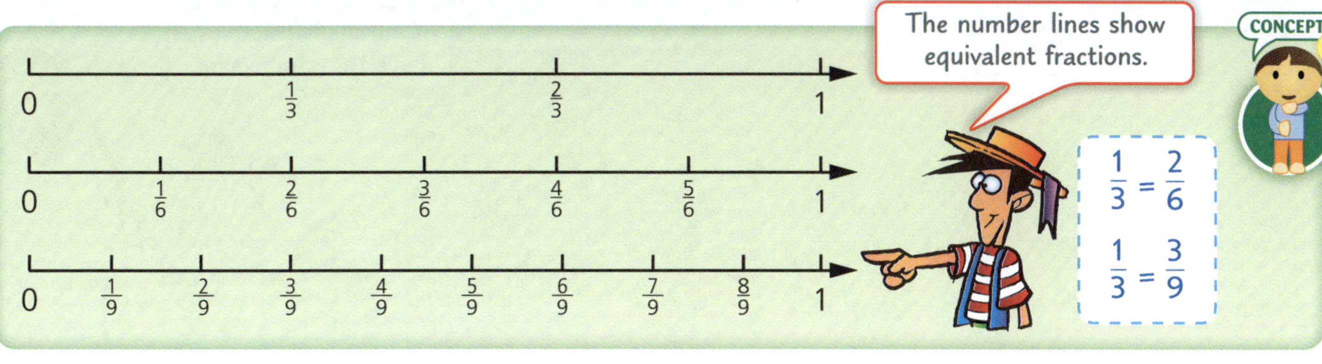

1 Use the number lines to show an equivalent fraction for:

a $\frac{1}{3}$ ☐ **b** $\frac{9}{9}$ ☐ **c** $\frac{3}{9}$ ☐ **d** $\frac{2}{3}$ ☐

e $\frac{2}{6}$ ☐ **f** $\frac{4}{6}$ ☐ **g** $\frac{6}{6}$ ☐ **h** $\frac{6}{9}$ ☐

2 Use the number lines above to answer **true** or **false**.

a $\frac{1}{6} = \frac{2}{9}$ ☐ **b** $\frac{2}{3} = \frac{6}{9}$ ☐ **c** $\frac{2}{3} = \frac{4}{6}$ ☐ **d** $\frac{6}{9} = \frac{4}{6}$ ☐

e $\frac{3}{3} = \frac{9}{9}$ ☐ **f** $\frac{3}{6} = \frac{5}{9}$ ☐ **g** $\frac{1}{3} = \frac{3}{9}$ ☐ **h** $\frac{5}{6} = \frac{2}{3}$ ☐

3 Complete the number lines.

a

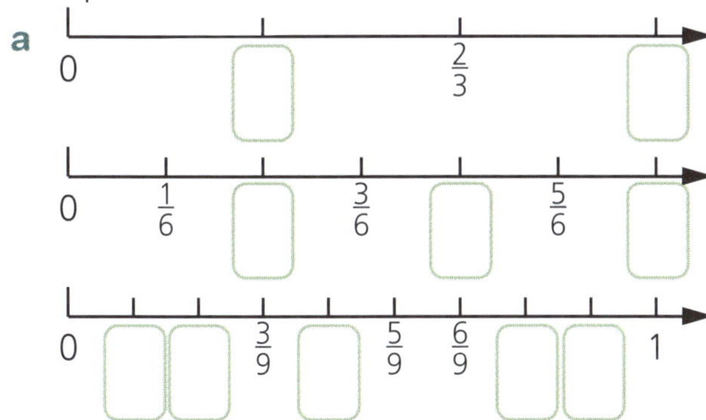

b

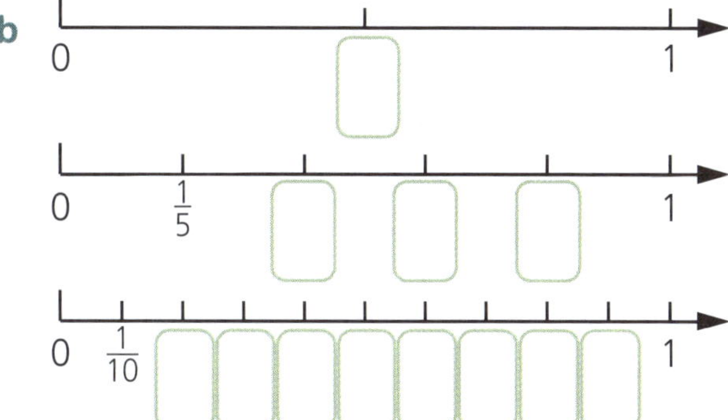

4 Use the number lines above to answer **true** or **false**.

a $\frac{1}{5} = \frac{2}{10}$ ☐ **b** $\frac{6}{9} = \frac{4}{6}$ ☐ **c** $\frac{1}{3} = \frac{1}{6}$ ☐ **d** $\frac{2}{5} = \frac{4}{10}$ ☐

e $\frac{2}{3} = \frac{4}{6}$ ☐ **f** $\frac{3}{6} = \frac{6}{9}$ ☐ **g** $\frac{4}{5} = \frac{9}{10}$ ☐ **h** $\frac{3}{5} = \frac{8}{10}$ ☐

i $\frac{1}{5} = \frac{1}{10}$ ☐ **j** $\frac{2}{3} = \frac{6}{9}$ ☐ **k** $\frac{1}{2} = \frac{5}{10}$ ☐ **l** $\frac{5}{6} = \frac{8}{9}$ ☐

5 Use the number lines above to write an equivalent fraction for:

a $\frac{1}{3}$ ☐ **b** $\frac{4}{6}$ ☐ **c** $\frac{1}{2}$ ☐ **d** $\frac{6}{9}$ ☐

e $\frac{8}{10}$ ☐ **f** $\frac{3}{9}$ ☐ **g** $\frac{2}{3}$ ☐ **h** $\frac{1}{5}$ ☐

1:18 Equivalent fractions

$\frac{1}{2} = \frac{2}{4} = \frac{4}{8}$

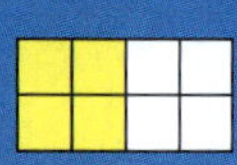

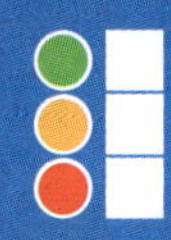

CONCEPT

1									
$\frac{1}{2}$	$\frac{1}{2}$								
$\frac{1}{4}$	$\frac{1}{4}$	$\frac{1}{4}$	$\frac{1}{4}$						
$\frac{1}{8}$	$\frac{1}{8}$	$\frac{1}{8}$	$\frac{1}{8}$	$\frac{1}{8}$	$\frac{1}{8}$	$\frac{1}{8}$	$\frac{1}{8}$		
$\frac{1}{5}$	$\frac{1}{5}$	$\frac{1}{5}$	$\frac{1}{5}$	$\frac{1}{5}$					
$\frac{1}{10}$	$\frac{1}{10}$	$\frac{1}{10}$	$\frac{1}{10}$	$\frac{1}{10}$	$\frac{1}{10}$	$\frac{1}{10}$	$\frac{1}{10}$	$\frac{1}{10}$	$\frac{1}{10}$

We can make equivalent fractions by multiplying the numerator and denominator by the same number.

$\frac{1}{2} \frac{(\times 5)}{(\times 5)} = \frac{5}{10}$

1 Complete these to make equivalent fractions.

a $\frac{1}{4} = \frac{\square}{8}$ **b** $\frac{2}{5} = \frac{\square}{10}$ **c** $\frac{3}{4} = \frac{\square}{8}$ **d** $\frac{1}{5} = \frac{\square}{10}$ **e** $\frac{1}{2} = \frac{\square}{4}$

f $\frac{3}{5} = \frac{\square}{10}$ **g** $\frac{2}{4} = \frac{\square}{8}$ **h** $\frac{4}{5} = \frac{\square}{10}$ **i** $\frac{1}{2} = \frac{\square}{8}$ **j** $1 = \frac{\square}{10}$

2 Complete these to make equivalent fractions.

a $\frac{1}{4} \frac{(\times 2)}{(\times 2)} = \frac{\square}{\square}$ **b** $\frac{1}{2} \frac{(\times 4)}{(\times 4)} = \frac{\square}{\square}$ **c** $\frac{1}{5} \frac{(\times 2)}{(\times 2)} = \frac{\square}{\square}$ **d** $\frac{3}{5} \frac{(\times 2)}{(\times 2)} = \frac{\square}{\square}$

e $\frac{3}{4} \frac{(\times 2)}{(\times 2)} = \frac{\square}{\square}$ **f** $\frac{4}{5} \frac{(\times 2)}{(\times 2)} = \frac{\square}{\square}$ **g** $\frac{1}{2} \frac{(\times 2)}{(\times 2)} = \frac{\square}{\square}$ **h** $\frac{2}{5} \frac{(\times 2)}{(\times 2)} = \frac{\square}{\square}$

i $\frac{1}{3} \frac{(\times 2)}{(\times 2)} = \frac{\square}{\square}$ **j** $\frac{1}{6} \frac{(\times 2)}{(\times 2)} = \frac{\square}{\square}$ **k** $\frac{2}{3} \frac{(\times 4)}{(\times 4)} = \frac{\square}{\square}$ **l** $\frac{4}{6} \frac{(\times 2)}{(\times 2)} = \frac{\square}{\square}$

3 Complete these to make equivalent fractions.

a $\frac{1}{3} \frac{(\times \quad)}{(\times \quad)} = \frac{4}{\square}$ **b** $\frac{3}{6} \frac{(\times \quad)}{(\times \quad)} = \frac{6}{\square}$ **c** $\frac{2}{3} \frac{(\times \quad)}{(\times \quad)} = \frac{8}{\square}$

d $\frac{2}{6} \frac{(\times \quad)}{(\times \quad)} = \frac{4}{\square}$ **e** $\frac{4}{10} \frac{(\times \quad)}{(\times \quad)} = \frac{8}{\square}$ **f** $\frac{3}{5} \frac{(\times \quad)}{(\times \quad)} = \frac{9}{\square}$

g $\frac{3}{5} \frac{(\times \quad)}{(\times \quad)} = \frac{6}{\square}$ **h** $\frac{1}{4} \frac{(\times \quad)}{(\times \quad)} = \frac{5}{\square}$ **i** $\frac{2}{7} \frac{(\times \quad)}{(\times \quad)} = \frac{6}{\square}$

j $\frac{7}{5} \frac{(\times \quad)}{(\times \quad)} = \frac{\square}{10}$ **k** $\frac{11}{3} \frac{(\times \quad)}{(\times \quad)} = \frac{\square}{9}$ **l** $\frac{5}{2} \frac{(\times \quad)}{(\times \quad)} = \frac{\square}{8}$

 ISBN 9780655708797

1:19 Equivalent fractions

$\frac{3}{5} = \frac{6}{10}$ Equivalent fractions have the same value.

CONCEPT

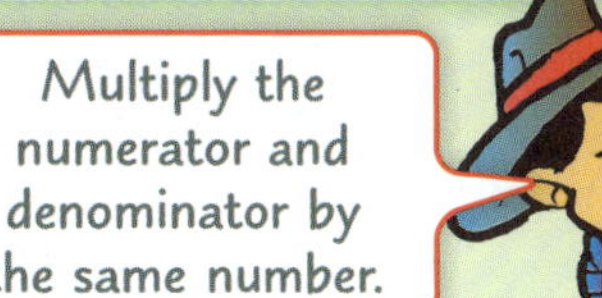

$\frac{1}{2}\,\frac{(\times 5)}{(\times 5)} = \frac{5}{10}$

Multiplying by $\frac{5}{5}$ is the same as multiplying by 1.

1 Write an equivalent fraction for each of these.

a $\frac{1}{3}\,\frac{(\times 2)}{(\times 2)} = \frac{\square}{\square}$ **b** $\frac{1}{4}\,\frac{(\times 3)}{(\times 3)} = \frac{\square}{\square}$ **c** $\frac{1}{2}\,\frac{(\times 5)}{(\times 5)} = \frac{\square}{\square}$ **d** $\frac{1}{5}\,\frac{(\times 3)}{(\times 3)} = \frac{\square}{\square}$

e $\frac{2}{5}\,\frac{(\times 3)}{(\times 3)} = \frac{\square}{\square}$ **f** $\frac{2}{3}\,\frac{(\times 4)}{(\times 4)} = \frac{\square}{\square}$ **g** $\frac{3}{4}\,\frac{(\times 2)}{(\times 2)} = \frac{\square}{\square}$ **h** $\frac{3}{5}\,\frac{(\times 3)}{(\times 3)} = \frac{\square}{\square}$

2 Complete these.

a $\frac{1}{2}\,\frac{(\times 4)}{(\times 4)} = \frac{\square}{\square}$ **b** $\frac{1}{5}\,\frac{(\times 2)}{(\times 2)} = \frac{\square}{\square}$ **c** $\frac{1}{3}\,\frac{(\times 3)}{(\times 3)} = \frac{\square}{\square}$ **d** $\frac{1}{6}\,\frac{(\times 2)}{(\times 2)} = \frac{\square}{\square}$

e $\frac{2}{3}\,\frac{(\times 2)}{(\times 2)} = \frac{\square}{\square}$ **f** $\frac{1}{2}\,\frac{(\times 3)}{(\times 3)} = \frac{\square}{\square}$ **g** $\frac{1}{5}\,\frac{(\times 4)}{(\times 4)} = \frac{\square}{\square}$ **h** $\frac{1}{3}\,\frac{(\times 4)}{(\times 4)} = \frac{\square}{\square}$

3 Multiply both the numerator and the denominator by 2.

a $\frac{1}{4} = \frac{\square}{\square}$ **b** $\frac{1}{6} = \frac{\square}{\square}$ **c** $\frac{1}{2} = \frac{\square}{\square}$ **d** $\frac{1}{5} = \frac{\square}{\square}$ **e** $\frac{1}{3} = \frac{\square}{\square}$

4 Multiply both the numerator and the denominator by 3.

a $\frac{1}{6} = \frac{\square}{\square}$ **b** $\frac{2}{3} = \frac{\square}{\square}$ **c** $\frac{1}{3} = \frac{\square}{\square}$ **d** $\frac{3}{4} = \frac{\square}{\square}$ **e** $\frac{4}{5} = \frac{\square}{\square}$

5 Multiply both the numerator and the denominator by 4.

a $\frac{1}{4} = \frac{\square}{\square}$ **b** $\frac{1}{5} = \frac{\square}{\square}$ **c** $\frac{1}{3} = \frac{\square}{\square}$ **d** $\frac{3}{4} = \frac{\square}{\square}$ **e** $\frac{2}{3} = \frac{\square}{\square}$

6 What number has been used to multiply the numerator and denominator in each pair of equivalent fractions below?

a $\frac{1}{2} = \frac{4}{8}$ ☐ **b** $\frac{1}{4} = \frac{3}{12}$ ☐ **c** $\frac{1}{3} = \frac{3}{9}$ ☐ **d** $\frac{1}{6} = \frac{2}{12}$ ☐ **e** $\frac{2}{3} = \frac{4}{6}$ ☐

f $\frac{3}{4} = \frac{6}{8}$ ☐ **g** $\frac{1}{5} = \frac{2}{10}$ ☐ **h** $\frac{3}{5} = \frac{6}{10}$ ☐ **i** $\frac{1}{2} = \frac{5}{10}$ ☐ **j** $\frac{1}{3} = \frac{4}{12}$ ☐

7 Complete these equivalent fractions.

a $\frac{1}{2} = \frac{\square}{4} = \frac{\square}{6} = \frac{\square}{8} = \frac{\square}{10} = \frac{\square}{12}$ **b** $\frac{1}{3} = \frac{\square}{6} = \frac{\square}{9} = \frac{\square}{12} = \frac{\square}{15} = \frac{\square}{18}$

1:20 Comparing decimals

$4.333 = $4.33 to the nearest cent.
$4.666 = $4.67 to the nearest cent.

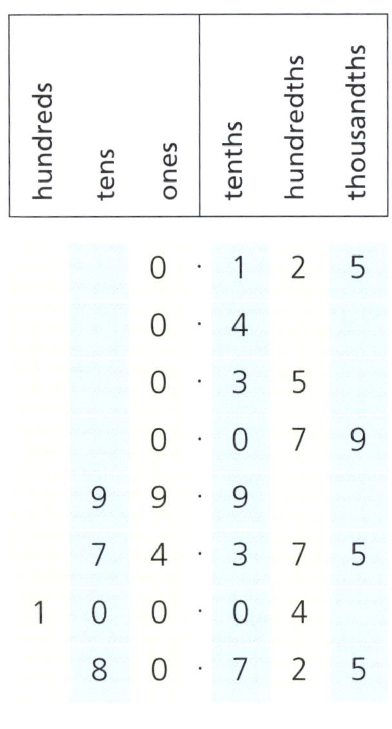

hundreds	tens	ones	·	tenths	hundredths	thousandths
		0	·	1	2	5
		0	·	4		
		0	·	3	5	
		0	·	0	7	9
	9	9	·	9		
	7	4	·	3	7	5
1	0	0	·	0	4	
	8	0	·	7	2	5

1 Order these from smallest to largest:

a 0·125, 0·4, 0·35, 0·079 (Use the diagram.)

b 99·9, 74·375, 100·04, 80·725 (Use the diagram.)

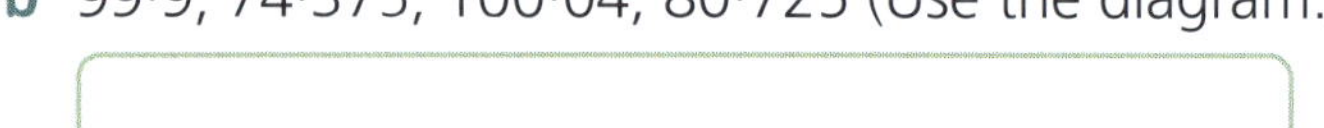

c 3·5, 3·49, 3·52, 3·095, 4, 4·2

d 0·066, 0·139, 0·3, 0·51, 1, 0·1

e 12·12, 1·212, 121·2, 1212, 0·1212

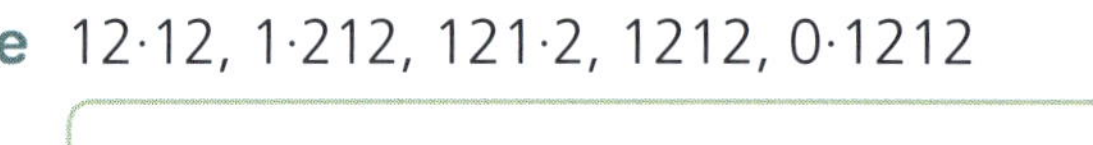

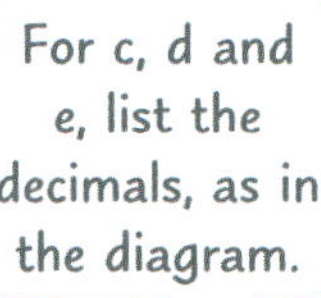

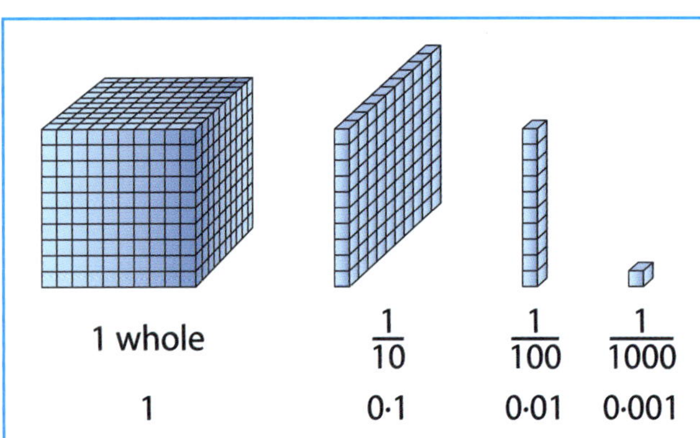

2 True (T) or false (F)?

a 10 × 0·001 = 0·01

b 10 × 0·01 = 0·1

c 10 × 0·1 = 1

d 1000 × 0·001 = 1

e 100 × 0·01 = 1

f 0·2 = 10 × 0·02

To round off a decimal to a given decimal place we look at the next digit. If it is 5 or more we round up. If it is less than 5, we round down.

3·128 rounds to 3·1 to 1 decimal place.

0·35 rounds to 0·4 to 1 decimal place.

3·128 rounds to 3·13 to 2 decimal places.

0·014 rounds to 0·01 to 2 decimal places.

3 Round each decimal to 1 decimal place, (that is, to the nearest tenth).

a 4·62 **b** 14·25 **c** 0·447

d 60·177 **e** 154·07 **f** 33·333

4 Round each decimal to 2 decimal places, (to the nearest hundredth).

a 9·627 **b** 14·253 **c** 0·145

d 35·288 **e** 65·043 **f** 0·415

See *Extra Support 6* (Comparing decimals).

1:21 Comparing decimals

60 ÷ 10 = 6
0·60 ÷ 10 = 0·06
so 0·6 ÷ 10 = 0·06

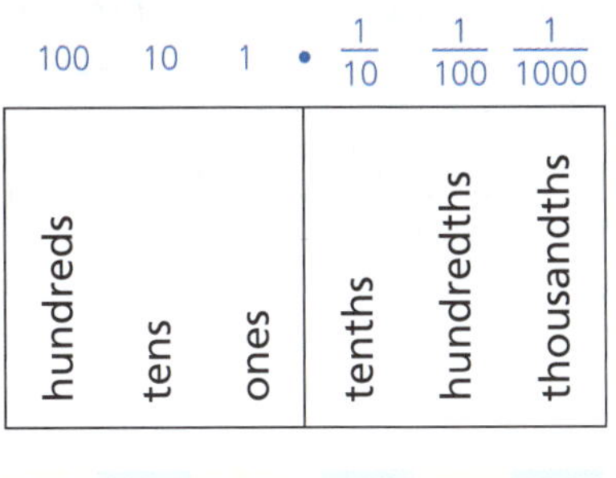

100	10	1	•	$\frac{1}{10}$	$\frac{1}{100}$	$\frac{1}{1000}$	
hundreds	tens	ones		tenths	hundredths	thousandths	
		0	·	1	0	0	0·1 = 100 thousandths
		0	·	0	1	0	0·01 = 10 thousandths
		0	·	0	0	1	0·001 = 1 thousandth
			·				
			·				length of koala in cm
			·				length of platypus in cm
			·				length of lizard in cm
			·				length of echidna in cm

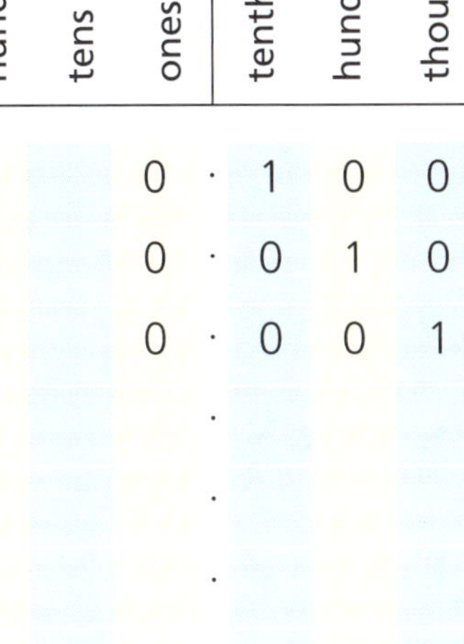

- Hundreds are 10 times smaller than tenths. 10 × 0·02 = 0·2
  Thousandths are 10 times smaller than hundredths. 10 × 0·002 = 0·02

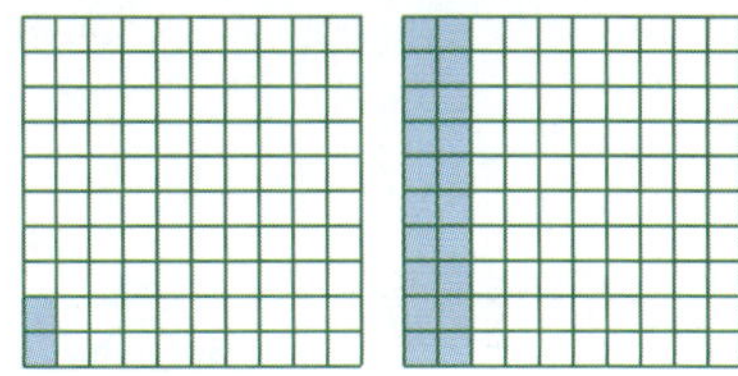

length = 60 cm

length = 42·15 cm

length = 82·125 cm

length = 29·4 cm

1 **a** Write the length of each animal on the table above.

b Write the length of each animal to the nearest centimetre.

koala ☐ platypus ☐ lizard ☐ echidna ☐

c Write the length of each animal in centimetres correct to 1 decimal place.

koala ☐ platypus ☐ lizard ☐ echidna ☐

d Order the numbers 60, 42·15, 82·125 and 29·4, from smallest to largest.

☐

2 A small part of the number line has been magnified.

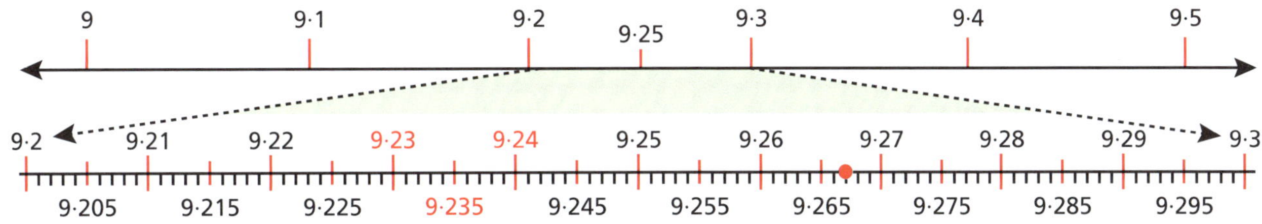

a A dot has been drawn at 9·267. Draw dots at 9·277, 9·24, 9·212, 9·4, 9 and 9·206.

b Write the number that is halfway between:

9·1 and 9·2 ☐ 9·21 and 9·22 ☐ 9·286 and 9·287 ☐

 • *AUSTRALIAN SIGNPOST MATHS 5* • ISBN 9780655708797

1:22 Subtraction from whole numbers

1 Complete, writing the answers as whole numbers or mixed numerals.

a $\frac{7}{8} + \frac{1}{8} =$ ☐ b $\frac{4}{6} + \frac{2}{6} =$ ☐ c $\frac{2}{3} + \frac{1}{3} =$ ☐ d $\frac{3}{4} + \frac{1}{4} =$ ☐

e $1\frac{1}{6} + \frac{5}{6} =$ ☐ f $2\frac{5}{8} + \frac{3}{8} =$ ☐ g $1\frac{7}{10} + \frac{3}{10} =$ ☐ h $2\frac{3}{5} + \frac{2}{5} =$ ☐

i $1\frac{3}{5} - \frac{3}{5} =$ ☐ j $2\frac{7}{10} - \frac{4}{10} =$ ☐ k $3\frac{3}{5} - \frac{1}{5} =$ ☐ l $2\frac{7}{12} - \frac{3}{12} =$ ☐

2 Complete.

a $1 - \frac{1}{6} =$ ☐ b $1 - \frac{1}{10} =$ ☐ c $1 - \frac{1}{8} =$ ☐ d $1 - \frac{1}{12} =$ ☐

e $1 - \frac{1}{5} =$ ☐ f $1 - \frac{3}{4} =$ ☐ g $1 - \frac{7}{10} =$ ☐ h $1 - \frac{2}{5} =$ ☐

i $1 - \frac{2}{3} =$ ☐ j $1 - \frac{5}{6} =$ ☐ k $1 - \frac{3}{8} =$ ☐ l $1 - \frac{5}{12} =$ ☐

3 Complete.

a $3 - \frac{1}{2} =$ ☐ b $2 - \frac{1}{3} =$ ☐ c $2 - \frac{1}{6} =$ ☐

d $3 - \frac{1}{5} =$ ☐ e $4 - \frac{1}{10} =$ ☐ f $4 - \frac{1}{12} =$ ☐

g $3 - \frac{1}{8} =$ ☐ h $4 - \frac{1}{4} =$ ☐ i $2 - \frac{3}{4} =$ ☐

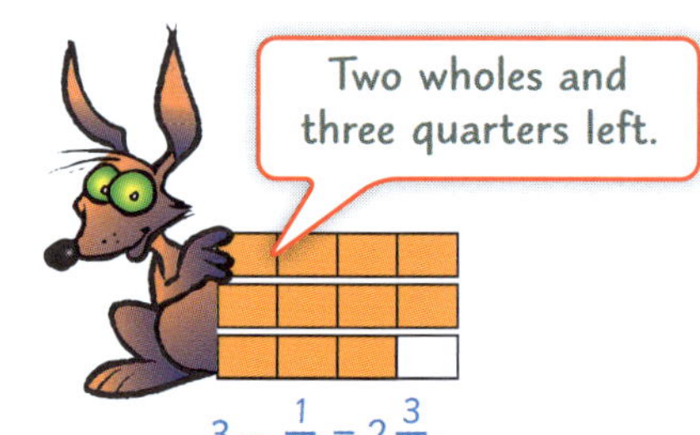

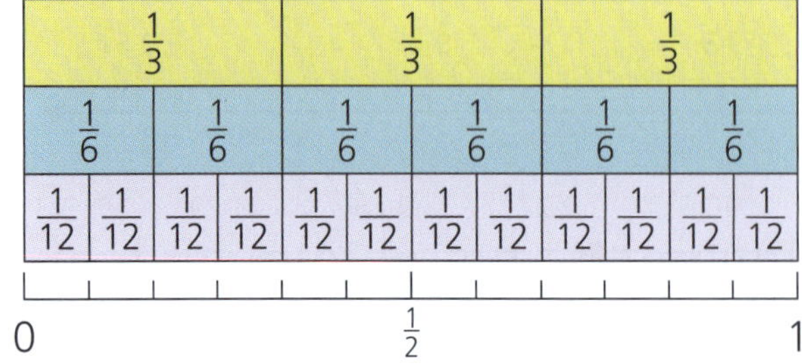

4 Use the diagram to show an equivalent fraction for:

a $\frac{2}{12} =$ ☐ b $\frac{10}{12} =$ ☐ c $\frac{4}{6} =$ ☐

d $\frac{2}{3} =$ ☐ e $\frac{8}{12} =$ ☐ f $\frac{3}{6} =$ ☐

5 Use the diagram in Question 4 to answer **true** or **false**.

a $\frac{1}{3} = \frac{4}{12}$ ☐ b $\frac{8}{12} = \frac{4}{6}$ ☐ c $\frac{2}{3} = \frac{6}{12}$ ☐ d $\frac{10}{12} = \frac{5}{6}$ ☐

6 Using the diagram, explain your answers to Questions 4 and 5 to a friend.

 • *AUSTRALIAN SIGNPOST MATHS 5* • ISBN 9780655708797

1:23 Using fractions

$\frac{1}{2} = \frac{2}{4} = \frac{3}{6} = \frac{4}{8} = \frac{5}{10}$

These are all equivalent fractions.

CONCEPT

- To order fractions, use equivalent fractions to give them the same denominator.

Order $\frac{3}{8}$, $\frac{3}{4}$, $\frac{1}{2}$ and $1\frac{1}{8}$ smallest first.

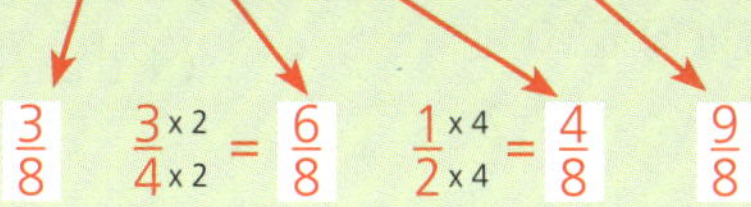

The order is: $\frac{3}{8}$, $\frac{1}{2}$, $\frac{3}{4}$ and $1\frac{1}{8}$.

- To add or subtract fractions, give them the same denominator.

$$\frac{3}{8} + \frac{1}{4} = \frac{3}{8} + \frac{1 \times 2}{4 \times 2}$$
$$= \frac{3}{8} + \frac{2}{8}$$
$$= \frac{5}{8}$$

In both, we changed the denominators to eighths.

1 Order these numbers from smallest to largest.

a $\frac{3}{4}$ $\frac{1}{2}$ $\frac{1}{4}$

b $\frac{3}{4}$ $1\frac{1}{4}$ $\frac{5}{8}$ $\frac{1}{2}$

c $\frac{1}{4}$ 1 $\frac{9}{8}$ $\frac{1}{8}$

d $\frac{3}{8}$ $\frac{1}{2}$ $\frac{3}{4}$ $\frac{1}{8}$

e $\frac{7}{10}$ $1\frac{1}{10}$ $\frac{1}{5}$ $\frac{1}{2}$

f $\frac{6}{10}$ $\frac{1}{5}$ $\frac{3}{2}$ $\frac{1}{10}$

2 Make the denominators the same before adding.

a $\frac{1}{4} + \frac{3}{8} = \frac{\square}{8} + \frac{3}{8} = \square$

b $\frac{1}{8} + \frac{1}{2} = \frac{1}{8} + \frac{\square}{8} = \square$

c $\frac{1}{2} + \frac{1}{4} = \square$

d $\frac{3}{4} + \frac{1}{2} = \square$

e $\frac{3}{4} + \frac{1}{8} = \square$

f $\frac{1}{10} + \frac{1}{5} = \square$

g $\frac{1}{8} + \frac{1}{4} = \square$

h $\frac{3}{5} + \frac{3}{10} = \square$

$\frac{7}{10} + \frac{7}{10} = \frac{14}{10}$ or $1\frac{4}{10}$

i $\frac{1}{4} + \frac{7}{8} = \square$

j $\frac{3}{5} + \frac{1}{10} = \square$

k $\frac{3}{10} + \frac{2}{5} = \square$

l $\frac{4}{5} + \frac{7}{10} = \square$

3 Make the denominators the same before subtracting.

a $\frac{3}{8} - \frac{1}{8} = \square$

b $\frac{5}{8} - \frac{1}{4} = \frac{5}{8} - \frac{\square}{8} = \square$

c $\frac{7}{8} - \frac{1}{2} = \frac{7}{8} - \frac{\square}{8} = \square$

d $\frac{5}{8} - \frac{1}{2} = \square$

e $\frac{9}{10} - \frac{1}{2} = \square$

f $\frac{7}{10} - \frac{2}{5} = \square$

g $\frac{3}{8} - \frac{1}{4} = \square$

h $\frac{7}{10} - \frac{1}{2} = \square$

i $\frac{6}{8} - \frac{1}{2} = \square$

j $\frac{9}{8} - \frac{3}{4} = \square$

k $\frac{9}{10} - \frac{1}{5} = \square$

l $\frac{3}{4} - \frac{3}{8} = \square$

m $\frac{7}{8} - \frac{3}{4} = \square$

n $\frac{4}{5} - \frac{6}{10} = \square$

o $\frac{3}{5} - \frac{1}{10} = \square$

p $\frac{11}{10} - \frac{1}{2} = \square$

q $\frac{9}{8} - \frac{1}{2} = \square$

r $\frac{3}{2} - \frac{7}{10} = \square$

s $\frac{7}{5} - \frac{7}{10} = \square$

 • *AUSTRALIAN SIGNPOST MATHS 5* • ISBN 9780655708797

1:24 Solving problems with fractions

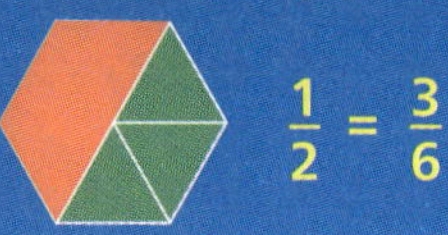

1. Half of a hexagonal garden has been used to plant seeds. Another sixth of the garden has mature plants. The rest has not been used. What fraction of the garden has not been used?

   ☐ of the garden

2. Our water tank was full yesterday, but my son left the tap running and one quarter of the water was wasted. How much of our water was left?

   ☐ of the tank

3. Three groups were allocated a section of the stage. We would all perform at the same time. Our group was allocated one sixth of the stage. How much was left for the other groups to use?

   ☐ of the stage

4. We had three strips of blue paper, each 12 cm long and 2 cm wide. Felicity used three quarters of a strip. I used five eighths of a strip. How much of the paper did we use?

   ☐ strips

5. Luis and his brother Tom climbed to the top of the Sydney Harbour Bridge. When Tom was halfway up, Luis was only three tenths of the way up. At that time, how much further up was Tom than Luis?

   ☐ of the way up

6. Jessica, Rhea and Lachlan entered the cross-country race. Yellow cones had been placed at the 1 km, 2 km and 3 km marks.

   a How far from the start is Lachlan, when he is two thirds of the way between the second and third cones?

   ☐ km

   b When Rhea had run three quarters of a kilometre, Jessica had run one and a half kilometres. How far apart were they?

   ☐ km

7. Rhonda bought 2 metres of tape. She used half a metre to make a one square-metre unit for measuring, and seven tenths of a metre to repair some books.

   a How much tape did she use?

   ☐ m

   b How much tape was not used?

   ☐ m

1:25 Using decimals

0·345 = 34·5%
0·087 = 8·7%
3·75m = 375 cm
4·8m = 480 cm

CONCEPT

We can use decimals to write large numbers in millions or billions.

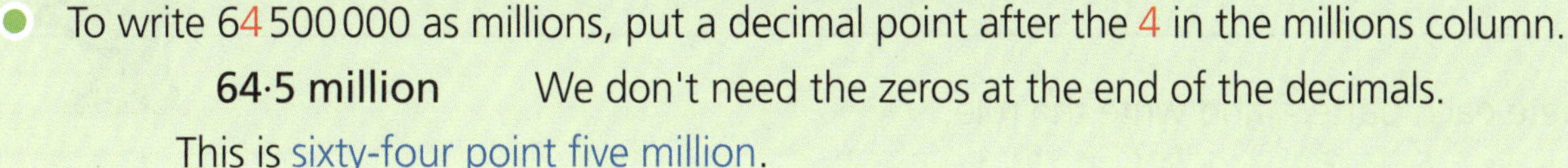
- To write 64 500 000 as millions, put a decimal point after the 4 in the millions column.

  64·5 million We don't need the zeros at the end of the decimals.

  This is sixty-four point five million.

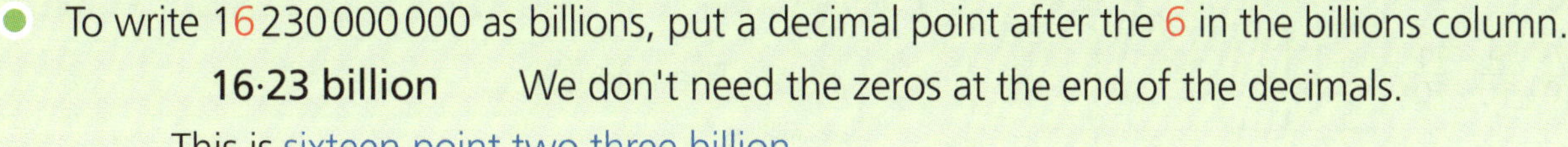
- To write 16 230 000 000 as billions, put a decimal point after the 6 in the billions column.

  16·23 billion We don't need the zeros at the end of the decimals.

  This is sixteen point two three billion.

Put the decimal point here for billions.

Put the point here for millions.

	Billions			Millions			Thousands			The rest		
A						5	6	0	0	0	0	0
B					2	5	6	5	0	0	0	0
C				1	2	5	6	0	0	0	0	0
D					6	8	4	0	0	0	0	0
E			3	9	0	0	0	0	0	0	0	0
F			7	1	8	0	0	0	0	0	0	0
G		6	2	4	4	0	0	0	0	0	0	0
H		1	3	7	0	0	0	0	0	0	0	0

1 Write as millions using a decimal.

a A ______ millions
b B ______ millions
c C ______ millions
d D ______ millions

2 Write as billions using a decimal.

a E ______ billions
b F ______ billions
c G ______ billions
d H ______ billions

CONCEPT

1 m = 1000 mm	1 L = 1000 mL	1 kg = 1000 g	1 km = 1000 m
4·29 m = 4290 mm	2·4 L = 2400 mL	9·22 kg = 9220 g	1·75 km = 1750 m
3750 mm = 3·75 m	3600 mL = 3·6 L	12 300 g = 12·3 kg	7700 m = 7·7 km

3 Complete these conversions.

a 3·9 m = ______ mm	**b** 12·7 kg = ______ g	**c** 45·6 km = ______ m
d 8·2 L = ______ mL	**e** 10·2 km = ______ m	**f** 11·48 L = ______ mL
g 5300 mm = ______ m	**h** 1850 g = ______ kg	**i** 6640 m = ______ km
j 5800 m = ______ km	**k** 4300 mL = ______ L	**l** 2675 g = ______ kg
m 0·145 = ______ %	**n** 0·125 = ______ %	**o** 0·3333 = ______ %

See *Extra Support 21* (Decimals!).

Patterns and percentages

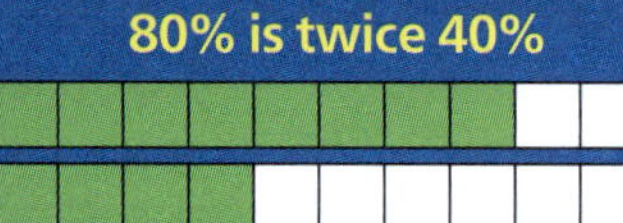

100% is one whole.
200% is two wholes.

70% means 70 out of every 100.

70% of 100 = 70
70% of 200 = 140

1 Complete each pattern and write the rule.

a 120%, 100%, 80%, ___, ___, ___ The rule is: ___

b $\frac{7}{10}$, $\frac{9}{10}$, $\frac{11}{10}$, ___, ___, ___, ___ The rule is: ___

c 4, $3\frac{8}{10}$, $3\frac{6}{10}$, ___, ___, ___, ___ The rule is: ___

d 0·85, 0·87, 0·89, ___, ___, ___ The rule is: ___

e 1·6, 1·5, 1·4, ___, ___, ___ The rule is: ___

f , … The rule is: ___

0·3, ___, ___, ___, ___, ___, ___

g 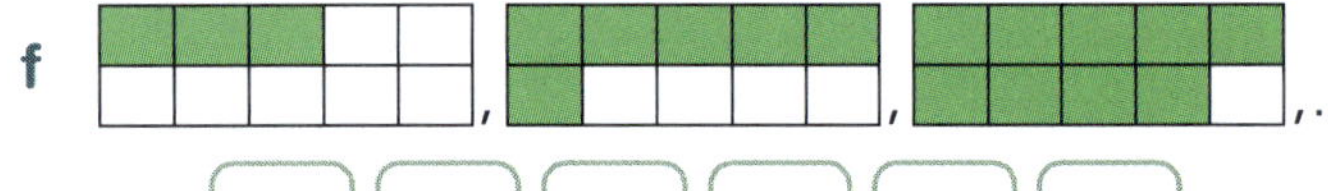

$\frac{1}{8}$,  ___, ___, ___, ___, ___, ___

The rule is: ___

h 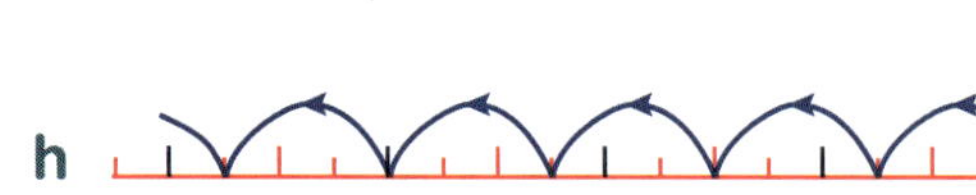

100%, ___, ___, ___, ___, …,

The rule is: ___

i 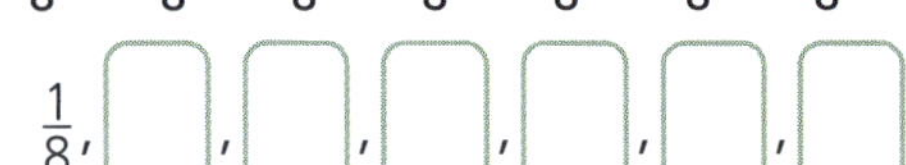, …

$\frac{1}{4}$, 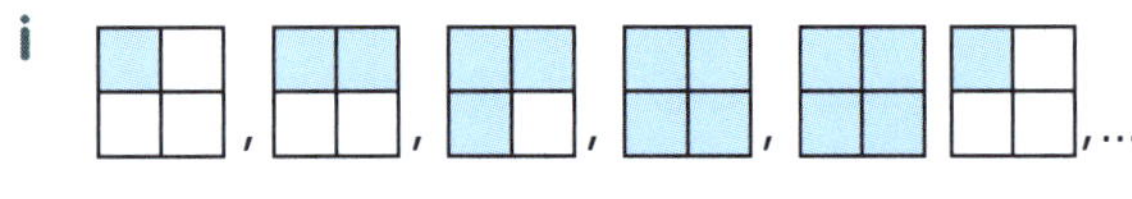 ___, ___, ___, ___, ___, ___

The rule is: ___

j 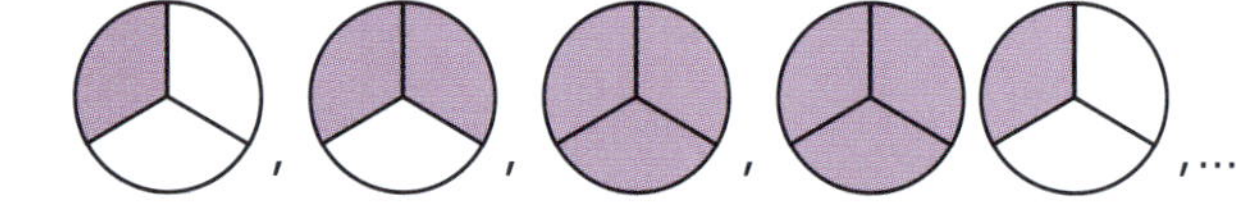, …

$\frac{1}{3}$,  ___, ___, ___, ___, ___, ___

The rule is: ___

2 Create your own percentage number pattern using jumps on the number line.

___, ___, ___, ___, ___, ___, ___

The rule is: ___

See *Extra Support 12* (Number patterns).

2:01 Number facts, ×6, ×7, ×8, ×9

Do you know these?

×	6	7	8	9
1	6	7	8	9
2	12	14	16	18
3	18	21	24	27
4	24	28	32	36
5	30	35	40	45
6	36	42	48	54
7	42	49	56	63
8	48	56	64	72
9	54	63	72	81
10	60	70	80	90

CONCEPT

The circle shows 8 × 9.

The product of 8 and 9 is 72.

9 × 8 = 8 × 9

The answer to a multiplication question is called the **product**.

1 Try to do these without using the table.

a 5 × 6 = ☐ **b** 3 × 8 = ☐ **c** 3 × 7 = ☐

d 4 × 9 = ☐ **e** 5 × 8 = ☐ **f** 7 × 9 = ☐

g 6 × 6 = ☐ **h** 7 × 7 = ☐ **i** 9 × 6 = ☐

j 8 × 9 = ☐ **k** 6 × 8 = ☐ **l** 8 × 6 = ☐

m 7 × 6 = ☐ **n** 8 × 7 = ☐

o 9 × 8 = ☐ **p** 9 × 9 = ☐

q 4 × 6 = ☐ **r** 8 × 8 = ☐

s The product of 2, 3 and 8 = ☐.

2

a

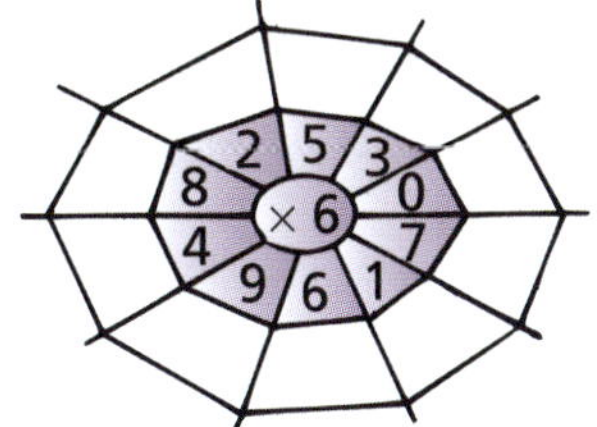

b

c

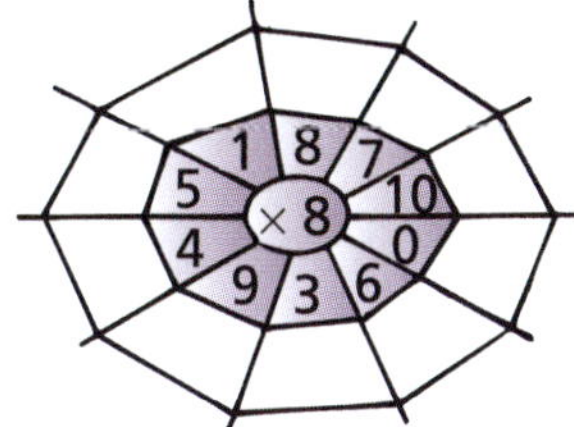

d

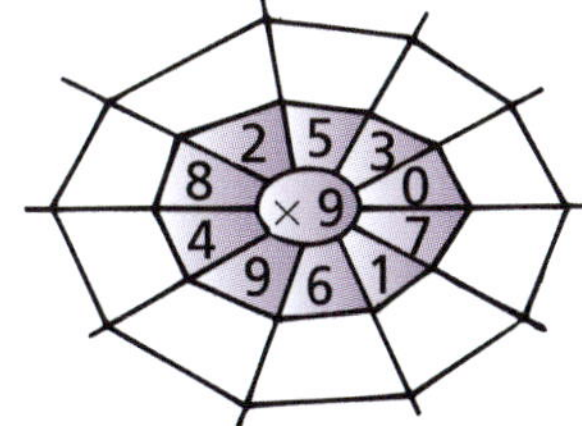

e

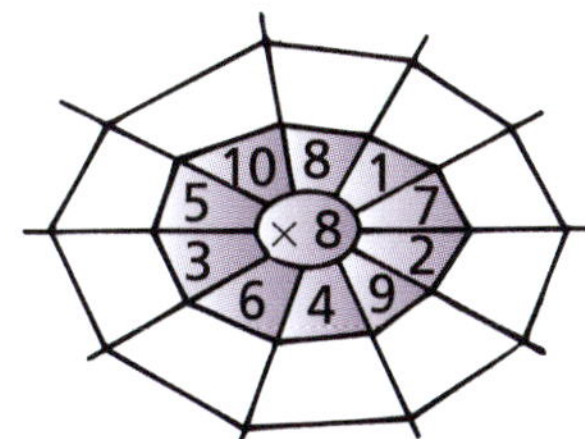

f

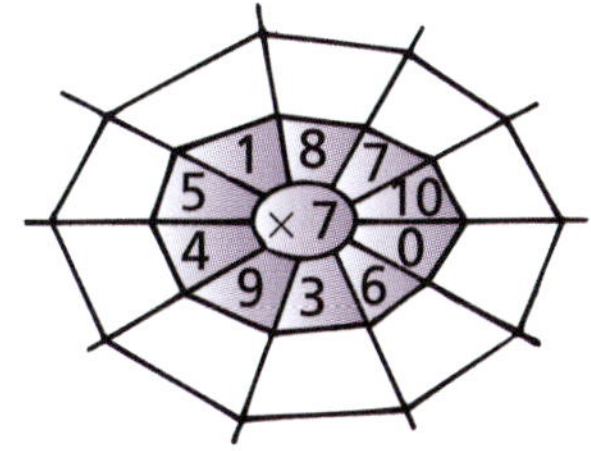

3 Write the first ten multiples of:

a 6 | 6 | ☐ | ☐ | ☐ | ☐ | ☐ | ☐ | ☐ | ☐ | ☐

b 7 | 7 | ☐ | ☐ | ☐ | ☐ | ☐ | ☐ | ☐ | ☐ | ☐

c 9 | 9 | ☐ | ☐ | ☐ | ☐ | ☐ | ☐ | ☐ | ☐ | ☐

See *Extra Support 7* (× 2, × 3, × 4, × 5, × 10 tables) and *Extra Support 8* (× 6, × 7, × 8, × 9 tables).

2:02 Learning your multiplication tables

CONCEPT

- Have someone test you.
- For each table you don't know, make a card with the question on one side and the answer on the other.
- Carry these cards with you, testing yourself until you know them.

1 Try to do these without using the table below.

a 3 × 3 = ☐ **b** 6 × 2 = ☐ **c** 4 × 3 = ☐ **d** 9 × 2 = ☐

e 8 × 3 = ☐ **f** 5 × 5 = ☐ **g** 4 × 6 = ☐ **h** 6 × 6 = ☐

i 4 × 4 = ☐ **j** 7 × 2 = ☐ **k** 9 × 3 = ☐ **l** 8 × 2 = ☐

m 5 × 3 = ☐ **n** 5 × 6 = ☐ **o** 8 × 8 = ☐ **p** 6 × 3 = ☐

q 9 × 6 = ☐ **r** 7 × 3 = ☐ **s** 10 × 6 = ☐ **t** 8 × 6 = ☐

u 7 × 7 = ☐ **v** 10 × 8 = ☐ **w** 7 × 6 = ☐ **x** 9 × 9 = ☐

2 **a**

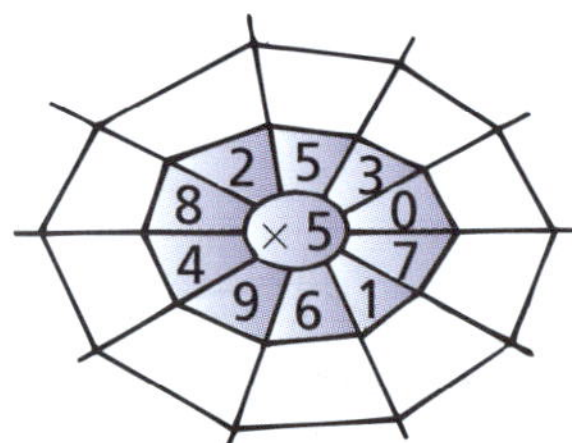

b

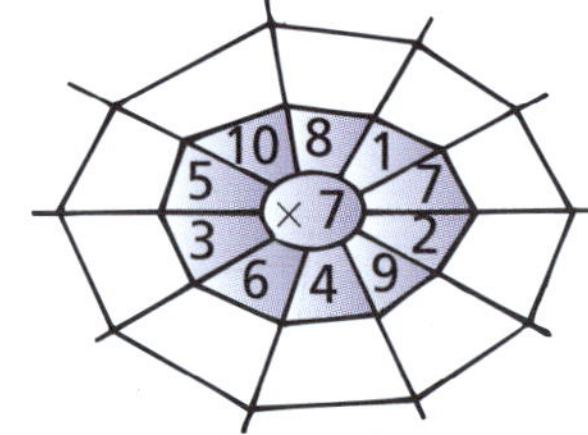

c

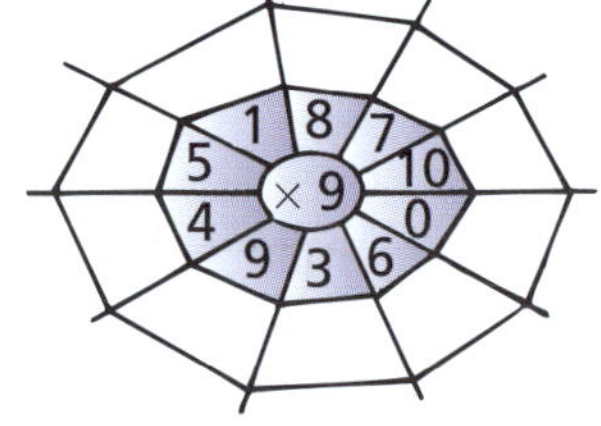

3 Write the first ten multiples of:

a 4 | 4 | ☐ | ☐ | ☐ | ☐ | ☐ | ☐ | ☐ | ☐ | ☐

b 8 | 8 | ☐ | ☐ | ☐ | ☐ | ☐ | ☐ | ☐ | ☐ | ☐

Can you see a connection between the multiples in parts **a** and **b**?

The multiples of 8 are ☐ the size of the multiples of 4.

0 × 1 = 0	0 × 2 = 0	0 × 3 = 0	0 × 4 = 0	0 × 5 = 0	0 × 6 = 0	0 × 7 = 0	0 × 8 = 0	0 × 9 = 0	0 × 10 = 0
1 × 1 = 1	1 × 2 = 2	1 × 3 = 3	1 × 4 = 4	1 × 5 = 5	1 × 6 = 6	1 × 7 = 7	1 × 8 = 8	1 × 9 = 9	1 × 10 = 10
2 × 1 = 2	2 × 2 = 4	2 × 3 = 6	2 × 4 = 8	2 × 5 = 10	2 × 6 = 12	2 × 7 = 14	2 × 8 = 16	2 × 9 = 18	2 × 10 = 20
3 × 1 = 3	3 × 2 = 6	3 × 3 = 9	3 × 4 = 12	3 × 5 = 15	3 × 6 = 18	3 × 7 = 21	3 × 8 = 24	3 × 9 = 27	3 × 10 = 30
4 × 1 = 4	4 × 2 = 8	4 × 3 = 12	4 × 4 = 16	4 × 5 = 20	4 × 6 = 24	4 × 7 = 28	4 × 8 = 32	4 × 9 = 36	4 × 10 = 40
5 × 1 = 5	5 × 2 = 10	5 × 3 = 15	5 × 4 = 20	5 × 5 = 25	5 × 6 = 30	5 × 7 = 35	5 × 8 = 40	5 × 9 = 45	5 × 10 = 50
6 × 1 = 6	6 × 2 = 12	6 × 3 = 18	6 × 4 = 24	6 × 5 = 30	6 × 6 = 36	6 × 7 = 42	6 × 8 = 48	6 × 9 = 54	6 × 10 = 60
7 × 1 = 7	7 × 2 = 14	7 × 3 = 21	7 × 4 = 28	7 × 5 = 35	7 × 6 = 42	7 × 7 = 49	7 × 8 = 56	7 × 9 = 63	7 × 10 = 70
8 × 1 = 8	8 × 2 = 16	8 × 3 = 24	8 × 4 = 32	8 × 5 = 40	8 × 6 = 48	8 × 7 = 56	8 × 8 = 64	8 × 9 = 72	8 × 10 = 80
9 × 1 = 9	9 × 2 = 18	9 × 3 = 27	9 × 4 = 36	9 × 5 = 45	9 × 6 = 54	9 × 7 = 63	9 × 8 = 72	9 × 9 = 81	9 × 10 = 90
10 × 1 = 10	10 × 2 = 20	10 × 3 = 30	10 × 4 = 40	10 × 5 = 50	10 × 6 = 60	10 × 7 = 70	10 × 8 = 80	10 × 9 = 90	10 × 10 = 100

See *Extra Support 7* (× 2, × 3, × 4, × 5, × 10 tables) and *Extra Support 8* (× 6, × 7, × 8, × 9 tables).

Division facts

4 × 8 = 32   32 ÷ 8 = 4
8 × 4 = 32   32 ÷ 4 = 8

This is called a multiplication fact family.

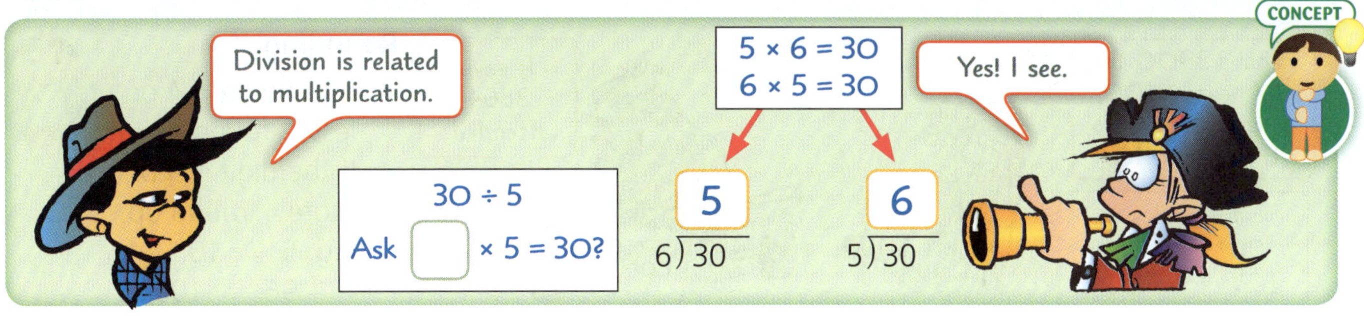

1 Use the multiplication table to answer the division questions.

a 4 × 10 = 40, so, 4)40 ☐ 10)40 ☐

b 5 × 8 = 40, so, 8)40 ☐ 5)40 ☐

c 7 × 3 = 21, so, 7)21 ☐ 3)21 ☐

d 9 × 8 = 72, so, 8)72 ☐ 9)72 ☐

e 8 × 9 = 72, so, 9)72 ☐ 8)72 ☐

f 4 × 9 = 36, so, 9)36 ☐ 4)36 ☐

2

a	☐ × 2 = 22	**b**	4 × ☐ = 40	**c**	☐ × 8 = 56	**d**	5 × ☐ = 10
e	☐ × 3 = 18	**f**	9 × ☐ = 81	**g**	☐ × 9 = 9	**h**	7 × ☐ = 0
i	☐ × 7 = 49	**j**	4 × ☐ = 32	**k**	☐ × 5 = 35	**l**	3 × ☐ = 27

3

a 18 ÷ 3 = ☐
Ask 3 × ☐ = 18

b 28 ÷ 4 = ☐
Ask 4 × ☐ = 28

c 40 ÷ 5 = ☐
Ask 5 × ☐ = 40

d 30 ÷ 3 = ☐
Ask 3 × ☐ = 30

e 42 ÷ 6 = ☐
Ask 6 × ☐ = 42

f 24 ÷ 4 = ☐
Ask 4 × ☐ = 24

4 Use the method in Question 3 to answer these.

a	18 ÷ 2 = ☐	**b**	25 ÷ 5 = ☐	**c**	18 ÷ 6 = ☐	**d**	24 ÷ 6 = ☐
e	30 ÷ 3 = ☐	**f**	4 ÷ 4 = ☐	**g**	35 ÷ 7 = ☐	**h**	27 ÷ 9 = ☐
i	0 ÷ 8 = ☐	**j**	48 ÷ 6 = ☐	**k**	16 ÷ 8 = ☐	**l**	36 ÷ 6 = ☐
m	27 ÷ 3 = ☐	**n**	25 ÷ 5 = ☐	**o**	63 ÷ 9 = ☐	**p**	45 ÷ 5 = ☐

5

a 15 ÷ ☐ = 3
Ask 3 × ☐ = 15

b 54 ÷ ☐ = 6
Ask 6 × ☐ = 54

c 49 ÷ ☐ = 7
Ask 7 × ☐ = 49

d 90 ÷ ☐ = 10
Ask 10 × ☐ = 90

e 55 ÷ ☐ = 11
Ask 11 × ☐ = 55

f 12 ÷ ☐ = 3
Ask 3 × ☐ = 12

g 81 ÷ ☐ = 9

h 42 ÷ ☐ = 7

i 36 ÷ ☐ = 4

 • *AUSTRALIAN SIGNPOST MATHS 5* • ISBN 9780655708797

2:04 Rounding

To round to the nearest hundred, look at the tens digit.
6743 becomes 6700

That's 3900 to the nearest 100, or that's 3860 to the nearest 10.

Examples:
96 ⟶ 100
527 ⟶ 500
4510 ⟶ 5000

Rounding

- If the digit is 4 or less … round down.
- If the digit is 5 or more … round up, e.g. 5 ⟶ 10, 96 ⟶ 100.

1 Round these numbers to the nearest ten.

a 37 ☐	**b** 82 ☐	**c** 111 ☐	**d** 126 ☐
e 305 ☐	**f** 927 ☐	**g** 792 ☐	**h** 329 ☐
i 1894 ☐	**j** 1895 ☐	**k** 1896 ☐	**l** 2067 ☐

2 Round these numbers to the nearest hundred.

a 742 ☐	**b** 381 ☐	**c** 151 ☐	**d** 853 ☐
e 937 ☐	**f** 679 ☐	**g** 405 ☐	**h** 249 ☐
i 3481 ☐	**j** 9048 ☐	**k** 4093 ☐	**l** 2145 ☐

3 Round these numbers to the nearest thousand.

a 2790 ☐	**b** 4281 ☐	**c** 8021 ☐	**d** 3724 ☐
e 7814 ☐	**f** 6930 ☐	**g** 1398 ☐	**h** 5316 ☐

4 **a** Circle the numbers that round to 3000.

3672	3196	2878
3945	2764	3285
3812	2246	3349

b Circle the numbers that round to 6000.

6249	5862	6591
5396	6478	6487
5723	6823	5734

5 **a** Circle the numbers that round to 3200.

3275	3227	3270
3249	3185	3175
3159	3129	3207

b Circle the numbers that round to 75 000.

75 247	75 672	74 503
74 820	75 981	75 199
74 498	74 981	74 500

6 Answer **true** or **false** for each statement.

a 7251 rounds to 7300. ☐

b 4500 rounds to 5000. ☐

c 6172 rounds to 6100. ☐

d 3409 rounds to 4000. ☐

Strategies, + and –

Partitioning 518 + 74

A problem may be solved using different strategies. Ask, 'Which method will work best?'

addition — 123 + 48

compensation strategy:
123 + 48
= 123 + 50 – 2
= 173 – 2
= 171

split strategy:
123 + 48
= (120 + 40) + (3 + 8)
= 160 + 11
= 171

algorithm strategy:

```
   1
  1 2 3
+   4 8
  1 7 1
```

jump strategy:
123 + 48
= 123 + 40 + 8
= 163 + (7 + 1)
= 171

subtraction — 123 – 48

compensation strategy:
123 – 48
= 123 – 50 + 2
= 73 + 2
= 75

split strategy: The trading makes the split strategy too difficult here.

algorithm strategy:

```
   11 13
  1̸  2̸  3̸
–    4  8
     7  5
```

jump strategy:
123 – 48
= 123 – 40 – 8
= 83 – 3 – 5
= 75

Practise these strategies on easier questions if you find them difficult.

Here are some of the strategies we have seen so far.

A	Looking for patterns	8 + 6 = 14 so 8 + 26 = 34,	3 + 8 = 11 so 300 + 800 = 1100	
B	Changing the order	115 + 137 + 15	= 115 + 15 + 137	= 130 + 137
C	Bridging to 10s	148 + 7	= 148 + 2 + 5	= 150 + 5
		9338 + 23	= 9338 + (2 + 20 + 1)	= 9361
D	Compensation	318 + 98	= 318 + 100 – 2	= 418 – 2
E	Split strategy	316 + 432	= (300 + 400) + (10 + 30) + (6 + 2)	= 700 + 40 + 8
F	Jump strategy	257 + 48	= 257 + 40 + 8	= 297 + 8
G	Compatible numbers	560 + 162 = (550 + 10) + (150 + 12) = 700 + 22		
H	Break up the number using place value	346 – 227	Step 1: 346 – **2**00 = 146 Step 2: 146 – **2**0 = 126 Step 3: 126 – **7** = 119	
I	Constant difference 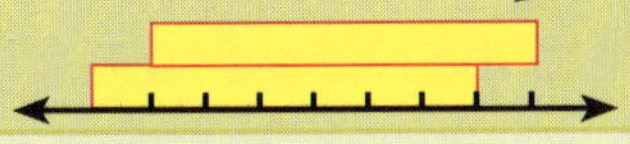	7000 – 4996 (+4 +4)	= 7012 + 5000	= 2012
		8140 – 2985 (+15 +15)	= 8155 – 3000	= 5155
J	Levelling	845 + 897 = 842 + 900 (+3 +3)		= 1742
	Take from one number and add it to the other	3988 + 955 = 3990 + 953 = 4000 + 943 = 4943 (+2 –2 +10 –10)		

1 Choose a strategy first.

a 376 + 195

b 362 + 137

c 456 – 290

d 643 – 104

 • *AUSTRALIAN SIGNPOST MATHS 5* • ISBN 9780655708797

2:06 Addition to 999

We can trade 10 ones for 1 ten.
We can trade 10 tens for 1 hundred.

CONCEPT

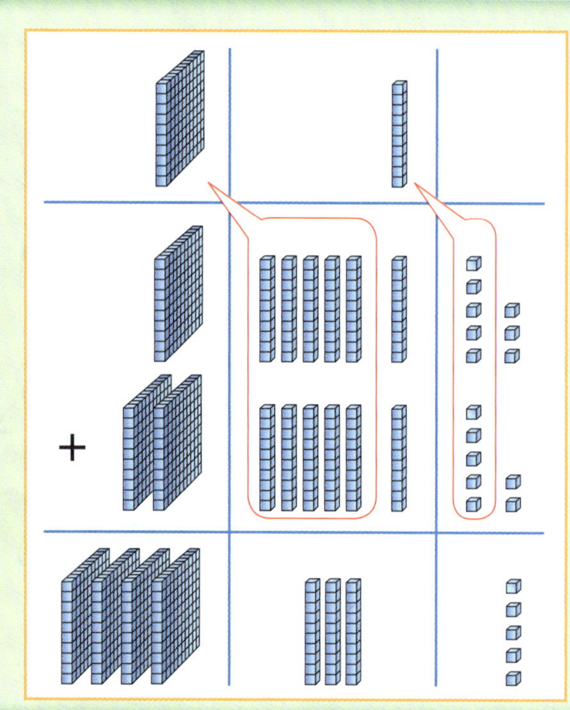

168 boys and 267 girls went on the excursion. How many students went on the excursion?

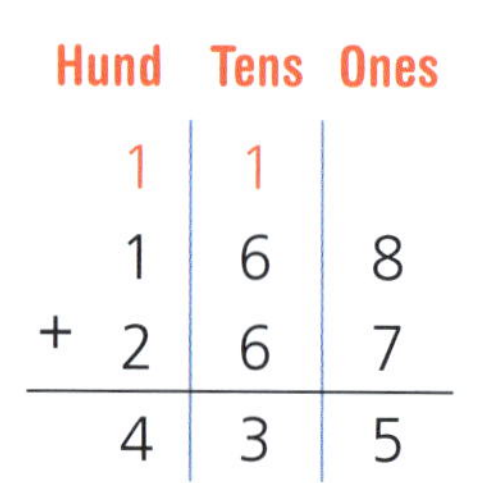

	Hund	Tens	Ones
	1	1	
	1	6	8
+	2	6	7
	4	3	5

or

$$\begin{array}{r} 100 + 60 + 8 \\ 200 + 60 + 7 \\ \hline 1\ \ 5 \\ 1\ \ 2\ \ 0 \\ +\ 3\ \ 0\ \ 0 \\ \hline 4\ \ 3\ \ 5 \end{array}$$

There are 435 students on the excursion.

We can check the answer by rounding to the nearest 100 (or 10).

$$200 + 300 = 500$$

435 is reasonably close to 500.

1

		H	T	U
a			8	4
	+	2	0	7
b			7	9
	+	1	7	5
c		7	0	9
	+		4	5
d		1	8	3
	+		6	5

e		2	5	5
	+	2	5	9
f		3	7	8
	+	6	7	6
g		5	7	2
	+	3	2	8
h		3	6	0
	+	2	5	6
i		4	7	3
	+	1	4	8
j		7	7	2
	+	1	1	9
k		5	3	7
	+	2	8	5
l		4	5	3
	+	4	6	8
m		2	7	3
	+	4	3	6
n		3	9	5
	+	3	3	6
o		2	5	6
	+	3	6	4
p		4	4	6
	+	3	4	9

2 Check your answers to Question 1, **m** to **p**, by rounding each number to the nearest 100.

(m)
	3	0	0
+	4	0	0

(n) ______

(o) ______

(p) ______

 • *AUSTRALIAN SIGNPOST MATHS 5* • ISBN 9780655708797

Addition to 999

We use rounding to estimate the answer. If the answer isn't close to the estimate we do the question again.

CONCEPT

Rounding rules

We round down if the digit is 4 or less. We round up if the digit is 5 or more.

When both numbers are rounded down the answer is an underestimate.	When both numbers are rounded up the answer is an overestimate.
319 + 443 = 762	482 + 257 = 739
300 + 400 = 700	**500 + 300 = 800**
The estimate is less than the actual answer.	The estimate is greater than the actual answer.

1

a
$$\begin{array}{rrrr} & H & T & U \\ & & 7 & 5 \\ + & 6 & 5 & 4 \\ \hline \end{array}$$

b
$$\begin{array}{rrrr} & H & T & U \\ & & 8 & 6 \\ + & 5 & 4 & 7 \\ \hline \end{array}$$

c
$$\begin{array}{rrrr} & H & T & U \\ & 6 & 6 & 5 \\ + & & 7 & 5 \\ \hline \end{array}$$

Estimate to quickly check your answers.

d
$$\begin{array}{rrrr} & 1 & 2 & 6 \\ + & 5 & 7 & 8 \\ \hline \end{array}$$

e
$$\begin{array}{rrrr} & 3 & 4 & 9 \\ + & 2 & 5 & 7 \\ \hline \end{array}$$

f
$$\begin{array}{rrrr} & 5 & 7 & 9 \\ + & 2 & 1 & 6 \\ \hline \end{array}$$

g
$$\begin{array}{rrrr} & 3 & 4 & 6 \\ + & 3 & 7 & 7 \\ \hline \end{array}$$

h
$$\begin{array}{rrrr} & 8 & 3 & 5 \\ + & 1 & 4 & 8 \\ \hline \end{array}$$

i
$$\begin{array}{rrrr} & 1 & 5 & 8 \\ + & 6 & 7 & 3 \\ \hline \end{array}$$

j
$$\begin{array}{rrrr} & 3 & 2 & 9 \\ + & 2 & 6 & 6 \\ \hline \end{array}$$

k
$$\begin{array}{rrrr} & 1 & 0 & 7 \\ + & 6 & 9 & 3 \\ \hline \end{array}$$

l
$$\begin{array}{rrrr} & 4 & 4 & 5 \\ + & 1 & 9 & 8 \\ \hline \end{array}$$

m
$$\begin{array}{rrrr} & 5 & 9 & 8 \\ + & 2 & 5 & 3 \\ \hline \end{array}$$

n
$$\begin{array}{rrrr} & 2 & 8 & 9 \\ + & 3 & 7 & 9 \\ \hline \end{array}$$

2 Use the strategy shown on the right to do these.

a 197 + 686

+ 3	− 3

b 445 + 198

−2	+ 2

c 407 + 369

d 295 + 288

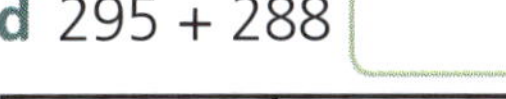

e 465 + 283

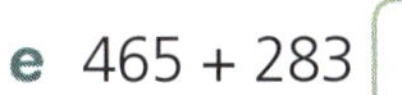

+ 3 − 20	− 3 + 20

f 378 + 188

Explain the strategy used here.

316 + 147 = (316 − 3) + (147 + 3)
= 313 + 150
= 463

 • *AUSTRALIAN SIGNPOST MATHS 5* • ISBN 9780655708797

2:08 Using the addition algorithm

The column values are ones, tens and hundreds.

583 apples and 179 oranges were sold. How many pieces of fruit were sold altogether?

All of these are ways of setting out the same sum.

```
  H  T  U
  1  1
  5  8  3
+ 1  7  9
---------
  7  6  2
```

```
  1  1
  5  8  3
+ 1  7  9
---------
  7  6  2
```

or

$$\begin{array}{r} 500 + 80 + 3 \\ 100 + 70 + 9 \\ \hline 1\quad 2 \\ 1\quad 5\quad 0 \\ +6\quad 0\quad 0 \\ \hline 7\quad 6\quad 2 \end{array}$$

or

583 + 179
= 583 + 179
(−1) (+1)
= 582 + 180
(−20) (+20)
= 562 + 200
= 762

762 pieces of fruit were sold altogether.

1

a 436 + 157	**b** 476 + 247	**c** 264 + 246	**d** 459 + 356
e 888 + 107	**f** 309 + 193	**g** 444 + 456	**h** 470 + 260
i 578 + 144	**j** 736 + 199	**k** 388 + 317	**l** 194 + 255

2 Estimate each answer, then use the estimate to check your answer to the problem.

a There were 375 men and 486 women employed in the company. How many people were employed in the company altogether? ☐ people

b We packed 563 boxes of toys on Thursday and 187 on Friday. How many boxes of toys did we pack altogether? ☐ boxes

c Last year I collected 267 swap cards. This year I collected 100 less than that. How many did I collect in the two years? ☐ cards

d I started a part-time job last week. I earned $274 last week and $198 this week. How much have I earned so far? ☐ dollars

e I need to travel to my grandparents' home and back today. They live 428 km away. How far must I travel? ☐ km

2:09 Subtraction with trading

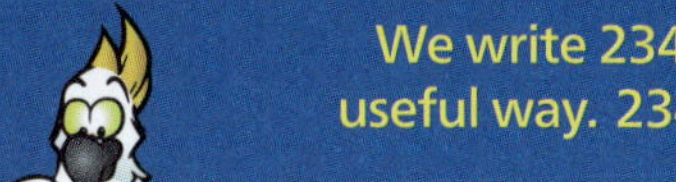

CONCEPT

John had 234 stamps but 18 were damaged. How many were left?

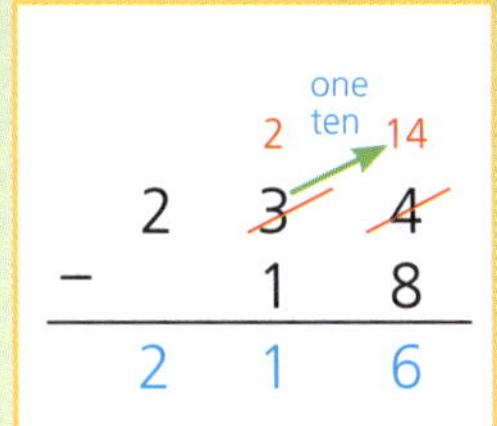

We can't take 8 from 4, so we trade 1 ten for 10 ones.

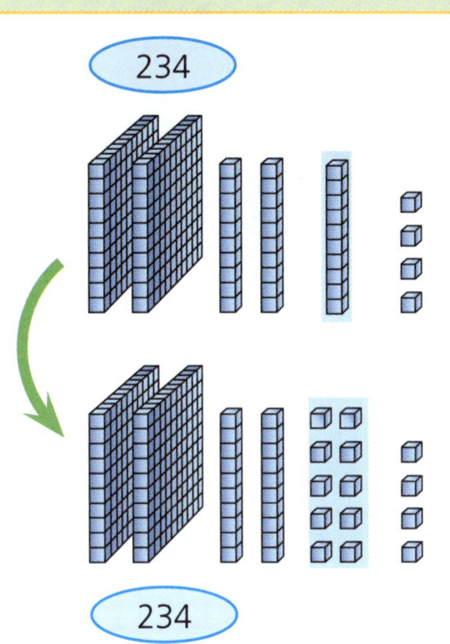

216 stamps were left.

1

	H	T	U
a		8	0
−		4	7
b		7	1
−		3	7
c	1	5	2
−		2	5
d	2	4	3
−		3	5
e	5	5	0
−	2	3	6
f	6	7	8
−	1	3	9
g	5	7	2
−	3	2	8
h	3	6	0
−	2	5	6
i	4	7	3
−	1	4	8
j	7	7	2
−	1	1	9
k	5	6	0
−	2	4	5
l	4	9	3
−	1	6	8
m	8	7	3
−	4	3	6
n	7	9	5
−	3	3	6
o	6	5	6
−	3	0	8
p	4	4	0
−	3	0	9

2 Check your answers to Question 1, **i** to **p**, by rounding each number to the nearest 100.

(i)	5	0	0
−	1	0	0
(j)	8	0	0
−	1	0	0
(k)	6	0	0
−	2	0	0
(l)			
−			
(m)			
−			
(n)			
−			
(o)			
−			
(p)			
−			

 • *AUSTRALIAN SIGNPOST MATHS 5* • ISBN 9780655708797

2:10 Number — Subtraction to 999

We can write 328 in another way.
328 = 200 + 120 + 8

CONCEPT

Mai had 328 flowers for sale. She sold 176. How many did she have left?

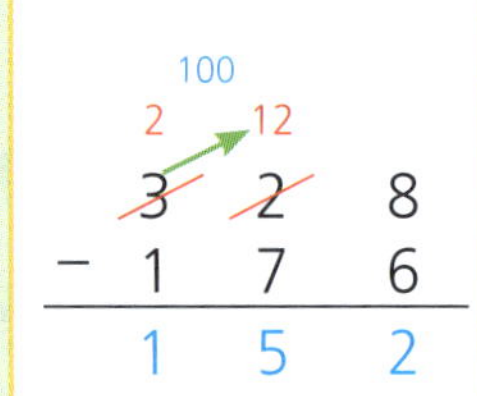

We can't take 7 tens from 2 tens. We trade 1 hundred for 10 tens.

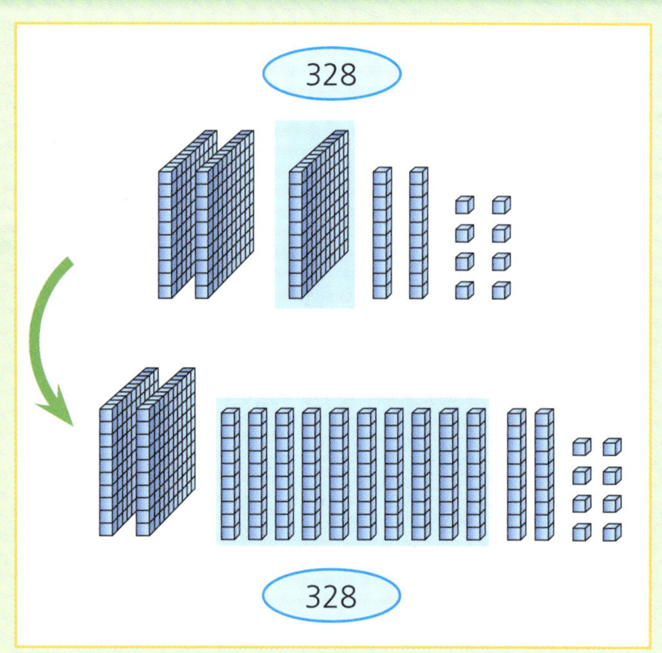

200 120
300 + 20 + 8
take away
100 + 70 + 6

152 flowers were left.

1

a 600 − 70	**b** 304 − 32	**c** 952 − 80	**d** 249 − 65
e 719 − 236	**f** 418 − 131	**g** 702 − 121	**h** 318 − 156
i 409 − 188	**j** 712 − 280	**k** 548 − 254	**l** 426 − 163
m 877 − 286	**n** 728 − 135	**o** 446 − 383	**p** 709 − 237

2 Use the strategy shown on the right to do these.

a 672 − 285 ☐

+ 5 + 10 | + 5 + 10

c 527 − 270 ☐

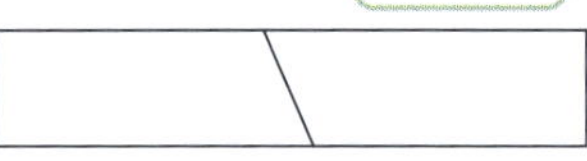

d 817 − 549 ☐

Discuss the strategy used here.

316 − 147 = (316 + 3) − (147 + 3)
= 319 − 150
= (319 + 50) − (150 + 50)
= 369 − 200
= 169

2:11 Multiples

A multiple of a counting number is found when you multiply that number by another counting number.

A multiple of 5 is found when you multiply it by a counting number.

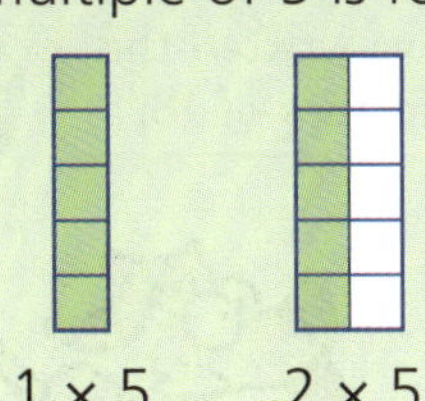
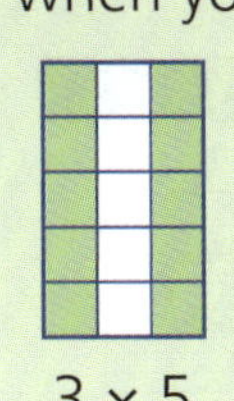

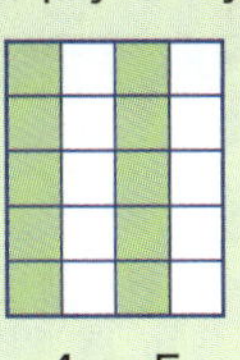
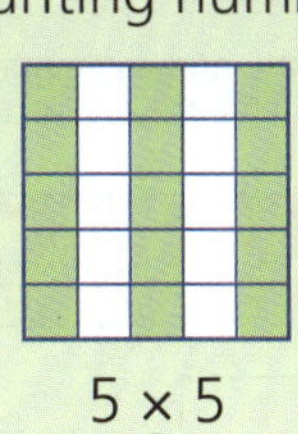

1 × 5 = 5, 2 × 5 = 10, 3 × 5 = 15, 4 × 5 = 20, 5 × 5 = 25

1 Complete these number sentences to find the first nine multiples of 5.

a 1 × 5 = ☐ b 2 × 5 = ☐ c 3 × 5 = ☐
d 4 × 5 = ☐ e 5 × 5 = ☐ f 6 × 5 = ☐
g 7 × 5 = ☐ h 8 × 5 = ☐ i 9 × 5 = ☐

The first ten multiples of 5 are 5, 10, ☐, ☐, ☐, ☐, ☐, ☐, ☐ and ☐.

2 Use skip counting to write down the first ten multiples of:

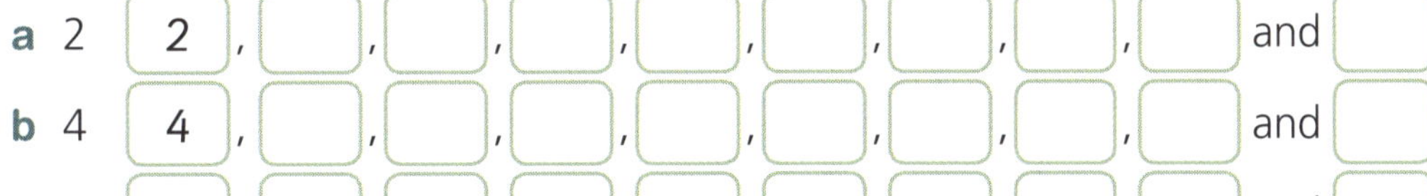
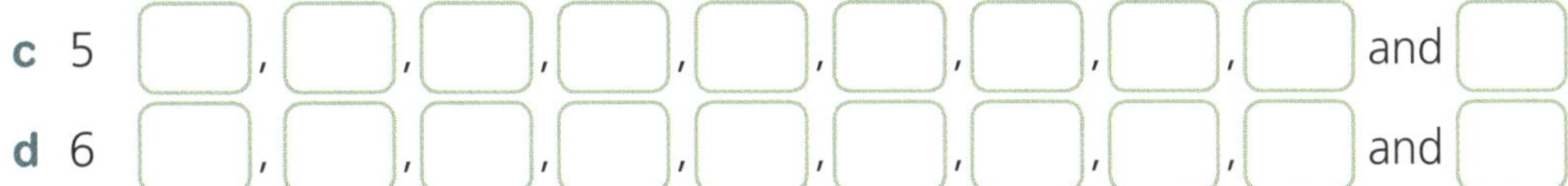
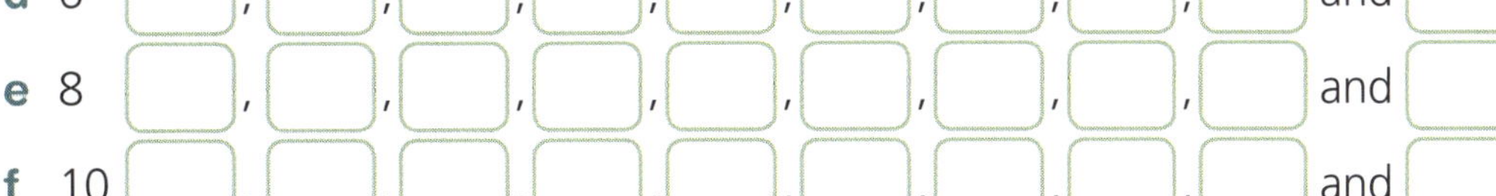

a 2 — 2, ☐, ☐, ☐, ☐, ☐, ☐, ☐, ☐ and ☐
b 4 — 4, ☐, ☐, ☐, ☐, ☐, ☐, ☐, ☐ and ☐
c 5 — ☐, ☐, ☐, ☐, ☐, ☐, ☐, ☐, ☐ and ☐
d 6 — ☐, ☐, ☐, ☐, ☐, ☐, ☐, ☐, ☐ and ☐
e 8 — ☐, ☐, ☐, ☐, ☐, ☐, ☐, ☐, ☐ and ☐
f 10 — ☐, ☐, ☐, ☐, ☐, ☐, ☐, ☐, ☐ and ☐

3 By looking at the answers in Question 2, find the smallest number that is a multiple of both:

a 2 and 5 ☐ b 5 and 6 ☐ c 6 and 10 ☐
d 5 and 8 ☐ e 2 and 10 ☐ f 4 and 10 ☐
g 6 and 8 ☐ h 4 and 5 ☐ i 8 and 10 ☐
j 2 and 8 ☐ k 4 and 8 ☐ l 5 and 10 ☐

4 Use different coloured connecting cubes to find the common multiples of 2 and 5.

The first 10 common multiples are:

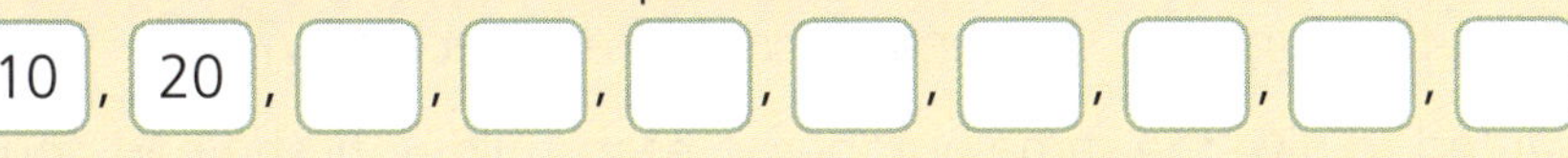

10, 20, ☐, ☐, ☐, ☐, ☐, ☐, ☐, ☐.

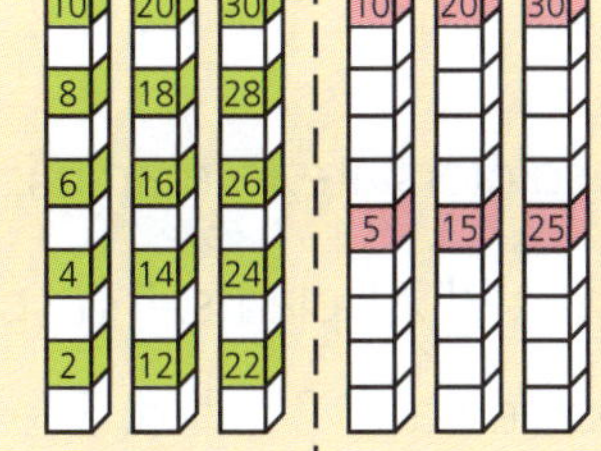

See *Extra Support 9* (Factors and multiples).

2:12 Factors

The factors of a counting number are all the counting numbers that divide it exactly.

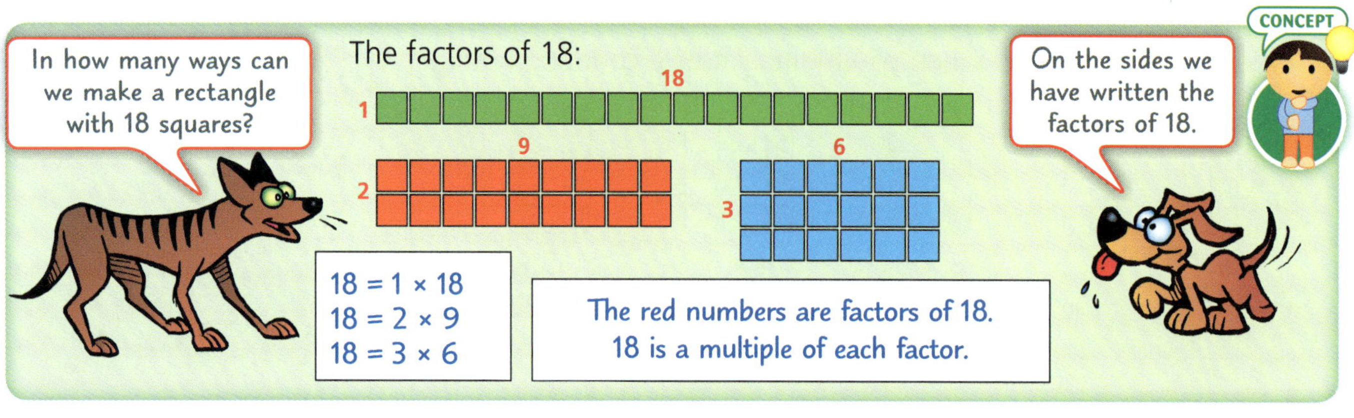

1. Use these rectangles to complete different number sentences below.

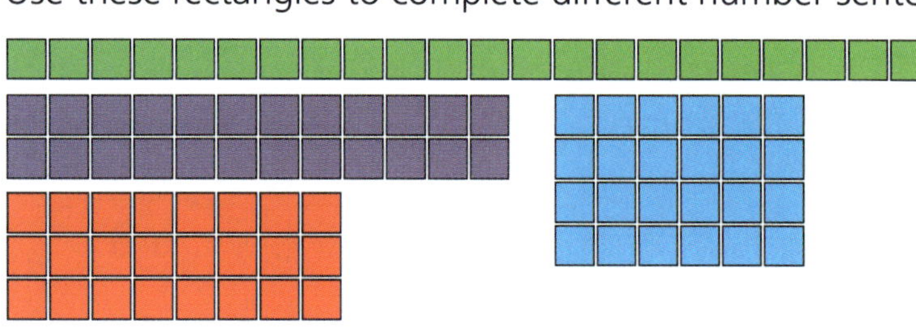

a 24 = ☐ × ☐   b 24 = ☐ × ☐   c 24 = ☐ × ☐

d 24 = ☐ × ☐   e The factors of 24 are ☐, ☐, ☐, ☐, ☐, ☐, ☐ and ☐.

2. Make rectangles using place-value blocks or square counters to find all factors of these numbers.

a 6: ☐, ☐, ☐, ☐

b 12: ☐, ☐, ☐, ☐, ☐, ☐

c 5: ☐, ☐

d 20: ☐, ☐, ☐, ☐, ☐, ☐

e 15: ☐, ☐, ☐, ☐

f 28: ☐, ☐, ☐, ☐, ☐, ☐

g 30: ☐, ☐, ☐, ☐, ☐, ☐, ☐, ☐

- Counting numbers that multiply to give a whole number are its **factors**.
- A number that has only two factors is called a **prime number**.
- A number that has more than two factors is called a **composite number**.

3. If 80 = 1 × 80, 80 = 2 × 40, 80 = 4 × 20, 80 = 5 × 16 and 80 = 8 × 10, then the factors of 80 are: ☐, ☐, ☐, ☐, ☐, ☐, ☐, ☐, ☐ and ☐.

4. a 16 soldiers are to march in equal rows. How wide could the rows be? ☐

b Sam had 21 plants. If he planted them in rows, how many could be in each row? ☐

c Debbie had 12 lollies. She wanted to give the same number to each child until she had none left. How many children might be given lollies? ☐

See *Extra Support 9* (Factors and multiples).

2:13 Factors and multiples

If a number ends in 0 or 5
it is a multiple of 5.
If it ends in 0, it is a multiple of 10.

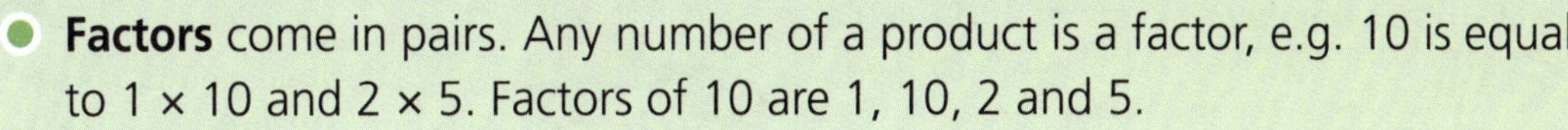

- **Factors** come in pairs. Any number of a product is a factor, e.g. 10 is equal to 1 × 10 and 2 × 5. Factors of 10 are 1, 10, 2 and 5.
- A **multiple** of a counting number is found when you multiply it by a counting number. The first 5 multiples of 7 are 7, 14, 21, 28 and 35.

1. Circle the factors of 21. 3 7 8 13 20 21
2. List the multiples of 2 that are less than 16. ______
3. What are the factors of 32? ___, ___, ___, ___, ___ and ___
4. What are the factors of 24? ___, ___, ___, ___, ___, ___, ___ and ___
5. What are the factors of 100? ___, ___, ___, ___, ___, ___, ___, ___, and ___
6. Write down the first ten multiples of:

   a 2 ___ ___ ___ ___ ___ ___ ___ ___ ___ ___

   b 4 ___ ___ ___ ___ ___ ___ ___ ___ ___ ___

   c 8 ___ ___ ___ ___ ___ ___ ___ ___ ___ ___

   d 10 ___ ___ ___ ___ ___ ___ ___ ___ ___ ___

2 is a factor of every even number.

7. Write the answer. Is it odd or even?

   a 4 × 4 = ___ which is ___ **b** 4 × 3 = ___ which is ___

   c 4 + 3 = ___ which is ___ **d** 4 + 6 = ___ which is ___

   e 7 × 2 = ___ which is ___ **f** 5 × 7 = ___ which is ___

8. Complete this for counting numbers.

   a even × even = ___ **b** even × odd = ___ **c** odd × odd = ___

INVESTIGATION

9. Give two examples to show that, for counting numbers:

   a even × even = even ______

   b even × odd = even ______

   c odd × odd = odd ______

   Discuss with others why this is so.

See *Extra Support 9* (Factors and multiples).

2:14 Addition of money

A decimal point (or full stop) separates the dollars and cents.
10 lots of 10 cents make 1 dollar.

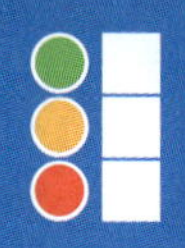

1

a $0.41 + $0.37	**b** $0.64 + $0.88	**c** $1.26 + $3.47	**d** $2.24 + $3.07	**e** $3.75 + $2.94
f $4.69 + $3.56	**g** $2.63 + $2.07	**h** $5.83 + $2.68	**i** $4.96 + $1.47	**j** $2.79 + $4.32
k $2.41 + $3.67	**l** $4.06 + $2.91	**m** $3.77 + $1.63	**n** $1.92 + $4.37	**o** $5.16 + $1.98

2 Write each as an algorithm or use a mental strategy to find your answer.

a $1.56 + $2.23 ______ **b** $4.01 + $1.76 ______

c $3.51 + $2.17 ______ **d** $5.03 + $3.65 ______

e $2.37 + $4.12 ______ **f** $6.45 + $2.03 ______

3 Find the total if I bought:

a a cake for $5.50 and a drink for $4.05. ______

b a dessert for $4.95 and a drink for $3.25. ______

c a sandwich for $7.30 and a drink for $1.55. ______

d a biscuit for $3.75 and a drink for $4.95. ______

4

a $2.21 + $0.85 + $1.82	**b** $1.61 + $3.17 + $4.05	**c** $4.68 + $1.83 + $2.86	**d** $5.91 + $1.45 + $1.65

2:15 Subtraction of money

Trade a ten-cent coin for 10 cents.
Trade $1 for 10 ten-cent coins.

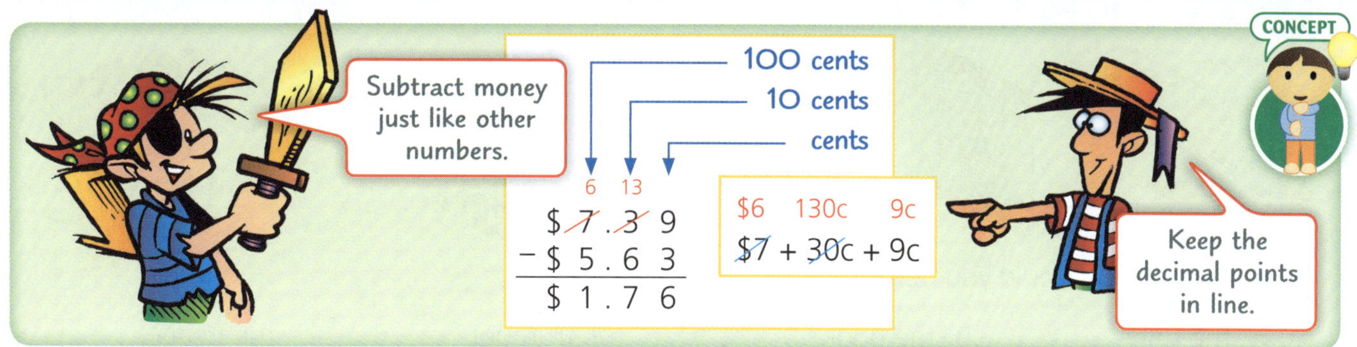

1

a $6.52 − $1.30	**b** $8.79 − $3.62	**c** $9.85 − $3.51	**d** $7.82 − $5.43	**e** $6.24 − $2.07
f $4.47 − $2.63	**g** $5.38 − $2.61	**h** $7.50 − $1.42	**i** $3.54 − $0.20	**j** $7.55 − $3.47
k $8.57 − $6.87	**l** $9.57 − $6.99	**m** $6.50 − $2.61	**n** $7.90 − $2.45	**o** $3.52 − $1.48

2 Write each as an algorithm or use a mental strategy to find your answer.

a $3.35 – $1.24 ______ **b** $8.98 – $4.00 ______

c $8.56 – $3.21 ______ **d** $4.54 – $4.49 ______

e $7.00 – $1.50 ______ **f** $3.50 – $1.99 ______

3 I started with $8.50. What do I have left if I buy:

a a book for $7.45? ______ **b** an icy pole for $2.30? ______

c a drink for $3.05? ______ **d** a keyring for $7.30? ______

e a pen for $4.95 ______ **f** marbles for $3.55? ______

First to $5

FUN SPOT

- Each player begins the game with $10 and takes turns to roll a dice.
- The number shown on each dice is multiplied by 10 and that number of cents is subtracted from the player's total.
- The game continues until one player reaches $5 or less.

2:16 Shopping

Trade 10 cents for a ten-cent coin.
Trade 10 ten-cent coins for $1.

$3.20

1 If you had $5, would you be able to buy:

a the hat? ☐ **b** the book? ☐ **c** the trumpet? ☐ **d** the bear? ☐

e the book and the bear? ☐ **f** the hat and the bear? ☐

g the hat and the trumpet? ☐ **h** the trumpet and the bear? ☐

2 Find the total of each bill.

a	hat	$2.90	**b**	hat	$2.90	**c**	book	$4.50
	bear	$1.70		book	$4.50		trumpet	$3.20
	total	____		total	____		total	____
d	book	$4.50	**e**	hat	$2.90	**f**	book	$4.50
	hat	$2.90		bear	$1.70		bear	$1.70
	bear	$1.70		trumpet	$3.20		trumpet	$3.20
	total	____		total	____		total	____

3 Find the amount of money left.

a $9.00 − $4.60 **b** $9.00 − $6.20 **c** $9.00 − $7.80 **d** $9.00 − $4.90 **e** $9.00 − $7.40

4 **a** $3.78 + $5.93 **b** $2.75 + $6.27 **c** $1.82 + $7.36 **d** $4.24 + $3.57 **e** $5.51 + $1.98

f $7.63 − $4.36 **g** $9.74 − $3.29 **h** $8.11 − $4.72 **i** $9.80 − $3.47 **j** $8.25 − $4.99

5 Round the answers from Question 4 to the nearest 5 cents.

a ☐ **b** ☐ **c** ☐ **d** ☐ **e** ☐

f ☐ **g** ☐ **h** ☐ **i** ☐ **j** ☐

2:17 Division with remainders

Sometimes we're asked for the remainder, sometimes we're not.

CONCEPT

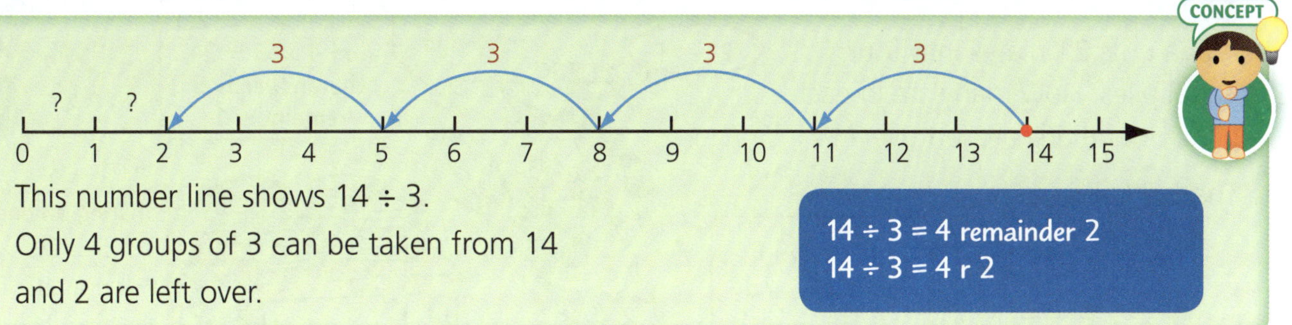

This number line shows 14 ÷ 3.

Only 4 groups of 3 can be taken from 14 and 2 are left over.

14 ÷ 3 = 4 remainder 2
14 ÷ 3 = 4 r 2

1 Use a number line to find the answers.

a 8 ÷ 3 = ☐ r ☐ **b** 9 ÷ 4 = ☐ r ☐ **c** 12 ÷ 5 = ☐ r ☐ **d** 14 ÷ 5 = ☐ r ☐

e 13 ÷ 5 = ☐ r ☐ **f** 11 ÷ 4 = ☐ r ☐ **g** 15 ÷ 4 = ☐ r ☐ **h** 15 ÷ 6 = ☐ r ☐

2 Use the pictures to answer these division questions.

	48
	80

a How many packets of 7 lollies in 48? 48 ÷ 7 = ☐ packets and ☐ remaining

b How many groups of 10 lollies in 48? 48 ÷ 10 = ☐ groups and ☐ remaining

c How many rows of 8 lollies in 48? 48 ÷ 8 = ☐ rows and ☐ remaining

d How many lots of 8 drops in 80? 80 ÷ 8 = ☐ lots and ☐ remaining

e How many lots of 10 drops in 80? 80 ÷ 10 = ☐ lots and ☐ remaining

f How many groups of 9 drops in 80? 80 ÷ 9 = ☐ groups and ☐ remaining

3 **a** How many groups of 3 hats can be made from 17 hats?

17 ÷ 3 = ☐ groups and ☐ remaining

b 17 ÷ 6 = ☐ groups of 6 and ☐ remaining

4 Use counters or place-value blocks to answer these.

a 10 pencils fill one tin. How many tins will 35 pencils fill? ☐ tins, 35 ÷ 10 = ☐ ,(r ☐)

b 33 books are in sets of 4. How many sets are there? ☐ sets, 33 ÷ 4 = ☐ ,(r ☐)

c 8 stamps fill a page. 42 stamps fill … ☐ pages, 42 ÷ 8 = ☐ ,(r ☐)

d 6 pens fill a box. 50 pens fill … ☐ boxes, 50 ÷ 6 = ☐ ,(r ☐)

2:18 Division of 2-digit numbers

Knowing your tables will make this easier.

CONCEPT

Alana puts 21 plates into four equal piles. How many are in each pile? How many are left over?

That's 21 divided by 4.

5 r 1

4) 21

That's 5 in each pile and 1 left over.

Sharing among 4:
4 × 5 = 20
(less than 21)
4 × 6 = 24
(too much)

1 You could use place-value blocks to answer these.

a r 2) 9	**b** r 3) 7	**c** r 2) 15	**d** r 4) 7	**e** r 5) 13
f r 4) 22	**g** r 5) 8	**h** r 6) 16	**i** r 3) 26	**j** r 10) 78
k r 4) 34	**l** r 10) 65	**m** r 7) 25	**n** r 10) 92	**o** r 8) 20
p r 9) 19	**q** r 5) 44	**r** r 6) 32	**s** r 8) 35	**t** r 7) 40

Share 60 sweets among 3 boys. How many sweets each? That's 60 divided by 3.

20

3) 60

Each boy has 20 sweets.

2

a 4) 40	**b** 2) 60	**c** 3) 30	**d** 5) 50	**e** 2) 40
f 3) 60	**g** 2) 20	**h** 3) 90	**i** 8) 80	**j** 6) 60

3 **a** We have 60 kg of rice to give away. How many people can be given 8 kg?

r
8) 60 ☐ people

b We wrapped 25 exercise books in packs of 4. How many packs did we wrap?

r
4) 25 ☐ packs

2:19 Using division facts

Division can be:
sharing … How many will each receive?
grouping… *How many groups can be made?*

How many teams of eight can be made with 52 students?

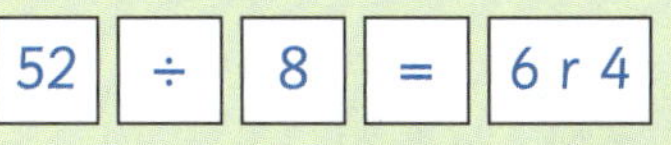

There are 6 teams of eight (and 4 students remaining).

CONCEPT

52 ÷ 8?
Since 6 × 8 = 48 and 7 × 8 = 56, the answer is 6 (remainder 4).

1 Use the first number sentence to fill in the other one.

a (6 × 3) + 2 = 20 20 ÷ 3 = ☐ r ☐ b (4 × 10) + 1 = 41 41 ÷ 10 = ☐ r ☐

c (7 × 9) + 2 = 65 65 ÷ 9 = ☐ r ☐

2

a 10 ÷ 4 = ☐ r ☐	b 13 ÷ 5 = ☐ r ☐	c 28 ÷ 6 = ☐ r ☐
d 40 ÷ 7 = ☐ r ☐	e 21 ÷ 2 = ☐ r ☐	f 17 ÷ 10 = ☐ r ☐
g 66 ÷ 8 = ☐ r ☐	h 43 ÷ 6 = ☐ r ☐	i 39 ÷ 5 = ☐ r ☐
j 14 ÷ 4 = ☐ r ☐	k 76 ÷ 9 = ☐ r ☐	l 53 ÷ 7 = ☐ r ☐

3 Write as a number sentence, showing remainders:

a 17 shared among 3.
☐ ÷ ☐ = ☐ r ☐

b 27 divided by 7.
☐ ÷ ☐ = ☐ r ☐

c 30 in groups of eight.
☐ ÷ ☐ = ☐ r ☐

d 25 oranges put into groups of 6. How many groups?
☐ ÷ ☐ = ☐ r ☐

e 53 cows put into herds of 10. How many herds?
☐ ÷ ☐ = ☐ r ☐

f 33 desks put into groups of 5. How many groups?
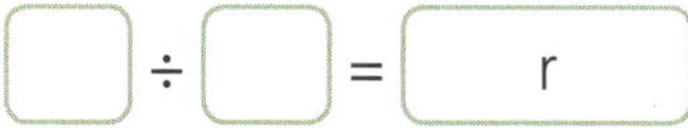

g 60 wombats shared among 9 zoos. How many in each zoo?
☐ ☐ ☐ = ☐ r ☐

h 36 biscuits put into rows of 8. How many rows?
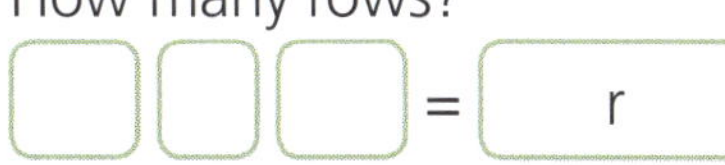

i 47 galahs living in groups of 6. How many groups?
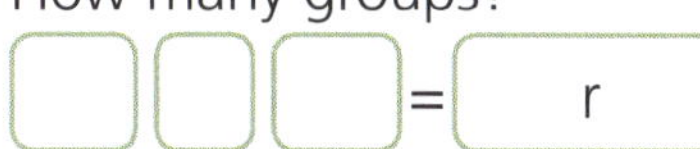

j 32 bottles put into 8 rows. How many in each row?
☐ ☐ ☐ = ☐ r ☐

k 29 birds flying in a flock. How many pairs?

l 53 days, 7 days in a week. How many weeks?
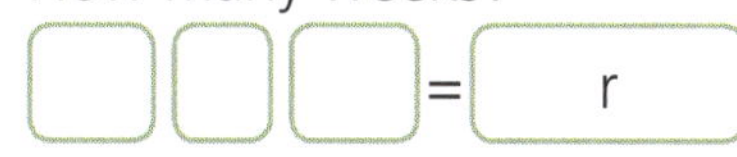

m 25 divided by 4.
☐ ☐ ☐ = ☐ r ☐

n 27 divided by 2.

o 46 divided by 5.
☐ ☐ ☐ = ☐ r ☐

4 How many teams of 5 can be made with 47 students? ☐

2:20 Subtraction to 999

435 = 300 + 120 + 15
− 100 − 80 − 9
= 200 + 40 + 6

CONCEPT

Abbie had 435 marbles. She gave her friend 189. How many were left?

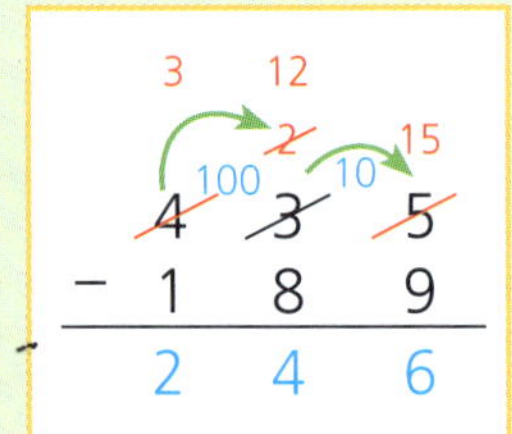

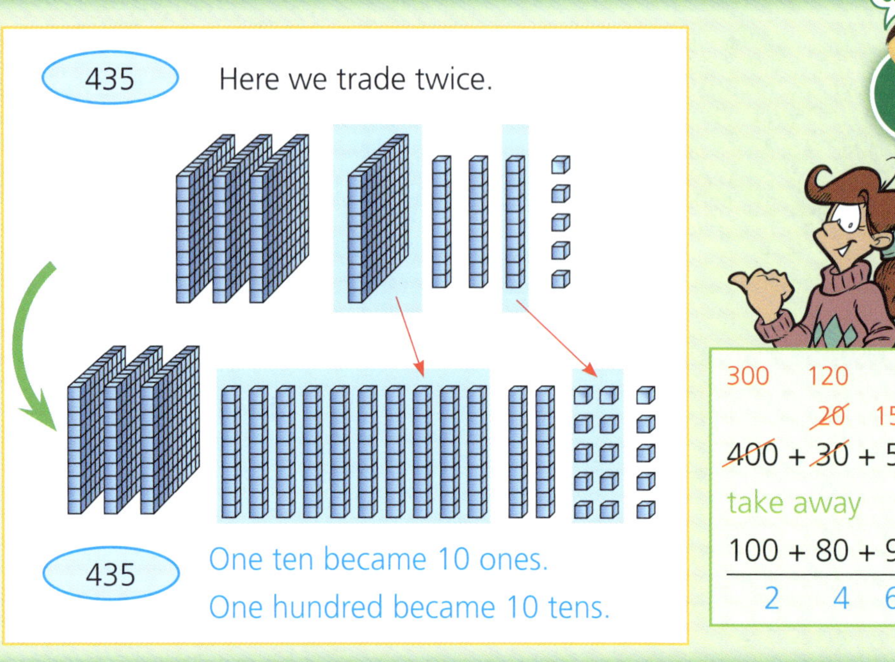

Abbie had 246 marbles left.

300	120	
	~~20~~	15
~~400~~ +	~~30~~ +	5
take away		
100 +	80 +	9
2	4	6

1

a 412 − 75
b 360 − 82
c 726 − 97
d 641 − 65

e 360 − 183
f 715 − 246
g 614 − 446
h 333 − 144

i 904 − 287
j 641 − 388
k 614 − 269
l 835 − 167

m 573 − 486
n 711 − 169
o 527 − 188
p 555 − 466

2 Use the strategy shown on the right to do these.

a 700 − 278 ☐
b 500 − 146 ☐

a 699 − ___ = ___ +1
b 499 − ___ = ___ +1

Discuss the strategy used here.

800 − 346 = 799 + 1 − 346

= 799 − 346 = 453 +1

= 454

2:21 Subtraction from hundreds

$600
= $500 + $90 + $10

Kim had saved $600. She gave $155 to help people affected by bushfires in Australia. How much did she have left?

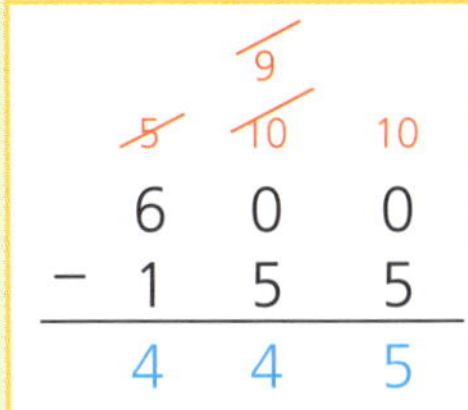

Kim had $445 left.

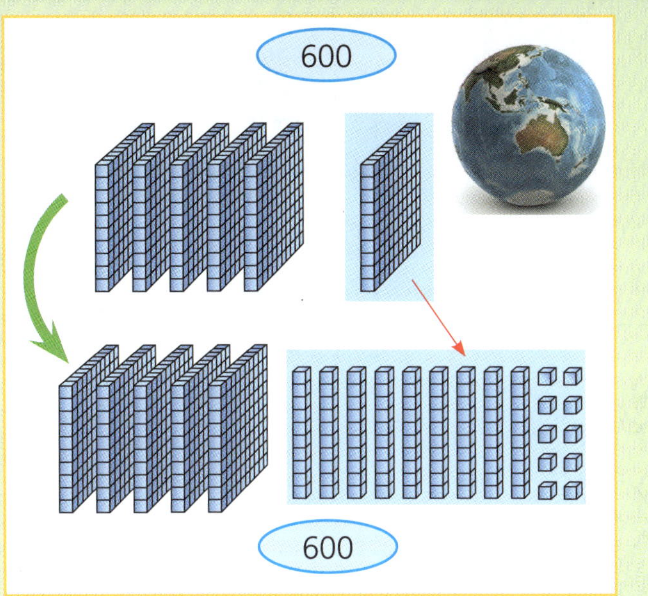

500 + 90 + 10
take away
100 + 50 + 5
400 + 40 + 5

1

a H T U
  1 0 0
−   2 7

b H T U
  2 0 0
−   3 8

c H T U
  9 0 0
−   6 1

d H T U
  6 0 0
−   5 5

e
  7 0 0
− 3 0 2

f
  9 0 0
− 7 9 3

g
  4 0 0
− 1 0 6

h
  3 0 0
− 2 5 3

2

a
  $ 6 . 0 0
− $ 5 . 3 4

b
  $ 5 . 0 0
− $ 3 . 9 9

c
  $ 8 . 0 0
− $ 6 . 7 4

d
  $ 7 . 0 0
− $ 6 . 6 8

3 Estimate each answer, then use the estimates to check your answers.

a Chloe needed 600 points to qualify for a state team. She earned only 487 points. How far short of her target was she?

b Blackburn Post Office was sent 900 stamp albums to sell. If 481 albums were sold in the first month, how many were left?

c In our class library we have 400 books. I have read 147. How many books have I not read?

d What is left if I had $10 and spent $3.65?

4 Use the strategy on the right to answer these.

a 700 − 182   **b** 400 − 279   **c** $900 − $528

 • *AUSTRALIAN SIGNPOST MATHS 5* • ISBN 9780655708797

2:22 Addition to 9999

Th means thousands. **T** means tens.
H means hundreds. **U** means ones.

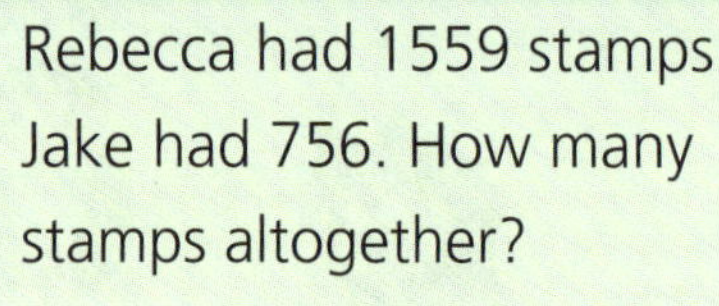

Rebecca had 1559 stamps. Jake had 756. How many stamps altogether?

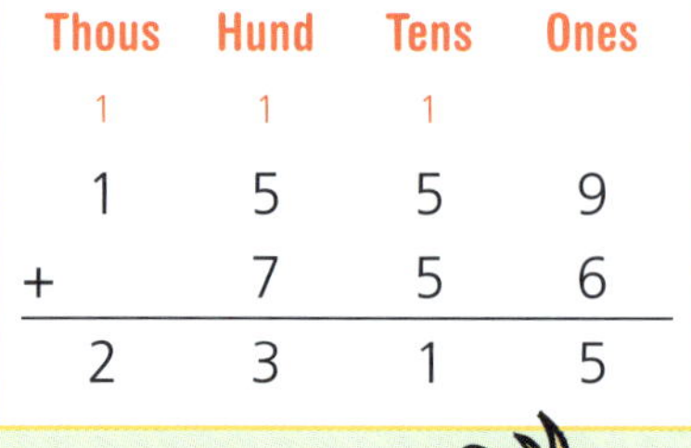

	Thous	Hund	Tens	Ones
	1	1	1	
	1	5	5	9
+		7	5	6
	2	3	1	5

2315 stamps altogether.

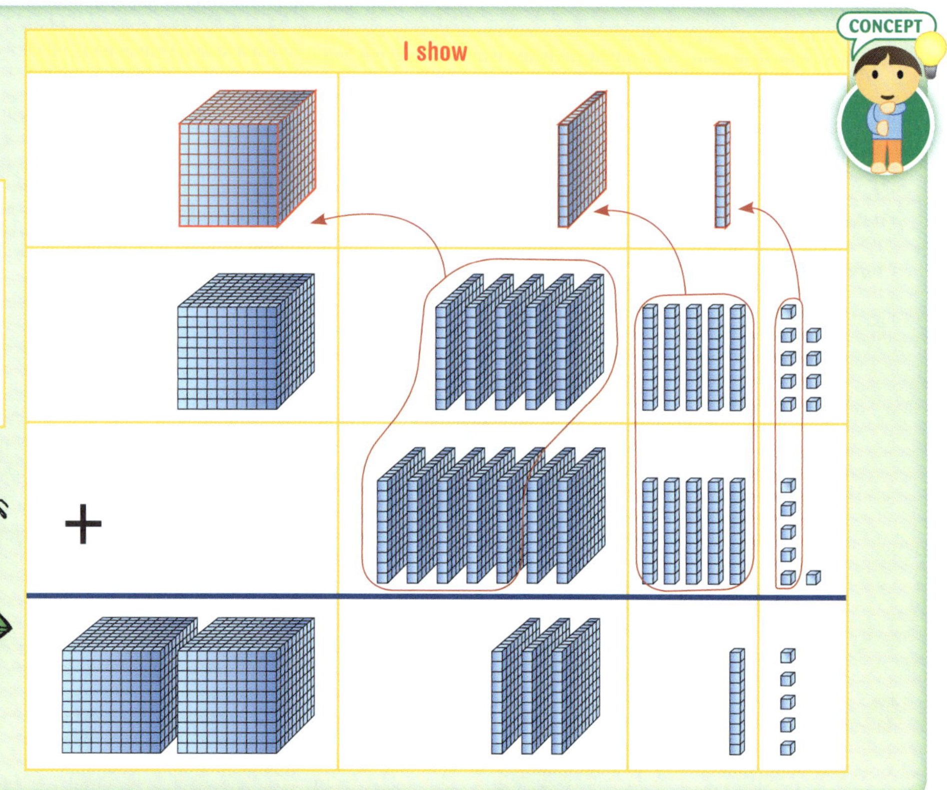

1

	Th H T U
a	3416 + 2052
b	8104 + 871
c	6318 + 1270
d	392 + 3406
e	35 + 7932
f	3418 + 2906
g	7950 + 650
h	6087 + 1164
i	946 + 2627
j	6492 + 1748

2

a	5071 + 2124
b	3831 + 1054
c	2516 + 1827
d	3195 + 5730
e	7041 + 978
f	4692 + 2813
g	7472 + 1809
h	479 + 3860
i	1793 + 5824
j	6097 + 1835

3

a	\$7542 + \$1607
b	\$6549 + \$1742
c	\$3581 + \$4328
d	\$2591 + \$3706
e	\$7059 + \$2371

2:23 Addition to 9999

13 hundreds
= 1 thousand + 3 hundreds

CONCEPT

I have three stamp albums. In the first is 3087 stamps, in the second 1872 stamps and in the third 4378. How many stamps have I got altogether?

How many stamps?

3087 + 1872 + 4378 = ☐

Answer

I have 9337 stamps.

	Thous	Hund	Tens	Ones
	1	2	1	
	3	0	8	7
	1	8	7	2
+	4	3	7	8
	9	3	3	7

1

a

	Th	H	T	U
	1	8	3	5
		4	0	8
+	5	3	1	8

b

	Th	H	T	U
		9	9	9
	4	2	5	6
+	1	6	8	0

c

	Th	H	T	U
	8	4	1	8
		6	4	7
+		7	5	3

d

	Th	H	T	U
	3	8	4	2
		7	0	6
+	2	9	3	4

2

a

```
   386
  2514
   977
+   27
```

b

```
   183
   964
  1863
+ 2098
```

c

```
  5142
   863
   744
+ 1088
```

d

```
  2099
  1847
  1935
+ 1207
```

3

a

```
  $61.29
  $13.91
+ $10.94
```

b

```
  $28.18
  $14.63
+ $ 9.72
```

c

```
  $ 8.47
  $60.08
+ $21.55
```

d

```
  $28.47
  $29.66
+ $28.67
```

4 Estimate then calculate. (E = estimate, A = answer)

a Residents were phoned at 3187 homes in Bendigo, 1394 in Ballarat and 914 in Geelong. How many residents were phoned? E = ☐ A = ☐

b A bookshop kept 3096 books in room A, 2515 in room B and 2845 in room C. How many books were in the three rooms? E = ☐ A = ☐

c Sandy spent $3245 renovating her laundry, $2188 on landscaping and $2840 on furniture. How much did she spend? E = ☐ A = ☐

2:24 Subtraction to 9999

1 thousand can be traded for 10 hundreds.

CONCEPT

2216 people started in a *Town To Surf* race, but 865 people dropped out before the finish. How many people finished the race?

- We can show 2216 with place-value blocks.
- Trade 1 hundred for 10 tens.
- Trade 1 thousand for 10 hundreds.
- Now we can subtract 865 by taking away 8 hundreds, 6 tens and 5 ones.

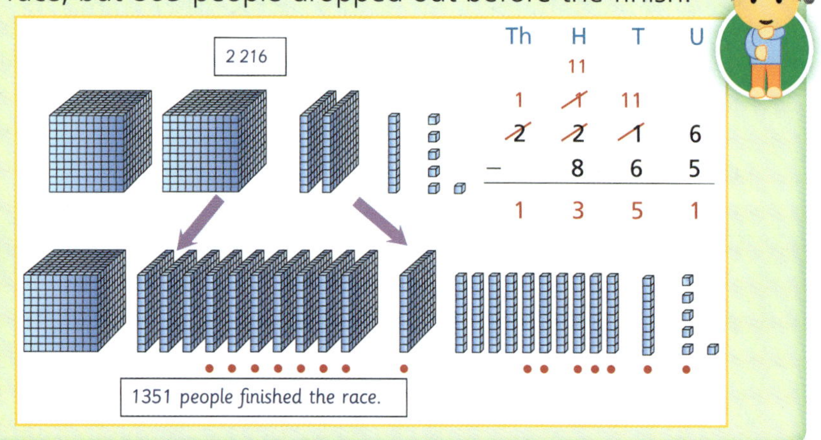

1

	a	b	c	d	e
	5695	7850	6925	8046	9388
−	1342	750	1505	46	3175

	f	g	h	i	j
	6450	2392	7500	6432	5299
−	380	1950	2180	129	3475

2

	a	b	c	d	e
	4381	2186	4506	7860	9945
−	1605	993	3800	870	6877

	f	g	h	i	j
	2315	6105	9031	7637	5455
−	1946	3827	7429	888	1966

3 a Stephanie made 9690 phone calls last year. If 7815 calls were related to her business, how many were not business calls?

b 3495 calls were on her mobile phone. How many were not on her mobile phone?

c During June, her business received $8475 and paid out $4816. How much money did her business make in June?

4 Tran bought 8095 bricks to pave part of his backyard. He used only 7186 bricks. How many were not used?

 • *AUSTRALIAN SIGNPOST MATHS 5* • ISBN 9780655708797

2:25

Subtraction from 1000s

1 thousand can be traded for 10 hundreds.

CONCEPT

We received 6000 books from the printers.
We sold 3721. How many have we got left?

	Th	H	T	U
		9	9	
	5	~~10~~	~~10~~	10
	~~6~~	~~0~~	~~0~~	~~0~~
−	3	7	2	1
	2	2	7	9

6000 has a zero in the units, tens and hundreds columns.

We trade 1 thousand for 10 hundreds, then trade 1 hundred for 10 tens, then trade 1 ten for 10 ones, and then subtract.

2279 books are left.

1

a $1000 - 436$

b $2000 - 301$

c $1000 - 897$

d $3000 - 725$

e $7000 - 1832$

f $4000 - 2860$

g $5000 - 3900$

h $9000 - 4427$

2

a $8000 - 3450$

b $6000 - 2988$

c $2000 - 1225$

d $7000 - 5355$

e $7000 - 4186$

f $4000 - 2695$

g $9000 - 8972$

h $8000 - 1367$

3

a The longest river is the Nile in North Africa (6690 km). Australia's longest river system is the Murray–Darling, which is 3370 km. How much shorter is this than the Nile?

b How much deeper is the Indian Ocean (7125 m at the Java Trench) than the Arctic Ocean (5450 m at the Eurasia Basin)?

c Mount Everest, the highest mountain on Earth, has an altitude of 8850 m. We needed to use a supply of oxygen as we climbed the last 5192 m of our ascent to the top. At what altitude did we begin to use oxygen?

d Tom McSeveny was born on 24 March 1916. How old was he on 24 March 2004?

e Lil Travers was born on 19 December 1919. How old was she on 28 December 2005?

Use estimation to check your answers.

 • *AUSTRALIAN SIGNPOST MATHS 5* • ISBN 9780655708797

2:26 Subtraction from 1000s strategy

8000:
7999 + 1

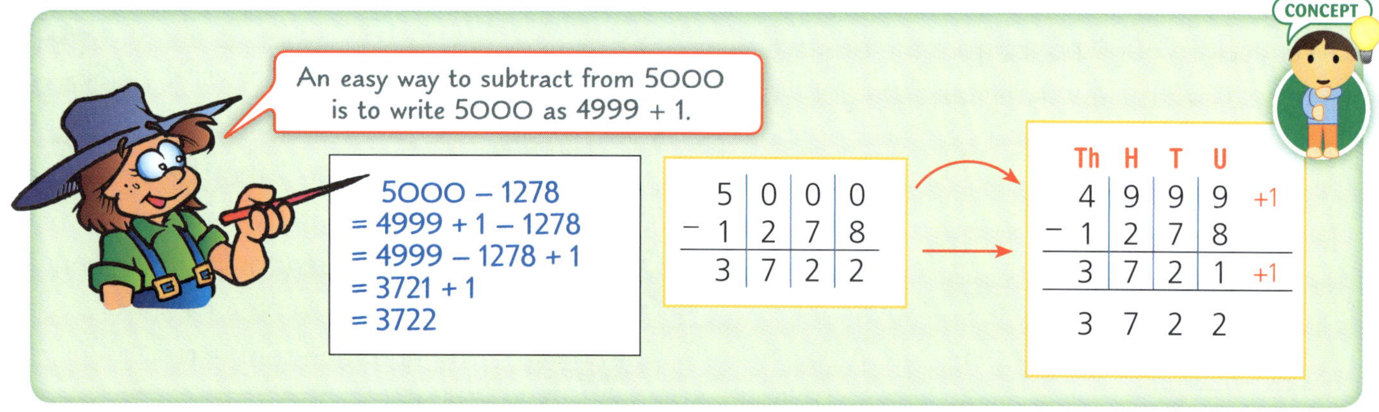

1 Use the strategy above to complete these.

a Th H T U
9 9 9 +1
~~1 0 0 0~~
− 3 8 2
+1
= ______

b Th H T U
3 9 9 9 +1
~~4 0 0 0~~
− 2 6 9 1
+1
= ______

c Th H T U
1 9 9 9 +1
~~2 0 0 0~~
− 1 9 8 3
+1
= ______

d Th H T U
2 9 9 9 +1
~~3 0 0 0~~
− 1 9 2 4
+1
= ______

e Th H T U
6 9 9 9 +1
~~7 0 0 0~~
− 3 4 8 1
+1
= ______

f Th H T U
5 9 9 9 +1
~~6 0 0 0~~
− 4 9 7 5
+1
= ______

g Th H T U
+1
~~$9 0 0 0~~
− $8 2 0 7
+1
= ______

h Th H T U
+1
~~$5 0 0 0~~
− $3 0 8 2
+1
= ______

i Th H T U
+1
~~$8 0 0 0~~
− $3 7 9 1
+1
= ______

2 Complete these on your own paper.

a 3000 – 1973 = ______

b 5000 – 1903 = ______

c 9000 – 2752 = ______

d 6000 – 2246 = ______

e I had $4000. I spent $2731. My change is ______.

3 **a** Solve 100 000 – 32 975 by changing 100 000 into 99 999 + 1. ______

b Solve 1 million – 237 345 by changing 1 million into 999 999 + 1. ______

2:27 Dividing 2-digit numbers

Divide the tens first, trade tens not used for ones, then divide the ones.

CONCEPT

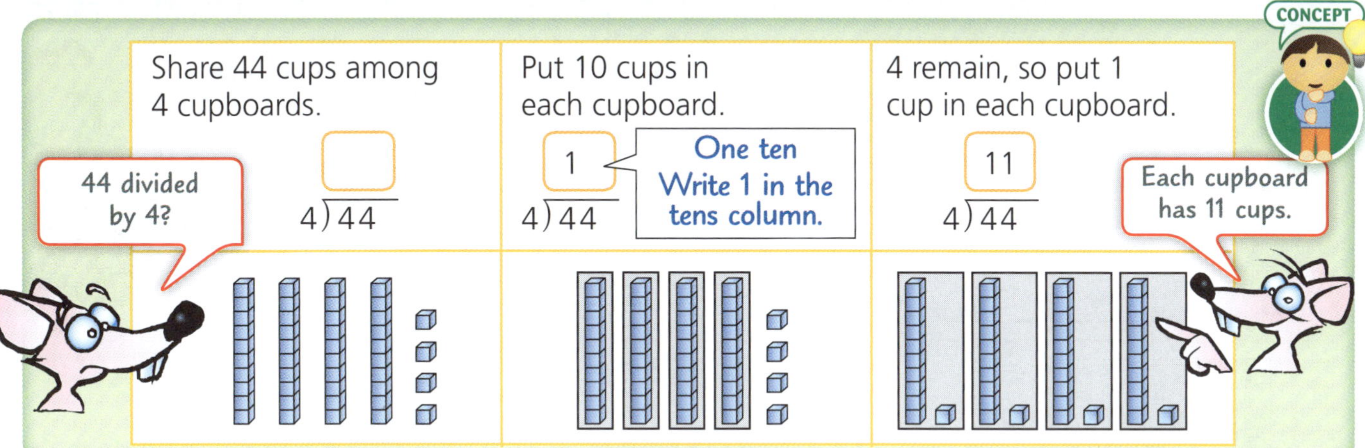

1 Here you won't need to trade tens for ones. Use a calculator to check your answers.

a	b	c	d	e	f
2)44	2)68	2)88	2)24	3)33	3)66

g	h	i	j	k	l
3)39	3)36	4)44	4)48	4)84	4)88

CONCEPT

Share 52 pens among 4 boxes.	Put 10 in each box and trade 1 ten for 10 ones.	12 remain, so put 3 in each box.

We can use place-value blocks to divide.

2 Use place-value blocks or mental strategies to do these. Use a calculator to check your answers.

a $34 \div 2 =$ ☐ b $45 \div 3 =$ ☐ c $92 \div 4 =$ ☐

d $54 \div 3 =$ ☐ e $65 \div 5 =$ ☐ f $68 \div 4 =$ ☐

FUN SPOT

Snakes and ladders

- Use the board on the right to play the game.
- Take turns to roll two dice. If one number divides the other exactly, divide, and move that number of spaces forward.

  If the dice show 6 and 2 (6 ÷ 2), move 3 spaces forward.
- The first to land on **Finish** wins.

2:28 Dividing 2-digit numbers

Divide the tens first, trade tens not used for ones, then divide the ones.

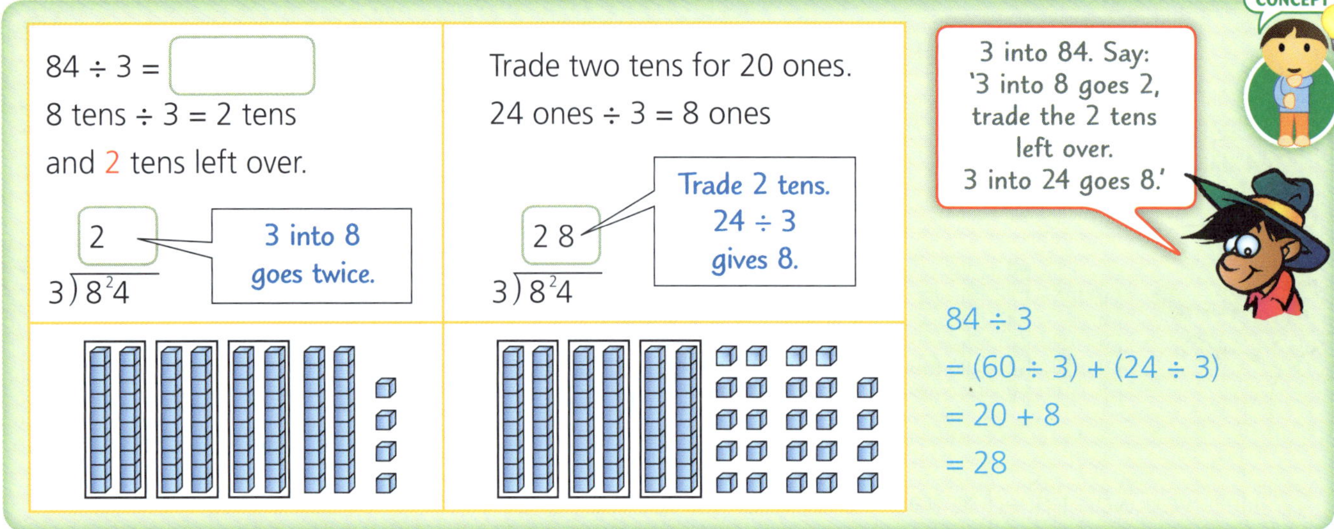

CONCEPT

84 ÷ 3 = ☐
8 tens ÷ 3 = 2 tens
and 2 tens left over.

$3\overline{)8^{2}4}$ with 2 above — 3 into 8 goes twice.

Trade two tens for 20 ones.
24 ones ÷ 3 = 8 ones

$3\overline{)8^{2}4}$ with 28 above — Trade 2 tens. 24 ÷ 3 gives 8.

3 into 84. Say: '3 into 8 goes 2, trade the 2 tens left over. 3 into 24 goes 8.'

84 ÷ 3
= (60 ÷ 3) + (24 ÷ 3)
= 20 + 8
= 28

1

a	b	c	d
2)46	5)55	4)84	2)82
e	**f**	**g**	**h**
3)90	2)24	2)68	6)66

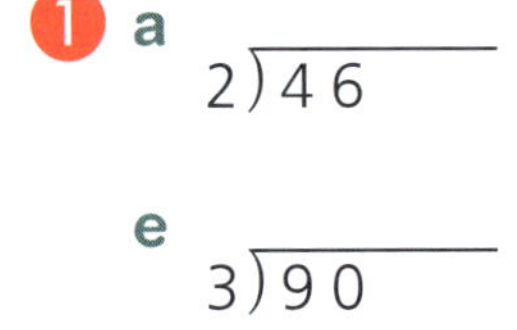

$4\overline{)7^{3}2}$ with 18 above

2 In these you need to trade 1 ten for 10 ones.

a	b	c	d
3)75	2)96	5)65	4)96
e	**f**	**g**	**h**
6)78	3)45	7)84	8)96

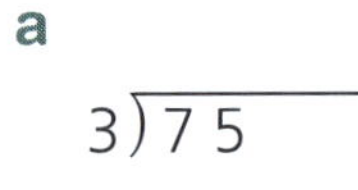

3 In these, you need to trade tens for ones.

a	b	c	d
3)54	7)98	5)70	4)68
e	**f**	**g**	**h**
5)85	5)95	6)96	3)87

280 ÷ 14
(divide both by 7)
40 ÷ 2 = 20

4 In each case, find one share.

a 52 brushes shared by 4.

4)52

One share = ☐

b 85 ladders shared by 5.

5)85

One share = ☐

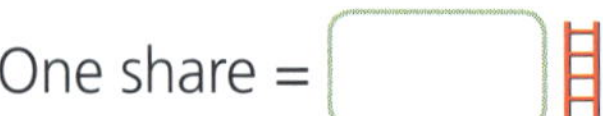

c 91 globes shared by 7.

7)91

One share = ☐

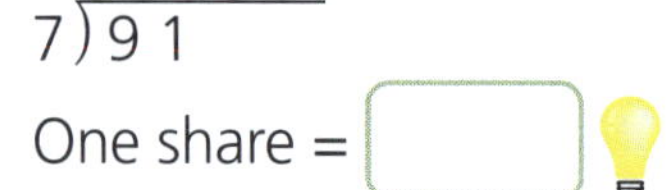

d 90 plants shared by 5.

5)90

One share = ☐

e 66 caps shared by 3.

3)66

One share = ☐

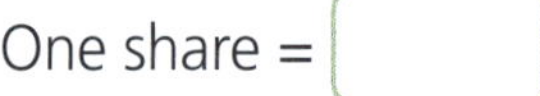

f 90 spades shared by 6.

6)90

One share = ☐

2:29 Dividing 2-digit numbers

Divide the tens first, trade tens not used for ones, then divide the ones.

CONCEPT

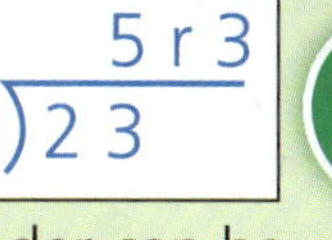

Share 23 pieces of toast between four people.

$4\overline{)23}$ = 5 r 3

In this case the remainder can be shared also.

$\frac{1}{4}$	$\frac{1}{4}$	$\frac{1}{4}$	$\frac{1}{4}$	$\frac{1}{4}$	$\frac{1}{4}$
$\frac{1}{4}$	$\frac{1}{4}$	$\frac{1}{4}$	$\frac{1}{4}$	$\frac{1}{4}$	$\frac{1}{4}$

Each person would be given an extra $\frac{3}{4}$ of a piece of toast.

$4\overline{)23}$ = $5\frac{3}{4}$

Each person receives $5\frac{3}{4}$ pieces of toast.

1 Show all remainders as fractions.

a $2\overline{)25}$ b $3\overline{)35}$ c $4\overline{)89}$

d $5\overline{)53}$ e $6\overline{)69}$ f $3\overline{)37}$

2 In these, you will need to trade 1 ten for 10 ones.

a $2\overline{)35}$ b $3\overline{)74}$ c $2\overline{)33}$

d $8\overline{)99}$ e $6\overline{)79}$ f $4\overline{)59}$

3 In these, you will need to trade 2 tens for 20 ones.

a $5\overline{)75}$ b $3\overline{)51}$ c $7\overline{)98}$ d $3\overline{)57}$

e $4\overline{)64}$ f $3\overline{)84}$ g $6\overline{)84}$ h $7\overline{)91}$

$3\overline{)8^{2}1}$ = 2 7

4 Here you will need to trade tens for ones.

a $5\overline{)85}$ b $6\overline{)96}$ c $4\overline{)76}$ d $5\overline{)90}$ e $2\overline{)96}$

f $2\overline{)74}$ g $5\overline{)80}$ h $3\overline{)81}$ i $4\overline{)72}$ j $6\overline{)90}$

5 a In two days I walked 36 km. What was the average distance walked each day?

b Seven people contributed a total of $84. What was the average amount given?

c Three towns in Australia recorded temperatures of 37°C, 15°C and 23°C. What was the average temperature for these towns?

d Five Goliath spiders were caught. The spans of their legs were 28 cm, 28 cm, 25 cm, 18 cm and 16 cm. What was the average span of their legs?

To find the average, find the total and divide by the number sharing.

2:30 Dividing 3-digit numbers

Divide the hundreds first, trade hundreds not used for tens, then divide the tens and ones.

CONCEPT

Amy was told to send the same number of glasses to six restaurants. What is the greatest number she can send to each if she has 897 glasses?

$$6\overline{)8^{2}9^{5}7} = 149\ r3$$

6 into **8** goes 1 time with 2 left over. Trade the 2.
6 into 2**9** goes 4 times with 5 left. Trade the 5.
6 into 5**7** goes 9 times with a remainder of 3.

Amy can send 149 glasses to each restaurant. She would then have 3 glasses left.

1 There are no remainders in these.

a $3\overline{)402}$ b $2\overline{)570}$ c $4\overline{)576}$ d $6\overline{)732}$ e $5\overline{)665}$

f $4\overline{)696}$ g $7\overline{)945}$ h $6\overline{)870}$ i $8\overline{)952}$ j $7\overline{)889}$

2 These have remainders.

a $6\overline{)887}$ b $5\overline{)706}$ c $4\overline{)937}$ d $7\overline{)824}$ e $3\overline{)772}$

f $8\overline{)939}$ g $4\overline{)786}$ h $6\overline{)814}$ i $5\overline{)918}$ j $8\overline{)951}$

3 a $4\overline{)324}$ b $5\overline{)250}$ c $3\overline{)216}$

d $6\overline{)378}$ e $8\overline{)264}$ f $9\overline{)657}$

4 a $4\overline{)169}$ b $5\overline{)155}$ c $8\overline{)649}$ d $7\overline{)800}$

e $4\overline{)300}$ f $8\overline{)900}$ g $9\overline{)400}$ h $7\overline{)200}$

i $9\overline{)342}$ j $4\overline{)196}$ k $5\overline{)335}$ l $3\overline{)282}$ m $7\overline{)588}$

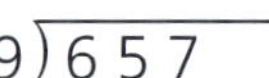

5 a The cheetah is the fastest land animal. If it can travel 105 metres in 5 seconds, how far could it travel in 1 second?

b The fastest animal is the peregrine falcon. It can fly 776 metres in 8 seconds. How far can it travel in 1 second?

 • *AUSTRALIAN SIGNPOST MATHS 5* • ISBN 9780655708797

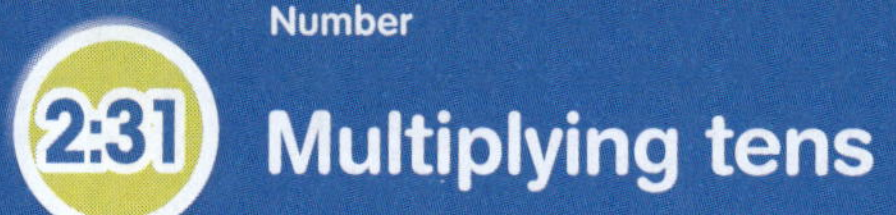

2:31 Multiplying tens

470 = 4 hundreds + 7 tens
= 47 tens

10 tens = 100

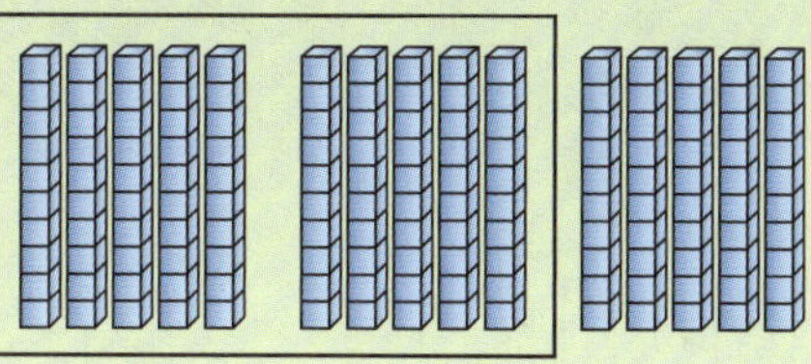

15 tens = 150 15 × 10 = 150

CONCEPT

To multiply by 10, put a zero at the end.

8 × 10 = 80
21 tens = 210
47 × 10 = 470

1
a 8 tens = ☐ b 9 tens = ☐ c 6 tens = ☐ d 4 tens = ☐
e 11 tens = ☐ f 14 tens = ☐ g 12 tens = ☐ h 13 tens = ☐
i 32 tens = ☐ j 21 tens = ☐ k 48 tens = ☐ l 85 tens = ☐
m 90 tens = ☐ n 77 tens = ☐ o 60 tens = ☐ p 99 tens = ☐

2
a 8 × 10 = ☐ b 7 × 10 = ☐ c 10 × 10 = ☐ d 9 × 10 = ☐
e 13 × 10 = ☐ f 18 × 10 = ☐ g 27 × 10 = ☐ h 22 × 10 = ☐
i 35 × 10 = ☐ j 61 × 10 = ☐ k 84 × 10 = ☐ l 75 × 10 = ☐

3
a 6 × 3 tens = ☐ tens = ☐
b 7 × 3 tens = ☐ tens = ☐
c 4 × 5 tens = ☐ tens = ☐
d 2 × 9 tens = ☐ tens = ☐
e 8 × 4 tens = ☐
f 5 × 8 tens = ☐
g 4 × 9 tens = ☐
h 7 × 6 tens = ☐

4
a 6 × 30 = 6 × 3 × 10 = ☐
b 8 × 50 = 8 × 5 × 10 = ☐
c 7 × 40 = 7 × 4 × 10 = ☐
d 5 × 40 = 5 × 4 × 10 = ☐

5
a 4 × 30 = ☐ b 3 × 60 = ☐ c 4 × 80 = ☐ d 7 × 50 = ☐
e 7 × $20 = ☐ f 9 × $60 = ☐ g 8 × $80 = ☐ h 6 × $60 = ☐

 • *AUSTRALIAN SIGNPOST MATHS 5* • ISBN 9780655708797

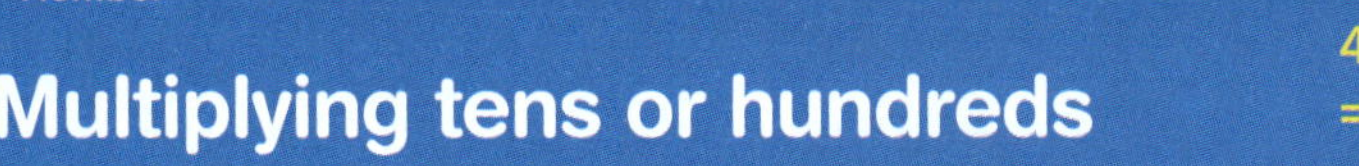

2:32 Multiplying tens or hundreds

4 × 7 hundreds (4 × 700)
= 28 hundreds (2800)

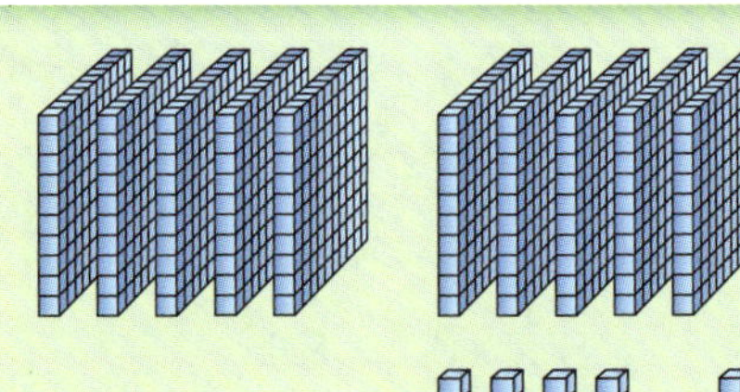

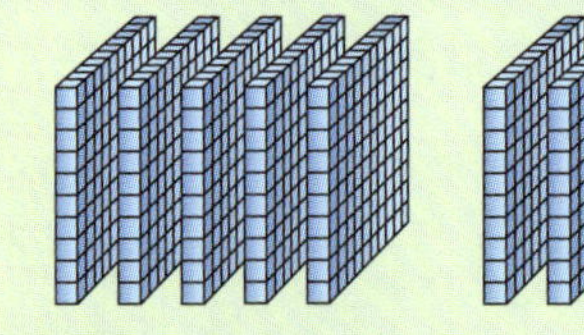

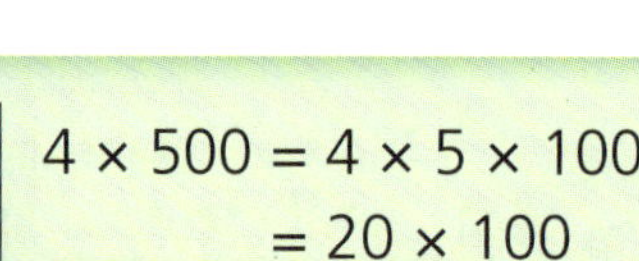

$4 \times 500 = 4 \times 5 \times 100$
$= 20 \times 100$
$= 2000$

$3 \times 40 = 3 \times 4 \times 10$
$= 12 \times 10$
$= 120$

	500
×	4
	2000

To multiply by 10, put a zero at the end of the number.

To multiply by 100, put 2 zeros at the end of the number.

1 a 7 tens = ☐ b 21 tens = ☐ c 9 hundreds = ☐
d 12 hundreds = ☐ e 10 hundreds = ☐ f 11 hundreds = ☐
g 25 hundreds = ☐ h 30 hundreds = ☐ i 49 hundreds = ☐

2 a 9 × 10 = ☐ b 27 × 10 = ☐ c 56 × 10 = ☐
d 6 × 100 = ☐ e 13 × 100 = ☐ f 25 × 100 = ☐

3 a 6 × 4 tens
= ☐ tens
= ☐

b 7 × 3 hundreds
= ☐ hundreds
= ☐

c 4 × 8 hundreds
= ☐ hundreds
= ☐

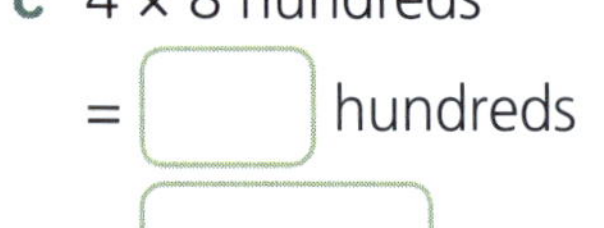

d 7 × 5 tens
= ☐ tens
= ☐

e 3 × 5 hundreds
= ☐ hundreds
= ☐

f 9 × 4 hundreds
= ☐ hundreds
= ☐

g 8 × 3 thousands
= ☐ thousands
= ☐

8 × 3000
= 24 × 1000
= 24 000

4 a 3 × 80 = ☐ b 7 × 50 = ☐ c 9 × 60 = ☐
d 4 × 200 = ☐ e 7 × 300 = ☐ f 5 × 600 = ☐

5

a

	H	T	U
		4	0
×			3

b

	H	T	U
		8	0
×			4

c

	H	T	U
		6	0
×			5

d

	Th	H	T	U
		3	0	0
×				6

e

	Th	H	T	U
		7	0	0
×				4

f

	Th	H	T	U
		9	0	0
×				8

You could use a calculator to check your answers.

2:33 Dividing 3-digit numbers by 10

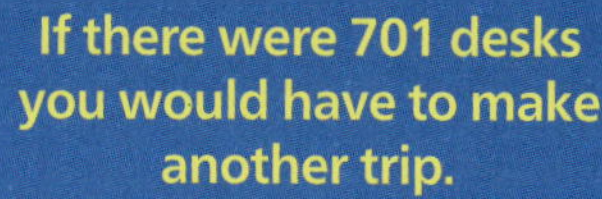

Ten eggs fill a carton. How many cartons can be filled with 593 eggs?

$$10\overline{)5\,9^9 3}\quad = 5\,9\text{ r}3$$

59 cartons can be filled. 3 eggs remain.

10 into 59 goes 5 with 9 over. Trade the 9. 10 into 93 goes 9 with remainder 3.

10 into 70 goes 7. 10 into 0 goes 0. The answer looks a bit like the question.

Ten desks fill our truck. How many trips would I need to make to transport 700 desks?

$$10\overline{)7\,0\,0}\quad = 7\,0$$

I would need to make 70 trips.

1 These have no remainder.

a $10\overline{)800}$	**b** $10\overline{)600}$	**c** $10\overline{)500}$	**d** $10\overline{)300}$	**e** $10\overline{)900}$
f $10\overline{)370}$	**g** $10\overline{)860}$	**h** $10\overline{)540}$	**i** $10\overline{)290}$	**j** $10\overline{)180}$
k $10\overline{)110}$	**l** $10\overline{)200}$	**m** $10\overline{)990}$	**n** $10\overline{)730}$	**o** $10\overline{)550}$

2 Most of these have remainders.

a $10\overline{)156}$	**b** $10\overline{)375}$	**c** $10\overline{)521}$	**d** $10\overline{)218}$	**e** $10\overline{)866}$
f $10\overline{)684}$	**g** $10\overline{)560}$	**h** $10\overline{)737}$	**i** $10\overline{)908}$	**j** $10\overline{)367}$
k $10\overline{)711}$	**l** $10\overline{)407}$	**m** $10\overline{)899}$	**n** $10\overline{)400}$	**o** $10\overline{)601}$

3
a Ashley has \$950. This is 10 times as much as Viv. How much has Viv got? \$ 

b The total number of runs I scored in 10 games is 510. What is my average number of runs scored per game? ☐ runs

c Mia used 470 mL of oil to fill ten identical lamps. How much was in each? ☐ mL

d Sarah has 200 g of sugar. Into how many cups could she place 10 g of it? ☐ cups

4 Find the missing digits.

a $10\overline{)\square\square\square} = 75$

b $10\overline{)\square\square\square} = 83\text{ r}1$

c $10\overline{)\square\square\square} = 60$

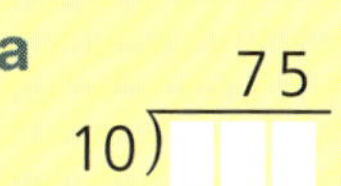

Hint: Multiplication family

$10 \times 60 = 600$
$60 \times 10 = 600$
$600 \div 10 = 60$
$600 \div 60 = 10$

2:34 Dividing with zero in the answer

Zero is a place holder.

1 Don't forget the zeros as you do these.

a $3\overline{)612}$ **b** $4\overline{)832}$ **c** $2\overline{)816}$ **d** $3\overline{)921}$ **e** $4\overline{)820}$

f $3\overline{)312}$ **g** $8\overline{)840}$ **h** $6\overline{)612}$ **i** $4\overline{)816}$ **j** $3\overline{)627}$

2 Some of these will have remainders.

a $5\overline{)505}$ **b** $3\overline{)306}$ **c** $4\overline{)408}$ **d** $2\overline{)806}$ **e** $3\overline{)609}$

f $8\overline{)802}$ **g** $5\overline{)508}$ **h** $2\overline{)609}$ **i** $7\overline{)708}$ **j** $6\overline{)605}$

3
a 864 sheep are in 8 paddocks. What is the average number per paddock? ☐

b How many groups of 6 tins are in 612 tins? ☐

c I caught 812 fish, 4 times as many as Peter. How many did Peter catch? ☐

d How many people can be given 4 sandwiches each if we have 416? ☐

e 6 bananas are needed to fill a bucket. How many buckets can be filled with 639 bananas? ☐

4 Round the first number to the nearest 100 to estimate, and write the estimate.

a 948 ÷ 3 ☐ **b** 782 ÷ 4 ☐

c 593 ÷ 6 ☐ **d** 987 ÷ 5 ☐

847 ÷ 4 becomes 800 ÷ 4 = 200

 • *AUSTRALIAN SIGNPOST MATHS 5* • ISBN 9780655708797

2:35 Divisibility

A number is divisible by 5, if there is no remainder when it is divided by 5.

Dividing by:	Divisibility test	Example
2	The number must be even.	578
3	The sum of the digits is divisible by 3.	267: 2 + 6 + 7 = 15
4	The last 2 digits are divisible by 4.	916: 16 ÷ 4 = 4
5	The last digit must be 0 or 5.	365
6	It is divisible by 2 and 3.	126
9	The sum of the digits is divisible by 9.	135: 1 + 3 + 5 = 9
10	The last digit is 0.	840
100	The last two digits are 00.	400

12 = 3 × 4, so to be divisible by 12, the number must be divisible by both 3 and 4

1 Circle the numbers which are:

a divisible by 2:	24	29	30	46	55	76	81	88	93	100
b divisible by 5:	30	44	45	60	73	75	86	95	120	135
c divisible by 3:	21	34	63	74	76	81	97	102	124	162
d divisible by 9:	24	36	56	72	684	693	115	126	154	234
e divisible by 4:	15	40	87	100	108	110	144	175	216	304
f divisible by 10:	15	40	82	100	110	111	172	183	220	333
g divisible by 100:	84	100	150	210	297	300	456	500	620	700

2 Write the numbers below in the columns of the table.
Some numbers can be placed in more than one column.

64 96 80 54 75 92 134 145 168
135 190 162 348 460 645 378 385 649

If a number is divisible by 9, then 9 is a **factor** of the number.

Divisible by 2	Divisible by 5	Divisible by 3	Divisible by 9

3 Write all the factors of each number.

a 8 ______ b 16 ______ c 35 ______
d 28 ______ e 49 ______ f 99 ______
g 24 ______ h 26 ______ i 28 ______

4 Do larger numbers have more factors? ______

2:36 Factors and multiples

The term *divisor* means *the number you are dividing by.*

1 Write down all factors of:

a 15 ☐ ☐ ☐ ☐ **b** 6 ☐ ☐ ☐ ☐

c 36 ☐ ☐ ☐ ☐ ☐ ☐ ☐ ☐ ☐

2 Write down the first ten multiples of:

a 6 ☐ ☐ ☐ ☐ ☐ ☐ ☐ ☐ ☐ ☐

b 9 ☐ ☐ ☐ ☐ ☐ ☐ ☐ ☐ ☐ ☐

c 7 ☐ ☐ ☐ ☐ ☐ ☐ ☐ ☐ ☐ ☐

Since 10 = 1 × 10 and 10 = 2 × 5, the factors of ten are 1, 10, 2 and 5.

ACTIVITY

- Some of the multiples of 6 are: 6, 12, 18, 24, 30, 36, 42, 48, 54, 60.
- The unit digits are: 6, 2, 8, 4, 0.
- We can draw the unit digit pattern like this. Begin and end at 6.

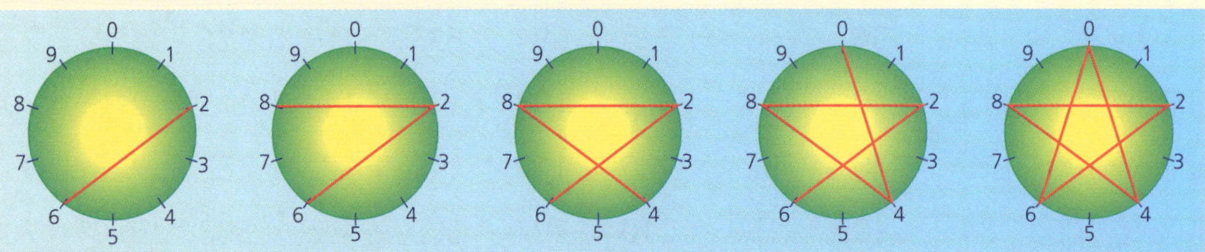

- Investigate the unit digit pattern for other multiples.

INVESTIGATION

Problem

Find all the factors of 64.

Solution

Use a calculator to divide 64 by 1, 2, 3, 4, etc.

Whole number answers, together with their divisors, are factors.

The factors of 64 are 1, 64, 2, 32, 4, 16 and 8.

Stop when the answer is less than the divisor.

3 Use this method to find all the factors of:

a 80 ☐ **b** 92 ☐ **c** 63 ☐

d 56 ☐ **e** 160 ☐ **f** 108 ☐

g 48 ☐ **h** 60 ☐ **i** 144 ☐

 • *AUSTRALIAN SIGNPOST MATHS 5* • ISBN 9780655708797

2:37 Using factors in multiplication

Factorising a number can make a question easier.

18 × 5
= 9 × 2 × 5
= 9 × 10
= 90

24 × 25
= 6 × 4 × 25
= 6 × 100
= 600

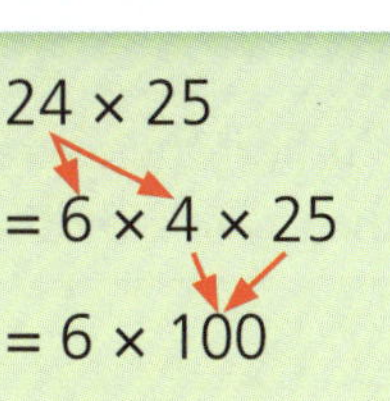

1 Complete each question to show how factors can be used.

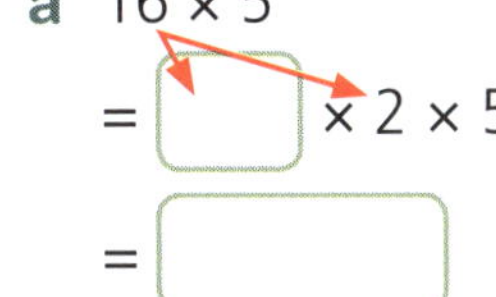

a 16 × 5 = ☐ × 2 × 5 = ☐

b 12 × 5 = ☐ × 2 × 5 = ☐

c 18 × 5 = ☐ × 2 × 5 = ☐

d 14 × 5 = ☐ × 2 × 5 = ☐

e 8 × 25 = ☐ × 4 × 25 = ☐

f 16 × 25 = ☐ × 4 × 25 = ☐

g 28 × 25 = ☐ × 4 × 25 = ☐

h 36 × 25 = ☐ × 4 × 25 = ☐

i 20 × 5 = ☐ × 2 × 5 = ☐

j 12 × 25 = ☐ × 4 × 25 = ☐

k 20 × 25 = ☐ × 4 × 25 = ☐

l 32 × 25 = ☐ × 4 × 25 = ☐

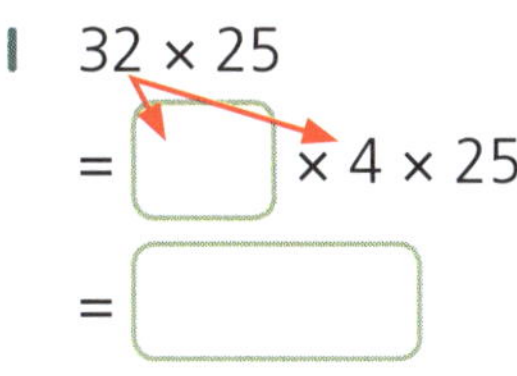

To multiply by 12, multiply by 6 and then double.

12 × 8
= 2 × 6 × 8
= 2 × 48
= 96

8 × 12
= 8 × 6 × 2
= 48 × 2
= 96

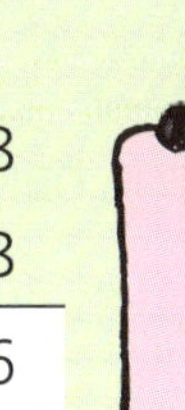

	4	8
+	4	8
	9	6

2

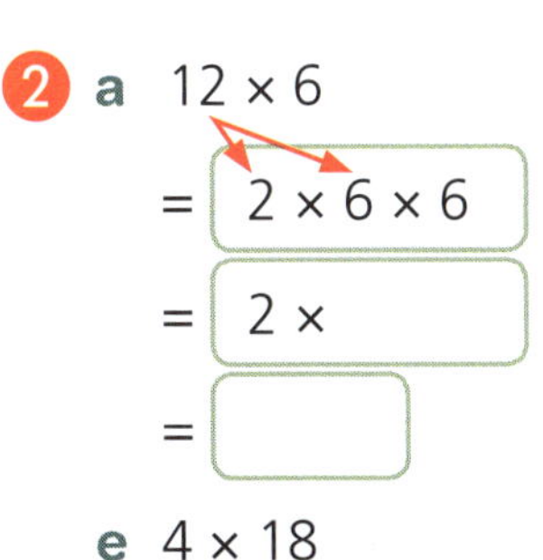

a 12 × 6 = 2 × 6 × 6 = 2 × ☐ = ☐

b 14 × 4 = 2 × ☐ × ☐ = 2 × ☐ = ☐

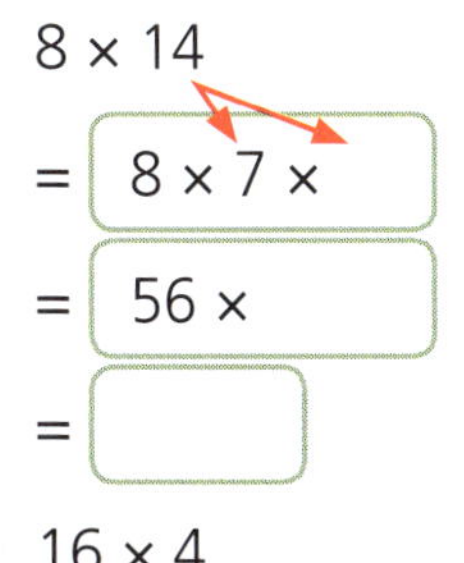

c 8 × 14 = 8 × 7 × ☐ = 56 × ☐ = ☐

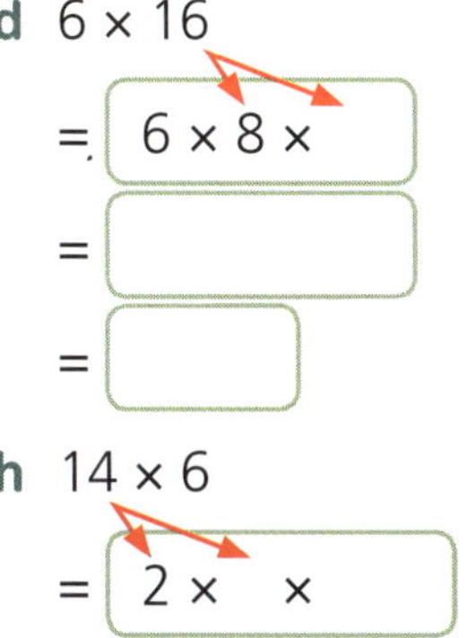

d 6 × 16 = 6 × 8 × ☐ = ☐ = ☐

e 4 × 18 = 2 × 2 × 18 = 2 × ☐ = ☐

f 20 × 9 = 2 × 10 × 9 = 2 × ☐ = ☐

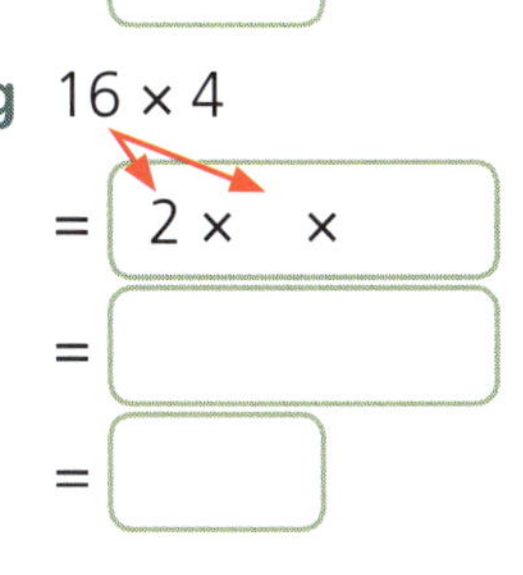

g 16 × 4 = 2 × ☐ × ☐ = ☐ = ☐

h 14 × 6 = 2 × ☐ × ☐ = ☐ = ☐

© PEARSON AUSTRALIA 2024 • *AUSTRALIAN SIGNPOST MATHS 5* • ISBN 9780655708797

To find the average, add the scores then divide by the number of scores.

An average is a fair share.

1 Measure the length of each nail.

a What is the average length of the nails? ______

b Tom needed two 4 cm long nails. He bought a packet of nails which said 'average length 4 cm'. These are the nails from that packet. Was he disappointed? Why or why not?

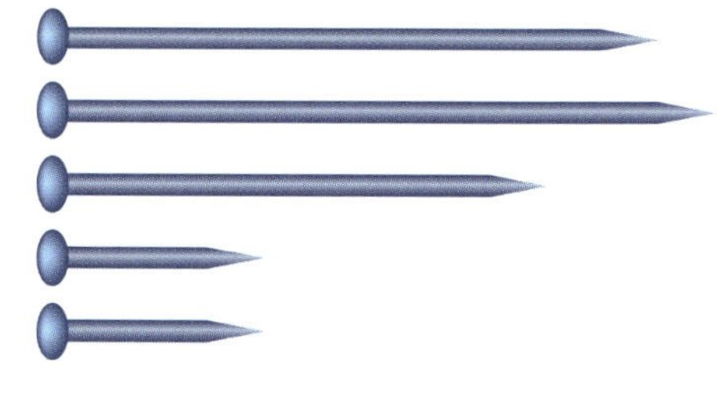

The average does not tell us about single cases, it gives the amount when shared.

2 **A** **B** **C** **D**

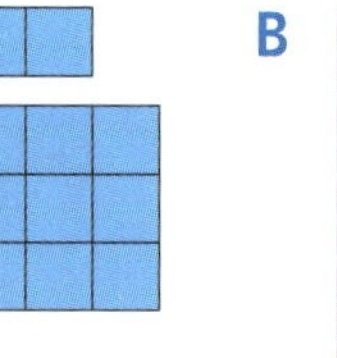

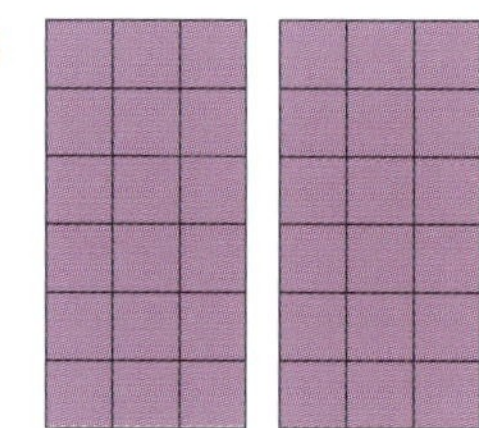

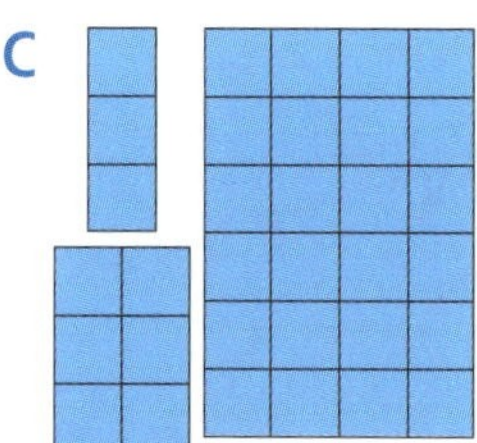

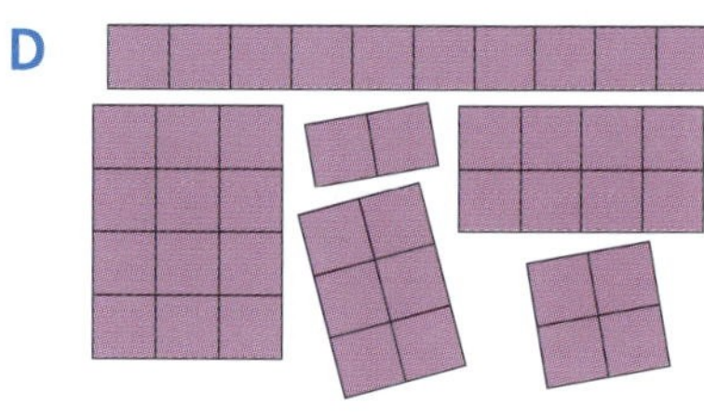

a Find the average number of small squares in each group of rectangles.

Average **A** = ______ Average **B** = ______ Average **C** = ______ Average **D** = ______

b What is the average height of the rectangles in **C**? ______

c What is the average width of the rectangles in **A**? ______

3 a Sam has \$40. I have \$28. What is the average of these amounts? ______

b In three days, I earned \$45, \$28 and \$17.
What were my average daily earnings? ______

c For our school play, 34 tickets were sold on the first day, 17 on the second, 25 on the third and 12 on the fourth. What was the average number of tickets sold per day? ______

An average can be written using a fraction or a decimal. Examples: Kim averaged $2\frac{1}{2}$ goals per game, I averaged 1·2 fish each hour.

4 Ben bought 2 tickets to the play, Sarah bought 4, Kuan bought 3 and Anna bought 1.

a What was the average number of tickets bought by these people? ______

b What was the average number of tickets bought by the two boys? ______

See *Extra Support 17* (Averages).

2:39 Mental strategies for multiplication

I like this strategy.

CONCEPT

13 students carried 9 bricks each. How many bricks were carried altogether?

Here we use known facts to find the answer.

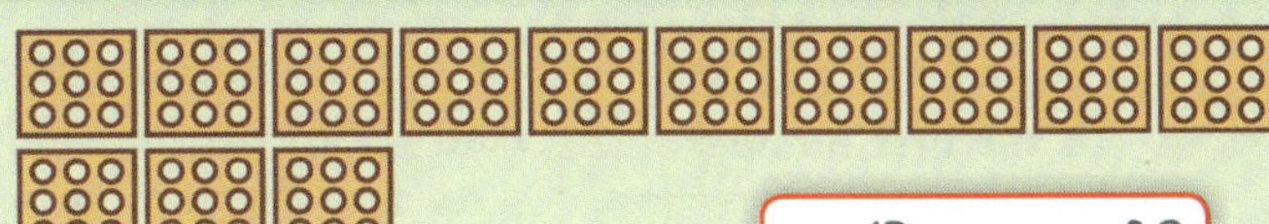

$13 \times 9 = (10 \times 9) + (3 \times 9)$
$= 90 + 27$
$= 117$

1 Use the mental strategy above to answer these questions.

a 14×8
$= (10 \times 8) + (4 \times 8)$
= ☐ + ☐
= ☐

b 12×4
$= (10 \times 4) + (2 \times 4)$
= ☐ + ☐
= ☐

c 15×6
$= (10 \times 6) + (5 \times 6)$
= ☐ + ☐
= ☐

d 19×5
$= (10 \times 5) + (9 \times 5)$
= ☐ + ☐
= ☐

e 17×9
$= (10 \times 9) + (7 \times 9)$
= ☐ + ☐
= ☐

f 16×8
$= (10 \times 8) + (6 \times 8)$
= ☐ + ☐
= ☐

4 groups of 16 is the same as
4 groups of 10 + 4 groups of 6.

2 Here we change the second number.

a 4×16
$= (4 \times 10) + (4 \times 6)$
= ☐ + ☐
= ☐

b 8×23
$= (8 \times 20) + (8 \times 3)$
= ☐ + ☐
= ☐

c 5×43
$= (5 \times 40) + (5 \times 3)$
= ☐ + ☐
= ☐

We can also use relationships between facts.
$23 \times 4 = 4 \times 23$, so double 23 and then double again.
(To double a number, we can add it to itself.)

$23 \times 4 = 2 \times (2 \times 23)$
$= 2 \times 46$
$= 92$

3 Use doubling to calculate these.

a $2 \times 23 =$ 46
$4 \times 23 = 2 \times$ 46
= ☐

b $51 \times 2 =$ ☐
$51 \times 4 = 2 \times$ ☐
= ☐

c $2 \times 21 =$ ☐
$4 \times 21 = 2 \times$ ☐
= ☐

2:40 Algebraic thinking

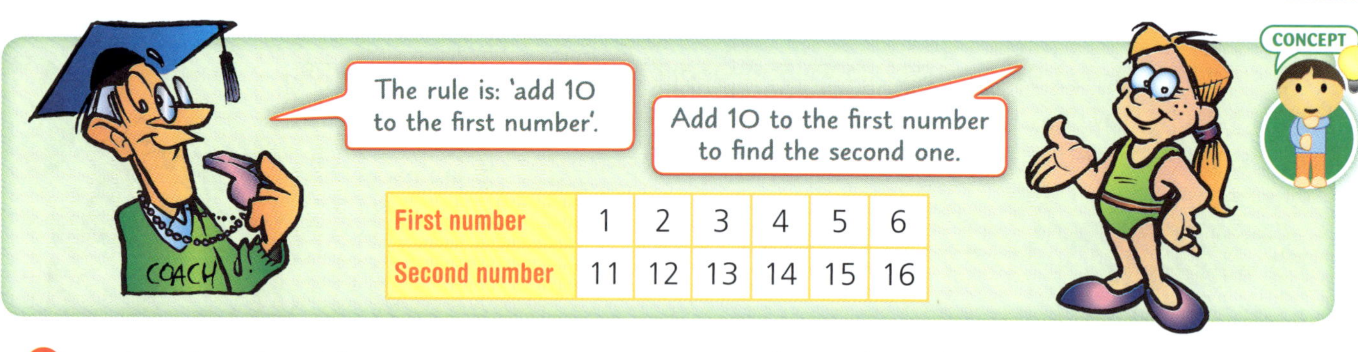

First number	1	2	3	4	5	6
Second number	11	12	13	14	15	16

1 a Complete the table.

First number	1	2	3	4	5	6
Second number	15	16	17	18		

b Write a rule to describe the pattern.

[ ] to the 1st number.

c What is the *Second number* if the *First number* is 9? [ ]

2 a Complete the table.

First number	1	2	3	4	5	6
Second number	4	8	12	16		

b Write a rule to describe the pattern.

[ ] the [ ] number by [ ].

c What is the *Second number* if the *First number* is 20? [ ]

3 a Complete the table.

First number	90	80	70	60	50	40
Second number	82	72	62	52		

b Write a rule to describe the pattern.

[ ] from the [ ] number.

c What is the *Second number* if the *First number* is 18? [ ]

4 a Complete the table.

Input number	36	46	56	66	76	86
Output number	43	53	63	73		

b Write a rule to describe the pattern.

[ ] to the input number.

c What is the *Output number* if the *Input number* is 8? [ ]

5 a Complete the table.

Input number	29	39	49	59	69	79
Output number	12	22	32			

b Write a rule to describe the pattern.

[ ] from the input number.

c What is the *Output number* if the *Input number* is 199? [ ]

ACTIVITY

6 Make your own number patterns using multiplication and addition.

a Multiply the first number by [ ].

First number	21	22	23	24	25	26
Second number						

b Add [ ] to the first number.

First number	1	2	3	4	5	6
Second number						

Algebraic thinking

Discuss: Mia is 7 years older that I am.
My age = Mia's age – 7.
What was my age when Mia was 11?

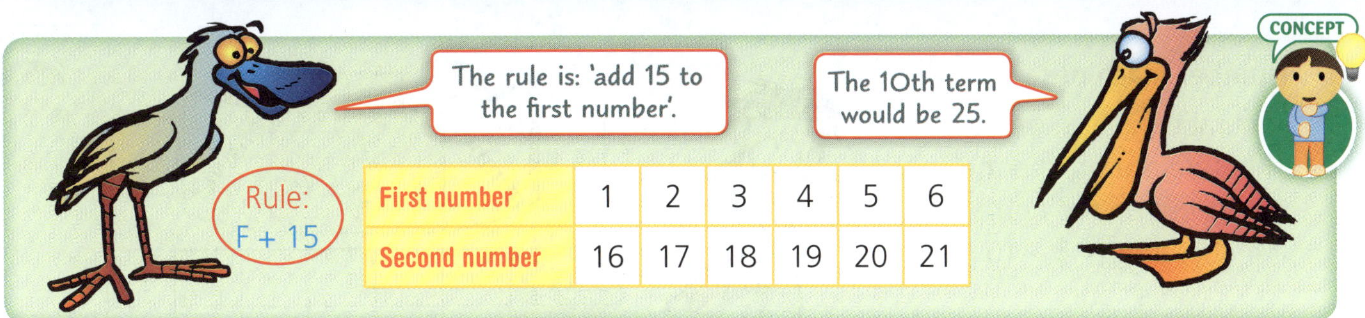

First number	1	2	3	4	5	6
Second number	16	17	18	19	20	21

1 Complete the tables and write a rule that connects the second number to the first number (F).

a

First number	1	2	3	4	5	6
Second number	7	14	21	28		

Rule: ☐ the first number by ☐ or F × ☐.

b

First number	1	2	3	4	5	6
Second number	9	18	27	36		

Rule: ☐ the first number by ☐ or F × ☐.

c

First number	1	2	3	4	5	6
Second number	24	25	26			

Rule: ☐ to the first number.

d

First number	1	2	3	4	5	6
Second number	36	37	38			

Rule: ☐ to the first number.

e

First number	35	45	55	65	75	85
Second number	27	37	47	57		

Rule: ☐

f

First number	92	82	72	62	52	42
Second number	104	94	84	74		

Rule: ☐

g

First number	2	4	6	7	10	12
Second number	6	12	18			

Rule: ☐

h

First number	1	2	3	4	5	6
Second number	9	19	29	39		

Rule: ☐

2 Find the *Second number* if the *First number (F)* is 10 and the *Rule* is:

a F + 7 ☐ **b** F – 6 ☐ **c** F × 3 ☐ **d** F ÷ 2 ☐

3 Find the *Second number* if the *First number (F)* is 8 and the *Rule* is:

a F × 2 + 10 ☐ **b** F ÷ 4 – 1 ☐ **c** F × 5 + 36 ☐ **d** (F – 1) × 10 ☐

4 Hiring a bike costs \$5 plus \$4 for every hour. The cost would be \$(4 × *n* + 5). What is the cost for:

a 2 hours? ☐ **b** 4 hours? ☐ **c** 10 hours? ☐ **d** 5 hours? ☐

5 European dress size = Australian dress size + 30. Convert these dress sizes.

a Australian size 8 is European size ☐. **b** European size 39 is Australian size ☐.

 • *AUSTRALIAN SIGNPOST MATHS 5* • ISBN 9780655708797

Algebraic thinking

Rule: $7 + 2 \times n$

Do × and ÷ then + and −.

CONCEPT

Number machines

A number goes in on the left. The **Rule** is used and the answer comes out on the right.
If 4 goes in, 4 × 3 + 10 = 22, so 22 comes out.

The rule is: $n \times 3 + 10$

Answer = 3 × number + 10

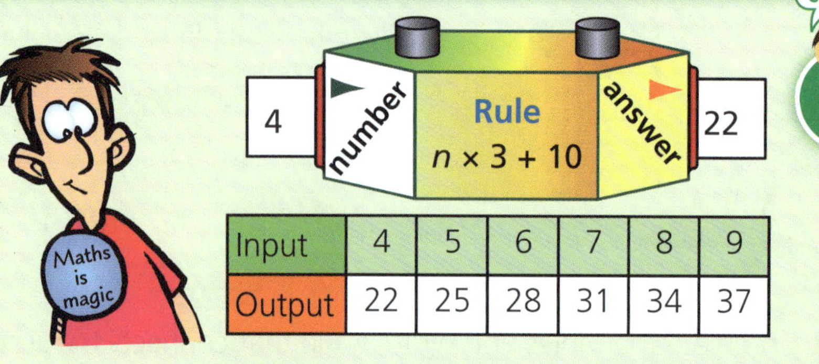

Input	4	5	6	7	8	9
Output	22	25	28	31	34	37

We can say that **Output = Input × 3 + 10.**

1 Use the rule for each number machine to complete the table. Rewrite the rule underneath.

a

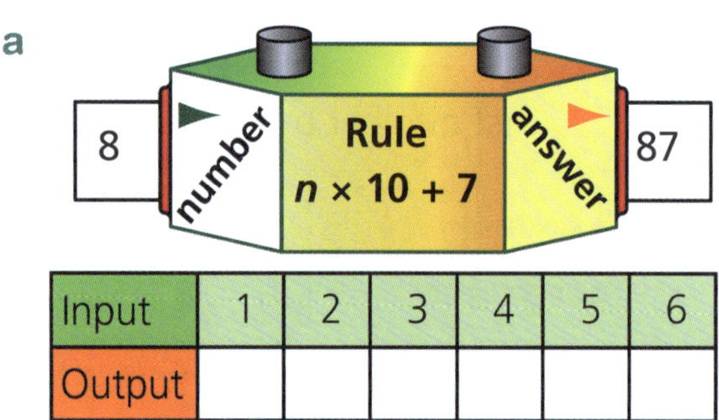

Input	1	2	3	4	5	6
Output						

If the input is 10, the output = ☐.

b

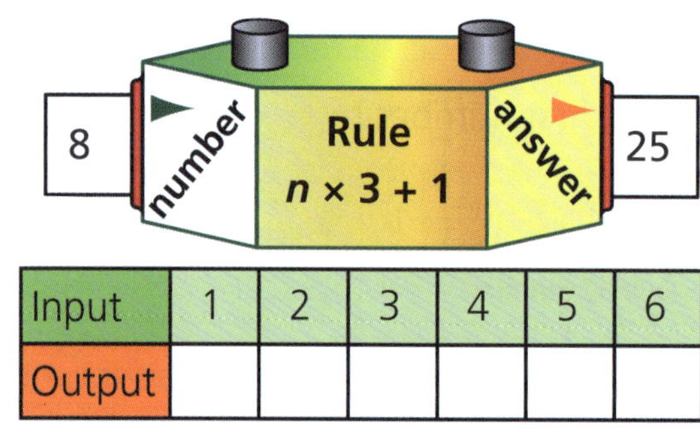

Input	1	2	3	4	5	6
Output						

If the input is 10, the output = ☐.

c

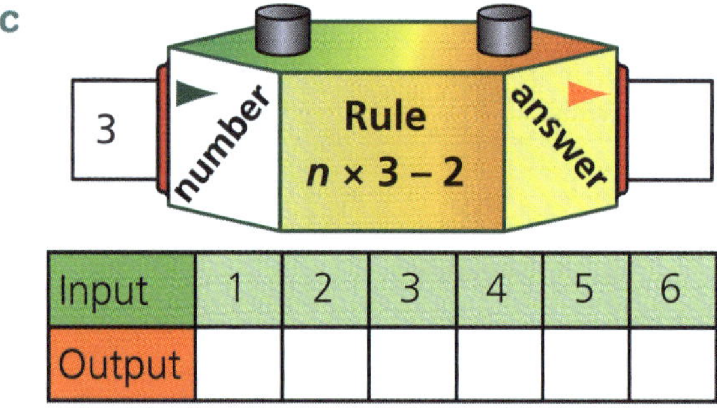

Input	1	2	3	4	5	6
Output						

If the input is 10, the output = ☐.

d

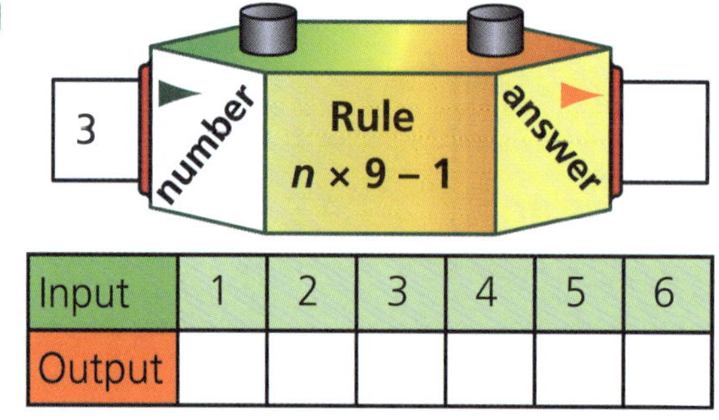

Input	1	2	3	4	5	6
Output						

If the input is 10, the output = ☐.

2 The rule $12 \times n$ gives the number of eggs if there are n cartons. How many eggs are in:

a 2 cartons? ☐ **b** 3 cartons? ☐ **c** 10 cartons? ☐ **d** 4 cartons? ☐

3 The rule $\$15 + 5 \times n$ gives the cost of hiring a boat for n hours. What is the cost for:

a 2 hours? ☐ **b** 4 hours? ☐ **c** 6 hours? ☐ **d** 10 hours? ☐

4 A term in the pattern 9, 11, 13, 15, ... can be found using the rule 7 + 2 x the term number. The 4th term is 7 + (2 × 4). The 10th term is 7 + (2 × 10). What is the:

a 2nd term? ☐ **b** 8th term? ☐ **c** 20th term? ☐ **d** 100th term? ☐

 ISBN 9780655708797

2:43 Multiplying 2-digit numbers

3 × 72:
3 groups of 70 plus
3 groups of 2

CONCEPT

3 × 72
= 3 groups of 72
= (3 × 7 tens) + (3 × 2 ones)
= 210 + 6
= 216
There are 216 pegs.

1 **a** 2 × 43 = (2 × 4 tens) + (2 × 3 ones)
= ☐ + ☐
= ☐

b 5 × 15 = (5 × 1 ten) + (5 × 5 ones)
= ☐ + ☐
= ☐

c 6 × 38 = (6 × 3 tens) + (6 × 8 ones)
= ☐ + ☐
= ☐

d 4 × 29 = (4 × 2 tens) + (4 × 9 ones)
= ☐ + ☐
= ☐

2 **a** 2 × 85
= (2 × 80) + (2 × 5)
= ☐ + ☐
= ☐

b 4 × 28
= (4 × 20) + (4 × 8)
= ☐ + ☐
= ☐

c 6 × 32
= (6 × 30) + (6 × 2)
= ☐ + ☐
= ☐

d 7 × 16
= (7 × 10) + (7 × 6)
= ☐ + ☐
= ☐

e 9 × 31
= (9 × 30) + (9 × 1)
= ☐ + ☐
= ☐

f 8 × 23
= (8 × 20) + (8 × 3)
= ☐ + ☐
= ☐

g 5 × 44
= (5 × 40) + (5 × 4)
= ☐ + ☐
= ☐

h 3 × 82
= (3 × 80) + (3 × 2)
= ☐ + ☐
= ☐

i 4 × 93
= (4 × 90) + (4 × 3)
= ☐ + ☐
= ☐

See *Extra Support 10* (Extended multiplication).

 • *AUSTRALIAN SIGNPOST MATHS 5* • ISBN 9780655708797

2:44 The extended form of multiplication

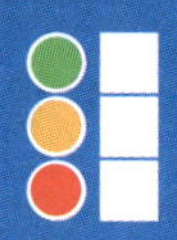

CONCEPT

We have 8 tennis balls. Each has a mass of 57 g. What is their total mass?

$8 \times 57 = (8 \times 50) + (8 \times 7)$
$= 400 + 56$
$= 456$

	H	T	U	
		5	7	
×			8	
		5	6	←(8 × 7)
	4	0	0	←(8 × 50)
	4	5	6	

8 lots of 7,
8 lots of 50.

Total mass is 456 grams.

1

a

	H	T	U
		4	3
×			5

b

	H	T	U
		7	3
×			4

c

	H	T	U
		2	7
×			8

d

	H	T	U
		7	7
×			3

e

	H	T	U
		7	9
×			6

f

	H	T	U
		9	1
×			2

g

	H	T	U
		3	8
×			7

h

	H	T	U
		1	9
×			8

2

a

	H	T	U
		4	9
×			3

b

	H	T	U
		3	2
×			9

c

	H	T	U
		5	4
×			6

d

	H	T	U
		7	5
×			5

e

	H	T	U
		9	6
×			4

f

	H	T	U
		4	4
×			7

g

	H	T	U
		3	7
×			8

h

	H	T	U
		2	1
×			9

3 Use rounding to check your answers in Questions 1 and 2.

See *Extra Support 10* (Extended multiplication).

2:45 The extended form of multiplication

5 × 7 = 35
5 × 70 = 350
5 × 700 = 3500

CONCEPT

Gabriela was given $175 but her mother was given 5 times as much. How much was her mother given?

H	T	U	
$ 1	7	5	
×		5	
	2	5	← (5 × 5)
3	5	0	← (5 × 70)
5	0	0	← (5 × 100)
$ 8	7	5	

5 lots of 5, 5 lots of 70, 5 lots of 100.

Her mother was given $875.

1

a

H	T	U
4	2	1
×		2

b

H	T	U
3	1	9
×		3

c

H	T	U
1	2	9
×		7

d

H	T	U
3	9	5
×		2

e

H	T	U
1	3	4
×		6

f

H	T	U
1	1	5
×		8

g

H	T	U
2	1	7
×		4

h

H	T	U
1	7	5
×		5

i

H	T	U
2	3	6
×		4

j

H	T	U
3	0	8
×		3

k

H	T	U
1	4	1
×		7

l

H	T	U
1	7	9
×		7

2

a Jordan needed to buy new horseshoes for her 48 horses. How many shoes must she buy if she needs one for each hoof? ☐ horseshoes

b Alana bought six 128-page books. How many pages did she buy? ☐ pages

c Rhonda carried four boxes of eggs to the car. In each box there were 144 eggs. How many eggs did she carry? ☐ eggs

d A father gave his younger son three times as much money as his older son. If he gave his older son $297, how much did he give the younger? ☐ dollars

3 Check your answers to Question 2 by using rounding.

 • *AUSTRALIAN SIGNPOST MATHS 5* • ISBN 9780655708797

2:46 The contracted form of multiplication

Multiply the units, then the tens, then the hundreds.

CONCEPT

Flood lights cost $142 each. I bought seven. How much did I pay?

Extended form

1	4	2
×		7
	1	4
2	8	0
7	0	0
9	9	4

Contracted form

H	T	U
1	4	2
× ₂	₁	7
9	9	4

What is traded goes here.

- 7 × 2 ones is 14 ones. Write 4 in the units column and put a small 1 in the tens column.
- 7 × 4 tens plus the 1 traded is 29 tens. Write 9 in the tens column and a small 2 in the hundreds column.
- 7 × 1 hundred plus the 2 traded is 9 hundreds. Write the 9 in the hundreds column.

Use the contracted form to answer these and check your answers with a calculator.

1
- a 20 × 8
- b 31 × 7
- c 83 × 3
- d 39 × 2
- e 18 × 5
- f 27 × 3
- g 63 × 5
- h 57 × 6
- i 46 × 10
- j 75 × 8
- k 57 × 4
- l 81 × 10
- m 40 × 3
- n 79 × 2
- o 14 × 4
- p 98 × 6

2
- a 128 × 3
- b 346 × 2
- c 117 × 5
- d 209 × 4
- e 325 × 3
- f 130 × 6
- g 121 × 8
- h 293 × 3
- i 484 × 2
- j 170 × 4
- k $1.98 × 5
- l $1.27 × 7
- m $1.53 × 6
- n $1.06 × 8
- o $1.35 × 7

© PEARSON AUSTRALIA 2024 • *AUSTRALIAN SIGNPOST MATHS 5* • ISBN 9780655708797

2:47 The contracted form of multiplication

× the units, then the tens.

4 × 3 hundreds plus 2 hundreds gives 14 hundreds.

	Th	H	T	U
		3	5	2
×		2		4
	1	4	0	8

14 hundreds is 1 thousand and 4 hundreds.

Use the contracted form to answer these.

1

a	b	c	d	e
630 × 3	811 × 6	700 × 8	824 × 2	933 × 3

f	g	h	i	j
583 × 2	419 × 4	407 × 9	312 × 8	971 × 6

k	l	m	n	o
546 × 5	768 × 10	369 × 7	257 × 9	498 × 10

p	q	r
609 × 7	850 × 9	999 × 6

3 × 2 thousands plus 1 thousand gives 7 thousands.

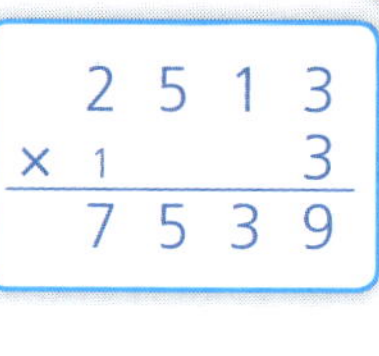

2

a	b	c
3021 × 3	2112 × 4	3033 × 3

d	e	f	g
1602 × 4	501 × 7	1810 × 5	2186 × 3

h	i	j	k
4974 × 2	2324 × 4	1650 × 6	3258 × 2

l	m	n	o	p
$13.85 × 7	$17.99 × 5	$12.47 × 6	$11.66 × 8	$41.35 × 10

2:48 Problems involving change of units

1·5 m
= 150 cm

CONCEPT

Anna bought 2 m of wire and used 135 cm of it to repair her aviary. How much wire was left?
We must first change 2 m to cm.
2 m – 135 cm → 200 cm – 135 cm

Length	Mass	Capacity	Time
1 m = 100 cm	1 kg = 1000 g	1 L = 1000 mL	1 min = 60 s
1 km = 1000 m		1 kL = 1000 L	1 h = 60 min
			1 day = 24 h

kilo (k) means 1000

1 **a** I bought 2 kg of seed and mice ate all but 750 g. How much was eaten?

b A jug holds 750 mL of milk. How many litres are needed to fill the jug four times?

c Eight children shared 2 kg of clay. How much clay was each child given?

d A movie on TV runs for 2 hours. Every 10 minutes, six advertisements are shown. How many ads are shown altogether between the start and finish?

2 **a** Nasha needed rice to prepare three meals. She needed 830 g for the first, 2480 g for the second and 1320 g for the third meal. How much rice must she buy if it is sold only in one kilogram packets?

b Every minute, 875 L of water flows into our dam. How many litres would flow into it in 8 minutes?

c How many 200 g packets of rice can we make if we have a 1 kg bag of rice?

How many 200 g packets of rice can we make if we have a 1850 kg sack of rice?

d Lee had four lengths of wire: 65 cm, 1 m 20 cm, 86 cm and 3 m 39 cm. How many metres of wire did she have altogether?

3 **a** The distance around a circular island is 5 km, while the distance across the middle is 1600 m. Robinson Crusoe and Man Friday wanted to get from one side (**A**), to the opposite (**B**). If Robinson Crusoe walked around the island and Man Friday walked across the middle, how much further would Robinson Crusoe walk?

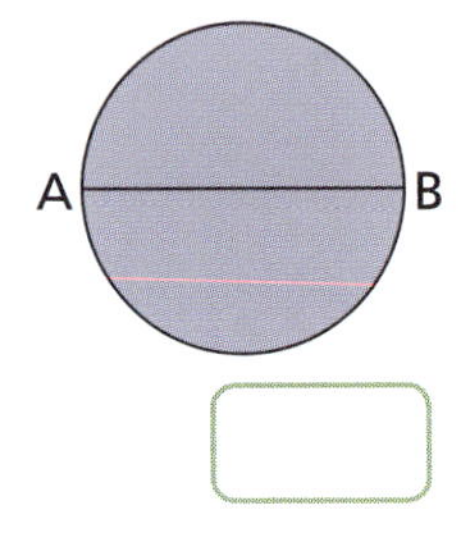

b Indu had to wait 7 days to have a leaking pipe repaired. How much water was lost if 6 L of water was lost each hour?

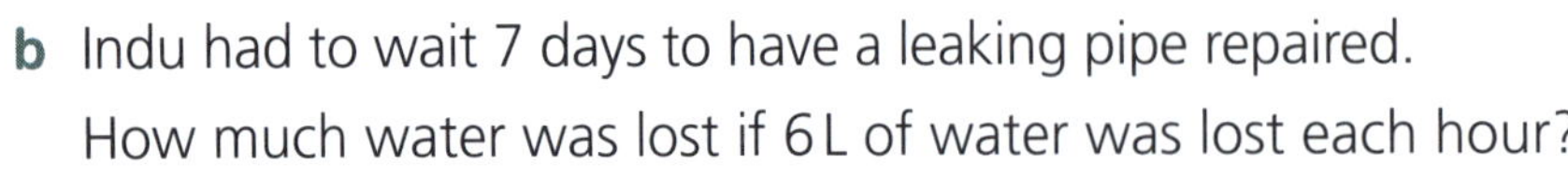

c If the value of a gram of gold is $11.43, what is the value of 1 kg of gold?

2:49 Estimating by rounding

If the next digit is 5 or more, round up. ... 850 → 900.
If it is less than 5, round down.

Round to the nearest 100 to estimate 339 + 850.

Estimate = 300 + 900
= 1200

The answer is 1189.

An estimate should be near the real answer. It is a good guess.

1 Round each number to the nearest 10 then work out the estimate.

a 157 + 31
E = 160 + 30
E = ☐

b 84 – 77
E = 80 – 80
E = ☐

c 63 + 88
E = ☐ + ☐
E = ☐

d 174 – 52
E = ☐ – ☐
E = ☐

2 Use the jump strategy or a calculator to write the answers to Question 1.

a ☐ b ☐ c ☐ d ☐

3 Round each number to the nearest 100 then work out the estimate.

a 325 + 189
E = 300 + 200
= ☐

b 608 – 518
E = ☐ – ☐
= ☐

c 751 + 427
E = ☐ + ☐
= ☐

d 846 – 749
E = ☐ – ☐
= ☐

4 Use the jump strategy or a calculator to write the answers to Question 3.

a ☐ b ☐ c ☐ d ☐

5 Round each number to the nearest 1000 then work out the estimate.

a 3804 + 621
E = 4000 + 1000
= ☐

b 7299 – 4106
E = ☐ – ☐
= ☐

c 6337 + 3904
E = ☐ + ☐
= ☐

6 Use the jump strategy or a calculator to write the answers to Question 5.

a ☐ b ☐ c ☐

7

Estimate which **two numbers** above should be added to give the answer closest to:

a 3000 ☐ b 7000 ☐ c 6000 ☐

d 11 000 ☐ e 12 000 ☐ f 16 000 ☐

g Was it necessary to add all of the pairs of numbers? ☐

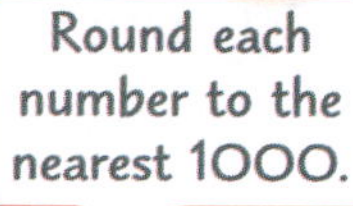

Round each number to the nearest 1000.

See *Extra Support 11* (Estimating products).

 • *AUSTRALIAN SIGNPOST MATHS 5* • ISBN 9780655708797

2:50 Estimating by rounding

It's the same for 1000s.
5551 is closer to 6000.

CONCEPT

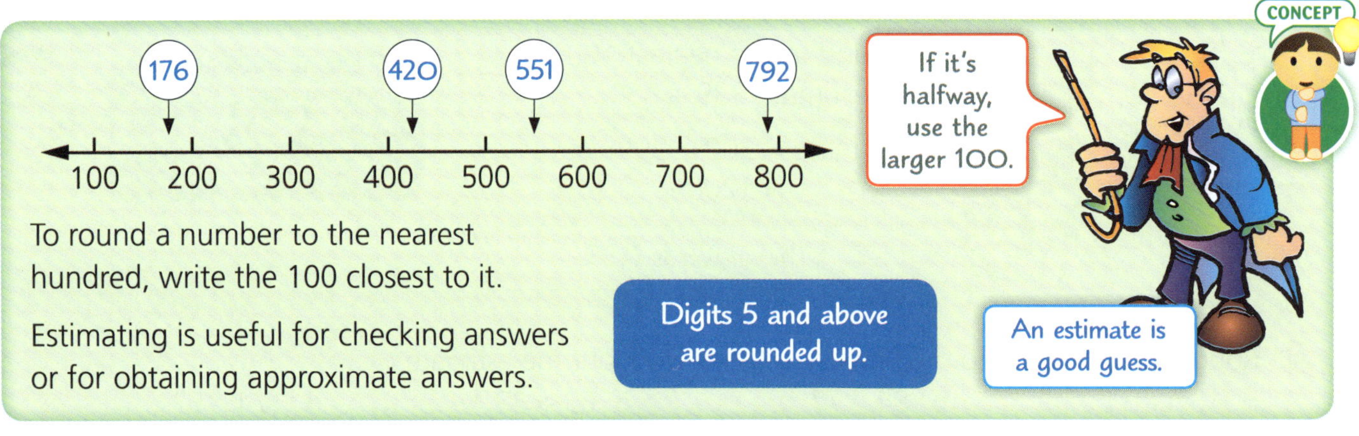

To round a number to the nearest hundred, write the 100 closest to it.

Estimating is useful for checking answers or for obtaining approximate answers.

Digits 5 and above are rounded up.

An estimate is a good guess.

1 Round these numbers to the nearest hundred.

a 297		**b** 306		**c** 541		**d** 183		**e** 748	
f 418		**g** 853		**h** 660		**i** 928		**j** 573	

2 **a** Is 48 × 6 closer to 50 × 5, 50 × 10 or 40 × 5?

b Is 94 × 7 closer to 90 × 5, 90 × 10 or 100 × 10?

c Is 351 × 8 closer to 400 × 5, 400 × 10 or 300 × 10?

It could be closer if one number goes up and the other goes down.

3 Circle the best answer from those given. Use your calculator to find the actual answer and compare this with your estimate.

	Question	Estimate
a	35 + 74 + 68 + 27	190, 210, 250
b	579 – 228	300, 400, 500
c	832 – 196	500, 600, 700
d	95 + 127 + 261 + 301	750, 790, 860

	Question	Estimate
e	28 × 6	100, 180, 210
f	156 ÷ 5	30, 50, 90
g	41 × 9	300, 400
h	401 ÷ 10	40, 60, 80

4 **a** Estimate the cost of 12 meals if they cost \$9.50 each.

b Tennis lessons cost \$9.80 each. Estimate how much it costs for 21 lessons.

c Estimate the cost of 33 litres of petrol at \$1.97 per litre.

INVESTIGATION

Estimate the number of grocery items needed to fill a shopping trolley.

Estimate the cost of the items in this shopping trolley.

Circle the estimate that is closest to yours.

\$150–\$200	\$200–\$250	\$250–\$300	\$300–\$350	\$350–\$400

See *Extra Support 11* (Estimating products).

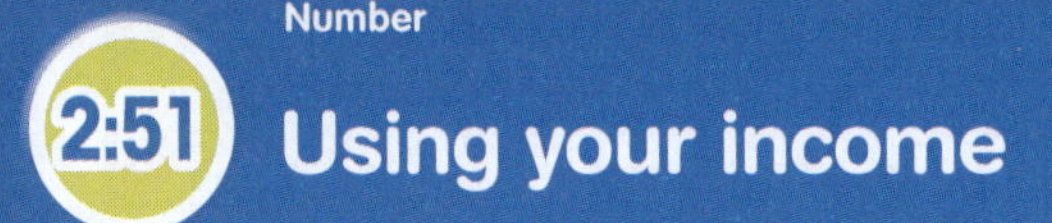

If costs exceed income you have a big problem.

Hannah and Yuri are working out their household accounts. At the end of each week any money left over is banked. Each person's payslip, expenses and bank balance are shown.

Hannah's accounts

1 **a** Estimate of Hannah's expenses: $ ______ **b** Hannah's actual expenses: $ ______

c At the end of the week, what must she deposit or withdraw from her bank account? $ ______

d The new bank balance is $ ______.

Yuri's accounts

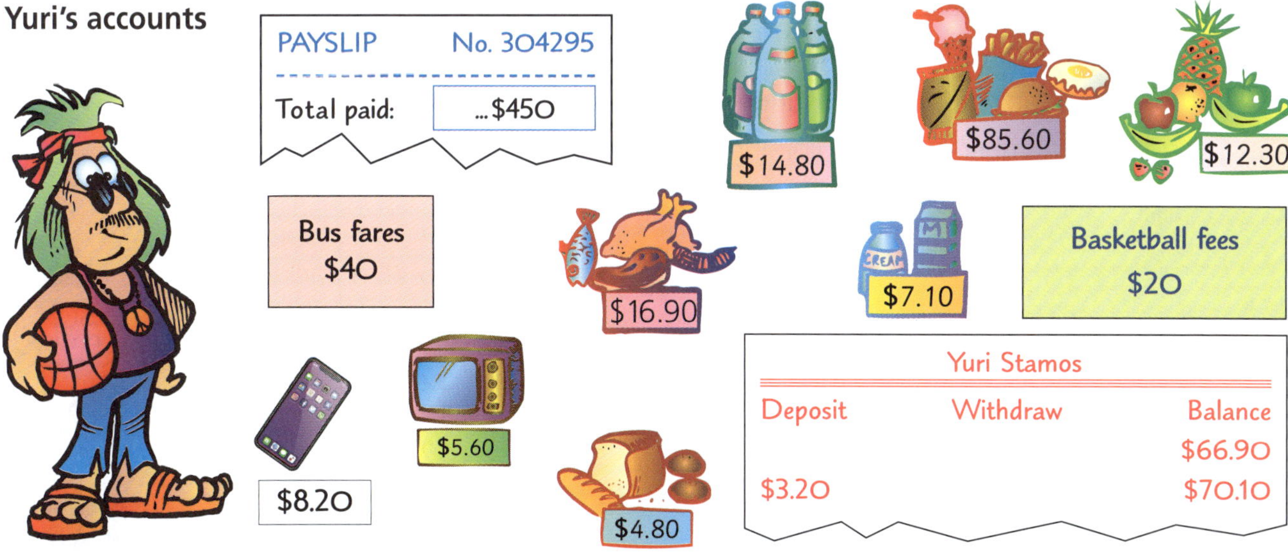

2 **a** Estimate of Yuri's expenses: $ ______ **b** Yuri's actual expenses: $ ______

c At the end of the week, what must Yuri deposit or withdraw from his bank account? ______

d The new bank balance is $ ______.

2:52 Making a budget

Once you know the cost, you can plan to find the money.

CONCEPT

A budget is a way of working out how much a plan will cost. Work out what you need and the cost of each item. Add them to find the total cost.

1 You plan to set up a class fish tank.
Decide what you want to buy.
Complete the table to find your budget.

Item	Number	Cost
tank		
filter		
stones		
food		
fish		
Total budget		

What you need:

tank $35 inc GST
filter $16.30 inc GST
stones $7.20 + GST = $7.92
fish food $10.80 inc GST
fish $3.50 each inc GST

GST (10%)
$7.20
+ .72
$7.92

Optional extras:

cave $10.20 inc GST
plant $3.40 each inc GST

2 You plan to organise a class party.
Decide how much you want to buy.
Complete the table to find your budget.
Consider the number of people coming.

Item	Number	Cost
Total budget		

Food:

soft drink $3 per litre inc GST
juice $3.50 per litre inc GST
chips $4 a packet inc GST
donuts $6 a dozen + GST = $ ______
lollies $4.30 a packet inc GST
popcorn $5.25 a packet inc GST

GST (10%)
$6.00
+ .60
______

Equipment:

serviettes $2 for 20 inc GST
plates $4.40 for 40 inc GST
party hats $2 for 10 inc GST

Other items:

 • *AUSTRALIAN SIGNPOST MATHS 5* • ISBN 9780655708797

2:53 Using operations to solve problems

Answers must include units.

1. Ten people booked on a trip missed the bus. As they had already paid, they were given a $2330 refund to share. How much did each receive? ______ dollars

2. Caroline is paid $153 per week. From this amount $19 is deducted for tax and other items. How much money does she receive in four weeks? ______ dollars

3. The cost of hiring a hall for a Boys' Brigade display was shared by six leaders. If the cost was $774, how much did each leader pay? ______ dollars

4. A truck has to move 400 tonnes of soil. On each trip, it carries a load of 18 tonnes. It makes 8 trips before it breaks down. How much soil was moved before it broke down? ______ tonnes

   How much soil was not moved? ______ tonnes

5. Charity workers expected to raise $1000 from three functions. The first raised $271, the second $406 and the third $590. How much more money did they raise than was expected? ______ dollars

6. A person laying bricks is paid to lay 960 bricks. Each hour 185 bricks are laid. How many bricks will be laid in 3 hours? ______ bricks

7. A book store sold 576 books in 8 hours. On average, how many books were sold each hour? ______ books

8. I can travel 9 km on a litre of fuel. How much would I use to travel 72 km? ______ litres

   What would be the cost of that fuel if I pay 160 cents per litre for it? ______ dollars

9. After travelling for $6\frac{1}{2}$ hours, I had travelled 495 km of the 875 km to my home. If the trip takes 12 hours, how far did I still have to travel? ______ km

   How many more hours should it take me? ______ hours

10. A farmer sold some cattle for $2360. He paid an agent $236 and a carrier $179. How much did he have left from the sale? ______ dollars

ACTIVITY

The unit pattern for multiples of 2 is 2, 4, 6, 8, 0; 2, 4, 6, 8, 0.

11. Draw the unit digit patterns for the numbers below.

a multiples of 4

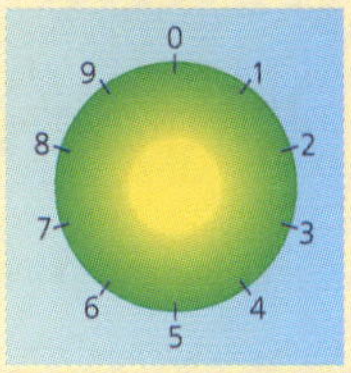
0
1
2
3
4
5
6
7
8
9

b multiples of 3

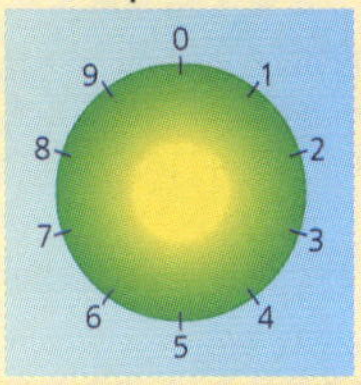
0
1
2
3
4
5
6
7
8
9

c multiples of 7

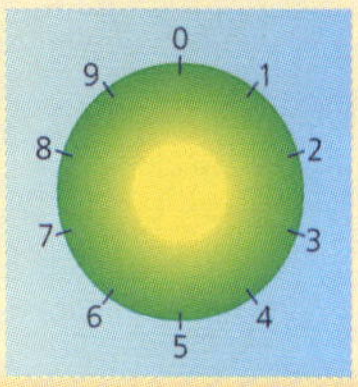
0
1
2
3
4
5
6
7
8
9

You saw these on page 62.

See *Extra Support 13* (Problem solving with algorithms), and *Extra Support 14 to 16* (Problem-solving strategies).

2:54 Estimating products

Write the zeros, then multiply the rest. 400 × 50 = 20 000

78 × 34
Estimate
80 × 30
= 2400

Round each number and multiply.

If a number ends in 5, use the higher ten.

1 Round each of these to the nearest ten.

a 27 ☐ **b** 49 ☐ **c** 83 ☐ **d** 47 ☐ **e** 25 ☐

f 91 ☐ **g** 65 ☐ **h** 48 ☐ **i** 71 ☐ **j** 62 ☐

2 Round each of these to the nearest hundred.

a 680 ☐ **b** 340 ☐ **c** 295 ☐ **d** 864 ☐ **e** 922 ☐

f 505 ☐ **g** 526 ☐ **h** 716 ☐ **i** 333 ☐ **j** 367 ☐

3 Find an estimate for each product by rounding each number first.

a 82 × 11
E = 80 × 10
= ☐

b 63 × 27
E = ☐ × ☐
= ☐

c 54 × 65
E = ☐ × ☐
= ☐

d 91 × 33
E = ☐ × ☐
= ☐

e 38 × 12
E = ☐ × ☐
= ☐

f 72 × 46
E = ☐ × ☐
= ☐

g 47 × 19
E = ☐ × ☐
= ☐

h 63 × 43
E = ☐ × ☐
= ☐

The **product** is the answer when you multiply.

Ask: Is the answer reasonable?

4 Round each number to its first digit and multiply to find an estimate.

a 43 × 631
E = 40 × 600
= ☐

b 36 × 194
E = ☐ × ☐
= ☐

c 82 × 666
E = ☐ × ☐
= ☐

d 58 × 749
E = ☐ × ☐
= ☐

43 × 461
Estimate
= 40 × 500
= 20 000

5 True or false?

a Approximating 27 × 7 with 30 × 10 will result in an estimate that is **larger** than the actual result. ☐

b Approximating 23 × 5 with 20 × 5 will result in an estimate that is **smaller** than the actual result. ☐

6 Estimate the answer, then check your estimate with a calculator. (E = estimate; A = answer)

ICT

a 94 × 37
E = ☐
A = ☐

b 65 × 31
E = ☐
A = ☐

c 57 × 347
E = ☐
A = ☐

d 625 × 47
E = ☐
A = ☐

 • *AUSTRALIAN SIGNPOST MATHS 5* • ISBN 9780655708797

2:55 Strategies for multiplication

Add the areas of the parts to find the area of the whole.

CONCEPT

The area model for 6 × 137

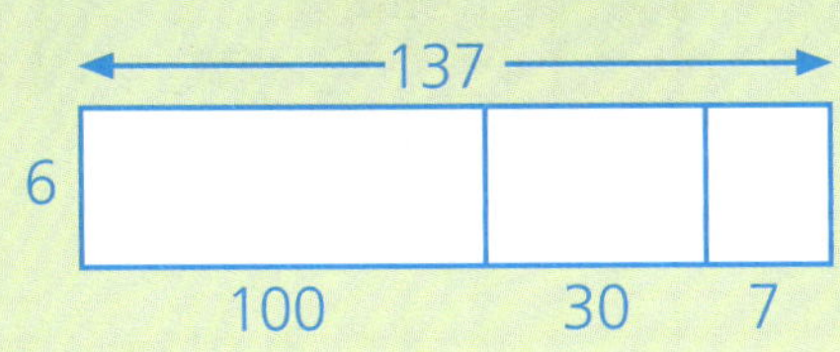

6 × 137
= (6 × 100) + (6 × 30) + (6 × 7)
= 600 + 180 + 42
= 822

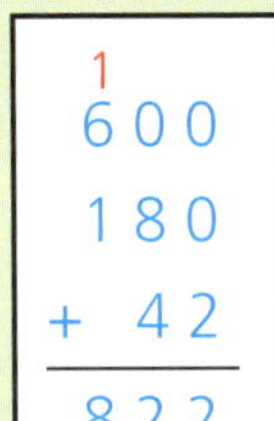

The area model for 25 × 28

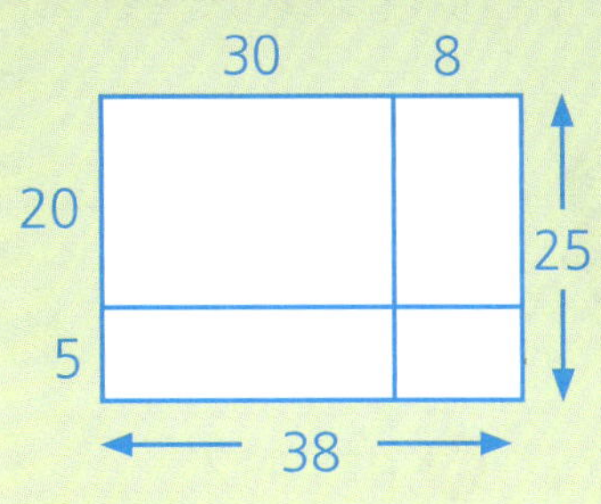

Break the whole into parts. Find each area, then add.

25 × 38
= (20 × 30) + (20 × 8) + (5 × 30) + (5 × 8)
= 600 + 160 + 150 + 40
= 950

1 Use the area model to find:

a 4 × 321

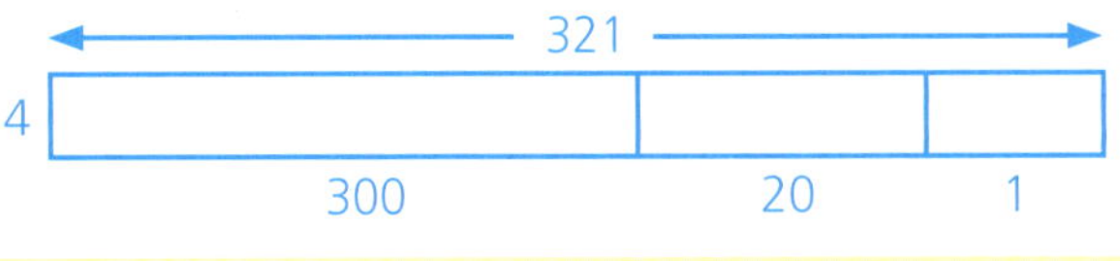

b 9 × 432

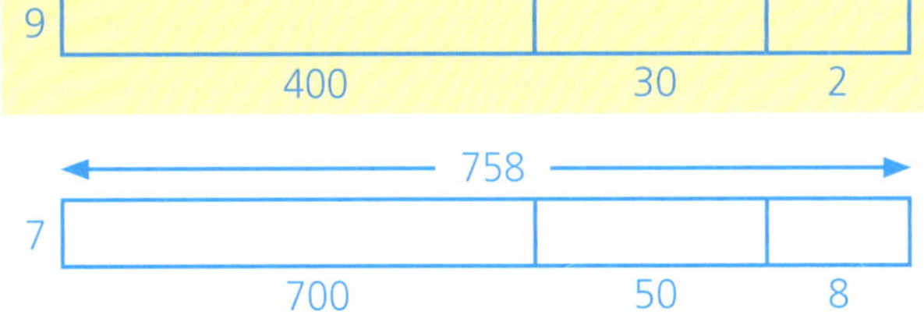

c 7 × 758

758
7
700
50
8

2 Use the area model to find:

a 34 × 57
= (30 × ☐) + (30 × ☐) + (4 × ☐) + (4 × ☐)
= ☐ + ☐ + ☐ + ☐
= ☐

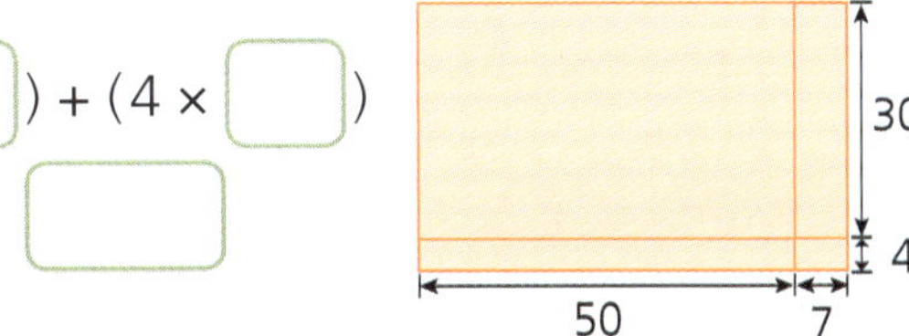

b 62 × 28
= (☐) + (☐) + (☐) + (☐)
= ☐ + ☐ + ☐ + ☐
= ☐

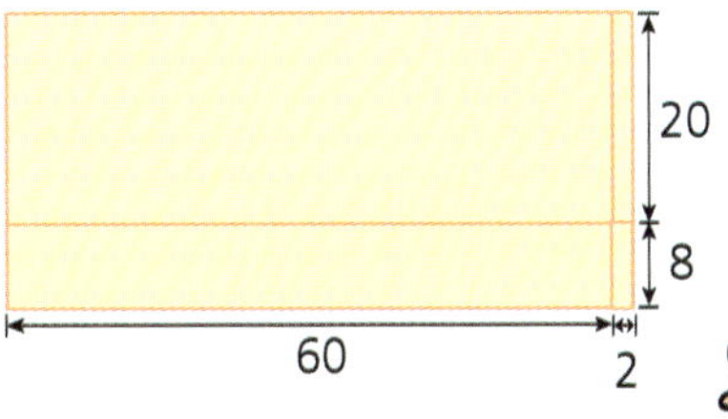

c 57 × 16
= (☐) + (☐) + (☐) + (☐)

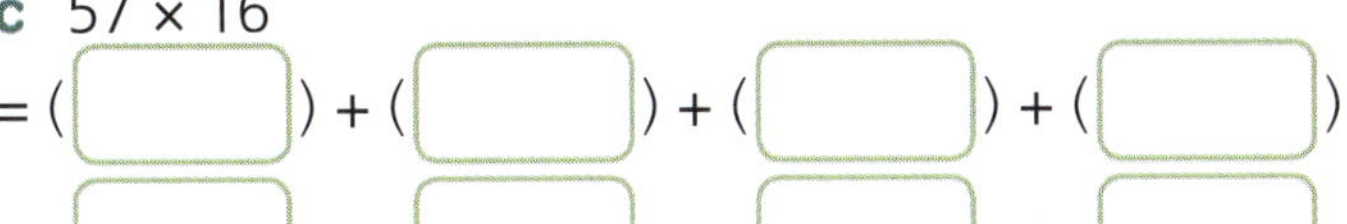

= ☐ + ☐ + ☐ + ☐
= ☐

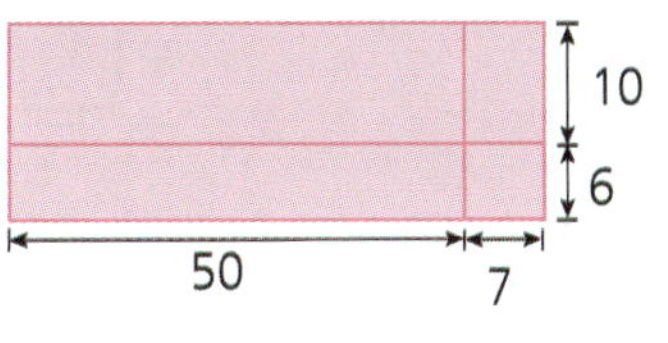

2:56 Multiplication by 2-digit numbers

34 × 86 = (30 × 86) + (4 × 86)

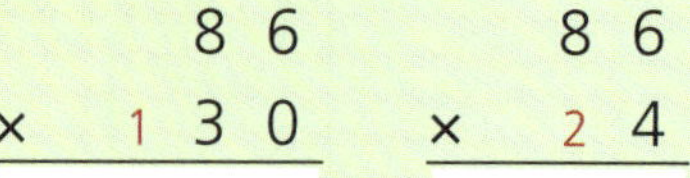

```
         8 6          8 6
    ×  1 3 0      ×   2 4
34 × 86 = 2 5 8 0  +  3 4 4  = 2924
```

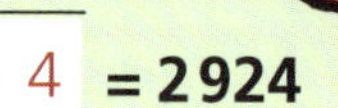

To multiply by 30, put down the 0 and multiply by 3.

1

a
```
  4 2
× 3 0
```
b
```
  5 6
× 2 0
```
c
```
  8 1
× 4 0
```
d
```
  4 3
× 3 0
```

e 40 × 65 [ ] f 70 × 92 [ ] g 90 × 27 [ ]

2

a 17 × 61 = (10 × 61) + (7 × [ ])

b 16 × 95 = (10 × [ ]) + (6 × 95)

c 31 × 53 = (30 × [ ]) + (1 × [ ])

d 46 × 66 = (40 × [ ]) + (6 × [ ])

e 72 × 37 = ([ ] × 37) + ([ ] × 37)

f 29 × 48 = ([ ] × 48) + ([ ] × 48)

g 49 × 59 = ([ ] × [ ]) + ([ ] × [ ]) = [ ] + [ ] = [ ]

h 72 × 64 = ([ ] × [ ]) + ([ ] × [ ]) = [ ] + [ ] = [ ]

3

a 63 × 10, 63 × 5: 15 × 63 = + = [ ]

b 74 × 20, 74 × 8: 28 × 74 = + = [ ]

c 92 × 40, 92 × 6: 46 × 92 = + = [ ]

d 81 × 50, 81 × 2: 52 × 81 = + = [ ]

e 75 × 70, 75 × 5: 75 × 75 = + = [ ]

f 88 × 60, 88 × 9: 69 × 88 = + = [ ]

g 52 × 30, 52 × 5: 35 × 52 = + = [ ]

h 96 × 40, 96 × 2: 42 × 96 = + = [ ]

i 28 × 50, 28 × 7: 57 × 28 = + = [ ]

j 84 × 60, 84 × 3: 63 × 84 = + = [ ]

4 Each night for two weeks, Anika's dad read 35 pages of the book 'Watership Down'. How many pages were read in the two weeks? [ ]

2:57 Multiplication by 2-digit numbers

To multiply by 60 put down the zero and multiply by 6.

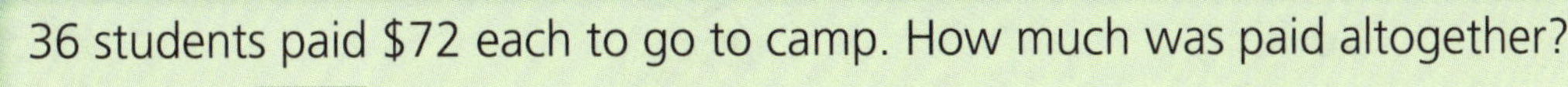

CONCEPT

36 students paid $72 each to go to camp. How much was paid altogether?

36 × 72 = ☐

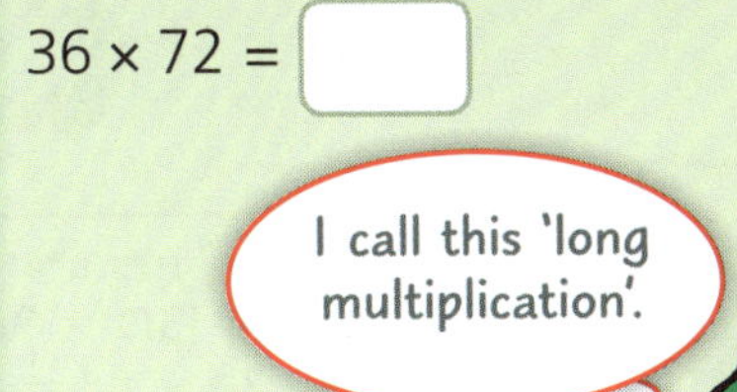


```
   7 2         7 2
×  3 0   +  ×    6
 2 1 6 0     4 3 2
```

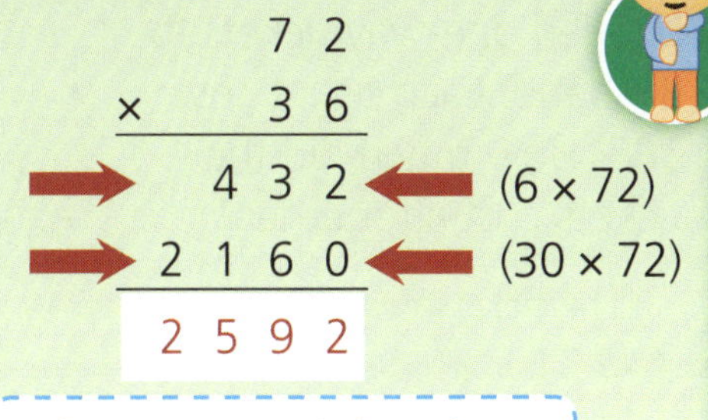

```
      7 2
×     3 6
    4 3 2   (6 × 72)
  2 1 6 0   (30 × 72)
  2 5 9 2
```

$2592 was paid altogether.

1

a
```
   3 2
×  1 4
        (4 × 32)
_____   (10 × 32)
```

b
```
   5 3
×  3 2
        (2 × 53)
_____   (30 × 53)
```

c
```
   9 3
×  5 1
        (1 × 93)
_____   (50 × 93)
```

d
```
   6 2
×  3 4
        (4 × ☐)
_____   (30 × ☐)
```

e
```
   7 1
×  4 4
        (4 × ☐)
_____   (40 × ☐)
```

f
```
   4 3
×  3 1
        (☐ × 43)
_____   (☐ × 43)
```

g
```
   9 4
×  2 2
        (☐ × 94)
_____   (☐ × 94)
```

2 Write out the algorithm and use it to find the answer.

a 12 × 89
```
   8 9
×  1 2
        (2 × ☐)
_____   (10 × ☐)
```

b 53 × 27
```
   2 7
×  5 3
        (3 × ☐)
_____   (50 × ☐)
```

c 63 × 56
```
   5 6
×
        (☐ × ☐)
_____   (☐ × ☐)
```

d 18 × 49
```
×
        (☐ × ☐)
_____   (☐ × ☐)
```

e 37 × 95
```
×
        (2 × ☐)
_____   (10 × ☐)
```

f 72 × 33
```
×
        (3 × ☐)
_____   (50 × ☐)
```

g 25 × 73
```
×
        (☐ × ☐)
_____   (☐ × ☐)
```

h 46 × 53
```
×
        (☐ × ☐)
_____   (☐ × ☐)
```

3 a One small bottle of correction fluid contains 18 mL. How much correction fluid would be contained in 56 small bottles? ☐

b In a box that weighed 200 g, Lucy sent 36 Christmas balls to Camha. If each ball weighed 14 g, what was the gross weight of the package? ☐

2:58 Multiplication by 2-digit numbers

$$\begin{array}{r} 88 \\ \times\ {}_3 4 \\ \hline 352 \end{array}$$

4 x 8 = 32, put down the 2, and trade 30 for 3 tens.

CONCEPT

34 members of our club booked one-way tickets to Brisbane. Each ticket cost $88. How much did the tickets cost altogether?

The tickets cost $2992.

Working

$$\begin{array}{rl} 88 & \\ \times\ 34 & \\ \hline 352 & 4 \times 88 \\ 2640 & 30 \times 88 \\ \hline 2992 & \end{array}$$

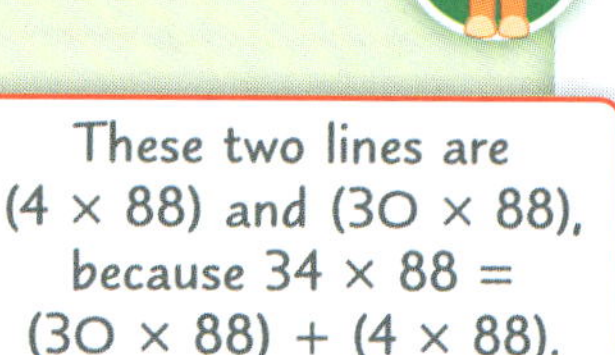

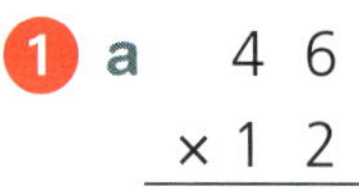

These two lines are (4 × 88) and (30 × 88), because 34 × 88 = (30 × 88) + (4 × 88).

1

a $\begin{array}{r} 46 \\ \times\ 12 \\ \hline \end{array}$ b $\begin{array}{r} 93 \\ \times\ 11 \\ \hline \end{array}$ c $\begin{array}{r} 81 \\ \times\ 24 \\ \hline \end{array}$ d $\begin{array}{r} 75 \\ \times\ 32 \\ \hline \end{array}$ e $\begin{array}{r} 67 \\ \times\ 12 \\ \hline \end{array}$

f 53 × 41 = $\begin{array}{r} 41 \\ \times\ 53 \\ \hline \end{array}$ g 62 × 27 = $\begin{array}{r} 27 \\ \times\ 62 \\ \hline \end{array}$ h 14 × 99 = $\begin{array}{r} 99 \\ \times\ 14 \\ \hline \end{array}$ i 25 × 18 = $\begin{array}{r} 18 \\ \times\ 25 \\ \hline \end{array}$ j 32 × 94 = $\begin{array}{r} 94 \\ \times\ 32 \\ \hline \end{array}$

k 16 × 52 ×

l 33 × 69 ×

m 28 × 31 ×

n 95 × 42 ×

2

a Each month Rhonda sends $38 to World Vision. How much does she send in a year?

b A gift shop purchased 36 teapots for $54 each and sold them for $87 each.
How much did the teapots cost the gift shop altogether?
What was the total amount the shop received by selling all the teapots?
How much profit did the gift shop make?

c Complete this table for other items sold by the gift shop.

Item	Number of items	Cost of one	Total cost	Selling price of one	Total from sales	Total profit
sugar bowl	65	$14		$28		
oval tray	43	$22		$35		
cup/saucer	76	$28		$47		

 • *AUSTRALIAN SIGNPOST MATHS 5* • ISBN 9780655708797

Multiplication by 2-digit numbers

Amir bragged that his stamp collection was 28 times larger than his brother's. His brother had 168 stamps. How many stamps did Amir say he had?

```
    1 6 8
×     2 8
  1 3 4 4  ← (8 × 168)
  3 3 6 0  ← (20 × 168)
  4 7 0 4
```

28 times as many!

1

a 429 × 13

b 153 × 27

c 362 × 45

d 287 × 72

e 803 × 75

f 740 × 56

g 904 × 34

h 610 × 89

i 311 × 68

j 17 × 952 (952 × 17)

k 38 × 750

l 26 × 5800

2

a Through air, sound travels at 330 metres each second. How far would it travel in 35 seconds?

Through sea water, sound travels 4 times faster. How far does it travel through sea water in 35 seconds?

b The platform of the Assyrian palace of Sargon covered about 11 hectares and was 15 metres high. It would have taken 8600 people 14 years to construct the platform. If one person could do all this work, how long would it take them?

FUN SPOT

Estimating the number of blocks in a jar

- Take turns to fill (or partly fill) a jar with place-value ones.
- Estimate the number of layers of ones in the jar.
- Look underneath to estimate the number in each layer.
- Multiply, to estimate the number of ones in the jar.
- See whose estimate is closest.

2:60 Finding missing numbers

Have you learned your addition and multiplication tables?

CONCEPT

$3 \times 4 = \square$ $4 \times \square = 12$ $12 \div \square = 3$

$\square \times 3 = 12$ $12 \times \square = 4$ $12 - \square = 3$ $12 = 7 + \square$

1 Find the missing numbers. Use a calculator to check your answers.

a $\square \times 8 = 24$ **b** $\square \times 7 = 42$ **c** $\square \times 6 = 36$

d $1 \times \square = 87$ **e** $11 \times \square = 99$ **f** $12 \times \square = 72$

g $9 \times \square = 63$ **h** $6 \times \square = 48$ **i** $5 \times \square = 55$

2 **a** Michaela had 93 coins in a bag. She drew out 15. How many were left? □

b There are 45 jars in 9 equal rows. How many are in each row? □

c 1000 trees were planted in 8 equal columns. How many were in one column? □

d In the game of Pludo there are 28 counters in each of four colours. After dropping them all in the car, I found 86. How many were still missing? □

Find the missing numbers.

3 **a** $\square + 37 = 40$ **b** $\square + 63 = 100$ **c** $\square + 70 = 180$

d $\square + 140 = 360$ **e** $\square + 156 = 365$ **f** $\square + 200 = 471$

g $311 + \square = 490$ **h** $517 + \square = 995$ **i** $840 + \square = 965$

4 **a** $\square - 8 = 7$ **b** $\square - 9 = 10$ **c** $\square - 6 = 5$

d $16 - \square = 7$ **e** $9 - \square = 4$ **f** $15 - \square = 7$

g $90 - \square = 30$ **h** $180 - \square = 60$ **i** $100 - \square = 31$

5 **a** $\square \div 6 = 5$ **b** $\square \div 4 = 8$ **c** $\square \div 7 = 6$

d $\square \div 9 = 9$ **e** $\square \div 3 = 36$ **f** $\square \div 2 = 45$

g $100 \div \square = 20$ **h** $60 \div \square = 10$ **i** $54 \div \square = 6$

6 **a** $\square = 436 \div 4$ **b** $\square + 14 = 36$ **c** $17 = \square - 14$

d $56 = \square - 37$ **e** $9 \times \square = 72$ **f** $8 = 32 \div \square$

g $\square = 50 \times 7$ **h** $\square - 27 = 63$ **i** $110 = \square + 36$

See *Extra Support 18* (Finding missing numbers).

3:01 Kilometres

Find something 1 km from your school.
This can be your benchmark for 1 km.

km means kilometre.
1 km = 1000 metres

This is her personal benchmark for 1 km.

1 To measure these distances, would you use metres or kilometres?

a the length of a skipping rope ______ **b** the height of a chimney ______

c the distance to the next town ______ **d** the distance to Fiji ______

e the distance you would walk in one day ______ **f** the distance around a house ______

g the perimeter of the school fence ______ **h** the length of the classroom ______

2 How many metres in:

a 2 km? ______ **b** 5 km? ______ **c** 4 km? ______ **d** 10 km? ______

3 How many kilometres in:

a 6000 m? ______ **b** 10 000 m? ______ **c** 7000 m? ______ **d** 9000 m? ______

4 Use the scale on the map to find the shortest distance by road (in **km**) from:

a the police station to the school ______

b the police station to the hospital ______

c the school to the post office ______

d the school to the shop ______

e the post office to the shop ______

f the church to the service station ______

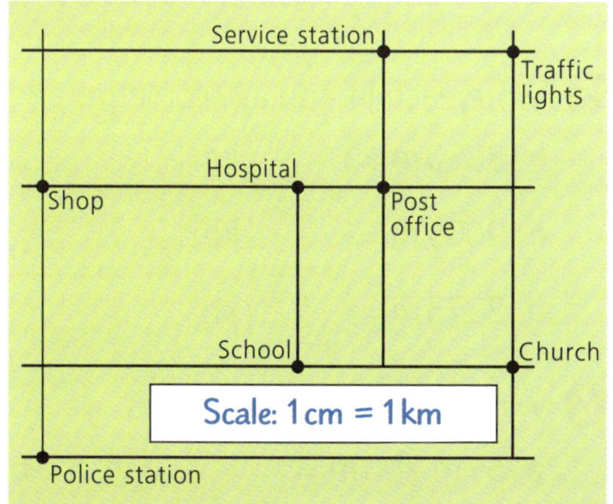

Researching distance

- Create a table to show distances to nearby towns or suburbs or distances between capital cities in Australia.
- Research how the metric system began (SI units).

3:02 Kilometres and metres

1 km = 1000 m
half a km = 500 m

1 Write as metres.

a 4 km ☐ b 7 km ☐ c 9 km ☐
d 6 km ☐ e 2 km ☐ f 3 km ☐
g 5 km ☐ h 10 km ☐ i 14 km ☐

km means kilometre.

kilometre
km

1000 m = 1 km

2 Write as kilometres.

a 3000 m ☐ b 9000 m ☐ c 5000 m ☐
d 7000 m ☐ e 12 000 m ☐ f 16 000 m ☐

3 Choose the most suitable unit (**km**, **m**, **cm**, **mm**) to measure:

a the length of a road ☐ b the height of a house ☐
c the width of your hand ☐ d the length of an ant ☐
e the depth of a lake ☐ f the distance to Melbourne ☐
g the height of a flagpole ☐ h the width of Torres Strait ☐

4 Write each speed as kilometres per hour (**km/h**).

a 60 km travelled in one hour ☐
b 95 km travelled in one hour ☐
c 140 km travelled in two hours ☐
d 200 km travelled in four hours ☐

80 km in 2 hours is 40 km in 1 hour.

110 km/h

5 Write each length as kilometres and metres.

a 3850 m = ☐ km ☐ m b 1056 m = ☐ km ☐ m
c 9005 m = ☐ km ☐ m d 5600 m = ☐ km ☐ m
e 3275 m = ☐ km ☐ m f 8241 m = ☐ km ☐ m

6 Write each length as metres.

a 5 km 200 m = ☐ m b 1 km 341 m = ☐ m c 4 km 750 m = ☐ m
d 8 km 5 m = ☐ m e 10 km 30 m = ☐ m f 7 km 38 m = ☐ m

ACTIVITY

Measure how many of your steps would equal:

a 1 m ☐ b 10 m ☐ c 100 m ☐
d Multiply the answer for 100 m by 10 to find how many of your steps make 1 km. ☐

 • *AUSTRALIAN SIGNPOST MATHS 5* • ISBN 9780655708797

Perimeter

Perimeter is the length of the boundary of a shape.

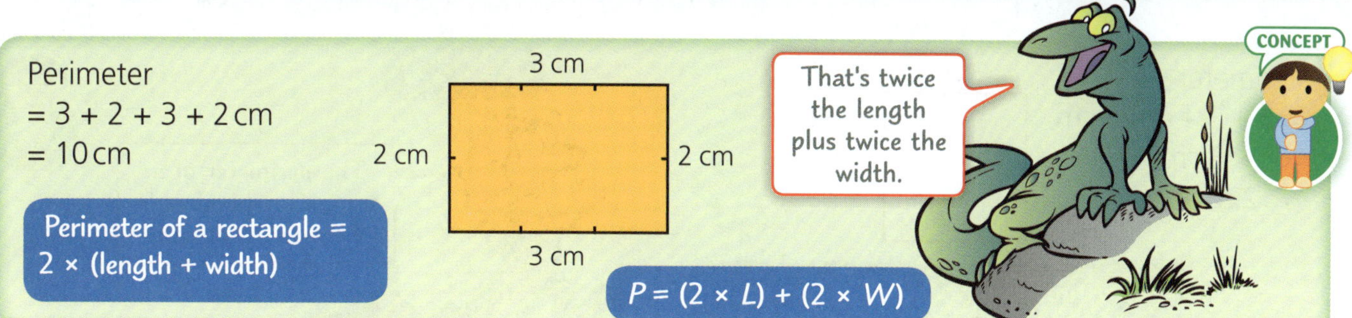

1 Measure the length and width and find the perimeter.

	Length	Width	Perimeter
a			
b			
c			
d			

2 Draw the following shapes and find the perimeter of each. You could use grid paper.

a A rectangle with sides 4 cm and 3 cm ☐ **b** A square with 4 cm sides ☐

c A rectangle with sides 5 cm and 4 cm ☐ **d** A square with 5 cm sides ☐

e A rectangle with sides 6 cm and 4 cm ☐ **f** A square with 6 cm sides ☐

3 Find the perimeter of each rectangle.

a
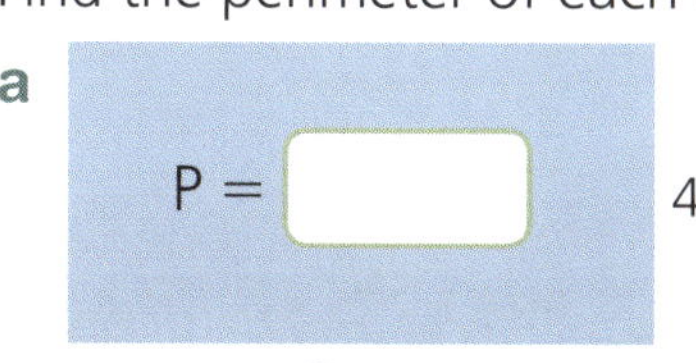

b

c
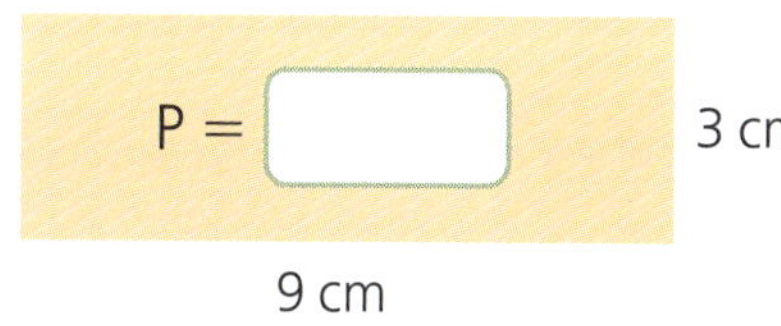

d

e
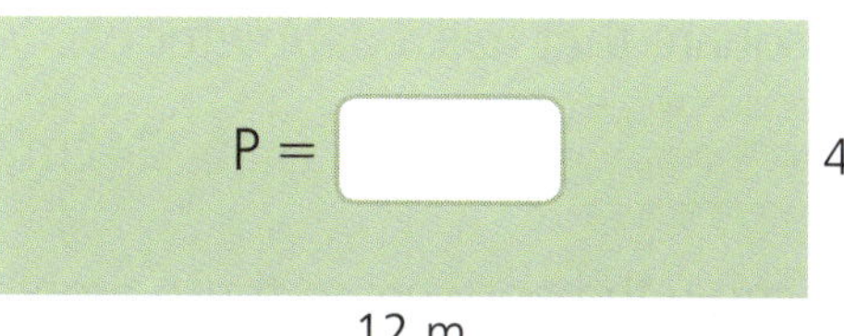

f
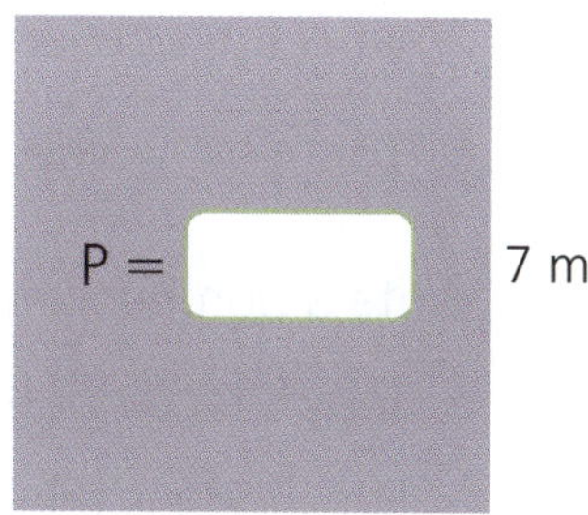

4 What are the dimensions and the perimeter (P) of the concept box above, correct to the nearest centimetre? L = ☐ W = ☐ P = ☐

 • *AUSTRALIAN SIGNPOST MATHS 5* • ISBN 9780655708797

3:04 Perimeter

Length, width and height are called dimensions.

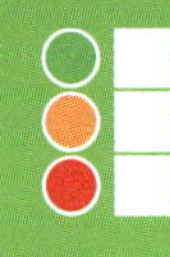

CONCEPT

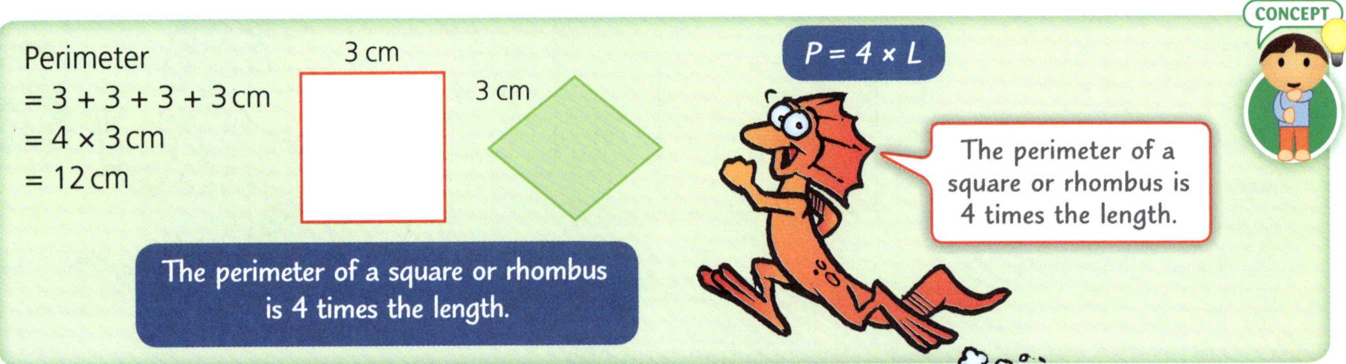

1 Find the perimeter (P) of each square or rhombus.

a

P = ☐ cm

b

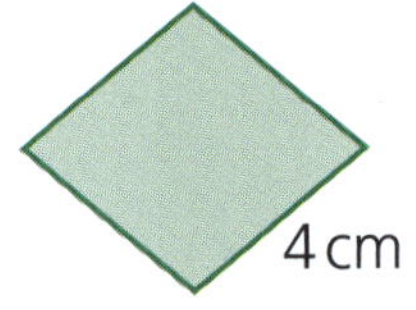

P = ☐ cm

c

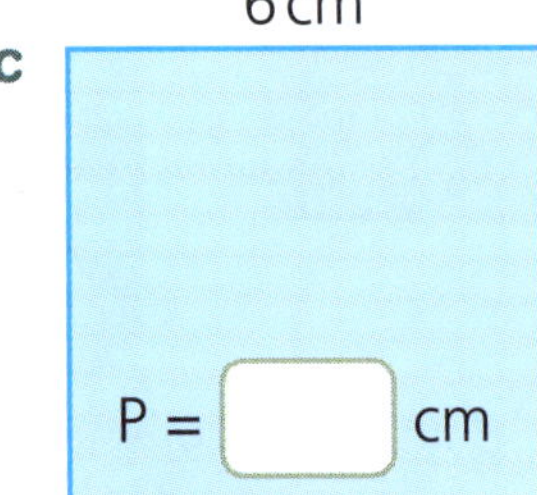

P = ☐ cm

d

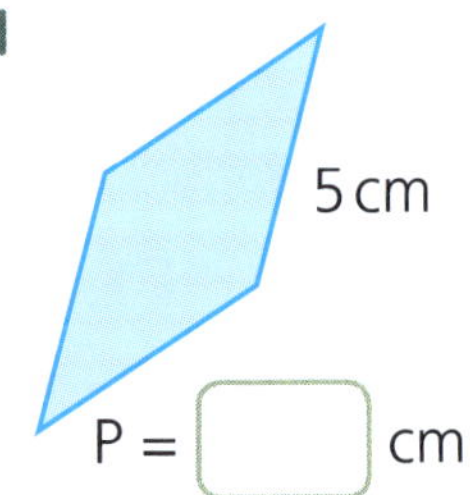

P = ☐ cm

2 Find the perimeter of these rectangles.

	Length	Width	Perimeter
a	7 cm	6 cm	
b	10 cm	7 cm	
c	12 cm	10 cm	
d	15 cm	7 cm	
e	20 cm	16 cm	

3 Find the perimeter of these squares.

	Length	Perimeter
a	9 cm	
b	12 cm	
c	15 cm	
d	20 cm	
e	25 cm	

A square has 4 equal sides.

4 What are the dimensions of a rectangle that has a perimeter of:

a 18 cm? Length = ☐ Width = ☐

b 30 cm? Length = ☐ Width = ☐

Perimeter of a rectangle = 2 × (length + width)

5 What is the side length of a square that has a perimeter of:

a 16 cm? Side length = ☐

b 24 cm? Side length = ☐

6 Write a number sentence to show the answers to these problems.

a Toby's rectangular paddock is 50 m long and 25 m wide.
How long is the fence that runs around his paddock? ☐

b Chadna wants to sew a lace border around her square handkerchief.
What length of lace will she need if her handkerchief is 20 cm long? ☐

Calculating area

8 cm² is the same as 8 square centimetres.

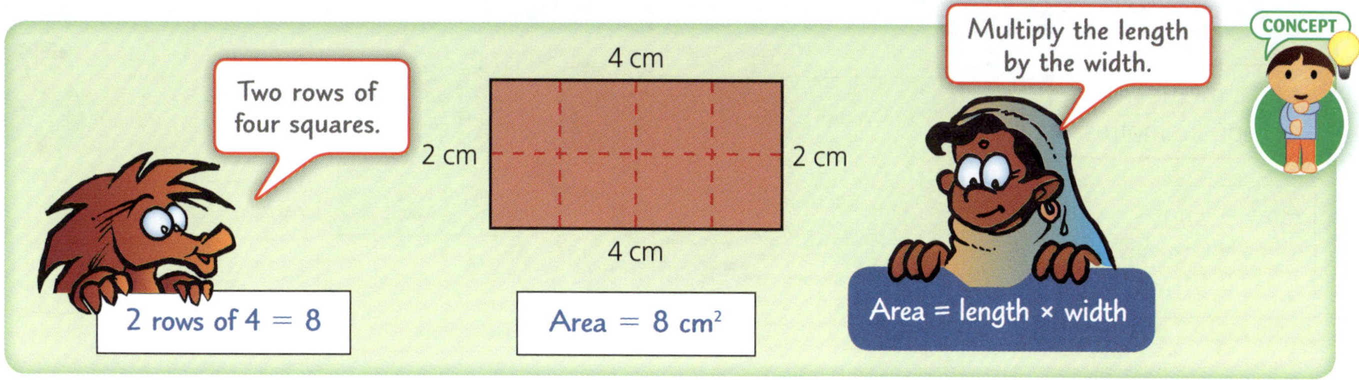

1 Find the area of these rectangles.

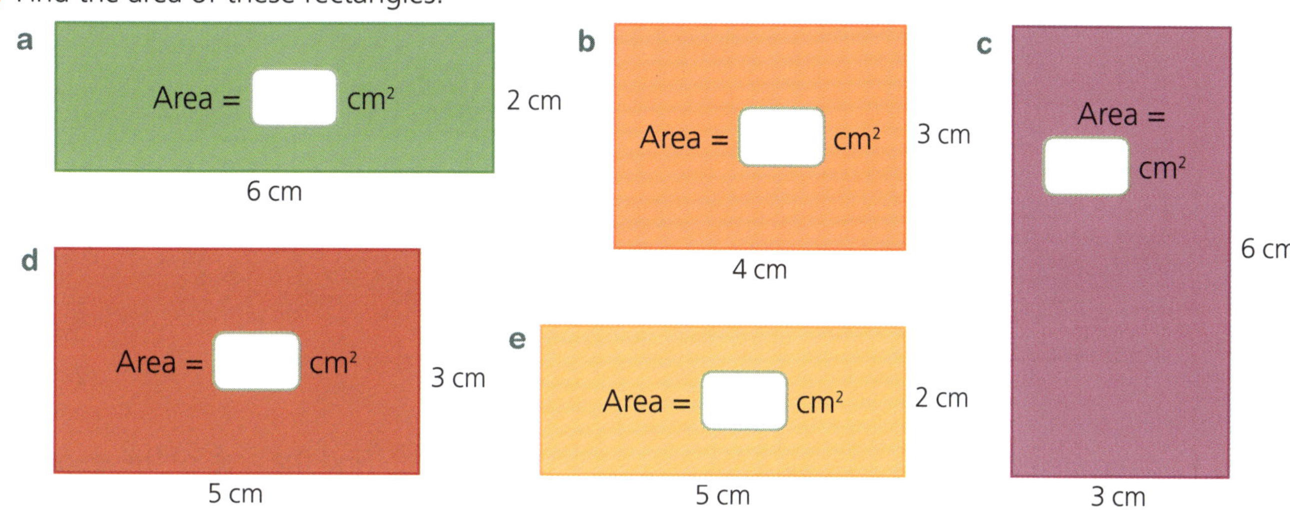

2 Measure the dimensions of the cover of this book to the nearest centimetre. Estimate the area.

a Length = ☐ cm b Width = ☐ cm

c The area of the cover is about ☐ cm²

cm² means square centimetres.

3 Write number sentences to show the solution to these problems.

a Lydia made a wristband that is 2 cm wide and 16 cm long.

i What is the top area of her wristband? ☐

ii How many 2 cm square stickers will she need to decorate the top area? ☐

b Camille's garden is 2 m by 6 m. She divides the area equally to grow tomatoes, spinach, leeks and cabbages. How much area does each vegetable use? ☐

c Jadee's piece of cardboard is 30 cm long and 20 cm wide. How many cards can she make if each card is made from a piece that is 14 cm long and 10 cm wide?

☐

d Leo is designing a label for the top of a gift box that is 40 cm long and 20 cm wide. What will be the size of his label? ☐

Square metres

1 m
1 m

A square metre is an area the size of a square with sides 1 metre.

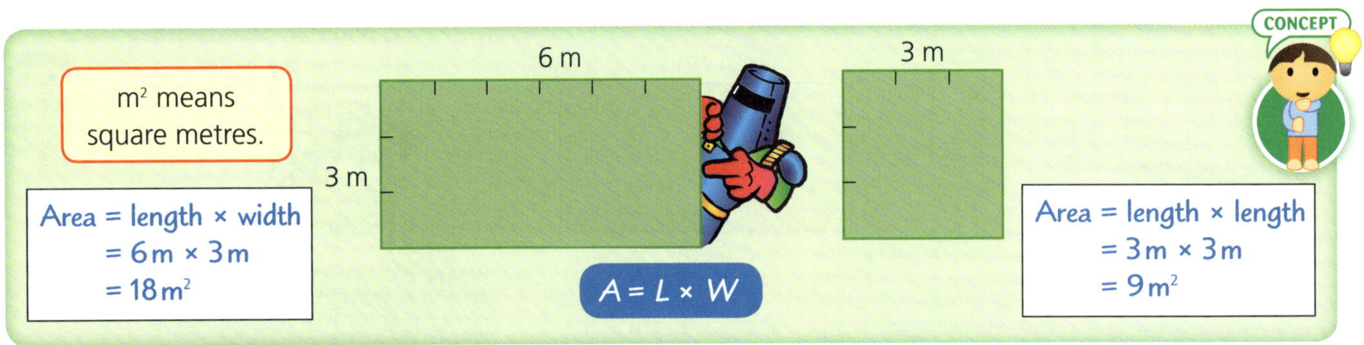

m² means square metres.

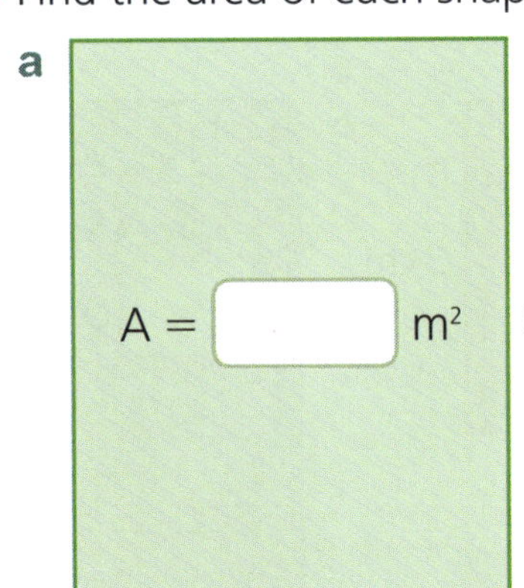

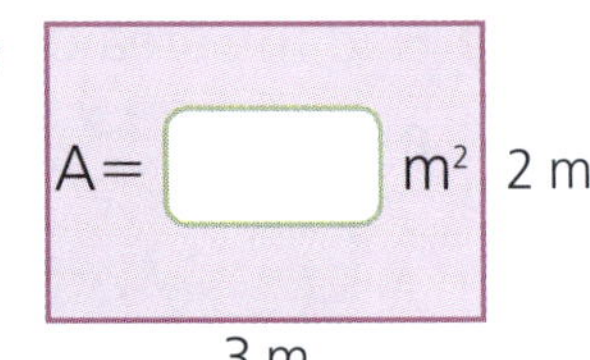

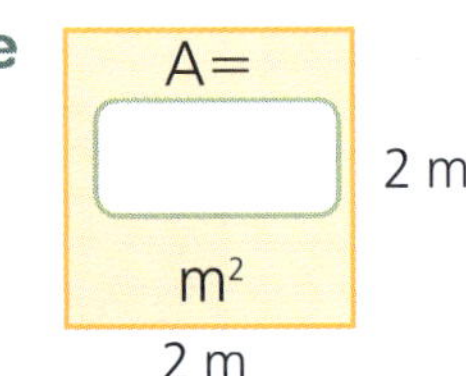

1 Find the area of each shape.

a A = ☐ m^2 (5 m by 4 m)

b A = ☐ m^2 (2 m by 5 m)

c A = ☐ m^2 (2 m by 3 m)

d A = ☐ m^2 (2 m by 7 m)

e A = ☐ m^2 (2 m by 2 m)

2 Find the area of rectangles with these dimensions.

	Length	Width	Area
a	9 m	4 m	m^2
b	7 m	6 m	m^2
c	10 m	8 m	m^2
d	8 m	7 m	m^2
e	9 m	6 m	m^2

3 Find the area of these squares.

	Length	Area
a	7 cm	
b	6 cm	
c	9 cm	
d	8 cm	
e	10 cm	

4 Circle the correct area for the rectangle with dimensions:

a length 9 m, width 7 m.
Area: $16\ m^2$ $63\ m^2$ $32\ m^2$

b length 8 m, width 6 m.
Area: $48\ m^2$ $14\ m^2$ $86\ m^2$

5 Measure the dimensions of the classroom. ☐

Use these to estimate the amount of carpet needed to cover the floor. ☐ m^2

6 **a** Chrissy wants to cover one wall with wallpaper. How much wallpaper will she need if the wall is 5 m long and 3 m high? ☐ m^2

b How much wallpaper would she need to cover a wall 7 metres long and 3 metres high if it has a window 2 m long and 1 m high? ☐ m^2

 • *AUSTRALIAN SIGNPOST MATHS 5* • ISBN 9780655708797

Area

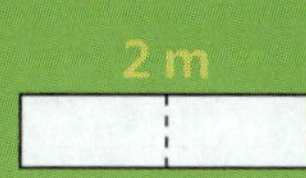

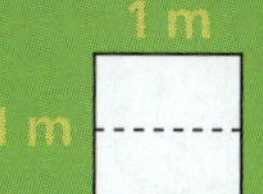

This area is still 1 m^2 when it is cut into parts.

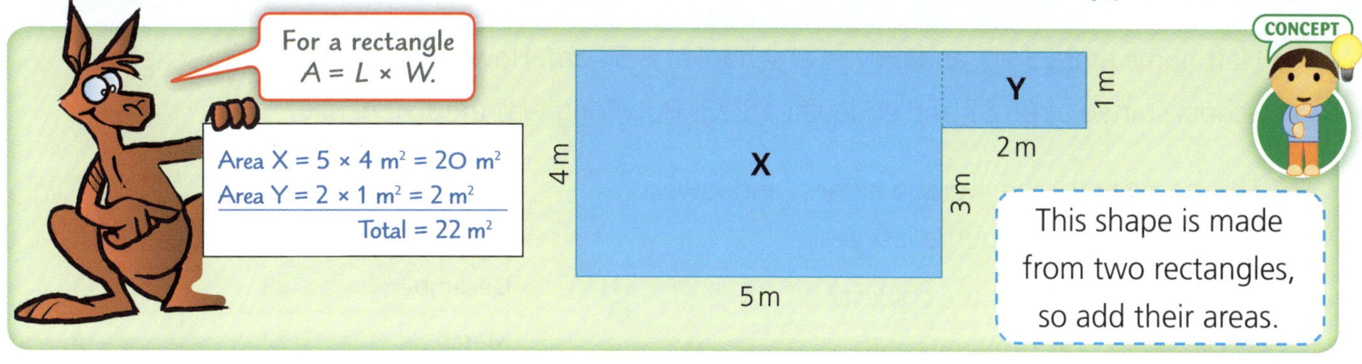

1 Find the area of each shape.

a

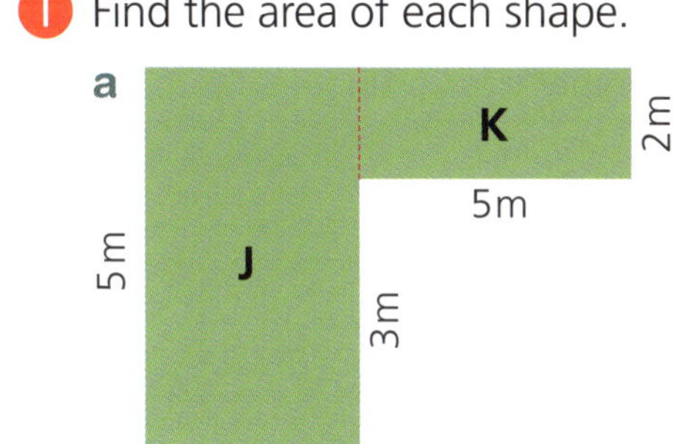

Area **J** = ☐ m^2

Area **K** = ☐ m^2

Total area = ☐ m^2

b

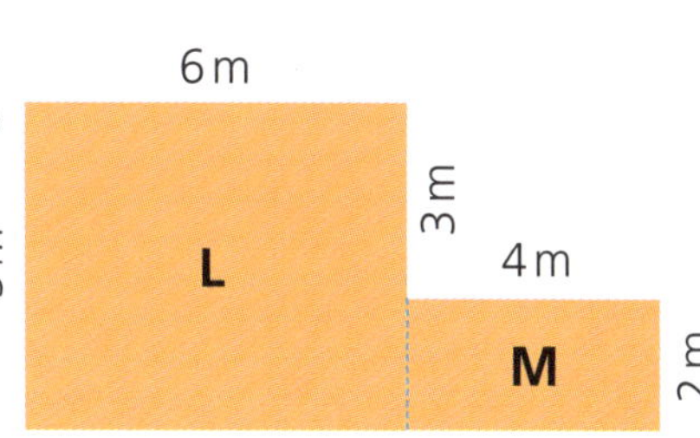

Area **L** = ☐ m^2

Area **M** = ☐ m^2

Total area = ☐ m^2

c

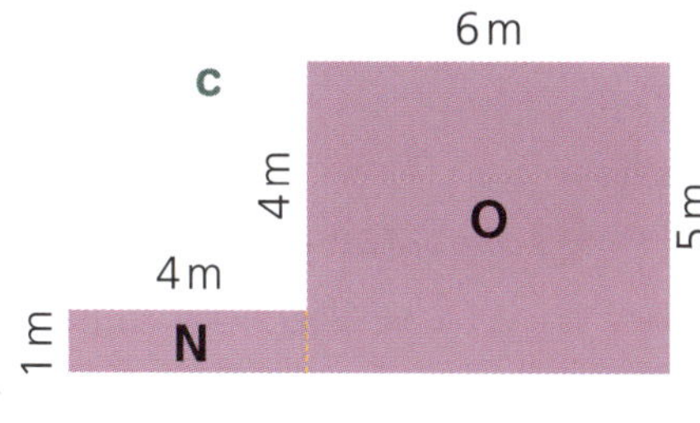

Area **N** = ☐ m^2

Area **O** = ☐ m^2

Total area = ☐ m^2

d

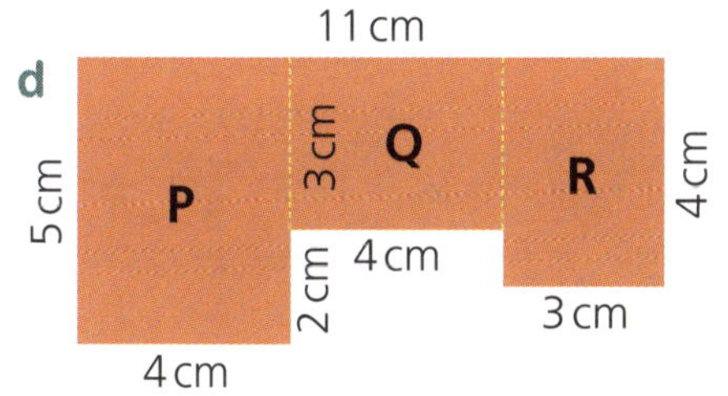

Area **P** = ☐ m^2

Area **Q** = ☐ m^2

Area **R** = ☐ m^2

Total area = ☐ m^2

e

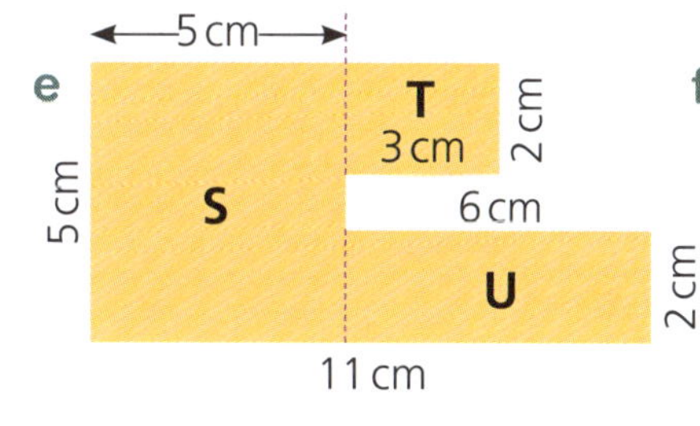

Area **S** = ☐ m^2

Area **T** = ☐ m^2

Area **U** = ☐ m^2

Total area = ☐ m^2

f

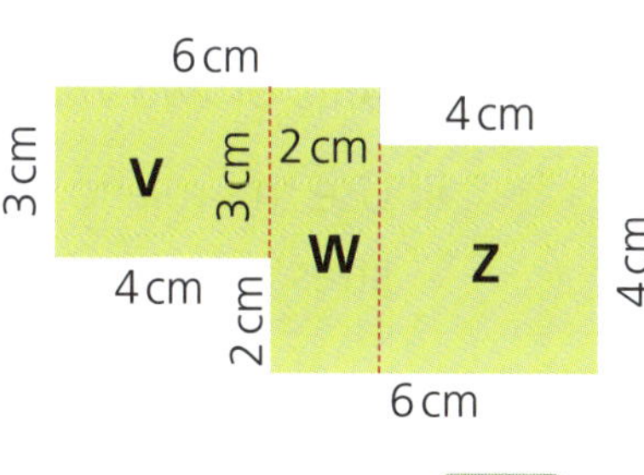

Area **V** = ☐ m^2

Area **W** = ☐ m^2

Area **Z** = ☐ m^2

Total area = ☐ m^2

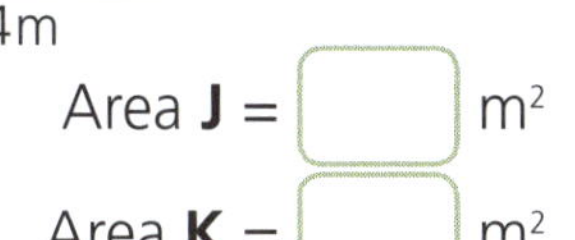
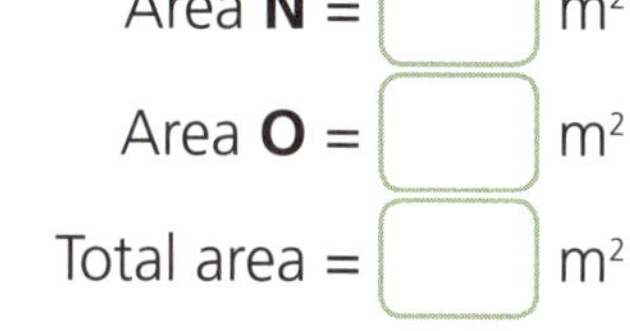

2 Write the dimensions (in whole cm) of three rectangles that have an area of:

a 12 cm^2 ☐, ☐, ☐

b 20 cm^2 ☐, ☐, ☐

3 Write the most appropriate unit of measure (cm^2 or m^2).

a a classroom floor = 150 ☐

b a ruler = 150 ☐

c gift card = 165 ☐

d a postage stamp = 6 ☐

e a garden = 600 ☐

f a whiteboard = 8 ☐

 • *AUSTRALIAN SIGNPOST MATHS 5* • ISBN 9780655708797

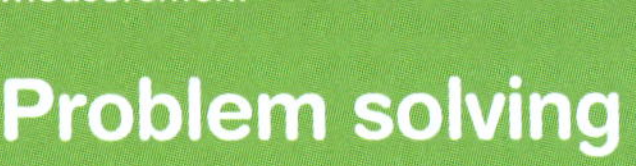

3:08 Problem solving

A floor plan is like an aerial map.

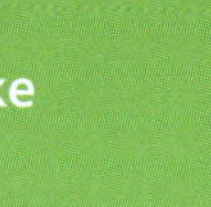

1. I left home at 8:25 am and arrived at school at 8:54 am. How long was the trip to school? [ ]
   School started at 08:57 and ended at 15:23. How long was the school day? [ ]

2. This table shows the average highest and lowest temperature in Melbourne last year.

Month	Average highest temperature (°c)	Average lowest temperature (°c)
December	23	13
March	22	14
June	13	7
September	16	9

   a Which month was the coldest? [ ]

   b Which month shown had the greatest difference between the average highest and lowest temperature?
   [ ]

3. a Sarah plans to lay new carpet in her bedroom.
   Use this floor plan to find how much carpet is needed.
   Area **A** = [ ] m^2 Area **B** = [ ] m^2 Area **C** = [ ] m^2

   Total area = [ ] m^2

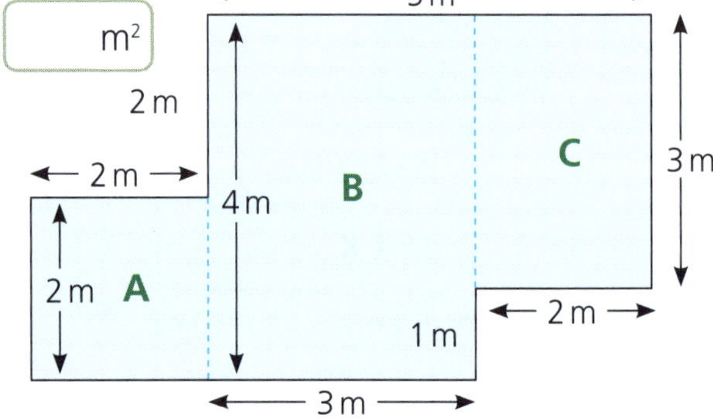

   b Sarah plans to paint 2 coats of paint on two feature walls. The dimensions of both walls are 5 m by 3 m

   i Area of one wall = [ ] m^2

   ii Area of two walls = [ ] m^2

   iii Use this rule to find how many litres of paint she will need.

   [ ] ÷ 15 × 2 = [ ] L

   She will need [ ] L of paint.

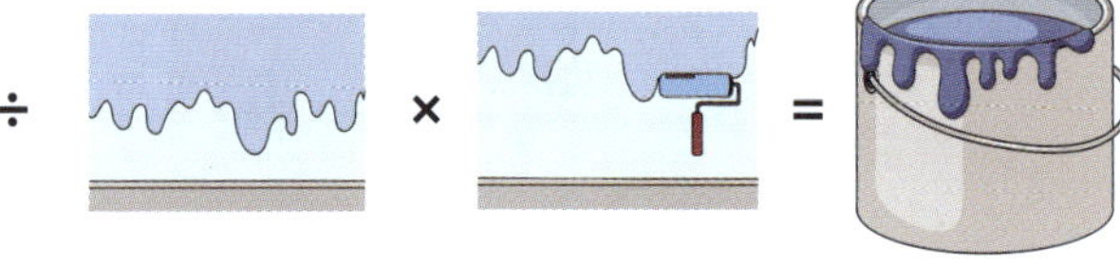

Total area (m^2) ÷ Spreading rate of paint (15 m^2/L) × Number of coats = Total litres required

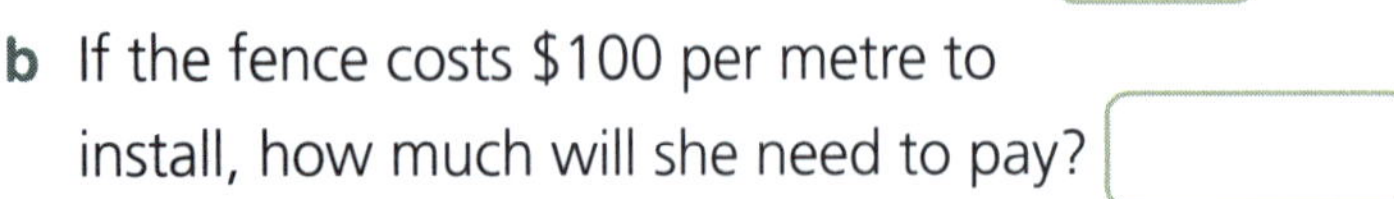

4. Rosie plans to install a fence around her pool.

   a Use this diagram to calculate the length of fencing she needs to install. [ ] m

   b If the fence costs $100 per metre to install, how much will she need to pay? [ ]

   c What is the surface area of her pool? [ ] m^2

   d What is the area inside Rosie's pool fence? [ ] m^2

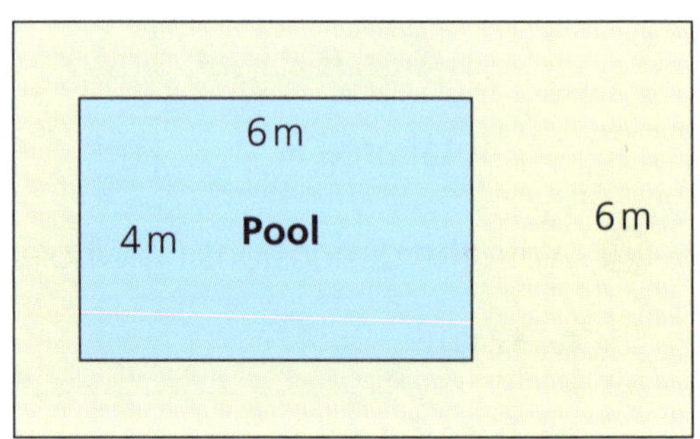

   e Rosie plans to lay tiles in the area around her pool, inside the pool fence. How many square metres of tiles will she need? [ ] m^2

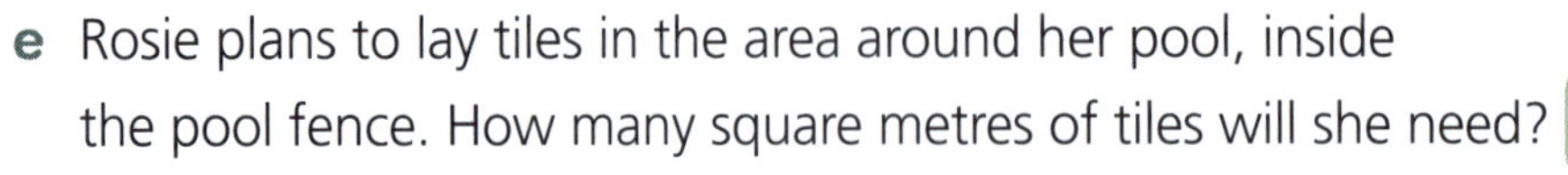

   f 1 metre must be left between the pool and the fence.
   What is the longest pool that could be inside this fence? [ ] m

 ISBN 9780655708797

3:09 Time units

How long from 3:45 to 4:12?
3:45 to 4:00 - 15 minutes } 15 + 12 = 27
4:00 to 4:12 - 12 minutes } 27 minutes

This year is: ____

A millennium is 1000 years.

We live in the 3rd millennium.

A century is 100 years.

We live in the 21st century.

The date today is: ____

All these units allow us to record and measure time.

CONCEPT

A decade is 10 years.
A year has 12 months.
A year is 52 weeks.
A fortnight is 2 weeks.
A week is 7 days.
A day is 24 hours.
An hour is 60 minutes.
A minute is 60 seconds.

1 Complete the following.

a 3 weeks = ☐ days	**b** 2 days = ☐ hours	**c** 7 minutes = ☐ seconds
d 180 minutes = ☐ hours	**e** 4 hours = ☐ minutes	**f** 6 fortnights = ☐ weeks
g 4 years = ☐ months	**h** 50 years = ☐ decades	**i** 120 minutes = ☐ hours
j 56 days = ☐ weeks	**k** 700 days = ☐ weeks	**l** 28 weeks = ☐ fortnights
m 84 days = ☐ fortnights	**n** 3 years = ☐ weeks	**o** 600 seconds = ☐ minutes

2 How much time has passed from:

a 8 am to 8:35 am? ☐
b 4:10 pm to 4:36 pm? ☐
c 5:13 am to 6:19 am? ☐
d 9 am to 10:49 am? ☐
e 7:08 pm to 9:52 pm? ☐
f 6:30 pm to 8:36 pm? ☐

3 If it is 8:17 am, how long will Graham have to wait until:

a school starts at 9 am? ☐
b sport starts at 10:30 am? ☐
c lunch starts at 1:05 pm? ☐
d school ends at 3:05 pm? ☐
e tennis coaching at 4:15 pm? ☐
f his dad gets home at 7:20 pm? ☐

4 At 8 am, Jessica was looking forward to her party at 8:30 pm that night. Write how long she has to wait in:

a hours and minutes ☐
b hours ☐
c minutes ☐
d seconds ☐

INVESTIGATION

First Nations Australian methods for identifying time and season

First Nations Australians have used many ways of keeping time, including observing patterns in the movements of stars and planets, and changes in the seasons. Search the internet for information about Aboriginal and Torres Strait Islander astronomy and seasonal calendars.

3:10 24-hour time

am means before noon. **Midnight** is **12:00 am**.
pm means after noon. **Noon** is **12:00 pm**.

1 These watches show 24-hour time. Use **am** or **pm** to rewrite each time.

a 

b 

c 

d 

e 

f 

g 

h 

i 

j 

2 Write each time in 24-hour form.

a 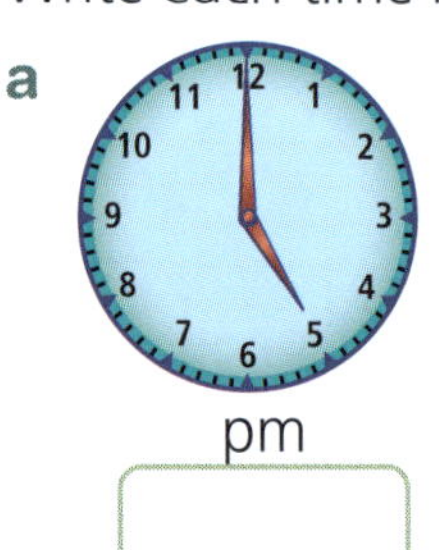
pm

b 
am

c 
pm

d 
pm

e 
am

3 Use 24-hour time to write the time one hour after:

a 3:00 pm ______ **b** 7:00 am ______ **c** 6:00 pm ______
d 9:00 pm ______ **e** 1:00 am ______ **f** 8:00 pm ______
g 11:00 am ______ **h** 11:00 pm ______ **i** 4:00 pm ______

- Use the internet to research where 24-hour time is used.
- Explain why you think 24-hour time is used.

 • *AUSTRALIAN SIGNPOST MATHS 5* • ISBN 9780655708797

Using 12- and 24-hour time

There are 24 hours in a day.

Timeline of a day

00:00 (or 0000) — **Midnight** (or 12 am)
04:00 (or 0400) — 4 am
Noon (or 12 pm)
15:00 (or 1500) — 3 pm
00:00 (or 0000) — **Midnight** (or 12 am)

CONCEPT

The 24-hour clock uses the numbers 00:00 to 23:59.

7:30 am = 07:30 or 0730

zero seven thirty hours

5 pm = 17:00 or 1700

seventeen-hundred hours

1 Write each time in two other ways.

a	5 pm =	17:00	or		**b**	0800 =	08:00	or	
c	0300 =		or		**d**	2 am =		or	
e	7 pm =		or		**f**	0100 =		or	
g	1100 =		or		**h**	0400 =		or	
i	10 pm =		or		**j**	6 pm =		or	
k	0900 =		or		**l**	12 am =		or	

2 What is the time:

a 2 hours after 11 am? ______

b 2 hours after 13:25? ______

c 3 hours before 7 am? ______

d 3 hours before 12:04? ______

e 4 hours after 9 am? ______

f 4 hours after 15:57? ______

g 3 hours before 6 pm? ______

h 2 hours before 08:41? ______

i 5 hours before 11 pm? ______

j 4 hours before 10:29? ______

FUN SPOT

Start at 00:00 and colour a pathway to finish at 00:00.

	07:00	09:00	04:00	09:00	10:00	11:00	12:00	14:00	20:00	21:00	23:00	
	06:00	02:00	03:00	11:00	09:00	10:00	13:00	15:00	19:00	22:00	20:00	
Start ►	**00:00**	01:00	04:00	07:00	08:00	11:00	14:00	17:00	18:00	23:00	**00:00**	◄ **Finish**
	02:00	08:00	05:00	06:00	07:00	13:00	15:00	16:00	19:00	20:00	21:00	

 • *AUSTRALIAN SIGNPOST MATHS 5* • ISBN 9780655708797

3:12 24-hour time problems

00:00 is midnight.
12:00 is noon.
13:00 is 1 pm.

1 This train timetable shows departure times from South Bank to Domestic Airport.

Train timetable, Saturday				
South Bank	12:50	13:20	13:50	14:20
Central	13:01	13:32	14:01	14:32
International Airport	13:22	13:53	14:22	14:53
Domestic Airport	13:25	13:56	14:25	14:56
Duration time for that train				

a Calculate the duration of each service from South Bank to Domestic Airport.

b How long does the 12:50 train take to travel from Central to the Domestic Airport?

c How much longer does the 13:20 train take to travel from South Bank to the Domestic Airport, than from South Bank to the International Airport?

d When is the latest train you could catch from South Bank to get to the International Airport before 2 pm?

e The 14:20 train from South Bank was delayed at Central for 12 minutes. At what time is the train likely to arrive at Domestic Airport?

f How often does a train travel from South Bank to Domestic Airport?

2 This bus timetable shows arrival times at bus stops from Flinders St to Camberwell. A bus travelling this route leaves Flinders St bus stop every 10 minutes.

Bus timetable, Monday	
Flinders St	12:52
Richmond	12:55
Burnley	12:58
Hawthorn	13:00
Glenferrie	13:02
Auburn	13:04
Camberwell	13:06

a How long does it take to travel on this route from Flinders St to Camberwell?

b Levi catches the bus from Flinders St at 12:52. At what time would he reach Glenferrie?

c Joshua misses the 12:52 bus from Flinders St and takes the next bus instead. At what time would he expect to arrive at Auburn bus stop?

d At what time would the 13:12 bus expect to arrive at Camberwell bus stop?

- Look up 24-hour bus and train timetables. Plan a trip with a specific time and destination in mind.

Using measurement scales

Discuss where scales are used.

CONCEPT

We usually record the measurements to the nearest unit mark, unless told otherwise.

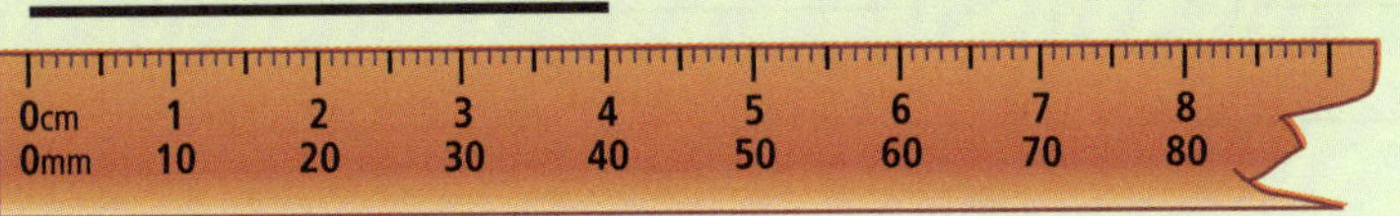

The measured length would be recorded as 40 mm or 4 cm.

1. Use the scale on each ruler to record the length of each bar.

a
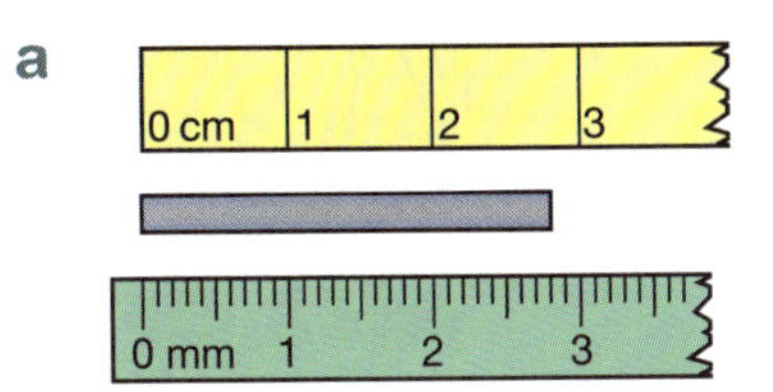

cm

mm

b
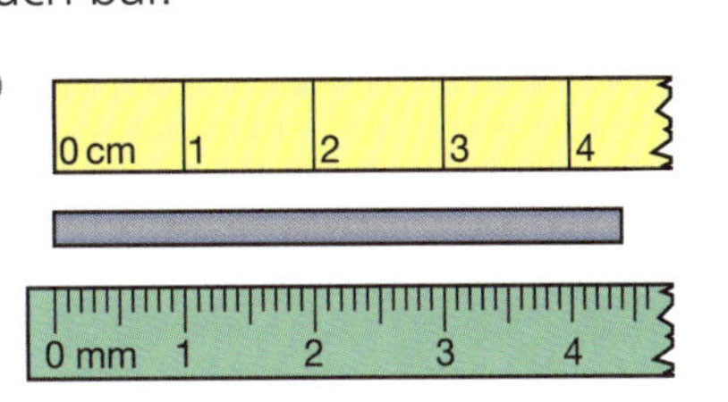

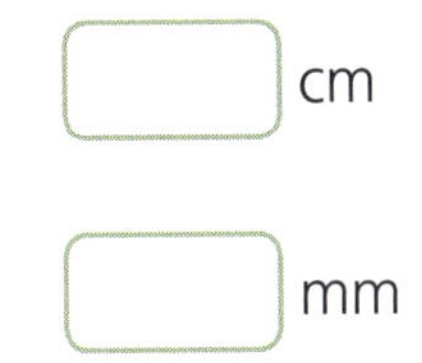
cm

mm

2. Record each measure shown.

a
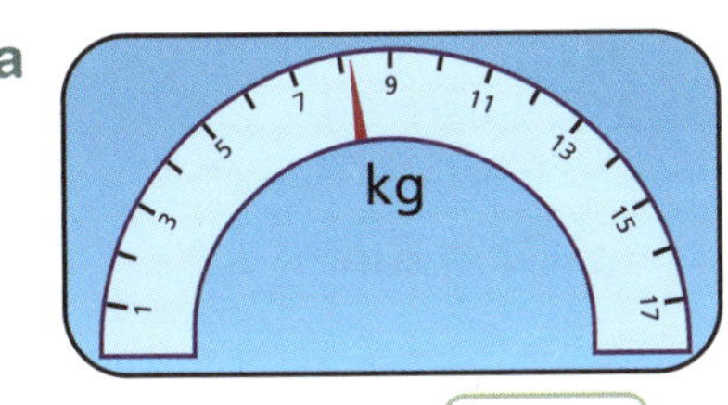

The measure is [ ] kg.

b
The measure is [ ] kg.

c
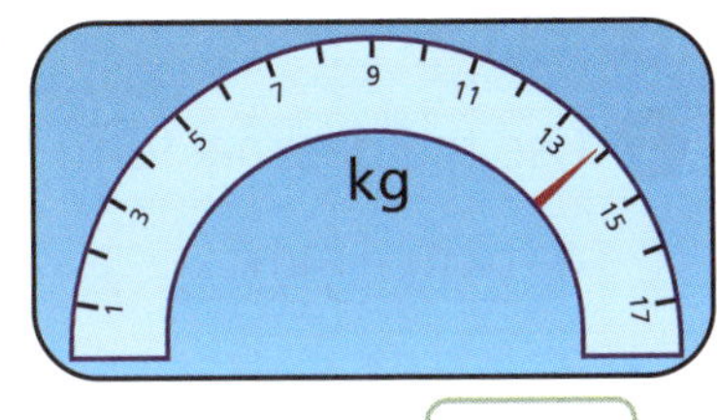

The measure is [ ] kg.

d
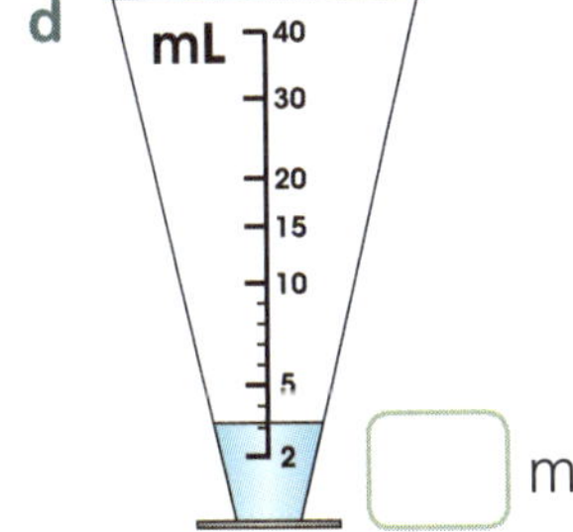

mL

e
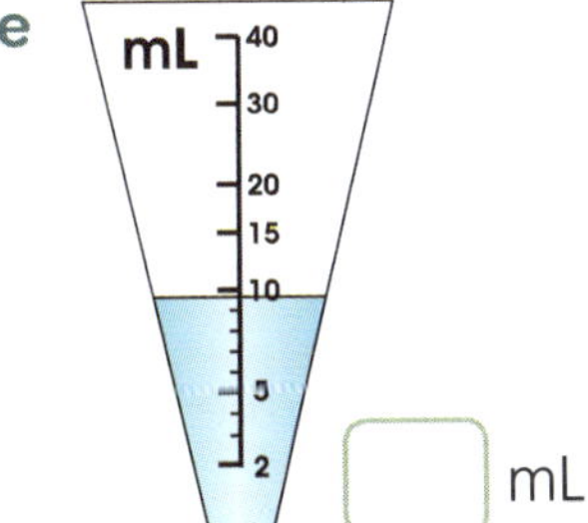

mL

f
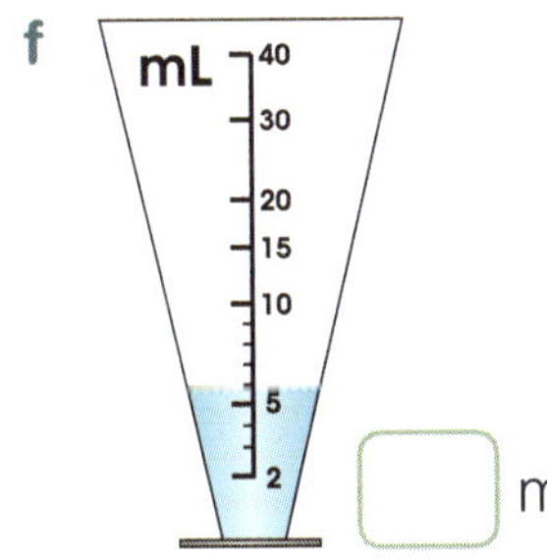

mL

g
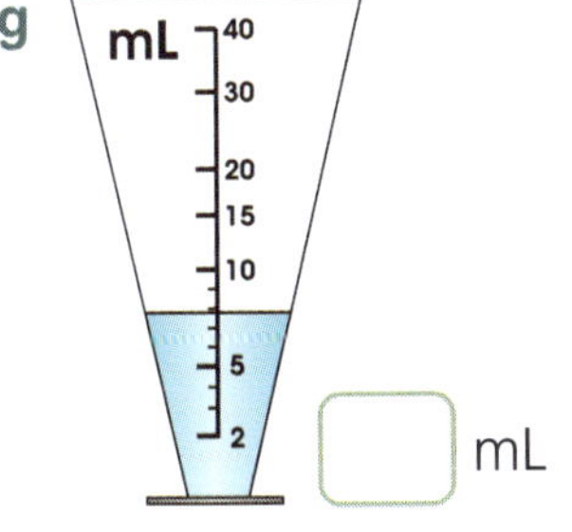

mL

h
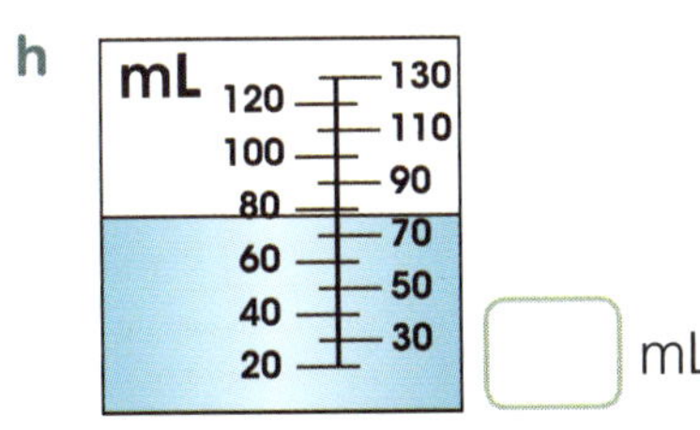

mL

i
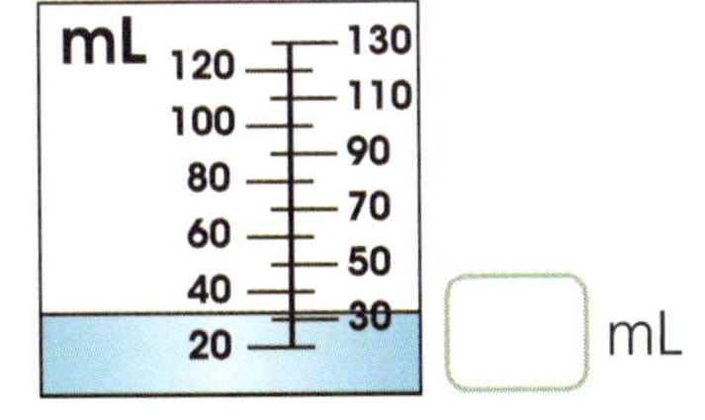

mL

j
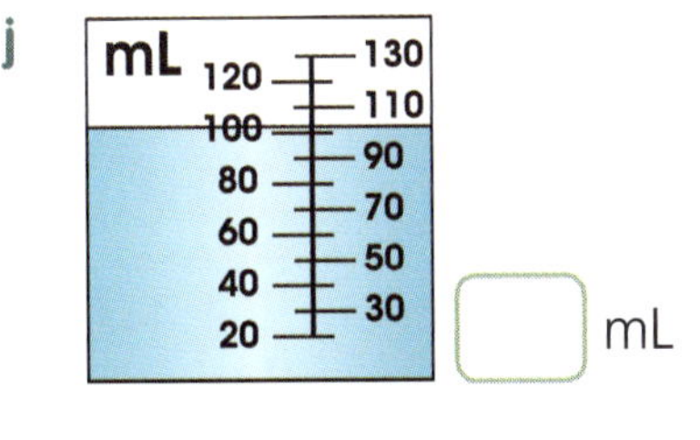

mL

k
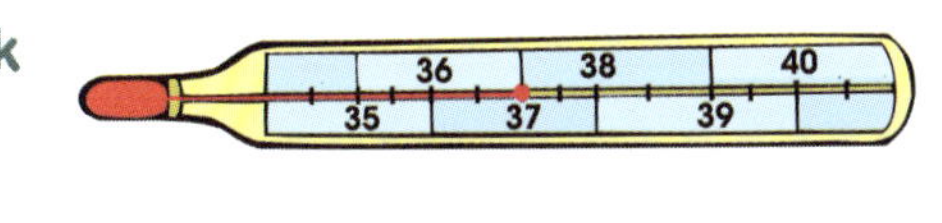

°C

l
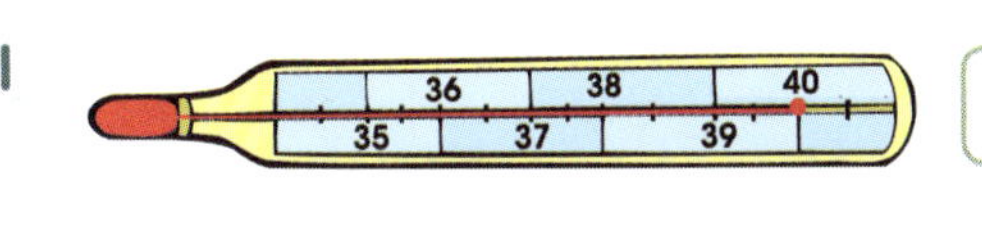
°C

m
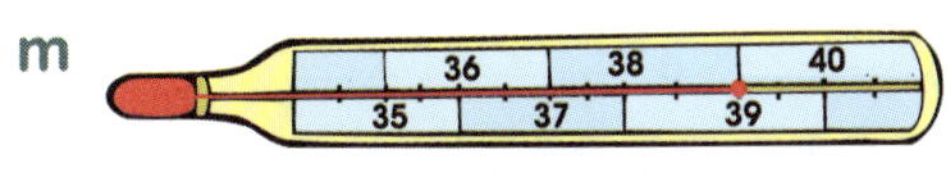
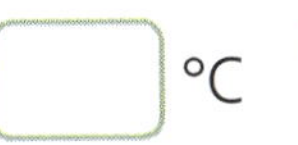
°C

n
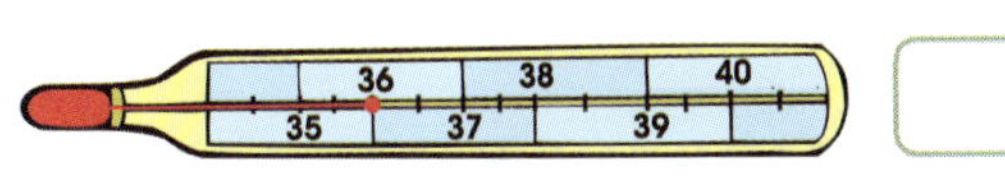
°C

3. The maximum temperature on Sunday was 35°, on Monday 27° and on Tuesday 29°.

a Which day was the warmest?

b Find the difference between the maximum temperatures on Sunday and Monday.

 • *AUSTRALIAN SIGNPOST MATHS 5* • ISBN 9780655708797

3:14 Millimetres

Perimeter is the total length around a shape.

1. Measure each interval to the nearest millimetre.

a ____ b ____ c ____ d ____ e ____ f ____

2. Arrange the lengths in ascending order. ____

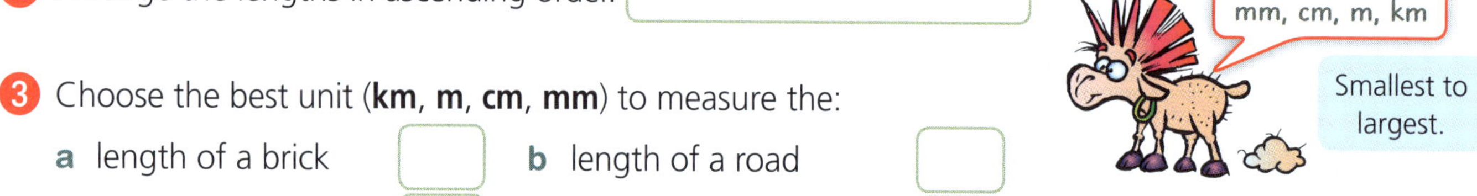

3. Choose the best unit (**km**, **m**, **cm**, **mm**) to measure the:

a length of a brick ____ b length of a road ____

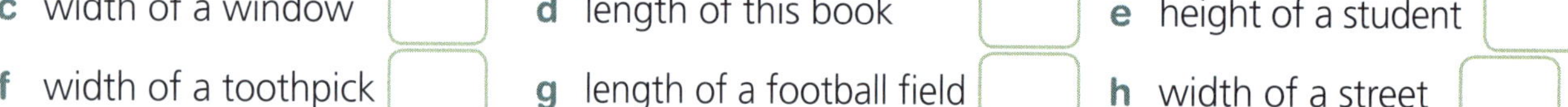

c width of a window ____ d length of this book ____ e height of a student ____

f width of a toothpick ____ g length of a football field ____ h width of a street ____

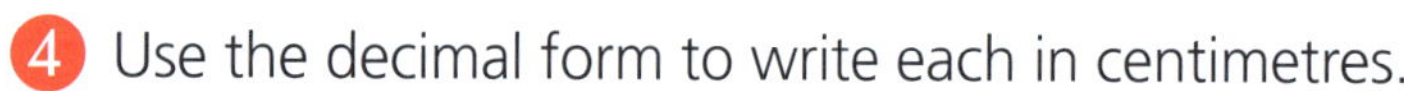

4. Use the decimal form to write each in centimetres.

a 6 cm 4 mm ____ b 8 cm 3 mm ____ c 3 cm 6 mm ____

d 4 cm 1 mm ____ e 9 cm 2 mm ____ f 5 cm 9 mm ____

5. Use the decimal form to write each in centimetres.

a 39 mm ____ b 65 mm ____ c 43 mm ____ d 82 mm ____

e 76 mm ____ f 91 mm ____ g 162 mm ____ h 158 mm ____

6. What is the perimeter of each shape? Answer correct to the nearest millimetre.

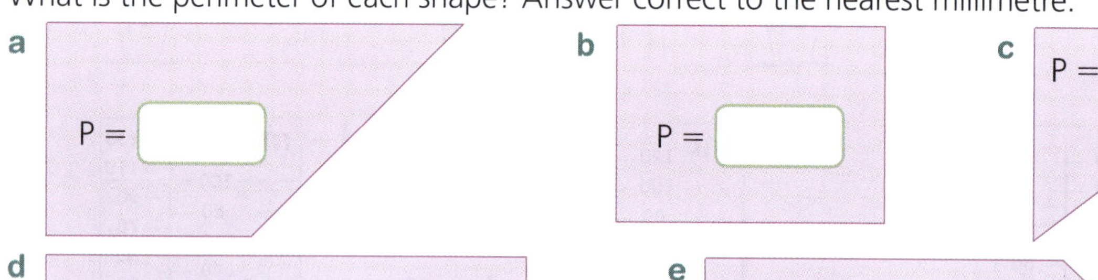

7. Calculate the perimeter for each shape.

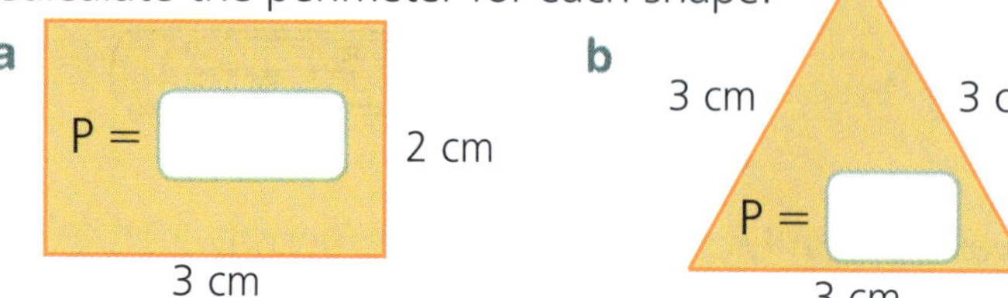

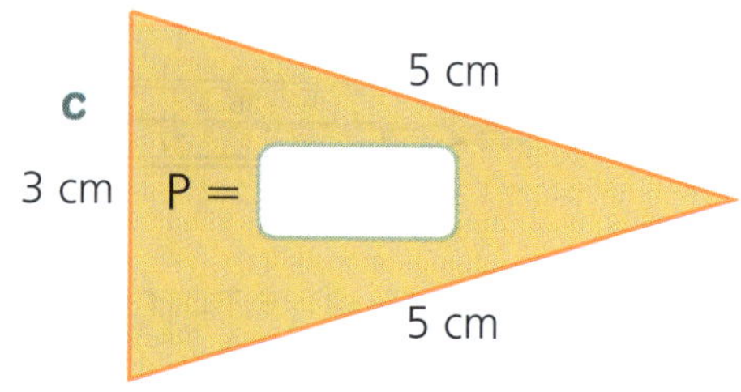

d Discuss shortcut methods to find the perimeters of these shapes.

 • *AUSTRALIAN SIGNPOST MATHS 5* • ISBN 9780655708797

3:15 Converting length measurements

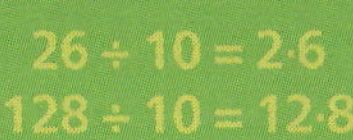

We can convert millimetres to centimetres by dividing by 10.

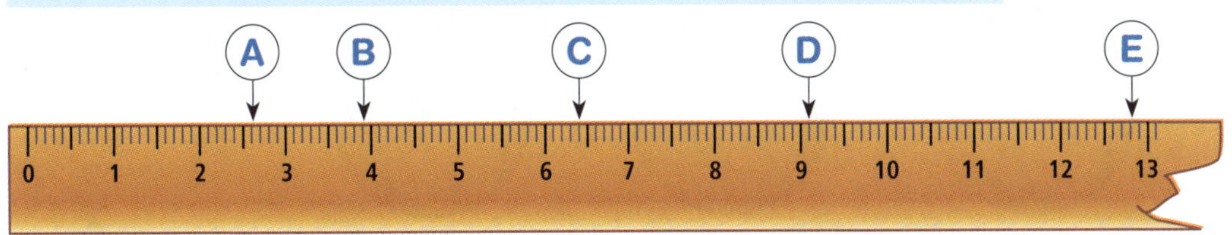

34 ÷ 10 = 3·4

1 Record the lengths shown on the ruler.

A	☐ mm	**B**	☐ mm	**C**	☐ mm	**D**	☐ mm	**E**	☐ mm
	☐ cm		☐ cm		☐ cm		☐ cm		☐ cm

2 Use the decimal form to write these as centimetres.

a 49 mm ☐ **b** 64 mm ☐ **c** 83 mm ☐ **d** 51 mm ☐

e 92 mm ☐ **f** 75 mm ☐ **g** 108 mm ☐ **h** 123 mm ☐

3 Use the decimal form to write these as metres.

a 251 cm ☐ **b** 829 cm ☐ **c** 375 cm ☐ **d** 642 cm ☐

e 563 cm ☐ **f** 925 cm ☐ **g** 1021 cm ☐ **h** 1165 cm ☐

4 Write these as centimetres.

a 3·16 m ☐ **b** 8·31 m ☐ **c** 4·65 m ☐ **d** 9·54 m ☐

e 5·27 m ☐ **f** 2·95 m ☐ **g** 7·45 m ☐ **h** 10·75 m ☐

5 Choose the most suitable unit (**km**, **m**, **cm**, **mm**) to measure:

a the length of a plane ☐ **b** the width of a road ☐

c the length of a river ☐ **d** the length of a classroom ☐

e the thickness of a match ☐ **f** the distance to Perth ☐

6 Order m, km, mm and cm in order from smallest unit to longest unit. ☐

- Measure objects that are less than 1 m.
- Record your measurements in millimetres and in centimetres.

Object measurement	mm	cm
pencil sharpener length	26 mm	2·6 cm

 • *AUSTRALIAN SIGNPOST MATHS 5* • ISBN 9780655708797

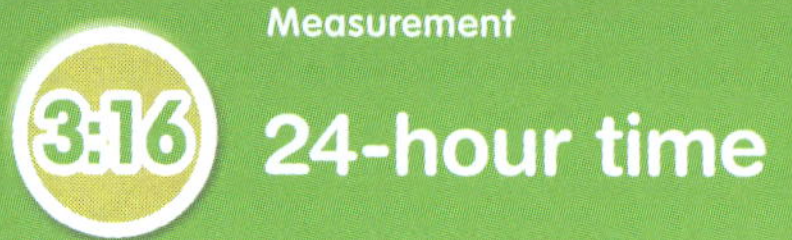

3:16 24-hour time

6 pm = 18:00 or 1800
11:45 pm = 23:45 or 2345

1. Write each time in 24-hour time.

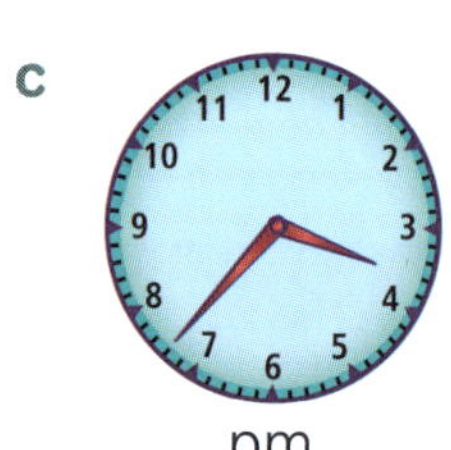

a pm
b am
c pm
d am

e pm
f pm
g am
h am

2. Use am or pm to write these 24-hour times.

a 19:51 ☐ b 02:37 ☐ c 06:13 ☐ d 16:24 ☐
e 05:49 ☐ f 13:06 ☐ g 18:27 ☐ h 08:59 ☐

3. Use 24-hour time to write:

a 3:54 pm ☐ b 9:32 am ☐ c 12:38 pm ☐ d 10:09 pm ☐
e 6:18 am ☐ f 5:47 pm ☐ g 8:14 am ☐ h 1:26 am ☐

How long is it from 1:37 pm to 3:15 pm?
1:37 + 23 mins → **2 pm, 2 pm** + 1 hr → **3 pm, 3 pm** + 15 mins → **3:15**.

Time passed: 23 mins + 1 hr + 15 mins = 1 hr 38 mins

4. Find the difference in time between:

a 3:21 am and 5:06 am ☐ b 12:34 pm and 5:19 pm ☐
c 6:48 am and 11:23 am ☐ d 10:56 am and 2:07 pm ☐

How long is it from 15:25 to 18:29?
15:25 + 3 hrs → **18:25, 18:25** + 4 mins → **8:29**.

Time passed: 3 hrs + 4 mins = 3 hrs 4 mins

5. Find the difference in time between:

a 13:45 and 14:09 ☐ b 15:27 and 16:13 ☐
c 22:18 and 23:38 ☐ d 18:03 and 19:46 ☐

Problems involving time

Timelines show how time passes between events.

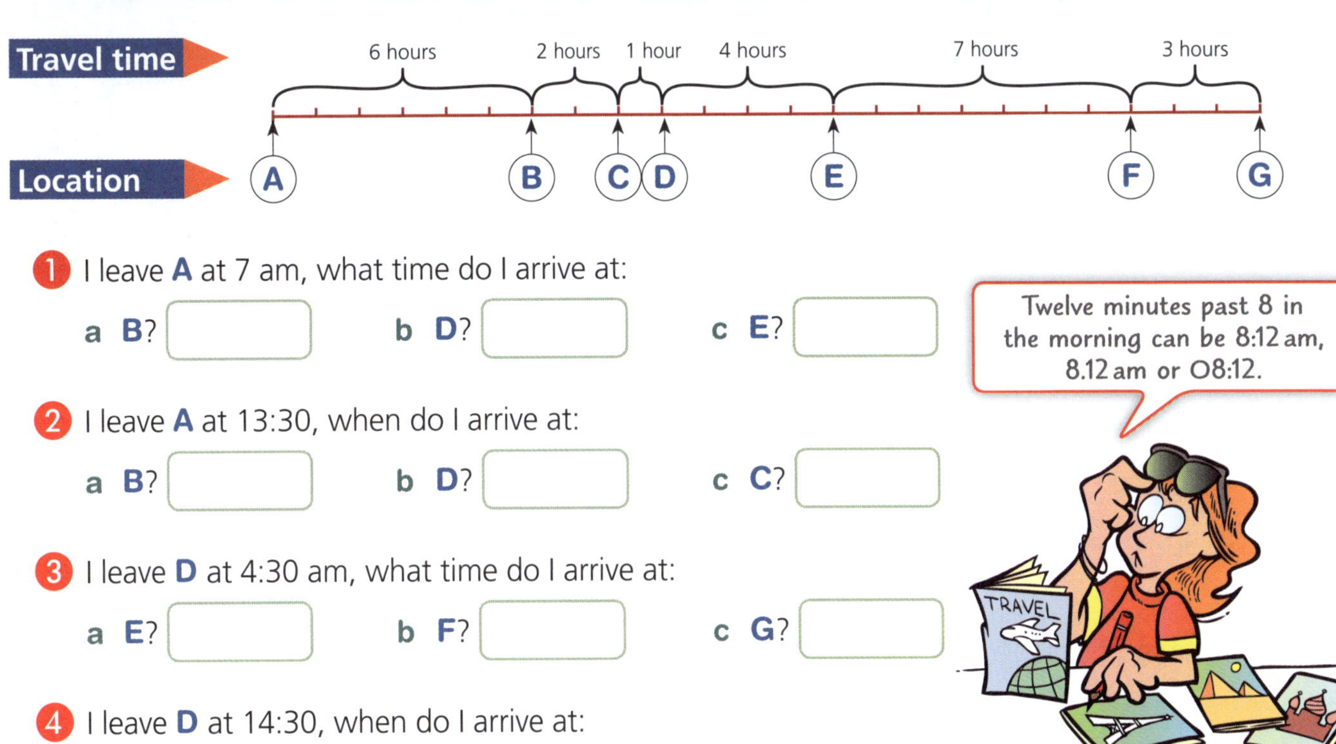

1 I leave **A** at 7 am, what time do I arrive at:

a **B**? ____ b **D**? ____ c **E**? ____

2 I leave **A** at 13:30, when do I arrive at:

a **B**? ____ b **D**? ____ c **C**? ____

3 I leave **D** at 4:30 am, what time do I arrive at:

a **E**? ____ b **F**? ____ c **G**? ____

4 I leave **D** at 14:30, when do I arrive at:

a **E**? ____ b **F**? ____ c **G**? ____

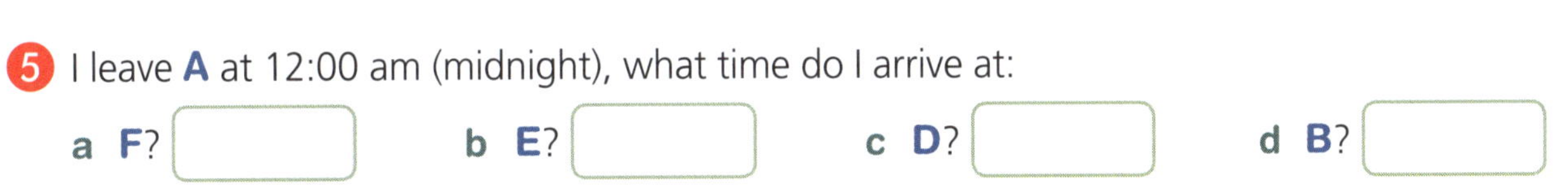

5 I leave **A** at 12:00 am (midnight), what time do I arrive at:

a **F**? ____ b **E**? ____ c **D**? ____ d **B**? ____

6 I leave **C** at 00:00, when do I arrive at:

a **D**? ____ b **E**? ____ c **F**? ____ d **G**? ____

7 Tell a story about the timeline at the top of the page.

8 Answer these problems.

a Our trip took $3\frac{1}{2}$ hours. When did we arrive if we left at 4:30 pm? ____

b We left home at 13:30. The trip took 5 hours. When did we reach our destination? ____

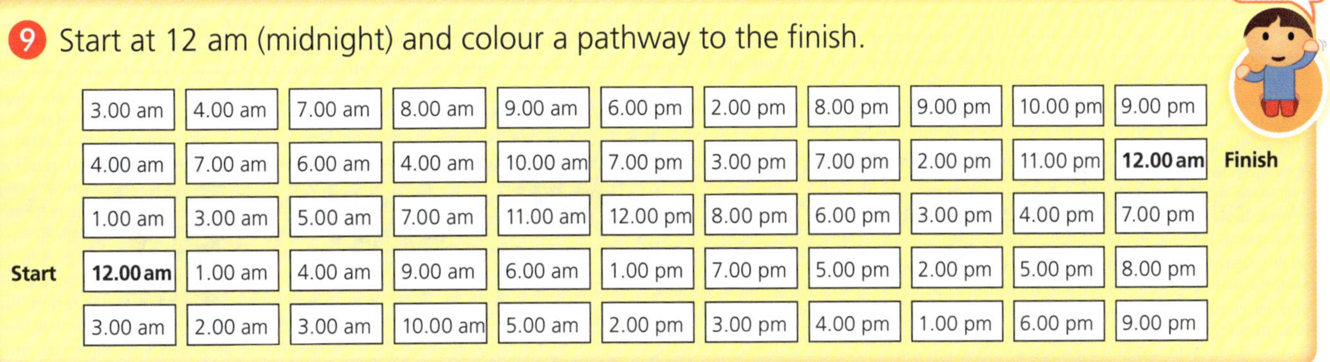

FUN SPOT

9 Start at 12 am (midnight) and colour a pathway to the finish.

	3.00 am	4.00 am	7.00 am	8.00 am	9.00 am	6.00 pm	2.00 pm	8.00 pm	9.00 pm	10.00 pm	9.00 pm	
	4.00 am	7.00 am	6.00 am	4.00 am	10.00 am	7.00 pm	3.00 pm	7.00 pm	2.00 pm	11.00 pm	**12.00 am**	**Finish**
	1.00 am	3.00 am	5.00 am	7.00 am	11.00 am	12.00 pm	8.00 pm	6.00 pm	3.00 pm	4.00 pm	7.00 pm	
Start	**12.00 am**	1.00 am	4.00 am	9.00 am	6.00 am	1.00 pm	7.00 pm	5.00 pm	2.00 pm	5.00 pm	8.00 pm	
	3.00 am	2.00 am	3.00 am	10.00 am	5.00 am	2.00 pm	3.00 pm	4.00 pm	1.00 pm	6.00 pm	9.00 pm	

3:18 Grams and kilograms

1000 g = 1 kg
2356 g = 2·356 kg
2356 g = 2 kg 356 g

1 Find how many grams (**g**) there are in:

a 7 kg ______ b 4 kg ______ c 8 kg ______

d 1 kg 625 g ______ e 3 kg 750 g ______ f 2 kg 125 g ______

g 3·5 kg ______ h 9·5 kg ______ i 7·5 kg ______

2 Rewrite the following as kilograms (**kg**) and grams (**g**).

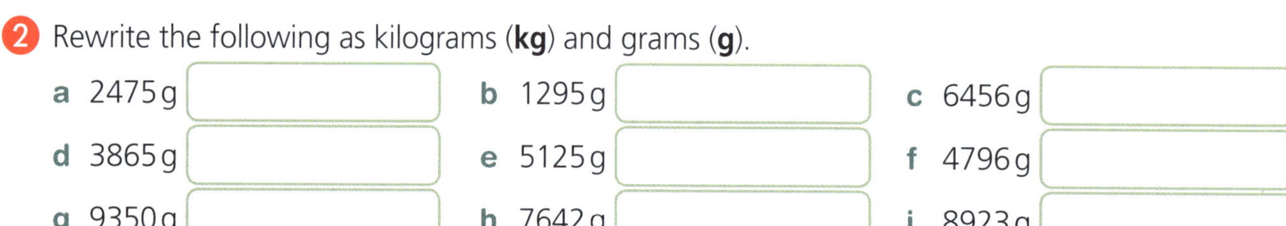

a 2475 g ______ b 1295 g ______ c 6456 g ______

d 3865 g ______ e 5125 g ______ f 4796 g ______

g 9350 g ______ h 7642 g ______ i 8923 g ______

3 Tick the most suitable unit of mass to measure the following.

	Mass	g	kg	t
a	a snail			
b	a semi-trailer			
c	a girl			
d	a man			
e	an elephant			
f	a lunch box			
g	a train			
h	a pencil case			

1000 kg is 1 tonne.

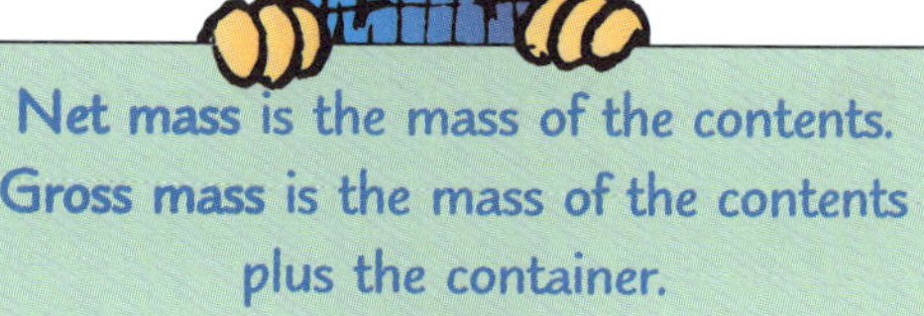

4 Write true or false for each statement. < means 'less than'. (The arrow points to the smaller side.)

a 1 kg > 500 g ______ b 5 kg > 4999 g ______ c 600 g > 600 kg ______

d 2·5 kg > 2600 g ______ e 12 kg < 15 000 g ______ f 2 kg > 1980 g ______

ACTIVITY

- Compare different measuring devices, e.g. standard balance scales, kitchen scales, bathroom scales, spring scales.
- Discuss the purposes for which each is used.
- Practise using different measuring devices to measure the mass of objects.

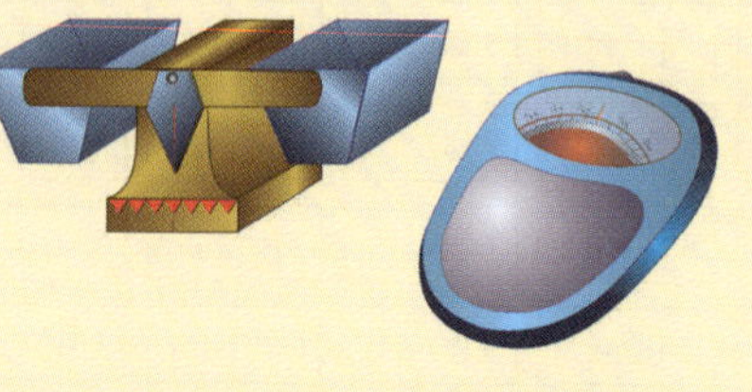

 • *AUSTRALIAN SIGNPOST MATHS 5* • ISBN 9780655708797

3:19 Measuring mass

1 L of milk has a mass of about 1 kg.

1 Find how many grams (**g**) there are in:

a 6 kg ☐ b 3 kg ☐ c 11 kg ☐

d 7 kg ☐ e 4 kg ☐ f 17 kg ☐

1000 g = 1 kg
7060 g = 7·060 kg
7060 g = 7 kg 60 g

2 Write how many kilograms are in:

a 4000 g ☐ b 8000 g ☐ c 2000 g ☐

d 6000 g ☐ e 9000 g ☐ f 5000 g ☐

3 Rewrite the following as kilograms (**kg**) and grams (**g**).

a 4376 g ☐ b 5463 g ☐ c 7355 g ☐

d 5367 g ☐ e 4260 g ☐ f 3500 g ☐

4 a Use a set of scales to measure and compare objects in the classroom.
Complete the table. In the right column, order the objects from lightest (1) to heaviest (4).

Object		Estimate	Mass (g)	Mass (kg and g)	Order
A					
B					
C					
D					

b Were your estimates accurate? ☐ *If not, discuss how you could improve your accuracy.*

c Which object was heaviest? ☐ d Which object was lightest? ☐

e The difference in mass between the heaviest and lightest object in the table is ☐.

5 a The ingredients needed to make 2 loaves of bread are shown in the table. Complete the table.

Ingredients	1 loaf	2 loaves	4 loaves	10 loaves
warm water		500 mL		
sugar		110 g		
yeast		15 g		
salt		7·5 g		
oil		125 mL		
flour		720 g		

For 2 loaves of bread:

b what is the total mass of the water and oil? ☐

c what is the total mass of the dry ingredients? ☐

d at what temperature do they need to be baked? ☐

Procedure: Place the flour, yeast and salt into a bowl. Mix together. Stir the water, oil and sugar separately. Combine with the dry ingredients. Knead the dough for 5 mins. Place the dough in an oiled tin. Leave to rise for 1 hour. Cook the dough in the oven at 180°C for 30 minutes. Allow to cool.

3:20 Perimeter

65 mm = 6·5 cm
137 mm = 13·7 cm

1. Measure the length of each interval to the nearest millimetre.

a ___ mm **b** ___ mm

c ___ mm **d** ___ mm

e ___ mm **f** ___ mm

2. Measure the perimeter of each shape in millimetres, then convert your answers to cm.

a P = ___ mm = ___ cm

b P = ___ mm = ___ cm

c P = ___ mm = ___ cm

d P = ___ mm = ___ cm

3. On this 5 mm grid paper, draw the following shapes.

a square with 3·5 cm sides

b rectangle with sides 2·5 cm and 4·5 cm

c rectangle with sides 3·5 cm and 5 cm

d What is the perimeter of the square in part **a**?

ACTIVITY

- Measure the perimeters of three different books to the nearest centimetre.
- Order the perimeters in size from smallest to largest.
- Measure the perimeters of other objects, such as tables or windows. Discuss the best unit of measure for this purpose.

Object	Perimeter	Order
Book A		
Book B		
Book C		

Object	Perimeter

Perimeter of a rectangle = 2 × length + 2 × width.

© PEARSON AUSTRALIA 2024 • *AUSTRALIAN SIGNPOST MATHS 5* • ISBN 9780655708797

Exploring perimeter and area

Perimeter
Area

1 Explore what happens to the area of a rectangle if we double its dimensions.

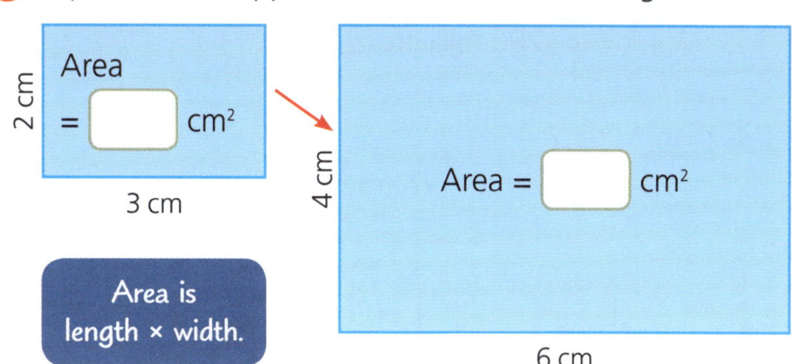

Area is length × width.

a When we doubled the dimensions, the area was multiplied by ☐.

b Double the dimensions of other rectangles. What happened? The area was multiplied by ☐.

2 Explore what happens to the area of a square if we double its dimensions.

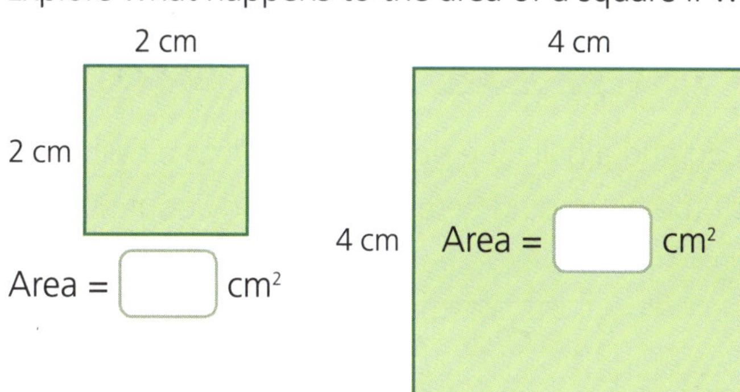

a When we doubled the dimensions of a square, we multiplied the area by ☐.

b Double the dimensions of other squares. The area is multiplied by ☐.

The length + the width is half the perimeter.

3 Investigate the connection between the perimeter and the area of a rectangle.
John drew six rectangles with a perimeter of 24 mm. Measure each to complete the table.

Rectangle		Perimeter	Length	Height	Area
A		24 mm			
B		24 mm			
C		24 mm			
D		24 mm			
E		24 mm			
F		24 mm			

a Which rectangle has the smallest area? ☐

b Which rectangle has the largest area? ☐

c What is your conclusion? ☐

$P = (2 \times L) + (2 \times W)$
$A = L \times W$

4 a Ben has a 200-centimetre length of wood to make a frame. Write the dimensions of the frame that would allow for a painting with the largest area. ☐

b Samson wants to build a window frame with the largest possible area. He has a 12-metre length of wood. What should be the dimensions of his window? ☐

3:22 Measuring volume in mL

175 mL is halfway between 150 mL and 200 mL.

1 Write each amount in short form.

a 6 litres ☐ b 8 litres ☐ c 200 millilitres ☐

2 Underline the items that would hold less than 1 litre.

can of lemonade kitchen sink mug ice tray fridge

ACTIVITY

A 200 mL 100 mL

B 200 mL 100 mL

C 200 mL 100 mL

3 Lilli wanted to compare the volume of an egg and a ball. She poured water into a calibrated container. She estimated that the volume of the ball would be the larger, and about 90 mL.

a How much water is in each picture above? ☐

b What is the water level on picture: **B**? ☐ **C**? ☐

c What is the difference between the measurements in pictures **A** and **B**? ☐

d What is the difference between the measurements in pictures **A** and **C**? ☐

e What is the volume of: the egg? ☐ the ball? ☐

f Which item has the larger volume? ☐

g Capacity is the amount a container can hold. Volume is the space it takes up. Is the capacity of an egg the same as the volume? ☐ Why or why not?

☐

h If an object has a larger volume, can we be sure it will weigh more? ☐

i Repeat this experiment with a balloon that will fit into your calibrated container and a rock, to compare the volume of the items. Compare the mass of each object. What did you find? ☐

☐

4 Ethan filled a jar with water and placed it in a large, empty container. He placed a bouncy ball in the jar and water overflowed into the container. He measured the water that overflowed and it was 25 mL.

What is the volume of the bouncy ball? ☐

Repeat this experiment to find the volume of other small items.

 • *AUSTRALIAN SIGNPOST MATHS 5* • ISBN 9780655708797

Capacity and volume

Capacity is the amount a container can hold. Volume is the space an object takes up.

CONCEPT

We immersed a thousands block into a calibrated container with 1 L of water (**A**). The water level rose to the 2 L mark (**B**). The thousands block took up 1 L of space.

A thousands block is 1000 ones blocks which equals 1000 cubic centimetres.

1 L = 1 000 blocks so 1 ones block = 1 mL.
1 mL = 1 cubic centimetre

1 This model was immersed into the container.

2 layers of 6 ones blocks = ☐ ones blocks

What is the volume of this model?

☐ mL or ☐ cubic centimetres

2 Convert to cubic centimetres.

a 42 mL ☐ cubic centimetres

b 327 mL ☐ cubic centimetres

c 608 mL ☐ cubic centimetres

3 Convert to millilitres.

a 15 cubic centimetres ☐ mL

b 138 cubic centimetres ☐ mL

c 569 cubic centimetres ☐ mL

INVESTIGATION

4 a Marika immersed an orange into a calibrated container with 1 L (1000 mL) of water. The water level rose to the 1250 mL mark. What is the volume of the orange? ☐ mL

b She took the orange out, peeled it and placed only the skin in. The water level rose to 1070 mL. What is the capacity of the orange skin? ☐ mL

c Calculate the capacity of the flesh of the orange. ☐ mL

The *flesh* of fruit is the part you eat.

4 Investigate the capacity of a banana.

a Immerse a whole banana into a calibrated container with 1 L (1000 mL) of water.

The water level rose to about ☐ mL.

What is the volume of the whole banana? about ☐ mL

b Peel the banana, then immerse only the banana skin.

The water level rose to about ☐ mL.

What is the volume of the banana skin? about ☐ mL

c What would be the volume of the flesh of the banana? about ☐ mL

3:24 Measuring capacity

1 L = 1000 mL
7·2 L = 7200 mL = 7 L 200 mL

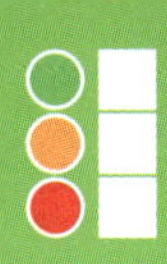

1 The contents of each full container was poured into the empty calibrated measuring container. Read the scale to find the capacity of each emptied container.

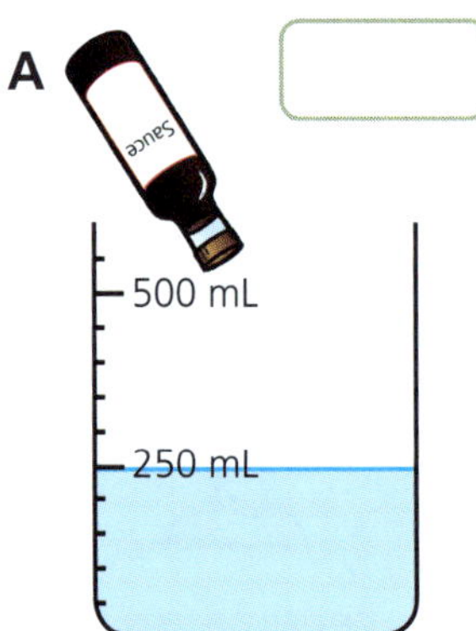

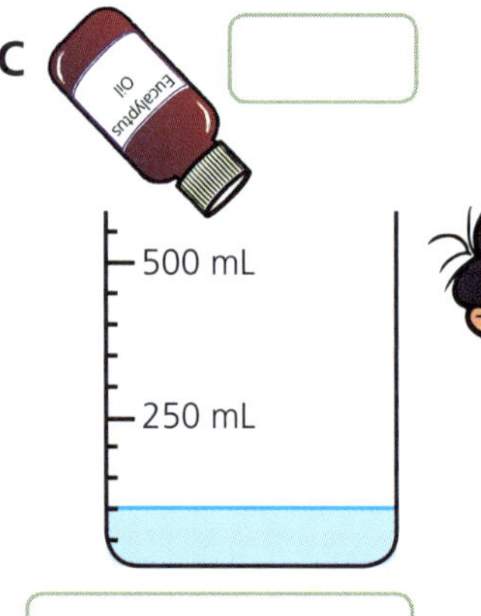

Order containers **A**, **B** and **C** from smallest to largest capacity.

2 Would you use millilitres (mL) or litres (L) to measure the capacity of:

a a bath? **b** a cup? **c** a sink? **d** a drink bottle?

3 How many millilitres are in:

a 4 L ___ mL **b** 10 L ___ mL **c** 22 L ___ mL
d 5·3 L ___ mL **e** 7·4 L ___ mL **f** 3·6 L ___ mL

4 How many litres are in:

a 9000 mL ___ L **b** 5000 mL ___ L **c** 3000 mL ___ L
d 1500 mL ___ L **e** 6800 mL ___ L **f** 2600 mL ___ L

5 Write these in millilitres.

a 1 L 600 mL **b** 1 L 950 mL **c** 2 L 300 mL

6 Write these as litres and millilitres.

a 7530 mL **b** 1075 mL **c** 35 700 mL

7 What could be a benchmark for 1 L?

ACTIVITY

Use a calibrated 1 L container to measure the capacity of these objects. Complete the table.

	Container	Estimate	Measure	Order
A	large mixing bowl			
B	bucket			
C	large vase			
D	tub			

 • *AUSTRALIAN SIGNPOST MATHS 5* • ISBN 9780655708797

3:25 Hectares

100 m

100 m

A hectare is the size of a square with sides 100 m.

1 Calculate how many square metres (**m²**) there are in:

a 2 ha ____ b 5 ha ____ c 7 ha ____ d 4 ha ____

e 6 ha ____ f 9 ha ____ g 3 ha ____ h 8 ha ____

2 Calculate how many hectares (**ha**) there are in:

a 10 000 m² ____ b 50 000 m² ____ c 30 000 m² ____ d 60 000 m² ____

e 40 000 m² ____ f 20 000 m² ____ g 90 000 m² ____ h 70 000 m² ____

3 Would you use square metres (**m²**) or hectares (**ha**) to find the area of:

a an airport? ____ b a sandpit? ____ c a door? ____

d a large farm? ____ e a national park? ____ f the kitchen floor? ____

g a city block? ____ h a large beach? ____ i a squash court? ____

4 Groups of students measured different areas of their playground. Use a calculator to find if each area is *less than*, *equal to* or *more than* a hectare. Complete the table.

		Length	Width	Area (m²)	Compared to 1 ha
a	Group 1	100 m	100 m		
b	Group 2	350 m	20 m		
c	Group 3	200 m	50 m		
d	Group 4	450 m	30 m		
e	Group 5	400 m	25 m		

ACTIVITY

- Use a suitable measuring instrument and markers to measure a 1 ha area. Remember this area so it can be your personal benchmark for 1 hectare.

3:26 Square kilometres

1 km × 1 km = 1 km^2

A square kilometre is the size of a square with sides 1000 m (or 1 km).

CONCEPT

We need a larger unit than the hectare to measure very large areas. We use **square kilometres**. One square kilometre contains 100 hectares.

1 square kilometre = 100 hectares

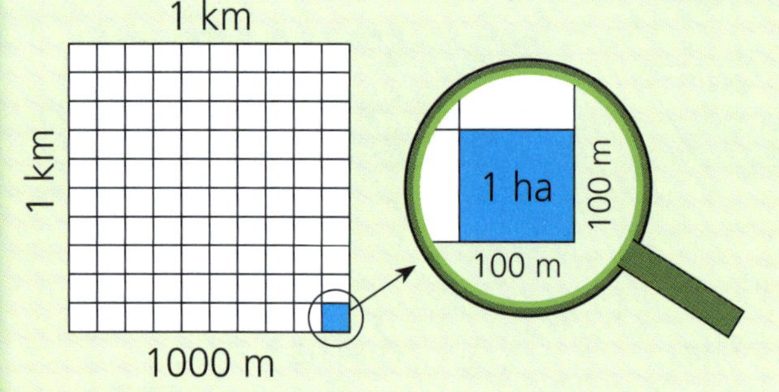

1 hectare
= 10 000 m^2
1 square kilometre
= 1000 m × 1000 m
= 1 000 000 m^2
= **100 ha**

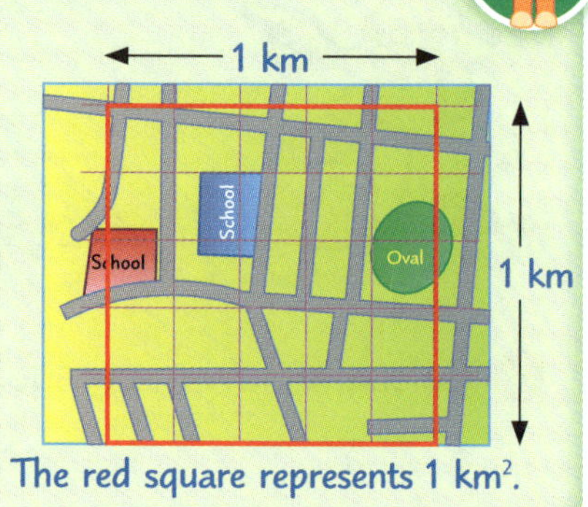

The red square represents 1 km^2.

1 Convert the following to hectares (**ha**).

a 1 km^2 ____ b 4 km^2 ____ c 2 km^2 ____
d 7 km^2 ____ e 3 km^2 ____ f 9 km^2 ____
g 10 km^2 ____ h 13 km^2 ____ i 15 km^2 ____

2 Convert the following to square kilometres (**km²**).

a 100 ha ____ b 300 ha ____ c 700 ha ____ d 200 ha ____
e 600 ha ____ f 900 ha ____ g 1300 ha ____ h 2700 ha ____

3 Write the most suitable unit of measure (**m²**, **ha**, **km²**) to record the area of:

a a garden ____ b a car park ____ c the Great Barrier Reef ____
d Queensland ____ e the ceiling ____ f a classroom floor ____
g a big paddock ____ h Tasmania ____ i a large school ____

4

Country / state / territory	Area
Australia	7 656 127 km^2
Northern Territory	1 334 404 km^2
Queensland	1 723 030 km^2
New South Wales	801 137 km^2
Australian Capital Territory	2358 km^2
Victoria	227 038 km^2
Tasmania	64 519 km^2
South Australia	979 651 km^2
Western Australia	2 523 924 km^2

Use the information in the table to find:

a the largest state or territory of Australia ____

b a state larger than Queensland ____

c the total area of Victoria and Tasmania ____

d the state that is about twice as large as New South Wales. ____

 ISBN 9780655708797

Can you draw the net of a didgeridoo?

1 Write **true** or **false** for these.

a A football has the shape of a cube.

b In any pyramid, every face is a triangle except perhaps the base.

c In any prism, every side is a rectangle except perhaps the two ends.

d The cross-section of any sphere is a circle.

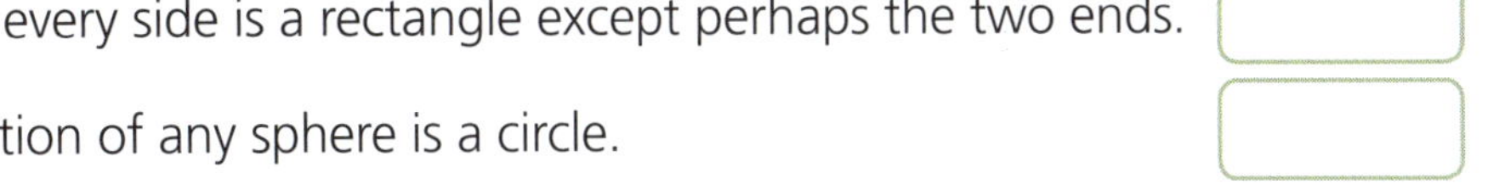

2 What 3D object can be made from each net?

a

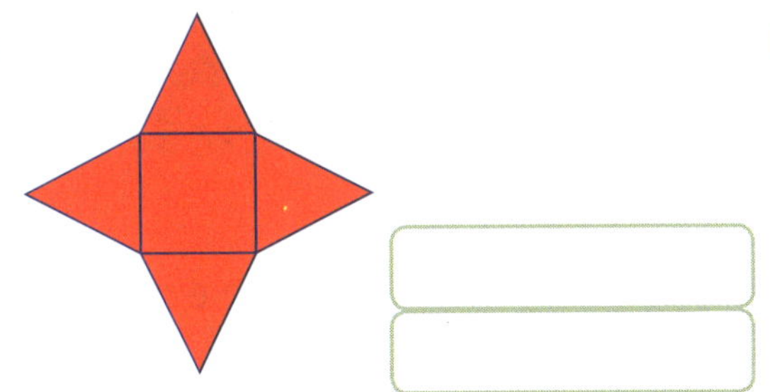

b

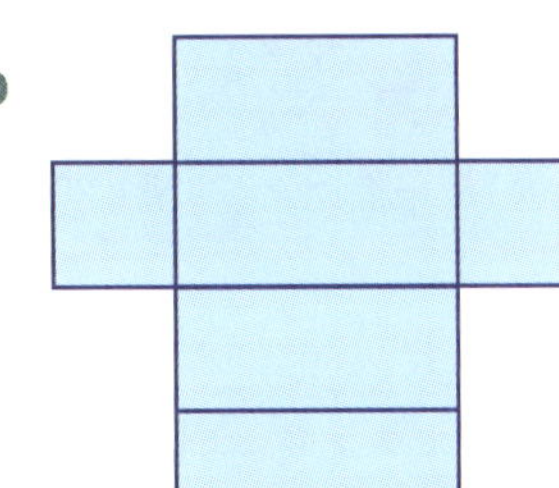

A didgeridoo has the shape of a ______.

3 Use the method shown below to draw two prisms and two pyramids on your own paper.

The two sides of a ruler can be used to draw parallel lines.

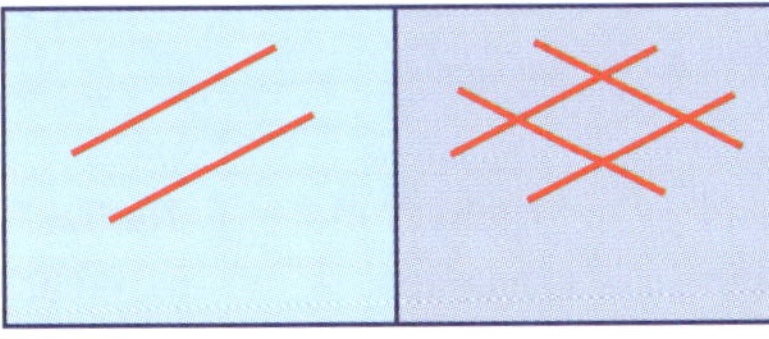

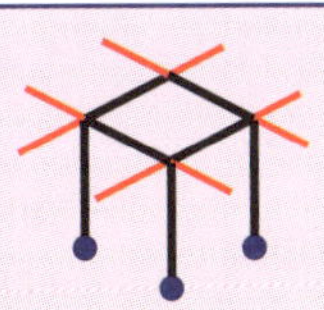

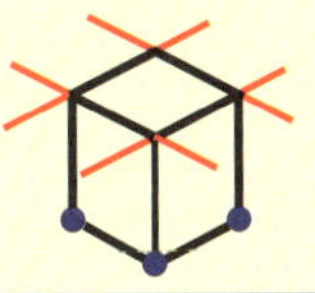

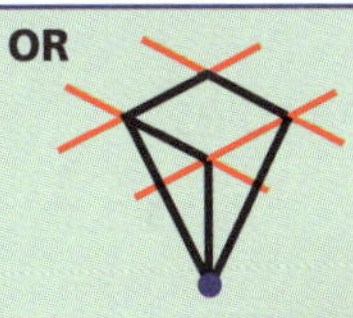

4 Draw the front, the top and the side views of each solid.

a

Object	Front view	Top view	Side view

b

Object	Front view	Top view	Side view

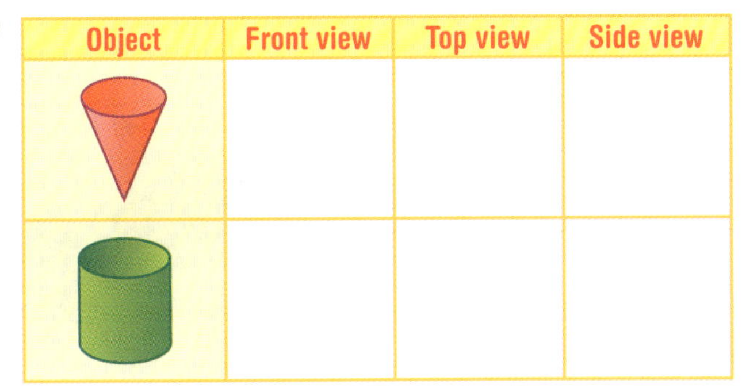

5 Jim studied this block.

a How many faces does it have?

b How many corners?

c How many edges?

He then cut along the vertical edges of his own box. He then flattened out the cardboard. Has he made the net of a cube? ______ Discuss.

 • *AUSTRALIAN SIGNPOST MATHS 5* • ISBN 9780655708797

4:02 Prisms and pyramids

A cube has ☐ faces, ☐ corners and ☐ edges.

- Prisms and pyramids are named according to the shape of their bases.
- The cross-sections of prisms and pyramids that are parallel to the base have the same shape as the base.

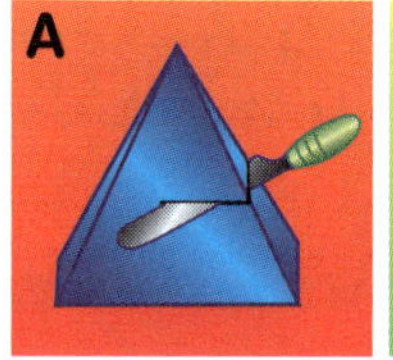

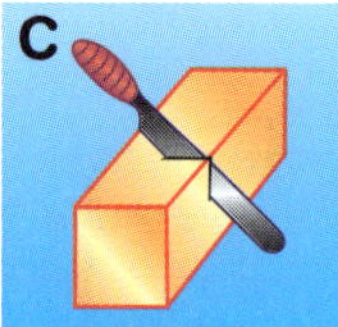

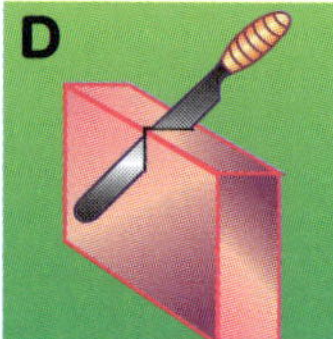

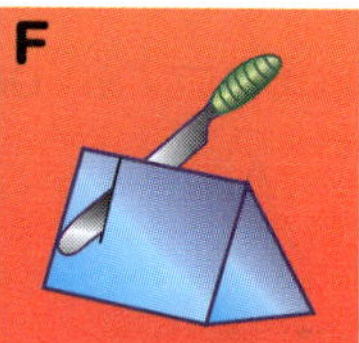

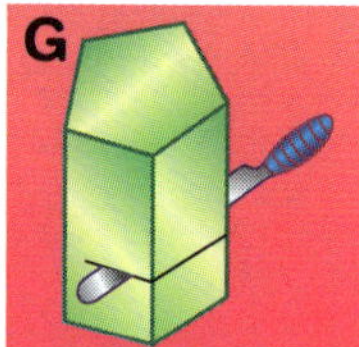

1 Which object is:

a a triangular prism? ☐ **b** a hexagonal pyramid? ☐ **c** a square prism? ☐

d a triangular pyramid? ☐ **e** a rectangular prism? ☐ **f** a square pyramid? ☐

2 Which of the objects **A** to **G** have cross-sections (parallel to the base) that are:

a smaller than the base? ☐ **b** the same size as the base (uniform)? ☐

3 Complete these tables.

Object	Number of corners	Number of edges	Number of faces
A			
B			
C			

Object	Number of corners	Number of edges	Number of faces
D			
E			
F			

Look for a rule that connects the number of corners and faces with the number of edges.

Corners + faces – edges = ☐

4 What object can be made from each set of faces?

a ________________

b ________________

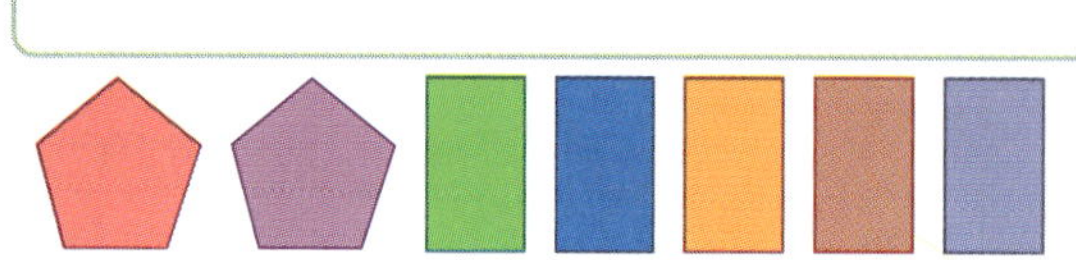

c ________________

 • *AUSTRALIAN SIGNPOST MATHS 5* • ISBN 9780655708797

Reflection, translation, rotation

Orientation stays the same for **translation**.

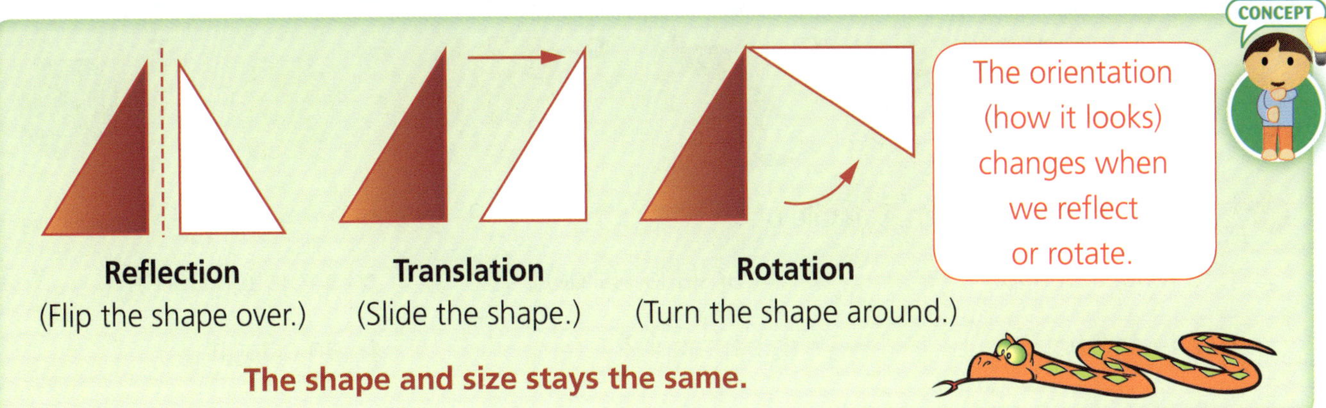

1 Write **yes** or **no** to show how transformations affect the way the triangle above is moved.

Transformation	Figure changes position	Figure changes shape	Figure changes size	Figure changes orientation
translation				
reflection				
rotation				

Orientation is the direction something is facing or pointing.

2 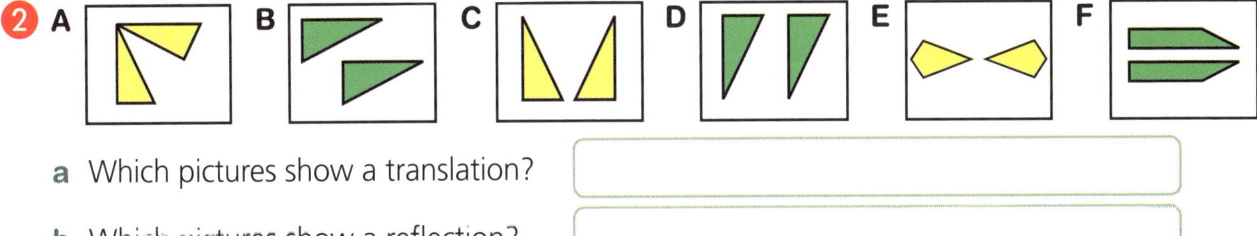

a Which pictures show a translation?

b Which pictures show a reflection?

For a rotation, the direction of movement is anticlockwise, unless told otherwise.

3 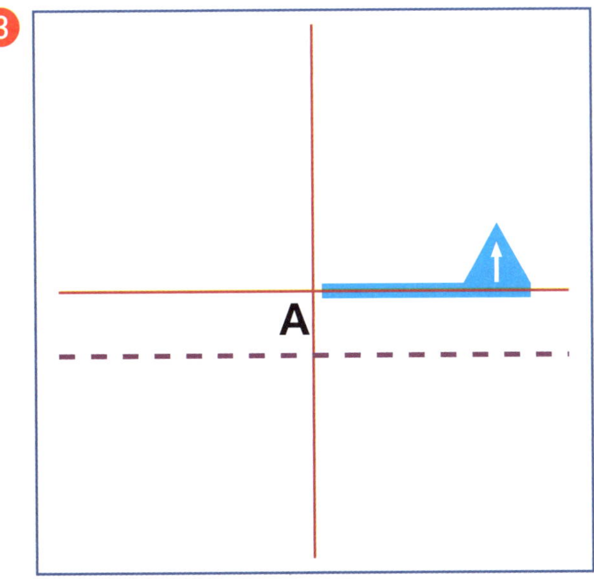

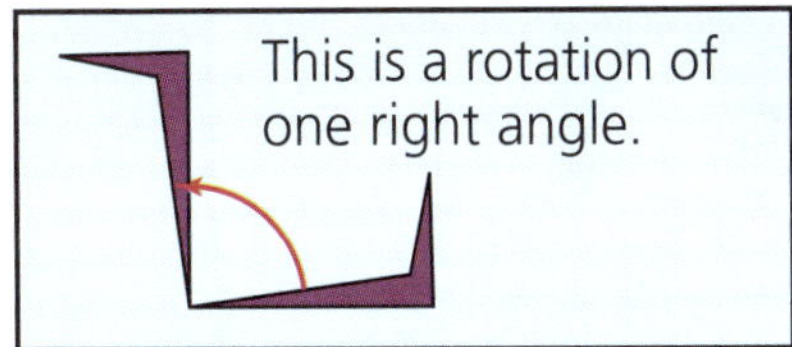

Draw the blue flag in its new position after:

a a reflection (flip) about the dotted line

b a translation (slide) of 2 cm up

c a rotation (turn) of one right angle around **A** (anticlockwise)

d a rotation of two right angles around **A**.

See *Extra Support 19 and 20* (Extension: enlargements).

4:04 Flip, slide, turn

A  B  C 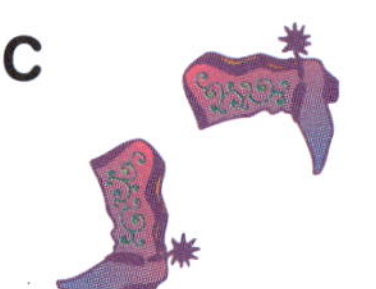 D 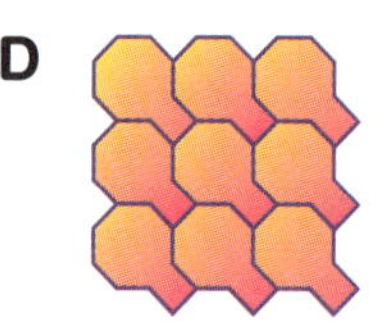 E 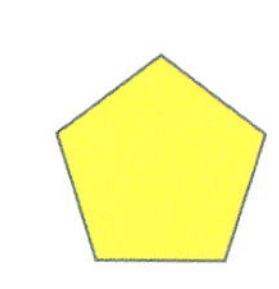 F 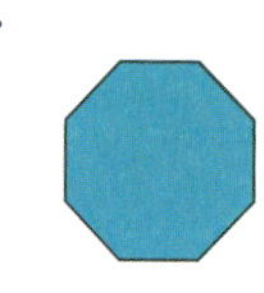

1 Which picture above is an example of:

a a reflection (flip)? ☐ b a translation (slide)? ☐ c a rotation (turn)? ☐
d a tessellation? ☐ e a pentagon? ☐ f an octagon? ☐

2 How many axes of symmetry has picture:

a **A**? ☐ b **B**? ☐ c **C**? ☐ d **E**? ☐ e **F**? ☐

3 a

Shade squares to reflect this shape about the green line.

b Rotate this shape clockwise through a right angle about **O**.

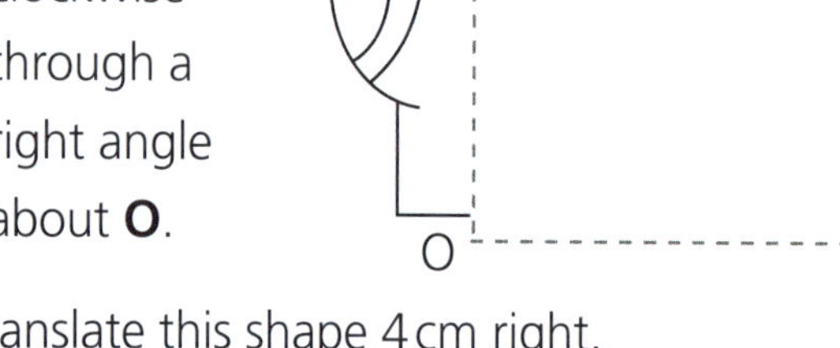

c Reflect this shape about the line.

d Translate this shape 4 cm right.

4 Complete these symmetrical designs.

a

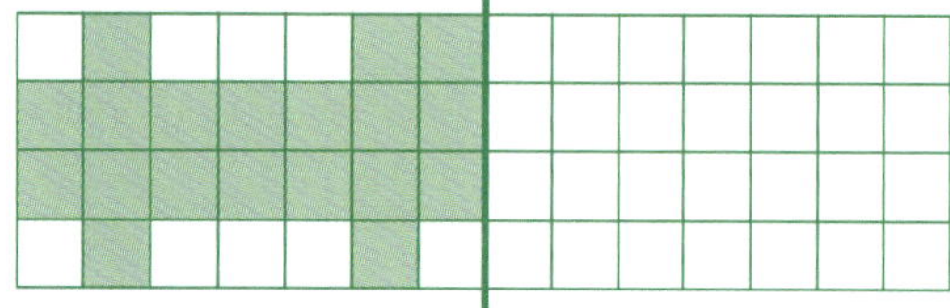

symmetry about a vertical line

b

symmetry about a horizontal line

5
- Translate the triangle 2 rectangles to the right, then rotate this image a quarter turn around the red dot.
- Next, reflect the last image in the dotted red line.

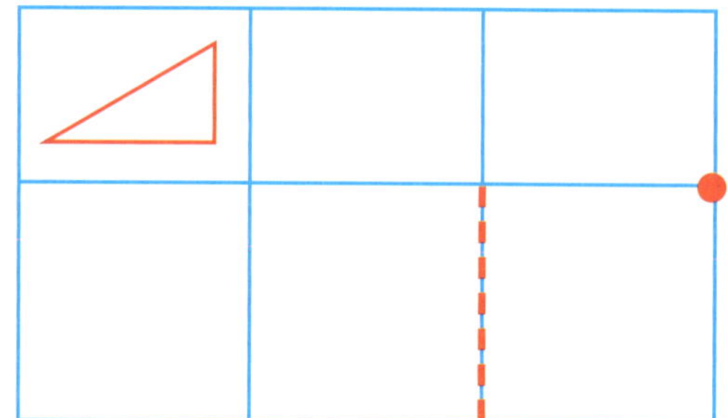

Use a computer program to make designs using translations, reflections and rotations.

See *Extra Support 19 and 20* (Extension: enlargements).

Nets

A net allows us to see all of the faces of a solid at once.

1 Match each object to its net. Circle the nets that do not match one of the objects.

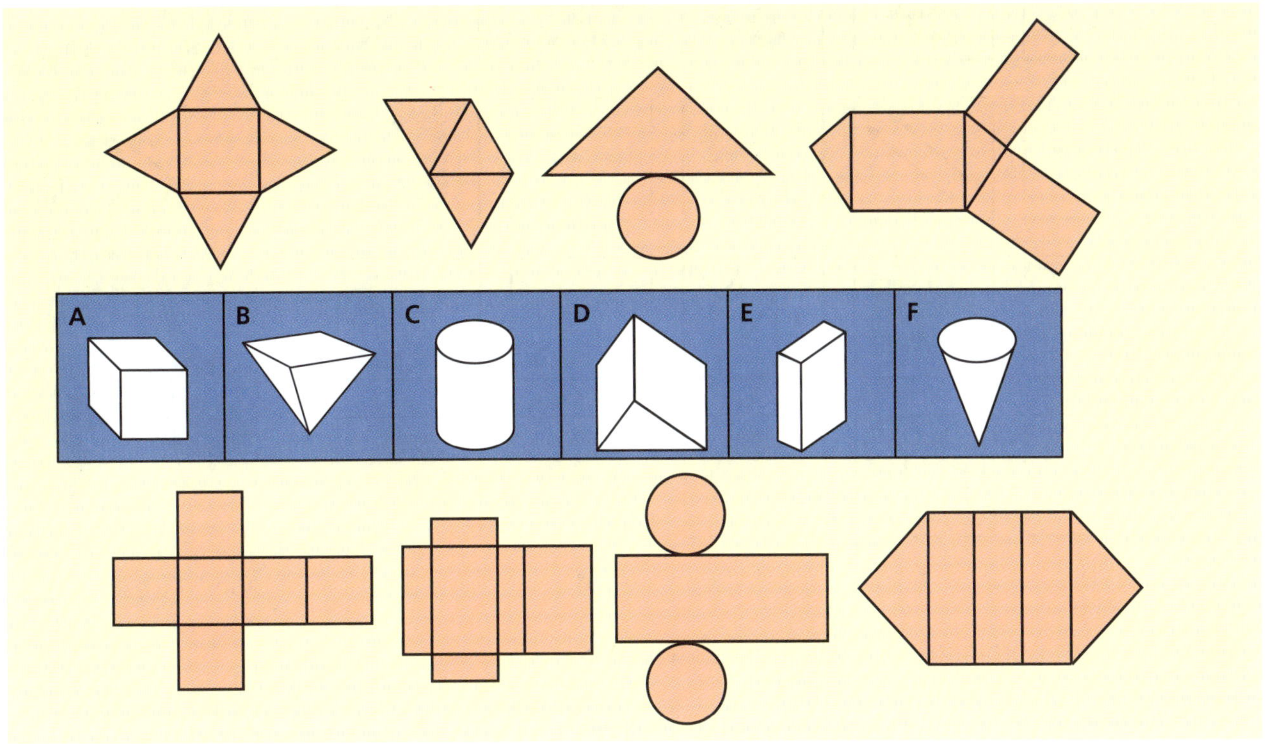

2 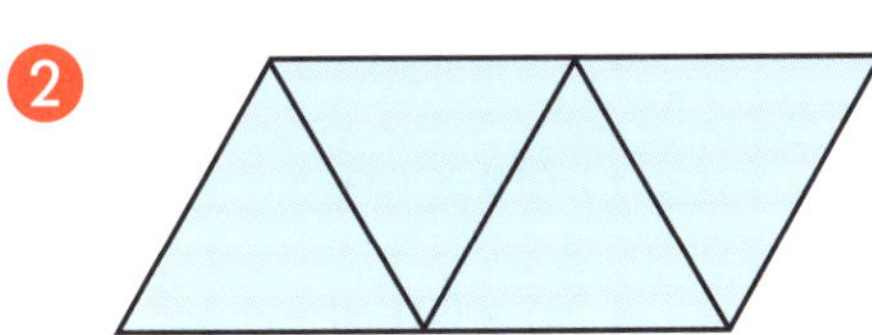

a This is the net of a ______________.

b Copy this net, making the side lengths four times as big.

c Use the net to make a model of the 3D object.

3 Complete the net of each 3D object.

a 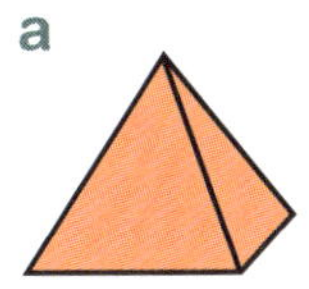 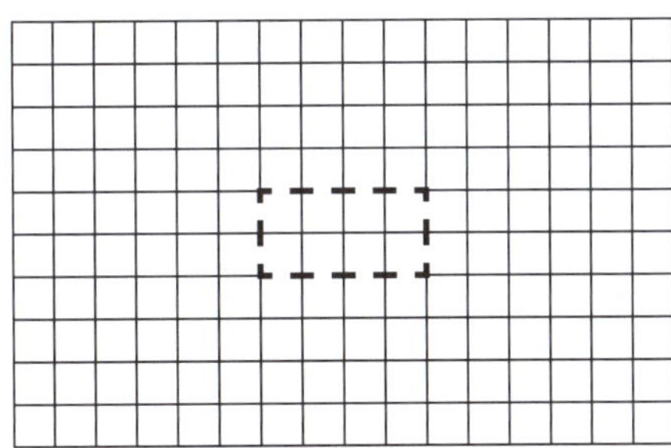

b 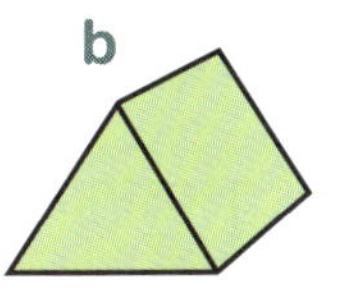 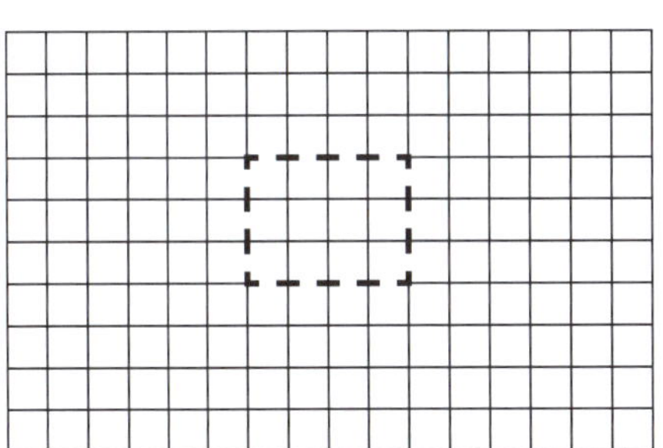

INVESTIGATION

- Cut up a box to make its net. Compare your net with others.

4 Circle the nets below that would be the net of a box.

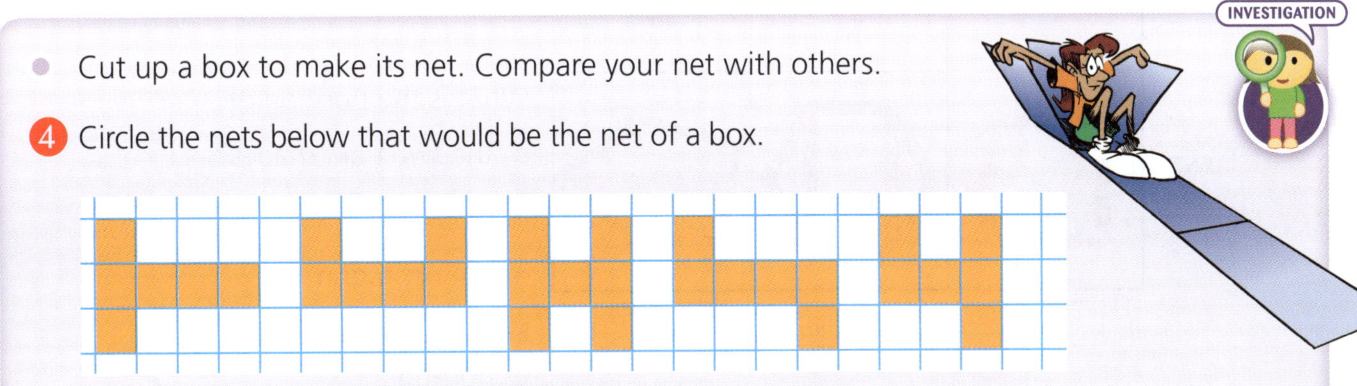

 • *AUSTRALIAN SIGNPOST MATHS 5* • ISBN 9780655708797

4:06 Describing position

We write the horizontal coordinate first.

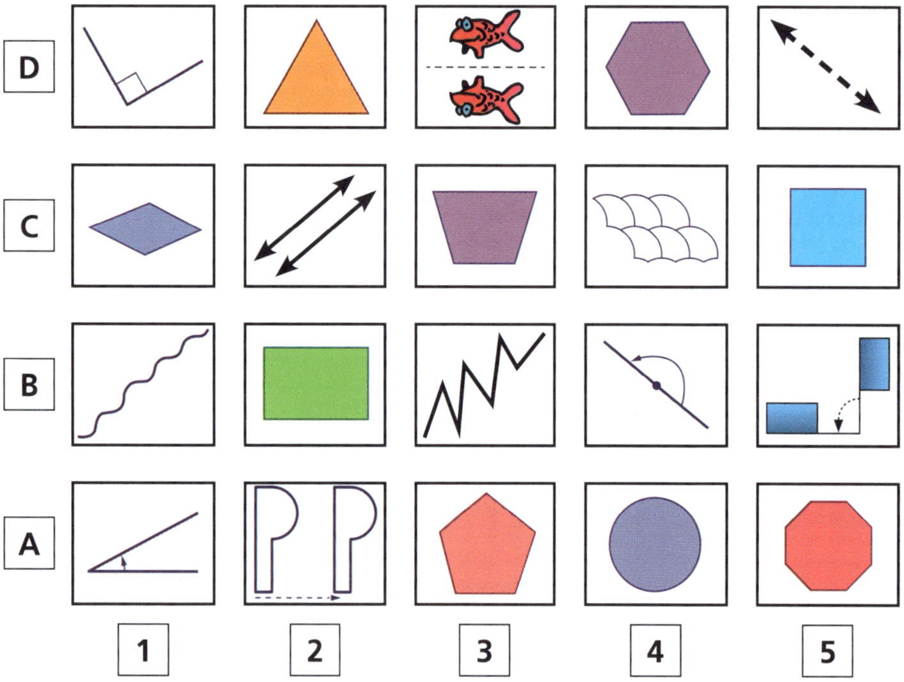

	1	2	3	4	5
D					
C					
B					
A					

A regular pentagon is at 3A.

Quadrilaterals have 4 straight sides.

1 Write the coordinates of the picture that shows:

a parallel lines ☐ b a straight angle ☐ c the right angle ☐

d the smallest angle ☐ e a circle ☐ f a rectangle ☐

g a rhombus ☐ h a trapezium ☐ i a pentagon ☐

j a hexagon ☐ k an octagon ☐ l a tessellation ☐

m a flip (reflection) ☐ n a slide (translation) ☐ o a turn (rotation) ☐

p each of the quadrilaterals ☐ q a zigzag line ☐

2 The models below are made of geostrips. (You could make them.)

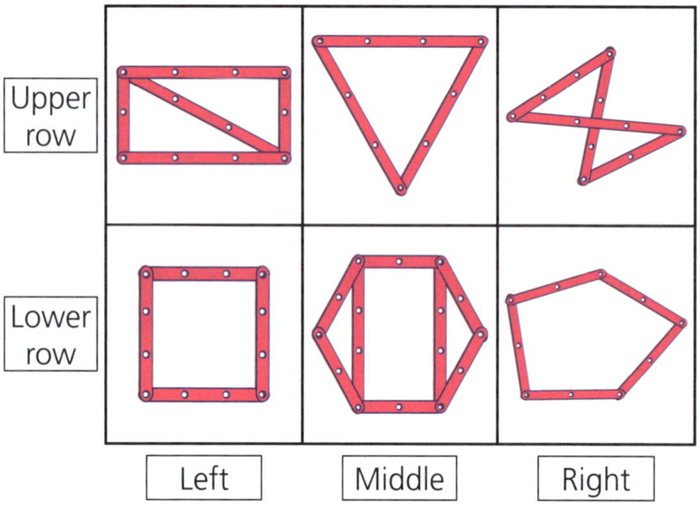

	Left	Middle	Right
Upper row			
Lower row			

What shape is the model with position:

a middle upper? ☐

b right lower? ☐

c left lower? ☐

What is the position of:

d the two rigid shapes? ☐

e the pentagon? ☐

Is the pentagon rigid or non-rigid? ☐

4:07 Using a protractor

Less than a right angle
acute

between a right angle and a straight angle
obtuse

CONCEPT

- Angles are measured in degrees and shown by the symbol °. This measure gives the amount of turning.
- A protractor has:
  1. a base line
  2. a centre point where the 90° line meets the base line
  3. two scales, one on the inside and one on the outside. Each scale goes from 0° to 180°.

1 Write down the size of each angle and say whether it is **acute** or **obtuse**.

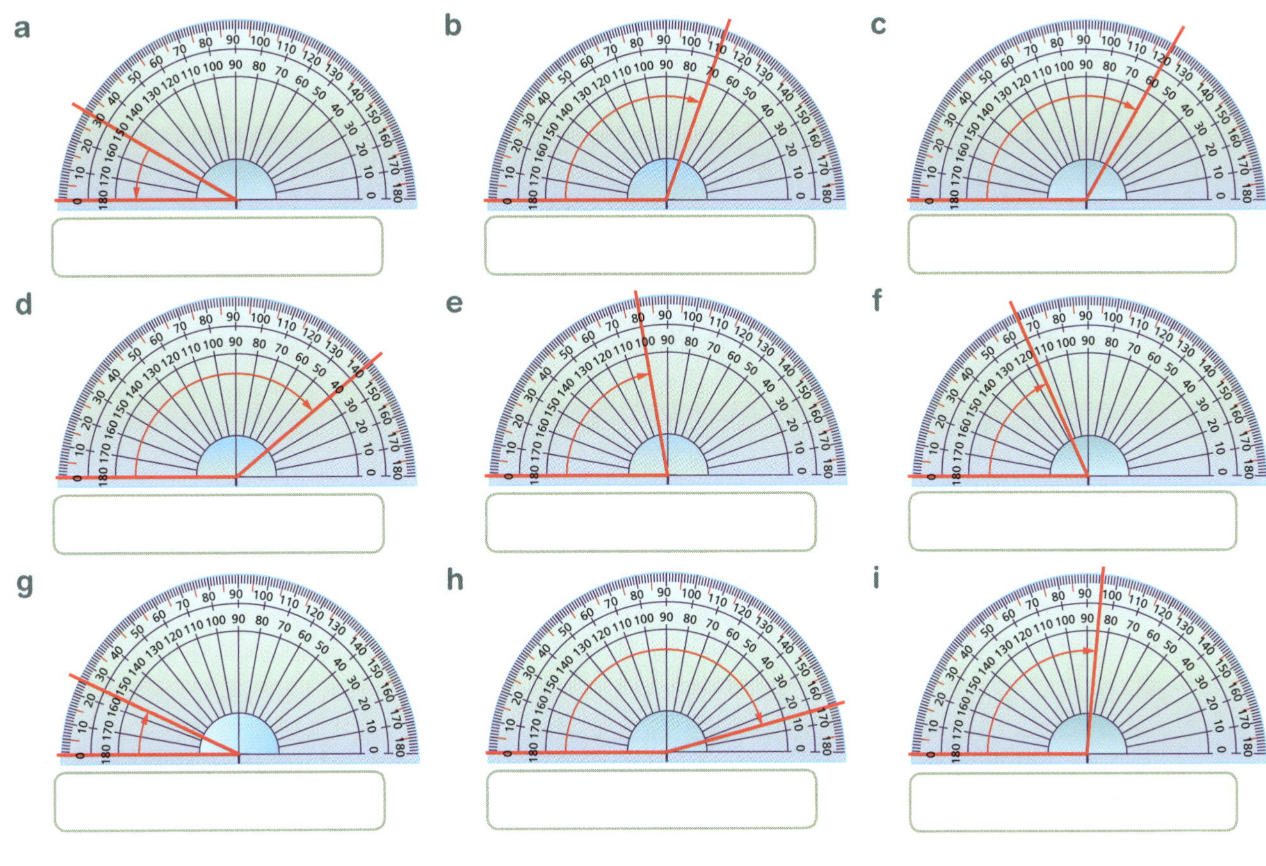

2 How many degrees has a:

a right angle? ______ b straight angle? ______ c revolution? ______

3 Describe how you would use a protractor to measure this angle.

4 Measure the angles on this block.

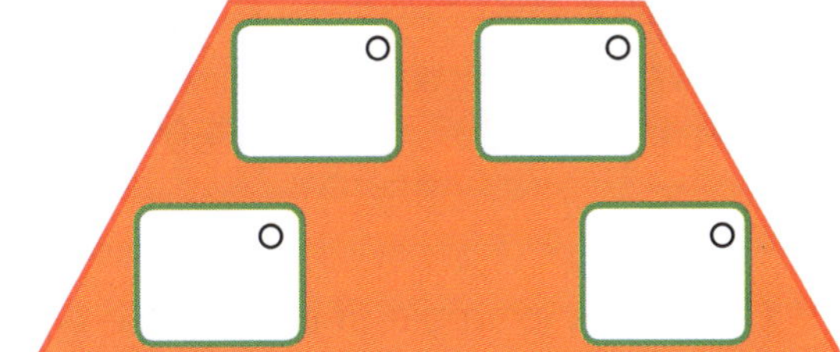

Angle types in degrees

reflex angles — between a straight angle and a full turn

1 Write the size of each angle. (The size is the amount of turn.)

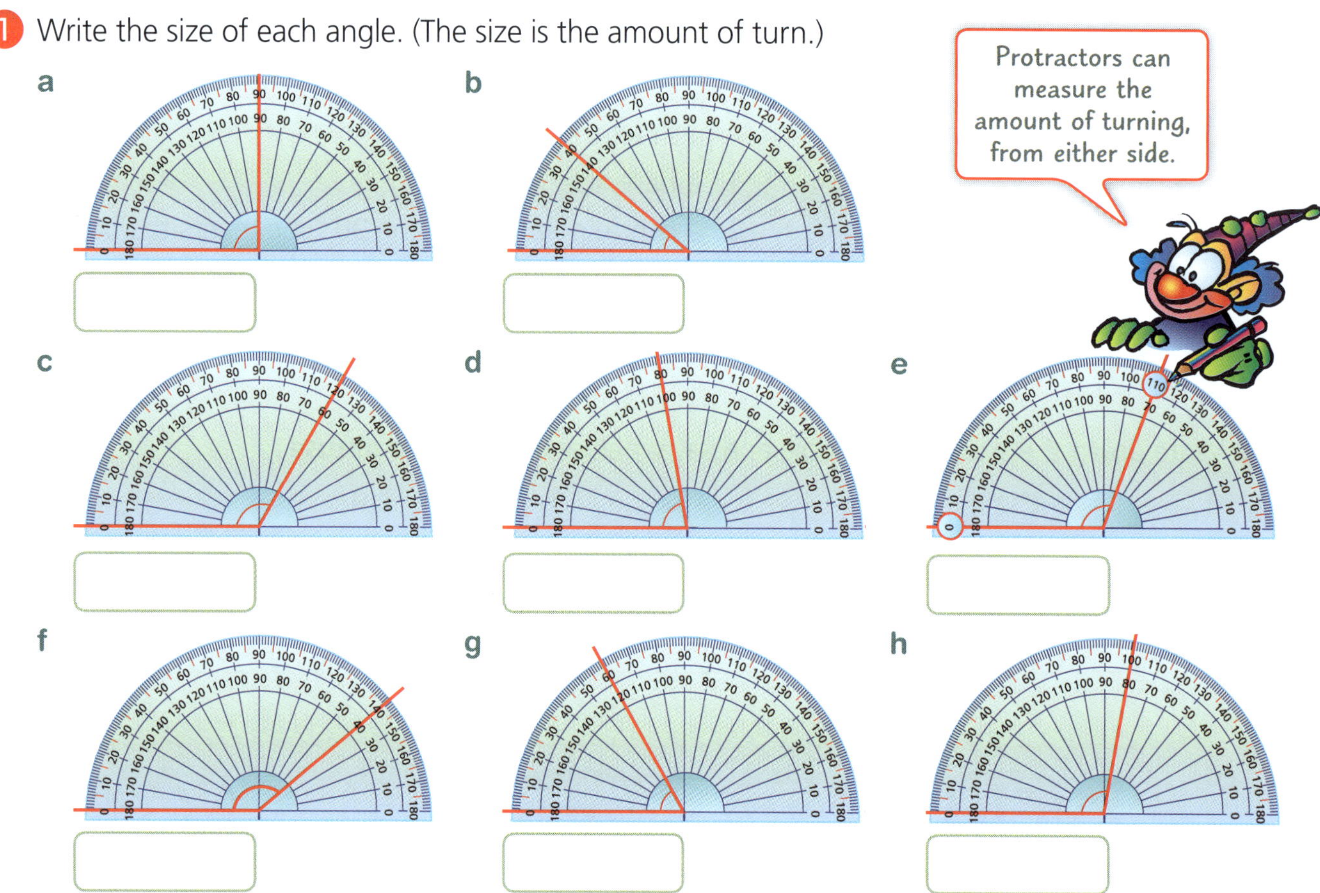

2 Complete the table by writing the type of angle. (If you need help, see page 122.)

Picture						
Type	acute					revolution (full turn)
Size	between 0° and 90°	90°	between 90° and 180°	180°	between 180° and 360°	360°

3 Give the type of angle if its size is:

a 35° ______ b 180° ______ c 360° ______ d 100° ______

e 75° ______ f 200° ______ g 90° ______ h 150° ______

i 5° ______ j 350° ______ k 340° ______ l 160° ______

m 15° ______ n 60° ______ o 194° ______

4 Draw an example of each angle type in Question 2.

4:09 Using a protractor

Estimate by comparing angles to a right angle (90°).

ACTIVITY

- Cut out a photocopy of this protractor. Also cut out the inside part, so you can see the arms of the angle you want to measure.
- You may have to turn the protractor to place one arm on the baseline.

1 Estimate the size of the angle, then use a protractor to measure its size correct to the nearest 10°. Draw the arms longer if necessary.

a

b

c

d

e

f

g

h

i

j

k

l

Drawing angles

ACTIVITY

- Draw one arm of the angle and place this arm of the angle along the baseline, with its end at the centre.
- Follow the scale from zero to the measure you want. Mark the spot, remove the protractor and join the point to the end of the arm.
- Use this method to draw the following angles.

40°	60°	20°	90°
100°	10°	120°	140°
170°	70°	180°	50°

This is how you draw an angle of 110°.

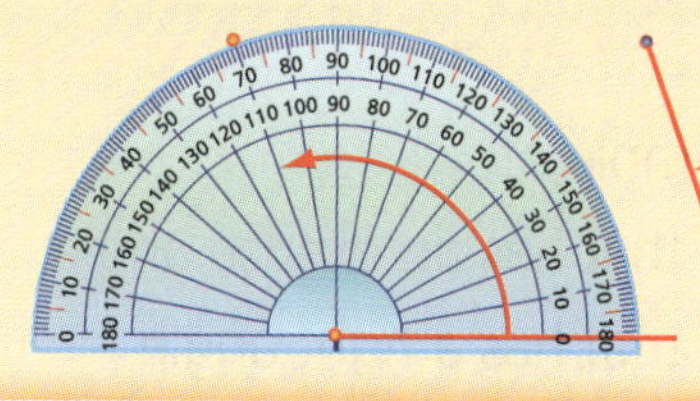

4:10 Classifying angles

The size of an angel is the amount of turn from one arm to the other.

Picture						
Type	acute	right	obtuse	straight	reflex	revolution (full turn)
Size	between 0° and 90°	90°	between 90° and 180°	180°	between 180° and 360°	360°

1. Name each type of angle.

a 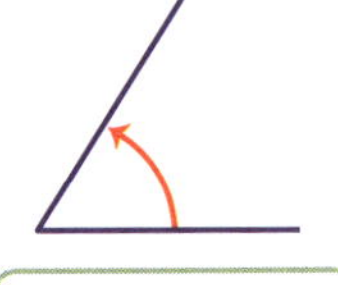

b 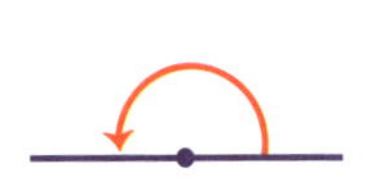

c 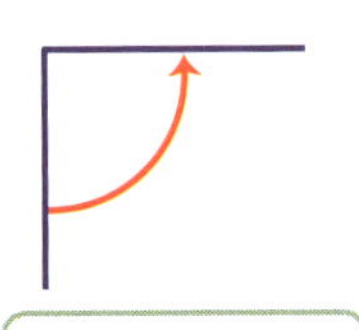

d 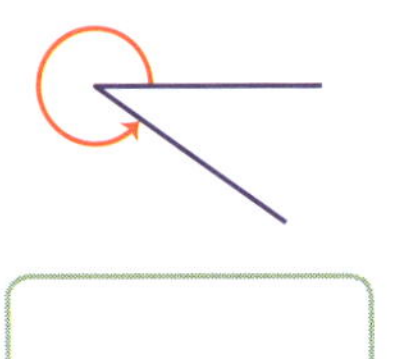

e 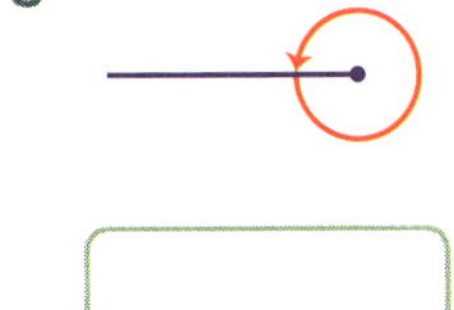

f 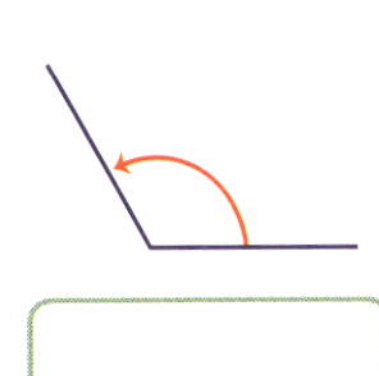

g 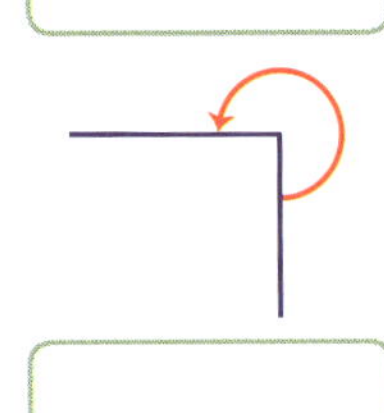

h 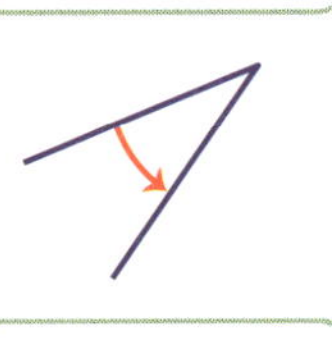

2. The diagram on the right is called a **flow chart**.
Flow charts help to organise our thinking.
Does it work for all angles up to one revolution?

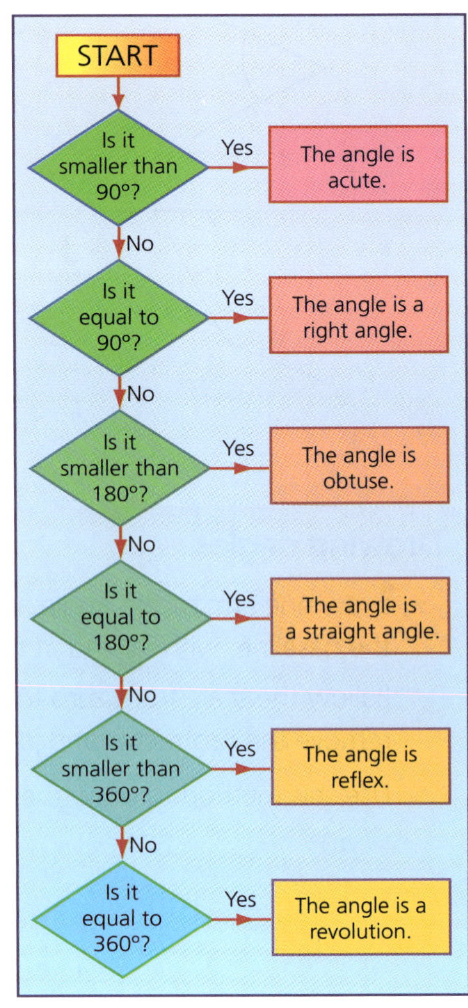

3. Give the angle type if its size is:

a 2° **b** 360°
c 180° **d** 120°
e 90° **f** 307°
g 139° **h** 92°

4. Give the name of a shape that has:

a all angles right angles
b all angles obtuse angles
c all angles acute angles

5. Draw an example of:

a a triangle that has an obtuse angle
b a triangle that has a right angle.

4:11 Compass directions

A compass needle always points north.

CONCEPT

Australia

Darwin
Derby
Fitzroy Crossing
Karumba
Coral Bay
Alice Springs
Rockhampton
Longreach
Brisbane
Kalgoorlie
Ceduna
Perth
Adelaide
Sydney
Canberra
Melbourne
Hobart
N
NW
NE
W
E
SW
SE
S

Scale:
1 cm = 300 km

Queensland is north of Tasmania.

- Halfway between north and east is **north-east**.
- Halfway between north and west is **north-west**.
- Halfway between south and east is **south-east**.
- Halfway between south and west is **south-west**.

- South Australia is in the south.
- Western Australia is in the west.
- The Northern Territory is in the north.

1 Give the direction of each place from Alice Springs. (Use N, E, W, S, NE, SE, NW or SW.)

a Coral Bay	**b** Ceduna	**c** Rockhampton	**d** Darwin
e Derby	**f** Canberra	**g** Karumba	**h** Kalgoorlie
i Sydney	**j** Perth	**k** Longreach	**l** Fitzroy Crossing

2 Give the direction of Alice Springs from:

a Coral Bay	**b** Ceduna	**c** Rockhampton	**d** Darwin
e Derby	**f** Canberra	**g** Karumba	**h** Kalgoorlie
i Sydney	**j** Perth	**k** Longreach	**l** Fitzroy Crossing

3 Name the place that is:

a north of Longreach	**b** east of Kalgoorlie
c north-east of Adelaide	**d** north-west of Kalgoorlie
e north-west of Ceduna	**f** south-west of Darwin
g south-west of Canberra	**h** south-east of Karumba

4 Which is the opposite direction to:

a north?	**b** east?	**c** south-west?
d south-east?	**e** north-east?	**f** north-west?

4:12 Reading a map

The scale allows us to find the distance between places.

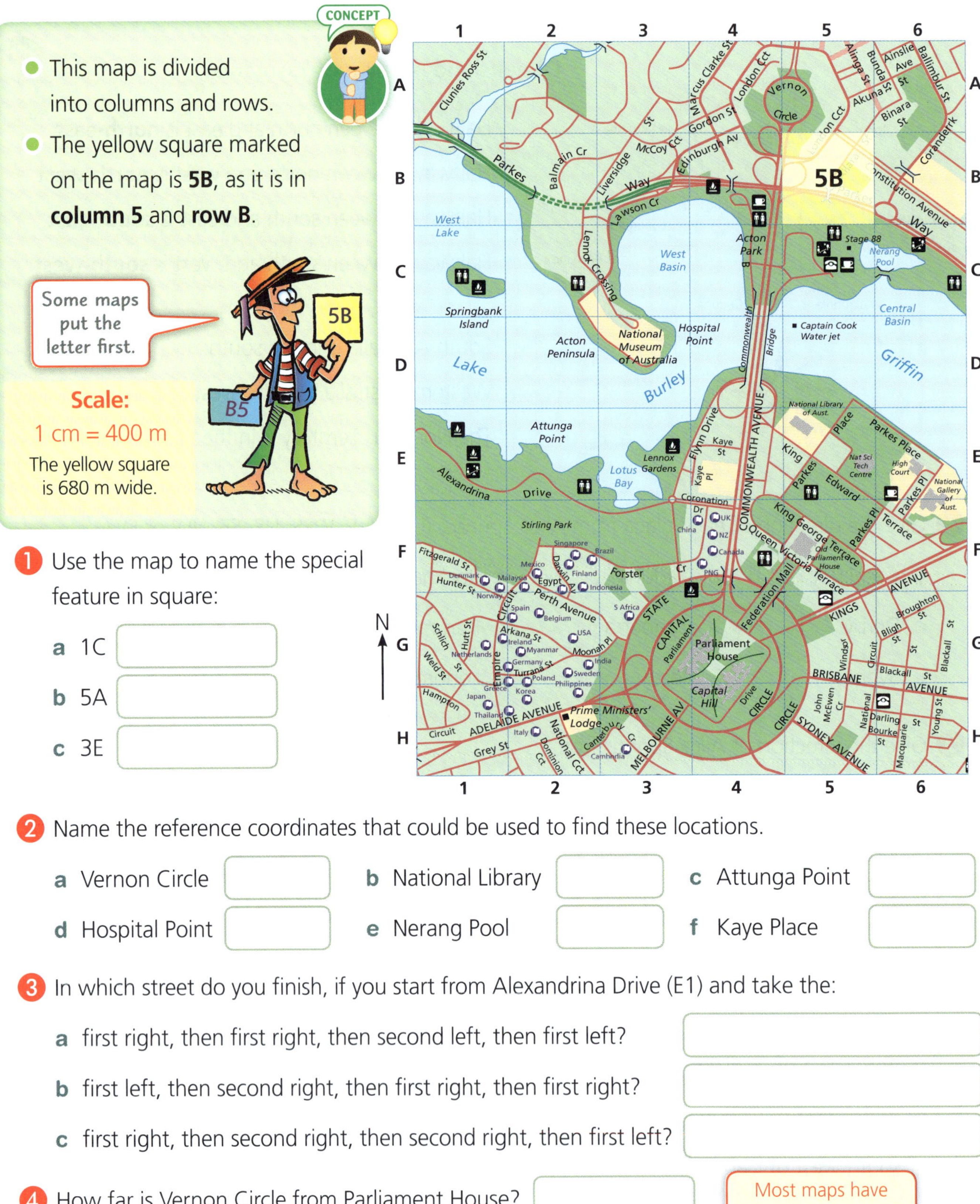

- This map is divided into columns and rows.
- The yellow square marked on the map is **5B**, as it is in **column 5** and **row B**.

Scale:
1 cm = 400 m
The yellow square is 680 m wide.

1 Use the map to name the special feature in square:

a 1C
b 5A
c 3E

2 Name the reference coordinates that could be used to find these locations.

a Vernon Circle
b National Library
c Attunga Point
d Hospital Point
e Nerang Pool
f Kaye Place

3 In which street do you finish, if you start from Alexandrina Drive (E1) and take the:

a first right, then first right, then second left, then first left?
b first left, then second right, then first right, then first right?
c first right, then second right, then second right, then first left?

4 How far is Vernon Circle from Parliament House?

Most maps have north at the top.

ACTIVITY

- Create a grid reference system for the classroom and use it to locate objects.
- Describe routes from one object to another.

Rotational symmetry

Spin this flower around its centre.

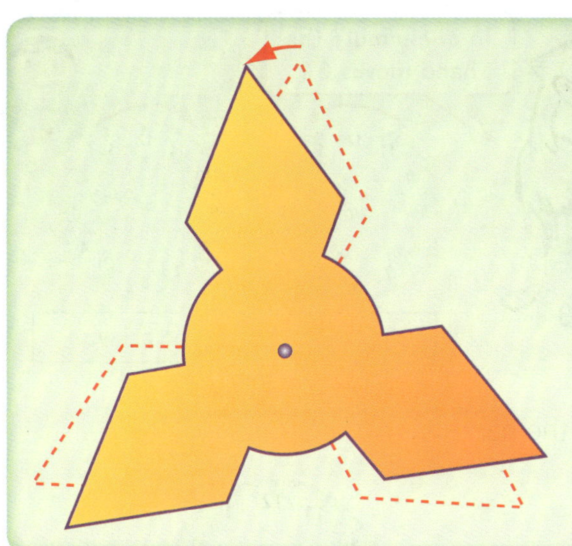

CONCEPT

A shape is said to have **rotational symmetry** if a tracing of the shape matches it after the tracing is rotated part of a full turn around the centre.

- If it is rotated about its centre, this shape will match its original position 3 times in one revolution.
- This shape has rotational symmetry of **order 3**.

1 Shape **A**

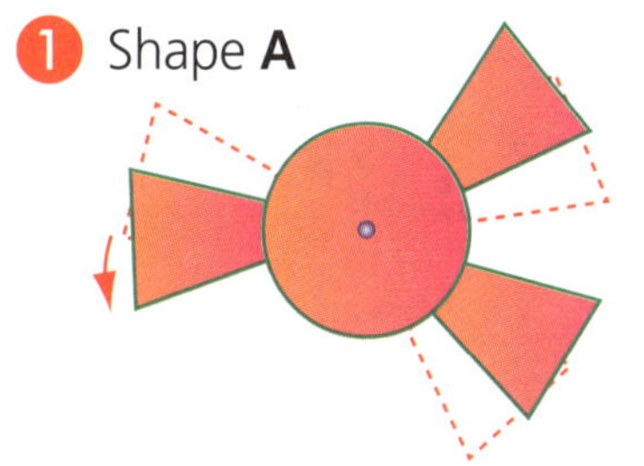

Shape **B**

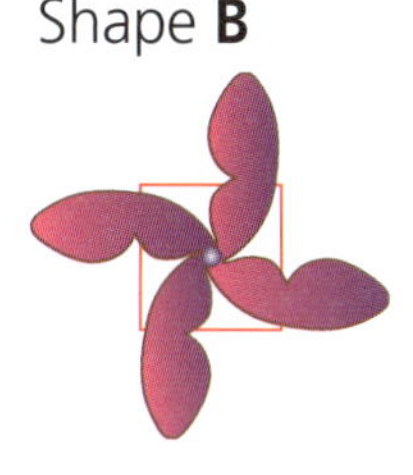

a Does shape **A** have line symmetry?

Does it have rotational symmetry?

b Does shape **B** have line symmetry?

Does it have rotational symmetry?

2 Which of the shapes below have rotational symmetry?

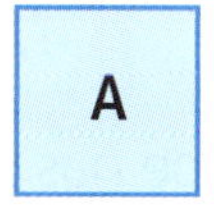

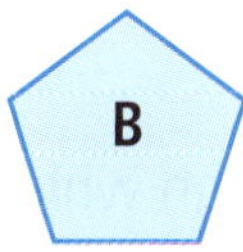

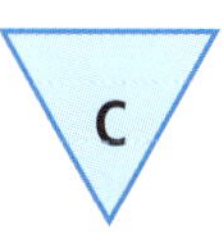

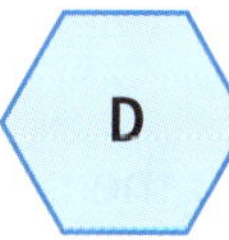

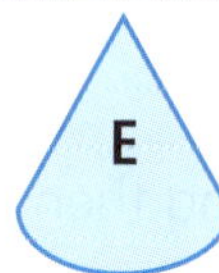

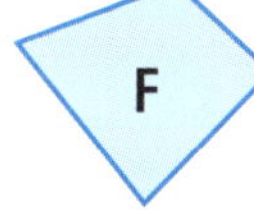

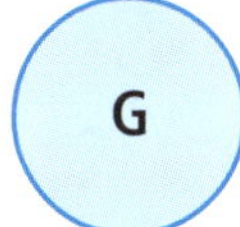

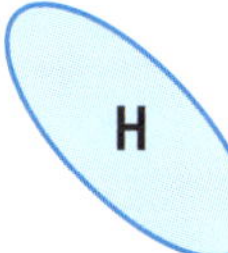

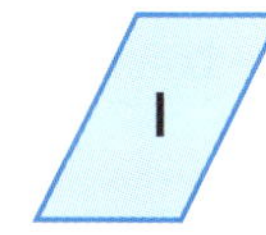

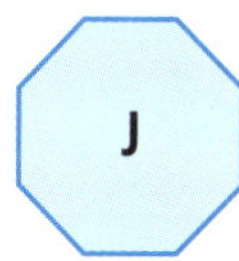

3 Which of the shapes above have line symmetry?

4 Do the patterns below have rotational symmetry (**Yes** or **No**)?
If so, what is the order of rotational symmetry? (It must be greater than 1.)

a

b
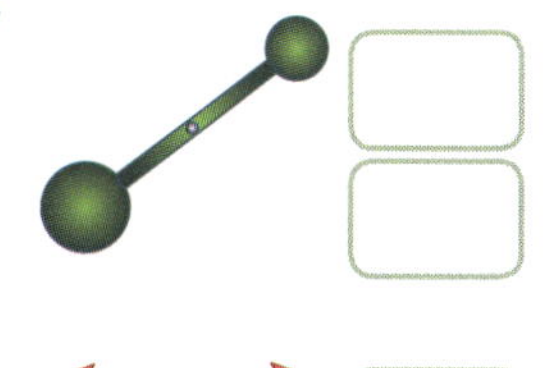

c

d
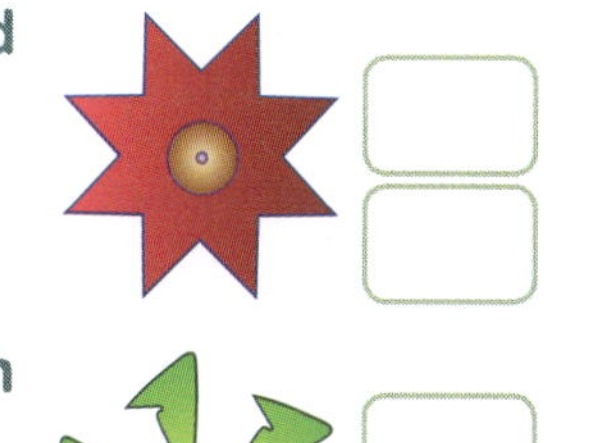

e

f
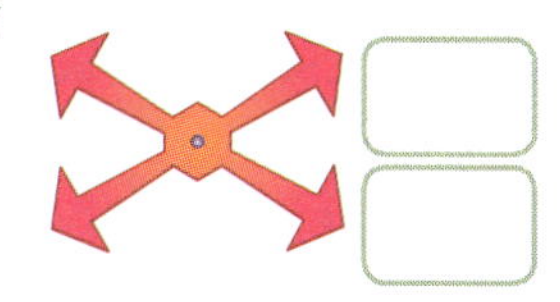

g
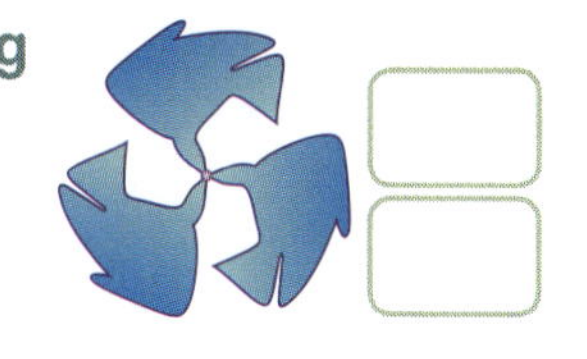

h

4:14 Measuring angles of rotation

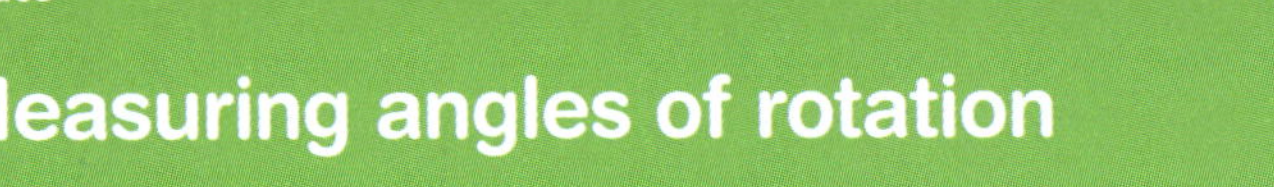

1. Use a protractor to measure the angle through which the hand has turned clockwise.

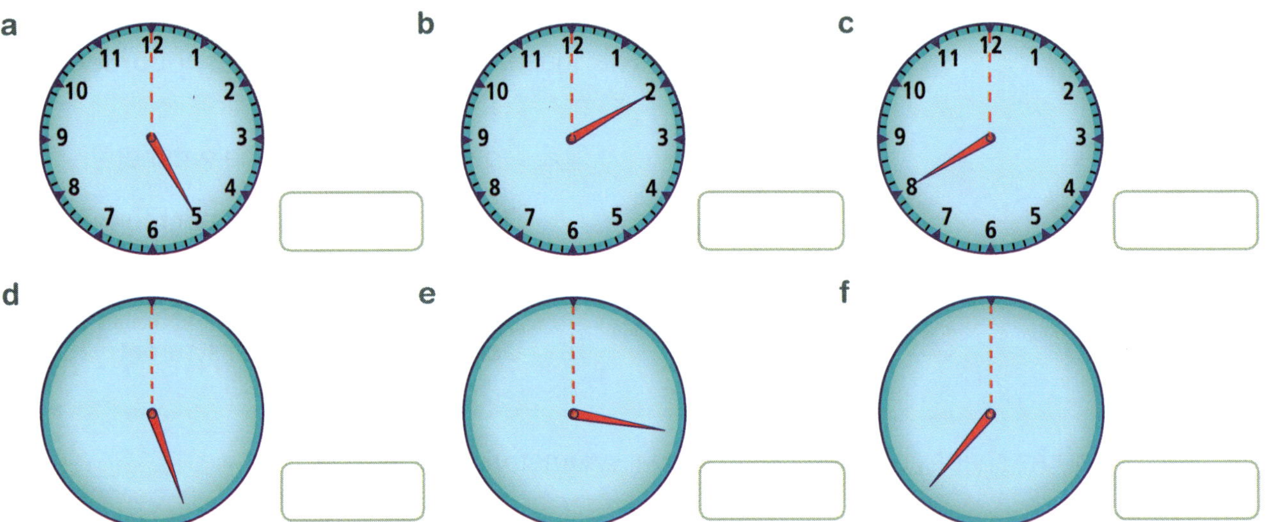

2. Estimate (E) and then measure (to the nearest 10°) the angle through which the shape has been rotated.

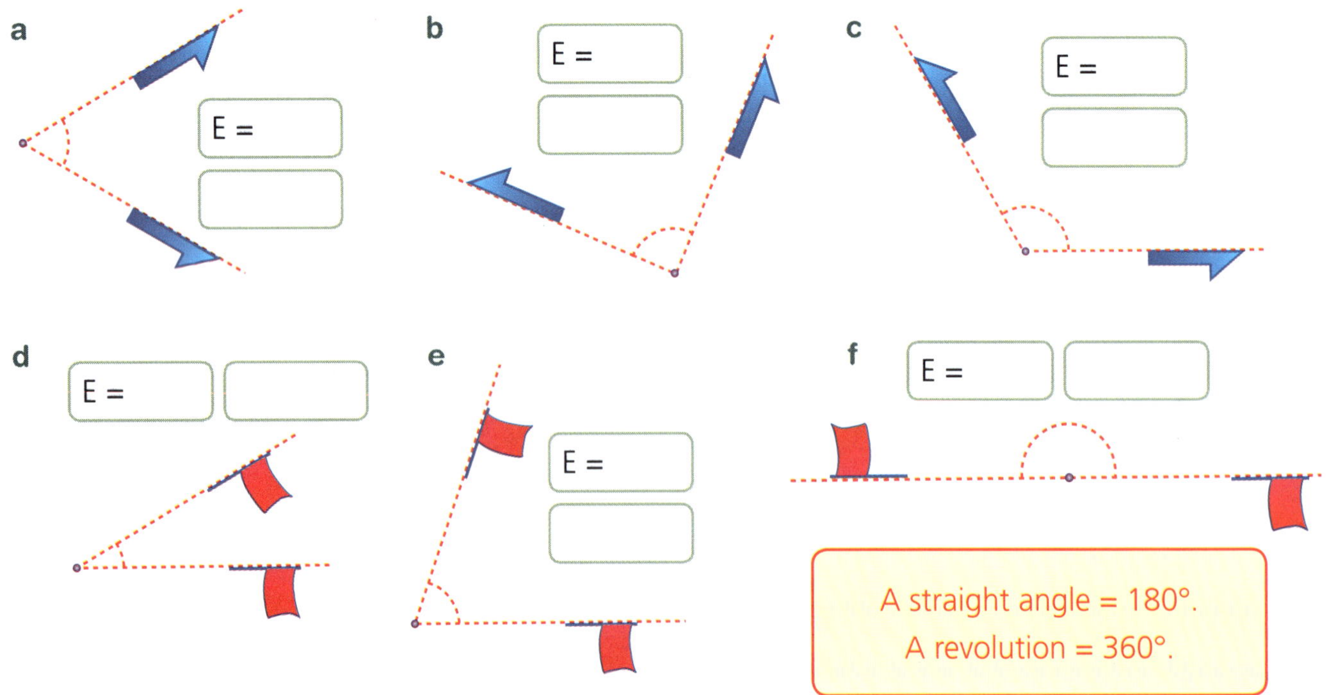

Rotational symmetry

Tick those with rotational symmetry:

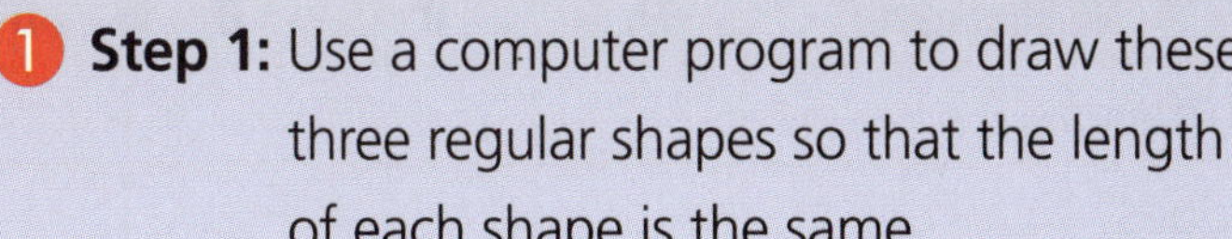

1 **Step 1:** Use a computer program to draw these three regular shapes so that the length of each shape is the same.

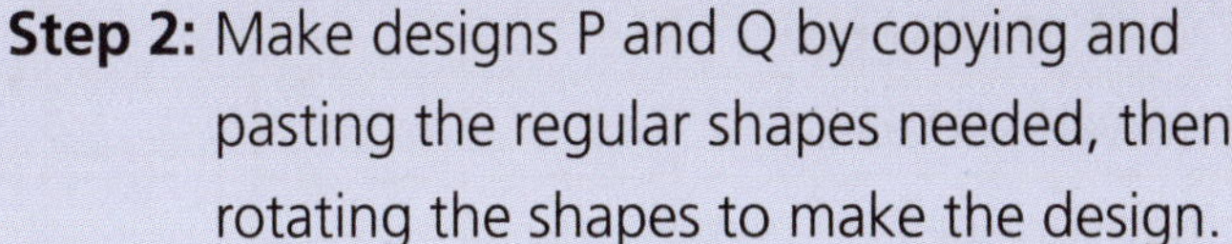

Step 2: Make designs P and Q by copying and pasting the regular shapes needed, then rotating the shapes to make the design.

Step 3: Group your design, then make a second copy of it.

Step 4: Use the rotate tool on your computer to find how many different times a copy of the design would fit exactly onto the original design as you turn through a full revolution.

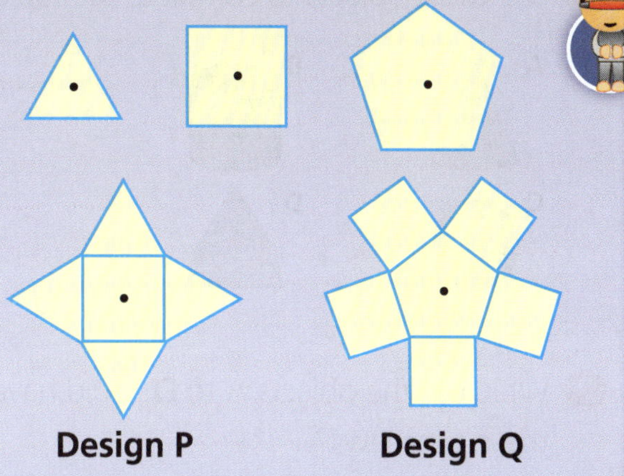

The number of times a copy would exactly fit the original in one revolution of turn is called the order of rotational symmetry.

a Design **P:** ☐ times **b** Design **Q:** ☐ times

Check: Print out 2 copies of your designs. Cut out one of each design and place each on the matching design. Turn the top design at the centre dot to see how many times it matches the bottom design in one revolution.

---

2 Use a computer program to choose a picture. Make a pattern by copying and pasting the picture, rotating it by 90° each time (**A**). Make other patterns using 60° (**B**) or 45° (**C**).

A (90 degrees)

(90°, 180°, 270°, 360° to a full revolution.)

B (60 degrees)

(60°, 120°, 180°, 240°, 300°, 360° to a full revolution.)

C (45 degrees)

(45°, 90°, 135°, 180°, 225°, 270°, 315°, 360° to a full revolution.)

3 Try making other designs using the rotate tool.

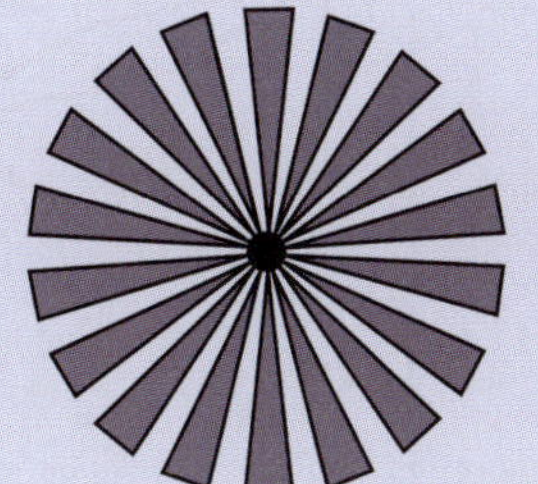

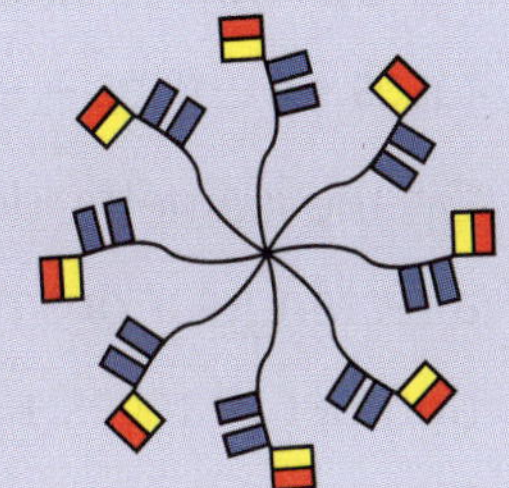

4:16 Views and nets of 3D objects

The sphere does not have a net.

1 Use these objects to complete the table.

A 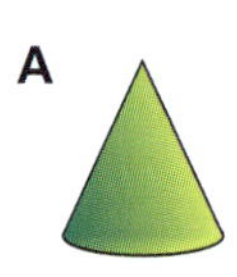

B 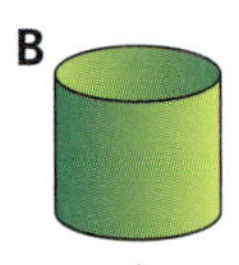

C 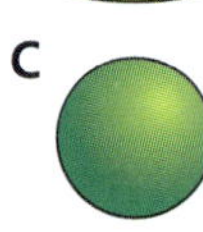

D 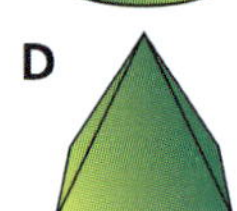

Number of:	A	B	C	D
surfaces				
edges				
vertices (corners)				
curved surfaces				
flat surfaces				

2 Which of the objects A to D could have these top views?

a b c

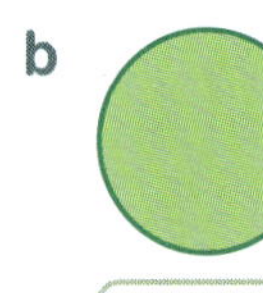

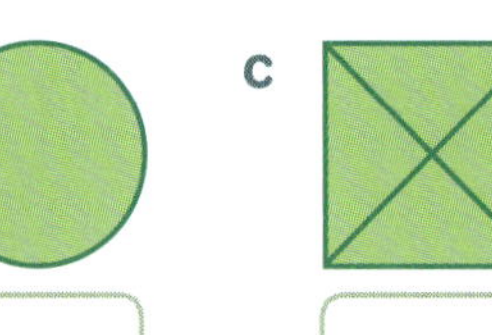

3 Which of the objects A to D could have these front views?

a b c

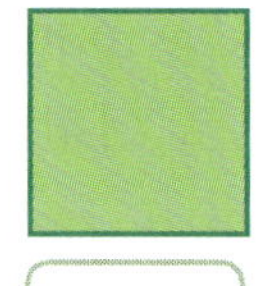

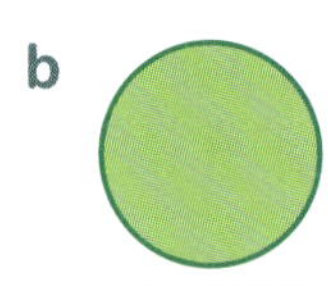

4 On the right is the net of an open cube. (It has no lid.)

Which of the nets below are of an open cube?

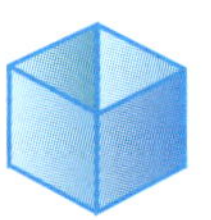

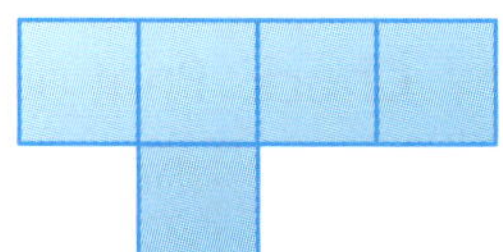

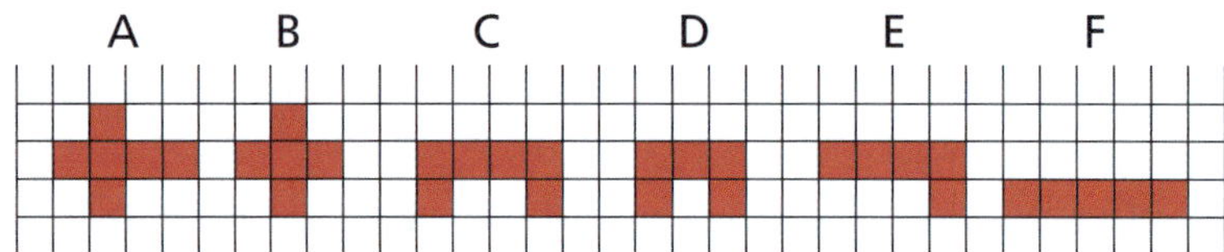

Copy one of the nets above to make an open cube with side lengths of 3 cm.

5 Which of the nets below are of an open rectangular prism?

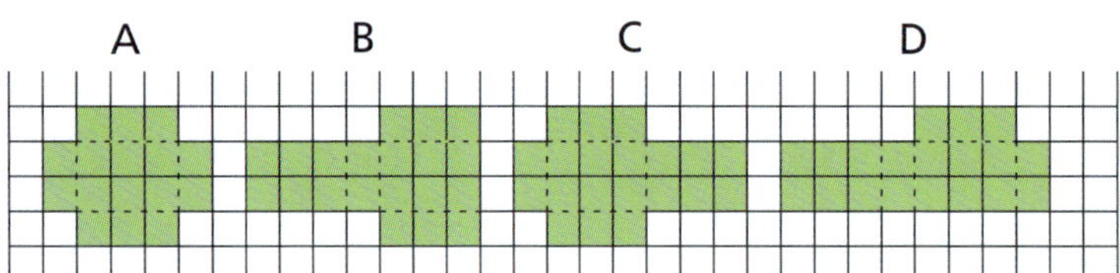

Copy one of them to make an open rectangular prism with a height of 2 cm and with a base 6 cm long and 4 cm wide.

6 a What is the name of the 3D object drawn on these isometric dots?

b For this object, find the number of faces + vertices – edges.

c On the isometric dot paper, draw a cube and a rectangular prism. For each object, find the number of faces + vertices – edges.

Cube: Rectangular prism:

Vertices are corners.

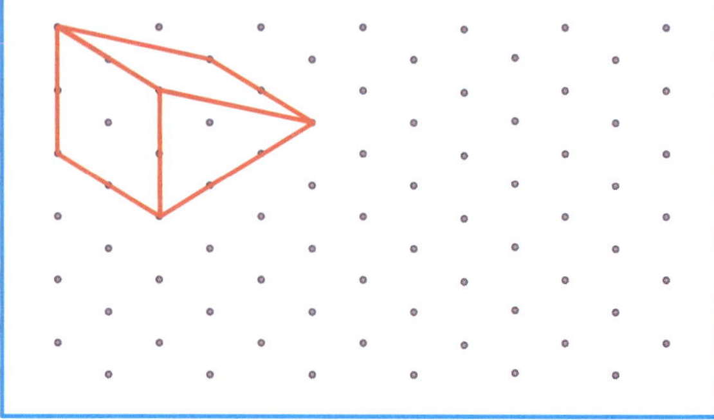

Coordinates on the number plane

At (1, 4) is a dog.
At (3, 2) is a lizard.

CONCEPT

Grid references

- On some maps we used a letter and a number to name a square. Here we name points.
- We use a number line as each axis to refer to a point.
- (2, 5) refers to 2 on the horizontal axis and 5 on the vertical axis. **(0, 0) is called the origin.** These coordinates are called **a number pair**.

1 What is found at:

a (1, 2)?

b (5, 7)?

c (1, 6)?

d (0, 0)?

e (2, 7)?

f (4, 1)?

g (5, 4)?

h (6, 6)?

i (5, 1)?

7
6
(2, 5)
5
4
3
2
1
0
0 1 2 3 4 5 6

2 Give the coordinates for the:

a emu
b triangular pyramid
c trapezium
d hexagon
e triangular prism
f lizard
g cockatoo
h right angle
i turtle

3 a Draw a red dot at each of the coordinates:
(0, 1), (6, 1), (4, 2), (6, 4), (6, 7), (4, 6), (3, 7), (0, 7), (4, 4), (2, 2) and (0, 1) again.
Join these points in order to create a closed shape. Name your shape.

4:18 Using coordinates

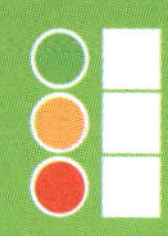

Guyana is at (5, 14).
The longest country in the world is at (2, 3).

CONCEPT

- The coordinates used here refer to the intersection of grid lines.
- (1, 12) means go up from 1 on the horizontal axis and across from 12 on the vertical axis.

I'm a llama.
I come from (1, 12).

South America

Scale: 1 cm = 500 km

Panama, Venezuela, Guyana, Suriname, French Guiana, Colombia, Ecuador, (1, 12), Peru, Brazil, Bolivia, Paraguay, Argentina, Uruguay, Chile, N

Horizontal axis: 0 1 2 3 4 5 6 7 8 9 10
Vertical axis: 0 1 2 3 4 5 6 7 8 9 10 11 12 13 14 15 16

1. Write down the countries that have these coordinates.
   - a (2, 14)
   - b (0, 15)
   - c (7, 10)
   - d (4, 7)
   - e (5, 9)
   - f (6, 7)
   - g (2, 11)
   - h (1, 13)
2. Which of the coordinates should we use for Guyana?
3. Give the coordinates of:
   - a Uruguay
   - b Ecuador
   - c Suriname
   - d Paraguay
4. Give three sets of coordinates for Colombia.
5. Give three sets of coordinates for Bolivia.
6. Give the greatest distance (to the nearest 100 km) across each country (west to east).
   - a Uruguay
   - b Bolivia
   - c Brazil
   - d Colombia
7. Which country is approximately:
   - a 1500 km south of Colombia?
   - b 800 km west of Suriname?
8. Use a grid to draw a map of Tasmania using a simple scale.

 • *AUSTRALIAN SIGNPOST MATHS 5* • ISBN 9780655708797

Drawing angles

Name the angles.

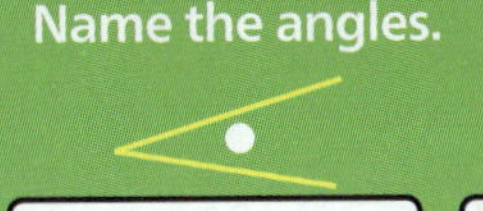

CONCEPT

Drawing an angle

1 Draw one arm of the angle.
2 Place the protractor so that the arm of the angle is on the baseline with one end at the centre.
3 Follow the scale from zero to the measure you want. Mark the spot.
4 Join this mark to the end of the arm to make the angle.

1 Use the method shown above to draw each angle on the left of the line.

a 50°

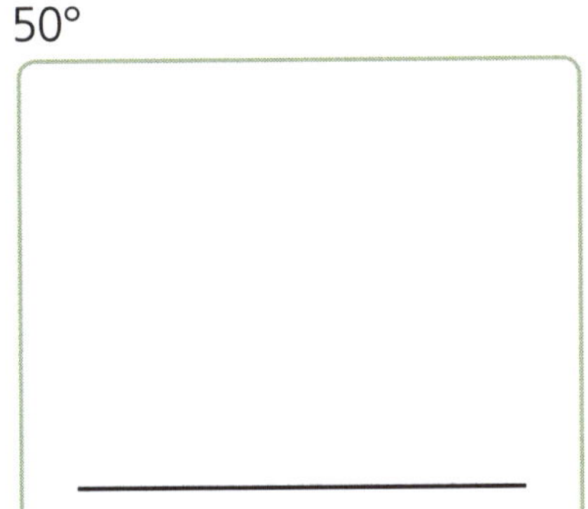

b 40°

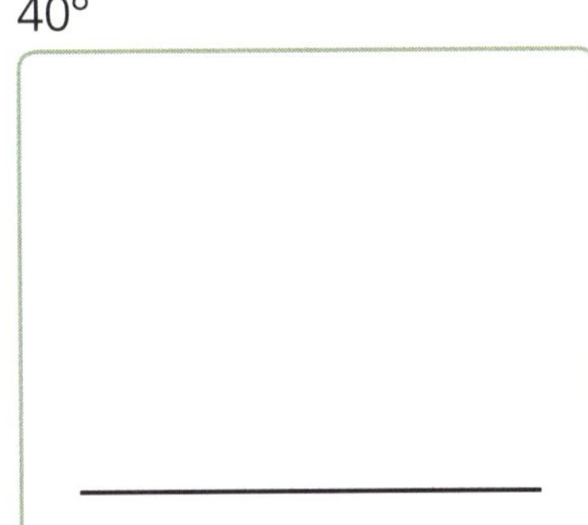

c 65°

d 120°

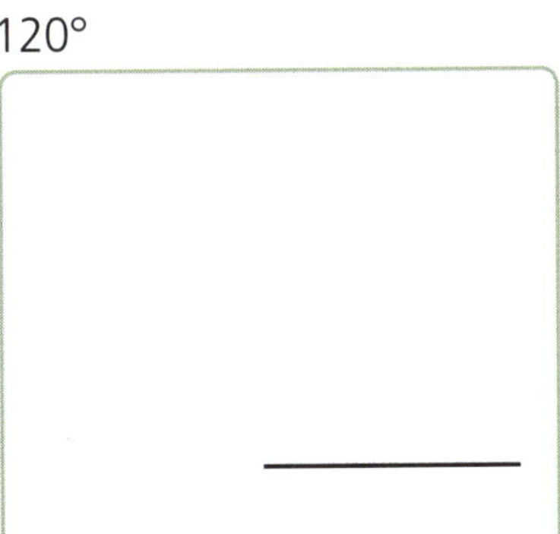

e 105°

f 147°

2 On your own paper draw an angle of:

a 30°	b 90°	c 135°	d 45°	e 165°
f 73°	g 118°	h 93°	i 14°	j 172°

How to draw a reflex angle

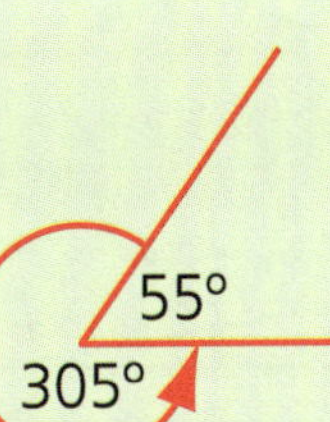

1 To draw an angle of 305°, calculate 360° – 305° (= 55°).
2 Draw the 55° angle.
3 Mark the reflex angle (305°) on the other side of 55°.

3 Draw the reflex angle:

a 300°	b 270°
c 190°	d 355°
e 225°	f 317°

A **reflex angle** is between a half turn and a full turn.

4:20 Angles greater than 180°

Practise reading a protractor correct to the nearest degree.

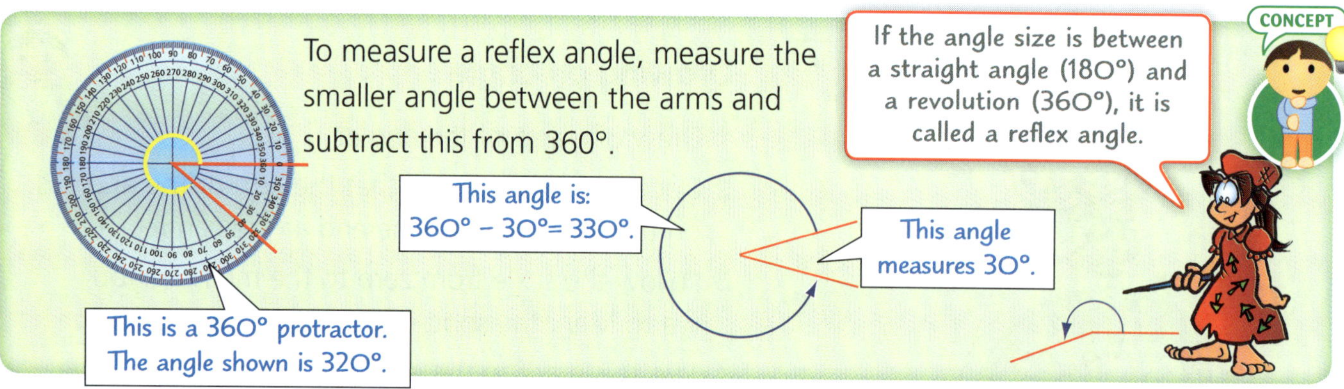

1 Write the angle shown on each 360° protractor.

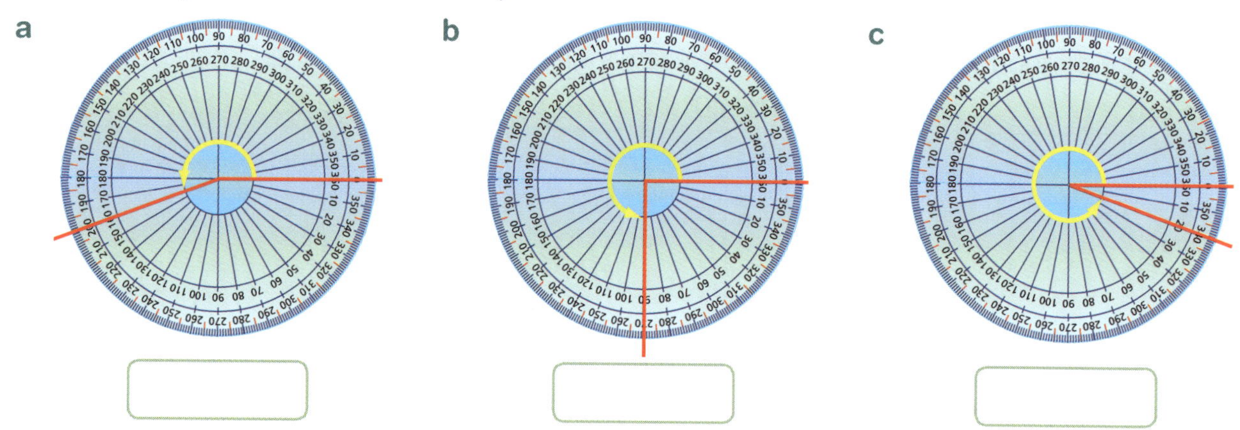

2 Angles at a point make a revolution (add up to 360°).

For each part of Question 1, find the size of the smaller angle at the point.

a ______ b ______ c ______

3 The size of the smaller angle is given. Find the size of each reflex angle.

a
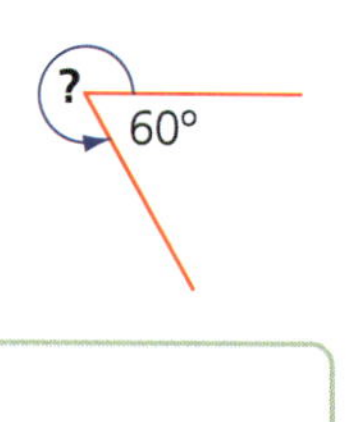

b
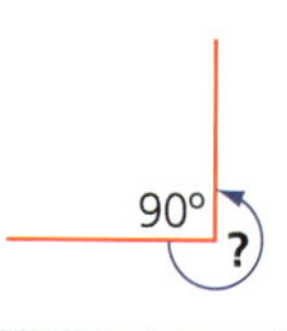

c
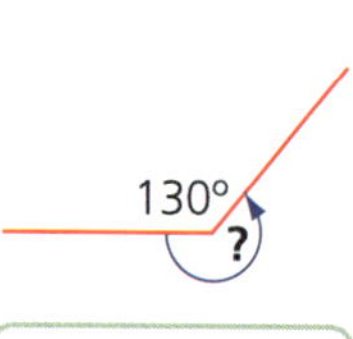

d
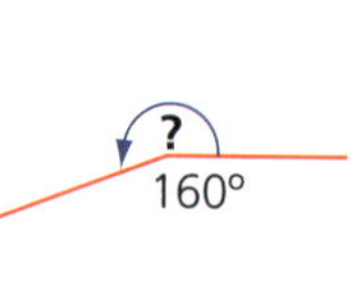

e
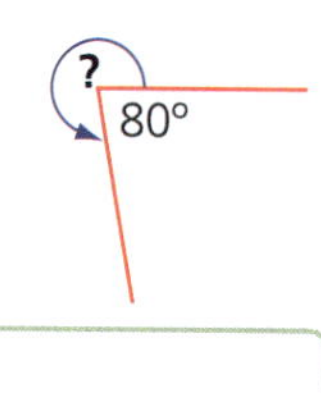

4 Measure each of these reflex angles correct to the nearest 10°.

a
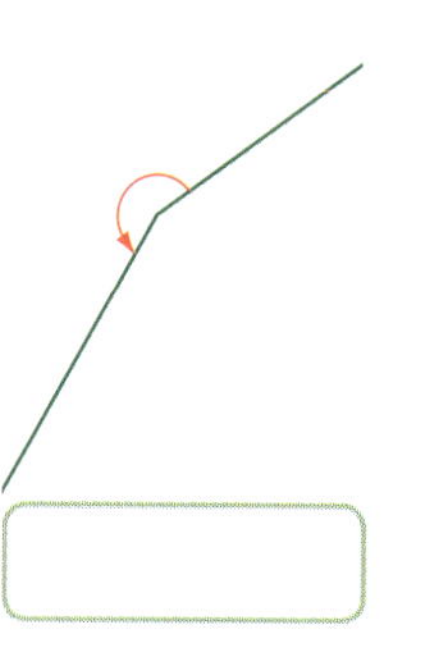

b
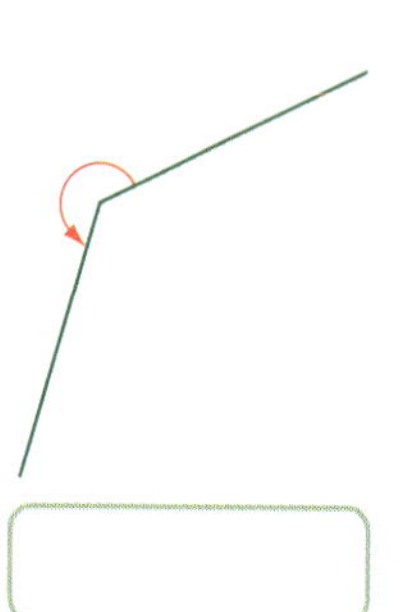

c
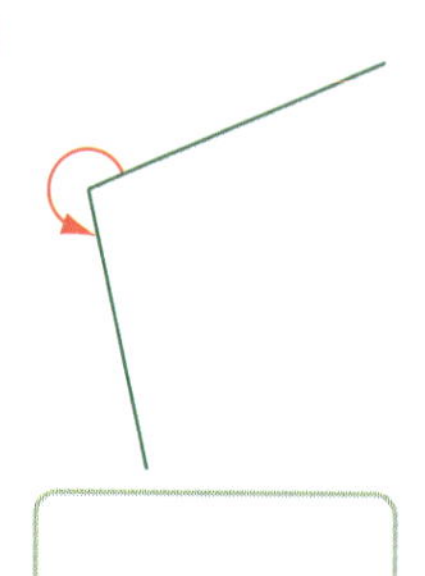

d
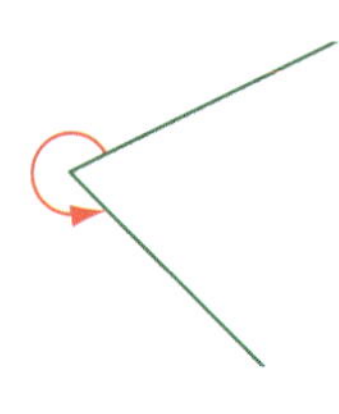

e
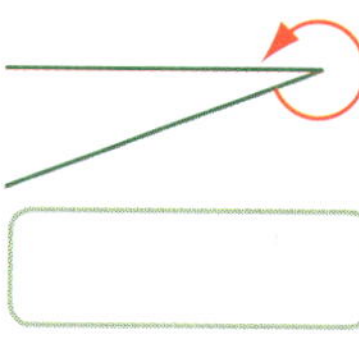

f

4:21 Mapping Australia

Karumba is at (10, 11).
Canberra is at (12, 4).

Use a ruler to measure length.

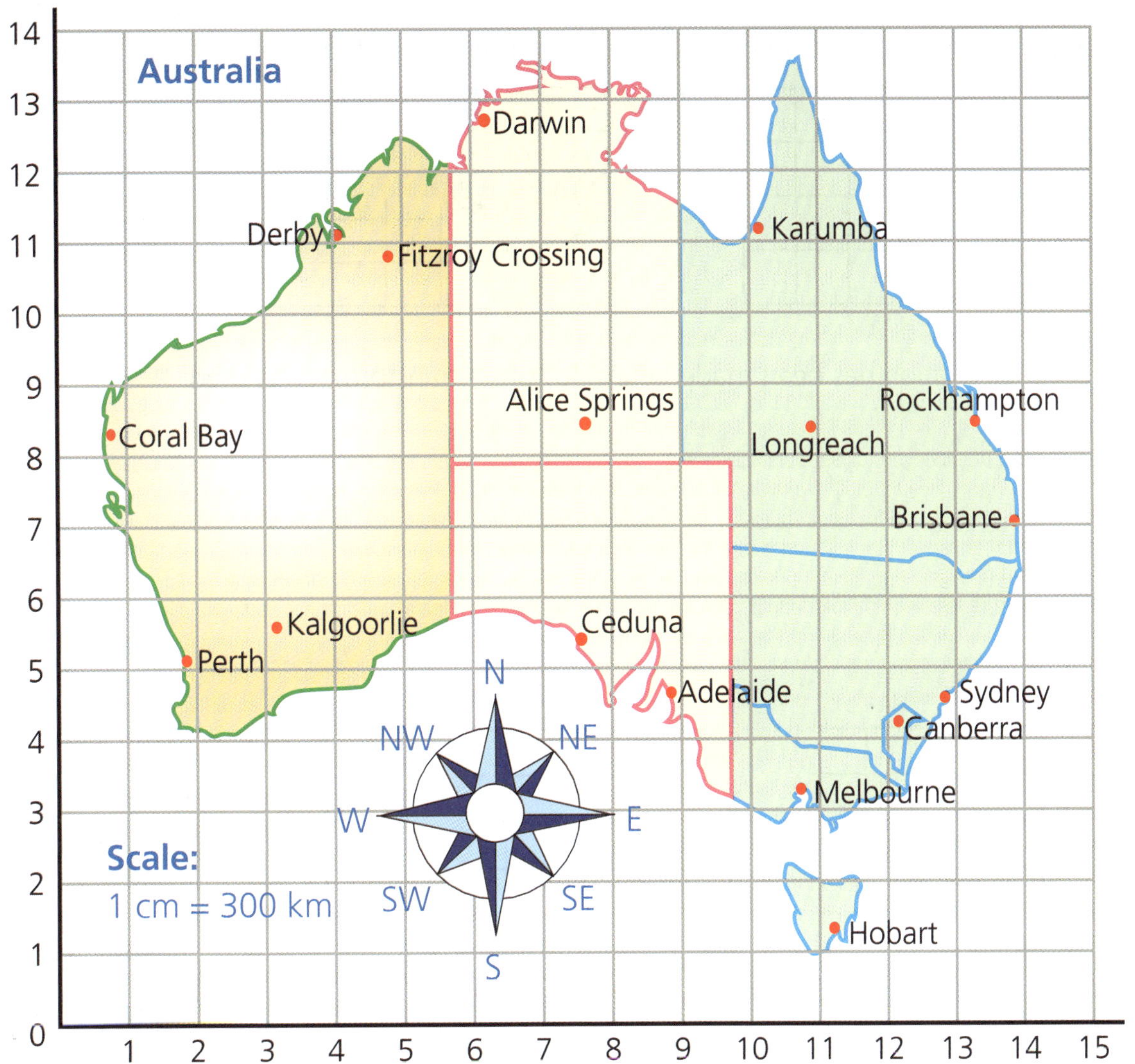

1 What is the nearest grid coordinate to:

a Darwin?

b Longreach?

c Hobart?

d Brisbane?

e Kalgoorlie?

f Perth?

2 What is the nearest place shown on the map that is about:

a 900 km south of Alice Springs?

b 1800 km north-east of Adelaide?

c 1200 km south-west of Derby?

3 a Use the scale on the map to find the length of Australia (east to west).

b Use the scale on the map to find the length of Australia (north to south).

c What is the distance between Perth and Sydney?

4:22 Using transformations

The transformations are reflection, translation and rotation.

1. Continue each tessellation, using its grid as a guide, then use pattern blocks to make your own.

a 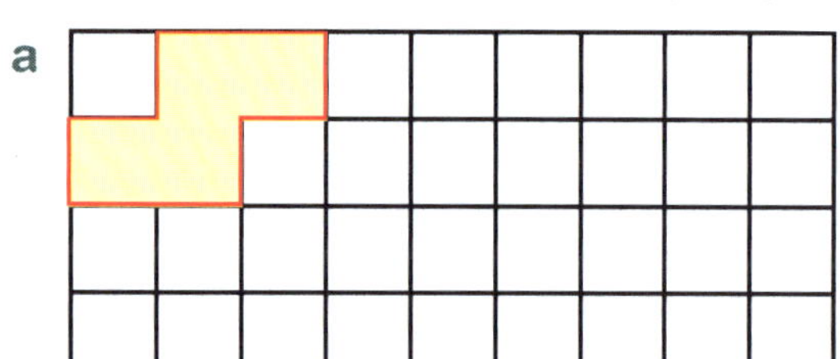

b 

2. Explain how each tessellation has been made, referring to the transformations used.

a

b

3. a 

Which transformations would move D to E?

b 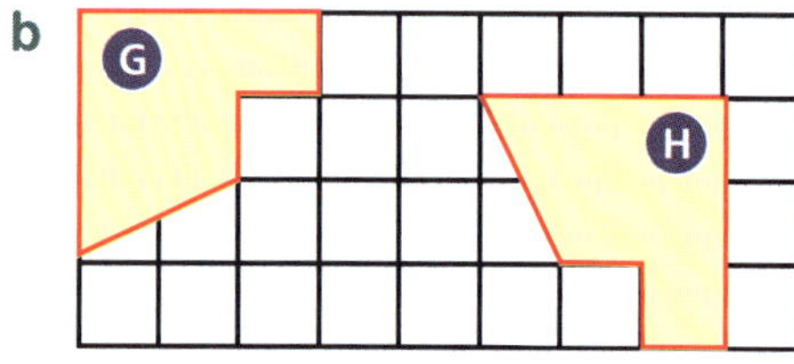

Which transformations would move G to H?

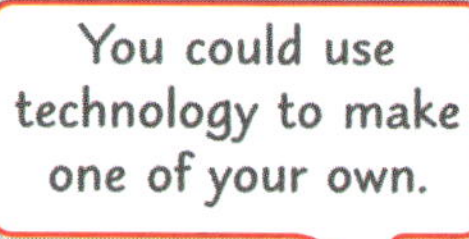

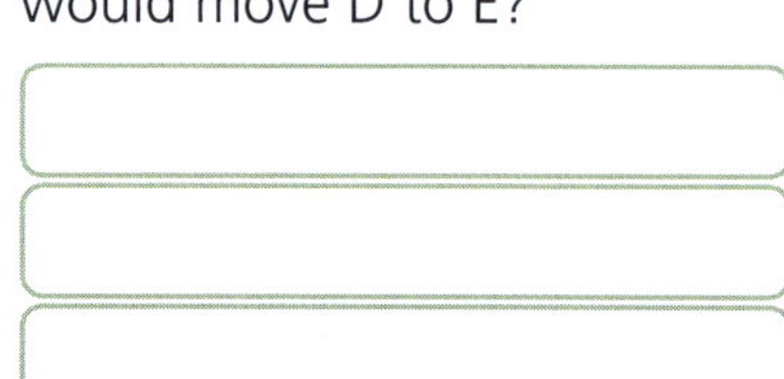

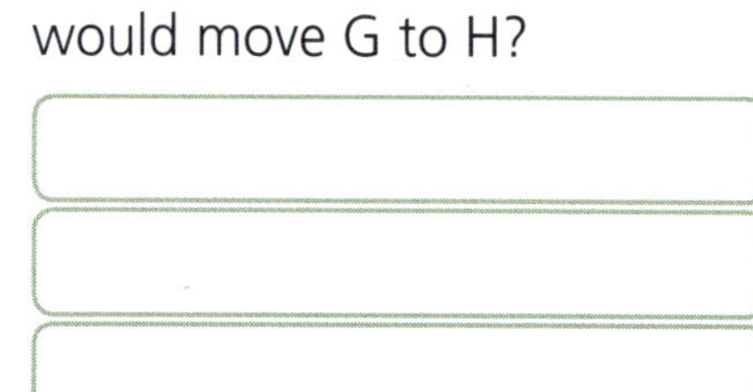

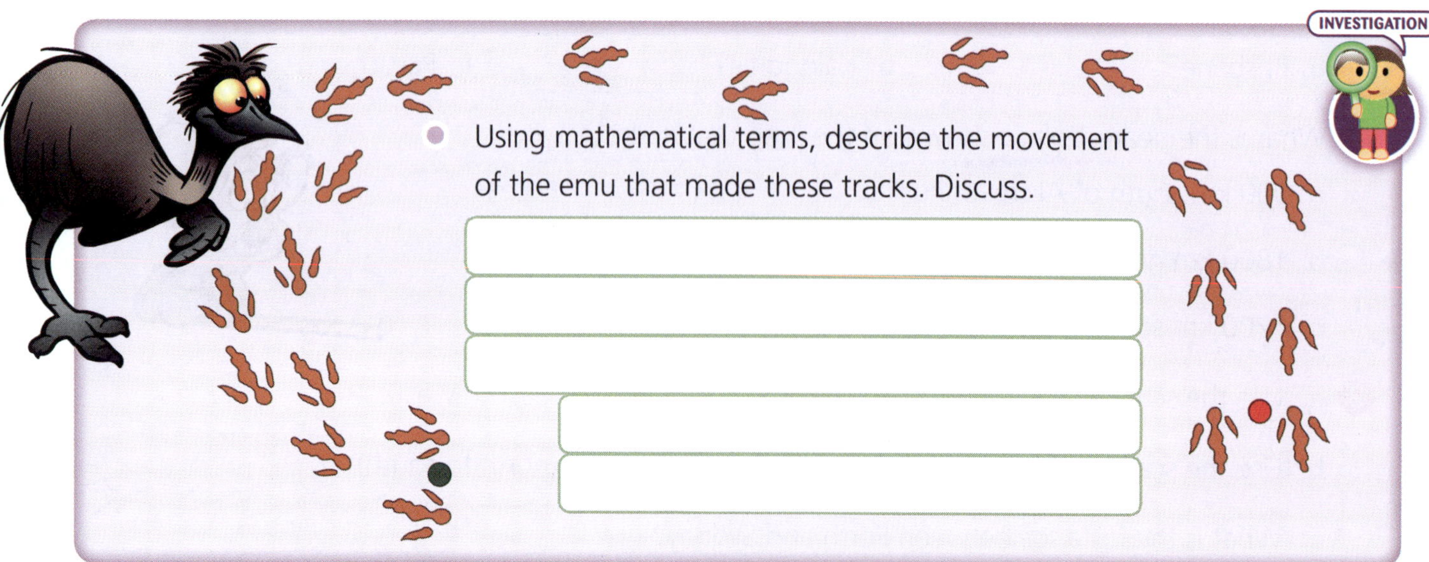

- Using mathematical terms, describe the movement of the emu that made these tracks. Discuss.

 • *AUSTRALIAN SIGNPOST MATHS 5* • ISBN 9780655708797

Using angles

Estimate the size of angles around you.

1 Use a protractor to draw the pair of acute angles at the left, and then right, of each end of the line. Extend the angle arms until the angles meet. What is the closest letter to their point of intersection?

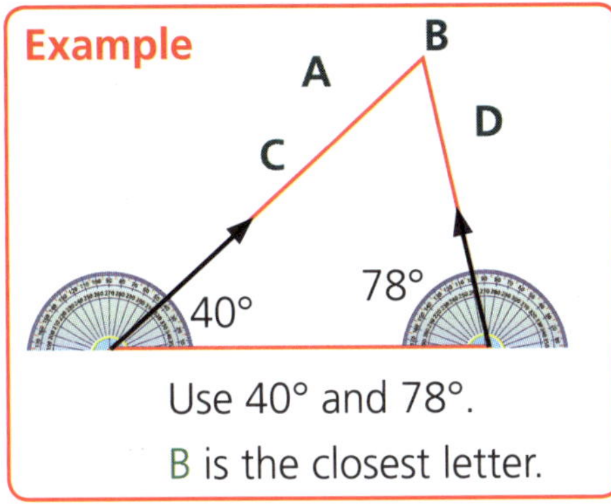

Use 40° and 78°.
B is the closest letter.

a 30° and 30° ☐

b 40° and 60° ☐

c 45° and 35° ☐

d 20° and 82° ☐

e 54° and 37° ☐

2 Draw a triangle that has a base of 4 cm and base angles of:

a 45° and 30°

b 20° and 75°

c 50° and 88°

3 **Triangulation**

1 My brother and I could see our sister.

2 We stood 100 metres apart (100 mm on our diagram). We each drew a line on the ground from our position towards our sister. We measured the angles we had made with the road. I measured 43°. Joe measured 45°.

3 We drew those angles on our diagram and extended the angle arms to find out where she was.
Our sister will be where the lines intersect.

4 Once we knew where she was, we measured (on our diagram) her distance from the road in millimetres. The real distance will be the same number, written as metres (53 m).

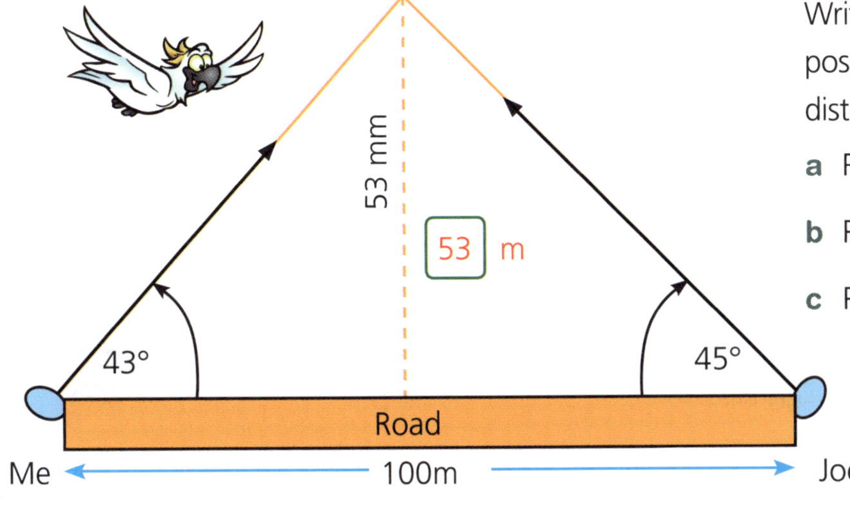

Write letters on this diagram to show the position of each place, and calculate its distance to the road.

a Place A: 70°, 40°. ☐ m to the road

b Place B: 25°, 35°. ☐ m to the road

c Place C: 43°, 57°. ☐ m to the road

5:01 Reading graphs

We may have to estimate when one unit stands for many.

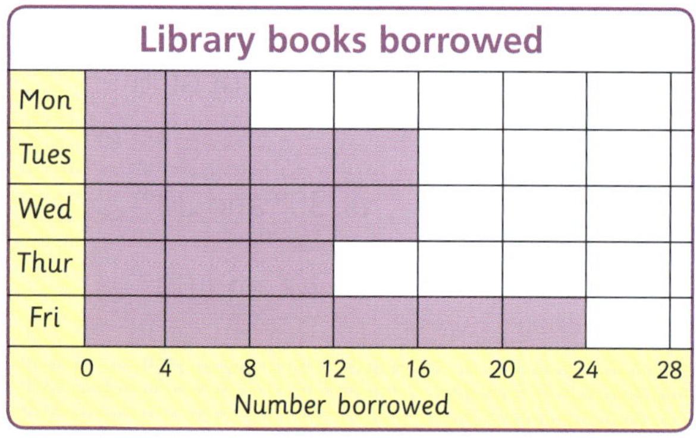

1 a How many books were borrowed on Thursday?

b On what day was the least number of books borrowed?

c On what days were the same number borrowed?

d One rectangle represents how many borrowed books? Scale: 1 unit =

e What was the total number of books borrowed during this week?

f Why would more books be borrowed on Friday?

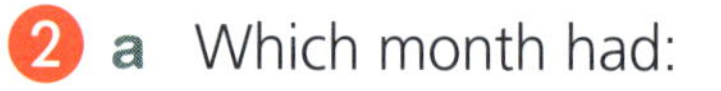

2 a Which month had:

i most sales?

ii least sales?

b How many sales occurred in:

i summer (Dec, Jan, Feb)?

ii autumn?

iii winter? iv spring?

v the first half of the year? vi the second half of the year?

c What was the total number of cars sold in the year?

Sale of cars

50, 40, 30, 20, 10, 0

Jan, Feb, Mar, Apr, May, Jun, Jul, Aug, Sep, Oct, Nov, Dec

Month of the year

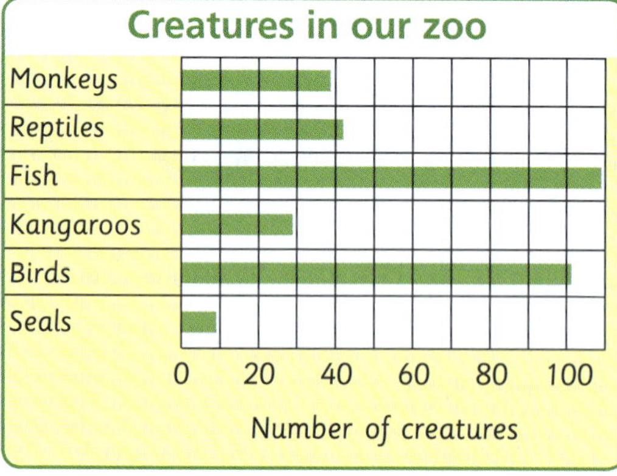

3 a Is it easy to tell the numbers of each creature?

b Give answers, correct to the nearest ten, for the approximate number of:

i monkeys ii fish

iii birds iv seals

c What is the approximate number of creatures in our zoo altogether?

d Why do you think there are more fish and birds in the zoo?

Noughts and Crosses

4 To win at Noughts and Crosses using a four-by-four grid you need three in a line, across, down or diagonally.

How many ways are there to get three in a line?

		O	
	O		
O			
	X	X	X

Drawing graphs

These are column graphs.

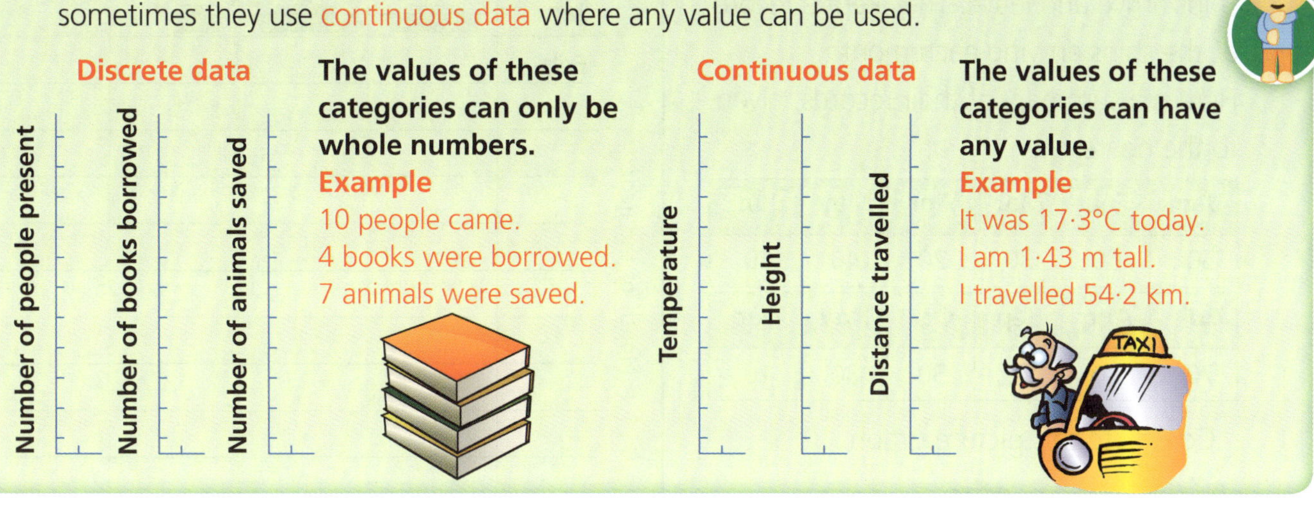

1 Year 5 teacher, Mrs Foster, had to choose three project topics for her class to do. She asked the librarian how many books covered each topic. The librarian, Mrs McSeveny, found that there were 6 books on wheat, 16 on wool, 4 on clouds, 13 on convicts, 18 on whales, 2 on ants and 8 on bees.

a Draw a column graph of this information.

b Which three topics do you think Mrs Foster would choose? Give a reason for your answer.

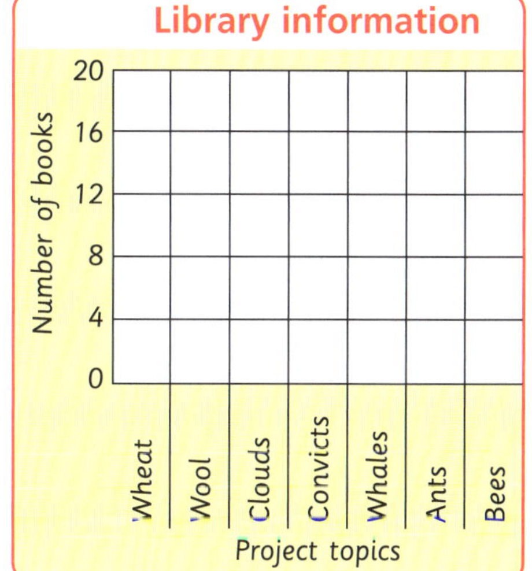

2 A tourist agency asked 2000 people to give the main method of travel they used when going on their last holiday.

They recorded the following responses:

bus: 334; ship: 240; car: 748; plane: 121; train: 517.

Some people said that they had never had a holiday away from their home.

a Complete the graph to show the types of holiday travel. (Estimate, as best you can, the height for each column.)

b How many people had never had a holiday away from home? (You can use a calculator.)

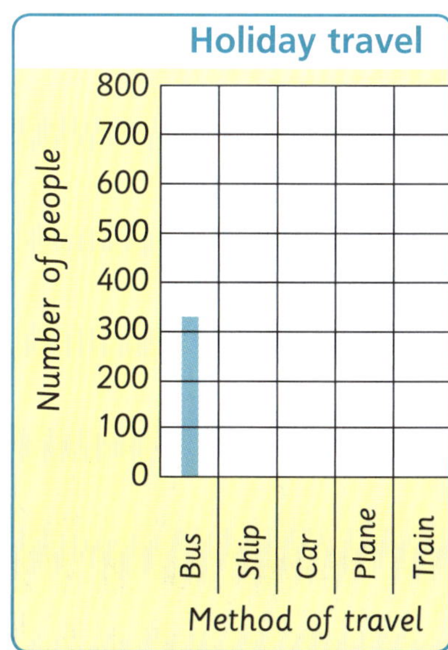

3 **a** Is the data used in Question 1 discrete or continuous?

b Is the data used in Question 2 discrete or continuous?

Drawing picture graphs

The symbol used for the key needs to be easily made into parts.

1 Elizabeth and Amber loved to watch the ships arrive and leave. They kept a record of the ships arriving each month.
Here is a summary of their records, given to the nearest ten.

Jan	Feb	Mar	Apr	May	Jun
50	60	30	20	40	60

Jul	Aug	Sep	Oct	Nov	Dec
70	80	60	50	30	10

Complete this picture graph.

Use this key:  = 20 ships

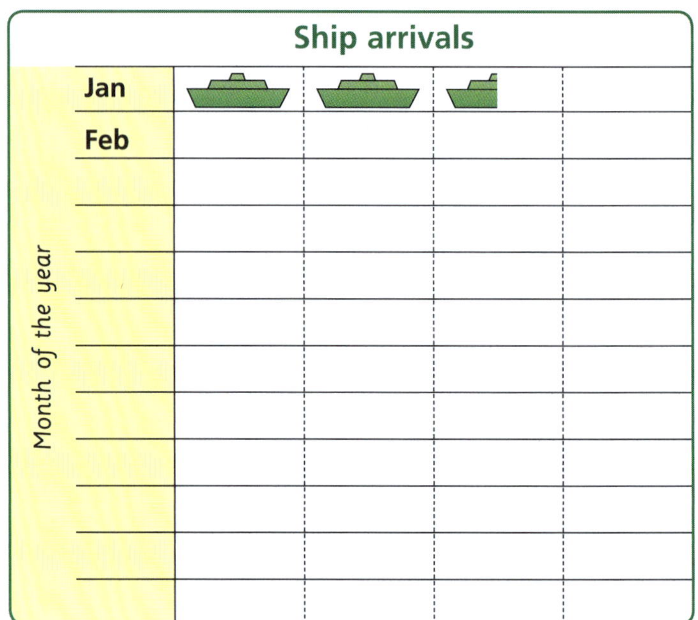

2 Use the information on the column graph to complete the picture graph on the right.

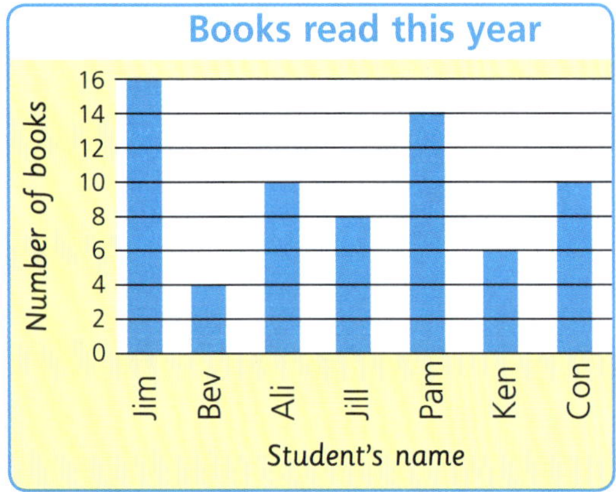

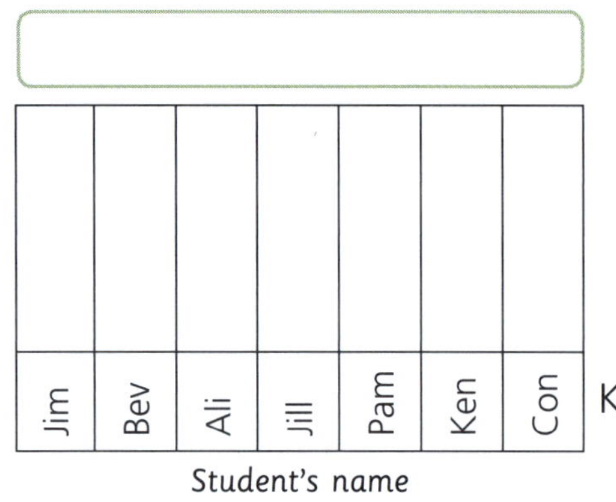

Key: = 4 books

Which type of graph do you think is the best for this data? Why?

3 Ms Travers, the Year 5 teacher, gave stamps for good bookwork.
She kept a tally of the stamps given to her six best students.
Fill in the **Total** column in the tally below.
Use this information to complete the picture graph on the right.

Name	Tally	Total
Alana	卌 卌 卌 卌 卌 |||	
Rachel	卌 卌 卌 卌 ||	
Naomi	卌 卌 卌 卌 卌 卌 卌 卌	
Luke	卌 卌 卌 卌 卌 卌	
Heather	卌 卌 卌 卌 卌 卌 卌		
Sandy	卌 卌 卌 卌 卌 卌 ||	

Stamps for bookwork

Alana	★ ★ ★
Rachel	
Naomi	
Luke	
Heather	
Sandy	

Key: ★ = 10 stamps
= 2 stamps

 • *AUSTRALIAN SIGNPOST MATHS 5* • ISBN 9780655708797

You could give each person a slip of paper, or let them read the questions and tell you their choices.

Survey/questionnaire

1 How often do you watch sport?
(Tick one response.)

- a lot ☐
- often ☐
- sometimes ☐
- not at all ☐

2 Which activity do you like most?
(Tick one response.)

- playing sport ☐
- reading books ☐
- walking ☐
- watching sport ☐

5M filled out this survey and kept this tally.

Category	Tally
1 a lot	卌
often	卌 卌 |
sometimes	卌 |||
not at all	|||
2 playing sport	卌 卌
reading books	卌 ||
walking	卌 |
watching sport	||||

When categories are used, the data is called categorical data.

1 In response to Question 1, how many students:

a ticked *often*? ☐ **b** ticked *not at all*? ☐

c did not tick *a lot*? ☐

2 **a** Which activity in **2** was selected seven times? ☐

b What was the most popular activity listed in **2**? ☐

c Which category was selected least in **1**? ☐

3 Use the results from the survey above to complete these column graphs.

a **Frequency of watching sport by 5M**

	0	2	4	6	8	10
a lot						
often						
sometimes						
not at all						

b **Activities chosen by 5M**

	0	2	4	6	8	10
playing sport						
reading books						
walking						
watching sport						

4 Use the survey above to conduct your own survey. Record your results on the table provided and complete your own graphs on the right.

- Which were the most popular categories in your survey? ☐ ☐

My investigation

Category	Tally
1 a lot	
often	
sometimes	
not at all	
2 playing sport	
reading books	
walking	
watching sport	

Frequency of watching sport

	0	2	4	6	8	10
a lot						
often						
sometimes						
not at all						

Activities chosen

	0	2	4	6	8	10
playing sport						
reading books						
walking						
watching sport						

Choosing at random

At random: Each ball is just as likely to be chosen.

CONCEPT

When we choose so that each item has the same chance of being selected, it is called a random choice.

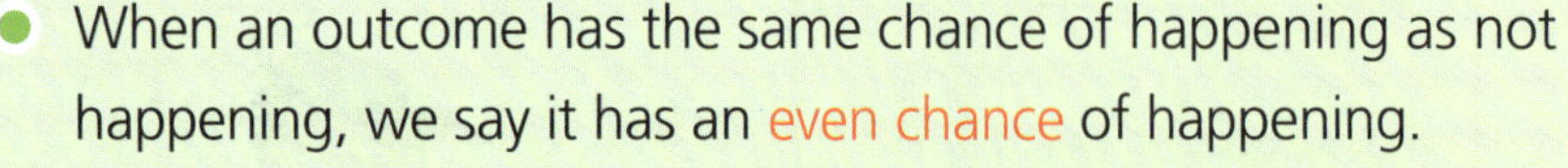

- When an outcome has the same chance of happening as not happening, we say it has an even chance of happening.
- When two or more outcomes have the same chance of happening, we say they have an equal chance of happening.

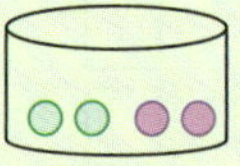

an even chance of being chosen

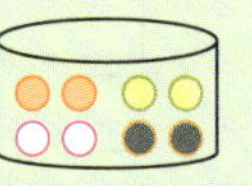

an equal chance of being chosen

Categories:

impossible, unlikely, even chance, likely, certain

1. Use the categories above to describe the chance that the boy will choose:
   - **a** a black peg ______ **b** a red peg ______
   - **c** a blue peg ______ **d** a coloured peg ______
2. Which colour has an even chance of being chosen? ______
3. Which colour has the least chance of being chosen? ______
4. We decided to toss a dice to decide which one of these six movies we would watch. We gave each movie one of the numbers found on the dice (**1** Mary Poppins, **2** Sound of Music, **3** Toy Story, **4** Matilda, **5** Annie, **6** Frozen).
   We now toss the dice and watch the movie that has that number.
   - **a** Are we choosing the movie at random? ______
   - **b** Are all movies equally likely to be chosen? ______
   - **c** Is there an even chance of watching a movie that has a girl's name in the title? ______
5. What does it mean, 'to choose at random'? ______

FUN SPOT

Rules: Place your counter on 'Start'. Toss a dice once. Follow the instructions to find where you end up.

- Read the directions on the game. On how many spaces can you end up? ______
- Which is the space you are most likely to end on? ______
- Play the game 10 times. Is it possible to end on 5, ten times in a row? ______ Is this likely? ______

Start	1 Move 1 space forward.	2	3 Move 1 space back.	4 Move 2 spaces back.	5	6 Move 1 space back.

 • *AUSTRALIAN SIGNPOST MATHS 5* • ISBN 9780655708797

5:06 Fair or unfair?

List the outcomes if a fair dice is tossed.

CONCEPT

A game is said to be fair if the chance of success is the same for all players.

- The rules should give each player the same chance of success.

Example

Each player tosses a dice. The player who tosses the highest number wins. If players toss the same number, they continue tossing until one throws a higher number than the other.

Is this game fair or unfair?

1 Tossing a dice

a I win if a 6 is tossed. You win if a 1 is tossed. Is this a fair game?

b I win if the number is 3 or more.
You win if the number is less than 3. Is this a fair game?

2 A dice has the numbers 1, 2 and 3 stuck on its 6 faces.
All 6 sides of the dice are shown in the diagrams on the right.

a Which number has the best chance of being tossed?

b Is there an even chance that a 3 will be tossed?

c Is there an equal chance that a 1, 2 and 3 will be tossed?

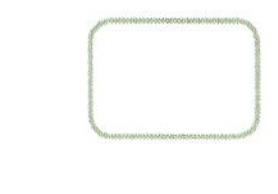

d Ben wins if 1 is tossed. Jim wins if 2 is tossed. I win if 3 is tossed. Is this a fair game?

e Would 1 and 2 have an equal chance of being tossed?

Explain your answer.

3 When an old penny is tossed, there is an even chance of a head or a tail. When two pennies are tossed, we could get 2 heads, 2 tails, or a head and a tail. Naomi wins if 2 heads are tossed, Luke wins if two tails are tossed, and Alana wins if a head and a tail are tossed. Toss two coins 50 times to see if this is fair. Is it fair or unfair?

CONCEPT

Competitive games

- The rules of a game may be fair, but the strategy used by each player and their skill at playing the game are far more likely to determine the outcome than chance.
- Even though I have played tennis for years, I would have little chance of beating a professional tennis player.
- Games depending purely on chance can be called fair or unfair, but the terms do not apply to games of skill. We use the term 'unfair' in these games only if someone is breaking the rules.

5:07 Comparing the chances

one half

one sixth

Am I more likely to toss a head on a coin or throw a 5 on a dice?

- There is one chance out of two that I will toss a head on a coin.
  I am likely to do this half of the time.
- There is one chance out of six that I will toss a five on a dice.
  I am likely to do this one sixth of the time.

Which is more likely?

1. I must choose one of Blinky's cards at random (without looking).
   Is it ***impossible***, ***unlikely***, an ***even chance***, ***likely*** or ***certain*** that I will choose:
   - **a** the number 3?
   - **b** a number less than 4?
   - **c** the number 1?
   - **d** the number 2?

2. **a** If I choose one of Blinky's cards at random, what number is more likely to be chosen?
   b If I choose two of Blinky's cards, what two numbers do you think are more likely to be chosen, two twos or a two and a three? ____ and ____
   c Take two twos and one three from a pack of cards. Shuffle these and choose two at random. Repeat this 20 times, keeping a tally of the results as you go. What outcome occurred more, two twos or a two and a three? ____ and ____

Numbers	Tally	Total
2, 2		
2, 3		

3. If a six is tossed on a dice, one point is earned. The first to roll 3 sixes wins.
   Jo and Mia take turns, but Mia goes first. Mia always tosses one dice. Jo always tosses two dice.
   a Who do you think has the better chance of winning?
   Why?
   b Play this game 3 times. How many times would Jo have won?

4. The supermarket gives me a domino each time I shop.
   This domino is given to me at random, being one of twenty-one possible dominos.
   a Would it be likely that my second domino would be the same as my first?
   b Once I have 18 different dominos, would it be likely that the next domino the supermarket gives me is one that I have not got?

 • *AUSTRALIAN SIGNPOST MATHS 5* • ISBN 9780655708797

Dot plots

The mode is the score that occurred the most.

Scores:
1, 2, 2, 2, 1, 4
The mode is 2.

CONCEPT

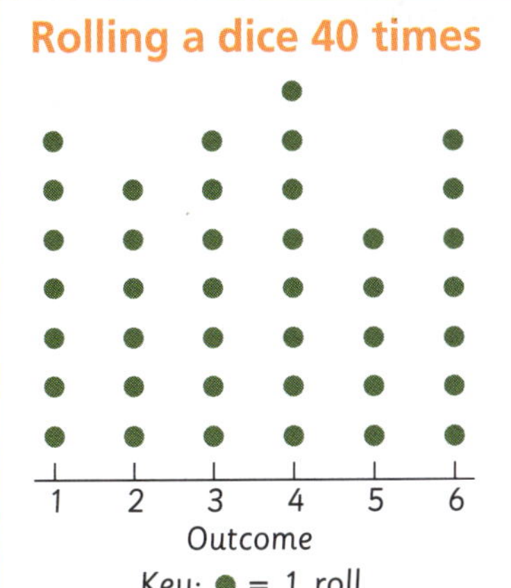

- This is a **dot plot**.
- Here, one dot has been drawn for each roll.
- 4 was rolled 8 times.
- When a dice is rolled, the possible outcomes are 1, 2, 3, 4, 5, and 6.
- The mode is ☐.

Do these results support the idea that each number on a dice is equally likely? ☐

Explain why.

1 Two dice were rolled 25 times. The totals are shown here.

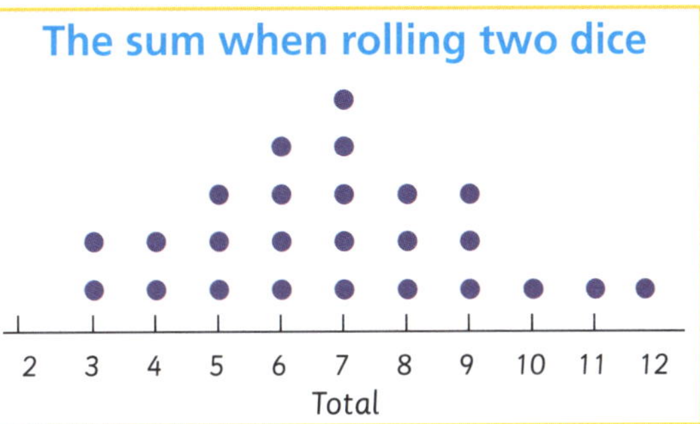

a Which total occurred most often? ☐

b Why is this?

2

Test results: 5M

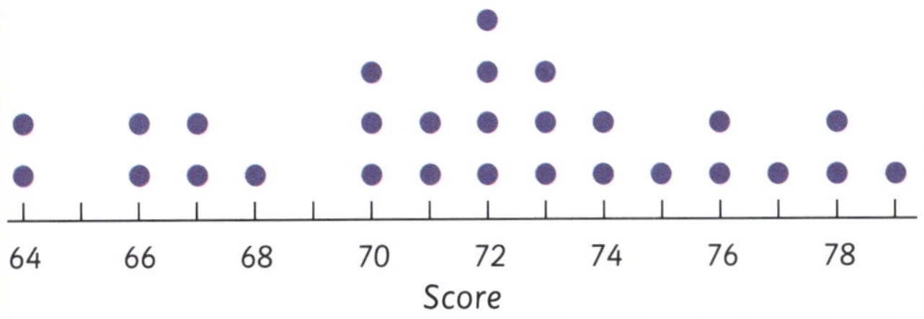

(Dot plot — Score axis 64 to 79, labelled 64, 66, 68, 70, 72, 74, 76, 78)

Score

a What is the mode of these scores? ☐

b The scores of the bottom quarter of the class were from ☐ to ☐.

c The scores of the middle half of the class were from ☐ to ☐.

d Use the dot plot to complete the table.

Test results: 5M																
Score	64	65	66	67	68	69	70	71	72	73	74	75	76	77	78	79
Number																

3 a Show the data below on this dot plot.

Finger widths (in cm) of students in 5M

2·0 1·8 2·0 1·7 2·1 1·8 2·1 1·7 2·2
1·6 2·0 1·5 1·7 1·6 2·0 1·9 2·1 1·7

b This data has two modes (two scores that share the highest score).

The two modes are ☐ and ☐.

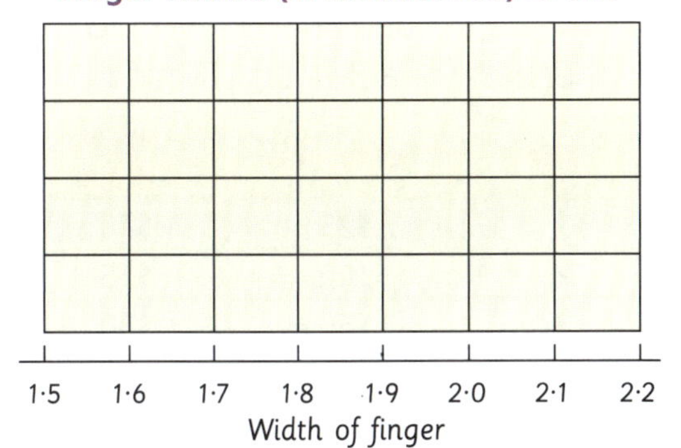

More line graphs

The vertical axis in each question uses continuous data.

1 Andy planted lawn seeds and graphed the growth at the end of each day for 14 days.

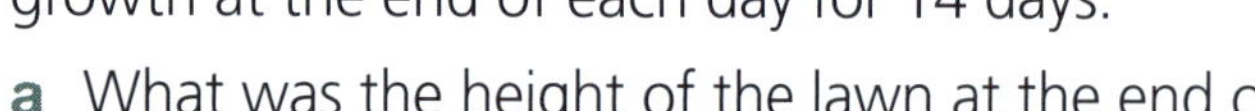

a What was the height of the lawn at the end of:

i day 7? ☐ ii day 2? ☐

iii day 14? ☐ iv day 13? ☐

b On what day was the height:

i 2 cm? ☐ ii 9 cm? ☐

iii 9·5 cm? ☐ iv 6 cm? ☐

c When did Andy first see the lawn? ☐

d On which day was the growth the greatest? ☐

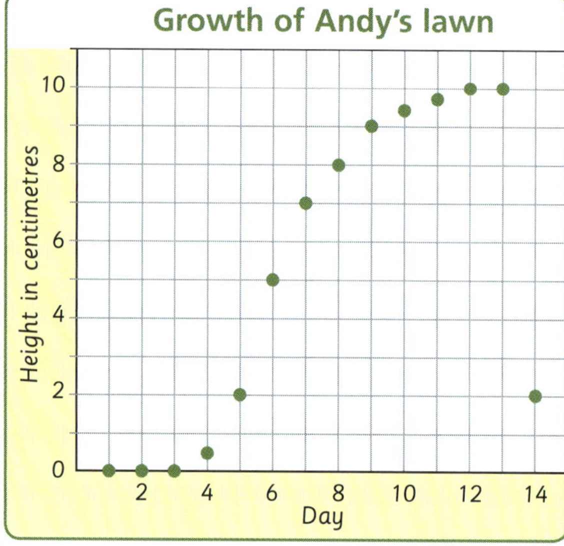

e By joining the dots, draw a line graph.

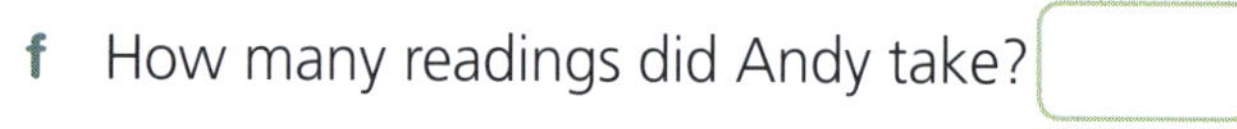

f How many readings did Andy take? ☐

g On which day did he mow the lawn? ☐

h On which day was the height 4 cm? ☐

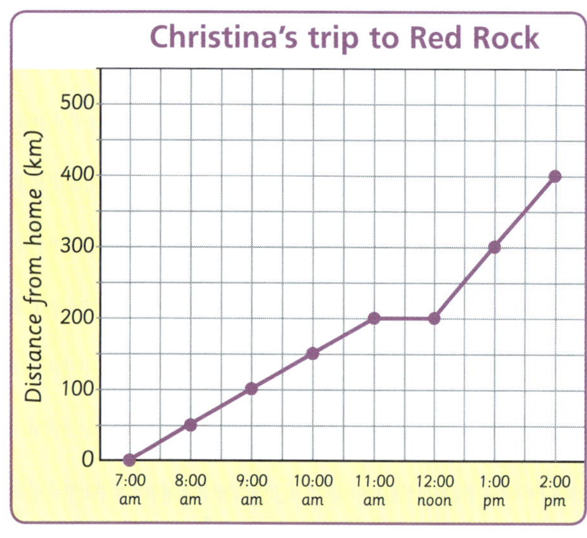

2 Christina left home early to travel on a straight road to Red Rock. This graph shows her progress.

a When did she leave home? ☐

b How far was she from home at:

i 9:00 am? ☐ ii 10:00 am? ☐

iii 1:00 pm? ☐ iv 2:00 pm? ☐

v 11:00 am? ☐ vi 12 noon? ☐

c When did she stop for lunch? ☐

d How long did she take for lunch? ☐

e How far did she travel between 10:00 am and 11:00 am? ☐

f How far did she travel between 12 noon and 1:00 pm? ☐

INVESTIGATION

3 Rhonda needed an electrician to fix her stove. Use the table to decide which quote is cheapest for a 3-hour, 15-min or $1\frac{1}{2}$-hour job.

Quote	Fee to arrive	Cost per 15 min	Cost for parts to be replaced	a 3-hour job	b 15-min job	c $1\frac{1}{2}$-hour job
1	$25	$40	$80			
2	$100	$15	$115			
3	$50	$30	$70			

The cheapest quote would be: a ☐ b ☐ c ☐

 • *AUSTRALIAN SIGNPOST MATHS 5* • ISBN 9780655708797

Reading line graphs

The conversion graphs use continuous data on both axes.

1 Leslie measured the mass of different amounts of sugar and graphed her findings. She joined the points to get this line graph.

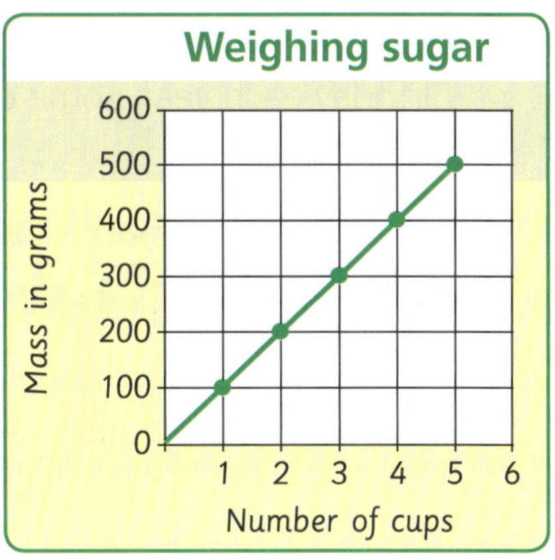

a What is the mass of:

i 2 cups? ☐ **ii** 4 cups? ☐

iii $1\frac{1}{2}$ cups? ☐ **iv** $3\frac{1}{2}$ cups? ☐

b How many cups of sugar have a mass of:

i 300 g? ☐ **ii** 500 g? ☐

iii 100 g? ☐ **iv** 50 g? ☐

c What would be the mass of 6 cups of sugar? ☐

We can often extend a line graph to gain further information.

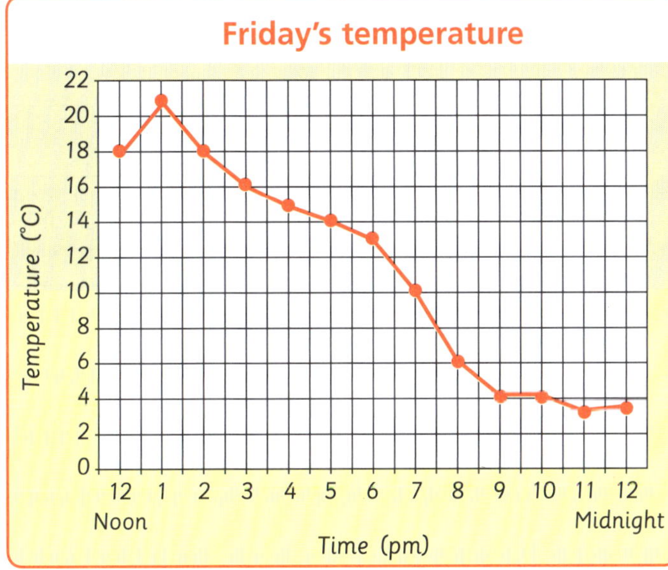

2 On Friday, Jasmine recorded the temperature every hour from noon until midnight. She then drew this graph.

a What was the temperature at:

i 2 pm? ☐ **ii** 11 pm? ☐

b What was the highest temperature recorded? What was the time then?

☐

c At what time was it:

i 10°C? ☐ **ii** 18°C? ☐

d Estimate the temperature at:

i 2:30 pm ☐ **ii** 7:30 pm ☐

iii 8:30 pm ☐ **iv** 10:30 pm ☐

Be cool, be cool!

Because the temperature changes steadily, we can estimate the temperature at other times.

Conversion graph: hours – minutes

Hours: 0, 1, 2, 3, 4, 5

Minutes: 60, 120, 180, 240, 300

3 We can change 2 hours to minutes by following the arrows shown on the graph. We could change 120 minutes to hours by coming back the other way.

a Use the graph to convert these into minutes.

i 5 hours ☐ **ii** 3 hours ☐

iii $1\frac{1}{2}$ hours ☐ **iv** $4\frac{1}{2}$ hours ☐

b Use the graph to convert these to hours.

i 180 minutes ☐ **ii** 240 minutes ☐ **iii** 150 minutes ☐ **iv** 270 minutes ☐

5:11 Drawing line graphs

In Questions 1 and 2, elapsed time is shown on the horizontal axis (the one going across).

1 Alan's parents measured his height on his birthday each year. Some of those measurements are shown below.

Alan's height

0 years	2 years	4 years	6 years	8 years
50 cm	90 cm	100 cm	120 cm	130 cm

10 years	12 years	14 years	16 years	18 years
140 cm	150 cm	170 cm	175 cm	180 cm

Alan's height

Height in centimetres: 0, 20, 40, 60, 80, 100, 120, 140, 160, 180, 200

Age in years: 0, 2, 4, 6, 8, 10, 12, 14, 16, 18

a Draw a line graph for these facts.

b Use the graph to estimate Alan's height at:

i 1 year ______ **ii** 5 years ______ **iii** 13 years ______ **iv** 11 years ______

c Six months before birth, Alan's height was 10 cm. Show this on the graph.

2 Redraw this column graph as a line graph.

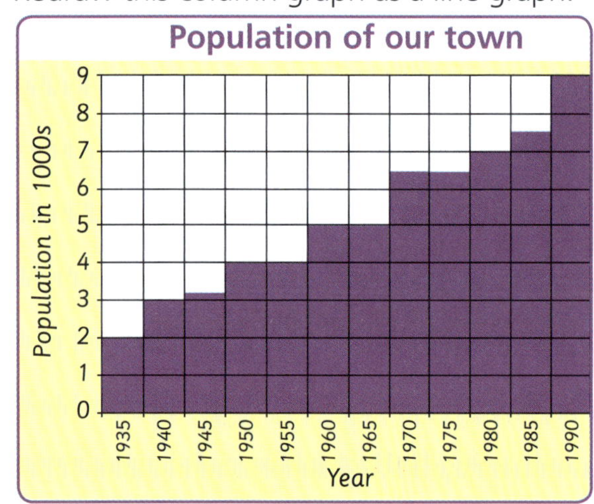

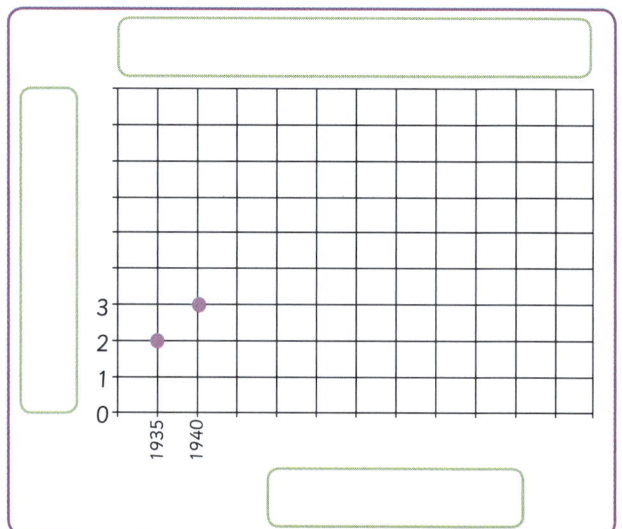

3 To draw a conversion graph we need two points. We then join these with a straight line.

0 acres = 0 hectares	40 acres = 16 hectares

a Use the information above to draw the graph.

b Use your graph to convert these to hectares.

i 20 acres ______ **ii** 15 acres ______

c Use your graph to convert these to acres.

i 12 hectares ______ **ii** 2 hectares ______

d Which is greater:

i 15 acres or 7 hectares? ______

ii 6 hectares or 16 acres? ______

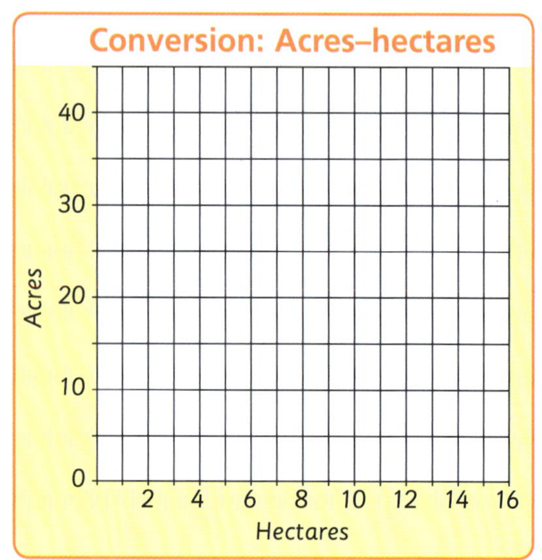

Matching graphs with stories

These graphs use percentages on the vertical axis.

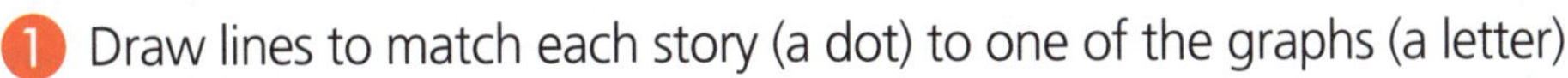

1 Draw lines to match each story (a dot) to one of the graphs (a letter).

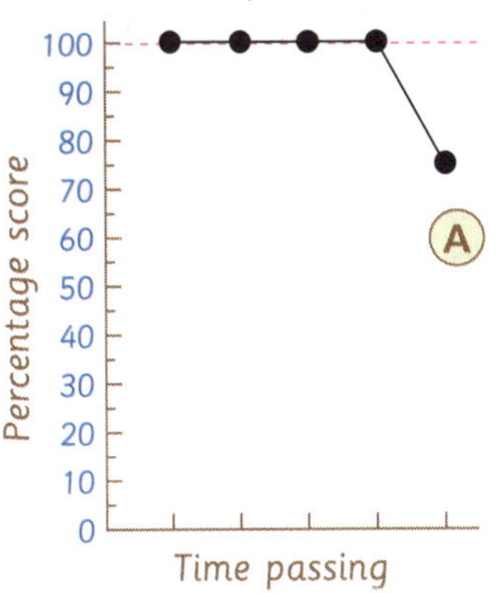

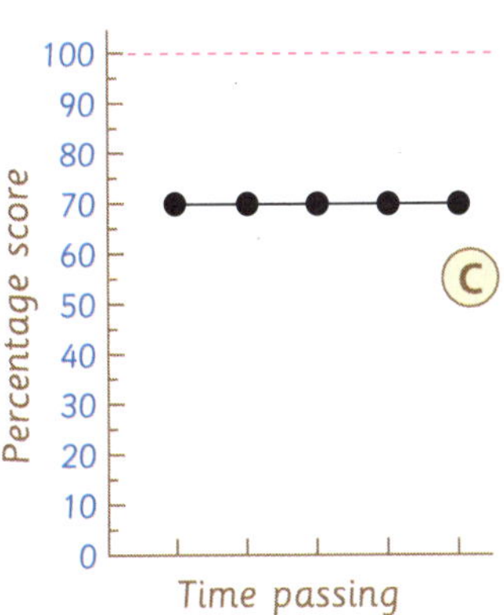

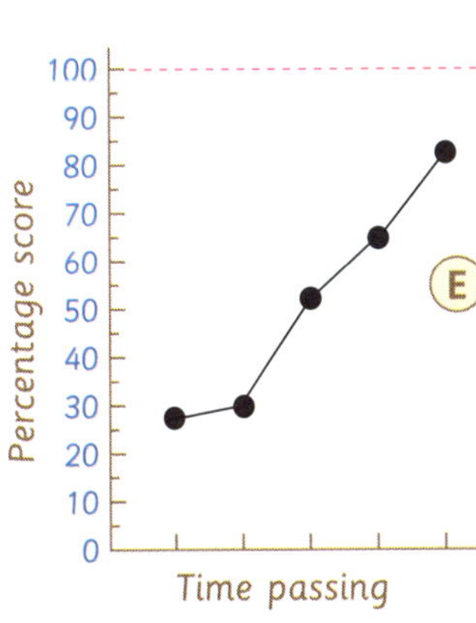

Stories

For five weeks, one after the other, I scored the same score for my writing assignment.

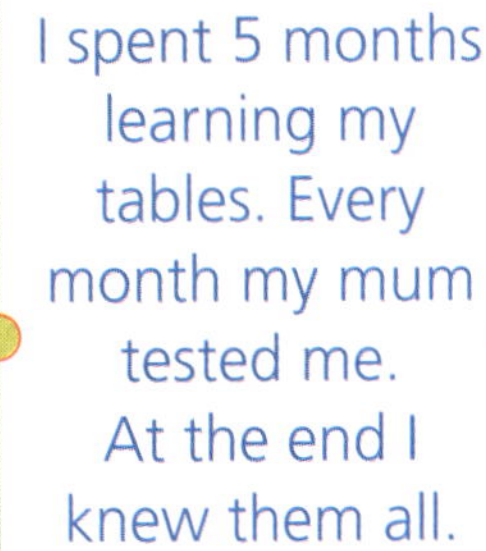

I spent 5 months learning my tables. Every month my mum tested me. At the end I knew them all.

I knew the name of 100 students in my year at school. I moved away and each year my memory faded.

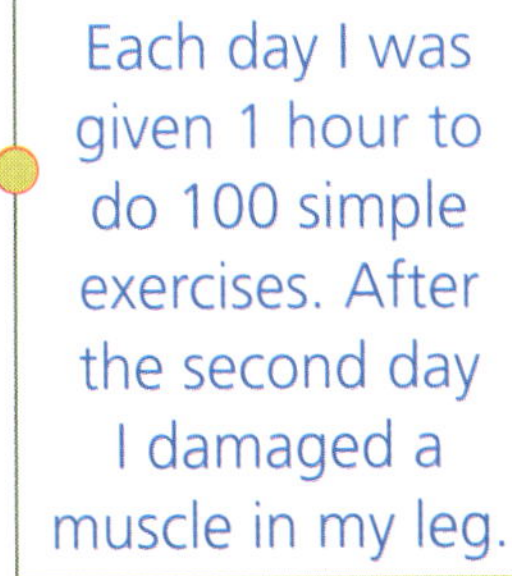

Each day I was given 1 hour to do 100 simple exercises. After the second day I damaged a muscle in my leg.

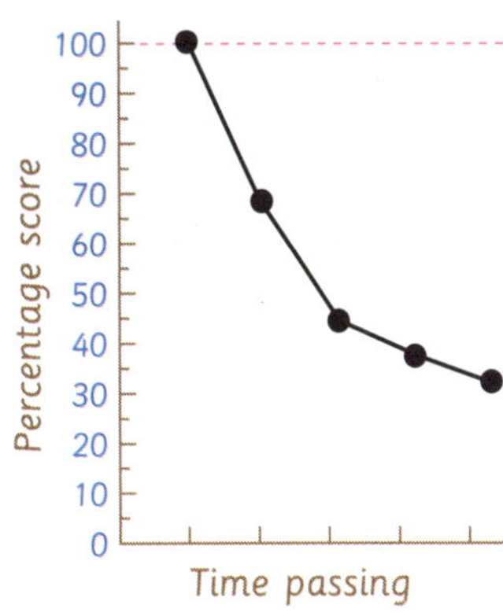

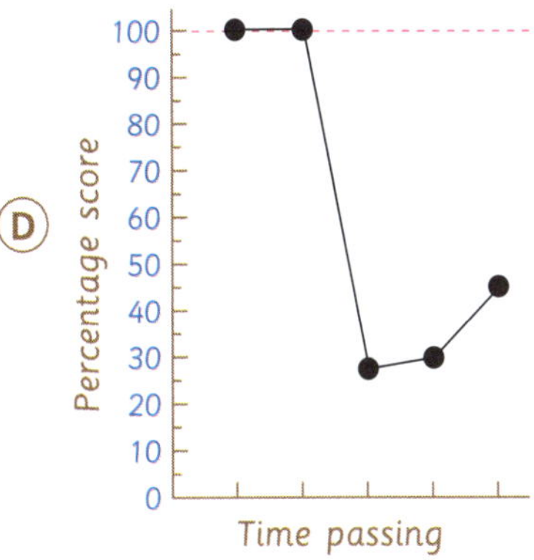

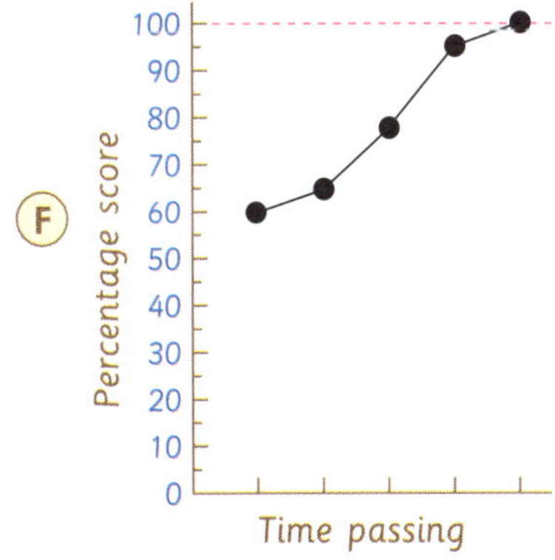

2 Write stories to match the two unmatched graphs in Question 1.

- Graph ◯:
- Graph ◯:

5:13 Chance, as a fraction

The total of the probabilities of the outcomes equals one.

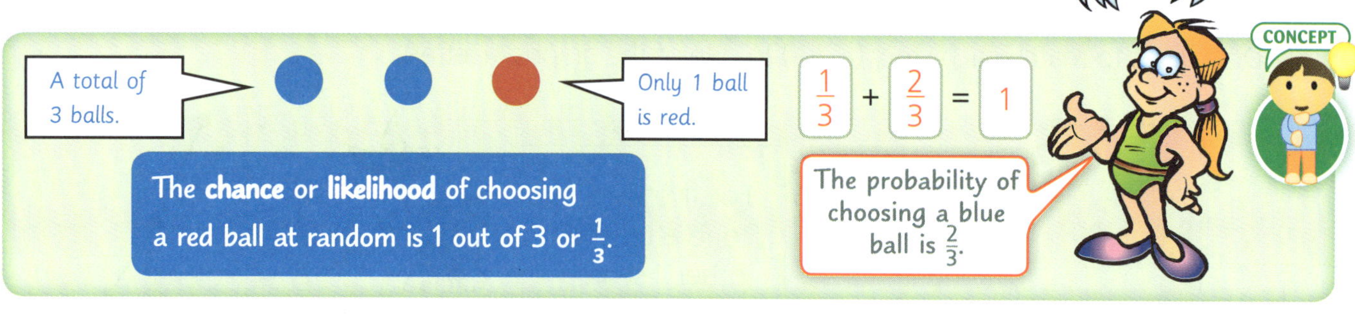

The **chance** or **likelihood** of choosing a red ball at random is 1 out of 3 or $\frac{1}{3}$.

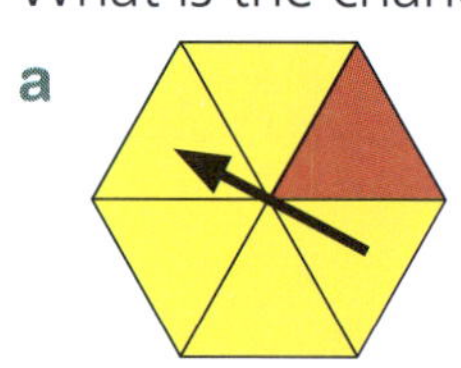
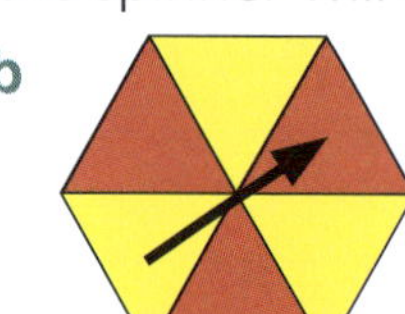

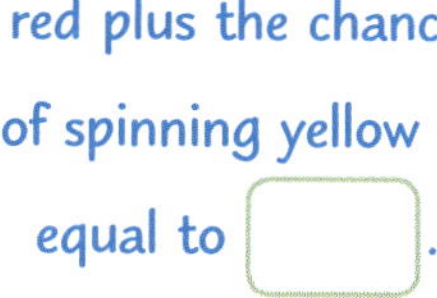

1 What is the chance, as a fraction, that the spinner will stop on:

a red? ☐ yellow? ☐

b red? ☐ yellow? ☐

c red? ☐ yellow? ☐

d red? ☐ yellow? ☐

In Question 1, the chance of spinning red plus the chance of spinning yellow is equal to ☐.

2 What is the likelihood, as a fraction, that the dice will show:

a 1? ☐ b 6? ☐ c 5? ☐

d 3? ☐ e an even number? ☐

3 What is the chance, as a fraction, that the spinner will stop on:

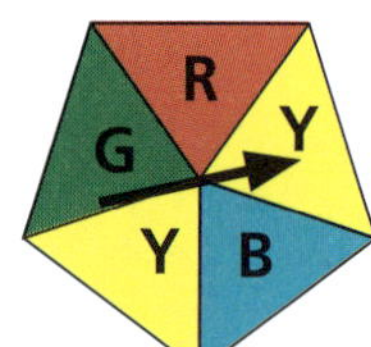
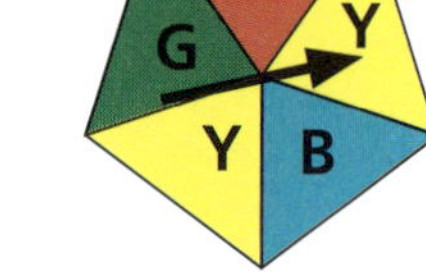

a red? ☐ b yellow? ☐ c green? ☐

d blue? ☐ e yellow or blue? ☐

4 The spinner is divided into ten equal sectors.
What is the chance (written as a fraction) of spinning:

a R ☐ b B ☐ c O ☐ d G ☐

5 What is the chance, as a fraction, that a ball drawn at random from the bag will be:

a red? ☐ b yellow? ☐ c blue? ☐ d red or green? ☐

e green? ☐ f not red? ☐ g not blue? ☐ h red or blue? ☐

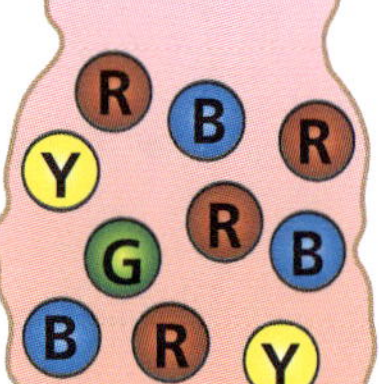

Chance

The chance of throwing a 5 is $\frac{1}{6}$,
but I haven't thrown a 5 in twenty throws.

1 Joey collected the 15 toys above. He will choose one at random.
What is the chance (written as a fraction) that he will choose:

a a standing soldier? ☐ **b** a knight on a horse or a nurse? ☐

c a knight on a horse? ☐ **d** a nurse or a standing soldier? ☐

e a toy? ☐ **f** a ball? ☐ **g** a nurse? ☐

A probability of $\frac{1}{15}$ means that there is one chance in 15 of choosing that outcome.

2 20 coloured pegs were placed in a paper bag as shown.

a Which colour is most likely to be drawn from the bag? ☐

b Which colour is least likely to be drawn from the bag? ☐

c Are we more likely to draw a blue peg or a red peg? ☐

d Order the colours from least likely to be selected, to most likely.

☐

6 blue, 9 green, 2 red, 3 yellow

Write as a fraction, the chance of choosing a peg that is:

e yellow ☐ **f** green ☐ **g** red ☐ **h** blue ☐

3 Rohan and Aminah played a dice game. Each threw two dice. Rohan won if the difference between the numbers on the dice was zero. Aminah won if the difference was 1.

a Who do you think will win more often? ☐ Is the game fair? ☐

Why or why not? ☐

b Play this game 20 times. Do your results agree with your answers above? ☐

FUN SPOT

4 What has this chance of being chosen from the bag?

a $\frac{1}{2}$ ☐

b 1 ☐

c $\frac{5}{40}$ ☐

d 0 ☐

e $\frac{10}{40}$ ☐

In this bag are 40 metal figures:
5 toy soldiers
20 convicts
5 nurses
10 farmers

5:15 Collecting chance data

Unequal chances?

1 Elena tossed a coin many times.

She kept this tally of the results.

	Throwing a coin	Total
Heads	𝍸 ||||	
Tails	𝍸 𝍸		

a How many times did she toss the coin? ☐

b What fraction of the time did she toss:

i a head? ☐ ii a tail? ☐

2 If two coins are tossed we could get two heads, two tails, or a head and a tail.

a Toss two coins 40 times. Record the results.

b Which result occurred most often?

c What fraction of the time did you toss:

		Total
Two heads		
Two tails		
Head and tail		

i two heads? ☐ ii two tails? ☐ iii a head and a tail? ☐

To take a counter **at random** from a bag means to take a counter without looking.

3 5 red counters, 3 blue counters and 1 yellow counter are placed in a bag.

A counter is chosen at random from the bag.

What is the chance (as a fraction) that it will be:

I'm not looking.

a red? ☐ b blue? ☐ c yellow? ☐

d Put 1 yellow, 3 blue and 5 red counters into a container.
- Take a counter.
- Record its colour.
- Return the counter to the container.

Do this many times.

Keep a tally of your results.

Red		
Blue		
Yellow		

What have you discovered?

CONCEPT

- If a fair coin has been tossed 19 times in a row and gets a head every time, what would be the chance of tossing a head on the 20th toss and why?
- Melbourne Storm played the Parramatta Eels in the first match of the 2023 NRL season. Melbourne Storm had won their first match in each of the previous 21 seasons. What do you think their chance of winning this match would be and why?

5:16 Collecting data

Work out the probability then see if what is expected actually happens.

1 Stickers were stuck on a dice so that the faces showed three 3s, two 5s and one 1. Write as a fraction the probability of rolling a:

a 3 ☐ **b** 5 ☐ **c** 1 ☐ **d** 6 ☐

e Which number would you expect to roll most often? ☐

2 Carry out the experiment in Question 1. Record your results in the table as you roll the dice 20 times.

a Which number was rolled most often? ☐

b What fraction of the time did you roll a:

i 3? ☐ **ii** 5? ☐ **iii** 1? ☐

Result	Tally	Total
1		
3		
5		

3 If you threw three coins 60 times, how often would you expect to throw three heads? ☐

Check your guess by carrying out the experiment.

Result	Tally	Total
No heads		
1 head		
2 heads		
3 heads		

4 A bag contains 20 lollies. They are wrapped in identical wrappings. There are 10 chocolates, 6 caramels, 3 candies and 1 licorice.

a If one lolly is taken at random from the bag, which type is:

i least likely to be chosen? ☐ **ii** most likely to be chosen? ☐

b Write as a fraction the chance of choosing a:

i chocolate ☐ **ii** caramel ☐ **iii** candy ☐ **iv** licorice ☐

5 Instead of using lollies, use counters (or cards) to carry out the experiment in Question 4.

- Mark 10 counters with an A, 6 with a B, 3 with a C and 1 with a D.
- Put these in a hat, choose one, record the result and then return it to the hat. Do this 60 times.
- Do you think this experiment is a good model of the one in Question 4? ☐

	Result	Tally	Total
A	Chocolate		
B	Caramel		
C	Candy		
D	Licorice		

6 **Dice soccer:** Two dice are rolled. The ball (a counter) is placed on start and is moved one place towards Goal A if the total is less than 7, and one place towards Goal B if 7 or more.

Who do you think should win? ☐

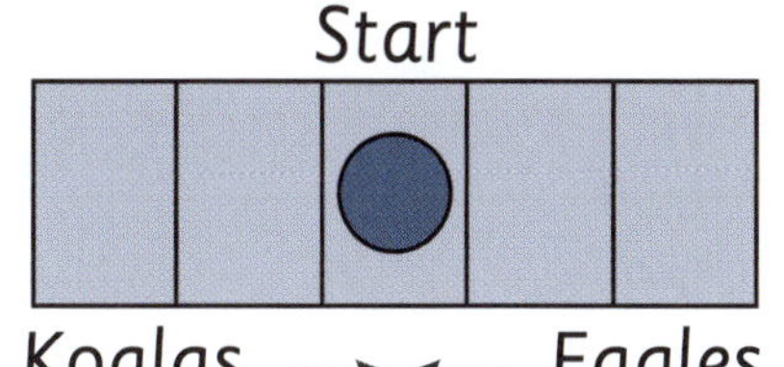

 • *AUSTRALIAN SIGNPOST MATHS 5* • ISBN 9780655708797

5:17 Data collected over time

Maximum means highest. Minimum means lowest.

1 **a** What was the maximum temperature for:

i Monday? ☐ **ii** Thursday? ☐

b What was the minimum temperature for:

i Monday? ☐ **ii** Wednesday? ☐

c On which day was the difference between the maximum and minimum greatest? ☐

Maximum and minimum temperatures

Degrees Celsius: 10, 12, 14, 16, 18, 20, 22

Day: Mon, Tue, Wed, Thu, Fri

Daily maximum

Daily minimum

2 Use the internet to find the maximum and minimum temperatures over 5 days.

a Record the temperatures in the table below.

	Mon	Tues	Wed	Thurs	Fri
Highest temp.					
Lowest temp.					

b Graph the results, as in Question 1.

c Describe and explain the results.

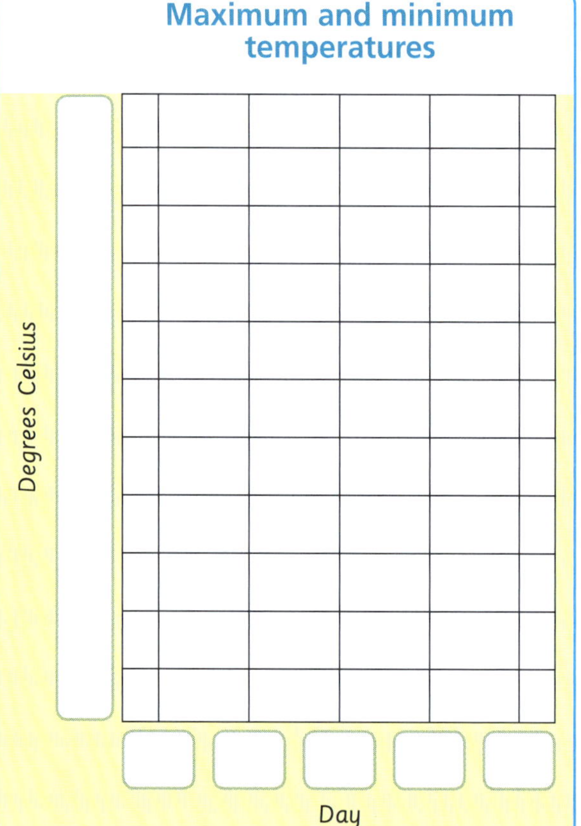

Insect diversity in the playground

INVESTIGATION

- Choose an area in the playground that has an insect population.
- Tape a 1-metre square border on the playground.
- Record the type and number of insects in the square at different times.

Time	Number of insects	Description of insects

Conclusions:

5:18 Data investigation

°C stands for degrees Celsius.
0°C is the freezing point of water.
100°C is the boiling point of water.

INVESTIGATION

1 Work in small groups to complete this investigation.

Step 1

Choose a topic to investigate.

Topic: How will the temperature change during the day?

Step 2

Decide when and how you will measure the changes.

When will the temperature be measured and how?

Step 3

Decide how you will record your measurements.

Time	Temperature	Comments

What do you expect to discover?

Step 4

Write down what you found and explain your conclusions.

Enter the results in a computer spreadsheet program such as Microsoft® Excel®.
Report on your results by using computer-generated graphs.

 • *AUSTRALIAN SIGNPOST MATHS 5* • ISBN 9780655708797

5:19 Using spreadsheets

The coordinates of the pink square are D6.

× 6 and × 7 tables

O	A	B	C	D	E	F	G	H	I	J
1	× 6 tables					× 7 tables				
2	1		6			1		7		
3	2		12			2		14		
4	3		18			3		21		
5	4		24			4		28		
6	5		30	(pink)		5		35		
7	6		36			6		42		
8	7		42			7		49		
9	8		48			8		56		
10	9		54			9		63		
11	10		60			10		70		
12	11		66			11		77		
13	12		72			12		84		
14				Test results					Test results	
15			× 6 tables	Test 1 23.4.24	Test 2 30.4.24			× 7 tables	Test 1 14.5.24	Test 2 21.5.24
16			Diane	8	12			Diane	7	12
17			Luke	10	12			Luke	9	12

1 These are the tables Diane and Luke were asked to learn. The spreadsheet shows the results of four tests they were given, and the dates on which the tests were held.

a What is the title?

b When was the second × 6 test held?

c In which month were the × 7 tables tests held?

d Use the spreadsheet to find:

- 8 × 7
- 9 × 6

e Did Diane and Luke know their tables completely before the testing began?

2 Pretend you are the teacher. Write a report about the progress shown by Diane and Luke in learning their 6 and 7 times tables.

3 **Step 1:** Use a spreadsheet program such as *Numbers* or *Excel* to make a spreadsheet, copying the information in *Rows 14, 15, 16* and *17* of the spreadsheet above.

Step 2: Add a line below these lines that shows your name in *Column C* and *Column H*.

Step 3: Get a friend to give you the test on the next line and record your score in *Column D*.

(1) 2 × 6 (2) 5 × 6 (3) 4 × 6 (4) 7 × 6 (5) 1 × 6 (6) 9 × 6 (7) 10 × 6 (8) 3 × 6 (9) 6 × 6 (10) 8 × 6 (11) 11 × 6 (12) 12 × 6

Step 4: Get a friend to give you the test on the next line and record your score in *Column I*.

(1) 2 × 7 (2) 5 × 7 (3) 4 × 7 (4) 7 × 7 (5) 1 × 7 (6) 9 × 7 (7) 10 × 7 (8) 3 × 7 (9) 6 × 7 (10) 8 × 7 (11) 11 × 7 (12) 12 × 7

Step 5: Learn these tables completely.

Step 6: Do the test in *Step 3* again and record the results in *Column E*. Did you improve?

Step 7: Do the test in *Step 4* again and record the results in *Column J*. Did you improve?

5:20 Bar and sector graphs

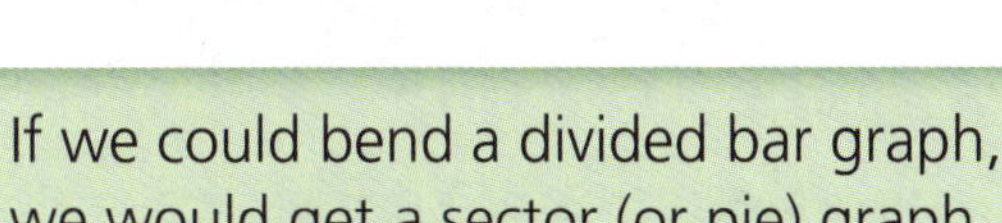

If we could bend a divided bar graph, we would get a sector (or pie) graph.

Big cats at the zoo

Tigers 20%	Leopards 30%	Lions 50%

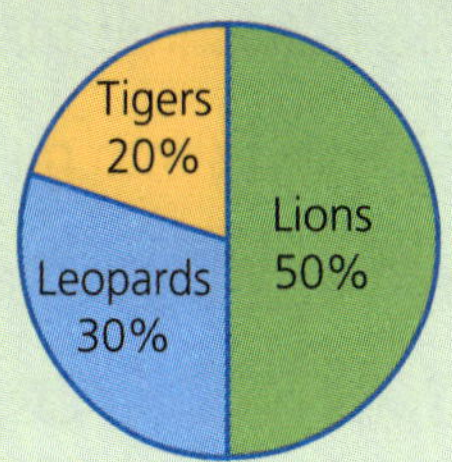

1 Use the graphs above to answer these questions.

a What kind of big cat is most plentiful at the zoo?

b What kind is least plentiful?

c What percentage of big cats in the zoo are leopards?

d If there are 20 big cats in the zoo, how many are tigers?

e What percentage of the big cats are not tigers?

f Are there any other types of big cat at the zoo?

How do you know?

100% means all of them.

Sector graph

Qld NSW Vic

2 The bar graph below is divided into three unequal parts.

Give this graph a title.

Canaries	Quail	Finches

Naomi and Hae have 100 birds, so Hae drew a bar 100 mm long so that each millimetre stood for one bird.

a How long, to the nearest millimetre, is the part of the graph showing:

i canaries? ii quail? iii finches?

b Of these birds owned by Hae and Naomi, how many were:

i canaries? ii quail? iii finches?

c Measuring in millimetres, what fraction of the graph shows:

i canaries? ii quail? iii finches?

d Measuring in centimetres what fraction of the graph shows:

i canaries? ii quail? iii finches?

e What percentage of the birds are:

i canaries? ii quail? iii finches?

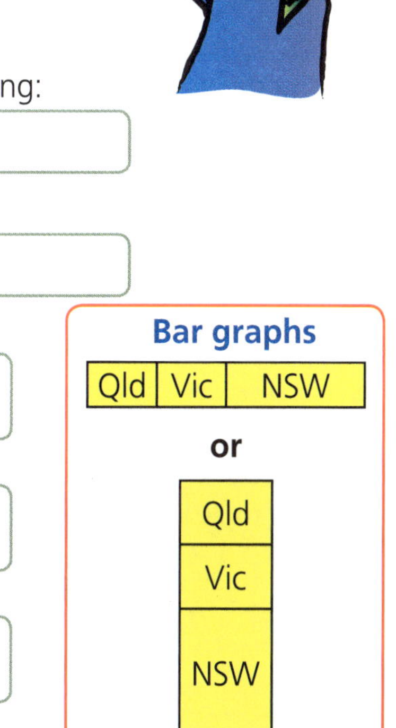

5:21 Reasoning with graphs

Is the data in Question 3 discrete or continuous?

1 In the USA, distance is measured in miles. Use the graph to convert:

a 40 kilometres into miles

b 60 kilometres into miles

c 12·5 miles into kilometres.

Which is the greater distance:

d 30 miles or 50 kilometres?

e 20 miles or 30 kilometres?

f Howler monkeys can be heard up to 16 km away. What is this distance in miles?

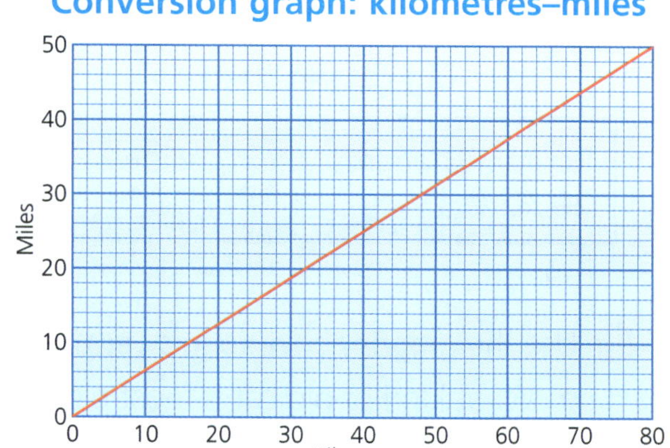

Discuss why each graph has been used to show the data.

2 Ed drew a graph of how he passed the time on his birthday.

a What activity took up most time?

b Was more time spent working or playing?

c Was less time spent working than sleeping?

d Which two categories used the same time?

e Which category used $\frac{1}{4}$ of the day?

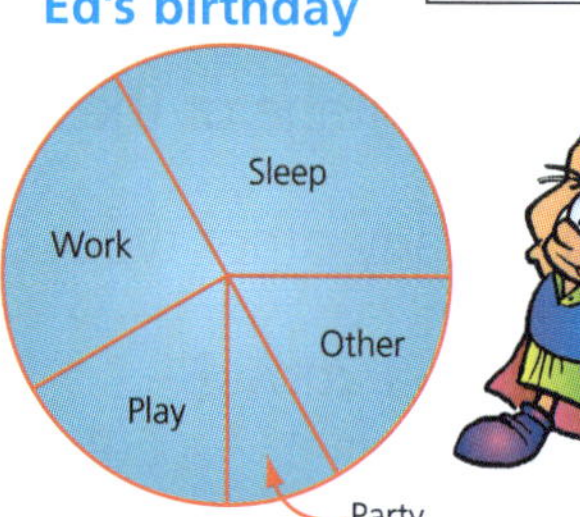

3 Heights of Year 6 students were measured to the nearest centimetre.

a How many had heights from 121 to 130 cm?

b How many had heights from 171 to 180 cm?

c How many had heights from 141 to 180 cm?

d Which category had the greatest number of people in it?

e Is it possible to tell how many people were 100 cm tall?

f How many Year 6 students were measured?

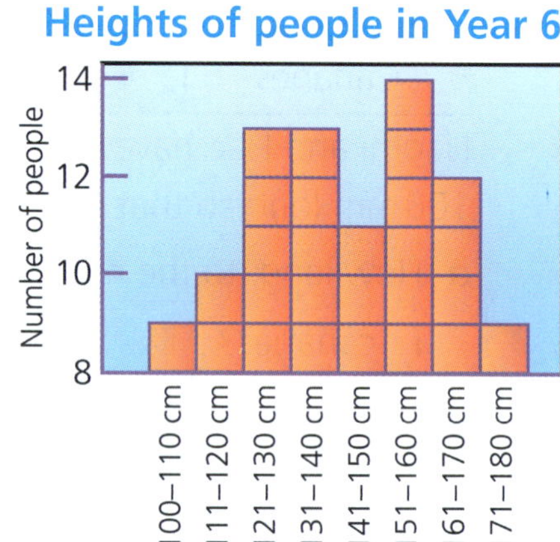

Tally of Year 5 test results

Mark group					
1 to 10	𝍸				
11 to 20	𝍸	𝍸	||||		
21 to 30	𝍸	𝍸	𝍸	𝍸	||
31 to 40	𝍸	𝍸	|||		

4 **a** How many students scored 11 to 20 marks?

b How many students scored less than 21?

c How many scored more than 20?

d How many students were in Year 5?

e Do we know how many people scored 40?

5:22 Selecting a graph to use

Do you want detail?
Do you want pictures?
Do you want to impress?

We can use the information in the table to create these two graphs.

Water in the tank

Day	Mon	Tue	Wed	Thurs	Fri
Litres	4	10	8	4	8

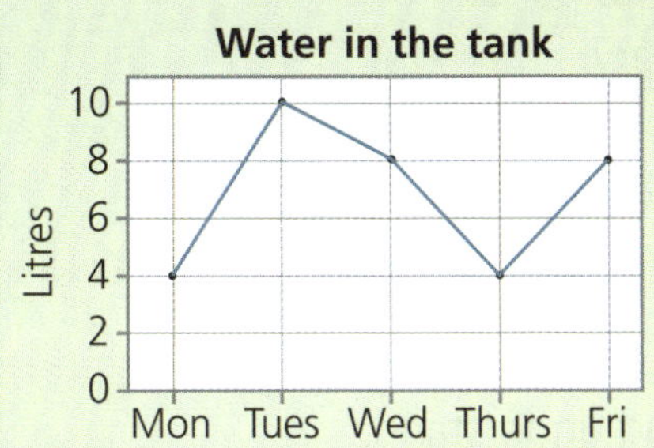

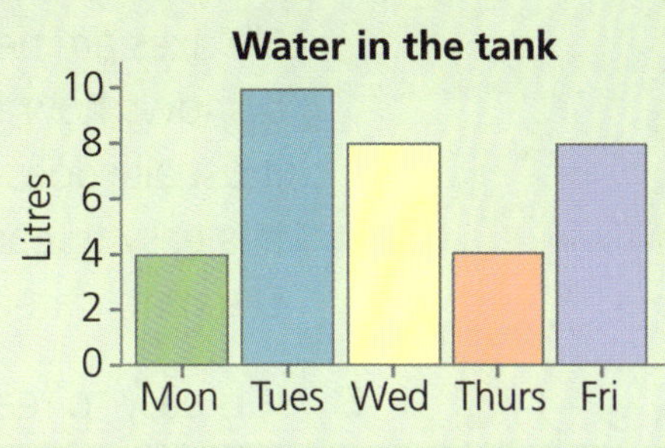

CONCEPT

Can the information be displayed on a sector graph? Discuss.

1 Use the information given in the tables to draw these graphs.
Circle the graph you think is the best way to present the data.

a **Have been to Perth**

Yes	5
No	95

Have been to Perth
(Line, picture or bar graph)

Have been to Perth
(Sector graph)

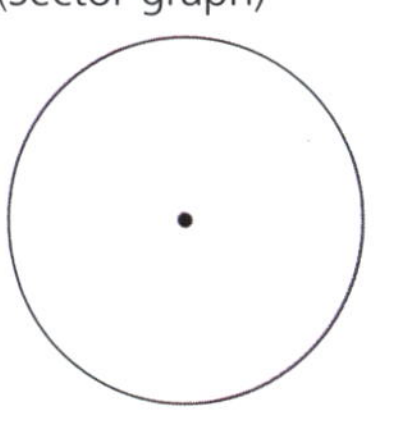

b **Jan's holiday**

Where	Days spent
Coast	2
Home	5
Country	3

Jan's holiday
(Divided bar graph)

Jan's holiday
(Column, picture or line graph)

c **Daisy's mass from birth**

Weeks	0	2	4	6
Mass (kg)	3·4	4	5·2	5·6

Daisy's mass from birth
(Line graph)

Daisy's mass from birth
(Column graph)

2 Write the best type of graph for the data in each table. Discuss the reasons for your answers.

a **Money in the bank**

Month	Jan	Feb	Mar	Apr	May	Jun	Jul
Money ($)	48	62	35	7	33	69	54

b **Favourite pet**

Dog	40
Cat	12

5:23 Comparing types of graphs

Match your needs to a graph.

Which of the graphs below (column, sector, picture, divided bar and line) are best suited to show the 'Sales of books'?

1 Name each graph and match each with its description.

1

______ graph

2

______ graph

3

______ graph

4

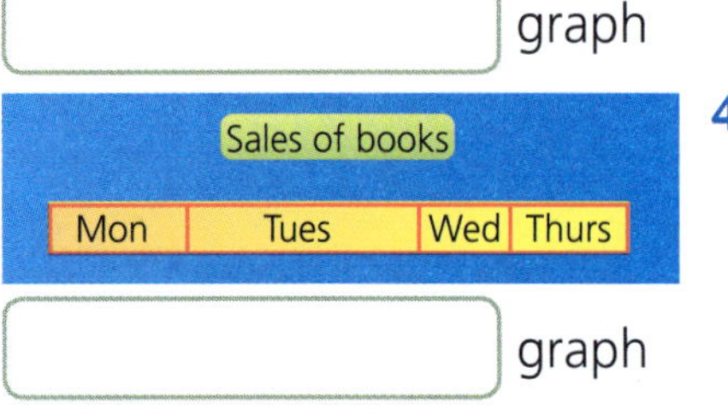

______ graph

5

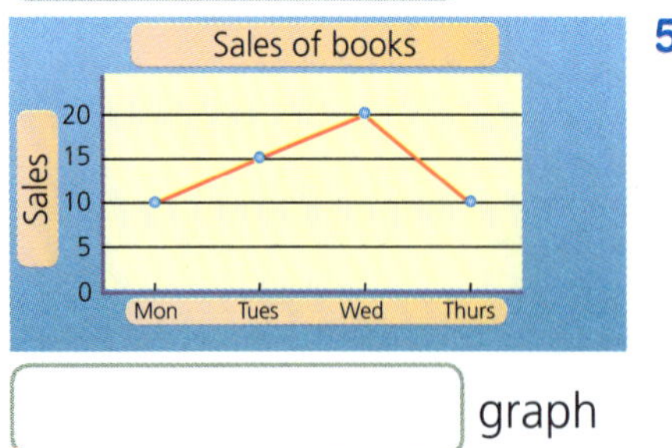

______ graph

A A circle is divided into parts.
No axes are necessary.
It shows how the whole is divided into parts.
It usually does not give details.
It is easy to compare the size of categories.
Uncomplicated and takes up little space.

B It is easy to read and understand.
It is easy to draw.
Two axes are used.
It is impressive in appearance.
It allows comparisons to be made at a glance.
It shows more detail than most graphs.

C It is more attractive than most graphs.
It does not give detailed information.
It allows us to compare the sizes of each category easily.
It uses a key.
Only one axis is necessary.
It is easy to understand.

D It shows more detail than most graphs.
All points on the line should have some meaning.
Each point has a reading on both axes.
A line is used to show trends and relationships.
Two axes are used.

E No axes are necessary.
It is uncomplicated and takes up little space.
It shows how the whole is divided into parts.
It often does not give details.
It is easy to compare the size of categories.
A rectangle is divided into parts.

2 Make a list of the advantages of using tables.

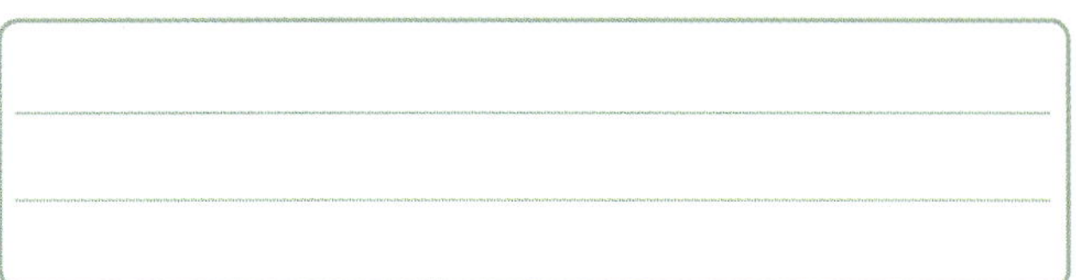

3 On your own paper, use a column graph to graph the sales of books in this table.

Sales of books				
Day	Mon	Tues	Wed	Thurs
Sales	35	48	44	63

 • *AUSTRALIAN SIGNPOST MATHS 5* • ISBN 9780655708797

Decimals

$0.17 is 17 cents. This is 17 hundredths of a dollar.

$0.35 is 35 cents.
$1.00 is 100 cents.

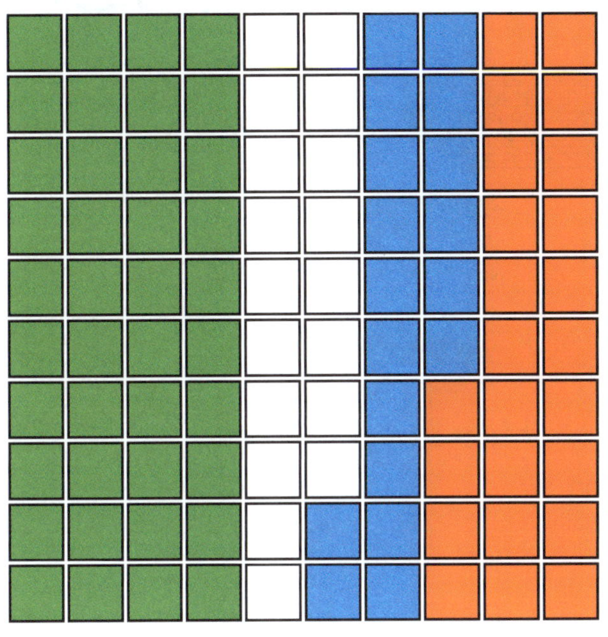

1 How many squares are grouped together? [ ]

2 What part of the group of squares:

a is green? [ ] out of 100 [ ]/100 0·[ ]

b is white? [ ] out of 100 [ ]/100 0·[ ]

c is blue? [ ] out of 100 [ ]/100 0·[ ]

3 Write the fraction and decimal that is coloured.

a [ ] 0·[ ]

b 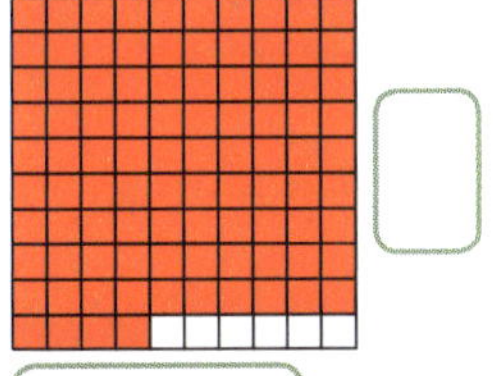 [ ] 0·[ ]

c 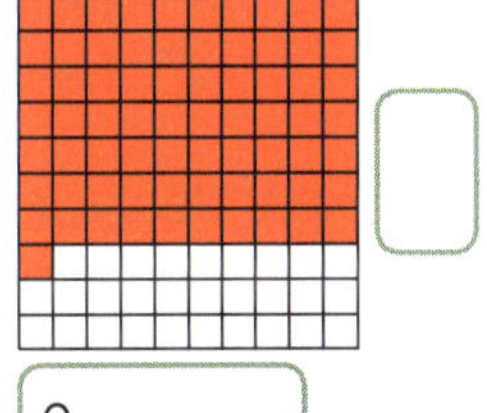 [ ] 0·[ ]

d 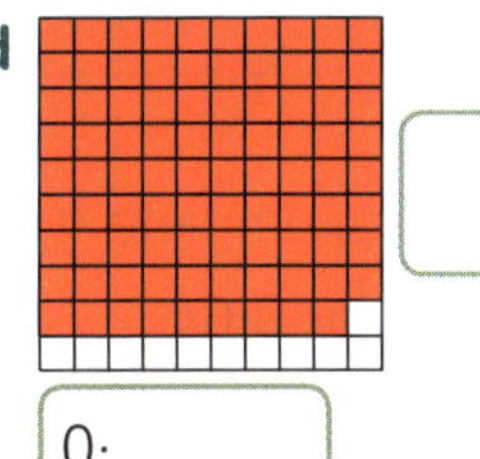 [ ] 0·[ ]

e 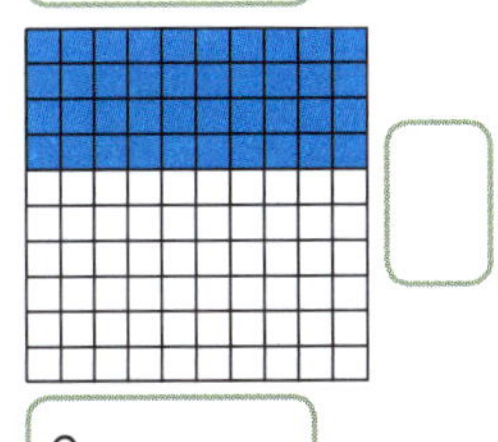 [ ] 0·[ ]

f 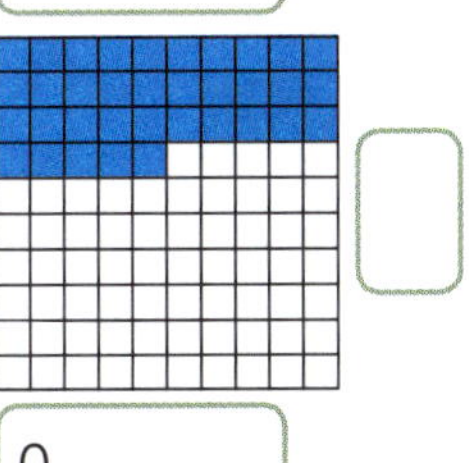 [ ] 0·[ ]

g 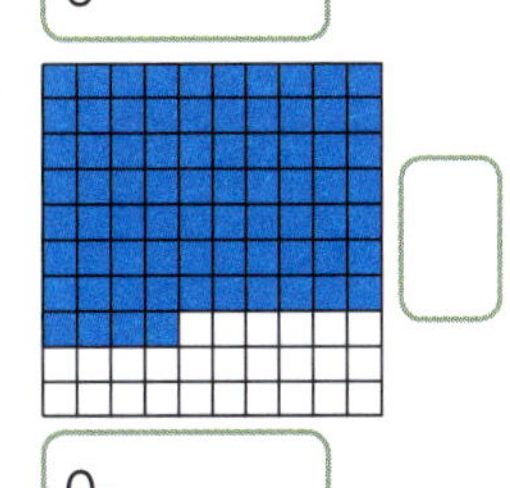 [ ] 0·[ ]

h 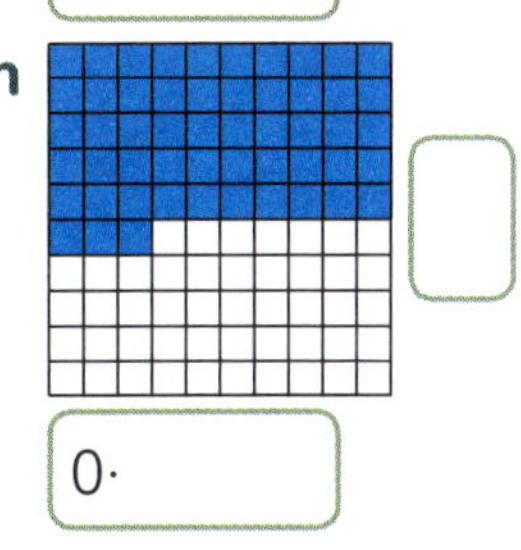 [ ] 0·[ ]

4 Write each in decimal form and as a fraction of one dollar.

a 15 cents $[ ] $ ——

b 83 cents 

c 90 cent 

d 37 cents [ ] [ ]

See 1:06 (Mixed numbers).

 • *AUSTRALIAN SIGNPOST MATHS 5* • ISBN 9780655708797

Place value in decimals

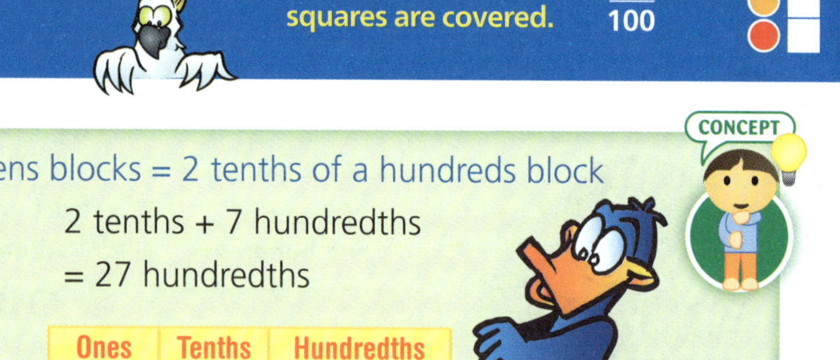

27 out of 100.

2 tens blocks = 2 tenths of a hundreds block

2 tenths + 7 hundredths

= 27 hundredths

Ones		Tenths	Hundredths
0	·	2	7

27 out of 100 is 27%.

1 Complete the label for each model.

a

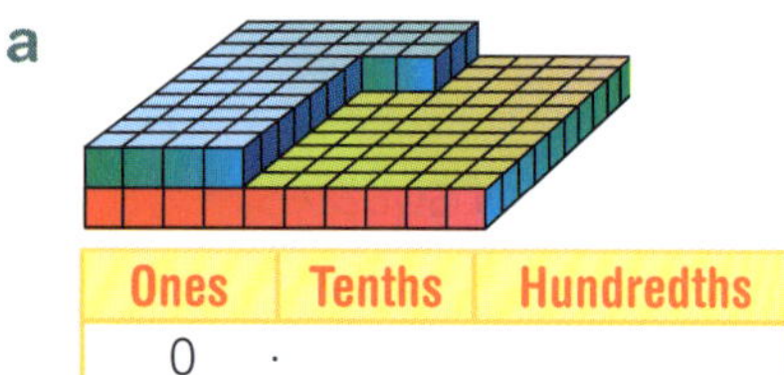

Ones		Tenths	Hundredths
0	·		

b

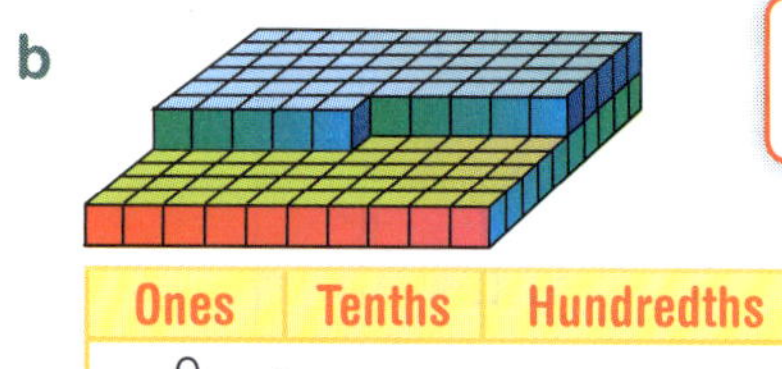

Ones		Tenths	Hundredths
0	·		

This is one whole and twenty-eight hundredths.

c

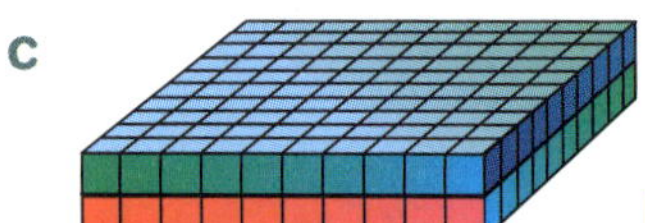

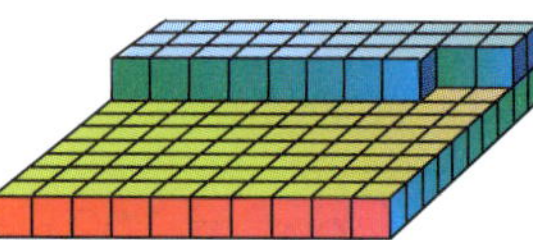

Ones		Tenths	Hundredths
	·		

2 Draw a line from each decimal to the correct fraction.

a

$1\frac{73}{100}$	0·17
$\frac{17}{100}$	1·73
$1\frac{53}{100}$	1·53

b

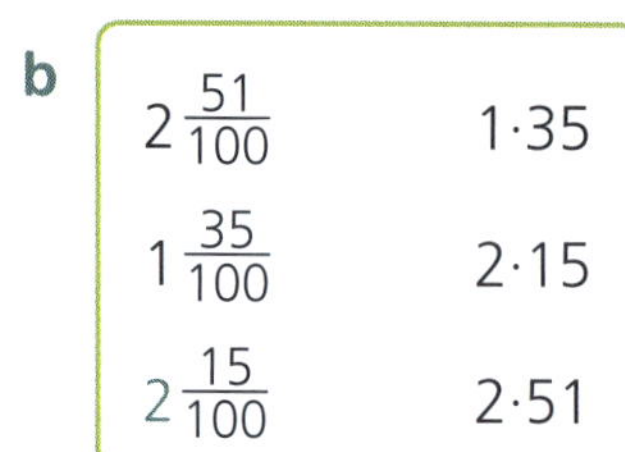

$2\frac{51}{100}$	1·35
$1\frac{35}{100}$	2·15
$2\frac{15}{100}$	2·51

c

$\frac{10}{100}$	3·49
$2\frac{49}{100}$	0·1
$3\frac{49}{100}$	2·49

3 Complete the numeral expanders for each decimal then write each as a percentage.

a 0·64

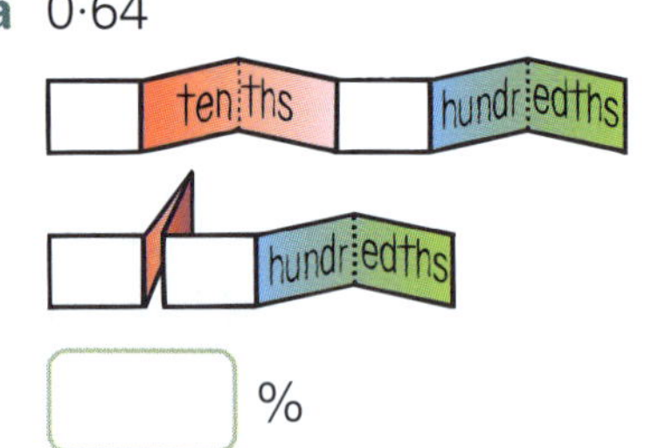

☐ %

b 0·32

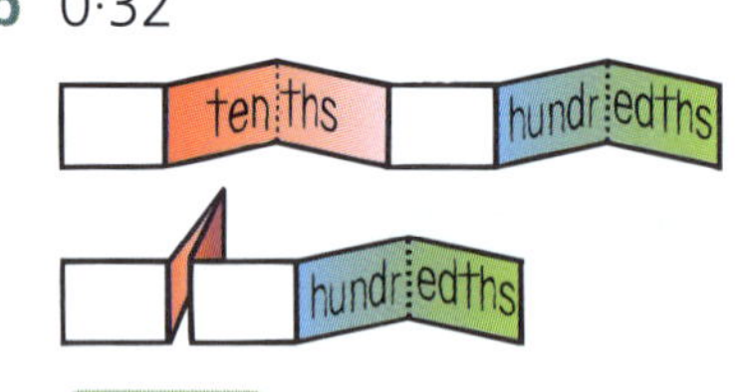

☐ %

c 0·19

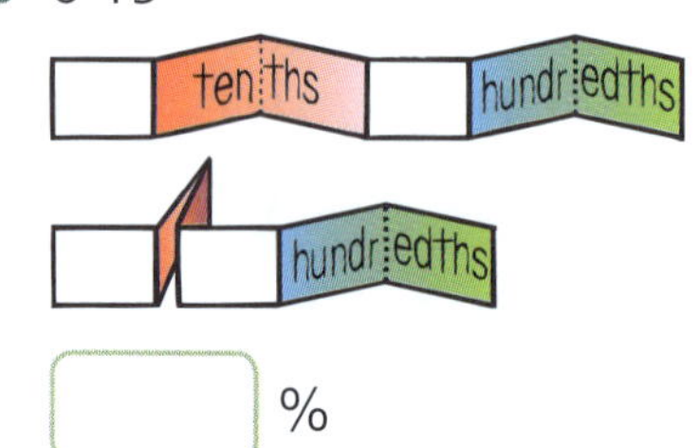

☐ %

d 0·08

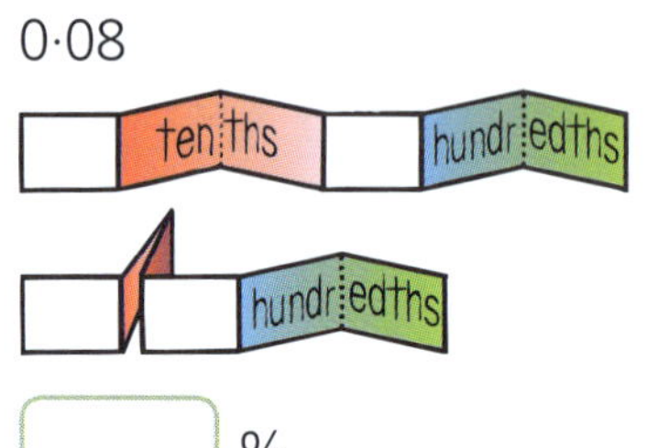

☐ %

e 0·7

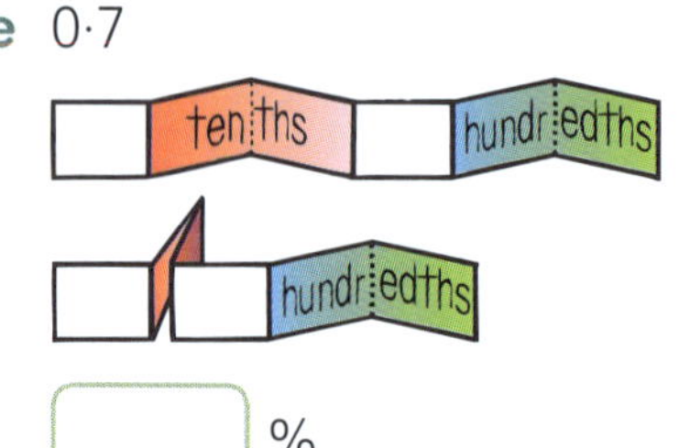

☐ %

f 0·93

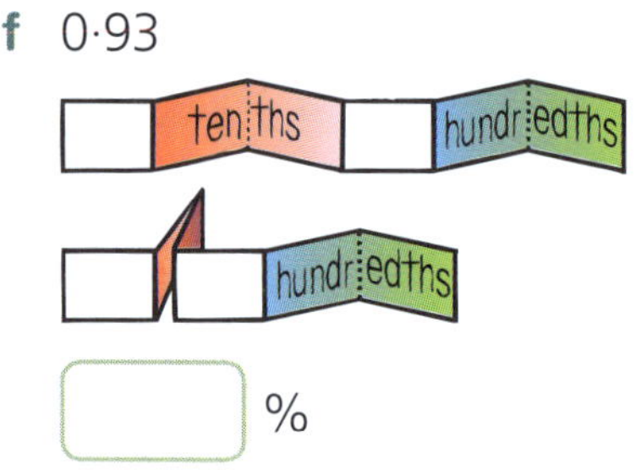

☐ %

See 1:07 (Tenths and hundredths) and 1:08 (Percentages).

Reading and writing decimals

The value of the 6 in 13·65 is 0·6 or 6 tenths.

1 Write the numeral for the number shown on each abacus.

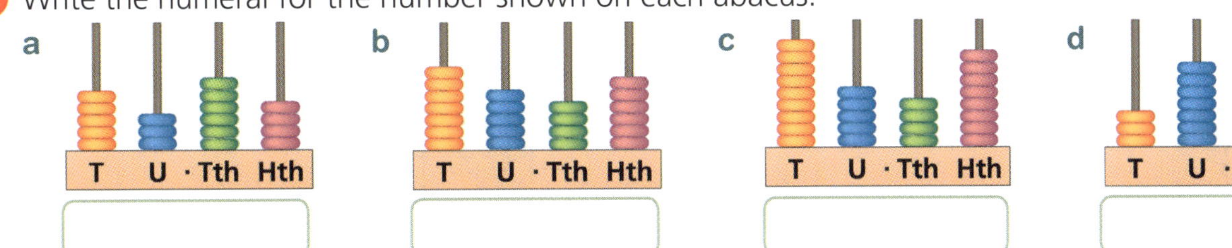

2 Use numerals to write:

a fifteen point seven five

b eighty point three six

c twenty-seven point nine two

d ninety point zero eight

e sixty-two point seven three

f seventy-one point nine nine

3 Complete the following.

a 0·91 = ☐ tenths and ☐ hundredth

b 0·40 = ☐ tenths and ☐ hundredths

c 0·09 = ☐ tenths and ☐ hundredths

4 Write the number represented by:

Each of these needs a decimal point.

decimal point

a 5 hundreds, 8 tens, 3 units, 2 tenths and 7 hundredths

b 6 hundreds, 0 tens, 3 units, 0 tenths and 2 hundredths

c 5 hundreds, 6 tens, 3 units and 8 tenths

d 4 hundreds, 1 ten, 0 units, 3 tenths and 9 hundredths

e six and nine tenths

f four and two tenths

g five and three tenths

h nine and one tenth

5 Write the value of each coloured digit.

a 273·61

b 651·93

c 911·42

d 827·04

e 129·93

f 372·14

g 740·51

h 391·72

i 692·76

j 509·73

k 233·21

l 609·49

See 1:15 (Place value and decimals).

 • *AUSTRALIAN SIGNPOST MATHS 5* • ISBN 9780655708797

+ and – of fractions

$\frac{46}{100} + \frac{22}{100} = \frac{\square}{100}$

1. Add or subtract these fractions. Colour part of the last grid to match your answer.

a 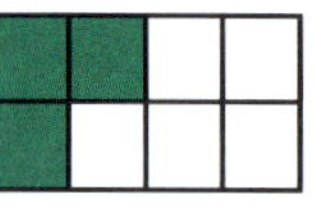 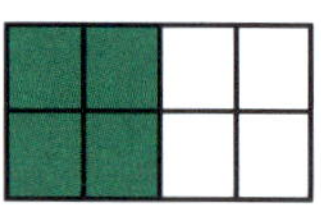 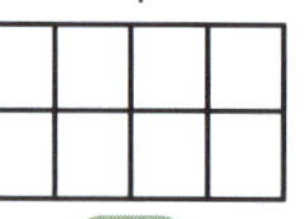

$\frac{3}{8} + \frac{4}{8} = \square$

b 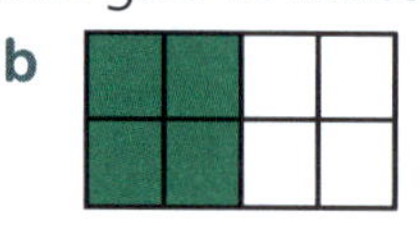 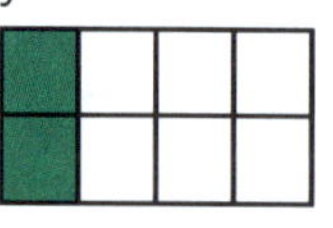 

$\frac{4}{8} + \frac{2}{8} = \square$

c 

$\frac{2}{10} + \frac{5}{10} = \square$

d 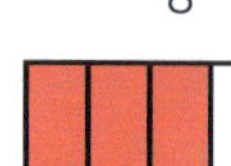 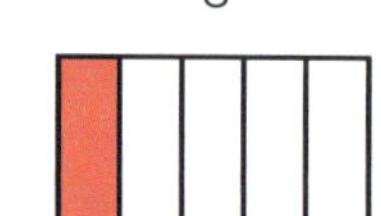 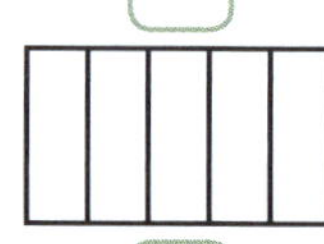

$\frac{3}{5} + \frac{1}{5} = \square$

e 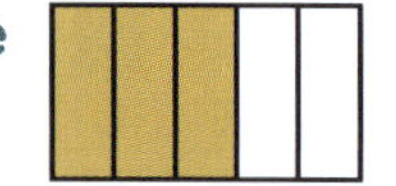 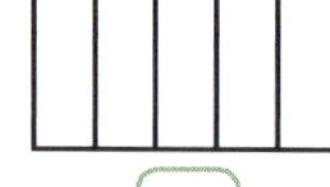

$\frac{3}{5} - \frac{2}{5} = \square$

f 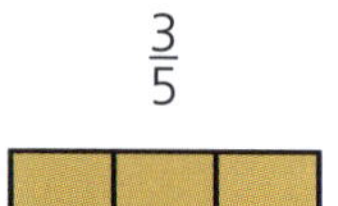   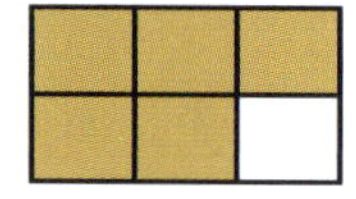 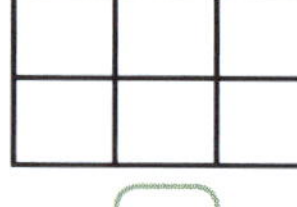

$\frac{5}{6} - \frac{3}{6} = \square$

g  

$\frac{8}{10} - \frac{5}{10} = \square$

h  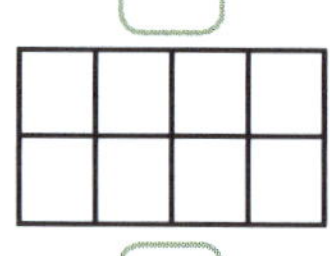

$\frac{7}{8} - \frac{5}{8} = \square$

2. Use the fraction card to find the answers.

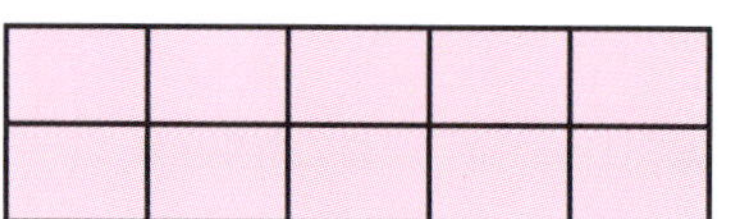

a $\frac{6}{10} - \frac{5}{10} = \square$ **b** $\frac{4}{10} - \frac{1}{10} = \square$ **c** $\frac{8}{10} - \frac{3}{10} = \square$ **d** $\frac{6}{10} - \frac{4}{10} = \square$

e $\frac{7}{10} - \frac{5}{10} = \square$ **f** $\frac{5}{10} - \frac{4}{10} = \square$ **g** $\frac{9}{10} - \frac{3}{10} = \square$ **h** $\frac{8}{10} - \frac{6}{10} = \square$

3. Use the hundred square to find the answers.

a $\frac{13}{100} + \frac{10}{100} = \square$ **b** $\frac{8}{100} + \frac{4}{100} = \square$ **c** $\frac{7}{100} + \frac{16}{100} = \square$

d $\frac{30}{100} + \frac{60}{100} = \square$ **e** $\frac{20}{100} + \frac{50}{100} = \square$ **f** $\frac{22}{100} + \frac{16}{100} = \square$

g $\frac{43}{100} + \frac{17}{100} = \square$ **h** $\frac{26}{100} + \frac{28}{100} = \square$ **i** $\frac{35}{100} + \frac{47}{100} = \square$

4. Use > or < to make each number sentence true.

a $\frac{3}{8} \square \frac{1}{8}$ **b** $\frac{7}{8} \square \frac{3}{8}$ **c** $\frac{2}{8} \square \frac{5}{8}$ **d** $\frac{4}{8} \square \frac{5}{8}$

e $\frac{1}{10} \square \frac{3}{10}$ **f** $\frac{9}{10} \square \frac{4}{10}$ **g** $\frac{7}{10} \square \frac{2}{10}$ **h** $\frac{3}{10} \square \frac{4}{10}$

The arrow of < and > points to the smaller part.

5. Explain your answers to Question 4 to a friend.

See 1:13 (Subtraction of fractions).

Place value to thousandths

Comparing decimals: Compare units, then tenths, then hundredths, …

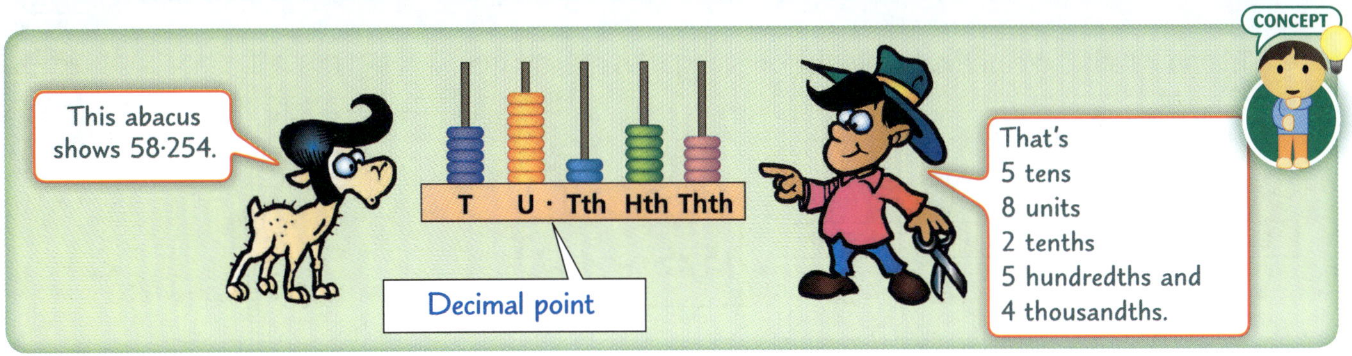

1 Write the value of each coloured digit.

a 34·629 ☐ b 97·638 ☐ c 79·035 ☐

d 75·351 ☐ e 52·746 ☐ f 21·917 ☐

g 64·007 ☐ h 83·579 ☐ i 48·102 ☐

2 Write the decimal for each fraction.

a $\frac{47}{100}$ = ☐ b $\frac{359}{1000}$ = ☐ c $\frac{7}{10}$ = ☐

d $\frac{206}{1000}$ = ☐ e $\frac{6}{10}$ = ☐ f $\frac{8}{1000}$ = ☐

The length of a decimal does not indicate its relative size.

3 Write the fraction for each decimal.

a 0·36 = ☐ b 0·417 = ☐ c 0·5 = ☐ d 0·875 = ☐

e 0·03 = ☐ f 0·48 = ☐ g 0·745 = ☐ h 0·625 = ☐

4 Circle the larger number and explain why.

a 0·6 or 0·276 because $\frac{6}{10}$ is greater than $\frac{2}{10}$.

b 0·723 or 0·75 because $\frac{75}{100}$ is greater than …

c 0·999 or 0·998 because …

Ordering decimals

Compare the whole numbers, then tenths, then hundredths, then thousandths.

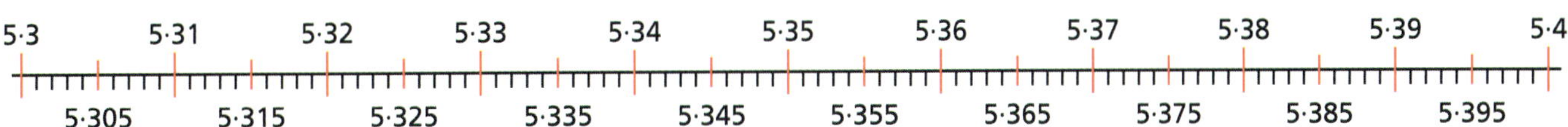

5 Write 5·34, 5·345, 5·35, 5·303 in order, smallest to largest. ☐

6 What is halfway between:

a 5·3 and 5·4? ☐ b 5·32 and 5·33? ☐ c 5·38 and 5·39? ☐

See 1:14 (Place value to thousandths).

Comparing decimals

< means is less than.
> means is greater than.
5 < 6 means 5 is less than 6.

CONCEPT

- To find which is greater, compare the ones first. 5 is greater than 4.

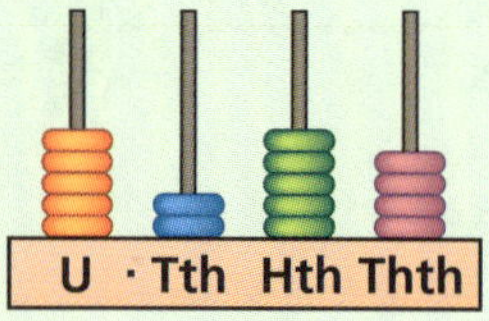

U · Tth Hth Thth — 5·254

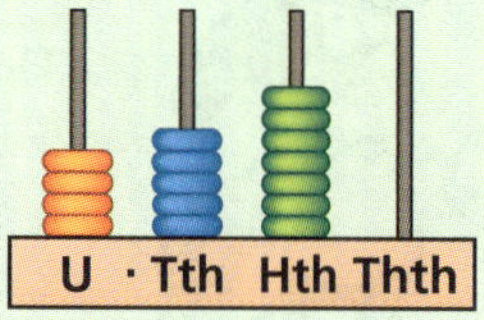

U · Tth Hth Thth — 4·570 or 4·57

5·254 > 4·57

- 6·8 4 3
  6·8 5
  5 > 4; same; same

  So 6·85 > 6·843

1. Write the numeral for the number shown on each abacus.

   a 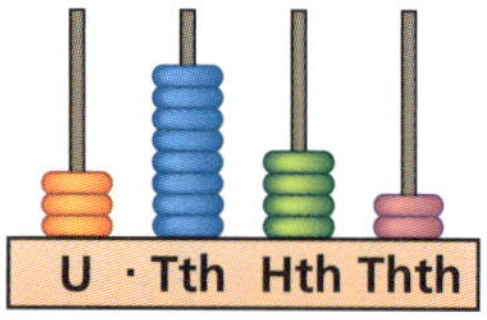 U · Tth Hth Thth
   b 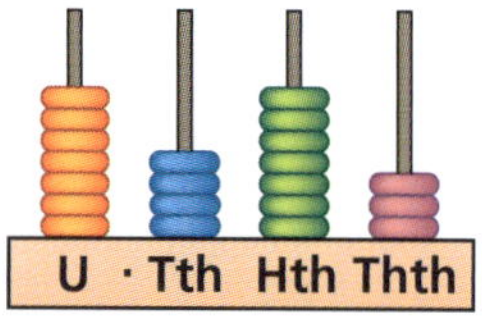 U · Tth Hth Thth
   c 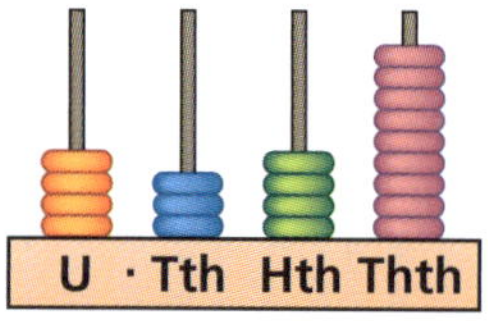 U · Tth Hth Thth
   d U · Tth Hth Thth

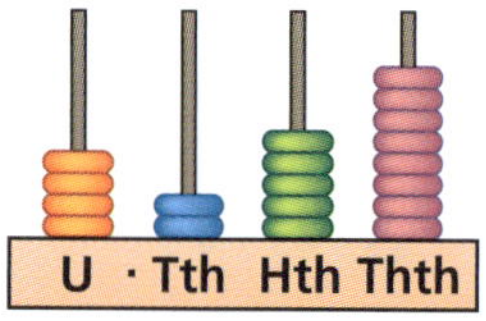

2. a Circle the picture showing the largest decimal in Question 1.
   b Write the answers to Question 1 in order, least to greatest.

3. Write the numeral for the number shown on each abacus.

   a 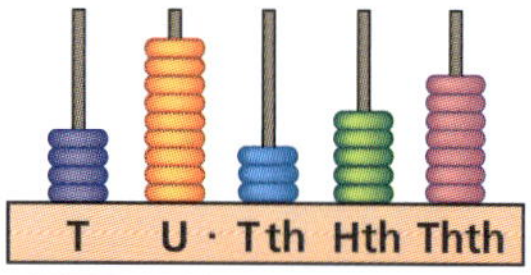 T U · Tth Hth Thth
   b 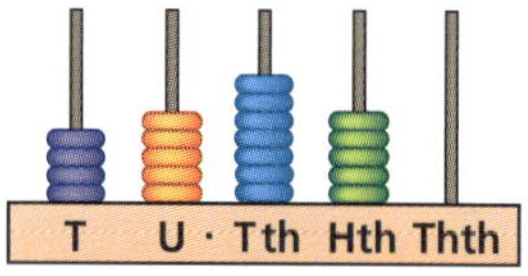 T U · Tth Hth Thth
   c T U · Tth Hth Thth

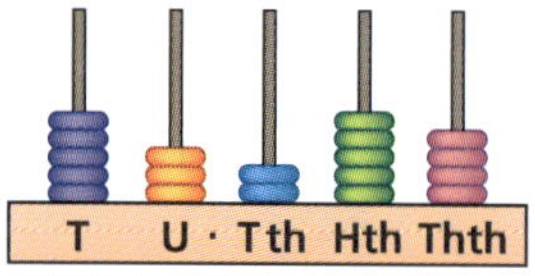

   Parts **a** and **c** have 5 digits. Part **b** has 4 digits.

4. Order from least to greatest.
   a 0·2, 0·125, 0·35
   b 1·2, 1·02, 1·002
   c 0·7, 0·007, 0·07
   d 1·4, 1·85, 2

5. Why is 2 greater than 1•85?

6. For each statement write **true** or **false**.
   a 6·735 < 6·603
   b 9·345 > 9·245
   c 8·238 < 8·304

7. Use < or > to make these number sentences true.
   a 3·619 ☐ 4·207
   b 9·138 ☐ 9·56
   c 4·196 ☐ 5·231
   d 8·953 ☐ 7·641
   e 1·403 ☐ 1·936
   f 6·925 ☐ 5·863
   g 5·306 ☐ 5·638
   h 7·612 ☐ 7·59

See 1:20 (Comparing decimals).

×2, ×3, ×4, ×5, ×10 tables

Do you know these?

×	2	3	4	5
1	2	3	4	5
2	4	6	8	10
3	6	9	12	15
4	8	12	16	20
5	10	15	20	25
6	12	18	24	30
7	14	21	28	35
8	16	24	32	40
9	18	27	36	45
10	20	30	40	50

CONCEPT

The circle shows 6 × 4.

The product of 6 and 4 is 24.

6 × 4 = 4 × 6

1 Try to do these without using the table.

a 9 × 3 = ☐   b 8 × 5 = ☐   c 8 × 4 = ☐

d 5 × 4 = ☐   e 7 × 5 = ☐   f 8 × 3 = ☐

g 7 × 2 = ☐   h 7 × 4 = ☐   i 3 × 5 = ☐

j 6 × 5 = ☐   k 6 × 3 = ☐   l 6 × 4 = ☐

2 Find the product of:

a 5 and 5 ☐   b 9 and 4 ☐

c 3 and 3 ☐   d 1 and 1 ☐

e 2 and 5 ☐   f 9 and 5 ☐

g 2, 5 and 4 ☐   h 3, 2 and 4 ☐

The answer to a multiplication question is called the **product**.

3

a
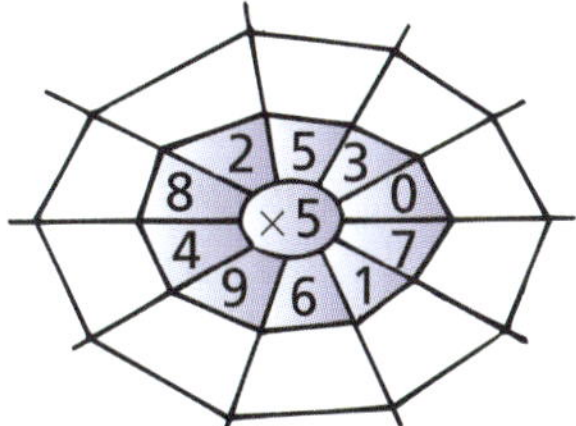

b
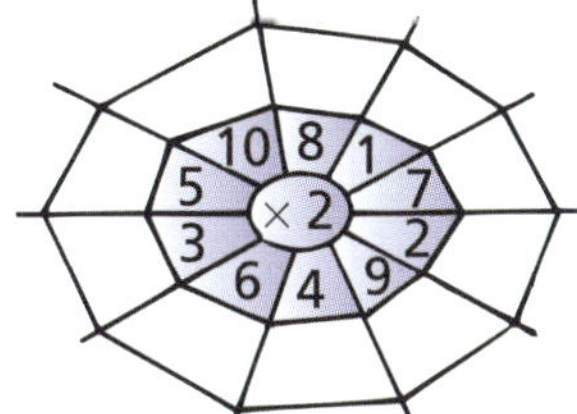

c
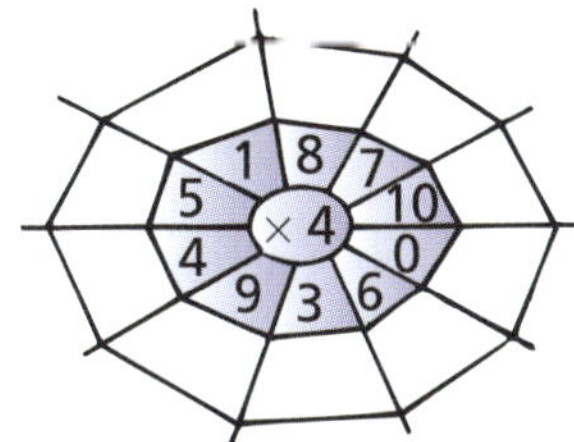

d
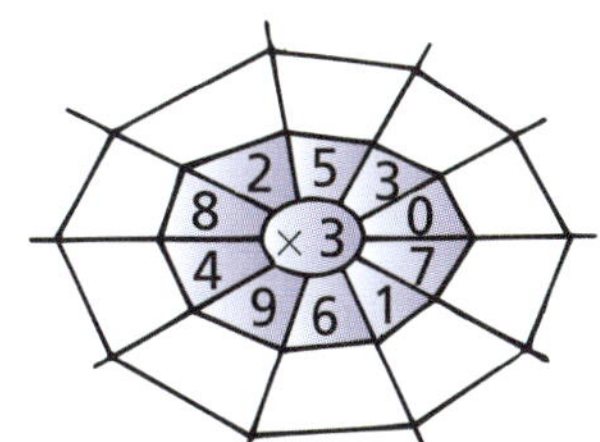

e
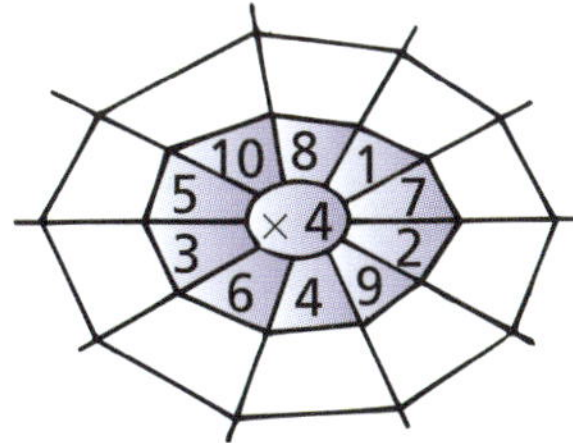

f
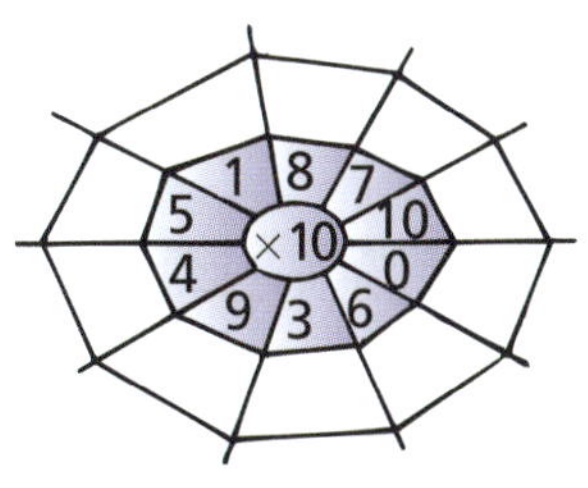

4 Write the first ten multiples of:

a 3 | 3 | ☐ | ☐ | ☐ | ☐ | ☐ | ☐ | ☐ | ☐ | ☐

b 4 | 4 | ☐ | ☐ | ☐ | ☐ | ☐ | ☐ | ☐ | ☐ | ☐

c 5 | 5 | ☐ | ☐ | ☐ | ☐ | ☐ | ☐ | ☐ | ☐ | ☐

See 2:01 (Number facts, × 6, × 7, × 8, × 9); 2:02 (Learning your multiplication tables) and *Extra Support 8* (× 6, × 7, × 8, × 9 tables).

 • *AUSTRALIAN SIGNPOST MATHS 5* • ISBN 9780655708797

× 6, × 7, × 8, × 9 tables

Rub out the pencil lines and do the questions again.

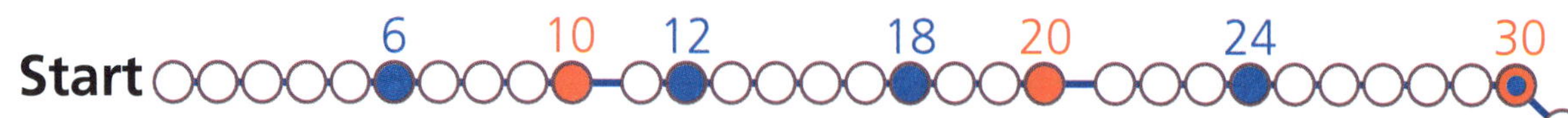

CONCEPT

- When multiplying by 3 or 6, the sum of the digits will be divisible by 3.
  8 × 3 = 24 (2 + 4 = 6), 8 × 6 = 48 (4 + 8 = 12), 9 × 6 = 54 (5 + 4 = 9).
- To multiply by 6, you could multiply by 3, then double. 6 x 3 = 18 so 6 × 6 = 2 × 18 = 36.
- If you know that 7 × 8 = 56, then you know that 8 × 7 = 56.

1 Join each question to its answer, using a pencil and ruler.

a

× 6	
2 × 6	48
5 × 6	0
8 × 6	12
0 × 6	54
6 × 6	30
1 × 6	36
9 × 6	24
4 × 6	60
3 × 6	6
7 × 6	18
10 × 6	42

b

× 7	
6 × 7	0
0 × 7	42
4 × 7	63
1 × 7	35
9 × 7	70
2 × 7	7
5 × 7	28
10 × 7	49
8 × 7	14
7 × 7	21
3 × 7	56

c

× 8	
10 × 8	48
3 × 8	40
6 × 8	8
1 × 8	80
5 × 8	0
8 × 8	24
0 × 8	72
4 × 8	16
9 × 8	64
2 × 8	56
7 × 8	32

× 2
× 4
× 8
answers end in: 8, 6, 4, 2, or 0.

× 10
answers end in: 0.

× 5
answers end in: 5 or 0.

d

× 9	
2 × 9	81
9 × 9	54
0 × 9	18
6 × 9	63
10 × 9	45
1 × 9	0
7 × 9	9
4 × 9	90
8 × 9	27
3 × 9	36
5 × 9	72

e

×	
5 × 5	48
6 × 9	49
7 × 7	35
5 × 4	25
8 × 6	54
7 × 5	20
9 × 3	63
9 × 7	28
3 × 6	32
7 × 4	27
4 × 8	18

f

×	
7 × 9	28
7 × 4	63
6 × 8	36
6 × 6	24
8 × 3	72
8 × 9	16
4 × 4	48
9 × 6	12
4 × 8	30
5 × 6	32
4 × 3	54

24 is:
8 × 3
4 × 6
3 × 8

3 4 4 4 5 5 6 6 7 7

See 2:01 (Number facts, × 6, × 7, × 8, × 9), 2:02 (Learning your multiplication tables) and *Extra Support 7* (× 2, × 3, × 4, × 5, × 10 tables).

Factors and multiples

12 × 1 = 12, 2 × 6 = 12, 3 × 4 = 12 so the factors of 12 are: 1, 12, 2, 6, 3 and 4.

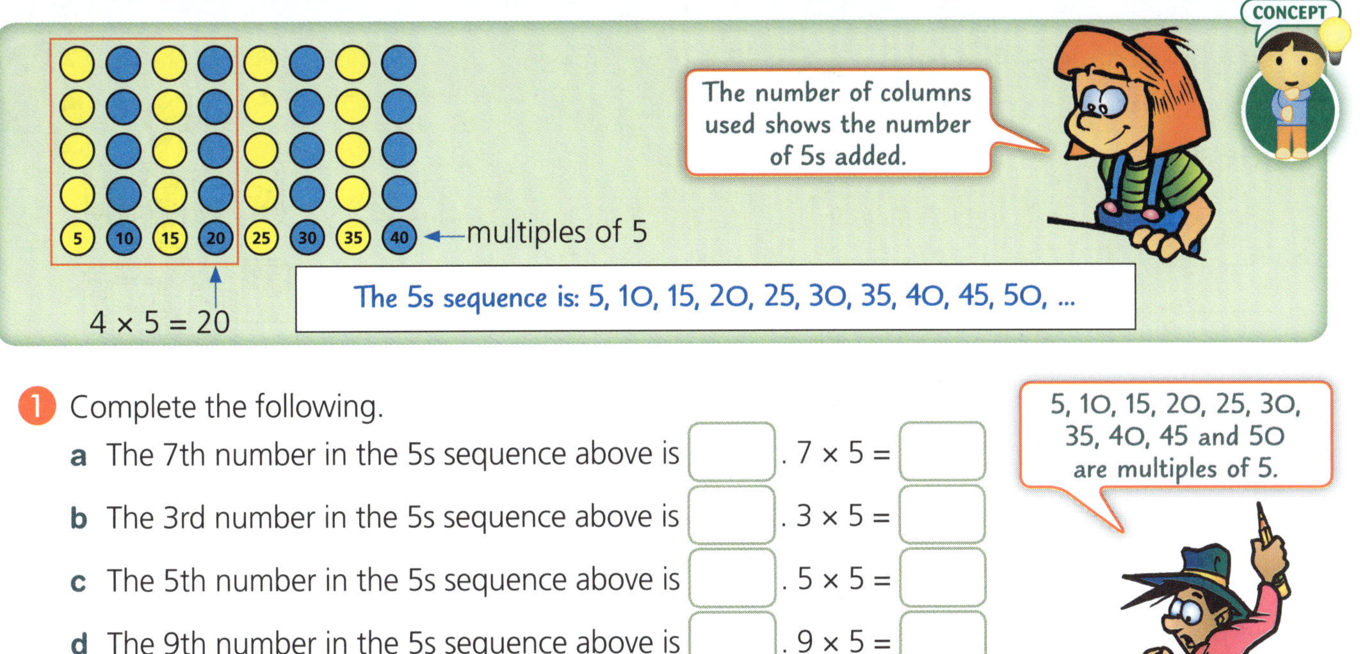

1 Complete the following.

a The 7th number in the 5s sequence above is ☐. 7 × 5 = ☐

b The 3rd number in the 5s sequence above is ☐. 3 × 5 = ☐

c The 5th number in the 5s sequence above is ☐. 5 × 5 = ☐

d The 9th number in the 5s sequence above is ☐. 9 × 5 = ☐

e The 6th number in the 5s sequence above is ☐. 6 × 5 = ☐

f The 8th number in the 5s sequence above is ☐. 8 × 5 = ☐

5, 10, 15, 20, 25, 30, 35, 40, 45 and 50 are multiples of 5.

2 Continue the patterns.

a 30, 35, 40, 45, ☐, ☐, ☐, ☐, ☐, ☐.

b 14, 16, 18, 20, ☐, ☐, ☐, ☐, ☐, ☐.

c 70, 80, 90, 100, ☐, ☐, ☐, ☐, ☐, ☐.

d 58, 60, 62, 64, ☐, ☐, ☐, ☐, ☐, ☐.

3 From the numbers 12, 14, 21, 24, 28, 35, 42 and 70, find two numbers that are multiples of both:

a 2 and 7 ☐ and ☐

b 5 and 7 ☐ and ☐

c 2 and 3 ☐ and ☐

d 3 and 7 ☐ and ☐

4 **a** 10 will be a factor of any number ending in ☐.

b 5 will be a factor of any number ending in ☐ or ☐.

c 2 will be a factor of any number ending in ☐, ☐, ☐, ☐ or ☐.

ICT

5 Using a calculator, fill in the next nine multiples.

a 36, 42, 48, ☐, ☐, ☐, ☐, ☐, ☐, ☐, ☐, ☐

b 63, 72, 81, ☐, ☐, ☐, ☐, ☐, ☐, ☐, ☐, ☐

See 2:11 (Multiples), 2:12 (Factors), 2:13 (Factors and multiples).

Extended multiplication

3 × 72 :
3 groups of 70 plus
3 groups of 2

CONCEPT

The 6 boxes of pegs each held 32 pegs. How many pegs were there altogether?

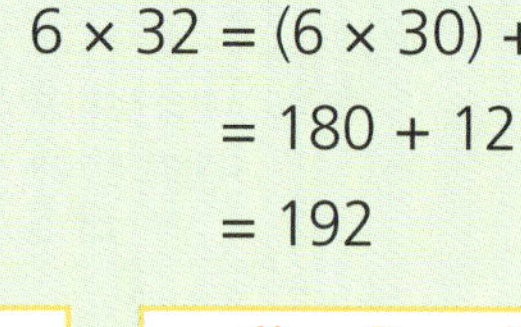

$6 \times 32 = (6 \times 30) + (6 \times 2)$
$= 180 + 12$
$= 192$

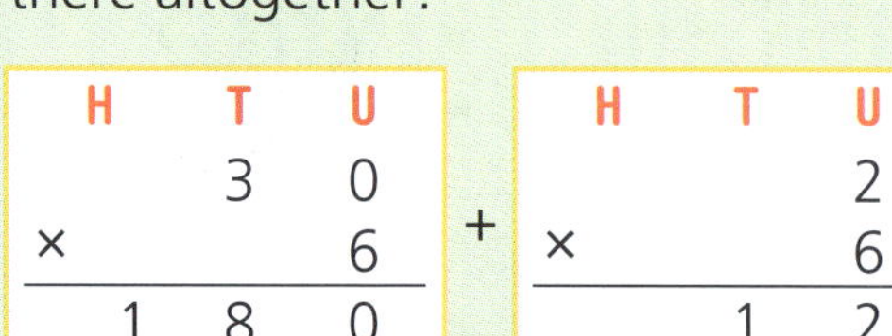

	H	T	U
		3	0
×			6
	1	8	0

\+

	H	T	U
			2
×			6
		1	2

=

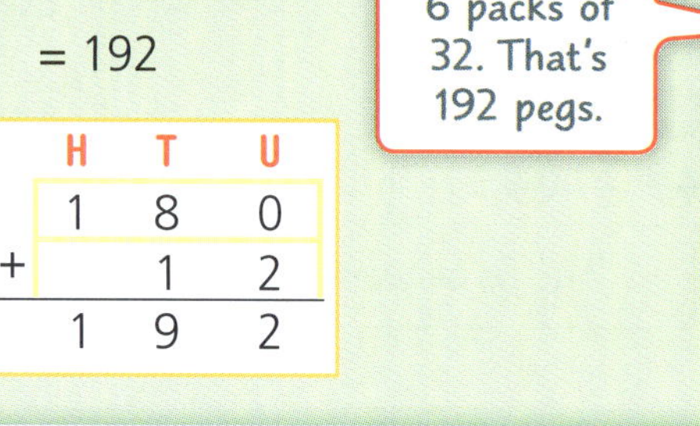

	H	T	U
	1	8	0
+		1	2
	1	9	2

1 One tin holds 25 blocks. How much would six tins hold?

6 × 25 blocks
= (6 × 20) + (6 × 5)
= ☐ + ☐
= ☐ blocks

	H	T	U
		2	0
×			6
	☐		

\+

	H	T	U
			5
×			6
	☐		

=

	H	T	U
	☐		
+	☐		
	☐		

2 I bought 7 tickets for $38 each. How much did it cost altogether?

7 × $38
= (7 × 30) + (7 × 8)
= ☐ + ☐
= ☐ dollars

	H	T	U
		3	0
×			7
	☐		

\+

	H	T	U
			8
×			7
	☐		

=

	H	T	U
	☐		
+	☐		
	☐		

3 There were 16 people in 9 boats. How many people were there?

9 × 16 people
= (9 × 10) + (9 × 6)
= ☐ + ☐
= ☐ people

	H	T	U
		1	0
×			9
	☐		

\+

	H	T	U
			6
×			9
	☐		

=

	H	T	U
	☐		
+	☐		
	☐		

4 73 students were each given $8. How much was given altogether?

73 × $8
= (70 × 8) + (3 × 8)
= ☐ + ☐
= ☐ dollars

	H	T	U
		7	0
×			8
	☐		

\+

	H	T	U
			3
×			8
	☐		

=

	H	T	U
	☐		
+	☐		
	☐		

See 2:43 (Multiplying 2-digit numbers) and 2:44 (The extended form of multiplication).

Estimating products

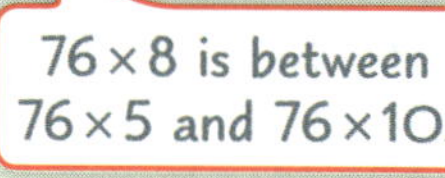

Estimate 76 × 8.

76 × 8 < 76 × 10 but 76 × 8 > 76 × 5,
so 76 × 8 is between 380 and 760.
(76 × 5 is half of 76 × 10.)

1 Circle the correct answers in each case.

a	47 × 7 is less than:	47 × 10	47 × 5	470	235
	47 × 7 is greater than:	47 × 10	47 × 5	470	235
b	58 × 8 is less than:	58 × 10	58 × 5	290	580
	58 × 8 is greater than:	58 × 10	58 × 5	290	580

47 × 10 = 470
58 × 10 = 580

2 Use the method in the concept box to find an upper and lower estimate.

a Estimate 73 × 9. 73 × 9 < [73 × 10] but > [73 × 5],
so 73 × 9 is between [ ] and [ ].

b Estimate 62 × 6. [ ] < [ ] but > [ ],
so 62 × 6 is between [ ] and [ ].

c Estimate 95 × 7. [ ] < [ ] but > [ ],
so 95 × 7 is between [ ] and [ ].

d Estimate 81 × 8. [ ] < [ ] but > [ ],
so 81 × 8 is between [ ] and [ ].

e Estimate 79 × 9 [ ] < [ ] but > [ ],
so 79 × 9 is between [ ] and [ ].

f Estimate 86 × 6 [ ] < [ ] but > [ ],
so 86 × 6 is between [ ] and [ ].

To find a × 5 answer, halve the × 10 answer.

Numbers in history

Roman numerals are used in some books and on clocks.

- LX means 50 and 10.
- XL means 10 less than 50.

Number	1	5	10	50	100	500	1000
Symbol	I	V	X	L	C	D	M

Examples: CCCXX = 320 CD = 400 DCC = 700 CM = 900 MMM = 3000 MDCXCI = 1691

3 Write our numeral for:

a CCCXL [ ] **b** CDLXIV [ ] **c** DCLXXV [ ] **d** MMCDIX [ ]

4 Write the Roman numeral for:

a 346 [ ] **b** 862 [ ] **c** 928 [ ] **d** 1263 [ ]

See 2:50 (Estimating by rounding).

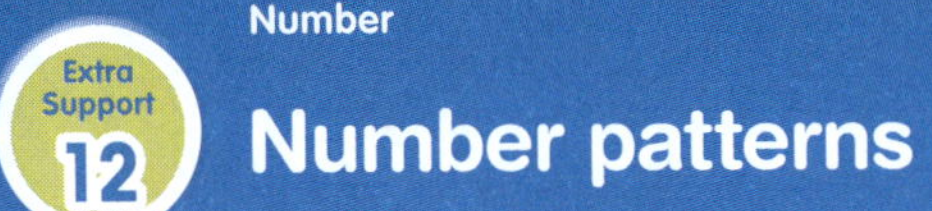

Number patterns

There are all sorts of patterns.

1 Complete each pattern and write the rule.

a 7, 10, 13, ☐, ☐, ☐, ☐ The rule is: ☐

b 7, 19, 31, ☐, ☐, ☐, ☐ The rule is: ☐

c 87, 78, 69, ☐, ☐, ☐, ☐ The rule is: ☐

d 53, 46, 39, ☐, ☐, ☐, ☐ The rule is: ☐

2 Write and continue the pattern made by the jumps on the number line. Write the rule for each.

a 120 140 160 180

120, ☐, ☐, ☐, ☐

The rule is: ☐

b 90 100 110 120 130

135, ☐, ☐, ☐, ☐

The rule is: ☐

3 Create your own number pattern using jumps on the number line. Write the rule.

a

☐, ☐, ☐, ☐, ☐, ☐ The rule is: ☐

4 Write and continue the pattern shown in these diagrams. Write the rule for each.

a The number of small squares

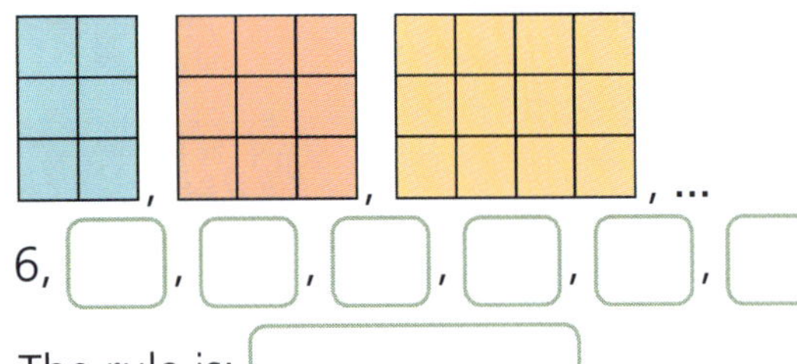

6, ☐, ☐, ☐, ☐, ☐, ☐

The rule is: ☐

b The number of star points

5, ☐, ☐, ☐, ☐, ☐, ☐

The rule is: ☐

c The number of small triangles

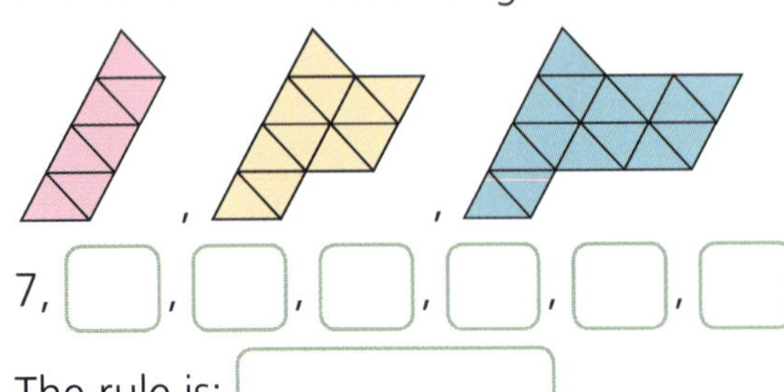

7, ☐, ☐, ☐, ☐, ☐, ☐

The rule is: ☐

d The number of sides drawn

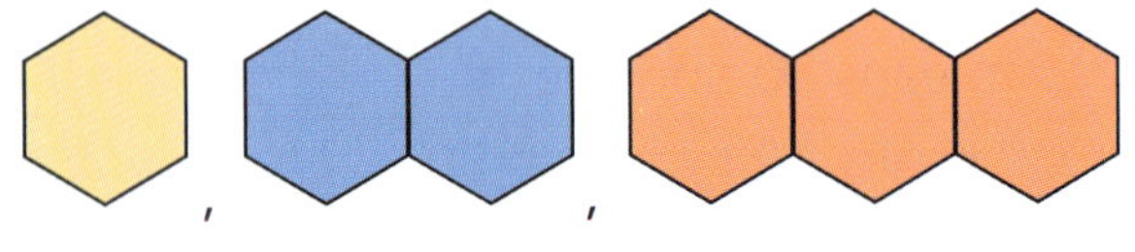

6, ☐, ☐, ☐, ☐, ☐, ☐

The rule is: ☐

See 1:26 (Patterns and percentages).

 ISBN 9780655708797

Problem solving with algorithms

These records are on the internet.

Deaths from traffic accidents, 2003							
Type of road user	NSW	Vic	Qld	SA	WA	Tas	Total
Drivers of motor vehicles	284	188	138	71	78	16	
Motor cyclists	55	56	53	22	23	9	
Pedal cyclists	14	7	5	3	6	0	
Passengers	124	89	88	40	48	4	
Pedestrians	95	58	37	18	24	6	
Other	–	–	–	–	1	–	
Total							

Source: Australian Transport Safety Bureau

1. Use the table above to answer the following.
   - **a** Fill in all the totals using the algorithm strategy.
   - **b** Which state had the smallest number of deaths?
   - **c** Which state had the most deaths?
   - **d** What was the total number of passengers killed in the six states?
   - **e** What was the total number of pedal cyclists killed in the six states?

Why is NSW higher?

What do you think?

2. What was the difference between the total number of road deaths in New South Wales and Tasmania?
3. In Victoria, how many more drivers of motor vehicles died than passengers?
4. What was the difference between the total number of motor cyclists and pedal cyclists who died?
5. What was the total number of cyclists who died from traffic accidents in New South Wales?
6. Which two states had a combined total number of deaths of 501?
7. Which two states had a difference in the total number of deaths of 119?

ACTIVITY

- The information above reports that over 6600 people died on Australian roads in 2003. The population then was 19 827 000. The population 20 years later in 2023 was 26 334 000.
  - Do you think the number of road deaths would have declined or increased in that time?
  - Research the correct answer on the internet to find out. Was your answer correct?

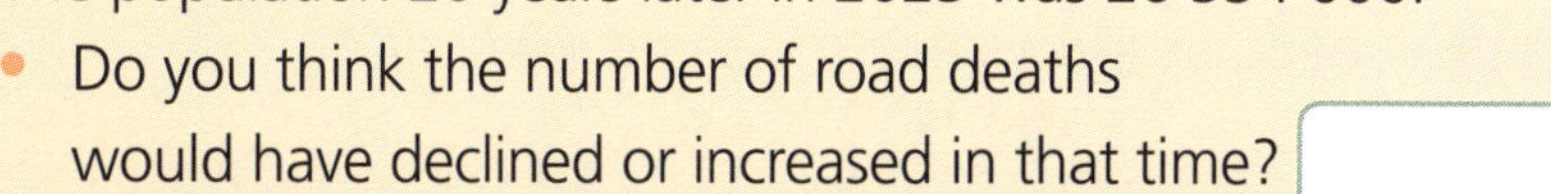

- Investigate safety measures which could be taken to reduce the number of traffic deaths. Discuss at least two safety measures for:
  - drivers
  - motor cyclists
  - pedal cyclists
  - passengers
  - pedestrians

See 2:53 (Using operations to solve problems).

Problem-solving strategies

Read, think, draw then calculate.

CONCEPT

How many faces would be showing if 22 cubes were placed on a table, end to end in a straight line?

Solution and reasoning

- Consider how many faces would show using 4 cubes. The two end cubes each have 4 faces showing. The two inside cubes each have 3 faces showing.
- Consider how many faces would show using 22 cubes. Each end cube would show 4 faces. Each inside cube would show 3 faces. The number of faces showing using 22 cubes: $(2 \times 4) + (20 \times 3) = 68$.

Altogether, 68 faces would be showing.

1. Matches are used to form squares end to end as shown.
   - **a** How many matches would be needed to form 70 squares? ☐
   - **b** How many matches would be used in the perimeter of this line of 70 squares? ☐ (Hint: Consider what is needed for each additional square.)

2. Matches are used to form triangles in a line as shown.
   - **a** How many would be needed to form 45 triangles? ☐
   - **b** How many would be used in the perimeter of this line of 45 triangles? ☐

3. Children's blocks (triangular prisms) are placed on a desk as shown.
   How many faces would be visible if there are:
   - **a** 5 blocks? ☐
   - **b** 50 blocks? ☐
   - **c** 132 blocks? ☐

4. Hexagonal paving bricks are stacked as shown.
   How many faces would be visible if we stacked:
   - **a** 3 bricks? ☐
   - **b** 20 bricks? ☐
   - **c** 37 bricks? ☐

Look for a pattern in the simpler case.

CONCEPT

How many 2-digit numbers can be made using the digits 2, 3, 4 and 5 if each digit is used only once in any one number?

Solution and reasoning

- List numbers starting with 2, 3, 4 then 5.

23	32	42	52
24	34	43	53
25	35	45	54

- No digit has been used twice in the same number.

Twelve 2-digit numbers can be made.

5. How many 2-digit numbers can be made using the digits:
   - **a** 5, 6, 7, 8 and 9 if each digit is used only once in any one number? ☐
   - **b** 0, 1, 2 and 3 if each digit is used only once in any one number? ☐
   - **c** 0, 1, 2, 3 and 4 if each digit can be used more than once in any one number? ☐

See 2:53 (Using operations to solve problems).

 • *AUSTRALIAN SIGNPOST MATHS 5* • ISBN 9780655708797

Problem-solving strategies

Even *trial and error* is a strategy.

Use this diagram of 5 dots to find how many intervals can be drawn that join pairs of dots.

Solution and reasoning

- Start at one point. Draw intervals to each of the other points.
- From the next point, draw any additional intervals possible.
- Do this at all other points, counting the intervals as you draw them.

4 + 3 + 2 + 1 = 10 Ten intervals can be drawn.

start

1. Use this diagram of 6 dots to find how many intervals can be drawn that join pairs of dots. ______

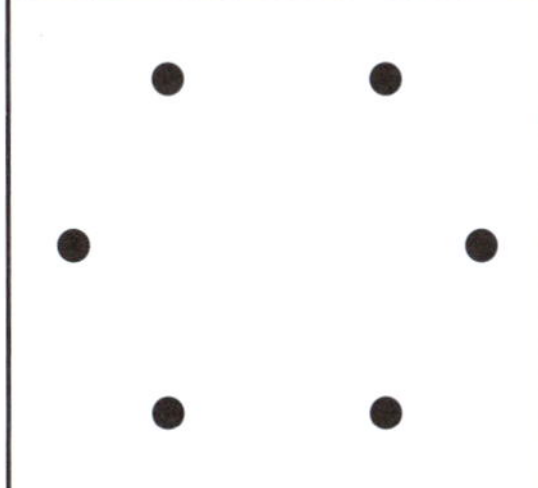

2. Use this diagram of 8 dots to find how many intervals can be drawn that join pairs of dots. ______

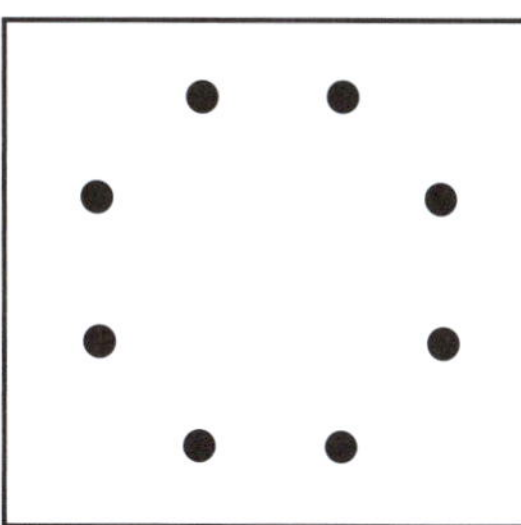

3. a Use the diagram of 9 dots to find the number of intervals that can be drawn from the centre to the other dots. ______

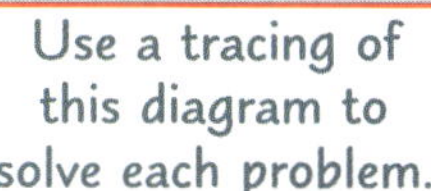

b How many intervals can be drawn from just one corner dot to any other dot, if the interval does not pass through a third dot? ______

c How many intervals can be drawn if each interval joins two dots and does not pass through a third dot? ______

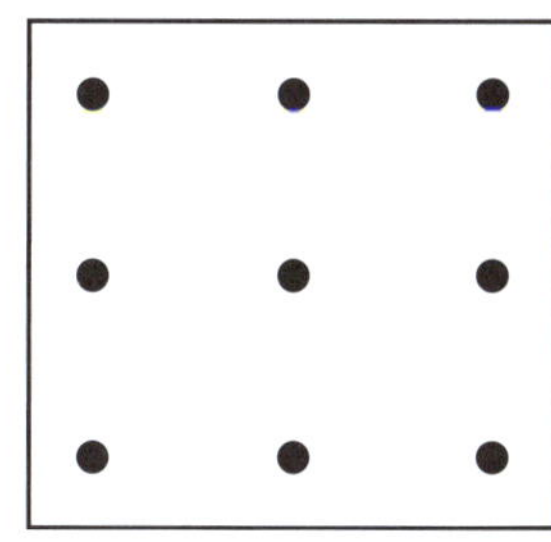

4. Use the diagram of 9 dots to find the number of squares that can be drawn using four of the dots as corners. ______

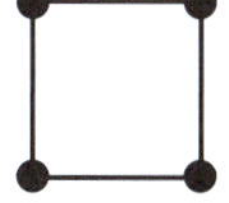

5. Write each of the numbers 1 to 24 in its proper place on this Venn diagram.

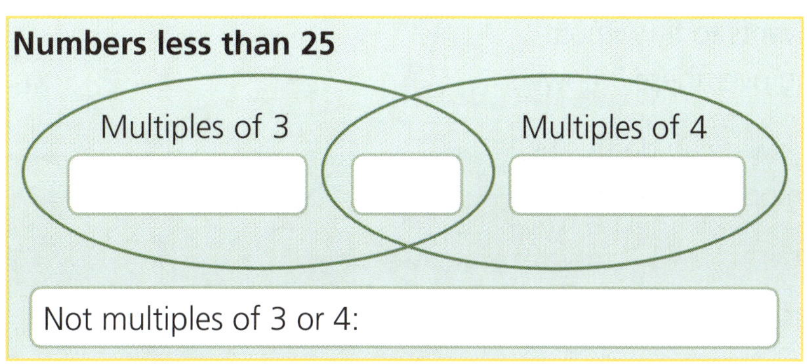

6. Does the height of a person depend on age? Explain your answer.

See 2:53 (Using operations to solve problems) and Extra Support 14 and 16 (Problem solving strategies).

Problem solving

Thinking outside the box means thinking in an original or creative way.

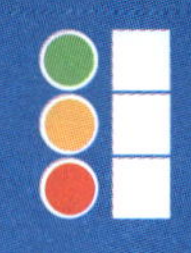

CONCEPT

Three different coloured cubes are used to make a tower. How many differently coloured towers is it possible to make?

Solution
These are the towers that can be built.

Answer
There are 6 different coloured towers.

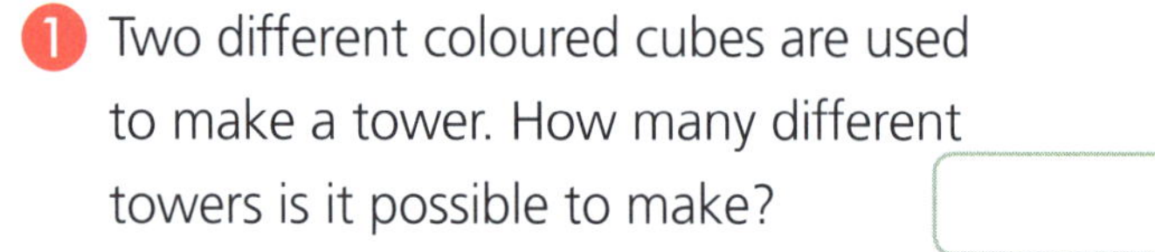

1. Two different coloured cubes are used to make a tower. How many different towers is it possible to make? ☐
2. Three different coloured cubes are used to make a tower which is two blocks high. How many towers is it possible to make? ☐
3. Four different coloured cubes are used to make a tower which is three blocks high. How many towers is it possible to make? ☐

4. Using only the coins shown above, list all the different ways you can make:
   - **a** 25 cents ☐
   - **b** 40 cents ☐
   - **c** 65 cents ☐
5. Using only the coins shown above, what is the least number of coins needed to make:
   - **a** 35 cents? ☐ **b** 60 cents? ☐ **c** 75 cents? ☐ **d** $1.25? ☐

FUN SPOT

6. A bee wants to fly without stopping over these 9 flowers.

   Show how it can do this by flying in only 4 straight lines.

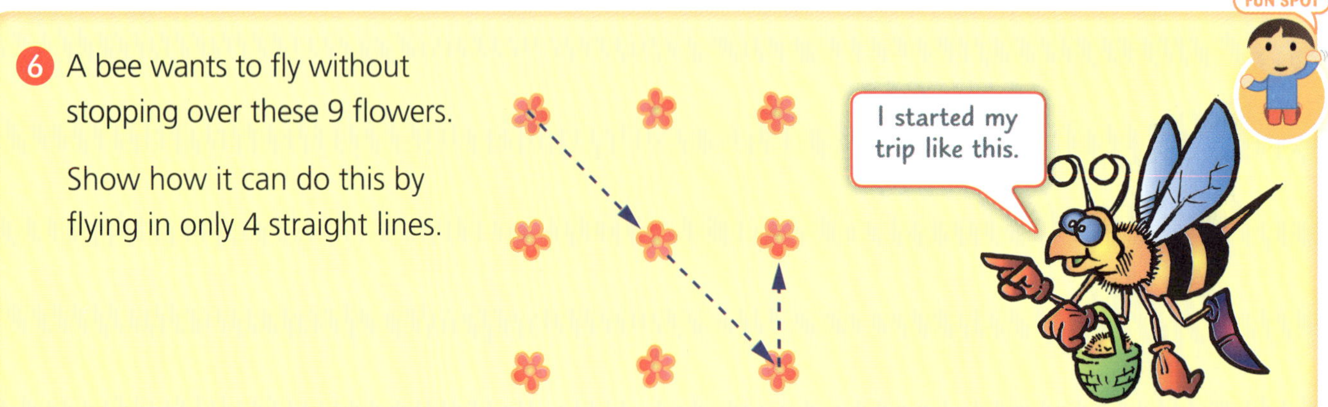

See 2:53 (Using operations to solve problems) and *Extra Support 14 to 15* (Problem-solving strategies).

 • *AUSTRALIAN SIGNPOST MATHS 5* • ISBN 9780655708797

Averages

What is the average of 2 L, 3 L and 700 mL?

We need the same unit in each.
Average = (2000 + 3000 + 700) ÷ 3 mL

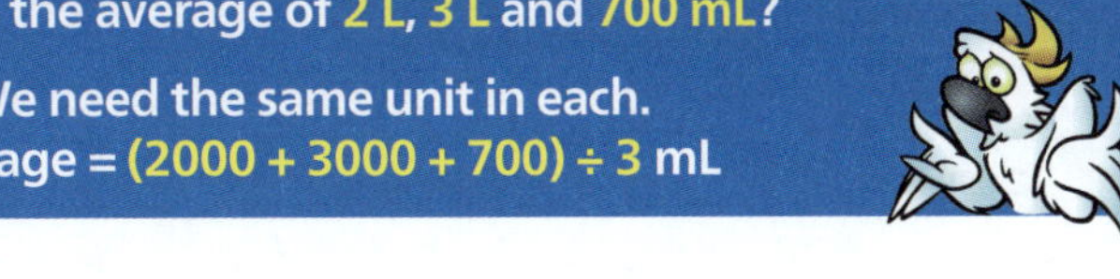

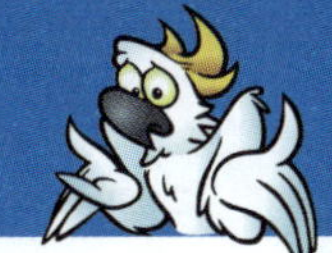

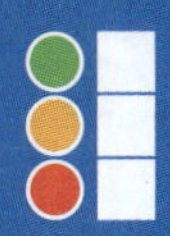

CONCEPT

120 marbles
30 marbles
60 marbles
Naomi
Sandy
Luke

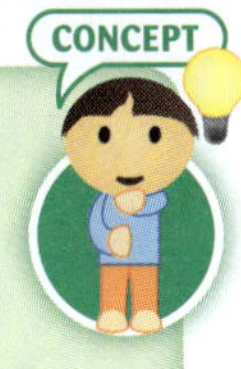

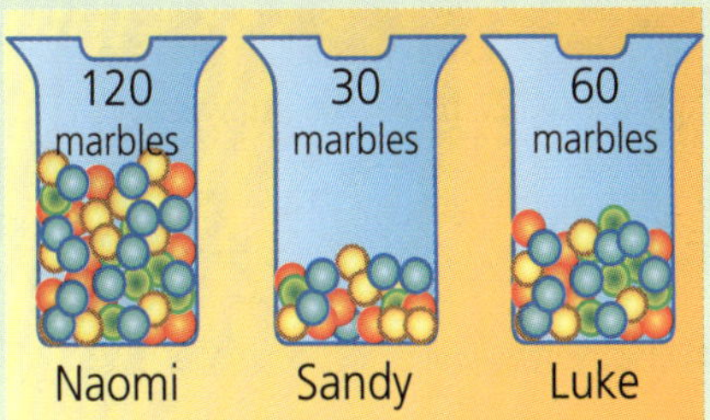

Find the average number of marbles in the three containers.

- Let's share the marbles.
  Step 1: Naomi gives Sandy 40.
  Step 2: Naomi gives Luke 10.

  70 is a fair share.

N	S	L
80	70	60
70	70	70

- Another way to share is to divide the total number of marbles by 3.
  The average = (120 + 30 + 60) ÷ 3

$$3 \overline{)\,210} = 70$$

The average is 70 marbles.

The average (or mean) is an **equal share**.

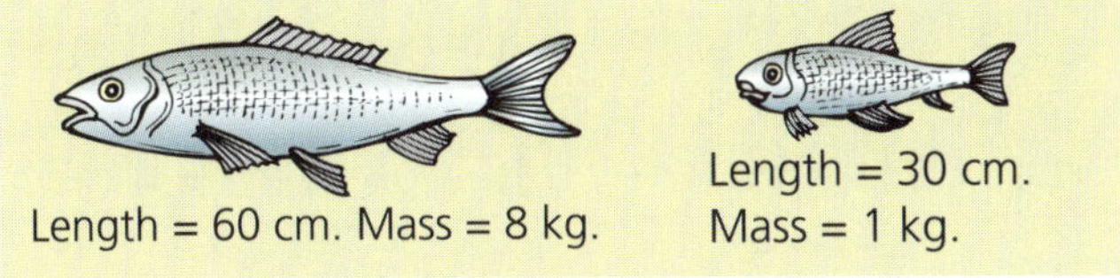

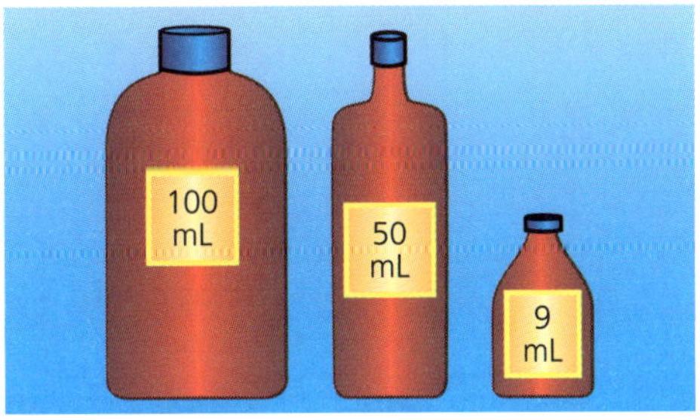

Length = 60 cm. Mass = 8 kg.
Length = 30 cm.
Mass = 1 kg.

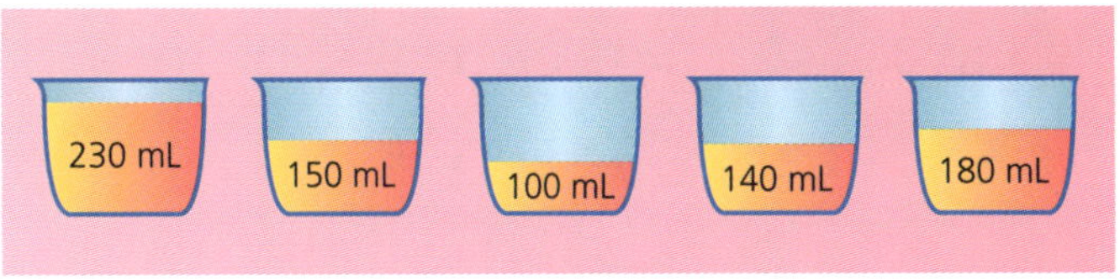

230 mL
150 mL
100 mL
140 mL
180 mL

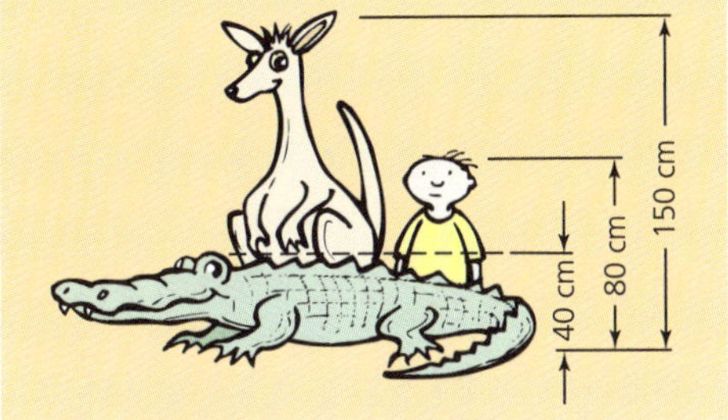

150 cm
80 cm
40 cm

100 mL
50 mL
9 mL

1 a Find the average length of the two fish.

b Find the average mass of the two fish.

c Find the average height of the kangaroo, the boy and the crocodile.

d What is the average contents of the bottles?

e What is the average contents of the cups?

f The contents of the cups are shared among five. How much does each receive?

2 At Heather's birthday party, the children played 'find the chocolates'. Alana found 12, Rachel 15, Naomi 10, Luke 6 and Miranda 12.

a If they shared all fairly, how many would each child receive?

b What was the average number of chocolates each found?

Always estimate first.

3 Within these rectangles, each small square has a length of 3 mm.

a What is the average width of these rectangles?

b What is the average height of these rectangles?

c What is the average number of small squares?

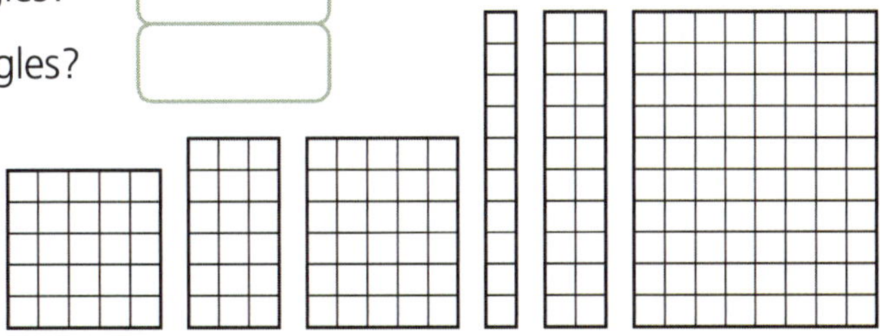

See 2:38 (Averages).

Finding missing numbers

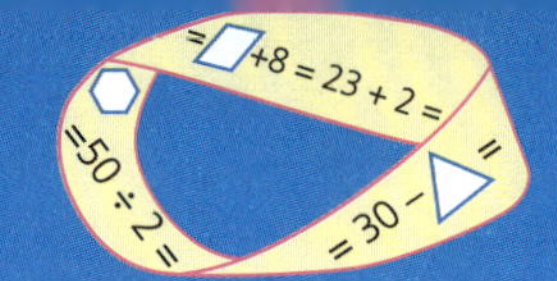

Write the missing number in each sentence.

1
a □ + 8 = 10 b □ + 3 = 7 c □ + 8 = 15
d 9 + □ = 12 e 8 + □ = 17 f 10 + □ = 10
g □ + 11 = 15 h □ + 9 = 14 i □ + 12 = 12
j 14 + □ = 20 k 18 + □ = 23 l 17 + □ = 19
m □ + 9 = 20 n □ + 15 = 25 o □ + 11 = 40

2
a 8 – □ = 1 b 9 – □ = 0 c 15 – □ = 10 d 10 – □ = 10
e □ – 3 = 7 f □ – 10 = 10 g □ – 7 = 8 h □ – 5 = 4
i 11 – □ = 4 j 11 – □ = 7 k 14 – □ = 6 l 14 – □ = 8
m □ – 8 = 4 n □ – 3 = 9 o □ – 1 = 19 p □ – 11 = 20

3
a □ × 6 = 18 b □ × 5 = 35 c □ × 4 = 24 d □ × 3 = 27
e 4 × □ = 20 f 7 × □ = 21 g 9 × □ = 90 h 8 × □ = 40
i □ × 10 = 80 j □ × 6 = 36 k □ × 4 = 28 l □ × 5 = 35
m 7 × □ = 56 n 8 × □ = 72 o 5 × □ = 45 p 9 × □ = 63

4
a □ ÷ 2 = 8 b □ ÷ 4 = 3 c □ ÷ 5 = 8
d 24 ÷ □ = 3 e 24 ÷ □ = 4 f 24 ÷ □ = 8
g □ squared = 9 h □ squared = 64
i □ squared = 100 j □ squared = 49

To square a number, multiply it by itself.

5
a 6 + 7 + □ = 15 b 3 – 1 + □ = 12 c 8 + 7 + □ = 20
d 4 × 2 + □ = 10 e 6 × 5 – □ = 26 f 21 ÷ 3 + □ = 13
g 2 × □ + 1 = 9 h 3 × □ + 2 = 17 i 2 × □ + 1 = 7

6
a 5 × (4 + 6) = (5 × □) + (5 × 6) b 3 × (9 + □) = (3 × 9) + (3 × 2)
c 7 × (3 + 4) = (7 × 3) + (7 × □) d 4 × (□ + 2) = (4 × 8) + (4 × 2)

See 2:60 (Finding missing numbers).

Extension: enlargements

Orientation stays the same but size changes

CONCEPT

Each point on the large shape is three times as far from centre **O** as the same point on the smaller shape. We have drawn an **enlargement** of the small shape.

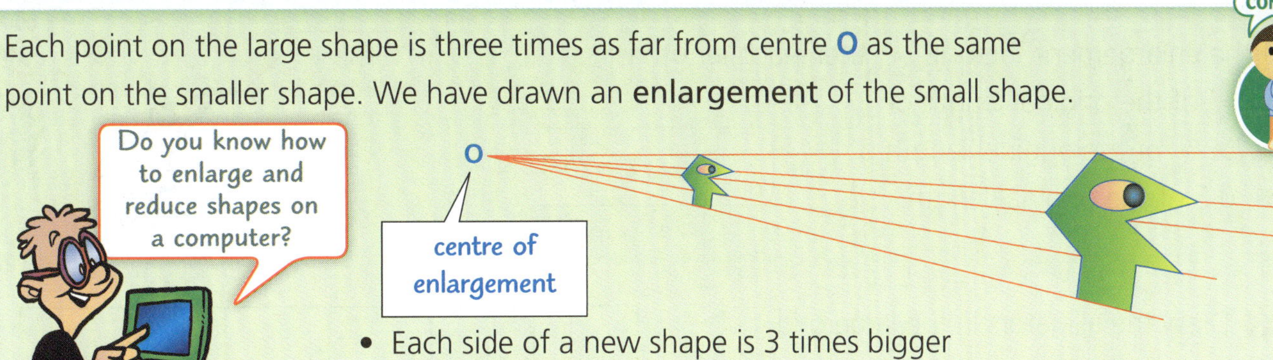

- Each side of a new shape is 3 times bigger than that side on the small shape.
- The enlargement factor is 3 (or 300%).

1. By doubling the distance of each point from the centre, draw a shape that has been enlarged by a scale factor of 2.

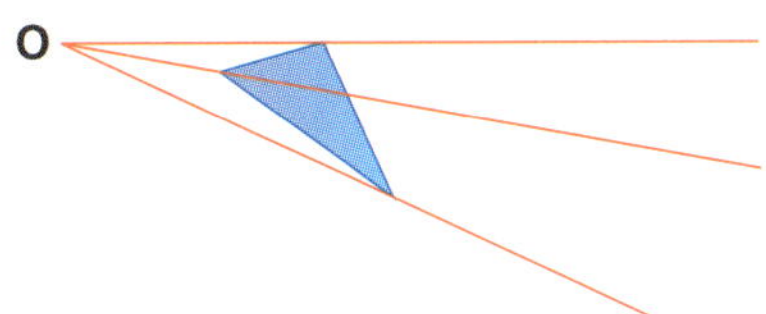

In each case the enlargement factor of the new shape is ______.

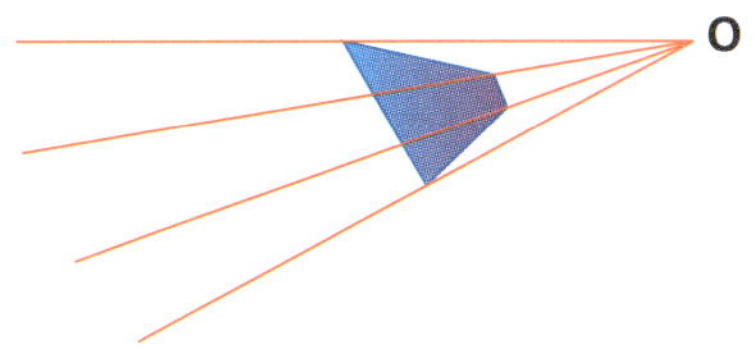

2. Here the centre of enlargement is inside the shape. Enlarge each shape by a scale factor of 3.

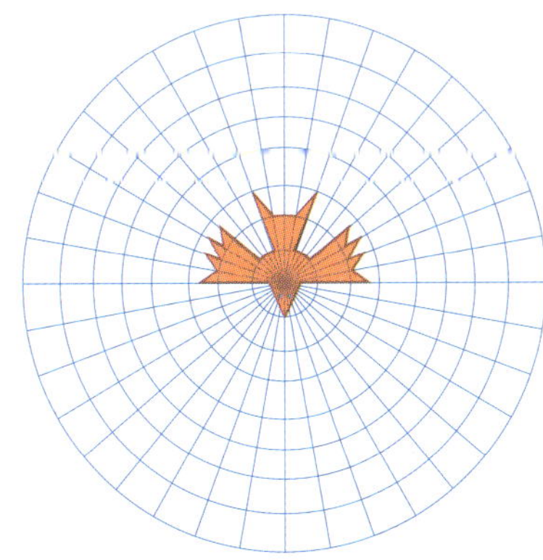

In each case the enlargement factor of the new shape is ______.

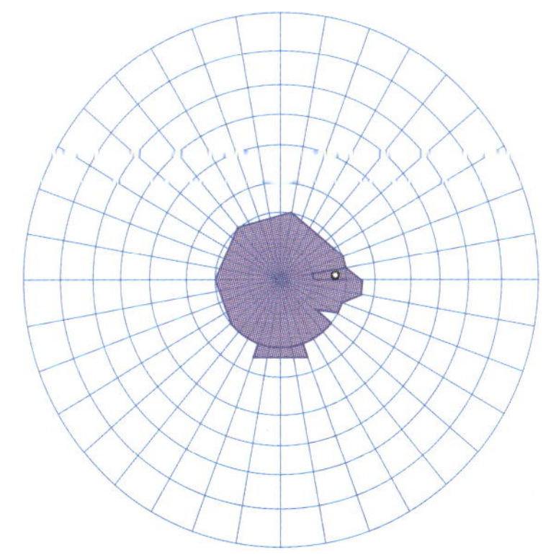

3. Each of these rectangles has the same shape.
   - **a** What is the enlargement factor of B if A is the original? ______
   - **b** What is the enlargement factor of C if A is the original? ______
   - **c** What is the enlargement factor of C if B is the original? ______
   - **d** What is the enlargement factor of A if B is the original? ______

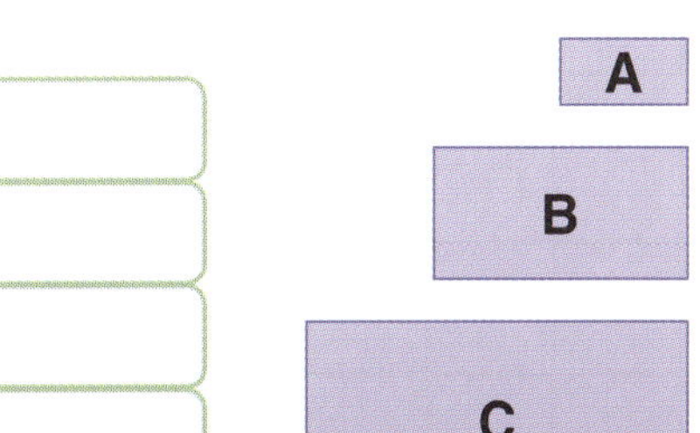

- Using a graphics program on your computer, enlarge and reduce a variety of shapes.

See 4:03 (Reflection, translation, rotation) and 4:04 (Flip, slide, turn).

Extension: enlargements

Orientation stays the same but size changes

CONCEPT

If the enlargement factor is $\frac{1}{2}$, then each length is:

- $\frac{1}{2}$ of the original length or
- 50% of the original length or
- 0·5 of the original length.

$\frac{1}{2}$ = 50% = 0·5

1 Draw the alligators in the large grid by copying one square at a time.

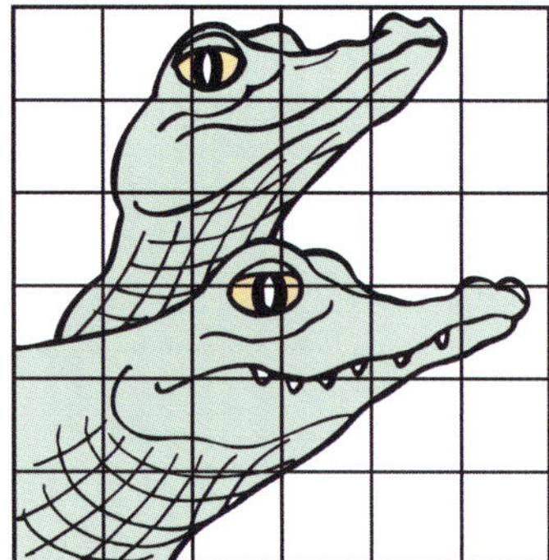

What enlargement factor has been used to make the larger drawing? ☐

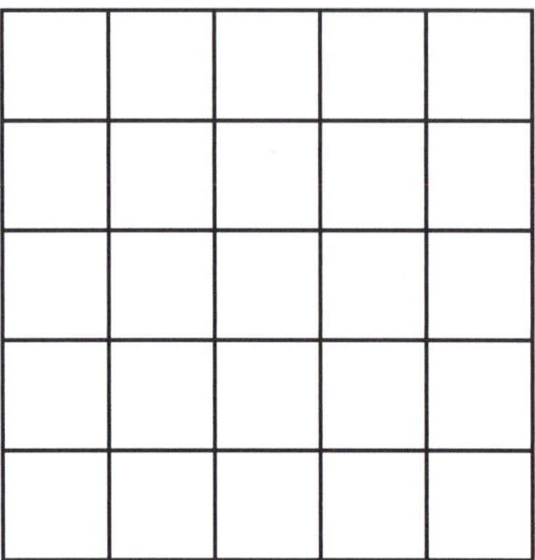

2 Copy the frog onto the grid below it. What enlargement factor has been used on the copy you are making? ☐

3 Copy the camel onto the smaller grid beside it. Here the enlargement factor is $\frac{2}{3}$ or $\frac{4}{6}$. It is a reduction.

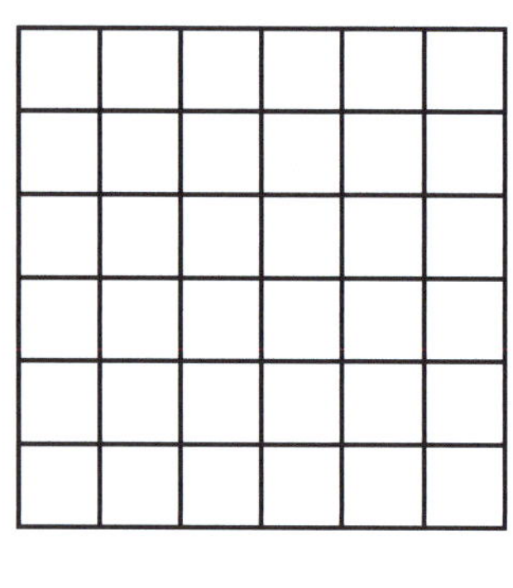

4 Draw a grid on a picture of your own and copy it.

See 4:03 (Reflection, translation, rotation) and 4:04 (Flip, slide turn).

 • *AUSTRALIAN SIGNPOST MATHS 5* • ISBN 9780655708797

Decimals!

What does a million look like?
Ha!
What does one millionth look like?

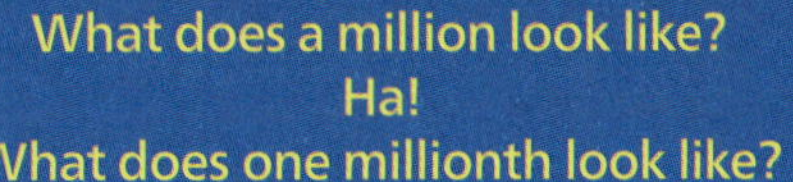

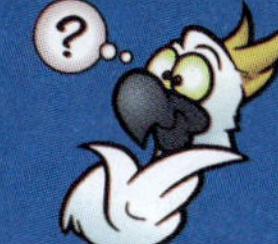

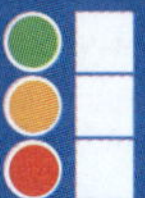

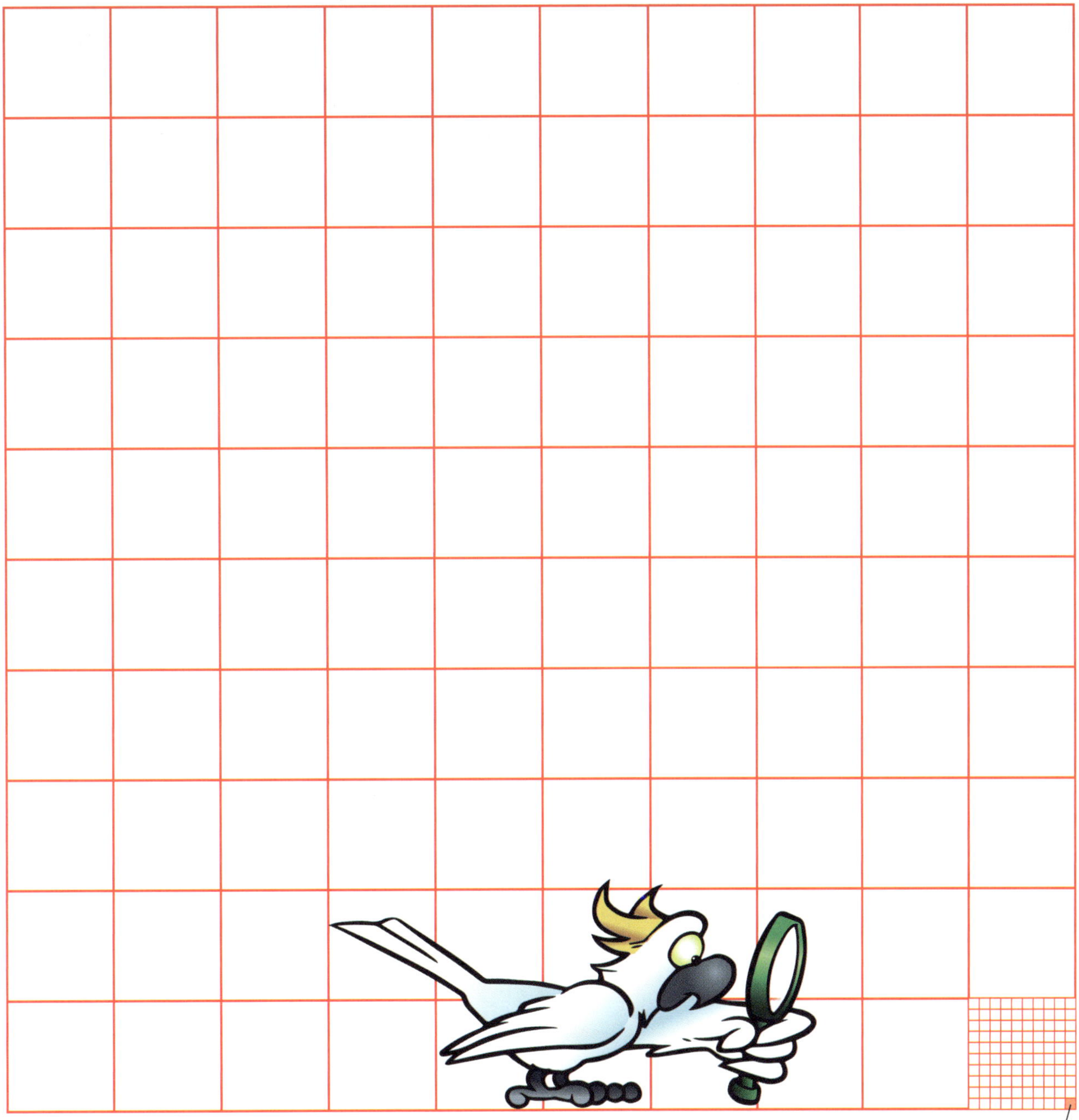

This hundred square represents 1 whole.

- Each part of the hundred square is *one hundredth* of the whole.
  That is *0·01 of the whole*.

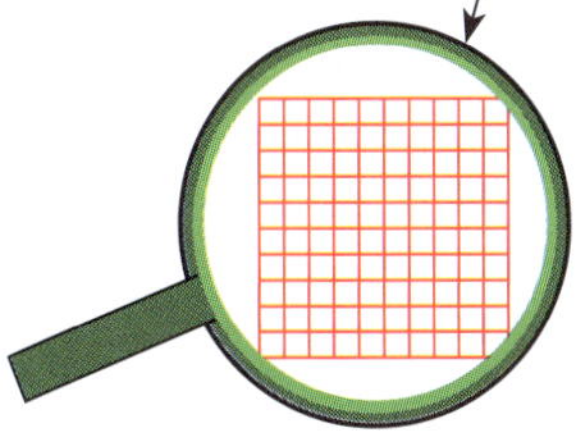

- The square in the bottom corner (0·01) has been cut into 100 parts.
  Each small square is *one ten-thousandth* of the whole. That is *0·0001 of the whole*.
  10 000 small squares would fit into the large hundred square.
- One of these very small squares (0·0001) has been cut into 100 parts. It is hard to see the separate parts. Each of these tiny squares is one millionth of the original hundred square. That's 0·000 001 of the whole. One million tiny squares make up the whole hundred square.

See 1:01 (Numbers using millions), 1:02 (Large numbers) and 1:25 (Using decimals).

 • *AUSTRALIAN SIGNPOST MATHS 5* • ISBN 9780655708797

Answers

1:01

1

	Ten millions	Millions	Hundred thousands	Ten thousands	Thousands	Hundreds	Tens	Ones
A			8	6	9	0	0	0
B		4	8	0	1	6	4	9
C	3	6	3	4	1	5	7	5
D	1	5	6	5	0	0	0	0

a A, B, D, C b 18 650 000 c 37 841 575

2 a 6 372 840 b 7 500 000 c 18 120 452
d 36 752 000 e 5 360 000 f 6 829 000

1:02

1

	Billions	Millions	Thousands	Ones
A			564	027
B		10	215	982
C		250	940	000
D	36	814	000	000
E	12	655	700	000

Order: A, B, C, E, D

2 a 860 000 000 b 70 000 000
c 14 000 000 000 d 2 000 000 000
e 308 000 000 f 100 000 000 000
g 150 238 000 km h 1 417 792 656
i 40 208 000 000 km j 1 071 360 000 km

1:03

Header: 5000, 5000, 6000, 6000

Concept: 17 000

1 a 6 949 271 b 17 302 689
c 8 905 784 d 99 999 000

2 a 3 000 000 + 400 000 + 70 000 + 5000 + 600
b 800 000 + 40 000 + 7000 + 200 + 30 + 1
c 20 000 000 + 6 000 000 + 800 000 + 9000 + 50
d 80 000 000 + 500 000 + 20 000 + 300

3 a 76 000 000 b 33 000 000
c 10 000 000 d 90 000 000

4 a 7350 b 16 423

5 a 307 350 b 516 423

1:04

1 a 100 b 43 c $\frac{57}{100}$ d 7 e 10

2 a 1 b $\frac{3}{4}$ c $\frac{1}{3}$
d 1 e $\frac{5}{8}$ f $\frac{6}{10}$

3 a $\frac{1}{4}$ b $\frac{3}{10}$ c $\frac{3}{8}$
d $\frac{2}{5}$ e $\frac{1}{10}$ f $\frac{5}{8}$

4 a

Three small rectangles will be coloured. 3

b 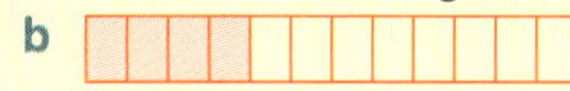

Four small rectangles will be coloured. 4

c $\frac{1}{3}$

d 3 rectangles will be coloured red.
5 rectangles will be coloured blue.

1:05

1 a 0, $\frac{1}{4}$, $\frac{1}{2}$, 1 $\frac{1}{2} > \frac{1}{4}$ b 0, $\frac{1}{10}$, $\frac{1}{3}$, 1 $\frac{1}{10} < \frac{1}{3}$

c 0, $\frac{1}{8}$, $\frac{1}{2}$, 1 $\frac{1}{2} > \frac{1}{8}$ d 0, $\frac{1}{6}$, $\frac{1}{3}$, 1 $\frac{1}{6} < \frac{1}{3}$

e 

$\frac{1}{10} < \frac{1}{5}$

2 a $\frac{1}{5}$, $\frac{1}{4}$, $\frac{1}{2}$ b $\frac{1}{100}$, $\frac{1}{20}$, $\frac{1}{10}$
c $\frac{1}{8}$, $\frac{1}{3}$, $\frac{1}{2}$ d $\frac{1}{12}$, $\frac{1}{8}$, $\frac{1}{4}$, $\frac{1}{2}$

3 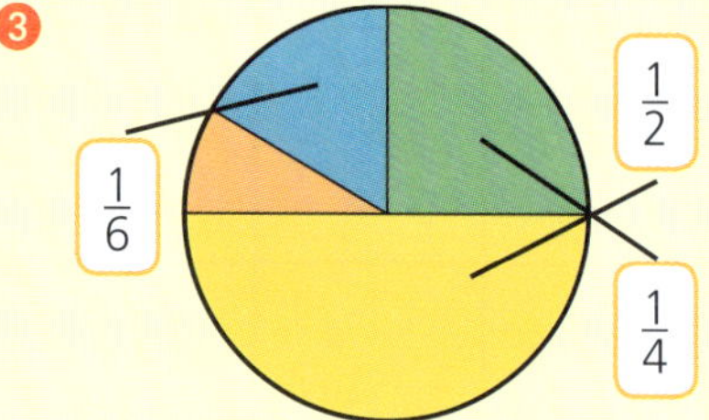

4 

5 smaller

6 $\frac{3}{4}$

1:06

1 a $\frac{78}{100}$ or 0·78 b $\frac{56}{100}$ or 0·56
c $\frac{63}{100}$ or 0·63 d $\frac{39}{100}$ or 0·39

2 a $2\frac{60}{100}$ or 2·6 b $1\frac{54}{100}$ or 1·54
c $2\frac{87}{100}$ or 2·87 d $1\frac{15}{100}$ or 1·15

3 a 2·37 b 1·76 c 6·08
d 9·95 e 7·81 f 5·03

4 a $6\frac{25}{100}$ b $3\frac{4}{100}$ c $9\frac{42}{100}$

5 $2\frac{75}{100}$

6 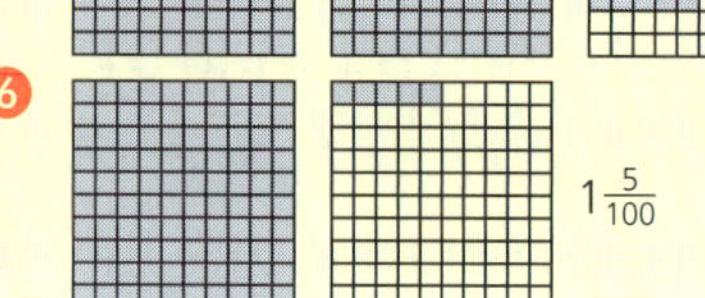

1:07

Header: 0·7 is the larger decimal

1 a 0·8 b 0·3 c 0·9 d 0·4 e 0·8
f 0·3 g 1·0 h 1·6 i 2·5 j 7·9

2 a $\frac{5}{10}$ — 0·5 | $\frac{8}{10}$ — 0·2 | $\frac{2}{10}$ — 0·8
b $2\frac{3}{10}$ — 2·03 | $2\frac{93}{100}$ — 2·93 | $2\frac{3}{100}$ — 2·3
c $4\frac{6}{10}$ — 4·5 | $4\frac{5}{100}$ — 4·6 | $4\frac{5}{10}$ — 4·05

3 a 0·9 b 0·5 c 0·12 d 0·34 e 0·4
f 1·6 g 2·3 h 1·12 i 3·8 j 3·02
k 6·9 l 2·87

4 a

0	$\frac{1}{10}$	$\frac{2}{10}$	$\frac{3}{10}$	$\frac{4}{10}$	$\frac{5}{10}$	$\frac{6}{10}$	$\frac{7}{10}$	$\frac{8}{10}$	$\frac{9}{10}$	1
0	0·1	0·2	0·3	0·4	0·5	0·6	0·7	0·8	0·9	1·0

b

3	$3\frac{1}{10}$	$3\frac{2}{10}$	$3\frac{3}{10}$	$3\frac{4}{10}$	$3\frac{5}{10}$	$3\frac{6}{10}$	$3\frac{7}{10}$	$3\frac{8}{10}$	$3\frac{9}{10}$	4	$4\frac{1}{10}$
3	3·1	3·2	3·3	3·4	3·5	3·6	3·7	3·8	3·9	4·0	4·1

1:08

1 a 80% b 65% c 75% d 40% e 30%
f 45% g 95% h 90%

2 a 20% b 35% c 25% d 60% e 70%
f 55% g 5% h 10%

3 a $\frac{25}{100}$, 25% b $\frac{65}{100}$, 65% c $\frac{45}{100}$, 45%
d $\frac{80}{100}$, 80% e $\frac{50}{100}$, 50% f $\frac{20}{100}$, 20%
g $\frac{60}{100}$, 60% h $\frac{35}{100}$, 35% i $\frac{75}{100}$, 75%
j $\frac{55}{100}$, 55% k $\frac{95}{100}$, 95% l $\frac{40}{100}$, 40%

1:09

Header: 75%

1 a b c d e f g h

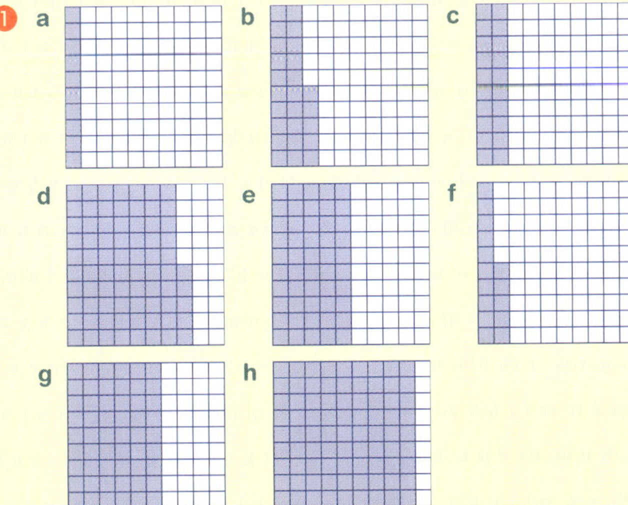

2 a 90% b 75% c 80% d 25%
e 50% f 85% g 40% h 10%

3 a 0·17, 17% b 0·76, 76% c 0·27, 27%
d 0·49, 49% e 0·98, 98% f 0·81, 81%
g 0·31, 31% h 0·12, 12% i 0·34, 34%
j 0·28, 28% k 0·63, 63% l 0·94, 94%

4 a 0·65 b 0·15 c 0·95 d 0·45 e 0·75
f 0·25 g 0·05 h 0·6 i 0·8 j 0·4
k 0·1 l 0·37 m 0·91 n 0·2 o 1

1:10

1 a $\frac{2}{6}$ or $\frac{1}{3}$ b $\frac{2}{4}$ or $\frac{1}{2}$ c 1 d $\frac{2}{8}$ or $\frac{1}{4}$

2 a $\frac{3}{4}$ b $\frac{5}{8}$ c $\frac{1}{2}$ d $\frac{4}{5}$

3 a 1 ÷ 2 b 3 ÷ 4 c 2 ÷ 5 d 7 ÷ 8

Concept: Alfie is $\frac{1}{3}$ of the way to the finish.
Rona is $\frac{2}{3}$ of the way to the finish.
Answers will vary. Niki is less than half way up the ladder.

4 a $\frac{1}{3}$ b $\frac{2}{3}$

5 If Heather's cake was much larger than Tom's cake, $\frac{1}{4}$ of Heather's cake could be larger than $\frac{1}{2}$ of Tom's cake.

1:11

1 a $\frac{17}{4}$ b $\frac{5}{4}$ c $\frac{5}{2}$ d $\frac{17}{5}$ e $\frac{9}{5}$
f $\frac{11}{4}$ g $\frac{10}{4}$ h $\frac{8}{3}$ i $\frac{17}{10}$ j $\frac{32}{10}$
k $\frac{25}{10}$ l $\frac{48}{10}$

2 a $2\frac{1}{4}$ b $2\frac{1}{3}$ c $2\frac{1}{2}$ d $1\frac{3}{4}$ e $3\frac{2}{3}$
f $2\frac{2}{4}$ g $2\frac{4}{5}$ h $8\frac{1}{2}$ i $1\frac{7}{10}$ j $4\frac{1}{10}$
k $3\frac{6}{10}$ l $5\frac{5}{10}$

1:12

1 a $\frac{4}{8}$ b $\frac{7}{8}$ c $\frac{3}{5}$ d $\frac{4}{5}$

2 a $\frac{6}{10}$ b $\frac{7}{10}$ c $\frac{9}{10}$ d $\frac{9}{10}$
e $\frac{7}{10}$ f $\frac{9}{10}$ g $\frac{8}{10}$ h $\frac{9}{10}$

3 a $\frac{8}{8}$ or 1 b $\frac{11}{8}$ or $1\frac{3}{8}$ c $\frac{10}{8}$ or $1\frac{2}{8}$ d $\frac{9}{8}$ or $1\frac{1}{8}$

4 a true b false c false d false
e true f true g true h false

5 a $\frac{8}{12}$ b $\frac{1}{10}$

1:13

1 a $\frac{4}{8}$ b $\frac{5}{8}$ c $\frac{3}{10}$
d $\frac{5}{10}$ e $\frac{3}{6}$ f $\frac{3}{6}$

2 a $\frac{2}{10}$ b $\frac{2}{10}$ c $\frac{5}{10}$ d $\frac{4}{10}$
e $\frac{1}{10}$ f $\frac{5}{10}$ g $\frac{1}{10}$ h $\frac{3}{10}$

3 a $\frac{4}{8}$ b $\frac{2}{8}$ c $\frac{4}{8}$ d $\frac{3}{8}$ e $\frac{7}{8}$ f $\frac{2}{5}$

4 a true b false c true d true

1:14

1 a 5·753 b 4·957 c 5·748 d 9·358
e 8·254 f 2·574

2

	Units	·	10ths	100ths	1000ths
a	3	·	1	9	7
b	5	·	6	3	8
c	9	·	2	4	9
d	6	·	5	4	8
e	8	·	3	5	2
f	2	·	7	1	9

1:15

1 a 0·8 b 0·1 c 0·5 d 7·5 e 4·1
f 9·3 g 0·64 h 0·33 i 0·25 j 0·805
k 0·065 l 215·5 m 90·8 n 11·125 o 33·333
p 296·48 q 507·05 r $90.15 s $971.06

2 a & b

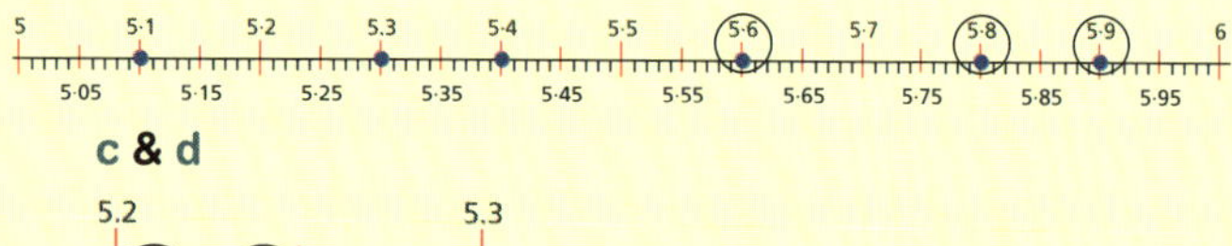

c & d

5.2 5.25 5.3

1:16

1 a $\frac{10}{8}$ b $\frac{9}{5}$ c $\frac{7}{4}$ d $\frac{7}{2}$ e $\frac{13}{5}$ f $\frac{19}{10}$

2 a $1\frac{3}{5}$ b $1\frac{1}{3}$ c $2\frac{1}{4}$ d $1\frac{1}{8}$

3 a $\frac{4}{8}$ b $\frac{3}{4}$ c $\frac{9}{10}$ d $\frac{4}{5}$ e $\frac{6}{5}$ f $\frac{8}{5}$
g $\frac{6}{5}$ h $\frac{9}{5}$ i $\frac{10}{10}$ j $\frac{16}{10}$ k $\frac{10}{10}$ l $\frac{13}{10}$
m $\frac{6}{8}$ n $\frac{4}{5}$ o $\frac{5}{10}$ p $\frac{9}{10}$

4 a $\frac{2}{4}$ b $\frac{2}{5}$ c $\frac{3}{10}$ d $\frac{2}{8}$ e $\frac{2}{5}$ f $\frac{6}{8}$
g $\frac{2}{3}$ h $\frac{1}{4}$ i $\frac{5}{10}$ j $\frac{9}{10}$ k $\frac{5}{10}$ l $\frac{6}{10}$

1:17

1 a $\frac{2}{6}$ or $\frac{3}{9}$ b $\frac{3}{3}$ or $\frac{6}{6}$ c $\frac{1}{3}$ or $\frac{2}{6}$
d $\frac{4}{6}$ or $\frac{6}{9}$ e $\frac{1}{3}$ or $\frac{3}{9}$ f $\frac{2}{3}$ or $\frac{6}{9}$
g $\frac{3}{3}$ or $\frac{9}{9}$ h $\frac{2}{3}$ or $\frac{4}{6}$

2 a false b true c true d true
e true f false g true h false

3 a

0 $\frac{1}{3}$ $\frac{2}{3}$ 1

0 $\frac{1}{6}$ $\frac{2}{6}$ $\frac{3}{6}$ $\frac{4}{6}$ $\frac{5}{6}$ 1

0 $\frac{1}{9}$ $\frac{2}{9}$ $\frac{3}{9}$ $\frac{4}{9}$ $\frac{5}{9}$ $\frac{6}{9}$ $\frac{7}{9}$ $\frac{8}{9}$ 1

b

0 $\frac{1}{2}$ 1

0 $\frac{1}{5}$ $\frac{2}{5}$ $\frac{3}{5}$ $\frac{4}{5}$ 1

0 $\frac{1}{10}$ $\frac{2}{10}$ $\frac{3}{10}$ $\frac{4}{10}$ $\frac{5}{10}$ $\frac{6}{10}$ $\frac{7}{10}$ $\frac{8}{10}$ $\frac{9}{10}$ 1

4 a true b true c false d true
e true f false g false h false
i false j true k true l false

5 a $\frac{2}{6}$ or $\frac{3}{9}$ b $\frac{2}{3}$ or $\frac{6}{9}$ c $\frac{5}{10}$ or $\frac{3}{6}$
d $\frac{2}{3}$ or $\frac{4}{6}$ e $\frac{4}{5}$ f $\frac{1}{3}$ or $\frac{2}{6}$
g $\frac{4}{6}$ or $\frac{6}{9}$ h $\frac{2}{10}$

1:18

1 a $\frac{2}{8}$ b $\frac{4}{10}$ c $\frac{6}{8}$ d $\frac{2}{10}$ e $\frac{2}{4}$
f $\frac{6}{10}$ g $\frac{4}{8}$ h $\frac{8}{10}$ i $\frac{4}{8}$ j $\frac{10}{10}$

2 a $\frac{2}{8}$ b $\frac{4}{8}$ c $\frac{2}{10}$ d $\frac{6}{10}$ e $\frac{6}{8}$
f $\frac{8}{10}$ g $\frac{2}{4}$ h $\frac{4}{10}$ i $\frac{2}{6}$ j $\frac{2}{12}$
k $\frac{8}{12}$ l $\frac{8}{12}$

3 a $\frac{1}{3}\ \frac{(\times4)}{(\times4)} = \frac{4}{12}$ b $\frac{3}{6}\ \frac{(\times2)}{(\times2)} = \frac{6}{12}$ c $\frac{2}{3}\ \frac{(\times4)}{(\times4)} = \frac{8}{12}$
d $\frac{2}{6}\ \frac{(\times2)}{(\times2)} = \frac{4}{12}$ e $\frac{4}{10}\ \frac{(\times2)}{(\times2)} = \frac{8}{20}$ f $\frac{3}{5}\ \frac{(\times3)}{(\times3)} = \frac{9}{15}$
g $\frac{3}{5}\ \frac{(\times2)}{(\times2)} = \frac{6}{10}$ h $\frac{1}{4}\ \frac{(\times5)}{(\times5)} = \frac{5}{20}$ i $\frac{2}{7}\ \frac{(\times3)}{(\times3)} = \frac{6}{21}$
j $\frac{7}{5}\ \frac{(\times2)}{(\times2)} = \frac{14}{10}$ k $\frac{11}{3}\ \frac{(\times3)}{(\times3)} = \frac{33}{9}$ l $\frac{5}{2}\ \frac{(\times4)}{(\times4)} = \frac{20}{8}$

1:19

1 a $\frac{2}{6}$ b $\frac{3}{12}$ c $\frac{5}{10}$ d $\frac{3}{15}$
e $\frac{6}{15}$ f $\frac{8}{12}$ g $\frac{6}{8}$ h $\frac{9}{15}$

2 a $\frac{4}{8}$ b $\frac{2}{10}$ c $\frac{3}{9}$ d $\frac{2}{12}$
e $\frac{4}{6}$ f $\frac{3}{6}$ g $\frac{4}{20}$ h $\frac{4}{12}$

3 a $\frac{2}{8}$ b $\frac{2}{12}$ c $\frac{2}{4}$ d $\frac{2}{10}$ e $\frac{2}{6}$

4 a $\frac{3}{18}$ b $\frac{6}{9}$ c $\frac{3}{9}$ d $\frac{9}{12}$ e $\frac{12}{15}$

5 a $\frac{4}{16}$ b $\frac{4}{20}$ c $\frac{4}{12}$ d $\frac{12}{16}$ e $\frac{8}{12}$

6 a 4 b 3 c 3 d 2 e 2
f 2 g 2 h 2 i 5 j 4

7 a $\frac{1}{2} = \frac{2}{4} = \frac{3}{6} = \frac{4}{8} = \frac{5}{10} = \frac{6}{12}$
b $\frac{1}{3} = \frac{2}{6} = \frac{3}{9} = \frac{4}{12} = \frac{5}{15} = \frac{6}{18}$

1:20

1 a 0·079, 0·125, 0·35, 0·4
b 74·375, 80·725, 99·9, 100·04
c 3·095, 3·49, 3·5, 3·52, 4, 4·2
d 0·066, 0·1, 0·139, 0·3, 0·51, 1
e 0·1212, 1·212, 12·12, 121·2, 1212

2 a true b true c true
d true e true f true

3 a 4·6 b 14·3 c 0·4
d 60·2 e 154·1 f 33·3

4 a 9·63 b 14·25 c 0·15
d 35·29 e 65·04 f 0·42

1:21

1 a Length of koala: 6 0
Length of lizard: 4 2 · 1 5
Length of platypus: 8 2 · 1 2 5
Length of echidna: 2 9 · 4

b Koala: 60
Lizard: 42
Platypus: 82
Echidna: 29

c Koala: 60·0
Lizard: 42·2
Platypus: 82·1
Echidna: 29·4

d 29·4, 42·15, 60, 82·125

 ISBN 9780655708797

2 a

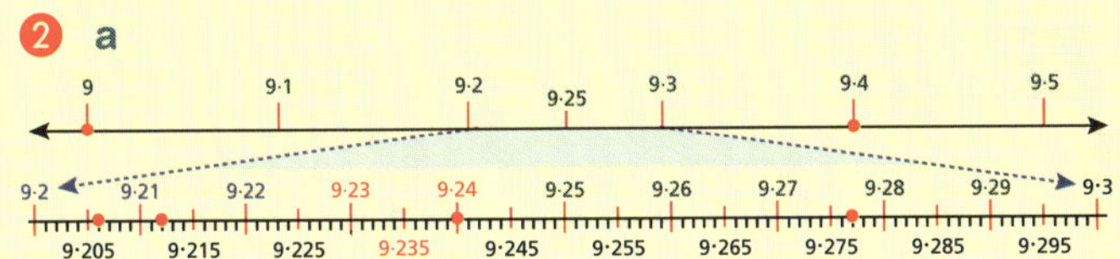

b 9·15, 9·215, 9·2865

1:22

1 a 1 b 1 c 1 d 1 e 2
f 3 g 2 h 3 i 1 j $2\frac{3}{10}$
k $3\frac{2}{5}$ l $2\frac{4}{12}$

2 a $\frac{5}{6}$ b $\frac{9}{10}$ c $\frac{7}{8}$ d $\frac{11}{12}$ e $\frac{4}{5}$ f $\frac{1}{4}$
g $\frac{3}{10}$ h $\frac{3}{5}$ i $\frac{1}{3}$ j $\frac{1}{6}$ k $\frac{5}{8}$ l $\frac{7}{12}$

3 a $2\frac{1}{2}$ b $1\frac{2}{3}$ c $1\frac{5}{6}$ d $2\frac{4}{5}$ e $3\frac{9}{10}$
f $3\frac{11}{12}$ g $2\frac{7}{8}$ h $3\frac{3}{4}$ i $1\frac{1}{4}$

4 a $\frac{1}{6}$ b $\frac{5}{6}$ c $\frac{2}{3}$ or $\frac{8}{12}$
d $\frac{4}{6}$ or $\frac{8}{12}$ e $\frac{4}{6}$ or $\frac{2}{3}$ f $\frac{6}{12}$ or $\frac{1}{2}$

5 a true b true c false d true

1:23

1 a $\frac{1}{4}, \frac{1}{2}, \frac{3}{4}$ b $\frac{1}{2}, \frac{5}{8}, \frac{3}{4}, 1\frac{1}{4}$ c $\frac{1}{8}, \frac{1}{4}, 1, \frac{9}{8}$
d $\frac{1}{8}, \frac{3}{8}, \frac{1}{2}, \frac{3}{4}$ e $\frac{1}{5}, \frac{1}{2}, \frac{7}{10}, 1\frac{1}{10}$ f $\frac{1}{10}, \frac{1}{5}, \frac{6}{10}, \frac{3}{2}$

2 a $\frac{5}{8}$ b $\frac{5}{8}$ c $\frac{3}{4}$ d $\frac{5}{4}$ or $1\frac{1}{4}$
e $\frac{7}{8}$ f $\frac{3}{10}$ g $\frac{3}{8}$ h $\frac{9}{10}$
i $\frac{9}{8}$ or $1\frac{1}{8}$ j $\frac{7}{10}$ k $\frac{7}{10}$ l $\frac{15}{10}$ or $1\frac{5}{10}$

3 a $\frac{2}{8}$ b $\frac{3}{8}$ c $\frac{3}{8}$ d $\frac{1}{8}$ e $\frac{4}{10}$ f $\frac{3}{10}$
g $\frac{1}{8}$ h $\frac{2}{10}$ i $\frac{2}{8}$ j $\frac{3}{8}$ k $\frac{7}{10}$ l $\frac{3}{8}$
m $\frac{1}{8}$ n $\frac{2}{10}$ o $\frac{5}{10}$ p $\frac{6}{10}$ q $\frac{5}{8}$ r $\frac{8}{10}$
s $\frac{7}{10}$

1:24

1 $\frac{2}{6}$ **2** $\frac{3}{4}$ **3** $\frac{5}{6}$
4 $1\frac{3}{8}$ or $\frac{11}{8}$ **5** $\frac{2}{10}$
6 a $2\frac{2}{3}$ km b $\frac{3}{4}$ km
7 a $1\frac{2}{10}$ m b $\frac{8}{10}$ m

1:25

1 a 5·6 millions b 25·65 millions
c 125·6 millions d 68·4 millions

2 a 3·9 billions b 7·18 billions
c 62·44 billions d 13·7 billions

3 a 3900 mm b 12 700 g c 45 600 m
d 8200 mL e 10 200 m f 11 480 mL
g 5·3m h 1·85 kg i 6·64 km
j 5·8 km k 4·3 L l 2·675 kg
m 14·5% n 12·5% o 33·33%

1:26

1 a 60%, 40%, 20% Rule: Subtract 20%.
b $\frac{13}{10}, \frac{15}{10}, \frac{17}{10}, \frac{19}{10}$ Rule: Add $\frac{2}{10}$.
c $3\frac{4}{10}, 3\frac{2}{10}, 3, 2\frac{8}{10}$ Rule: Subtract $\frac{2}{10}$.
d 0·91, 0·93, 0·95 Rule: Add 0·02.
e 1·3, 1·2, 1·1 Rule: Subtract 0·1.
f 0·6, 0·9, 1·2, 1·5, 1·8, 2·1 Rule: Add 0·3.
g $\frac{2}{8}, \frac{3}{8}, \frac{4}{8}, \frac{5}{8}, \frac{6}{8}, \frac{7}{8}$ Rule: Add $\frac{1}{8}$.
h 85%, 70%, 55%, 40% Rule: Subtract 15%.
i $\frac{2}{4}, \frac{3}{4}, \frac{4}{4}, \frac{5}{4}, \frac{6}{4}, \frac{7}{4}$ Rule: Add $\frac{1}{4}$.
j $\frac{2}{3}, \frac{3}{3}, \frac{4}{3}, \frac{5}{3}, \frac{6}{3}, \frac{7}{3}$ Rule: Add $\frac{1}{3}$.

2 Answers will vary.

2:01

1 a 30 b 24 c 21 d 36 e 40
f 63 g 36 h 49 i 54 j 72
k 48 l 48 m 42 n 56 o 72
p 81 q 24 r 64 s 48

2 a b

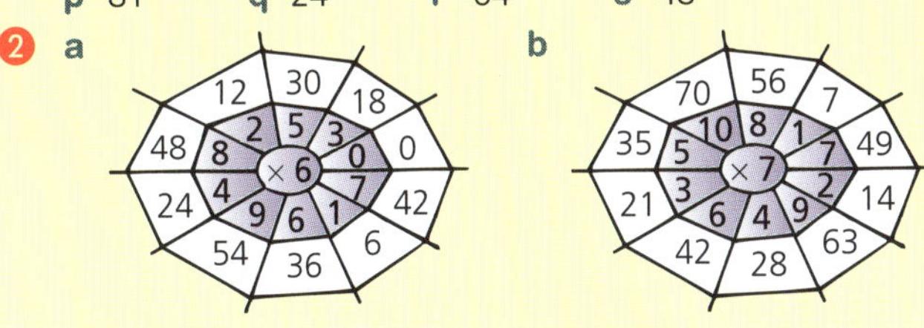

c d

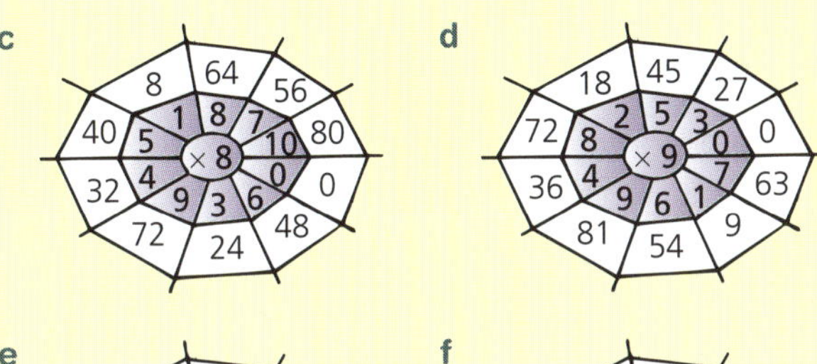

e f

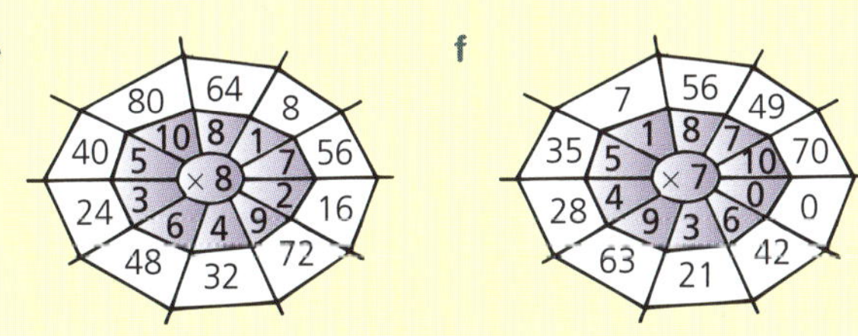

3 a 6, 12, 18, 24, 30, 36, 42, 48, 54, 60
b 7, 14, 21, 28, 35, 42, 49, 56, 63, 70
c 9, 18, 27, 36, 45, 54, 63, 72, 81, 90

2:02

1 a 9 b 12 c 12 d 18 e 24 f 25
g 24 h 36 i 16 j 14 k 27 l 16
m 15 n 30 o 64 p 18 q 54 r 21
s 60 t 48 u 49 v 80 w 42 x 81

2 a b

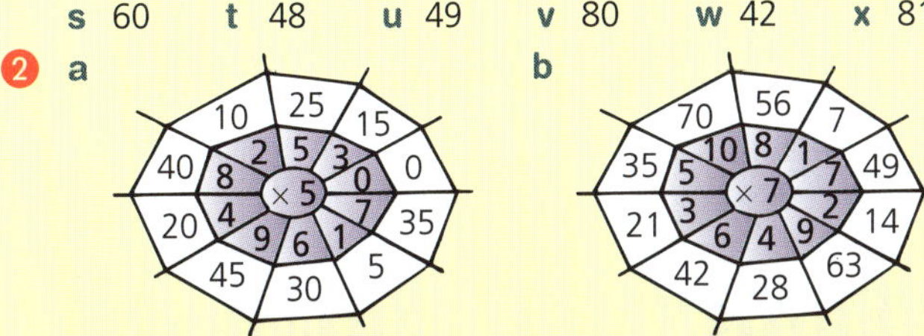

c

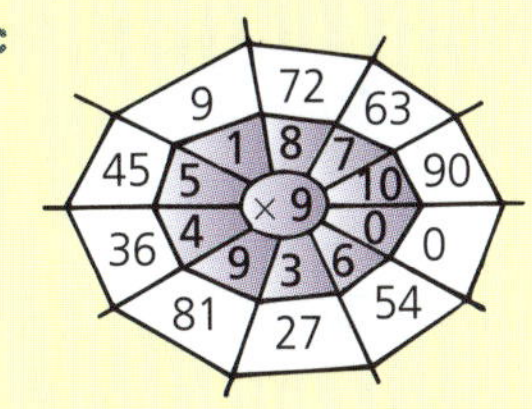

3 a 4, 8, 12, 16, 20, 24, 28, 32, 36, 40
b 8, 16, 24, 32, 40, 48, 56, 64, 72, 80
The multiples of 8 are **twice** the size of the multiples of 4.

2:03

1 a 10, 4 b 5, 8 c 3, 7
d 9, 8 e 8, 9 f 4, 9

2 a 11 b 10 c 7 d 2
e 6 f 9 g 1 h 0
i 7 j 8 k 7 l 9

3 a 6, 6 b 7, 7 c 8, 8
d 10, 10 e 7, 7 f 6, 6

4 a 9 b 5 c 3 d 4
e 10 f 1 g 5 h 3
i 0 j 8 k 2 l 6
m 9 n 5 o 7 p 9

5 a 5, 5 b 9, 9 c 7, 7
d 9, 9 e 5, 5 f 4, 4
g 9 h 6 i 9

2:04

1 a 40 b 80 c 110 d 130
e 310 f 930 g 790 h 330
i 1890 j 1900 k 1900 l 2070

2 a 700 b 400 c 200 d 900
e 900 f 700 g 400 h 200
i 3500 j 9000 k 4100 l 2100

3 a 3000 b 4000 c 8000 d 4000
e 8000 f 7000 g 1000 h 5000

4 a 3672 3196 2878
3945 2764 3285
3812 2246 3349
b 6249 5862 6591
5396 6478 6487
5723 6823 5734

5 a 3275 3227 3270
3249 3185 3175
3159 3129 3207
b 75 247 75 672 74 503
74 820 75 981 75 199
74 498 74 981 74 500

6 a true b true c false d false

2:05

1 a 571 b 499 c 166 d 539

2:06

1 a 291 b 254 c 754 d 248
e 514 f 1054 g 900 h 616
i 621 j 891 k 822 l 921
m 709 n 731 o 754 p 795

2 m 700 n 700 o 700 p 700

2:07

1 a 729 b 633 c 740 d 704
e 606 f 795 g 723 h 983
i 831 j 595 k 800 l 643
m 851 n 668

2 a 883 b 643 c 776 d 583
e 748 f 566

2:08

1 a 593 b 723 c 510 d 815
e 995 f 502 g 900 h 730
i 722 j 935 k 705 l 449

2 a 861 (people) b 750 (boxes) c 434 (cards)
d 472 (dollars) e 856 (km)

2:09

1 a 33 b 34 c 127 d 208
e 314 f 539 g 244 h 104
i 325 j 653 k 315 l 325
m 437 n 459 o 348 p 131

2 i 400 j 700 k 400 l 300
m 500 n 500 o 400 p 100

2:10

1 a 530 b 272 c 872 d 184
e 483 f 287 g 581 h 162
i 221 j 432 k 294 l 263
m 591 n 593 o 63 p 472

2 a 387 b 547 c 257 d 268

2:11

1 a 1 × 5 = 5 b 2 × 5 = 10
c 3 × 5 = 15 d 4 × 5 = 20
e 5 × 5 = 25 f 6 × 5 = 30
g 7 × 5 = 35 h 8 × 5 = 40
i 9 × 5 = 45

The first ten multiples of 5 are 5, 10, 15, 20, 25, 30, 35, 40, 45 and 50.

2 a 2, 4, 6, 8, 10, 12, 14, 16, 18 and 20
b 4, 8, 12, 16, 20, 24, 28, 32, 36 and 40
c 5, 10, 15, 20, 25, 30, 35, 40, 45 and 50
d 6, 12, 18, 24, 30, 36, 42, 48, 54 and 60
e 8, 16, 24, 32, 40, 48, 56, 64, 72 and 80
f 10, 20, 30, 40, 50, 60, 70, 80, 90 and 100

3 a 10 b 30 c 30 d 40 e 10 f 20
g 24 h 20 i 40 j 8 k 8 l 10

4 The first 10 common multiples are: 10, 20, 30, 40, 50, 60, 70, 80, 90, 100.

2:12

1 a–d Answers will include 1 × 24, 2 × 12, 3 × 8 and 4 × 6.
  e 1, 24, 2, 12, 3, 8, 4, and 6
2 a 1, 6, 2, 3 b 1, 12, 2, 6, 3, 4
  c 1, 5 d 1, 20, 2, 10, 4, 5
  e 1, 15, 3, 5 f 1, 28, 2, 14, 4, 7
  g 1, 30, 2, 15, 3, 10, 5, 6
3 1, 80, 2, 40, 4, 20, 5, 16, 8 and 10
4 a 1, 16, 2, 8 or 4 b 1, 21, 3 or 7 (assuming that you can have a row of 1)
  c 1, 12, 2, 6, 3 or 4

2:13

1 (3) (7) 8 13 20 (21)
2 2, 4, 6, 8, 10, 12, 14
3 1, 32, 2, 16, 4, 8
4 1, 24, 2, 12, 3, 8, 4, 6
5 1, 100, 2, 50, 4, 25, 5, 20, 10
6 a 2, 4, 6, 8, 10, 12, 14, 16, 18, 20
  b 4, 8, 12, 16, 20, 24, 28, 32, 36, 40
  c 8, 16, 24, 32, 40, 48, 56, 64, 72, 80
  d 10, 20, 30, 40, 50, 60, 70, 80, 90, 100
7 a 16, even b 12, even c 7, odd
  d 10, even e 14, even f 35, odd
8 a even b even c odd
9 Answers will vary.

2:14

1 a $0.78 b $1.52 c $4.73
  d $5.31 e $6.69 f $8.25
  g $4.70 h $8.51 i $6.43
  j $7.11 k $6.08 l $6.97
  m $5.40 n $6.29 o $7.14
2 a $3.79 b $5.77 c $5.68
  d $8.68 e $6.49 f $8.48
3 a $9.55 b $8.20 c $8.85
  d $8.70
4 a $4.88 b $8.83 c $9.37 d $9.01

2:15

1 a $5.22 b $5.17 c $6.34
  d $2.39 e $4.17 f $1.84
  g $2.77 h $6.08 i $3.34
  j $4.08 k $1.70 l $2.58
  m $3.89 n $5.45 o $2.04
2 a $2.11 b $4.98 c $5.35
  d $0.05 e $5.50 f $1.51
3 a $1.05 b $6.20 c $5.45
  d $1.20 e $3.55 f $4.95

2:16

1 a Yes b Yes c Yes d Yes
  e No f Yes g No h Yes
2 a $4.60 b $7.40 c $7.70 d $9.10
  e $7.80 f $9.40
3 a $4.40 b $2.80 c $1.20 d $4.10 e $1.60
4 a $9.71 b $9.02 c $9.18 d $7.81 e $7.49
  f $3.27 g $6.45 h $3.39 i $6.33 j $3.26
5 a $9.70 b $9.00 c $9.20 d $7.80 e $7.50
  f $3.25 g $6.45 h $3.40 i $6.35 j $3.25

2:17

1 a 2 r 2 b 2 r 1 c 2 r 2 d 2 r 4
  e 2 r 3 f 2 r 3 g 3 r 3 h 2 r 3
2 a 48 ÷ 7 = 6 packets and 6 remaining
  b 48 ÷ 10 = 4 groups and 8 remaining
  c 48 ÷ 8 = 6 rows and 0 remaining
  d 80 ÷ 8 = 10 lots and 0 remaining
  e 80 ÷ 10 = 8 lots and 0 remaining
  f 80 ÷ 9 = 8 groups and 8 remaining
3 a 17 ÷ 3 = 5 groups and 2 remaining
  b 17 ÷ 6 = 2 groups of 6 and 5 remaining
4 a 3 tins, 35 ÷ 10 = 3, (r 5)
  b 8 sets, 33 ÷ 4 = 8, (r 1)
  c 5 pages, 42 ÷ 8 = 5, (r 2)
  d 8 boxes, 50 ÷ 6 = 8, (r 2)

2:18

1 a 4 r 1 b 2 r 1 c 7 r 1 d 1 r 3 e 2 r 3
  f 5 r 2 g 1 r 3 h 2 r 4 i 8 r 2 j 7 r 8
  k 8 r 2 l 6 r 5 m 3 r 4 n 9 r 2 o 2 r 4
  p 2 r 1 q 8 r 4 r 5 r 2 s 4 r 3 t 5 r 5
2 a 10 b 30 c 10 d 10 e 20
  f 20 g 10 h 30 i 10 j 10
3 a 7 r 4, 7 people b 6 r 1, 6 packs

2:19

1 a 6 r 2 b 4 r 1 c 7 r 2
2 a 2 r 2 b 2 r 3 c 4 r 4 d 5 r 5
  e 10 r 1 f 1 r 7 g 8 r 2 h 7 r 1
  i 7 r 4 j 3 r 2 k 8 r 4 l 7 r 4
3 a 17 ÷ 3 = 5 r 2 b 27 ÷ 7 = 3 r 6
  c 30 ÷ 8 = 3 r 6 d 25 ÷ 6 = 4 r 1
  e 53 ÷ 10 = 5 r 3 f 33 ÷ 5 = 6 r 3
  g 60 ÷ 9 = 6 r 6 h 36 ÷ 8 = 4 r 4
  i 47 ÷ 6 = 7 r 5 j 32 ÷ 8 = 4 r 0
  k 29 ÷ 2 = 14 r 1 l 53 ÷ 7 = 7 r 4
  m 25 ÷ 4 = 6 r 1 n 27 ÷ 2 = 13 r 1
  o 46 ÷ 5 = 9 r 1
4 9 teams (9 r 2)

2:20

1 a 337 b 278 c 629 d 576
  e 177 f 469 g 168 h 189

i 617 j 253 k 345 l 668
m 87 n 542 o 339 p 89

2 a 422 b 354

2:21

1 a 73 b 162 c 839 d 545 e 398
f 107 g 294 h 47

2 a $0.66 b $1.01 c $1.26 d $0.32

3 a 113 points b 419 albums c 253 books
d $6.35

4 a 518 b 121 c $372

2:22

1 a 5468 b 8975 c 7588 d 3798 e 7967
f 6324 g 8600 h 7251 i 3573 j 8240

2 a 7195 b 4885 c 4343 d 8925
e 8019 f 7505 g 9281 h 4339
i 7617 j 7932

3 a $9149 b $8291 c $7909
d $6297 e $9430

2:23

1 a 7561 b 6935 c 9818 d 7482

2 a 3904 b 5108 c 7837 d 7088

3 a $86.14 b $52.53 c $90.10 d $86.80

4 a your estimate, 5495 b your estimate, 8456
c your estimate, $8273

2:24

1 a 4353 b 7100 c 5420 d 8000 e 6213
f 6070 g 442 h 5320 i 6303 j 1824

2 a 2776 b 1193 c 706 d 6990 e 3068
f 369 g 2278 h 1602 i 6749 j 3489

3 a 1875 b 6195 c $3659

4 909

2:25

1 a 564 b 1699 c 103 d 2275
e 5168 f 1140 g 1100 h 4573

2 a 4550 b 3012 c 775 d 1645
e 2814 f 1305 g 28 h 6633

3 a 3320 km b 1675 m c 3658 m
d 88 years old e 86 years old

2:26

1 a 617 + 1 = 618 b 1308 + 1 = 1309
c 16 + 1 = 17 d 1075 + 1 = 1076
e 3518 + 1 = 3519 f 1024 + 1 = 1025
g $792 + 1 = $793 h $1917 + 1 = $1918
i $4208 + 1 = $4209

2 a 1027 b 3097 c 6248
d 3754 e $1269

3 a 67 025 b 762 655

2:27

1 a 22 b 34 c 44 d 12
e 11 f 22 g 13 h 12
i 11 j 12 k 21 l 22

2 a 17 b 15 c 23
d 18 e 13 f 17

2:28

1 a 23 b 11 c 21 d 41 e 30
f 12 g 34 h 11

2 a 25 b 48 c 13 d 24 e 13
f 15 g 12 h 12

3 a 18 b 14 c 14 d 17 e 17
f 19 g 16 h 29

4 a 13 brushes b 17 ladders c 13 globes
d 18 plants e 22 caps f 15 spades

2:29

1 a $12\frac{1}{2}$ b $11\frac{2}{3}$ c $22\frac{1}{4}$ d $10\frac{3}{5}$
e $11\frac{3}{6}$ or $11\frac{1}{2}$ f $12\frac{1}{3}$

2 a $17\frac{1}{2}$ b $24\frac{2}{3}$ c $16\frac{1}{2}$ d $12\frac{3}{8}$
e $13\frac{1}{6}$ f $14\frac{3}{4}$

3 a 15 b 17 c 14 d 19
e 16 f 28 g 14 h 13

4 a 17 b 16 c 19 d 18 e 48
f 37 g 16 h 27 i 18 j 15

5 a 18 km b $12 c 25°C d 23 cm

2:30

1 a 134 b 285 c 144 d 122 e 133
f 174 g 135 h 145 i 119 j 127

2 a 147 r 5 b 141 r 1 c 234 r 1 d 117 r 5
e 257 r 1 f 117 r 3 g 196 r 2 h 135 r 4
i 183 r 3 j 118 r 7

3 a 81 b 50 c 72 d 63
e 33 f 73

4 a 42 r 1 b 31 c 81 r 1 d 114 r 2 e 75
f 112 r 4 g 44 r 4 h 28 r 4 i 38 j 49
k 67 l 94 m 84

5 a 21 m b 97 m

2:31

1 a 80 b 90 c 60 d 40
e 110 f 140 g 120 h 130
i 320 j 210 k 480 l 850
m 900 n 770 o 600 p 990

2 a 80 b 70 c 100 d 90
e 130 f 180 g 270 h 220
i 350 j 610 k 840 l 750

3 a 18 tens = 180 b 21 tens = 210
c 20 tens = 200 d 18 tens = 180
e 320 f 400 g 360 h 420

4 a 180 b 400 c 280 d 200
5 a 120 b 180 c 320 d 350
e $140 f $540 g $640 h $360

2:32

1 a 70 b 210 c 900 d 1200 e 1000
f 1100 g 2500 h 3000 i 4900
2 a 90 b 270 c 560 d 600 e 1300
f 2500
3 a 24 tens, 240 b 21 hundreds, 2100
c 32 hundreds, 3200 d 35 tens, 350
e 15 hundreds, 1500 f 36 hundreds, 3600
g 24 thousands, 24 000
4 a 240 b 350 c 540 d 800 e 2100
f 3000
5 a 120 b 320 c 300 d 1800 e 2800
f 7200

2:33

1 a 80 b 60 c 50 d 30 e 90
f 37 g 86 h 54 i 29 j 18
k 11 l 20 m 99 n 73 o 55
2 a 15 r 6 b 37 r 5 c 52 r 1 d 21 r 8 e 86 r 6
f 68 r 4 g 56 h 73 r 7 i 90 r 8 j 36 r 7
k 71 r 1 l 40 r 7 m 89 r 9 n 40 o 60 r 1
3 a $95 b 51 runs c 47 mL d 20 cups
4 a 750 b 831 c 600

2:34

1 a 204 b 208 c 408 d 307 e 205
f 104 g 105 h 102 i 204 j 209
2 a 101 b 102 c 102 d 403
e 203 f 100 r 2 g 101 r 3 h 304 r 1
i 101 r 1 j 100 r 5
3 a 108 sheep b 102 groups c 203 fish
d 104 people e 106 buckets (106 r 3)
4 a 900 ÷ 3 = 300 b 800 ÷ 4 = 200
c 600 ÷ 6 = 100 d 1000 ÷ 5 = 200

2:35

1 These numbers will be circled.
a 24, 30, 46, 76, 88, 100
b 30, 45, 60, 75, 95, 120, 135
c 21, 63, 81, 102, 162
d 36, 72, 684, 693, 126, 234
e 40, 100, 108, 144, 216, 304
f 40, 100, 110, 220
g 100, 300, 500, 700

2

Divisible by 2	Divisible by 5	Divisible by 3	Divisible by 9
64, 96, 80, 54, 92, 134, 168, 190, 162, 348, 460, 378	80, 75, 145, 135, 190, 460, 645, 385	96, 54, 75, 168, 135, 162, 348, 645, 378	54, 135, 162, 378

3 a 1, 8, 2, 4 b 1, 16, 2, 8, 4
c 1, 35, 5, 7 d 1, 28, 2, 14, 4, 7
e 1, 49, 7 f 1, 99, 3, 33, 9, 11
g 1, 24, 2, 12, 3, 8, 4, 6 h 1, 26, 2, 13
i 1, 28, 2, 14, 4, 7
4 no

2:36

1 a 1, 15, 3, 5 b 1, 6, 2, 3
c 1, 36, 2, 18, 3, 12, 4, 9, 6
2 a 6, 12, 18, 24, 30, 36, 42, 48, 54, 60
b 9, 18, 27, 36, 45, 54, 63, 72, 81, 90
c 7, 14, 21, 28, 35, 42, 49, 56, 63, 70
3 a 1, 80, 2, 40, 4, 20, 5, 16, 8, 10
b 1, 92, 2, 46, 4, 23
c 1, 63, 3, 21, 7, 9
d 1, 56, 2, 28, 4, 14, 7, 8
e 1, 160, 2, 80, 4, 40, 5, 32, 8, 20, 10, 16
f 1, 108, 2, 54, 3, 36, 4, 27, 6, 18, 9, 12
g 1, 48, 2, 24, 3, 16, 4, 12, 6, 8
h 1, 60, 2, 30, 3, 20, 4, 15, 5, 12, 6, 10
i 1, 144, 2, 72, 3, 48, 4, 36, 6, 24, 8, 18, 9, 16, 12

2:37

1 a 16 × 5 = 8 × 2 × 5 = 80
b 12 × 5 = 6 × 2 × 5 = 60
c 18 × 5 = 9 × 2 × 5 = 90
d 14 × 5 = 7 × 2 × 5 = 70
e 8 × 25 = 2 × 4 × 25 = 200
f 16 × 25 = 4 × 4 × 25 = 400
g 28 × 25 = 7 × 4 × 25 = 700
h 36 × 25 = 9 × 4 × 25 = 900
i 20 × 5 = 10 × 2 × 5 = 100
j 12 × 25 = 3 × 4 × 25 = 300
k 20 × 25 = 5 × 4 × 25 = 500
l 32 × 25 = 8 × 4 × 25 = 800
2 a 12 × 6 = 2 × 6 × 6 = 2 × 36 = 72
b 14 × 4 = 2 × 7 × 4 = 2 × 28 = 56
c 8 × 14 = 8 × 7 × 2 = 56 × 2 = 112
d 6 × 16 = 6 × 8 × 2 = 48 × 2 = 96
e 4 × 18 = 2 × 2 × 18 = 2 × 36 = 72
f 20 × 9 = 2 × 10 × 9 = 2 × 90 = 180
g 16 × 4 = 2 × 8 × 4 = 2 × 32 = 64
h 14 × 6 = 2 × 7 × 6 = 2 × 42 = 84

2:38

1 a 4 cm b Yes, because there were no 4 cm nails.
2 a A: 9, B: 18, C: 11, D: 7 b 4 units
c 4 units
3 a $34 b $30 c 22 tickets
4 a $2\frac{1}{2}$ or 2·5 tickets b $2\frac{1}{2}$ or 2·5 tickets

2:39

1 a 80 + 32 = 112 b 40 + 8 = 48 c 60 + 30 = 90
d 50 + 45 = 95 e 90 + 63 = 153 f 80 + 48 = 128

2 a 40 + 24 = 64 b 160 + 24 = 184 c 200 + 15 = 215

3 a 92
b 51 × 2 = 102
51 × 4 = 2 × 102
= 204
c 2 × 21 = 42
4 × 21 = 2 × 42
= 84

2:40

1 a

First number	1	2	3	4	5	6
Second number	15	16	17	18	19	20

b Add 14 to the 1st number.
c 23

2 a

First number	1	2	3	4	5	6
Second number	4	8	12	16	20	24

b Multiply the 1st number by 4.
c 80

3 a

First number	90	80	70	60	50	40
Second number	82	72	62	52	42	32

b Subtract 8 from the 1st number.
c 10

4 a

Input number	36	46	56	66	76	86
Output number	43	53	63	73	83	93

b Add 7 to the input number.
c 15

5 a

Input number	29	39	49	59	69	79
Output number	12	22	32	42	52	62

b Subtract 17 from the input number.
c 182

6 Answers will vary.

2:41

1 a

First number	1	2	3	4	5	6
Second number	7	14	21	28	35	42

Multiply the first number by 7 or F × 7.

b

First number	1	2	3	4	5	6
Second number	9	18	27	36	45	54

Multiply the first number by 9 or F × 9.

c

First number	1	2	3	4	5	6
Second number	24	25	26	27	28	29

Add 23 to the first number or F + 23.

d

First number	1	2	3	4	5	6
Second number	36	37	38	39	40	41

Add 35 to the first number or F + 35.

e

First number	35	45	55	65	75	85
Second number	27	37	47	57	67	77

Subtract 8 from the first number or F – 8.

f

First number	92	82	72	62	52	42
Second number	104	94	84	74	64	54

Add 12 to the first number or F + 12.

g

First number	2	4	6	7	10	12
Second number	6	12	18	21	30	36

Multiply the first number by 3 or F × 3.

h

First number	1	2	3	4	5	6
Second number	9	19	29	39	49	59

Multiply the first number by 10 and subtract 1, or F × 10 – 1.

2 a 17 b 4 c 30 d 5

3 a 26 b 1 g 76 h 70

4 a $13 b $21 c $45 d $25

5 a 38 b 9

2:42

1 a

Input	1	2	3	4	5	6
Output	17	27	37	47	57	67

Output = 107

a

Input	1	2	3	4	5	6
Output	4	7	10	13	16	19

Output = 31

a

Input	1	2	3	4	5	6
Output	1	4	7	10	13	16

Output = 28

a

Input	1	2	3	4	5	6
Output	8	17	26	35	44	53

Output = 89

2 a 24 b 36 c 120 d 48

3 a $25 b $35 c $45 d $65

4 a 11 b 23 c 47 d 207

 ISBN 9780655708797

2:43

1 a 80 + 6 = 86 b 50 + 25 = 75
c 180 + 48 = 228 d 80 + 36 = 116

2 a 160 + 10 = 170 b 80 + 32 = 112
c 180 + 12 = 192 d 70 + 42 = 112
e 270 + 9 = 279 f 160 + 24 = 184
g 200 + 20 = 220 h 240 + 6 = 246
i 360 + 12 = 372

2:44

1 a 215 b 292 c 216 d 231
e 474 f 182 g 266 h 152

2 a 147 b 288 c 324 d 375
e 384 f 308 g 296 h 189

2:45

1 a 842 b 957 c 903 d 790 e 804
f 920 g 868 h 875 i 944 j 924
k 987 l 1253

2 a 192 horseshoes b 768 pages
c 576 eggs d $891

2:46

1 a 160 b 217 c 249 d 78 e 90 f 81
g 315 h 342 i 460 j 600 k 228 l 810
m 120 n 158 o 56 p 588

2 a 384 b 692 c 585 d 836 e 975
f 780 g 968 h 879 i 968 j 680
k $9.90 l $8.89 m $9.18 n $8.48 o $9.45

2:47

1 a 1890 b 4866 c 5600 d 1648 e 2799
f 1166 g 1676 h 3663 i 2496 j 5826
k 2730 l 7680 m 2583 n 2313 o 4980
p 4263 q 7650 r 5994

2 a 9063 b 8448 c 9099 d 6408 e 3507
f 9050 g 6558 h 9948 i 9296 j 9900
k 6516 l $96.95 m $89.95 n $74.82 o $93.28
p $413.50

2:48

1 a 1 kg 250 g b 3 L
c 250 g d 66 ads

2 a 5 kg b 7000 L c 5 pkts, 9250 pkts
d 6·1 m

3 a 900 m b 1008 L
c $11 430

2:49

1 a 190 b 0
c 60 + 90 = 150 d 170 − 50 = 120

2 a 188 b 7 c 151 d 122

3 a 500 b 600 − 500 = 100
c 800 + 400 = 1200 d 800 − 700 = 100

4 a 514 b 90 c 1178 d 97

5 a 5000 b 7000 − 4000 = 3000
c 6000 + 4000 = 10 000

6 a 4425 b 3193 c 10 241

7 Estimates will vary.
a 2199 + 693 b 2199 + 4904 c 693 + 4904
d 2199 + 9251 e 4904 + 7057 f 7057 + 9251
g No. We can estimate to decide whether the two numbers would be close to the answer.

2:50

1 a 300 b 300 c 500 d 200 e 700
f 400 g 900 h 700 i 900 j 600

2 a 50 × 5 b 90 × 5 c 300 × 10

3 a 210 b 400 c 600 d 790
e 180 f 30 g 400 h 40

4 Estimates will vary. The actual answers are:
a $114 b $205.80 c $65.01

2:51

1 a Answers will vary. b $229.50
c $200.50 is deposited (banked). d $272.10

2 a Answers will vary. b $213.10
c $236.90 is deposited (banked). d $307

2:52

Answers will vary.

2:53

1 $233 2 $536 3 $129
4 144 tonnes, 256 tonnes 5 $267
6 555 bricks 7 72 books 8 8 L, $12.80
9 380 km, $5\frac{1}{2}$ hours 10 $1945

11 a b

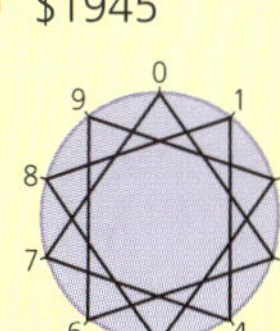

c

2:54

1 a 30 b 50 c 80 d 50
e 30 f 90 g 70 h 50
i 70 j 60

2 a 700 b 300 c 300 d 900
e 900 f 500 g 500 h 700
i 300 j 400

3 a 800 b 60 × 30 = 1800 c 50 × 70 = 3500
d 90 × 30 = 2700 e 40 × 10 = 400 f 70 × 50 = 3500
g 50 × 20 = 1000 h 60 × 40 = 2400

4 a 24 000 b 40 × 200 = 8000
c 80 × 700 = 56 000 d 60 × 700 = 42 000

5 a true b true

6 a E = 3600, A = 3478 b E = 2100, A = 2015
c E = 18 000, A = 19 779 d E = 30 000, A = 29 375

2:55

1 a (4 × 300) + (4 × 20) + (4 × 1) = 1284
b (9 × 400) + (9 × 30) + (9 × 2) = 3888
c (7 × 700) + (7 × 50) + (7 × 8) = 5306

2 a (30 × 50) + (30 × 7) + (4 × 50) + (4 × 7)
= 1500 + 210 + 200 + 28
= 1938
b (60 × 20) + (60 × 8) + (2 × 20) + (2 × 8)
= 1200 + 480 + 40 + 16
= 1736
c (50 × 10) + (50 × 6) + (7 × 10) + (7 × 6)
= 500 + 300 + 70 + 42
= 912

2:56

1 a 1260 b 1120 c 3240 d 1290
e 2600 f 6440 g 2430

2 a (10 × 61) + (7 × 61) b (10 × 95) + (6 × 95)
c (30 × 53) + (1 × 53) d (40 × 66) + (6 × 66)
a (70 × 37) + (2 × 37) f (20 × 48) + (9 × 48)
g (40 × 59) + (9 × 59) = 2360 + 531 = 2891
h (70 × 64) + (2 × 64) = 4480 + 128 = 4608

3 a 630 + 315 = 945 b 1480 + 592 = 2072
c 3680 + 552 = 4232 d 4050 + 162 = 4212
e 5250 + 375 = 5625 f 5280 + 792 = 6072
g 1560 + 260 = 1820 h 3840 + 192 = 4032
i 1400 + 196 = 1596 j 5040 + 252 = 5292

4 490 (pages)

2:57

1 a 448 b 1696 c 4743
d 2108 e 3124 f 1333 g 2068

2 a 1068 b 1431 c 3528 d 882
e 3515 f 2376 g 1825 h 2438

3 a 1008 mL b 704 g

2:58

1 a 552 b 1023 c 1944 d 2400
e 804 f 2173 g 1674 h 1386
i 450 j 3008 k 832 l 2277
m 868 n 3990

2 a $456 b $1944, $3132, $1188
c • $910, $1820, $910
• $946, $1505, $559
• $2128, $3572, $1444

2:59

1 a 5577 b 4131 a 16 290 d 20 664
e 60 225 f 41 440 g 30 736 h 54 290 i 21 148
j 16 184 k 28 500 l 150 800

2 a 11 550 m, 46 200 m b 120 400 years

2:60

Concept: 12, 3, 4, 4, 3, 9, 5

1 a 3 b 6 c 6 d 87 e 9
f 6 g 7 h 8 i 11

2 a 78 coins b 5 jars
c 125 trees d 26 counters

3 a 3 b 37 c 110 d 220 e 209
f 271 g 179 h 478 i 125

4 a 15 b 19 c 11 d 9 e 5
f 8 g 60 h 120 i 69

5 a 30 b 32 c 42 d 81 e 108
f 90 g 5 h 6 i 9

6 a 109 b 22 c 31 d 93 e 8
f 4 g 350 h 90 i 74

3:01

1 a metres b metres c kilometres
d kilometres e kilometres f metres
g metres h metres

2 a 2000 m b 5000 m c 4000 m
d 10 000 m

3 a 6 km b 10 km c 7 km d 9 km

4 a 4 km b 6 km c 3 km
d 5 km e 4 km f 5 km

3:02

1 a 4000 m b 7000 m c 9000 m
d 6000 m e 2000 m f 3000 m
g 5000 m h 10 000 m i 14 000 m

2 a 3 km b 9 km c 5 km d 7 km
e 12 km f 16 km

3 a km b m c cm d mm
e m f km g m h km

4 a 60 km/h b 95 km/h c 70 km/h
d 50 km/h

5 a 3 km 850 m b 1 km 56 m c 9 km 5 m
d 5 km 600 m e 3 km 275 m f 8 km 241 m

6 a 5200 m b 1341 m c 4750 m
d 8005 m e 10 030 m f 7038 m

3:03

1

	Length	Width	Perimeter
a	5 cm	2 cm	14 cm
b	4 cm	3 cm	14 cm
c	3 cm	3 cm	12 cm
d	6 cm	2 cm	16 cm

2 a 14 cm b 16 cm c 18 cm d 20 cm
e 20 cm f 24 cm

3 a 24 cm b 24 cm c 24 cm d 26 m
e 32 m f 28 m

4 L = 18 cm, W = 4 cm, P = 44 cm

3:04

1 a 16 cm b 16 cm c 24 cm d 20 cm

2 a 26 cm b 34 cm c 44 cm d 44 cm
e 72 cm

3 a 36 cm b 48 cm c 60 cm d 80 cm
e 100 cm

4 a Answers will vary. One answer is: L = 4 cm, B = 5 cm
b Answers will vary. One answer is: L = 9 cm, B = 6 cm

5 a 4 cm b 6 cm

6 a (2 × 50 m) + (2 × 25 m) = 150 m
The fence is 150 m long.
b 4 × 20 cm = 80 cm
She will need lace 80 cm long.

3:05

1 a 12 cm^2 b 12 cm^2 c 18 cm^2 d 15 cm^2
e 10 cm^2

2 a L = 28 cm b W = 21 cm
c About A = 588 cm^2

3 a i 32 cm^2 ii up to 8 b 3 m^2 c 4
d To cover the entire top the label should be 800 cm^2, so his label cannot exceed 800 cm^2.

3:06

1 a 20 m^2 b 10 m^2 c 6 m^2 d 14 m^2 e 4 m^2

2 a 36 m^2 b 42 m^2 c 80 m^2 d 56 m^2 e 54 m^2

3 a 49 cm^2 b 36 cm^2 c 81 cm^2
d 64 cm^2 e 100 cm^2

4 a 63 m^2 will be circled. b 48 m^2 will be circled.

5 Answers will vary.

6 a 15 m^2 of wallpaper b 19 m^2 of wallpaper

3:07

1 a Area J = 20 m^2 Area K = 10 m^2 Total area = 30 m^2
b Area L = 30 m^2 Area M = 8 m^2 Total area = 38 m^2
c Area N = 4 m^2 Area O = 30 m^2 Total area = 34 m^2
d Area P = 20 m^2 Area Q = 12 m^2 Area R = 12 m^2
Total area = 44 m^2
e Area S = 25 m^2 Area T = 6 m^2 Area U = 12 m^2
Total area = 43 m^2
f Area V = 12 m^2 Area W = 10 m^2 Area Z = 16 m^2
Total area = 38 m^2

2 a 12 cm by 1 cm, 2 cm by 6 cm, 3 cm by 4 cm
b 20 cm by 1 cm, 10 cm by 2 cm, 5 cm by 4 cm

3 a m^2 b cm^2 c cm^2
d cm^2 e m^2 f m^2

3:08

1 29 min, 6 h 26 min

2 a June b December

3 a Area A = 4 m^2, Area B = 12 m^2, Area C = 6 m^2
Total area = 22 m^2
b i 15 m^2 ii 30 m^2
iii 30 ÷ 15 × 2 = 4 L, She will need 4 L of paint.

4 a 32 m b $3200 c 24 m^2
d 60 m^2 e 36 m^2 f 8 m

3:09

1 a 21 b 48 c 420 d 3 e 240
f 12 g 48 h 5 i 2 j 8
k 100 l 14 m 6 n 156 o 10

2 a 35 min b 26 min c 1 h 6 min
d 1 h 49 min e 2 h 44 min f 2 h 6 min

3 a 43 min b 2 h 13 min c 4 h 48 min
d 6 h 48 min e 7 h 58 min f 11 h 3 min

4 a 12 h 30 min b 12·5 h
c 750 min d 45 000 s

3:10

1 a 1:00 pm b 3:00 pm c 8:00 pm d 9:00 am
e 6:00 pm f 7:00 am g 11:00 pm h 4:00 pm
i 2:00 pm j 9:00 pm

2 a 17:00 b 11:00 c 20:00 d 14:00 e 04:00

3 a 16:00 b 08:00 c 19:00 d 22:00 e 02:00
f 21:00 g 12:00 h 00:00 i 17:00

3:11

1 Answers may vary. Some are:
a 5 pm = 17:00 or 1700 b 0800 = 08:00 or 8 am
c 0300 = 03:00 or 3 am d 2 am = 02:00 or 0200
e 7 pm = 19:00 or 1900 f 0100 = 01:00 or 1 am
g 1100 = 11:00 or 11 am h 0400 = 04:00 or 4 am
i 10 pm = 22:00 or 2200 j 6 pm = 18:00 or 1800
k 0900 = 09:00 or 9 am l 12 am = 00:00 or 0000

2 a 1 pm or 13:00 b 15:25 or 3:25 pm
c 4 am or 04:00 d 09:04 or 9:04 am
e 1 pm or 13:00 f 19:57 or 7:57 pm
g 3 pm or 15:00 h 06:41 or 6:41 am
i 6 pm or 18:00 j 06:29 or 6:29 am

Fun spot:

	07:00	09:00	04:00	09:00	10:00	11:00	12:00	14:00	20:00	21:00	23:00	
	06:00	02:00	03:00	11:00	09:00	10:00	13:00	15:00	19:00	22:00	20:00	
Start	**00:00**	01:00	04:00	07:00	08:00	11:00	14:00	17:00	18:00	23:00	**24:00**	Finish
	02:00	08:00	05:00	06:00	07:00	13:00	15:00	16:00	19:00	20:00	21:00	

3:12

1 a the 12:50 train ... 35 min, the 13:20 train ... 36 min, the 13:50 train ... 35 min, the 14:20 train ... 36 min
b 24 min c 3 min d the 13:20 train
e 15:08 f every half hour

2 a 14 min b 13:02 c 13:14 (or 1:14 pm)
d 13:26 (or 1:26 pm)

3:13

1 a 3 cm, 28 mm b 4 cm, 44 mm
2 a 8 kg b 7 kg c 14 kg d 3 mL
e 10 mL f 6 mL g 8 mL h 80 mL
i 30 mL j 100 mL k 37°C l 40°C
m 39°C n 36°C
3 a Sunday b 8° (Celsius)

3:14

1 a 75 mm b 53 mm c 105 mm d 17 mm
e 26 mm f 98 mm
2 d, e, b, a, f, c
3 a cm b km c m or cm d cm
e cm f mm g m h m
4 a 6·4 cm b 8·3 cm c 3·6 cm d 4·1 cm
e 9·2 cm f 5·9 cm
5 a 3·9 cm b 6·5 cm c 4·3 cm d 8·2 cm
e 7·6 cm f 9·1 cm g 16·2 cm h 15·8 cm
6 a 148 mm b 120 mm c 108 mm d 162 mm
e 160 mm
7 a 10 cm b 9 cm c 13 cm d Discussion

3:15

1 (A) 26 mm, 2·6 cm (B) 39 mm, 3·9 cm
(C) 64 mm, 6·4 cm (D) 91 mm, 9·1 cm
(E) 128 mm, 12·8 cm
2 a 4·9 cm b 6·4 cm c 8·3 cm d 5·1 cm
e 9·2 cm f 7·5 cm g 10·8 cm h 12·3 cm
3 a 2·51 m b 8·29 m c 3·75 m d 6·42 m
e 5·63 m f 9·25 m g 10·21 m h 11·65 m
4 a 316 cm b 831 cm c 465 cm d 954 cm
e 527 cm f 295 cm g 745 cm h 1075 cm
5 a m b m c km d m
e mm f km
6 mm, cm, m, km

3:16

1 a 22:31 b 07:57 c 15:37 d 04:09 e 21:02
f 20:19 g 01:23 h 11:43
2 a 7:51 pm b 2:37 am c 6:13 am d 4:24 pm
e 5:49 am f 1:06 pm g 6:27 pm h 8:59 am
3 a 15:54 b 09:32 c 12:38 d 22:09
e 06:18 f 17:47 g 08:14 h 01:26
4 a 1 h 45 min b 4 h 45 min c 4 h 35 min d 3 h 11 min
5 a 24 min b 46 min c 80 min or 1 h 20 min
d 103 min or 1 h 43 min

3:17

1 a 1 pm b 4 pm c 8 pm
2 a 19:30 b 22:30 c 21:30
3 a 8:30 am b 3:30 pm c 6:30 pm
4 a 18:30 b 01:30 the next day
c 04:30 the next day
5 a 8 pm b 1 pm c 9 am d 6 am
6 a 01:00 b 05:00 c 12:00 d 15:00
7 Answers will vary.
8 a 8 b 18:30 (or 6:30 pm)
9 Start at 12 am (midnight) and colour a pathway to the finish.

	3.00 am	4.00 am	7.00 am	8.00 am	9.00 am	6.00 pm	2.00 pm	8.00 pm	9.00 pm	10.00 pm	9.00 pm	
	4.00 am	7.00 am	6.00 am	4.00 am	10.00 am	7.00 pm	3.00 pm	7.00 pm	2.00 pm	11.00 pm	**12.00 am**	Finish
	1.00 am	3.00 am	5.00 am	7.00 am	11.00 am	12.00 pm	8.00 pm	6.00 pm	3.00 pm	4.00 pm	7.00 pm	
Start	**12.00 am**	1.00 am	4.00 am	9.00 am	6.00 am	1.00 pm	7.00 pm	5.00 pm	2.00 pm	5.00 pm	8.00 pm	
	3.00 am	2.00 am	3.00 am	10.00 am	5.00 am	2.00 pm	3.00 pm	4.00 pm	1.00 pm	6.00 pm	9.00 pm	

3:18

1 a 7000 g b 4000 g c 8000 g
d 1625 g e 3750 g f 2125 g
g 3500 g h 9500 g i 7500 g
2 a 2 kg 475 g b 1 kg 295 g c 6 kg 456 g
d 3 kg 865 g e 5 kg 125 g f 4 kg 796 g
g 9 kg 350 g h 7 kg 642 g i 8 kg 923 g
3 a g b t c kg d kg
e t f g g t h g
4 a true b true c false
d false e true f true

3:19

1 a 6000 b 3000 c 11 000
d 7000 e 4000 f 17 000
2 a 4 b 8 c 2
d 6 e 9 f 5
3 a 4 kg 376 g b 5 kg 463 g c 7 kg 355 g
d 5 kg 367 g e 4 kg 260 g f 3 kg 500 g
4 Answers will vary.
5 a

Ingredients	1 loaf	2 loaves	4 loaves	10 loaves
warm water	250 mL	500 mL	1 L	2·5 L
sugar	55 g	110 g	220 g	550 g
yeast	7·5 g	15 g	30 g	75 g
salt	3·75 g	7·5 g	15 g	37·5 g
oil	62·5 mL	125 mL	250 mL	625 mL
flour	360 g	720 g	1420 g	3·6 kg

b 625 mL c 852·5 g d 180°C

3:20

1 a 48 mm b 74 mm c 95 mm d 27 mm
e 60 mm f 67 mm
2 a 134 mm, 13·4 cm b 122 mm, 12·2 cm
c 222 mm, 22·2 cm d 274 mm, 27·4 cm
3 The shapes will be drawn. d P = 14 cm

 • *AUSTRALIAN SIGNPOST MATHS 5* • ISBN 9780655708797

3:21

1. Area of smaller rectangle = 6 cm^2
   Area of larger rectangle = 24 cm^2
   a 4
   b 4
2. Area of small square = 4 cm^2.
   Area of larger square = 16 cm^2.
   a 4
   b 4
3.

Rectangle	Perimeter	Length	Height	Area
A	24 mm	11 mm	1 mm	11 mm^2
B	24 mm	10 mm	2 mm	20 mm^2
C	24 mm	9 mm	3 mm	27 mm^2
D	24 mm	8 mm	4 mm	32 mm^2
E	24 mm	7 mm	5 mm	35 mm^2
F	24 mm	6 mm	6 mm	36 mm^2

   a A **b** F (the square)
   c Answers will vary. (If the perimeter is fixed, the greatest area will be a square.)
4. **a** 50 cm by 50 cm **b** 3 m by 3 m

3:22

1. **a** 6 L **b** 8 L **c** 200 mL
2. Items underlined: can of lemonade, mug, ice tray
3. **a** 100 mL in each **b** B: 150 mL, C: 175 mL
   c 50 mL **d** 75 mL **e** egg: 50 mL, ball: 75 mL
   f ball **g** no, The shell would take up some of the space. The contents of the egg (the capacity) is slightly smaller than 50 mL.
   h no **i** Answers will vary but the balloon will have a greater volume than the rock but the rock will be heavier.
4. 25 mL (or 25 cubic centimetres)

3:23

1. 12 ones blocks, volume = 12 mL or 12 cubic centimetres
2. **a** 42 cubic centimetres **b** 327 cubic centimetres
   c 608 cubic centimetres
3. **a** 15 mL **b** 138 mL **c** 569 mL
4. **a** 250 mL **b** 70 mL **c** 180 mL
5. Answers will vary.

3:24

1. A: 250 mL, B: 400 mL, C: 100 mL C, A, B
2. **a** L **b** mL **c** L **d** mL
3. **a** 4000 mL **b** 10 000 mL **c** 22 000 mL
   d 5300 mL **e** 7400 mL **f** 3600 mL
4. **a** 9 L **b** 5 L **c** 3 L
   d 1·5 L **e** 6·8 L **f** 2·6 L
5. **a** 1600 mL **b** 1950 mL **c** 2300 mL
6. **a** 7 L 530 mL **b** 1 L 75 mL **c** 35 L 700 mL
7. Answers will vary. (You could use a litre carton of milk.)

3:25

1. **a** 20 000 m^2 **b** 50 000 m^2 **c** 70 000 m^2 **d** 40 000 m^2
   e 60 000 m^2 **f** 90 000 m^2 **g** 30 000 m^2 **h** 80 000 m^2
2. **a** 1 ha **b** 5 ha **c** 3 ha **d** 6 ha **e** 4 ha
   f 2 ha **g** 9 ha **h** 7 ha
3. **a** ha **b** m^2 **c** m^2 **d** ha **e** ha
   f m^2 **g** ha **h** ha **i** m^2
4. **a** 10 000 m^2, equal to 1 hectare
   b 7000 m^2, less than 1 hectare
   c 10 000 m^2, equal to 1 hectare
   d 13 500 m^2, more than 1 hectare
   e 10 000 m^2, equal to 1 hectare

3:26

1. **a** 100 ha **b** 400 ha **c** 200 ha
   d 700 ha **e** 300 ha **f** 900 ha
   g 1000 ha **h** 1300 ha **i** 1500 ha
2. **a** 1 km^2 **b** 3 km^2 **c** 7 km^2 **d** 2 km^2
   e 6 km^2 **f** 9 km^2 **g** 13 km^2 **h** 27 km^2
3. **a** m^2 **b** m^2 **c** km^2
   d km^2 **e** m^2 **f** m^2
   g ha **h** km^2 **i** ha
4. **a** Western Australia **b** Western Australia
   c 291 557 **d** Queensland

4:01

1. **a** false **b** true **c** true **d** true
2. **a** square pyramid **b** rectangular prism
   A didgeridoo has the shape of a cylinder.
3. Two prisms and two pyramids will be drawn.
4. **a**

Front	Top	Side
□	□	□
▭	▯	▭

   b

Front	Top	Side
▽	○	▽
▯	○	▯

5. **a** 6 **b** 8 **c** 12, the net of a cube should have exactly 6 faces

4:02

Header: 6 faces, 8 corners and 12 edges

1. **a** F **b** B **c** C **d** A **e** D **f** E
2. **a** A, B, E **b** C, D, F, G

3

Object	Number of corners	Number of edges	Number of faces
A	4	6	4
B	7	12	7
C	8	12	6
D	8	12	6
E	5	8	5
F	6	9	5

Corners + faces − edges = 2

a square pyramid **b** pentagonal prism

c cube

4:03

1

Transformation	Figure changes position	Figure changes shape	Figure changes size	Figure changes orientation
translation	yes	no	no	no
reflection	yes	no	no	yes
rotation	yes	no	no	yes

2 **a** B, D **b** C, E, F

3

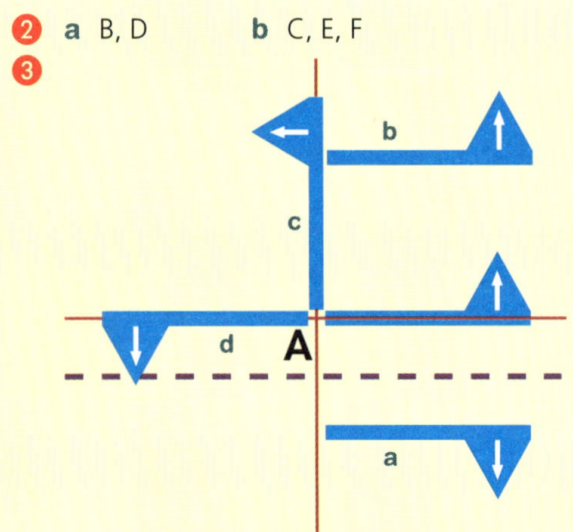

4:04

1 **a** B **b** A, D **c** C **d** D **e** E **f** F

2 **a** 0 **b** 1 **c** 0 **d** 5 **e** 8

3 **a**

b

c

d

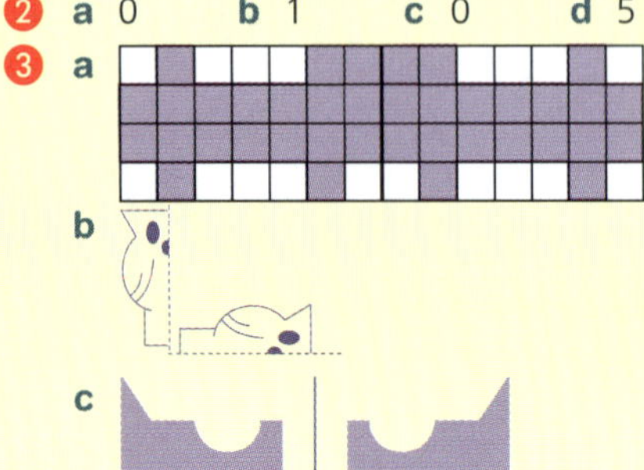

4 **a**

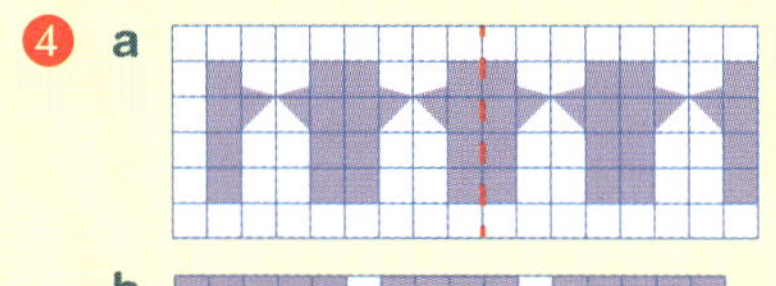

b

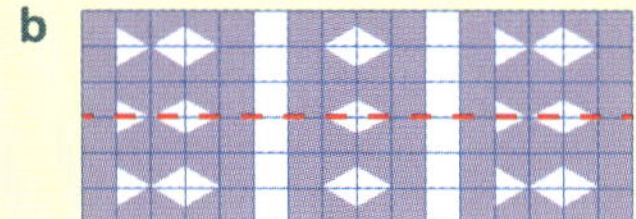

5

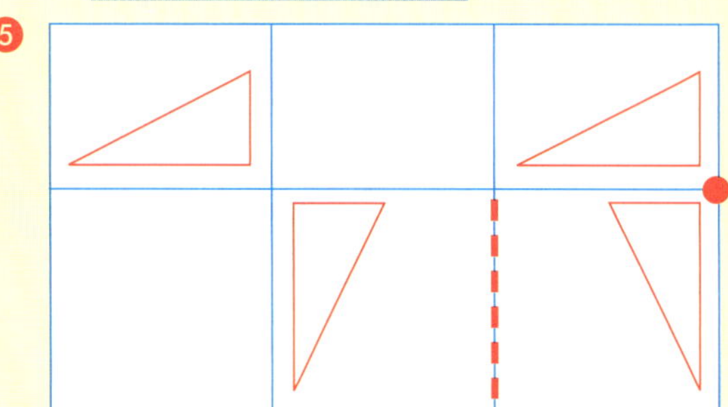

4:05

1

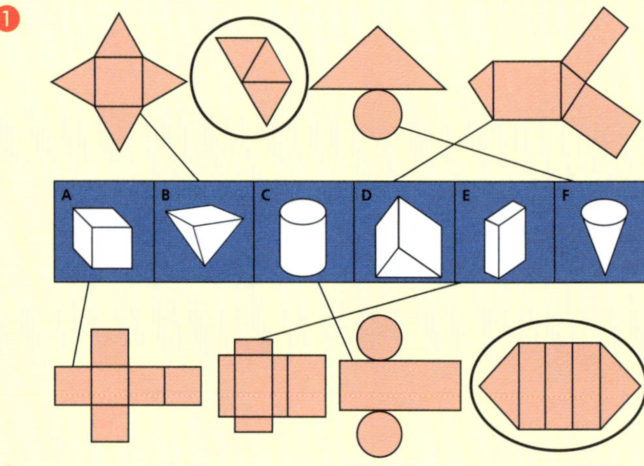

2 **a** triangular pyramid **b–c** A model will be made.

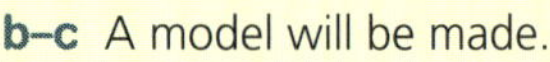

3 **a** **b**

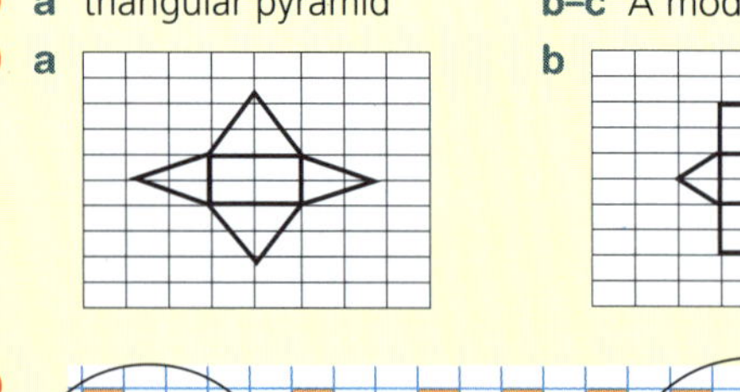

4

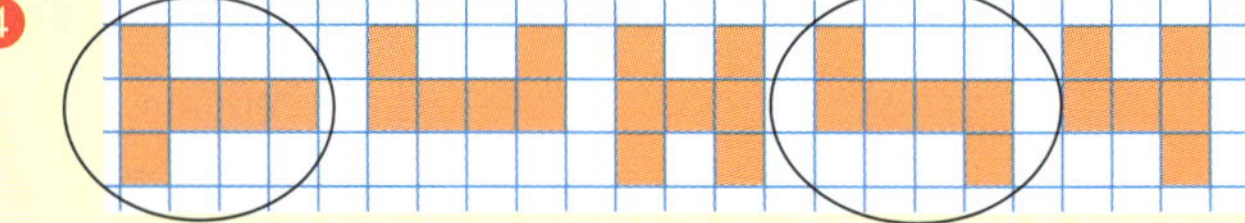

4:06

1 **a** 2C **b** 4B **c** 1D **d** 1A **e** 4A
f 2B **g** 1C **h** 3C **i** 3A **j** 4D
k 5A **l** 4C **m** 3D **n** 2A (or 2C)
o 5B **p** 1C, 2B, 3C, 5C **q** 3B

2 **a** triangle **b** pentagon **c** square
d left upper, middle upper **e** right lower, non-rigid

4:07

1 a 30°, acute b 110°, obtuse c 120°, obtuse
d 140°, obtuse e 80°, acute f 65°, acute
g 25°, acute h 165°, obtuse i 95°, obtuse

2 a 90 b 180 c 360

3 Answers will vary. The baseline of the protractor must be aligned with one of the arms of the angle with the centre point of the protractor over the vertex of the angle. The angle can be read off the outer scale. The second arm of the angle may need to be extended to aid this process.

4 120°, 120°, 60°, 60°

4:08

1 a 90° b 40° c 120° d 80°
e 110° f 140° g 60° h 100°

2

Picture						
Type	acute	right	obtuse	straight	reflex	revolution (full turn)
Size	between 0° and 90°	90°	between 90° and 180°	180°	between 180° and 360°	360°

3 a acute b straight c revolution (full turn)
d obtuse e acute f reflex g right
h obtuse i acute j reflex k reflex
l obtuse m acute n acute o reflex

4 One of each angle type in Question 2 will be drawn.

4:09

1 a 60° b 40° c 100° d 120°
e 50° f 20° g 120° h 40°
i 140° j 70° k 80° l 130°

4:10

1 a acute b straight c right d reflex
e revolution f obtuse g reflex h acute

2 Yes

3 a acute b revolution c straight d obtuse
e right f reflex g obtuse h obtuse

4 a square or rectangle
b regular pentagon, regular hexagon, regular octagon, etc.
c some triangles

5 Answers will vary.

4:11

1 a W b S c E d N e NW f SE
g NE h SW i SE j SW k E l NW

2 a E b N c W d S e SE f NW
g SW h NE i NW j NE k W l SE

3 a Karumba
b Ceduna, Sydney, Canberra or Adelaide
c Rockhampton, Brisbane or Longreach
d Coral Bay
e Derby, Fitzroy Crossing or Coral Bay
f Derby, Fitzroy Crossing or Coral Bay
g Melbourne
h Rockhampton or Brisbane

4 a south b west c north-east
d north-west e south-west f south-east

4:12

1 a Springbank Island b Vernon Circle
c Lennox Gardens (or Lotus Bay)

2 a 5A (or 4A) b 5E c 2E
d 3D e 6C (or 5C) f 4E

3 a Perth Avenue b Coronation Drive c Moonah Place

4 approximately 3600 m or 3 km 600 m

4:13

1 a Yes, No b No, Yes

2 A, B, C, D, G, H, I, J

3 A, B, C, D, E, G, H, J

4 a Yes, 4 b No c Yes, 2 d Yes, 8
e Yes, 6 f Yes, 2 g Yes, 3 h No

4:14

1 a 150° b 60° c 240°
d 160° e 100° f 220°

2 Estimates will vary.
a 60° b 90° c 120°
d 30° e 70° f 180°

4:15

Header: shapes 2 and 3 will be ticked

1 a 4 b 5

2–3 Answers will vary.

4:16

1

Number of:	A	B	C	D
surfaces	2	3	1	5
edges	1	2	0	8
vertices (corners)	1	0	0	5
curved surfaces	1	1	1	0
flat surfaces	1	2	0	5

2 a A b B, C c D

3 a B b C c A, D

4 B, E

5 A, B, D

6 a triangular prism b $5 + 6 - 9 = 2$
c cube = 2, rectangular prism = 2

4:17

1 a kangaroo b koala c cone
d rectangle e triangle f cylinder
g echidna h sphere i platypus

2 a 2, 1 b 6, 2 c 3, 0 d 0, 5 e 4, 3 f 3, 2
g 4, 5 h 0, 3 i 3, 4

3 a

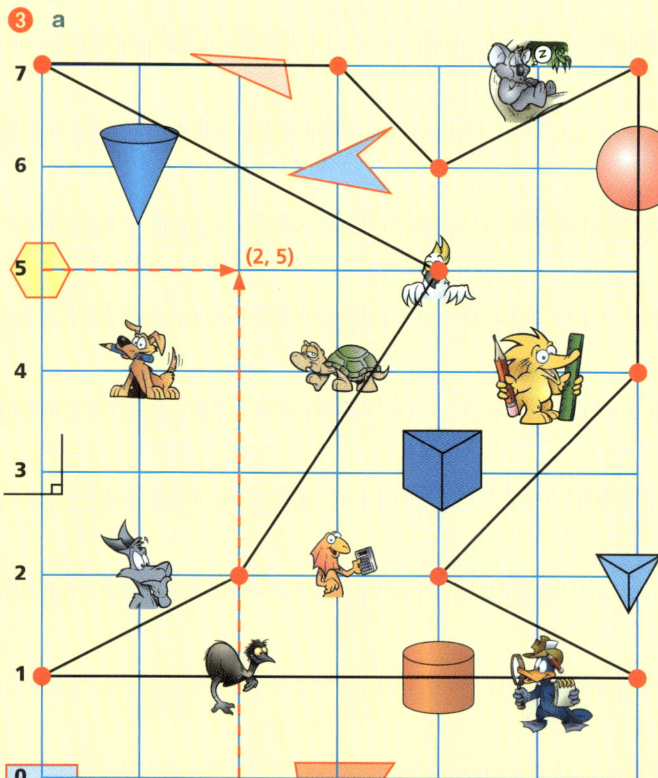

b decagon

4:18

1 a Colombia b Panama c Brazil d Argentina
e Paraguay f Uruguay g Peru h Ecuador

2 (5, 14)

3 a (6, 7) b (1, 13) c (6, 14) d (5, 9)

4 three of (2, 13), (2, 14), (2, 15) or (3, 14)

5 three of (3, 10), (3, 11), (4, 10), (4, 11) or (5, 10)

6 a 500 km b 1300 km c more than 4000 km
d 1300 km

7 a Chile (or Peru) b Venezuela (or Brazil)

4:19

Header: acute, obtuse

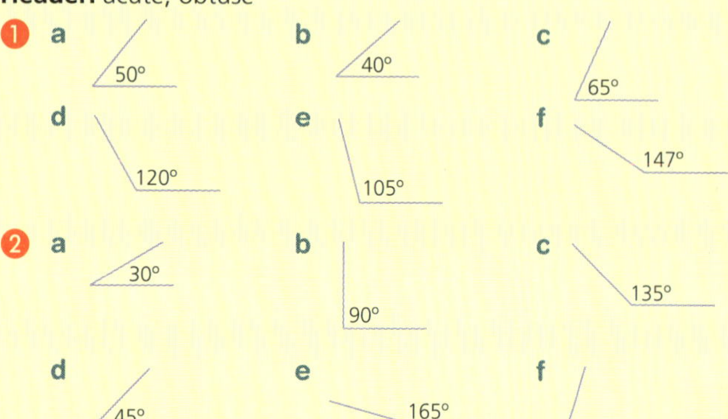

g 118° h 93° i 14°
j 172°

3 a 300° b 270° c 190°
d 355° e 225° f 317°

4:20

1 a 200° b 270° c 340°

2 a 160° b 90° c 20°

3 a 300° b 270° c 230°
d 200° e 280°

4 a 200° or 210° b 230° c 260°
d 290° e 340° f 350°

4:21

1 a (6, 13) b (11, 8) c (11, 1)
d 14, 7 e (3, 6) f 2, 5

2 a Ceduna b Rockhampton or Brisbane
c Coral Bay

3 a 4050 km b 3750 km c 3300 km

4:22

1 a

b

2 a The shape has been translated to the right and down
b Answers may vary. The shape has been translated to the right and reflected down.

3 a translation and rotation b translation and rotation

Investigation: The emu started at the green dot and walked forward (translation) and turned to the right (rotation) then started moving faster in a straight line (translation) then slowed down, turning to the right (rotation), then stopped at the red dot.

4:23

1 E L H J G F M K

a F b L
c G d J
e H

2 a b c

3 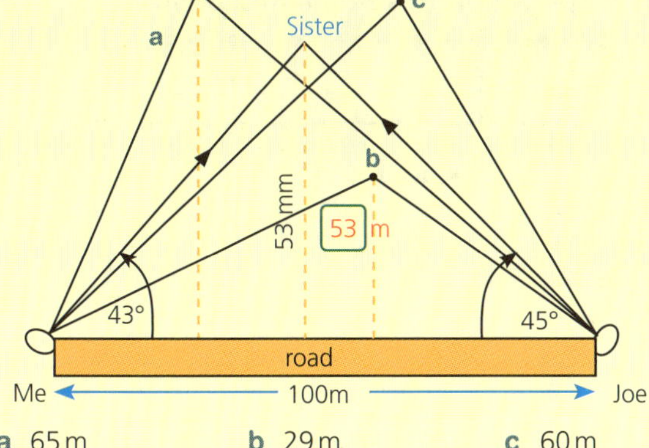

a 65m b 29m c 60m

5:01

1 a 12 b Monday
c Tuesday and Wednesday d 4, 4 books
e 76 f borrowed for the weekend

2 a i October ii February
b i 65 ii 85 iii 80 iv 105 v 130 vi 205
c 335

3 a No. The bars do not end on the lines of the horizontal scale.
b i 40 ii 110 iii 100 iv 10
c about 330
d They are small, cheap to feed and easy to care for.

4 24

5:02

1 a 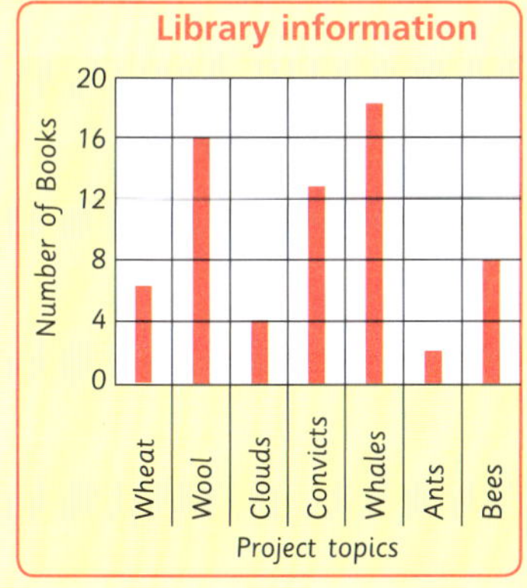

b Wool, convicts and whales. There are more books on these.

2 a 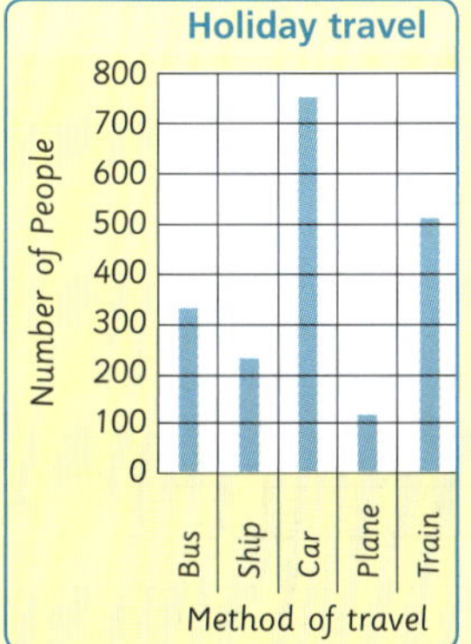

b 40

3 a Discrete b Discrete

5:03

1 **Ship arrivals**

Month of the year	
Jan	
Feb	
Mar	
Apr	
May	
June	
July	
Aug	
Sep	
Oct	
Nov	
Dec	

2 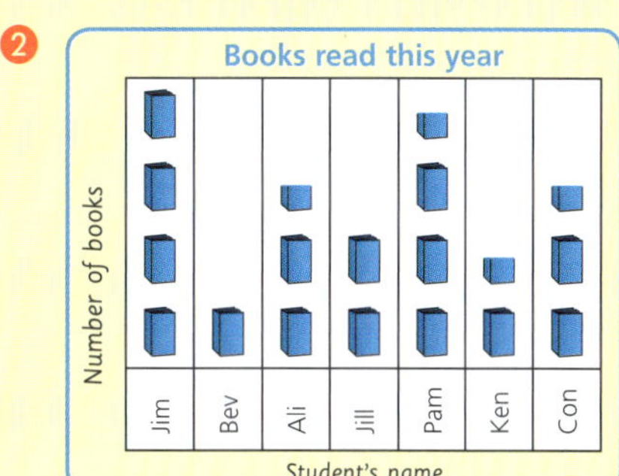

3

Name	Tally	Total
Alana	卌 卌 卌 卌 卌 |||	28
Rachel	卌 卌 卌 卌 ||	22
Naomi	卌 卌 卌 卌 卌 卌 卌 卌	40
Luke	卌 卌 卌 卌 卌 卌	30
Heather	卌 卌 卌 卌 卌 卌 卌		36
Sandy	卌 卌 卌 卌 卌 卌 ||	32

Stamps for bookwork

Alana	
Rachel	
Naomi	
Luke	
Heather	
Sandy	

Key: ★ = 10 stamps
= 2 stamps

5:04

1 a 11 b 3 c 22

2 a reading books b playing sport
c not at all

3 a 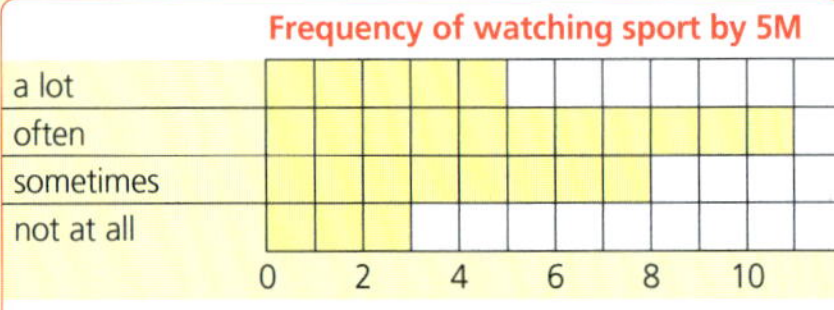

b
Activities chosen by 5M
playing sport
reading books
walking
watching sport
0 2 4 6 8 10

4 Answers will vary.

5:05

1 a impossible b even chance
c unlikely d certain
2 red
3 yellow
4 a yes b yes c yes
5 To choose at random means that each outcome has the same chance of being selected.

Fun spot: 2 (you can end up on 2 or 5), 2 (landing on 1,2,3 or 4 means you end up on 2), yes, not likely

5:06

Concept: yes
1 a yes b no
2 a 3 b yes c no d no
e No. The question mark stands for either a 1 or a 2, so one of these numbers will be present twice, the other once. They will not have an equal chance of being tossed.
3 unfair

5:07

Concept: toss a head on a coin
1 a unlikely b certain c impossible d likely
2 a 2 b answers will vary
c Drawing a two and a three is more likely.
3 a Jo. She is twice as likely to roll a 6 when she tosses.
b Answers will vary.
4 a no b no

5:08

Concept: The mode is 4. Answers will vary.
1 a 7
b There are more combinations that add to 7 (6 and 1, 2 and 5, 3 and 4) than any other number.
2 a 72 b 64 to 68 c 70 to 74
d

Test results: 5M

Score	64	65	66	67	68	69	70	71	72	73	74	75	76	77	78	79
Number	2	0	3	2	1	0	3	2	4	3	2	1	2	1	2	1

3 a Finger widths (in centimetres) of 5M
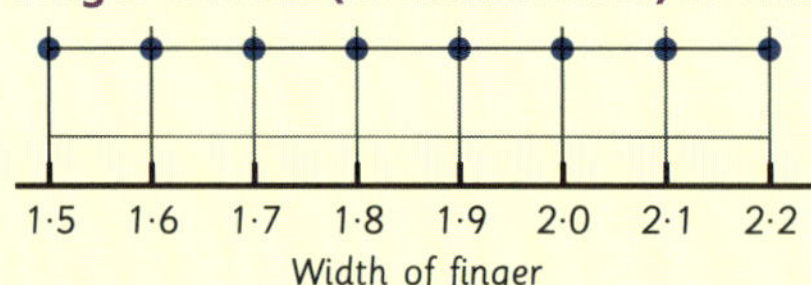

b 1·7 and 2·0

5:09

1 a i 7 cm ii 0 cm iii 2 cm iv 10 cm
b i day 5 and day 14 ii day 9 iii day 10
iv about halfway through day 7
c day 4 d day 6
e Students should draw a smooth graph passing through all points.
f 14 g day 14
h about halfway through day 6
2 a 7:00 am
b i 100 km ii 150 km iii 300 km
iv 400 km v 200 km vi 200 km
c 11:00 am d 1 hour e 50 km f 100 km
3

Quote	Fee to arrive	Cost per 15 min	Cost for parts to be replaced	a 3-hour job	b 15-min job	c $1\frac{1}{2}$-hour job
1	$25	$40	$80	$585	$145	$345
2	$100	$15	$115	$395	$230	$305
3	$50	$30	$70	$480	$150	$300

The cheapest quote would be: a 2 b 1 c 3

5:10

1 a i 200 g ii 400 g iii 150 g iv 350 g
b i 3 cups ii 5 cups iii 1 cup iv $\frac{1}{2}$ cup
c 600 g
2 a i 18°C ii 3°C b 21°C at 1 pm
c i 7 pm ii noon and 2 pm
d i 17°C ii 8°C iii 5°C iv 3·5°C
3 a i 300 min ii 180 min iii 90 min iv 270 min
b i 3 h ii 4 h iii $2\frac{1}{2}$ h iv $4\frac{1}{2}$ h

5:11

1 a 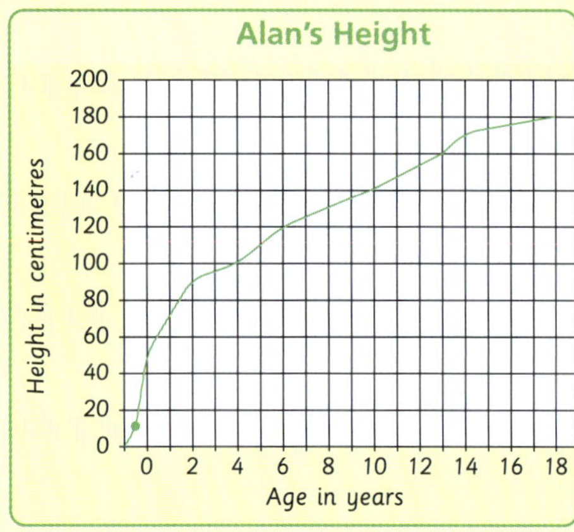

b i 70 cm ii 110 cm iii 160 cm iv 145 cm
c Alan's height 6 months before birth is marked on the graph.

2 Population

Population in 1000s

Year

3 a 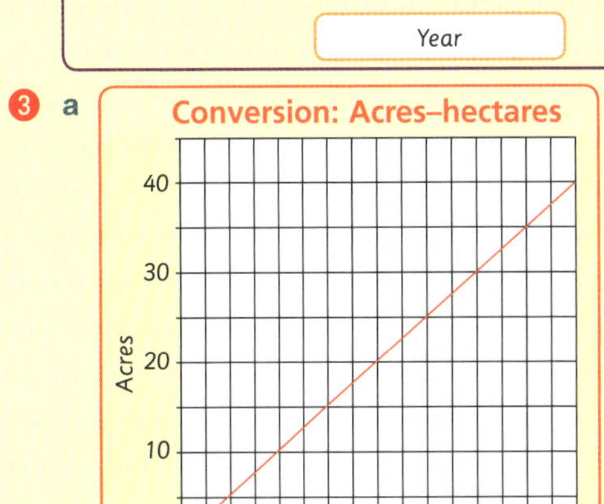

b i 8 ha ii 6 ha
c i 30 acres ii 5 acres
d i 7 hectares ii 16 acres

5:12

1 In order, from top down: C, F, B, D
2 Answers will vary

5:13

1 a $\frac{1}{6}, \frac{5}{6}$ b $\frac{3}{6}, \frac{3}{6}$ c $\frac{2}{6}, \frac{4}{6}$ d $\frac{5}{6}, \frac{1}{6}$
2 a $\frac{1}{6}$ b $\frac{1}{6}$ c $\frac{1}{6}$ d $\frac{1}{6}$ e $\frac{3}{6}$ or $\frac{1}{2}$
3 a $\frac{1}{5}$ b $\frac{2}{5}$ c $\frac{1}{5}$ d $\frac{1}{5}$ e $\frac{3}{5}$
4 a $\frac{1}{10}$ b $\frac{4}{10}$ c $\frac{3}{10}$ d $\frac{2}{10}$
5 a $\frac{4}{10}$ b $\frac{2}{10}$ c $\frac{3}{10}$ d $\frac{5}{10}$ or $\frac{1}{2}$
e $\frac{1}{10}$ f $\frac{6}{10}$ g $\frac{7}{10}$ h $\frac{7}{10}$

5:14

1 a $\frac{12}{15}$ b $\frac{3}{15}$ c $\frac{2}{15}$ d $\frac{13}{15}$
e $\frac{15}{15}$ f $\frac{0}{15}$ g $\frac{1}{15}$
2 a green b red c blue
d red, yellow, blue, green
e $\frac{3}{20}$ f $\frac{9}{20}$ g $\frac{2}{20}$ h $\frac{6}{20}$
3 a Aminah should win most of the time. No. Rohan has 6 ways of winning. Aminah has 10 (throwing a 2 and a 1 is a different throw to a 1 and a 2).
b Answers may vary.

4 a a convict; or not a convict
b a metal figure
c a nurse; or a toy soldier
d not a metal figure; or anything not in the bag
e a farmer; or a toy soldier or nurse

5:15

1 a 20 b i $\frac{9}{20}$ ii $\frac{11}{20}$
2 Answers will vary.
3 a $\frac{5}{9}$ b $\frac{3}{9}$ c $\frac{1}{9}$
d Answers may vary.

Concept:

- Even chance or 1 in 2 or $\frac{1}{2}$.
- Answers will vary. In this case it is not an even chance as many factors will contribute to the result (motivation, training, ability and determination).

5:16

1 a $\frac{3}{6}$ or $\frac{1}{2}$ b $\frac{2}{6}$ or $\frac{1}{3}$ c $\frac{1}{6}$
d $\frac{0}{6}$ or 0 e 3
2 Answers will vary. Discuss your results.
3 A good guess is about 7 or 8, since there are 8 different results that are equally likely, and 60 ÷ 8 = 7.5. Discuss your results.
4 a i licorice ii chocolate
b i $\frac{10}{20}$ or $\frac{1}{2}$ ii $\frac{6}{20}$ or $\frac{3}{10}$ iii $\frac{3}{20}$ iv $\frac{1}{20}$
5 Answers will vary. Discuss your results.
6 Koalas, because a total of 7 or more is more likely.

5:17

1 a i 16°C ii 22°C b i 11°C ii 14°C
c Thursday
2 Answers will vary.

5:18

1 Answers will vary.

5:19

1 a ×6 and ×7 tables b 30.4.24 c May
d 56, 54 e no
2 Answers will vary.
3 Answers will vary.

5:20

1 a lion b tiger c 30% d 4 e 80%
f No. The heading of the graph implies that these are all of the big cats.
2 Graph titles will vary. Sample title: 'Naomi and Hae's Birds'
a i 30 mm ii 20 mm iii 50 mm
b i 30 ii 20 iii 50
c i $\frac{30}{100}$ ii $\frac{20}{100}$ iii $\frac{50}{100}$
d i $\frac{3}{10}$ ii $\frac{2}{10}$ iii $\frac{5}{10}$
e i 30% ii 20% iii 50%

5:21

1. a 25 miles b 37·5 miles c 20 km d 50 km
   e 20 miles f 10 miles
2. a sleep b working c yes
   d play and other e work
3. a 13 b 9 c 46
   d 151 cm–160 cm
   e No. The category is 100 cm to 110 cm. f 91
4. a 14 b 19 c 35 d 54
   e No. The graph only shows scores in groups.

5:22

1. a Answers will vary and could include:

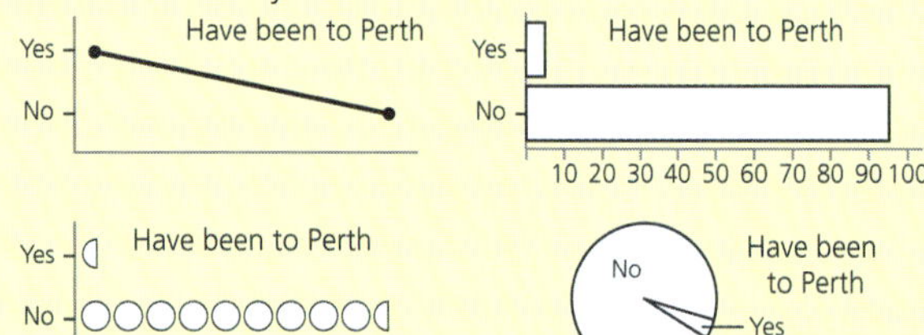

   b Answers will vary and could include:

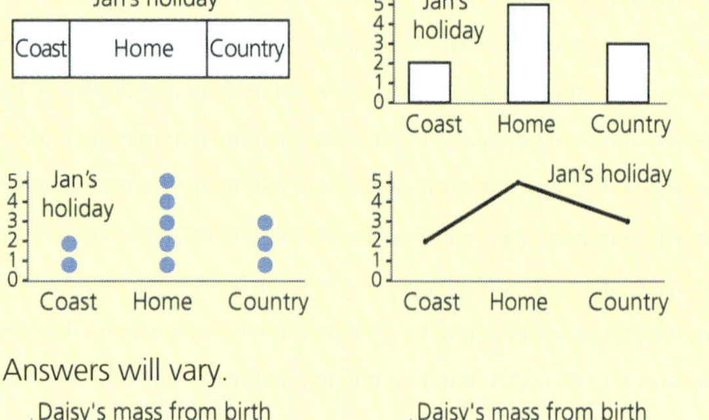

   c Answers will vary.

Daisy's mass from birth
Daisy's mass from birth

5:23

1. Column graph 1 joins B. Sector graph 2 joins A.
   Picture graph 3 joins C. Divided bar graph 4 joins E.
   Line graph 5 joins D.
2. Answers will vary. Tables clearly display all available data using a standard and simple format. Tables are easy to create and the information is easy to access. Tables take up little space.
3. A column graph will be drawn.

ES 1

1. 100
2. a 40 out of 100, $\frac{40}{100}$, 0·40 b 18 out of 100, $\frac{18}{100}$, 0·18
   c 18 out of 100, $\frac{18}{100}$, 0·18
3. a 0·49, $\frac{49}{100}$ b 0·94, $\frac{94}{100}$ c 0·71, $\frac{71}{100}$ d 0·89, $\frac{89}{100}$
   e 0·40, $\frac{40}{100}$ f 0·35, $\frac{35}{100}$ g 0·74, $\frac{74}{100}$ h 0·53, $\frac{53}{100}$
4. a \$0·15, \$$\frac{15}{100}$ b \$0·83, \$$\frac{83}{100}$
   c \$0·90, \$$\frac{90}{100}$ d \$0·37, \$$\frac{37}{100}$

ES 2

1. a

Ones		Tenths	Hundredths
0	·	4	6

   b

Ones		Tenths	Hundredths
0	·	5	5

   c

Ones		Tenths	Hundredths
1	·	2	8

2.

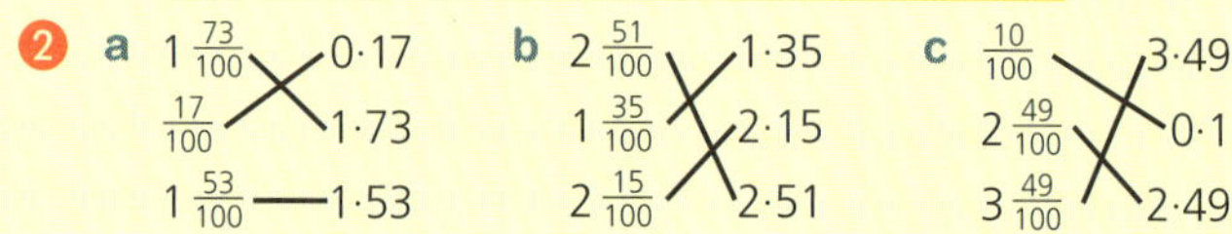

3.

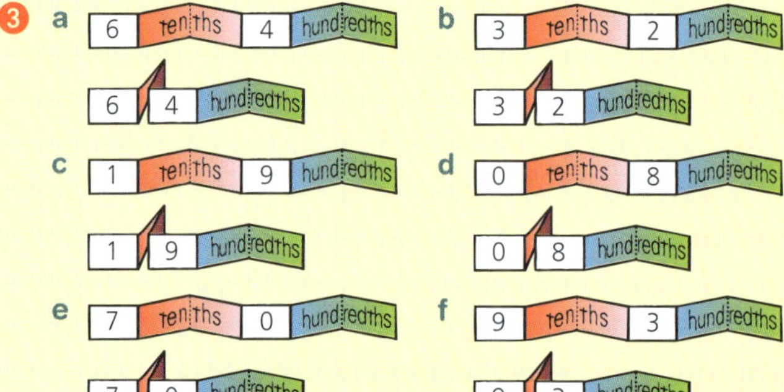

ES 3

1. a 53·64 b 75·46 c 95·48 d 37·90
2. a 15·75 b 80·36 c 27·92 d 90·08
   e 62·73 f 71·99
3. a 9 tenths and 1 hundredth
   b 4 tenths and 0 hundredths
   c 0 tenths and 9 hundredths
4. a 583·27 b 603·02 c 563·8 d 410·39
   e 6·9 f 4·2 g 5·3 h 9·1
5. a 3 b $\frac{9}{10}$ c 10 d 800
   e 20 f $\frac{4}{100}$ g 0 h $\frac{7}{10}$
   i $\frac{6}{100}$ j 500 k 30 l $\frac{9}{100}$

ES 4

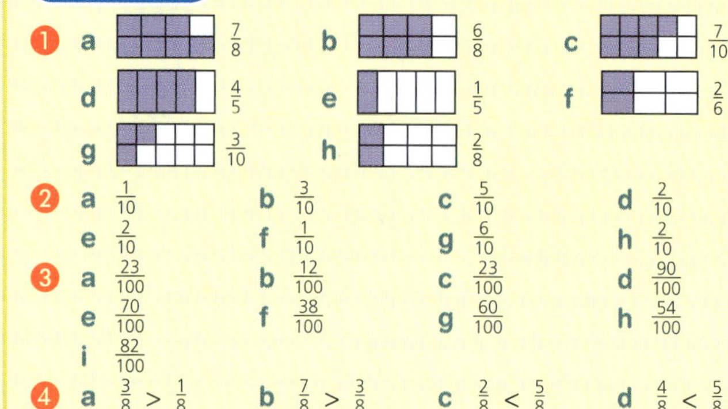

1. a $\frac{7}{8}$ b $\frac{6}{8}$ c $\frac{7}{10}$
   d $\frac{4}{5}$ e $\frac{1}{5}$ f $\frac{2}{6}$
   g $\frac{3}{10}$ h $\frac{2}{8}$
2. a $\frac{1}{10}$ b $\frac{3}{10}$ c $\frac{5}{10}$ d $\frac{2}{10}$
   e $\frac{2}{10}$ f $\frac{1}{10}$ g $\frac{6}{10}$ h $\frac{2}{10}$
3. a $\frac{23}{100}$ b $\frac{12}{100}$ c $\frac{23}{100}$ d $\frac{90}{100}$
   e $\frac{70}{100}$ f $\frac{38}{100}$ g $\frac{60}{100}$ h $\frac{54}{100}$
   i $\frac{82}{100}$
4. a $\frac{3}{8} > \frac{1}{8}$ b $\frac{7}{8} > \frac{3}{8}$ c $\frac{2}{8} < \frac{5}{8}$ d $\frac{4}{8} < \frac{5}{8}$
   e $\frac{1}{10} < \frac{3}{10}$ f $\frac{9}{10} > \frac{4}{10}$ g $\frac{7}{10} > \frac{2}{10}$ h $\frac{3}{10} < \frac{4}{10}$

 • *AUSTRALIAN SIGNPOST MATHS 5* • ISBN 9780655708797

ES 5

1. a 6 tenths b 8 thousandths c 3 hundredths
   d 5 hundredths e 4 hundredths f 9 tenths
   g 4 ones h 7 hundredths i 2 thousandths
2. a 0·47 b 0·359 c 0·7 d 0·206
   e 0·6 f 0·008
3. a $\frac{36}{100}$ b $\frac{417}{1000}$ c $\frac{5}{10}$ d $\frac{875}{100}$
   e $\frac{3}{100}$ f $\frac{48}{100}$ g $\frac{745}{1000}$ h $\frac{625}{1000}$
4. a 0·6 because $\frac{6}{10}$ is greater than $\frac{2}{10}$
   b 0·75 because $\frac{75}{100}$ is greater than $\frac{72}{100}$
   c 0·999 because $\frac{999}{1000}$ is greater than $\frac{998}{1000}$
5. 5·303, 5·34, 5·345, 5·35
6. a 5·35 b 5·325 c 5·385

ES 6

1. a 3·842 b 7·473 c 4·349 d 4·258
2. a Part b in Question 1 will be circled.
   b 3·842, 4·258, 4·349, 7·473
3. a 49·357 b 45·750 c 53·254
4. a 0·125, 0·2, 0·35 b 1·002, 1·02, 1·2
   c 0·007, 0·07, 0·7 d 1·4, 1·85, 2
5. The whole number 2 is greater than the whole number 1.
6. a false b true c true
7. a 3·619 < 4·207 b 9·138 < 9·56 c 4·196 < 5·231
   d 8·953 > 7·641 e 1·403 < 1·936 f 6·925 > 5·863
   g 5·306 < 5·638 h 7·612 > 7·59

ES 7

1. a 27 b 40 c 32 d 20 e 35
   f 24 g 14 h 28 i 15 j 30
   k 18 l 24
2. a 25 b 36 c 9 d 1 e 10
   f 45 g 40 h 24
3. a

   ×5: 2→10, 5→25, 3→15, 0→0, 7→35, 1→5, 6→30, 9→45, 4→20, 8→40

   b

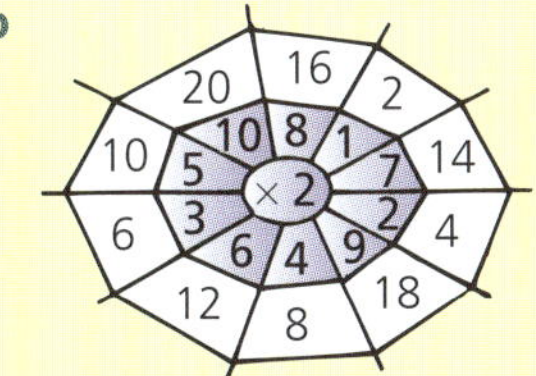

   c

   ×4: 8→32, 7→28, 10→40, 0→0, 6→24, 3→12, 9→36, 4→16, 5→20, 1→4

   d

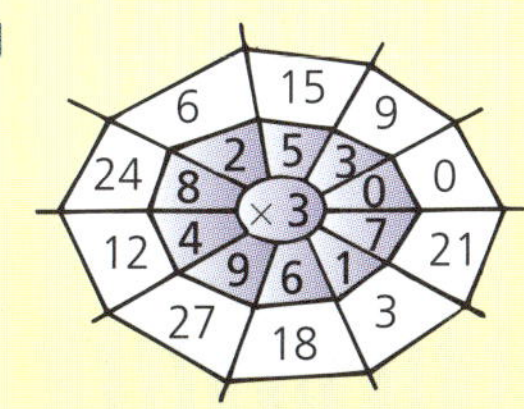

   e

   ×4: 8→32, 1→4, 7→28, 2→8, 9→36, 4→16, 6→24, 3→12, 5→20, 10→40

   f

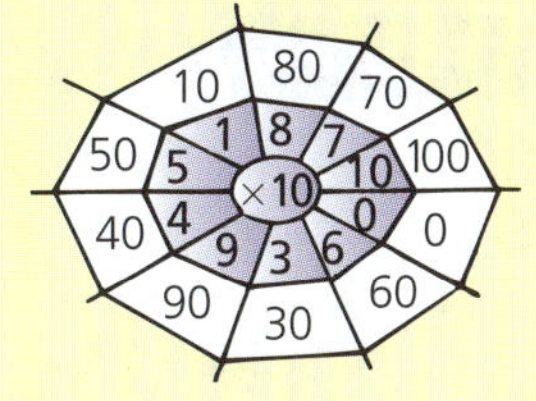

4. a 3, 6, 9, 12, 15, 18, 21, 24, 27, 30
   b 4, 8, 12, 16, 20, 24, 28, 32, 36, 40
   c 5, 10, 15, 20, 25, 30, 35, 40, 45, 50

ES 8

1. a

× 6	
2 × 6	48
5 × 6	0
8 × 6	12
0 × 6	54
6 × 6	30
1 × 6	36
9 × 6	24
4 × 6	60
3 × 6	6
7 × 6	18
10 × 6	42

b

× 7	
6 × 7	0
0 × 7	42
4 × 7	63
1 × 7	35
9 × 7	70
2 × 7	7
5 × 7	28
10 × 7	49
8 × 7	14
7 × 7	21
3 × 7	56

c

× 8	
10 × 8	48
3 × 8	40
6 × 8	8
1 × 8	80
5 × 8	0
8 × 8	24
0 × 8	72
4 × 8	16
9 × 8	64
2 × 8	56
7 × 8	32

d

× 9	
2 × 9	81
9 × 9	54
0 × 9	18
6 × 9	63
10 × 9	45
1 × 9	0
7 × 9	9
4 × 9	90
8 × 9	27
3 × 9	36
5 × 9	72

e

×	
5 × 5	48
6 × 9	49
7 × 7	35
5 × 4	25
8 × 6	54
7 × 5	20
9 × 3	63
9 × 7	28
3 × 6	32
7 × 4	27
4 × 8	18

f

×	
7 × 9	28
7 × 4	63
6 × 8	36
6 × 6	24
8 × 3	72
8 × 9	16
4 × 4	48
9 × 6	12
4 × 8	30
5 × 6	32
4 × 3	54

ES 9

1. a 35, 7 × 5 = 35
   b 15, 3 × 5 = 15
   c 25, 5 × 5 = 25
   d 45, 9 × 5 = 45
   e 30, 6 × 5 = 30
   f 40, 8 × 5 = 40
2. a 50, 55, 60, 65, 70, 75
   b 22, 24, 26, 28, 30, 32
   c 110, 120, 130, 140, 150, 160
   d 66, 68, 70, 72, 74, 76
3. a any two of 14, 28, 42 and 70
   b 35 and 70
   c any two of 12, 24 and 42
   d 21 and 42
4. a 0 b 5, 0 c 2, 4, 6 ,8, 0
5. a 54, 60, 66, 72, 78, 84, 90, 96, 102
   b 90, 99, 108, 117, 126, 135, 144, 153, 162

ES 10

1. 120 + 30 = 150 blocks

	H	T	U
		2	0
×			6
	1	2	0

\+

	H	T	U
			5
×			6
		3	0

=

	H	T	U
	1	2	0
+		3	0
	1	5	0

2 210 + 56 = 266 dollars

	H	T	U		H	T	U		H	T	U
		3	0				8		2	1	0
×			7	×			7	+		5	6
	2	1	0	+		5	6	=	2	6	6

3 90 + 54 = 144 people

	H	T	U		H	T	U		H	T	U
		1	0				6			9	0
×			9	×			9	+		5	4
		9	0	+		5	4	=	1	4	4

4 560 + 24 = 584 dollars

	H	T	U		H	T	U		H	T	U
		7	0				3		5	6	0
×			8	×			8	+		2	4
	5	6	0	+		2	4	=	5	8	4

ES 11

1 a 47 × 10 47 × 5 470 235
47 × 10 47 × 5 470 235
b 58 × 10 58 × 5 290 580
58 × 10 58 × 5 290 580

2 a 73 × 9 < 73 × 10 but > 73 × 5 so 73 × 9 is between 730 and 365.
b 62 × 6 < 62 × 10 but > 62 × 5 so 62 × 6 is between 620 and 310.
c 95 × 7 < 95 × 10 but > 95 × 5 so 95 × 7 is between 950 and 475.
d 81 × 8 < 81 × 10 but > 81 × 5 so 81 × 8 is between 810 and 405.
e 79 × 9 < 79 × 10 but > 79 × 5 so 79 × 9 is between 790 and 395.
f 86 × 6 < 86 × 10 but > 86 × 5 so 86 × 6 is between 860 and 430.

3 a 340 b 464 c 675 d 2409

4 a CCCXLVI b DCCCLXII c CMXXVIII
d MCCLXIII

ES 12

1 a 16, 19, 22, 25 Rule: add 3
b 43, 55, 67, 79 Rule: add 12
c 60, 51, 42, 33 Rule: subtract 9
d 32, 25, 18, 11 Rule: subtract 7

2 a 120, 135, 150, 165, 180; add 15
b 135, 125, 115, 105, 95; subtract 10

3 Answers will vary.

4 a 6, 9, 12, 15, 18, 21, 24; add 3
b 5, 10, 15, 20, 25, 30, 35; add 5
c 7, 11, 15, 19, 23, 27, 31; add 4
d 6, 11, 16, 21, 26, 31, 36; add 5

ES 13

1 a

Deaths from traffic accidents, 2003

Type of road user	NSW	Vic	Qld	SA	WA	Tas	Total
Drivers of motor vehicles	284	188	138	71	78	16	775
Motor cyclists	55	56	53	22	23	9	218
Pedal cyclists	14	7	5	3	6	0	35
Passengers	124	89	88	40	48	4	393
Pedestrians	95	58	37	18	24	6	238
Other	-	-	-	-	1	-	1
Total	**572**	**398**	**321**	**154**	**180**	**35**	**1660**

b Tasmania c New South Wales
d 393 e 35

2 537 3 99 4 183 5 69

6 Qld and WA 7 SA and Tas

ES 14

1 a 211 matches b 142 matches
2 a 91 matches b 47 matches
3 a 12 faces b 102 faces c 266 faces
4 a 19 faces b 121 faces c 223 faces
5 a 20 b 9 c 20

ES 15

1 15 

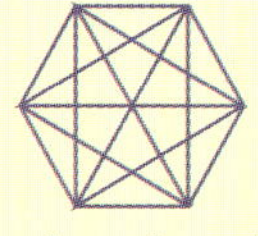

2 28

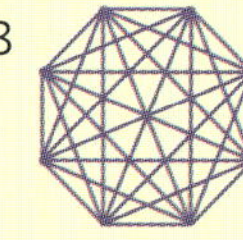

3 a 8

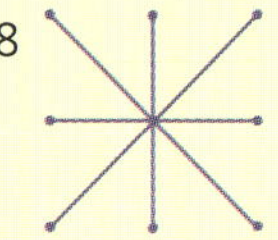

b 5

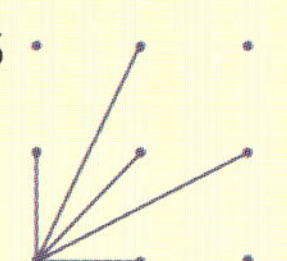

c 28

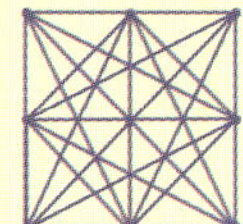

4 6

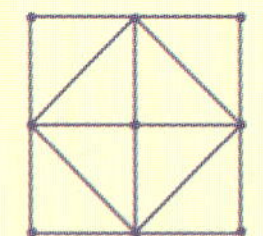

5

Numbers less than 25

Multiples of 3 only	Multiples of 3 and 4	Multiples of 4 only
3, 6, 9, 15, 18, 21	12, 24	4, 8, 16, 20

Outside both: 1, 2, 5, 7, 10, 11, 13, 14, 17, 19, 22, 23

6 Not necessarily. Answers will vary.

ES 16

1 2 2 6 3 24

4 a 20c + 5c, 10c + 10c + 5c, 10c + 5c + 5c + 5c
b 20c + 20c, 20c + 10c + 10c, 20c + 10c + 5c + 5c, 10c + 10c + 10c + 5c + 5c

c 50c + 10c + 5c, 50c + 5c + 5c + 5c, 20c + 20c + 20c + 5c, 20c + 20c + 10c + 10c + 5c, 20c + 20c + 10c + 5c + 5c + 5c, 20c + 10c + 10c + 10c + 5c + 5c + 5c

5 a 3 b 2 c 3 d 6

6

ES 17

1 a 45 cm b 4·5 kg or $4\frac{1}{2}$ kg c 90 cm
d 53 mL e 160 mL
f Each receives 160 mL.

2 a 11 chocolates b 11 chocolates

3 a 12 mm b $23\frac{3}{6}$ mm (or $23\frac{1}{2}$ mm)
c $30\frac{3}{6}$ (or $30\frac{1}{2}$ squares)

ES 18

1 a 2 b 4 c 7 d 3 e 9
f 0 g 4 h 5 i 0 j 6
k 5 l 2 m 11 n 10 o 29

2 a 7 b 9 c 5 d 0 e 10
f 20 g 15 h 9 i 7 j 4
k 8 l 6 m 12 n 12 o 20
p 31

3 a 3 b 7 c 6 d 9 e 5
f 3 g 10 h 5 i 8 j 6
k 7 l 7 m 8 n 9 o 9
p 7

4 a 16 b 12 c 40 d 8 e 6
f 3 g 3 h 8 i 10 j 7

5 a 2 b 10 c 5 d 2 e 4
f 6 g 4 h 5 i 3

6 a 4 b 2 c 4 d 8

ES 19

1

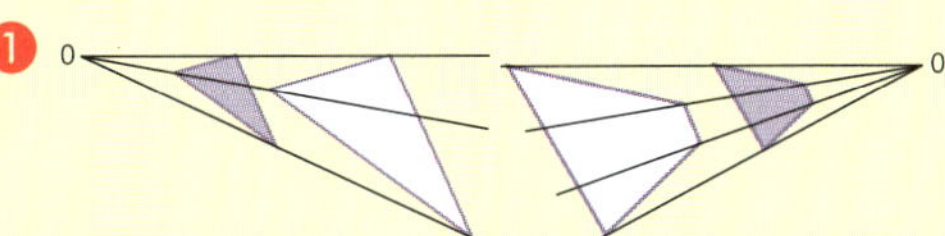

The enlargement factor is 2 or 200%.

2

The enlargement factor is 3 or 300%.

3 a 2 b 3 c $1\frac{1}{2}$ d $\frac{1}{2}$

ES 20

1 2, An enlargement of the alligators will be drawn.

2 1, A copy of the frog will be drawn.

3 The camel will be drawn on the smaller grid.

4 Answers will vary.

ES 21

Discussion will occur.